DECEPTION ON HIS MIND

Also by Elizabeth George

DECEPTION ON HIS MIND

Elizabeth George

BCA

LONDON NEW YORK SYDNEY TORONTO

This edition published 1997
by BCA
By arrangement with Hodder and Stoughton,
A division of Hodder Headline PLC

CN 1422

Typeset in Minion 11/13pt by
Palimpsest Book Production Limited,
Polmont, Stirlingshire

Printed and bound in Germany
by Graphischer Großbetrieb Pößneck GmbH

For Kossur
In friendship and with love

'Where is the man who has the power and skill
To stem the torrent of a woman's will?
For if she will, she will, you may depend on't;
And if she won't, she won't; so there's an end on't'

—*from the pillar erected on the Mount in the
Dane John Field, Canterbury*

Prologue

———❖———

To Ian Armstrong, life had begun its current downward slide the moment he'd been made redundant. He'd known when he'd been offered the job that it was only a temporary appointment. The advertisement he'd answered had not indicated otherwise and no offer of a contract had ever been made him. Still, when two years passed without a whisper of unemployment in the offing, Ian had unwisely learned to hope, which hadn't been such a good idea.

Ian's penultimate foster mother would have greeted the news of his job loss by munching a shortbread finger and proclaiming, 'Well, you can't change the wind, can you, my lad? When it blows over cow dung, a wise man holds his nose.' She would have poured tepid tea into a glass – she never used a cup – and she would have sloshed it down. She would have gone on to say, 'Ride the horse that's got its saddle on, lad,' and she would have returned to perusing her latest copy of *Hello!*, admiring its photos of well-groomed nobs living the good life in posh London flats and on country estates.

This would be her way of telling Ian to accept his fate, her unsubtle message that the good life was not for the likes of him. But Ian had never aspired to the good life. All he'd ever sought was acceptance, and he pursued it with the passion of an unadopted and unadoptable child. What he wanted was simple: a wife, a family, and the security of knowing that he had a future somewhat more promising than the grimness of his past.

These objectives had once seemed possible. He'd been good at his job. He'd arrived for work early every day. He'd laboured extra hours for no extra pay. He'd learned the names of all his fellow workers. He'd even gone so far as to memorise the names of their spouses and children, which was no mean feat. And the thanks he'd garnered for all this effort was a farewell office party drinking lukewarm squash and a box of handkerchiefs from Tie Rack.

Ian had tried to forestall and even to prevent the inevitable. He'd pointed out the services he'd rendered, the late hours he'd worked, and the sacrifices he'd made in not seeking other employment while occupying his temporary position. He'd sought compromise by making offers of working for a lower salary, and ultimately he'd begged not to be cut off.

The humiliation of grovelling in front of his superior was nothing to Ian if grovelling meant he could keep his position. Because keeping his position meant that the mortgage could continue to be paid on his new house. With that taken care of, he and Anita could move forward with their efforts to produce a sibling for Mikey, and Ian wouldn't have to send his wife out to work. More importantly, he also wouldn't have to see the scorn in Anita's eyes when he informed her he'd lost yet another job.

'It's this rotten recession, darling,' he'd told her. 'It goes on and on. Our parents had World War II as their trial by fire. This recession is ours.'

Her eyes had said derisively 'Don't give me philosophy. You didn't even *know* your parents, Ian Armstrong.' But what she said with an inappropriate and hence ominous amiability was, 'So it's back to the library for me, I suppose. Though I hardly see what help that'll be once I've arranged to pay someone to look after Mikey while I'm out. Or did you plan to look after him yourself instead of looking for work?' Her lips were tight with insincerity when she offered him a brittle smile.

'I hadn't thought –'

'That's the trouble with you, Ian. You never think. You never have a plan. We move from problem to crisis to the brink of disaster. We have a new house we can't pay for and a baby to feed and still you aren't thinking. If you'd planned ahead, if you'd cemented your position, if you'd threatened to leave eighteen months ago when the factory needed reorganisation and you were the *only* one in Essex who could do it for them –'

'That's not actually the case, Anita.'

'There you are! See?'

'What?'

'You're too humble. You don't put yourself forward. If you did, you'd have a contract now. If you ever once *planned*, you'd have demanded a contract then and there when they needed you most.'

There was no point in explaining business to Anita when she was in a state. And Ian really couldn't blame his wife for the state she was in. He'd lost three jobs in the six years they'd been married. And while she'd been supportive through his first two spates of unemployment, they'd lived with her parents then and hadn't the financial worries that menaced them now. If only things could be different, Ian thought. If only his job could have been secure. But residing in the twilight world of *ifs* did nothing to offer a solution to their problems.

So Anita had returned to work, a pathetic and ill-paying job at the town library where she reshelved books and helped pensioners locate magazines. And Ian began the humiliating process of seeking employment once again, in an area of the country long depressed.

He started each day by dressing carefully and leaving the house before his wife. He'd been as far north as Ipswich, as far west as Colchester. He'd been south to Clacton and had even ventured onward to Southend-on-Sea. He'd given it his best, but so far he'd managed nothing. Nightly he faced Anita's silent but growing contempt. When the weekends came, he sought escape.

Walking provided it, on Saturdays and Sundays. In the past few weeks, he'd come to know the entire Tendring Peninsula intimately. His favourite stroll was a short distance from the town, where a right turn past Brick Barn Farm took him to the track across the Wade. At the end of the lane he'd park the Morris, and when the tide was out, he put on his wellingtons and slopped across the muddy causeway to the lump of land called Horsey Island. There he watched the waterfowl and he poked about for shells. Nature gave him the peace that the rest of life denied him. And in the early weekend mornings, he found nature at her best.

On this particular Saturday morning, the tide was high, so Ian Armstrong chose the Nez for his walk. The Nez was an impressive promontory of gorse-tangled land that rose 150 feet above the North Sea and separated it from an area of tidal swamp called the Saltings. Like the towns along the coast, the Nez was fighting a battle against the sea. But unlike these towns, it had no line of breakwaters to guard it and no concrete slopes to serve as armour over the uneasy combination of clay, pebbles, and earth that caused the cliffs to crumble to the beach below them.

Ian decided to begin at the southeast end of the promontory, making his way round the tip and down the west side, where waders like redshanks and greenshanks nested and fed themselves from the shallow marsh pools. He waved a jaunty goodbye to Anita, who returned his farewell expressionlessly, and he wound his way out of the housing estate. Five minutes took him to Balford-le-Nez Road. Five minutes more and he was on Balford's High Street, where the Dairy Den Diner was serving up breakfast and Kemp's Market was arranging its vegetable displays.

He spun through the town and turned left along the seafront. Already, he could tell that the day was going to be yet another hot one, and he unrolled his window to breathe the balmy salt air. He gave himself over to an enjoyment of the morning and worked at forgetting the difficulties he faced. For a moment, he allowed himself to pretend all was well.

It was in this frame of mind that Ian rounded the curve into Nez Park Road. The guard's shack at the entrance to the promontory was empty so early in the morning, no attendant there to claim sixty pence for the privilege of a walk along the clifftop. So Ian bumped over the cratered terrain towards the car park above the sea.

That was when he saw the Nissan, a hatchback standing alone in the early-morning light, just a few feet from the boundary poles that marked the edge of the car park. Ian bounced towards it, avoiding pot holes as best he could. His mind on his walk, he thought nothing of the hatchback's presence until he noticed that one of its doors was hanging open and its bonnet and roof were beaded with dew not yet evaporated in the day's coming heat.

Ian frowned at this. He tapped his fingers against the steering wheel of the Morris and thought about the uncomfortable relationship between the top of a cliff and an abandoned car with its door left open. At the direction in which his thoughts began to head, he very nearly decided to turn tail for home. But human curiosity got the better of him. He edged the Morris forward until he was idling at the Nissan's side.

He said cheerily out of his open window, 'Good morning? I say, do you need any help in there?' in case someone was dossing in the car's back seat. Then he noted that the glove compartment was hanging open and that its contents appeared to be strewn upon the floor.

Ian made a quick deduction from this sight: someone had been searching for something. He got out of the Morris and leaned into the Nissan for a better look.

The search had been nothing if not thorough. The front seats were slashed, and the back seat was not only cut open but pulled forward as if in the expectation that something had been hidden behind it. The side panels of the doors appeared to have been roughly removed and then just as roughly returned to place; the console between the seats gaped open; the lining of the roof sagged down.

Ian adjusted his previous deduction with alacrity. Drugs, he thought. The harbours of Parkeston and Harwich were no great distance from this spot. Lorries, cars, and vast shipping containers arrived there by the dozen on ferries every day. They came from Sweden, Holland, and Germany, and the wise smuggler who managed to get past customs would be sensible to drive to a remote location – just like the Nez – before retrieving his contraband. This car was abandoned, Ian concluded, having served its purpose. He would have his walk and then phone the police to have it towed away.

He was childishly pleased with his insight. Amused at his first reaction to the sight of the car, he pulled his wellingtons from the boot of the Morris and as he squirmed his feet into them, he chuckled at the thought of a desperate soul attempting to end his troubles at this particular site. Everyone knew that the edge of the Nez's clifftop was perilously friable. A potential suicide wishing to fling himself into oblivion at this spot was far likelier to end up sliding with the clay, the gravel, and the silt on to the beach below as the cliffside collapsed beneath his weight in a dirty heap. He might break his leg, certainly. But end his life? Hardly. No one was going to die on the Nez.

Ian smacked the boot of the Morris shut. He locked the door and patted the vehicle's roof. 'Good old thing,' he said in an affable fashion. 'Thank you very much indeed.' The fact that the engine continued to turn over in the morning was a miracle that Ian's natural superstition told him he ought to encourage.

He picked up five papers that lay on the ground next to the Nissan and deposited them within the car's glove compartment from which they'd no doubt originally come. He swung the hatchback's door closed, thinking, No need to be untidy about things. Then he approached the steep old concrete steps that led down to the beach.

At the top of these steps, Ian paused. Even at this hour, the sky above him was a bright blue dome, unmarked by the presence of clouds, and the North Sea was tranquil with the calm of summer. A fog bank lay like a roll of cotton wool far out on the horizon, serving as distant backdrop for a fishing boat – perhaps half a mile off shore – that chugged in the direction of Clacton. A flock of gulls surrounded this like gnats round fruit. More gulls, Ian saw, were buzzing along the waterline at clifftop height. They flew in his direction from the north, from Harwich whose cranes he could glimpse even from this distance across Pennyhole Bay.

Ian thought of the birds as a welcoming committee, so intent did they seem upon him as a target. Indeed, they approached with such mindless determination that he found himself giving more than idle consideration to du Maurier's story, Hitchcock's film, and Tippi Hedren's avian torment. He was thinking about beating a hasty retreat – or at least doing something to shield his head – when as a single unit the birds arced and dived at a structure on the beach. This was a pillbox, a concrete fortification from World War II from which troops had watched and waited to defend their country from Nazi invasion. The structure had once stood on the top of the Nez, but as time and the sea had washed away the cliffside, it now sat on the sand below.

Ian saw that other gulls were already doing their web-footed tapdance on the pillbox's roof. From a hexagonal opening on this same roof, where a machine-gun emplacement once would have stood, more birds entered and exited the structure. They gabbled and cawed as if in communication, and their message seemed to pass telepathically to the birds off shore, for these began to leave the fishing boat and to head towards land.

Their decisive flight reminded Ian of a scene on the beach near Dover that he'd witnessed as a child. A big barking brute of a dog had been lured out to sea by a flock of similar birds. The dog had been playing at catching them from the water, but they had been deadly serious, and they'd circled farther and farther out into the sea until the poor animal was a quarter of a mile from the shore. No one's shouting or imprecations had brought the dog back. And no one had been able to control the birds. Had he not seen the gulls toying with the dog's ebbing strength – circling above him just out of his reach, cawing, approaching, then darting away – Ian would never have thought it reasonable to conclude that birds were creatures with murderous intentions. But he'd seen it that day and he'd believed it ever since. And he always kept a respectful distance from them.

He thought of that poor dog now. It was obvious that the gulls were toying with something and whatever that desolate something was, it was inside the old pillbox. Action was called for.

Ian descended the stairs. He said, 'Hey, there! I say!' and he waved his arms. This did little to deter the gulls that bobbed on the guano-streaked concrete rooftop and flapped their wings minaciously. But Ian wasn't about to be put off. The long-ago gulls in Dover had got the better of their canine pursuer, but these Balford gulls weren't about to get the better of Ian Armstrong.

He jogged in their direction. The pillbox was some twenty-five yards from the foot of the steps, and he was able to build up a fair amount of speed in that distance. Arms waving, he descended on the birds with a yowl, and he was pleased to see his efforts at intimidation bear fruit. The gulls took to the air, leaving Ian alone with the pillbox, and whatever it was that they had been investigating within it.

The entrance was a crawlhole less than three feet from the sand, the perfect height for a small seal to wriggle through, seeking shelter. And a seal was what Ian expected to find when he himself duck-walked through the short tunnel and emerged in the gloom of the pillbox's interior.

Cautiously, he stood. His head brushed the damp ceiling. A pervasive odour of seaweed and dying crustaceans seemed to rise from the ground and to seep from the walls. These were heavily embellished with graffiti, which at a glance appeared to be solely sexual in nature.

Light filtered in from embrasures, allowing Ian to note that the pillbox – which he'd never explored before this moment, despite his many trips to the Nez – was actually two concentric structures. It was shaped like a doughnut, and an opening in its internal wall acted as access to its centre. This was what had attracted the gulls, and finding nothing of substance on the rubbish-strewn ground, it was towards this aperture that Ian moved, calling out, 'Hello there? Anyone here?' without realising that an animal – wounded or otherwise – would hardly be likely to answer.

The air felt close. Outside, the cries of the birds rose and fell. As he reached the opening, Ian could hear wings flapping and webbed feet scuttling as the more intrepid gulls descended once again. This would not do, Ian thought grimly. He was the human, after all, master of the planet and king of all that he surveyed. It was unthinkable that a gang of hooligan birds could presume dominance over him.

He said, 'Shoo! Off with you! Get out of it!' and burst into the open air of the pillbox's centre. Birds rocketed skywards. Ian's gaze followed their flight. He said, 'That's better,' and pushed his coat sleeves towards his elbows to ready himself to deal with whatever the gulls had been tormenting.

It wasn't a seal and they hadn't done with their tormenting. He saw this at the same moment as his stomach lurched upward and his sphincter quivered.

A thin-haired young man sat upright with his back against the old concrete machine-gun emplacement. The fact that he was dead was demonstrated by the two remaining sea gulls who picked at his eyes.

Ian Armstrong took one step towards the body, his own feeling like ice. When he could breathe again and believe what he saw, he uttered only four words. 'Well, Jesus be praised.'

Chapter One

———◆———

Whoever said April is the cruellest month had never been in London in the midst of a summer heatwave. With air pollution dressing the sky in designer brown, diesel lorries draping the buildings – and the inside of noses – in basic black, and leaves wearing the very latest in dust and grit, London in late-June was the cruellest month. Indeed, it was a veritable hellhole. This was Barbara Havers' unsentimental evaluation of her nation's capital as she drove through it on Sunday afternoon, heading homeward in her rattling Mini.

She was ever so slightly – but nonetheless pleasantly – tanked up. Not enough to be a danger to herself or to anyone else on the streets, but enough to review the events of the day in the pleasant afterglow produced by expensive French champagne.

She was returning home from a wedding. It hadn't been the social event of the decade, which she'd long expected that the marriage of an earl to his longtime beloved was supposed to be. Rather, it had been a quiet affair in a tiny church close to said earl's home in Belgravia. And instead of bluebloods dressed to the nines, its guests had been only the earl's closest friends as well as a few of his fellow police officers from New Scotland Yard. Barbara Havers was one of this latter group. At times, she liked to think that she was also one of the former.

Upon reflection, Barbara realised that she should have expected of Detective Inspector Thomas Lynley just the sort of quiet wedding that he and Lady Helen Clyde had orchestrated. He'd been downplaying the Lord Asherton side of his life for as long as she'd known him, and the last thing he would have wanted in the way of nuptials was an ostentatious ceremony attended by a well-heeled crowd of Hooray Henrys. So instead of that, sixteen decidedly unHenrylike guests had assembled to watch Lynley and Helen take the marital plunge, after which they'd all repaired to *La Tante Claire* in Chelsea, where they'd tucked into six kinds of *hors d'oeuvres*, champagne, lunch, and more champagne.

Once the toasts were made and the couple seen off to a honeymoon destination which they had both laughingly refused to disclose, the rest of the wedding party disbanded. Barbara stood on the frying-pan pavement of Royal Hospital Road and exchanged a few words with the other guests, among them Lynley's best man, a forensic specialist called Simon St James. In best English fashion, they'd commented upon the weather first. Depending upon the speaker's level of tolerance for heat, humidity, smog, fumes, dust, and glare, the atmosphere was deemed wonderful, hideous, blessed, bloody awful, delightful, delectable, insufferable, heavenly, or plain effing hell. The bride was pronounced beautiful. The groom was handsome. The food was delicious. After this, there was a general pause in which the company decided upon two courses of action: talk that ventured beyond banalities or friendly farewells.

The group parted ways. Barbara was left with St James and his wife Deborah. Both were wilting in the merciless sun, St James dabbing a white handkerchief to his brow and Deborah fanning herself enthusiastically with an old theatre programme which she'd fished from her capacious straw bag.

'Will you come home with us, Barbara?' she asked. 'We're going to sit in the garden for the rest of the day, and I plan to ask Dad to turn the hose pipe on us.'

'That sounds just the ticket,' Barbara said. She rubbed her neck where sweat had soaked her collar.

'Good.'

'But I can't. To tell you the truth, I'm whacked.'

'Understandable,' St James said. 'How long has it been?'

Deborah added quickly, 'How stupid of me. I'm sorry, Barbara. I'd completely forgotten.'

Barbara doubted this. The bandages across her nose and the bruises on her face – not to mention her chipped front tooth – made it unlikely that anyone who saw her would miss the fact that she'd recently served sentence in hospital. Deborah was merely too polite to draw attention to this. 'Two weeks,' Barbara replied to St James' question.

'How's the lung?'

'Functioning.'

'And the ribs?'

'Only when I laugh.'

St James smiled. 'Are you taking time off?'

'Under orders, yes. I can't go back till I've got clearance from the doctor.'

'I'm sorry about it all,' St James said. 'It was a rotten piece of luck.'

'Yeah. Well.' Barbara shrugged. Heading part of a murder investigation for the first time, she'd been injured in the line of duty. It wasn't something she wanted to talk about. Her pride had taken as serious a blow as her body.

'So what will you do?' St James asked.

'Escape the heat,' Deborah advised her. 'Go to the Highlands. Go to the lakes. Go to the sea. I wish we could.'

Barbara tossed Deborah's suggestions round in her mind as she drove up Sloane Street. Inspector Lynley's final order to her at the conclusion of the investigation had directed her to take a holiday, and he'd repeated that order in a private moment between the two of them after his wedding.

'I meant what I said, Sergeant Havers,' he'd told her. 'You're due some time off, and I want you to take it. Are we clear on the subject?'

'We're clear, Inspector.'

But what they weren't clear on was what she was supposed to do with her enforced leisure. She'd greeted the idea of a period away from work with the horror of a woman who kept her private life, her wounded psyche, and her raw emotions in order by not having time to attend to them. In the past, she'd used her holidays from the Yard to deal with her father's failing health. After his death, she'd used her free hours to confront her mother's mental infirmities, the family home's renovation and sale, and her own move to her current digs. She didn't like to have time on her hands. The suggestion of a stretch of minutes dissolving into hours leaking into days extending into one week and maybe even two ... Her palms began to sweat at the very thought. Pains shot into her elbows. Every fibre of her short, stout being began to shriek, 'Anxiety attack.'

So as she veered through traffic and blinked against a particle of soot that floated in through her window on the blistering air, she felt like a woman on the edge of an abyss. It dropped down and away and into forever. It was signposted with the dread words *free time.* What would she do? Where would she go? How would she fill the endless hours? Reading romances? Washing the only three windows she possessed? Learning how to iron, to bake, to sew? How about melting away in the heat? This bloody heat, this miserable heat, this flaming, flipping, sodding heat, this –

Get a grip, Barbara told herself. It's a holiday you're doomed to, not solitary confinement.

At the top of Sloane Street, she waited patiently to make the turn into Knightsbridge. She'd listened to the television news in her hospital room day after day, so she knew that the exceptional weather had brought an even greater than normal influx of foreign tourists to London. But here she saw them. Hordes of shoppers wielding bottles of mineral water shoved their way along the pavement. Hordes more poured out of Knightsbridge tube station, bee-lining in every direction towards the trendy shops. And five minutes later when Barbara had managed to negotiate her way up Park Lane, she could see even more of them – along with her countrymen – baring their lily-skinned bodies to Apollo on the thirsty grass of Hyde Park. Under the scorching sun, double decker open-topped buses trundled along, carrying a full load of passengers who listened with rapt attention to tour guides speaking into microphones. And tour coaches disgorged Germans, Koreans, Japanese, and Americans at every hotel she saw.

All of us breathing the same air, she thought. The same torrid, noxious, used-up air. Perhaps a holiday was called for after all.

She bypassed the mad congestion of Oxford Street and instead headed northwest on the Edgware Road. The masses of tourists thinned out here, to be replaced by masses of immigrants: dark women in *saris, chādors,* and *hijabs;* dark men in everything from blue jeans to robes. As she crawled along in the flow of traffic, Barbara watched these one-time foreigners moving purposefully in and out of shops. She reflected on the changes that had come upon London in her thirty-three years. The food had undergone a distinct improvement, she concluded. But as a member of the police force, she knew that this polyglot society had engendered a score of polyglot problems.

She detoured to avoid the crush of humanity that always gathered round Camden Lock. Ten minutes more and she was finally cruising up Eton Villas, where she prayed to the Great Angel of Transport to grant her a parking space that was near her personal hovel.

The angel offered a compromise: a spot round the corner about fifty yards away. With some creative shoe-horning, Barbara squeezed her Mini into a space fit only for a motorbike. She trudged back the way she'd come and swung open the gate of the yellow brick Edwardian house behind which her bungalow sat.

In the long drive across town, the pleasant glow from the champagne had metamorphosed in the way of most pleasant glows arising from alcohol: she was killingly thirsty. She set her sights on the path that led along the side of the house to the back garden. At the bottom of this, her tiny bungalow looked cool and inviting in the shade of a false acacia.

Looks deceived as usual. When Barbara unlocked the door and stepped inside, heat engulfed her. The three windows were open in the hope of encouraging cross ventilation, but there was no breeze stirring without so the heavy air fell upon her lungs like a visitation of the plague on the unprepared.

'Bloody hell,' Barbara muttered. She threw her shoulder bag on the table and went to the fridge. A litre of Volvic looked like a tower block among its companions: the cartons and packages of leftover take-away and ready-to-eat meals. Barbara grabbed the bottle and took it to the sink. She swilled down five mouthfuls, then leaned over and poured half of what was left on to the back of her neck and into her cropped hair. The sudden rush of cold water against her skin made her eyeballs throb. It was perfect heaven.

'Bliss,' Barbara said. 'I've discovered God.'

'Are you having a bath?' a child's voice asked behind her. 'Shall I come back later?'

Barbara swung round to the door. She'd left it open, but she hadn't expected that its position might be interpreted as an invitation to casual visitors. She hadn't actually seen any of her neighbours since being discharged from the Wiltshire hospital where she'd spent several days. To avoid the potential of a chance encounter, she'd limited her comings and goings to periods when she knew the residents of the larger building were out.

But here stood one of them, and when the child ventured a hop-and-step closer, her liquid brown eyes grew round and large.

'Whatever have you done to your face, Barbara? Have you had a car crash? It looks perfectly dreadful.'

'Thanks, Hadiyyah.'

'Does it hurt? What happened? Where've you been? I've been ever so worried. I even phoned twice. I did that today. See. Your answer machine is blinking. Shall I play it for you? I know how. You taught me, remember?'

Hadiyyah skipped happily across the room and plopped herself on to Barbara's divan. The answer machine stood on a shelf by the tiny fireplace, and she confidently punched one of its buttons and beamed at Barbara as her own voice was played.

'Hello,' her message said. *'This is Khalidah Hadiyyah. Your neighbour. Up in the front of the house. In the ground-floor flat.'*

'Dad says I'm always supposed to identify myself whenever I ring someone,' Hadiyyah confided. 'He says it's only polite.'

'It's a good habit,' Barbara acknowledged. 'It reduces confusion on the other end of the line.' She reached for a limp tea towel hanging from a hook. She used it on her hair and the back of her neck.

'It's awfully hot, isn't it?' the message continued chattily. *'Where are you? I'm ringing to ask, d'you want to go for an ice cream? I've saved up so I have enough for two and Dad says I c'n invite anyone I like so I'm inviting you. Ring me back soon. But don't be afraid. I won't invite anyone else in the meantime. 'Bye now.'* And then a moment later, after the beep and an announcement of the time, another message from the same voice. *'Hello. This is Khalidah Hadiyyah. Your neighbour. Up in the front of the house. In the ground-floor flat. I still want to go for an ice cream. Do you? Ring me, please. If you can, that is. I'll pay. I can pay because I've saved up.'*

'Did you know who it was?' Hadiyyah asked. 'Did I tell you enough so you knew who it was? I wasn't sure how much I was s'posed to say, but it seemed like enough.'

'It was perfect,' Barbara said. 'I especially liked the information about the ground-floor flat. It's good to know where I can find your lolly when I need to steal it to buy some fags.'

Hadiyyah giggled. 'You wouldn't, Barbara Havers!'

'Never doubt me, kiddo,' Barbara said. She went to the table where she rooted in her bag for a packet of Players. She lit up and inhaled, wincing at the prick of pain in her lung.

'That's not good for you,' Hadiyyah noted.

'So you've told me before.' Barbara set the cigarette on the edge of an ashtray in which eight of its brothers had already been extinguished. 'I've got to shed this get-up, Hadiyyah, if you don't mind. I'm bloody boiling.'

Hadiyyah didn't appear to take the hint. She nodded, saying, 'You must be hot. Your face's gone all red,' and she squirmed on the divan to make herself more comfortable.

'Well, it's all girls, isn't it?' Barbara sighed. She went to the cupboard, and, standing in front of it, she yanked her dress over her head, putting her heavily taped chest on display.

'Were you in an accident?' Hadiyyah asked.

'Sort of. Yeah.'

'Did you break something? Is that why you're bandaged?'

'My nose. Three ribs.'

'That must've hurt awfully. Does it hurt still? Shall I help you change your clothes?'

'Thanks. I can cope.' Barbara kicked her shoes into the cupboard and peeled off her tights. In a lump beneath a black plastic mackintosh lay a pair of purple harem trousers with a drawstring waist. The very thing, she decided. She stepped into them and topped the outfit with a crumpled pink T-shirt. *Cock Robin Deserved It* was printed on the front. Thus garbed, she turned back to the little girl, who was thumbing curiously through a paperback novel she'd found on the table next to the bed. The previous evening, Barbara had reached the part where the eponymous lusty savage had been driven beyond human endurance by the sight of the heroine's firm, young – and conveniently stripped – buttocks as she delicately entered the river for her bath. Barbara didn't think Khalidah Hadiyyah needed to learn what happened next. She crossed the room and removed the book from her hands.

'What's a throbbing member?' Hadiyyah inquired, her brow furrowed.

'Ask your dad,' Barbara said. 'No. On second thoughts, don't.' She couldn't imagine Hadiyyah's solemn father fielding such a question with the same aplomb that she herself could muster. 'It's the official drum-beater for a secret society,' Barbara explained. 'He's the throbbing member. The other members sing.'

Hadiyyah nodded thoughtfully. 'But it said that she *touched* his –'

'What about that ice cream?' Barbara asked heartily. 'Can I accept the invitation straightaway? I could do with strawberry. What about you?'

'That's what I've come to see you about.' Hadiyyah slithered off the divan and earnestly clasped her hands behind her back. 'I've got to take back the invitation,' she said, hurrying to add, 'but it's not a forever taking back. It's just for now.'

'Oh.' Barbara wondered why her spirits took a downward slide at the news. Experiencing disappointment hardly made sense since enjoying ice cream with an eight-year-old child wasn't an event to emblazon upon her social calendar.

'Dad and I are going away, you see. It's just for a few days. We're leaving straightaway. But since I rang and invited you out for an ice cream, I thought I should tell you that we couldn't go till later. In case you rang me back. That's why I'm here.'

'Ah. Sure.' Barbara retrieved her cigarette from the ashtray and eased into one of the table's two accompanying chairs. She'd not yet opened yesterday's post, merely moving it on top of an old *Daily Mail*, and she saw that at the head of the pile was an envelope marked: *Looking for Love?* Aren't we all, she thought sardonically and screwed the fag into her mouth.

'That's okay, isn't it?' Hadiyyah asked anxiously. 'Dad said it was okay for me to come and tell you. I didn't want you to think I'd invite you somewhere and then not be round to see did you want to go. That would be mean, wouldn't it?'

A little line appeared between Hadiyyah's heavy black eyebrows. Barbara observed the weight of worry settle on her small shoulders, and she reflected on the way that life moulds people to be who they are. No eight-year-old girl with her hair still in plaits should have to trouble herself so much about others.

'It's more than okay,' Barbara said. 'But I plan to hold you to the invitation. Where strawberry ice cream's concerned, I draw the line at letting friends off the hook.'

Hadiyyah's face brightened. She gave a little skip. 'We'll go when Dad and I get back, Barbara. We're going away for a few days. Just a few days. Dad and I. Together. Did I already say?'

'You did.'

'I didn't know about it when I rang you, see. Only what happened is that Dad got a phone call and he said "What? *What?* When did this occur?" and the next thing I knew, he said we were going to the sea. Imagine, Barbara.' She clasped her hands to her bony little chest. 'I've never been to the sea. Have you?'

The sea? Barbara thought. Oh, yes indeed. Mildewed beach huts and suntan lotion. Donning damp swim suits with scratchy crotches. She'd spent every childhood summer holiday at the sea, trying for a tan and managing only a mixture of peeling skin and freckles.

'Not recently,' Barbara said.

Hadiyyah bounced to her. 'Why don't you come? With me and Dad? Why don't you come? It'd be *such* fun!'

'I don't really think –'

'Oh, it would, it would. We could make castles in the sand and swim in the water. We could play catch. We could run on the beach. If we take a kite, we could even –'

'Hadiyyah. Have you managed to say what you've come to say?'

Hadiyyah stilled herself at once and turned to the voice at the door. Her father stood there, watching her gravely.

'You said you would require only one minute,' he observed. 'And there is a point at which a brief visit to a friend becomes an intrusion upon her hospitality.'

'She's not bothering me,' Barbara said.

Taymullah Azhar appeared to observe her – rather than just notice her presence – for the first time. His slender shoulders shifted, the only indication of his surprise. 'What's happened to you, Barbara?' he asked quietly. 'Have you been in an accident?'

'Barbara broke her nose,' Hadiyyah informed him, going to her father's side. His arm went round her, his hand curved at her shoulder. 'And three of her ribs. She's got bandages all up and all down, Dad. I told her she should come with us to the sea. It'd be good for her. Don't you think?'

Azhar's face shuttered immediately at this suggestion. Barbara said quickly, 'A nice invitation, Hadiyyah. But my sea-going days are completely kaput.' And to the girl's father, 'A sudden trip?'

'He got a phone call,' Hadiyyah began.

Azhar interposed. 'Hadiyyah, have you said goodbye to your friend?'

'I told her how I didn't know we were going till you came in and said that –'

Barbara saw Azhar's hand tighten on his daughter's shoulder. 'You've left your suitcase open on your bed,' he told the child. 'Go and put it in the car at once.'

Hadiyyah lowered her head obediently. She said, ''Bye, Barbara,' and scampered through the door. Her father nodded at Barbara and began to follow.

'Azhar,' Barbara said. And when he stopped and turned back to her, 'Want a fag before you go?' She held the packet out towards him and met his eyes square on. 'One for the road?'

She watched him weigh the pros and cons of remaining another three minutes. She wouldn't have attempted to detain him had he not seemed so anxious to keep his daughter quiet about their journey. Suddenly Barbara's curiosity was piqued, and she sought a way to satisfy it. When he didn't answer, she decided that a prod was in order. She said, 'Heard anything from Canada?' as a form of coercion. But she hated herself the moment she'd said it. Hadiyyah's mother had been on holiday in Ontario for the eight weeks that Barbara had been acquainted with the child and her father. And daily Hadiyyah had scoured the post for cards and letters – and a birthday present – that never came. 'Sorry,' Barbara said. 'That was rotten of me.'

Azhar's face was what it always was: the most unreadable of any man's in Barbara's acquaintance. And he had no compunction about letting a silence hang between them. Barbara bore it as long as she could before she said, 'Azhar, I apologise. I was out of line. I'm always out of line. I do out of line better than anything else. Here. Have a fag. The sea will still be there if you leave five minutes later than you planned.'

Azhar relented, but slowly. His guard was up as he took the proffered packet and shook out a cigarette. While he lit it, Barbara used her bare foot to shove the other chair back from the table. He didn't sit.

'Trouble?' she asked him.

'Why should you think that?'

'A phone call, a sudden change of plan. In my business, that means only one thing: whatever the news is, it isn't good.'

'In your business,' Azhar pointed out.

'And in yours?'

He lifted his cigarette to his mouth and spoke behind it. 'A small family matter.'

'Family?' He'd never spoken of family. Not that he'd ever spoken of anything personal. He was as guarded a creature as Barbara had ever encountered outside the criminal fraternity. 'I didn't know you had family in this country, Azhar.'

'I have significant family in this country,' he said.

'But on Hadiyyah's birthday, no one –'

'Hadiyyah and I do not see my family.'

'Ah. I get it.' Except she didn't. He was rushing off to the sea on a small family matter concerning a significant family that he never saw?

'Well, how long d'you expect to be gone? Anything I can do for you here? Water the plants? Collect the post?'

He appeared to consider this far longer than the conventional politeness of the offer required. Finally he said, 'No. I think not. There's merely been a minor upheaval among my relations. A cousin phoned to give voice to his concerns, and I go to them to offer my support and my expertise in these matters. It is a question of a few days away. The . . .' He smiled. He had – when he used it – a most attractive smile, perfect white teeth gleaming against his pecan skin. 'The plants and the post can wait, I dare say.'

'Which direction are you heading in?'

'East.'

'Essex?' And when he nodded, she went on with, 'Lucky you, then, to be out of this heat. I've half a mind to follow and spend the next seven days with my bum firmly planted in the old North Sea.'

He didn't react other than to say, 'I'm afraid that Hadiyyah and I will see little of the water on this trip.'

'That's not what she thinks. She'll be disappointed.'

'She must learn to live with disappointment, Barbara.'

'Really? She seems a bit young to be racking up a score in the life's-bitter-lessons game, wouldn't you say?'

Azhar ventured closer to the table and put his cigarette out in the ashtray. He was wearing a short-sleeved cotton shirt and as he leaned past her, Barbara caught the crisp clean scent of his clothing and she saw the fine black hairs on his arm. Like his daughter, he was delicately boned. But he was darker in colouring. 'Unfortunately, we cannot dictate the age at which we learn how much life is going to deny us.'

'Is that what life did to you, then?'

'Thank you for the cigarette,' he said.

He was gone before she could get another dig in. And when he was gone, Barbara wondered why the hell she felt the need to dig at him at all. She told herself it was for Hadiyyah's sake: someone had to act in the child's best interests. But the truth was that Azhar's impermeable self-containment acted as a spur upon her, pricking at the sides of her need to know. Damn it all, who was the man? What was his solemnity all about? And how did he manage to hold the world at bay?

She sighed. The answers certainly wouldn't come from slouching sluglike at the dining table with a burning fag hanging from her lip. Forget it, she thought. It was too bloody hot to think about anything, let alone to come up with believable rationales for the behaviour of her fellow humans. Sod her fellow humans, she decided. In this heat, sod the whole flaming world. She reached for the small pile of envelopes on the table.

Looking for love? leered up at her. The question was superimposed upon a heart. Barbara slid her index finger under the flap and pulled out a single-page questionnaire. *Tired of trial-and-error dating?* it asked across the top. *Willing to take a chance that finding the Right Person is better handled by computer than by luck?* And then followed the questions, asking about age, about interests, about occupation, salary, and level of education. Barbara considered filling it out for her own amusement, but after she evaluated her interests and realised that she had virtually none worth mentioning – who really wanted to be computer-matched with a woman who read *The Lusty Savage* to lull herself to sleep? – she screwed up the questionnaire and lobbed it towards the rubbish bin in her matchbox kitchen. She gave her attention to the rest of the post: BT bill asking to be paid, an advert for private health insurance, and an offer of a deluxe week for two on a cruise ship described as a floating paradise of pampering and sensuality.

She could do with the cruise ship, she realised. She could do with a week of deluxe pampering, with or without the accompanying sensuality. But a glance at the brochure's photographs revealed slim and tanned young things perched on bar stools and lounging poolside, their fingernails painted and lips pouting glossily, attended by men with hirsute chests. Barbara pictured herself floating daintily among them. She sniggered at the thought. She hadn't been in a bathing suit in years, having come to believe that some things are better left to draperies, shrouds, and the imagination.

The brochure went the way of the questionnaire before it. Barbara stubbed out her cigarette with a sigh and looked about the bungalow for further employment. There wasn't any. She trundled over to the divan, searched out the television's remote, and decided to give herself over to an afternoon of channel surfing.

She pressed the first button. Here was the Princess Royal, looking slightly less equine than usual as she inspected a Caribbean hospital for disadvantaged children. Boring. Here was a documentary on Nelson Mandela. Another snore. She picked up the pace and surfed through an Orson Welles film, a Prince Valiant cartoon, two chat shows, and a golf tournament.

And then her attention was riveted to the sight of a phalanx of police constables facing down a mass of dark-skinned protestors. She thought she was about to settle in for a good wallow with either Tennison or Morse when a red band appeared at the bottom of the screen with the word LIVE superimposed on it. A breaking news story, she realised. She watched it curiously.

She told herself it was no different from an archbishop's attention being drawn to a story about Canterbury Cathedral. She was, after all, a cop. Still, she felt a twinge of guilt – she *was* supposed to be on holiday, wasn't she? – as she avidly watched the story unfold.

Which was when she saw *Essex* printed on the screen. Which was when she twigged that the dark-skinned faces below the protest signs were Asian. Which was when she upped the volume on the television.

'– body was found yesterday morning, apparently in a pillbox on the beach,' the young reporter was saying. She appeared to be one or two leagues out of her depth because as she spoke, she smoothed her carefully coiffed blonde hair into place and cast apprehensive glances at the swarm of people behind her, as if afraid they might seek to recoif her without her permission. She put a hand to her ear to block out the noise.

'Now! Now!' the protestors were shouting. Their signs – crudely lettered – called for *Justice At Once!* and *Action!* and *The Real Truth!*

'What began as a very special town council meeting ostensibly called to discuss redevelopment issues,' Blondie recited into her microphone, 'disintegrated into what you see behind me now. I've managed to make contact with the protest leader, and –' Blondie was jostled to one side by a burly constable. The picture veered crazily as the camera operator apparently lost his footing.

Angry voices shouted. A bottle soared in the air. A chunk of concrete followed. The phalanx of police constables raised their protective Plexiglas shields.

'Holy shit,' Barbara murmured. What the hell was happening?

The blonde reporter and the cameraman regained their footing. Blondie pulled a man into the camera's range. He was a muscular Asian somewhere in his twenties, long hair escaping from a ponytail, one sleeve ripped away from his shirt. He shouted over his shoulder, 'Get *away* from him, damn you!' before turning to the reporter.

She said, 'I'm standing here with Muhannad Malik, who –'

'We've no bloody intention of putting up with evasions, distortions,

21

and outright lies,' the man broke in, speaking into the microphone. 'The time has come for our people to demand equal treatment under the law. If the police won't see this death for what it is – a hate crime and an out-and-out murder – then we intend to seek justice in our own way. We have the power, and we have the means.' He swung away from the microphone and used a loud hailer to shout to the people in the crowd. 'We have the power! We have the means!'

They roared. They surged forward. The camera swung wildly and flickered. The reporter said, 'Peter, we need to get to safer ground,' and the picture switched to the station's news studio.

Barbara recognised the grave-faced newsreader at the pinewood desk. Peter Somebody. She'd always loathed him. She loathed all men with sculptured hair.

'To recap on the situation in Essex,' he said. And he did just that, as Barbara lit another cigarette.

The body of a man, Peter explained, had been discovered on Saturday in a pillbox on the beach by an early-morning walker in Balford-le-Nez. So far, the victim had been identified as one Haytham Querashi, recently arrived from Karachi, Pakistan, to wed the daughter of a wealthy local businessman. The town's small but growing Pakistani community was calling the death a racially motivated crime – hence, nothing short of murder – but the police had yet to declare what sort of investigation they were pursuing.

Pakistani, Barbara thought. *Pakistani*. Again she heard Azhar say, '. . . a minor upheaval among my relations.' Yes. Right. Among his *Pakistani* relations. Holy shit.

She looked back at the television, where Peter was continuing to drone on, but she didn't hear him. What she heard was the tumult of her own thoughts.

They told her that having a substantial Pakistani community outside a metropolitan area was such an anomaly in England that for there to be two such communities along the coast in Essex would be wildly coincidental. With Azhar's own words telling her that he was on his way to Essex, with his departure preceding this newsflash of what was clearly a riot-in-the-making, with Azhar heading off to deal with 'a minor upheaval' within his family . . . There was a limit to Barbara's tolerance of coincidence. Taymullah Azhar was on his way to Balford-le-Nez.

He planned, he'd said, to offer his 'expertise in these matters'. But *what* expertise? Brick throwing? Riot planning? Or did he expect to get involved in an investigation by the local police? Did he hope for access to the forensic lab? Or, more ominously, did he intend to become involved in the sort of community activism she'd just witnessed on the television, the sort that invariably led to major violence, arrest, and a stretch in the nick?

'Damn,' Barbara muttered. What in God's name was the man thinking? And what in bloody hell was he doing, taking a very special eight-year-old girl along for the ride?

Barbara gazed out of the door, in the direction Hadiyyah and her father had taken. She thought of Hadiyyah's bright smile and the plaits that twitched like living things when she skipped. Finally, she stubbed out her cigarette among the others.

She went to the clothes cupboard and pulled her haversack off the shelf.

Chapter Two

———◆———

Rachel Winfield decided to close the shop ten minutes early, and she didn't feel one twinge of guilt. Her mother had left at half-past three – it was the day of her weekly 'do' at the Sea and Sun Unisex Hairstylists – and although she'd left firm instructions about what constituted doing one's duty at the till, for the past thirty minutes not a single customer or even a browser had come inside.

Rachel had more important things to attend to than watching the second hand of the wall clock slowly circumnavigate the dial. So after carefully checking to make sure that the display cases were locked, she bolted the front door. She flipped the *Open* sign to *Closed* and went to the stockroom, where she took from its hiding place behind the rubbish bins a perkily wrapped box that she'd done her best to keep from her mother's eyes. Tucking it under her arm, she ducked into the alley where she kept her bike. The box she placed lovingly in the basket. Then she guided the bike round the corner to the front of the shop and took a moment to doublecheck the door.

There'd be hell to pay if she was caught leaving early. There'd be permanent damnation if she not only left early but also left without locking up properly. The bolt was old and sometimes it stuck. Common sense called for a quick, reassuring, and thankfully foiled attempt to get inside. Good, Rachel thought when the door didn't budge. She was in the clear.

Although it was late in the day, the heat still hadn't abated. The regular North Sea wind – which made the town of Balford-le-Nez so nasty in the depths of winter – wasn't gusting at all this afternoon. Nor had it gusted for the last two weeks. It wasn't even sighing enough to stir the bunting that hung dispiritedly across the High Street.

Beneath those crisscrossing red and blue triangles of manufactured gaiety, Rachel pedalled determinedly southward, heading for the upmarket part of the town. She wasn't going home. Had she been doing so, she would have been riding in the opposite direction, along the seafront and beyond the industrial estate to the three truncated streets of terraced houses where she and her mother lived in frequently strained good will. Rather, she was heading to the home of her oldest, best, and only true friend, upon whose life recent tragedy had fallen.

Must remember to be sympathetic, Rachel told herself sternly as she pedalled. Must remember *not* to mention Clifftop Snuggeries before I tell her how bad I feel. Although I don't feel bad like I ought to feel, do I? I feel like a door's been opened wide and I want to rush through it while I got the chance.

Rachel hiked her skirt above her knees to make the pedalling easier and to keep the thin, diaphanous material from becoming snagged in the greasy chain. She'd known she was going to pay a call on Sahlah Malik when she'd dressed this morning, so she probably should have worn something more suitable for a long bicycle ride in the late afternoon. But the length of the skirt she'd chosen favoured her best features – her ankles – and Rachel was a young woman who knew that, having been given so little to work with in the looks department by the Almighty, she had to accentuate what positives she had. So she regularly wore skirts and shoes that flattered her ankles, always hoping the casual gazes that fell upon her would overlook the mess of her face.

She'd heard every word in the book applied to her in her twenty years: *homely, arse-ugly, bagged out,* and *grotty* were the usual adjectives. *Cow, mare,* and *sow* were the nouns of choice. She'd been the butt of jokes and of ceaseless bullying throughout her schooldays, and she'd early learned that for people like her, life presented three clear choices: cry, run away, or learn to fight back. She'd chosen the third, and it was her willingness to take on all comers that had won her Sahlah Malik as a friend.

Her best friend, Rachel thought. Through thick and through thin. They'd had the thick of it since they were nine years old. For the past two months, they'd had the thin. But things were going to change for the two of them. Rachel was nothing if not certain of that.

She teetered up the slope of Church Road, past St John's graveyard where the flowers drooped from their stalks in the heat. She followed the curve by the railway station's grime-covered walls and panted up the sharp acclivity that led to the better neighbourhoods with their rolling lawns and leafy streets. This section of the town was called The Avenues, and Sahlah Malik's family lived on Second, a five-minute walk from the Greensward, that stretch of perfect lawn beneath which two rows of beach huts perched above the sea.

The Maliks' house was one of the grander residences in the neighbourhood, with wide lawns, gardens, and a small pear orchard where Rachel and Sahlah had shared childhood secrets. It was very English: tile-clad, half-timbered, and diamond-paned in the fashion of another century. Its worn front door was studded with iron, its multiple chimneys were reminiscent of Hampton Court, and its detached garage – tucked at the back of the property – resembled a medieval fortress. To look at it, one would never guess that it was less than ten years old. And while one might conclude that its inhabitants were among the wealthiest people in Balford, one would also never guess that those same inhabitants had originated in Asia, in a land of *mujahidin*, mosques, and *fiqh*.

Rachel's face was beaded with perspiration by the time she bumped over the kerb and opened the front gate. She gave a sigh of pure pleasure as she passed beneath the fresh-scented coolness of a willow tree. She stayed there a moment, telling herself it was to catch her breath but all the while knowing it was also to plan. In her twenty years, she'd never gone to the home of anyone who'd been recently bereaved in such a fashion as her friend. And now she had to concentrate on what to say, how to say it, what to do, and how to act. The last thing she wanted was to put a foot wrong with Sahlah.

Leaving her bike propped against a garden urn abloom with geraniums, Rachel plucked the wrapped package from her basket and advanced on the front door. Carefully, she sought the best opening remarks. *I'm so terribly sorry . . . I came as soon as I could . . . I didn't want to phone 'cause it seemed so impersonal . . . This changes things awfully . . . I know how you loved him . . .*

Except that last was a lie, wasn't it? Sahlah Malik hadn't loved her intended husband at all.

Well, it was no matter now. The dead couldn't come back to demand an accounting from the living, and there was very little point in dwelling upon her friend's lack of feeling for a man who'd been chosen from complete strangers to be her spouse. Of course, he wouldn't *be* her spouse now. Which nearly made one think . . . But no. Rachel forced all speculation from her mind. With her package tucked under her arm, she rapped on the door.

It swung open under her knuckles. As it did so, the unmistakable sound of cinematic background music rose over voices speaking a foreign tongue in the sitting room. The language was Urdu, Rachel guessed. And the film would be yet another catalogue purchase made by Sahlah's sister-in-law, who doubtless sat on a cushion in front of the video player in her usual fashion: with a bowl of soapy water in her lap and dozens of her gold bangles piled into it for a thorough wash.

Rachel wasn't far off the mark. She called out, 'Hullo? Sahlah?' and ventured to the sitting-room doorway. There she found Yumn, the young wife of Sahlah's brother, seeing not to the care of her copious jewellery, but rather to the mending of one of her many *dupattās*. Yumn was sewing industriously upon the hem of this scarf, and she was making an inexpert hash of the effort.

She gave a little shriek when Rachel cleared her throat. She threw her hands up and let the needle, the thread, and the scarf fly in three different directions. She was, unaccountably, wearing thimbles on every finger of her left hand. These flew off as well. 'How you frightened me!' she exclaimed energetically. 'Oh, my goodness, my goodness, Rachel Winfield. And on *this* of all days, when *nothing* on earth should discompose me. The female cycle is a delicate thing. Has no one told you that?'

Sahlah had always referred to her sister-in-law as born for RADA but bred for nothing. The former certainly appeared to be the truth. Rachel's entry had hardly been surreptitious. But Yumn seemed willing to milk it for whatever power its meagre spotlight offered. She was shining this light on her 'female cycle', as she called it, and she used her hands to cradle her stomach in the event that Rachel failed to catch her meaning. This was hardly likely. If Yumn ever thought or spoke of anything besides her intention of achieving a third pregnancy – within thirty-seven months of marriage and before her second son was eighteen months old – Rachel wasn't aware of it.

'Sorry,' she said. 'I didn't mean to startle you.'

'I do hope not.' Yumn looked about for her scattered sewing. She squinted at the scarf, using her good right eye and closing the left one, whose wandering she generally hid by draping a *dupattā* to cast a shadow over it. When she seemed intent upon returning to her work and ignoring Rachel indefinitely, Rachel spoke again.

'Yumn, I've come to visit Sahlah. Is she about?'

Yumn shrugged. 'She's always about, that girl. Although whenever I call for her, she goes stone deaf. She needs a proper beating, but there's nobody willing to give her one.'

'Where is she?' Rachel asked.

'"Poor little thing", they think,' Yumn continued. '"Leave her be. She's grieving." *Grieving*, mind you. What an amusing thought.'

Rachel felt alarmed at this remark, but out of loyalty to Sahlah she did her best to hide it. 'Is she here?' she asked patiently. 'Where is she, Yumn?'

'She's gone upstairs.' As Rachel turned from the sitting room, Yumn added, 'Where she's prostrate with mourning, no doubt,' with a malicious chuckle.

Rachel found Sahlah in the bedroom at the front of the house, the room that had been fitted out for Yumn's two small boys. She stood at an ironing board, where she was folding a mound of freshly dried nappies into perfect, neat squares. Her nephews – a toddler of twenty-seven months and his younger brother – lay in a single cot near the open window. They were fast asleep.

Rachel hadn't seen her friend for a fortnight. Their last words hadn't been pleasant ones, so despite her rehearsal of prefatory remarks, she felt gawky and overcome with awkwardness. This sensation didn't arise solely from the misunderstanding that had grown between them, however. Nor did it arise from the fact that in entering the Maliks' house, Rachel was aware of walking into another culture. Instead, it rose from the acute appreciation she had – refreshed each time she looked at her friend – of the physical differences between herself and Sahlah.

Sahlah was lovely. In deference to her religion and to the wishes of her parents, she wore the modest *shalwār-qamīs*. But neither the baggy trousers nor the tunic that hung below her hips managed to detract from her looks. She had nutmeg skin and cocoa eyes, with lashes that were thick and long. She wore her dark hair in one dense plait that hung to her waist, and when she raised her head as Rachel said her name, wispy curls like cobwebs fell round her face. The sole imperfection she possessed was a birthmark. It was strawberry in colour and strawberry in shape, high on her cheekbone like a tattoo. It darkened perceptibly when her eyes met Rachel's.

Rachel started at full view of Sahlah's face. Her friend looked ill, and Rachel immediately forgot everything she'd rehearsed. Impulsively, she held out the gift she'd brought. She said, 'This is for you. It's a present, Sahlah,' and at once felt like a miserable fool.

Slowly, Sahlah brushed the wrinkles from a nappy. She made the first fold in the material, lining up the corners with intense concentration.

Rachel said, 'I didn't mean any of it. What do *I* know about love anyway? Me, of all people. And I know even less about marriage, don't I? Especially when you consider my circumstances. I mean, my mum was married for about ten minutes once. And she'd done it for love, according to her. So there you have it.'

Sahlah made two more folds in the nappy and placed it on the pile at the end of the ironing board. She walked to the window and checked on her nephews. It seemed a needless thing to do, Rachel thought. They were sleeping like the dead.

Rachel winced at the mental figure of speech. She had – she absolutely *had* – to avoid using or even thinking that word for the duration of her visit to this house. She said, 'I'm sorry, Sahlah.'

'You didn't need to bring a gift,' Sahlah replied in a low voice.

'Do you forgive me? Please say that you forgive me. I couldn't bear it if you won't forgive me.'

'You don't need to apologise for anything, Rachel.'

'That means you don't forgive me, doesn't it?'

The delicately carved bone beads of Sahlah's earrings clicked together as she shook her head. But she said nothing.

'Will you take the present?' Rachel asked. 'When I saw it, I thought of you. Open it. Please.' She wanted so much to bury the acrimony that had coloured their last conversation. She was desperate to take back her words and her accusations because she wanted to be back on their old footing with her friend.

After a moment of reflection, Sahlah gave a gentle sigh and took the box. She studied the wrapping paper before she removed it, and Rachel was pleased to see her smile at the drawings of tumbling kittens in a tangle of wool. She touched a fingertip to one of them. Then she eased the ribbon off the package and slid her finger beneath the Sellotape. When she had the top off the package, she lifted out the garment and ran her fingers along one of its golden threads.

As a peace offering, Rachel knew she had chosen well. The *sherwani* coat was long. Its collar was high. It offered respect to Sahlah's culture as well as to her religion. Worn with trousers, it would cover her completely. Her parents – whose good will and understanding were essential to Rachel's plans – could only approve. But at the same time, the coat underscored the value that Rachel placed upon her friendship with Sahlah. It was silk, liberally threaded with strands of gold. Its cost declared itself everywhere, and Rachel had dipped deeply into her savings to pay for the garment. But that was of no account if it brought Sahlah back to her.

'The colour's what caught my eye,' Rachel said. 'Burnt sienna's perfect with your skin. Put it on.' She gave a forced little laugh as Sahlah hesitated, her head bent to the coat and her index finger circling the edge of one of its buttons. Real horn, those buttons, Rachel wanted to say. But she couldn't get the words out. She was too afraid. 'Don't be shy, Sahlah. Put it on. Don't you like it?'

Sahlah placed the coat on the ironing board and folded its arms as carefully as she had done the nappies. She reached for one of the dangling ornaments on her beaded necklace, and she held it like a talisman. 'It's too much, Rachel,' she finally said. 'I can't accept it. I'm sorry.'

Rachel felt sudden tears well in her eyes. She said, 'But we always ... We're friends. Aren't we friends?'

'We are.'

'Then –'

'I can't reciprocate. I haven't the money, and even if I had ...' Sahlah went back to folding the garment, letting her sentence hang.

Rachel finished it for her. She'd known her friend long enough to realise what she was thinking. 'You'd give it to your parents. You wouldn't spend it on me.'

'The money. Yes.' *It's what we generally do* was what she didn't add. She'd said it so often over the eleven years of their friendship – and she'd repeated it endlessly since first making Rachel aware of her intentions to marry a Pakistani stranger chosen by her parents – that there was no need for her to tack the sentence on to the declarations she'd already made.

Before coming to the house, Rachel hadn't considered the possibility that her visit to Sahlah might actually make her feel worse than she'd been feeling for the last few weeks. She'd seen her future as a form of syllogism: Sahlah's fiancé was dead; Sahlah was alive; ergo, Sahlah was free to resume her position as Rachel's best friend and the dearest companion of her future life. Apparently, however, this wasn't to be.

Rachel's stomach churned. She felt light in the head. After everything she'd done, after everything she'd known, after everything she'd been told and had loyally kept to herself because that's what friends did when they were best friends, right . . . ?

'I want you to have it.' Rachel strove for the sort of tone one used when paying a visit to a house where death had paid a visit first. 'I just came to say that I'm most awfully sorry about . . . well, about your . . . loss.'

'Rachel,' Sahlah said quietly. 'Please don't.'

'I understand how bereft you must be. Despite your having known him for so short a time, I'm sure you must have come to love him. Because –' She could hear her voice tightening. It would soon be shrill. 'Because I know you wouldn't marry anyone you didn't love, Sahlah. You always said you'd never do that. So it only stands to reason that when you first saw Haytham, your heart just flew to him. And when he put his hand on your arm – his damp clammy hand – you knew he was the one. That's what happened, isn't it? And that's why you're so cut up now.'

'I know it's hard for you to understand.'

'Except you don't look cut up. At least not about Haytham. I wonder why. Does your dad wonder why?'

She was saying things she didn't mean to say. It was as if her voice had a life all its own, and there was nothing she could do to bring it under control.

'You don't know what's going on inside me,' Sahlah declared quietly, almost fiercely. 'You want to judge me by your own standards, and you can't because they're different from mine.'

'Like I'm different from you,' Rachel added, and the words were bitter. 'Isn't that right?'

Sahlah's voice softened. 'We're friends, Rachel. We've always been and we'll always be friends.'

The assertion wounded Rachel more than any repudiation could have done. Because she knew the statement was just a statement. True though it may have been, it wasn't a promise.

Rachel fished in the breast pocket of her blouse and brought out the crumpled brochure she'd been carrying with her for more than two months. She'd looked at it so often that she'd memorised its pictures and their accompanying pitch for the Clifftop Snuggeries, two-bedroomed flats in three oblong brick buildings. As their name suggested, they sat above the sea on the South Promenade. Depending upon which model one chose, the flats had either balconies or terraces, but in either case they each had a view: the Balford pleasure pier to the north or the endless grey-green stretch of sea to the east.

'These are the flats.' Rachel unfolded the brochure. She didn't hand it over because somehow she knew that Sahlah would refuse to take it from her. 'I've got enough money saved to make the down payment. I could do that.'

'Rachel, won't you try to see how things are in my world?'

'I mean, I *want* to do that. I'd see to it that your name – as well as my own – went on the deed. Each month, you'd only have to pay –'

'I can't.'

'You *can*,' Rachel insisted. 'You only think you can't because of how you've been brought up. But you don't need to live like this for the rest of your life. No one else does.'

The elder boy stirred in the cot and whimpered in his sleep. Sahlah went back to him. Neither child was covered – it was far too warm in the room for that – so there was no adjustment to make in any bedclothes. Sahlah brushed her hand lightly against the boy's forehead. Asleep, he changed positions, his rump in the air.

'Rachel,' Sahlah said, keeping her eyes on her nephew, 'Haytham is dead, but that doesn't end my obligation to my family. If my father chooses another man for me tomorrow, I'll marry him. I must.'

'*Must*? That's mad. You didn't even know him. You won't know the next one. What about –'

'No. It's what I want to do.'

Her voice was quiet, but there was no mistaking what the firmness of her tone implied. She was saying *The past is dead* without saying it. But she'd forgotten one thing. Haytham Querashi was dead as well.

Rachel went to the ironing board and finished folding the coat. She was as careful about the task as Sahlah had been about folding the nappies. She brought the hem up to meet the shoulders. She formed the sides into thin wedges which she tucked into the waist. From the cot, Sahlah watched her.

When she had returned the coat to its box and tapped the lid on it, Rachel spoke again. 'We always talked about how it would be.'

'We were little then. It's easy to have dreams when you're just a child.'

'You thought I wouldn't remember them.'

'I thought you'd outgrow them.'

The remark smarted, probably much more than Sahlah intended. It indicated the extent to which she had changed, the extent to which the circumstances of her life had changed her. It also indicated the degree to which Rachel had not changed at all. 'Like you've outgrown them?' she asked.

Sahlah's gaze faltered under Rachel's. Her hand went to one of the bars on the children's cot, and her fingers grasped it. 'Believe me, Rachel. This is what I must do.'

She looked as if she was trying to say more, but Rachel had no ability to draw inferences. She tried to read Sahlah's face, to understand what emotion and meaning underlaid her statement. But she couldn't grasp them. So she said, 'Why? Because it's your way? Because your father insists? Because you'll be thrown out of your family if you don't do like you're told?'

'All of that's true.'

'But there's more, isn't there? Isn't there more?' Rachel hurried on. 'It doesn't matter if your family throw you out. I'll take care of you, Sahlah. We'll be together. I won't let anything bad happen to you.'

Sahlah let out a soft, ironic laugh. She turned to the window and looked at the afternoon sunshine that beat relentlessly down on the garden, drying the soil, desiccating the lawn, robbing the flowers of life. 'The bad's already happened,' she said. 'Where were you to stop it?'

The question chilled Rachel as no breath of cool wind could have done. It suggested that Sahlah had come to know the lengths to which Rachel had been willing to go in order to preserve their friendship. Her courage faltered. But she couldn't leave the house without knowing the truth. She didn't want to be faced with it, because if the truth was what she thought it might be, she would also be faced with the knowledge that she herself had been the cause of their friendship's demise. But there was no way round it that Rachel could see. She had barged her way in where she wasn't wanted. Now she would have to learn the cost.

'Sahlah,' she said, 'did Haytham . . .' She hesitated. How to ask it without admitting the ugly extent to which she'd been willing to betray her friend?

'What?' Sahlah asked. 'Did Haytham what?'

'Did he mention me at all to you? Ever?'

Sahlah looked so bewildered at the question that Rachel had her answer. It was accompanied by a swelling of relief so sweet that she tasted its sugar on the back of her tongue. Haytham Querashi had died saying nothing, she realised. For the moment, at least, Rachel Winfield was safe.

From the window, Sahlah watched her friend pedal off on her bicycle. She was riding towards the Greensward. She meant to return home by way of the seafront. Her route would take her directly past the Clifftop Snuggeries, where she'd harboured her dreams despite everything Sahlah had said and done to illustrate that they'd taken different paths.

At heart, Rachel was no different from the little girl she'd been at the junior school where she and Sahlah had first stumbled across each other. She'd had plastic surgery to build relatively reasonable features out of the disastrous face she'd been born with, but beneath those features, she was still the same child: always hopeful, eager, and filled with plans no matter how impractical.

Sahlah had done her best to explain that Rachel's master plan – the plan that they should purchase a flat and live together into old age like the two social misfits they were – could not be realised. Her father would not allow her to set up house in such a fashion, with another woman and away from the family. And even if, in a fit of madness, he decided to allow his only daughter to adopt such an aberrant lifestyle, Sahlah herself could not do it. She might have done, once. But now it was too late.

Each ticking moment made it later still. Haytham's death was in so many ways her own. If he had lived, nothing would have mattered. Now he was dead, everything did.

She clasped her hands beneath her chin and closed her eyes, wishing for a breath of sea air to cool her body and still her feverish mind. Once in a novel – kept carefully hidden from her father who wouldn't have approved – she had read the term 'her mind raced wildly' about a desperate heroine and had not understood how a mind could possibly accomplish such an unusual feat. But now she knew. For her mind had been racing like a herd of gazelles ever since she'd been told that Haytham was dead. She'd considered every permutation of what to do, where to go, who to see, how to act, and what to say from that moment forward. She'd come up with no answers. As a result, she'd become completely immobilised. Now she was the incarnation of waiting. But what she waited for she could not have said. Rescue, perhaps. Or a renewal of the ability to pray, something she'd once done five times a day with perfect devotion. It was lost to her now.

'Has the troll gone, then?'

Sahlah turned from the window to see Yumn lounging in the doorway, one shoulder against the jamb. 'Are you speaking about Rachel?' Sahlah asked her.

Her sister-in-law advanced into the room, arms raised languidly as she plaited her hair. The braid that resulted was insubstantial, barely the thickness of a woman's little finger. Yumn's scalp showed through it unappealingly in places. '"Are you speaking about Rachel?"' Yumn mimicked. 'Why do you always talk like a woman with a poker up her bum?' She laughed. She'd removed the *dupattā* she always wore, and without the scarf and with her hair pulled back and away from her face, her wandering eye looked more pronounced than usual. When she laughed, the eye seemed to skitter from side to side like the yolk of an uncooked egg. 'Rub my back,' she ordered. 'I want to be relaxed for your brother tonight.'

She went to the bed where her elder child would soon start sleeping, and she kicked off her sandals and sank on to the azure counterpane. She swung her legs up and lay on her side. She said, 'Sahlah, did you hear what I said? Rub my back.'

'Don't call Rachel a troll. She can't help what she looks like any more than . . .' Sahlah stopped herself short of the final two words. *Any more than you can* would be carried straight back to Muhannad, with a suitable amount of hysteria accompanying it. And Sahlah's brother would see that she paid for the insult to the mother of his sons.

Yumn observed her, smiling slyly. She so wanted Sahlah to complete the sentence. She'd enjoy nothing more than to hear the crack of Muhannad's palm on his younger sister's cheek. But Sahlah wouldn't give her the pleasure. Instead, she joined her at the bed and watched as Yumn removed her upper garments.

'I want the oil,' she instructed. 'The one that smells of eucalyptus. And warm it in your hands first. I can't bear it cold.'

Sahlah fetched it obediently as Yumn stretched out on her side. Her body was showing the strain of two pregnancies that had followed so quickly one after the other. She was only twenty-four, but already her breasts were sagging and the second pregnancy had stretched her skin and added more weight to her sturdy frame. In another five years, if she adhered to her intention of producing annual offspring for Sahlah's brother, it was likely that she'd be nearly as wide as she was tall.

She coiled her braid to the top of her head and fastened it

there with a hair pin she took from the bedside table. She said, 'Begin.'

Sahlah did so, pouring the oil first into her palms and smoothing them together to warm it. She hated the thought of having to touch the other woman's flesh, but as the wife of her elder brother, Yumn could make demands of Sahlah and could expect them to be carried out without protest.

Sahlah's marriage would have ended Yumn's suzerainty over her, not because of the mere fact of the marriage but because it would have taken Sahlah out of her father's house and out from under Yumn's spatulate thumb. And unlike Yumn who, despite her domineering ways, was forced to put up with a mother-in-law to whom she had to subjugate herself, Sahlah would have lived with Haytham alone, or at least until such a time as he began to send to Pakistan for his family. None of that would happen now. She was a prisoner, and everyone in the household on Second Avenue – save her two small nephews – was one of her gaolers.

'That's very nice,' Yumn sighed. 'I want my skin to gleam. He likes it that way, your brother, Sahlah. It arouses him. And when he's aroused . . .' She chuckled. 'Men. What children they are. The demands they make. The desires they have. How miserable they can make us, eh? They fill us with babies at the wink of an eye. We have one son and before he's six weeks old, his father is upon us, wanting another. How lucky you are to have escaped this miserable fate, *bahin*.' Her lips curved, as if she had a source of amusement to which only she was privy.

Sahlah could tell – as Yumn intended – that she felt no misery at her fate. Rather, she revelled in her ability to reproduce and how she could use that ability: to get what she wanted, to do what she desired, to manipulate, cajole, wheedle, and demand. How had her parents come to choose such a wife for their only son? Sahlah wondered. While it was true that Yumn's father had money and her generous dowry had paid for many improvements in the Malik family's business, there had to have been other suitable women available when the elder Maliks had decided it was time to seek a bride for Muhannad. And how could Muhannad bear to touch the woman? Her flesh was like dough and her scent was acrid.

'Tell me, Sahlah,' Yumn murmured, closing her eyes in contentment as Sahlah's fingers kneaded her muscles, '*are* you pleased? It's quite all right to tell me the truth. I won't speak a word to Muhannad about it.'

'Am I pleased about what?' Sahlah reached for more oil, poured it into the bowl of her palm.

'To have escaped doing your duty. Providing sons for a husband and grandchildren for your parents.'

'I've not thought about providing my parents with grandchildren,' Sahlah said. 'You're doing that well enough.'

Yumn chuckled. 'I can't believe I've gone all these months since Bishr's birth without another on the way. Muhannad only touches me and I usually come up pregnant the next morning. And what sons your brother and I have together! What a man among men Muhannad is.'

Yumn flipped on to her back. She cupped and lifted her heavy breasts. Her nipples were the size of saucers, as dark as the copperas collected from the Nez.

'Just look at what child bearing does to a woman's body, *bahin*. How lucky you are to be slim and untouched, to have escaped this.' She gestured listlessly. 'Look at you. No varicose veins, no stretch marks anywhere, no swellings or pains. So virginal, Sahlah. You look so lovely that it makes me wonder if you really wanted to marry at all. I dare say you didn't. You wanted nothing to do with Haytham Querashi. Isn't that right?'

Sahlah forced herself to meet her sister-in-law's challenging stare. Her heartbeat felt as if it was sending blood to her face. 'Do you want me to continue with the oil?' she asked. 'Or have you had enough?'

Ever so slowly, Yumn smiled. 'Enough?' she asked. 'Oh, no, *bahin*. I've not had enough.'

From the library window, Agatha Shaw watched her grandson getting out of his BMW. She looked at her watch. He was half an hour late. She didn't like that. Businessmen were supposed to be punctual, and if Theo wanted to be taken seriously in Balford-le-Nez as the scion of Agatha and Lewis Shaw – and subsequently a person to be reckoned with – then he was going to have to learn the importance of wearing a wrist watch instead of that ridiculous slave-thing he favoured. What a ghastly gewgaw. When she was his age, if a twenty-six-year-old man had worn a bracelet, he'd have found himself at the unfortunate end of a lawsuit in which the word *sodomite* was bandied about with rather more frequency than was particularly appealing.

Agatha stepped to the side of the window's embrasure and allowed the curtains to shield her from view. She studied Theo's approach.

There were days when everything about the young man set her teeth on edge, and this was one of them. He was too like his mother. The same blond hair, the same fair skin that freckled in summer, the same athletic build. She, thank God, had gone to whatever reward the Almighty reserved for Scandinavian sluts who lose control of cars and kill themselves and their husbands in the process. But Theo's presence in his grandmother's life served always to remind her that she'd lost her youngest and most beloved child twice: first to a marriage that resulted in his disinheritance, and second to a car crash that left her – Agatha – in charge of two unruly boys under the age of ten.

As Theo approached the house, Agatha considered all the aspects of him that prompted her disapproval. His clothes were utterly wrong for his position. He favoured loosely tailored linens: jackets with shoulder pads, shirts with no collars, trousers with pleats. And always in pastel colours or fawn or buff. He wore sandals rather than shoes. Whether he put on socks had always been a matter of chance. As if all this wasn't enough to prevent potential investors from taking him seriously, since the night of her death he'd worn his execrable mother's chain and gold cross, one of those ghastly, macabre Catholic things with a tiny crucified body stretched out on it. Just the thing to ask an entrepreneur to gaze upon while attempting to convince him to put his money into the restoration, renovation, and renaissance of Balford-le-Nez.

But there was no telling Theo how to dress, how to carry himself, or how to speak when presenting the Shaw plans for the town's redevelopment. 'People either believe in the project or they don't, Gran,' would be the way he received her suggestions.

The fact that she had to make suggestions in the first place also set her teeth on edge. This was *her* project. This was *her* dream. She'd got herself on to the Balford town council for four successive terms on the strength of her dreams for the future, and it was maddening that now – because of a single blood vessel's audacious rupturing within her brain – she had to step back and regain her strength, allowing her soft-spoken, addle-brained grandson to do her talking for her. The very thought was enough to send her into another seizure, so she tried not to think of it.

She heard the front door open. Theo's sandals slapped against the parquet floor, then were muffled as he reached the first of the Persian carpets. He exchanged a few words with someone in the entry – Mary Ellis, the daily girl, no doubt, whose borderline incompetence made Agatha wish she'd been born at a time when the hired help was flogged as a matter of course. Theo said, 'The library?' and came in her direction.

Agatha saw to it that she was upright when her grandson joined her. The tea things were laid out on the table, and she'd left them there with the sandwiches curling up at the edges and a dull-sheened skin forming on the surface of the tea. They would serve as an illustration of the fact that Theo was late again. Agatha grasped the handle of her walking stick with both hands and placed it in front of her so that its three prongs could bear the bulk of her weight. This effort to seem the mistress of her physical functions caused her arms to tremble, and she was grateful that she'd donned a cardigan despite the day's heat. At least the trembling was camouflaged by the thin folds of wool.

Theo paused in the doorway. His face was shiny with perspiration and his linen shirt clung to his torso, emphasising his wiry frame. He didn't speak. Instead, he walked to the tea tray and the three-tiered sandwich stand next to it. He scooped up three egg mayonnaise sandwiches, and he ate them in rapid succession without apparent regard for their lack of freshness. He didn't even seem to notice that the tea into which he dropped a lump of sugar hadn't been hot for the last twenty minutes.

'If the summer stays like this, we're in for a good run with the pier and arcade,' Theo said. But his words sounded cautious, as if there was something besides the pier on his mind. Agatha's antennae went up. But she said nothing as he continued. 'It's too bad we can't have the restaurant done before August, because we'd be in the black before we knew it. I spoke to Gerry DeVitt about the completion date, but he doesn't think there's much hope of hurrying things up a bit. You know Gerry. If it's to be done, it's to be done properly. No cutting corners.' Theo reached for another sandwich, cucumber this time. 'And, of course, no cutting costs.'

'Is that why you're late?' Agatha needed to sit – she could feel her legs beginning to tremble along with her arms – but she refused to allow her body to overrule what her mind had dictated for it.

Theo shook his head. He carried his cup of cold tea over to her and gave her a dry kiss on the cheek. 'Hullo,' he said. 'I'm sorry for ignoring the proprieties. I had no lunch. Aren't you hot in that cardigan, Gran? Do you want a cup of tea?'

'Stop fussing over me. I don't have either foot in the grave, no matter how much you might wish it.'

'Don't be silly, Gran. Here. Sit down. Your cheeks're getting damp and you're shaking. Can't you feel it? Come on. Sit.'

She pulled her arm away from him, saying, 'Stop treating me like an imbecile. I'll sit when I'm ready. Why are you acting so strangely? What happened at the council meeting?' It was where she herself should have been and would have been had not her stroke supervened ten months before. Heat or no heat, she would have been there, bending that band of myopic misogynists to the power of her will. It had taken ages – not to mention a hefty contribution to their campaign coffers – to talk them into a Sunday meeting to consider her redevelopment plans for the seafront, and Theo along with their architect and a city planner imported from Newport, Rhode Island, had been scheduled to make the presentation.

Theo sat, holding his tea cup between his knees. He sloshed the liquid round in it, then swallowed it in one fast gulp and placed the cup on the table next to his chair. 'You haven't heard, then?'

'Heard what?'

'I went to the meeting. We all went, just as you wanted.'

'I should certainly hope so.'

'But things got derailed and the redevelopment plans didn't come up.'

Agatha forced her legs to take the required steps without faltering. She stood in front of him. 'They didn't come up? Why not? Redevelopment was what the bloody meeting was all about.'

'Yes, it was,' he replied. 'But there was a . . . well, a serious disruption, I suppose you might call it.' Theo reached for the signet ring he wore – his father's ring, it was – and played his thumb across its engraved surface. He looked distressed, and Agatha's suspicions were immediately aroused. Theo didn't like conflict, and if he was acting uneasy at the moment, it had to be because he'd failed her. Blast the boy to hell and back! All she'd asked of him was to cope with the politics of a simple presentation and he'd managed to fluff it with his usual flair.

'We're being opposed,' she said. 'One of the council opposes us. Who? Malik? Yes, it's Malik, isn't it? That mule-faced upstart provides this town with a single patch of green that he calls a park – *and* names it after one of his heathen relatives – and suddenly he decides he's a man with a vision. It's Akram Malik, isn't it? And the council's backing him instead of falling on their knees and thanking God I've the money, the connections, and the inclination to put Balford back on the map.'

'It wasn't Akram,' Theo said. 'And it wasn't about the redevelopment.' For some reason, he looked away for a moment before he met her eyes squarely. It was as if he was gathering the nerve to go on. 'I can't believe you didn't hear what happened. It's all over town. It was about this other matter, Gran. About this business on the Nez.'

'Oh, piffle the Nez.' There was *always* something coming up about the Nez, mostly questions having to do with public access to a part of the coastline that was becoming increasingly fragile. But questions about the Nez came up on a regular basis, so why some long-haired ecologist would choose the redevelopment meeting – *her* redevelopment meeting, damn everyone – to blither on about speckle-bellied gorse sitters or some other fanciful form of wildlife was beyond her comprehension. This meeting had been in the pipeline for months. The architect had taken two days from his other projects to be here and the city planner had flown to England at her personal expense. Their presentation had been initiated, calculated, orchestrated, and illustrated to the last detail, and the fact that it could be derailed by anyone's concern about a crumbling promontory of land that could be discussed at any date, in any place, at any time . . . Agatha felt her trembling worsen. She worked her way to the sofa and lowered herself to it. 'How,' she asked her grandson, 'did you let this happen? Didn't you object?'

'I couldn't object. The circumstances –'

'What circumstances? The Nez will be there next week, next month, and next year, Theo. I fail to see how a discussion about the Nez was a burning necessity today of all days.'

'It wasn't about the Nez,' Theo said. 'It was about this death. The one that occurred out there. A delegation from the Asian community came to the meeting and demanded to be heard. When the council tried to fob them off till another time –'

'Heard about what?'

'About this man who died on the Nez. Come on, Gran. The story was all over the front page of the *Standard*. You must have read it. And I know Mary Ellis must have gossiped about it.'

'I don't listen to gossip.'

He went to the tea table and poured himself another cup of cold Darjeeling. He said, 'Be that as it may,' in a tone that told her he didn't believe her for an instant, 'when the council tried to turn away the delegation, they took over the hall.'

'They? Who?'

'The Asians, Gran. There were more of them outside, waiting for a signal. When they got it, they started putting on the pressure. Shouting. Brick throwing. It got ugly fast. The police had to break it up.'

'But this was *our* meeting.'

'Right. It was. But it turned into someone else's. There was no getting round it. We'll have to reschedule when things quieten down.'

'Stop sounding so unmercifully reasonable.' Agatha thumped her stick against the carpet. It made virtually no noise, which infuriated her. What she wanted was a good bout of pan throwing. A few broken pieces of crockery too wouldn't have gone amiss. "'We'll just have to reschedule . . .'"? Where do you think that sort of attitude will get you in life, Theodore Michael? This meeting was arranged to accommodate *our* needs. We requested it. We as good as stood in a queue tugging our forelocks to get it. And now you tell me that a puling group of uneducated coloureds who no doubt didn't even take time to *bathe* before presenting themselves –'

'Gran!' Theo's fair skin was flushing. 'The Pakistanis bathe quite as often as we do. And even if they didn't, their hygiene's hardly the point, is it?'

'Perhaps you'll tell me what the point is?'

He came back to his seat, opposite her. His tea cup rattled in its saucer in a manner that made her want to howl. *When* would he learn how to carry himself like a Shaw, for God's sake?

'This man – his name was Haytham Querashi –'

'I know that very well,' she snapped.

He lifted an eyebrow. 'Ah,' he said. He placed his tea cup carefully on the table and kept his attention on it, rather than on his grandmother, as he continued. 'Then you probably also know that he was due to marry Akram Malik's daughter next week. Evidently, the Asian community doesn't believe that the police are moving fast enough to get to the bottom of what happened to Querashi. They brought their grievance to the council meeting. They were especially hard . . . well, they were hard on Akram. He tried to control them. They walked all over him. He was fairly humiliated about the whole thing. I couldn't ask for another meeting after that. It wouldn't have been right.'

Despite what the disruption had done to her own plans, Agatha found herself taking pleasure in this piece of information. In addition to the man's raising her ire by forcing his way into her special passion – redeveloping Balford – she hadn't forgiven Akram Malik for taking her place on the town council. He hadn't actually run against her, but he hadn't turned down the appointment when someone was needed to fill her place until a by-election could be called. And when that by-election had been held and she herself had been too ill to stand for the seat, Malik had done so, campaigning as earnestly as if he'd been after a seat in the House of Commons. She was delighted, therefore, at the thought of the man's embarrassment at the hands of his own community.

She said, 'That must have got right up old Akram's nose, having his precious Pakis take the mickey out of him in a public forum. How I wish I'd been there.' She saw Theo wince. Mr Compassion. He always pretended to be such a bleeding heart. 'Don't tell me you don't feel the same, young man. You're a Shaw at the end of the day and you know it. We have our ways and they have theirs, and the world would be a better place if each of us kept to our own.' She rapped her knuckles on the table to get his attention. 'Just try to tell me you disagree. You had more than one run-in with coloured boys when you were at school.'

'Gran . . .' What was that note in Theo's voice? Impatience? Ingratiation? Mollification? Condescension? Agatha's eyes narrowed upon her grandson.

'What?' she demanded.

He didn't reply at once. He touched the rim of his tea cup in a meditative gesture, looking deep in thought. 'That's not all,' he said. 'I stopped at the pier. After what went on at the meeting, I thought it would be a good idea to make sure the attractions were running smoothly. That's why I'm late, by the way.'

'And?'

'And it was a good thing that I went. There was a dust-up between five blokes out on the pier, right outside the arcade.'

'Well, I hope to God you sent them packing, whoever they were. If the pier gets the reputation as a spot for the local hooligans to aggravate tourists, we may as well lay redevelopment to rest.'

'It wasn't hooligans,' Theo said. 'It wasn't tourists either.'

'Then who?' She was becoming agitated again. She could feel an ominous rush of blood in her ears. If her pressure was on the rise, there'd be hell to pay when she next saw the doctor. And no doubt another six months of enforced convalescence, which she didn't think she could endure.

'They were teenagers,' he said. 'Just kids from the town. Asian and English. Two of them had knives.'

'This is *just* what I was talking about. When people don't keep to their own, there's trouble. If one allows immigration from a culture with no respect for human life, then one can hardly discount the prospect of representatives from that culture walking about with knives. Frankly, Theo, you were lucky the little heathens weren't carrying scimitars.'

Theo got up abruptly. He walked to the sandwiches. He picked one up, then put it down. He set his shoulders.

'Gran, the English boys were the ones with the knives.'

She recovered quickly enough to say tartly, 'Then I hope you relieved them of them.'

'I did. But that's not actually the point.'

'Then kindly tell me what the point is, Theo?'

'Things are heating up. It's not going to be pleasant. Balford-le-Nez is in for some trouble.'

Chapter Three

———◆———

Finding a suitable route to get out to Essex was a case of damned if you do and damned if you don't. Barbara faced the choice of crossing most of London and weaving her way through mind-numbing traffic or risking the vehicular uncertainties of the M25, which orbited the megalopolis and even at the best of times required one to put all plans for a timely arrival at one's destination temporarily on hold. With either choice, she would get to sweat. For the coming of evening hadn't brought with it the slightest corresponding drop in temperature.

She chose the M25. And after throwing her haversack into the back seat and grabbing a fresh bottle of Volvic, a packet of crisps, a peach, and a new supply of Players, she set off on her prescribed holiday. The fact that it wasn't a bona fide holiday didn't bother her in the least. She'd be able to say airily, 'Oh, I've been to the sea, darling,' should anyone ask her how she'd spent her time away from New Scotland Yard.

She drove into Balford-le-Nez and passed St John's Church just as its tower bells were chiming eight o'clock. She found the seaside town little changed from what it had been during the annual summer holidays she'd spent here with her family and with her parents' friends: the corpulent and odoriferous Mr and Mrs Jenkins – Bernie and Bette – who yearly followed the Haverses' rust-spotted Vauxhall in their own compulsively polished Renault, all the way from their London neighbourhood in Acton east to the sea.

The approach to Balford-le-Nez hadn't altered at all in the years since Barbara had last been here. The wheat fields of the Tendring Peninsula gave way on the north of the Balford Road to the Wade, a tidal marsh into which flowed both the Balford Channel and a narrowing estuary called the Twizzle. When the tide was in, the water of the Wade created islands out of hundreds of boggy excrescences. When the tide was out, what remained in its ebb were flats of mud and sand across which green algae stretched slimy arms. To the south of the Balford Road, small enclaves of houses still stood. Stucco-walled and squat, with sparse untended gardens, these were some of the old summer cottages occupied by families who, like Barbara's own, came to escape the seasonal heat of London.

This year, however, there was no escaping. The wind that blew in at the Mini's window and ruffled Barbara's crop of ill-cut hair was nearly as hot as the wind she'd felt as she'd driven out of London a few hours earlier.

At the junction of the Balford Road and the High Street, she braked and considered her options. She had nowhere to stay, so there was that to see to. Her stomach was rumbling, so there was food to dig up. She was in the dark as to what kind of investigation into the Pakistani man's death was actually in progress, so there was that to suss out as well.

Unlike her superior officer who never seemed to manage a decent meal, Barbara wasn't one to deny her stomach its due. Accordingly, she turned left down the gentle slope of the High Street beyond which she had her first glimpse of sea.

As had been the case in her girlhood, there was no dearth of eating establishments in Balford, and most of them appeared not to have changed hands – or been painted – in the years since she had last been a visitor. She settled on the Breakwater Restaurant, which served its meals – perhaps with ominous intent – directly next door to D.K. Corney, a business establishment whose sign announced that its employees were Funeral Directors, Builders, Decorators, and Heating Engineers. Sort of one-stop shopping, Barbara decided. She parked the Mini with one of its front tyres on the kerb and went to see what the Breakwater had to offer.

Not much, she discovered, a fact that other diners must have been aware of, because although it was the dinner hour, she found herself alone in the restaurant. She chose a table near the door in the hope of catching an errant sea breeze should one fortuitously decide to blow. She plucked the laminated menu from its upright position next to a vase of plastic carnations. After using it to fan herself for a minute, she gave it the once-over and decided that the Mega-Meal was not for her despite its bargain price (£5.50 for pork sausage, bacon, tomato, eggs, mushrooms, steak, frankfurter, kidney, hamburger, lamb chops, and chips). She settled on the restaurant's declared speciality: buck rarebit. Always grateful to know venison wasn't involved – she drew the line at eating anything with antlers – she embraced this delicacy of a poached egg on Welsh rarebit. She placed her order with a teenaged waitress sporting an impressive blemish precisely in the middle of her chin, and a moment later she saw that the Breakwater Restaurant was going to provide her with one-stop shopping of another kind.

Next to the till lay a tabloid newspaper. Barbara crossed to fetch it, trying to ignore the unsavoury sucking sounds that her trainer-shod feet made as she trod the sticky restaurant floor.

The words *Tendring Standard* were printed across the masthead in blue. They were accompanied by a lion rampant and the boast 'Essex Newspaper of the Year'. Barbara took this journal back to her table and laid it on the plastic cloth, which was artfully embossed with tiny white flowers and splattered with the remains of a busy lunchtime.

The tabloid was a well-thumbed journal from the previous afternoon, and Barbara had to look no further than the front page because the death of Haytham Querashi was apparently the first 'suspicious demise' that had occurred on the Tendring Peninsula in more than five years. As such, it was getting the journalistic red carpet treatment.

The front page displayed a picture of the victim as well as a photo of the site where his body had been found. Barbara studied both pictures.

In life, Haytham Querashi had looked innocuous enough. His dark face was pleasant but largely forgettable. The caption beneath his picture indicated that he was twenty-five years old, but he looked older. This was the result of his sombre expression, and his balding head added to the effect. He was clean-shaven and moon-faced, and Barbara guessed that he would have been given to carrying too much extra weight in middle age, had he lived to see it.

The second picture depicted an abandoned pillbox sitting on the beach at the foot of a cliff. It was built of grey, pebble-studded concrete, hexagonal in shape with an entry that was low to the ground. Barbara had seen this structure before, years ago on a walk with her younger brother when they'd noticed a boy and a girl glancing round surreptitiously before crawling inside on an overcast day. Barbara's brother had innocently wondered if the two teenagers were intent on playing war. Barbara had commented ironically that an invasion was definitely what they had in mind. She'd steered Tony clear of the pillbox. 'I c'n make machine-gun noises for them,' he'd offered. She'd assured him that sound effects were not required.

Her dinner arrived. The waitress positioned the cutlery – which appeared to be indifferently washed – and settled the plate in front of her. She'd been scrupulous about avoiding scrutiny of Barbara's bandaged face when taking her order, but now the girl gave it an earnest look and said, 'C'n I ask? D'you mind?'

'Lemonade,' Barbara said in reply. 'With ice. And I don't suppose you have a fan you can turn on, have you? I'm about to wilt.'

'Broke yesterday,' the girl said. 'Sorry.' She fingered the blemish on her chin in an unappetising fashion. 'It's just that I was thinking of doing it myself, when I've got the money. So I was wondering: did it hurt much?'

'What?'

'Your nose. Haven't you had it fixed? Isn't that why you've got all those bandages?' She picked up the table's chrome napkin dispenser and studied her reflection. 'I want a bobbed one myself. Mum says to thank God for what I have, but I say why did God invent plastic surgery if we weren't meant to use it? I'm planning to do my cheekbones as well, but the nose comes first.'

'It wasn't surgery,' Barbara said. 'I broke it.'

'Lucky you!' the girl exclaimed. 'So you got a new one on the National Health! Now, I wonder . . .' Clearly, she was meditating on the prospect of walking rapidly into a door with proboscis at the ready.

'Yeah, well, they don't ask how you want it set,' Barbara said. 'Had they bothered to inquire, I would have requested a Michael Jackson. I've always been a slave to perpendicular nostrils.' And she crackled her newspaper meaningfully.

The girl – whose nametag identified her as Suzi – leaned one hand against the table, noted what Barbara was reading, and said confidentially, 'They should never've come here, you know. This's what happens when they go where they're not wanted.'

Barbara set down her paper and speared a portion of poached egg on her fork. She said, 'Pardon?'

Suzi nodded at the newspaper. 'Those coloureds. What're they doing here anyway? Besides raising a ruckus, which they did real proper this afternoon, as a matter of fact.'

'They're trying to improve their lot in life, I expect.'

'Hmph. Why don't they improve it somewheres else? My mum said there'd be trouble eventually if we let them settle round here, and look what's happened: one of them overdoses down on the beach and all the rest start carrying on and shouting it's murder.'

'It's a drug-related death?' Barbara began to scan the paragraphs of the story for the pertinent details.

'What else could it be?' Suzi asked. 'Everyone knows they swallow bags of opium and God knows what else back in Pakistan. They smuggle it into this country in their stomachs. Then when they get here, they get locked up in a house till they do a pooh and get it all out of their system. After that they're free to go. Didn't you know? I saw that on the telly once.'

Barbara recalled the description of Haytham Querashi that she'd heard on television. The newsreader *had* identified him as recently arrived from Pakistan, hadn't he? She wondered for the first time if she'd misread all her cues in dashing out to Essex on the strength of a televised demonstration and Taymullah Azhar's mysterious behaviour.

Suzi was continuing. 'Only in this case, one of the bags broke in this bloke's insides and he crawled in that pillbox to die. That way, he wouldn't disgrace his people. They're big on *that* as well, you know.'

Barbara returned to the article and began to read it in earnest. 'Has the post-mortem been released, then?' Suzi seemed so grounded in the certainty of her facts.

'We all *know* what happened. Who needs a post-mortem? But tell that to the coloureds. When it comes out that he died of an overdose, they'll blame it on us. Just you wait and see.'

She turned on her heel and headed towards the kitchen. Barbara called, 'My lemonade?' as the door swung shut behind her.

Alone again, Barbara read the rest of the article unimpeded. The dead man, she saw, had been the Production Manager at a local business called Malik's Mustards & Assorted Accompaniments. This concern was owned by one Akram Malik who, according to the article, was also a member of the town council. At the time of his death — which the local CID had declared took place on Friday night, nearly forty-eight hours before Barbara's arrival in Balford — Mr Querashi had been eight days away from marrying the Malik daughter. It was his future brother-in-law and local political activist Muhannad Malik who, upon the discovery of Querashi's body, had spear-headed the local outcry for a CID investigation. And although the enquiry had been handed over to the CID immediately, no cause of death had as yet been announced. As a result of this, Muhannad Malik promised that other prominent members of the Asian community would be joining him to dog the investigators. 'We would be foolish to pretend we are not aware of what "getting to the truth" means when it's applied to an Asian,' Malik was quoted as saying on Saturday afternoon.

Barbara laid the newspaper to one side as Suzi returned with her glass of lemonade in which a single piece of ice bobbed with hopeful intentions. Barbara nodded her thanks and ducked her head back to the paper to forestall any additional commentary. She needed to think.

She had little doubt that Taymullah Azhar was the 'prominent member of the Asian community' whom Muhannad Malik had promised to produce. Azhar's departure from London had followed too closely on the heels of this story for the situation to be otherwise. He had come here, and Barbara knew it was only a matter of time until she stumbled upon him.

She could only imagine how he would greet her intention to run interference between him and the local police. For the first time, she realised how presumptuous she was being, concluding that Azhar would need her intercession. He was an intelligent man – good God, he was a university professor – so he had to know what he was getting into. Hadn't he?

Barbara ran her finger down the moisture on the side of her lemonade glass and considered her own question. What she knew about Taymullah Azhar she knew from conversations with his daughter. From Hadiyyah's remark, 'Dad's got a late class tonight,' she had initially concluded that he was a student. This conclusion wasn't based so much on preconception as it was on the man's apparent age. He *looked* like a student, and when Barbara had discovered that he was a professor of microbiology, her amazement had resulted more from learning his age than from not having had a racial stereotype affirmed. At thirty-five, he was two years older than Barbara herself. Which was rather maddening since he looked ten years younger.

But age aside, Barbara knew there was a certain naïveté that accompanied Azhar's profession. The ivory tower aspect of his career protected him from the realities of day-to-day living. His concerns would revolve round laboratories, experiments, lectures, and impenetrable articles written for scientific journals. The delicate dance of policework would be as foreign to him as nameless bacteria viewed beneath a microscope would be alien to her. The politics of university life – which Barbara had come to know at a distance from working on a case in Cambridge the previous autumn – were nothing like the politics of policing. An impressive list of publications, appearances at conferences, and university degrees didn't have the same cachet as experience on the job and a mind for murder. Azhar would no doubt discover this fact the first moment he spoke to the officer in charge, if that indeed was his intention.

The thought of that officer sent Barbara back to the newspaper again. If she was going to muscle in with warrant card at the ready in the hope of buffering Taymullah Azhar's presence on the scene, it would help to know who was running the show.

She began a second related story on the third page of the paper. The name she was seeking was in the first paragraph. Indeed, the entire story was about the officer in charge. Because not only was this the first 'suspicious demise' that had occurred on the Tendring Peninsula in more than five years, it was also the first investigation to be headed by a woman.

She was the recently promoted Detective Chief Inspector Emily Barlow, and Barbara muttered, 'Holy hell hallelujah,' then allowed herself a delighted grin when she saw the name. For she had done her last three detective courses at the training school in Maidstone, right at Emily Barlow's side.

This, Barbara concluded, was surely a sign: a bolt from the blue, a message from the gods, handwriting – in red neon lights, if you will – scrawled on the wall of her own future. This wasn't just a case of already being acquainted with Emily Barlow and thereby having an entrée to the investigation based on a passing familiarity with the head of the team. This was also a case of the galloping meant-to-bes, having all the hallmarks of a spate of fortuitous on-the-job training that bore the potential of sending Barbara's career shooting off like a rocket. Because the simple fact was that nowhere was there a woman more competent, more suited for criminal investigations, and more gifted in the politics of policework than Emily Barlow. And Barbara knew that what she could learn by working at Emily's side for a week was more valuable than anything covered in a textbook on criminology.

Emily's sobriquet had been 'Barlow the Beast' during the detective courses they'd taken together. In a world in which men rose to positions of authority by simple virtue of being men, Emily had blasted her way through the ranks of the CID by proving herself equal to the opposite sex in every way. 'Sexism?' she'd said one night in answer to Barbara's question on the topic. She'd been exercising furiously on a rowing machine, and she didn't slow her pace even a fraction as she replied. 'It doesn't come up. Once blokes know you'll go for their cobblers if they step out of line, they don't. Step out of line, that is.'

And on she strode with one object in mind: attaining the position of Chief Constable of Police. Since Emily Barlow had made DCI at thirty-seven, Barbara knew that she would have no trouble reaching her goal.

Barbara bolted down the rest of her dinner, paid, and left Suzi a generous tip. Her spirits higher than they'd been in days, she went back to the Mini and started off with a roar. She could keep an eye on Hadiyyah now; she could see to it that Taymullah Azhar didn't cross any lines that could cause him trouble. And as an added bonus for her efforts, she could watch Barlow the Beast at work on a case and hope that something of the DCI's remarkable stardust might rub off on to a sergeant's shoulders.

'Do I need to send Presley to assist you, Inspector?'

DCI Emily Barlow heard the pointed question from her Detective Superintendent and translated it mentally prior to answering. What he really meant was 'Did you manage to placate the Pakistanis? Because if you didn't, I have another DCI who can do the job adequately in your place.' Donald Ferguson was up for promotion to the assistant chief constable's position, and the last thing he wanted was the heretofore well-greased pathway of his career to become suddenly cratered by political potholes.

'I don't need anyone's assistance, Don. The situation's under control.'

Ferguson barked a laugh. 'I've got two men in hospital and a pod of Pakis ready to blow. Don't tell me what's under control, Barlow. Now how do things stand?'

'I told them the truth.'

'That's a brilliant move.' On the other end of the telephone line, Ferguson's voice was honeyed with sarcasm. Emily pondered why the Super was still at work at this time of the evening since the Pakistani demonstrators had long since dispersed and the superintendent had never been a man for burning the midnight oil. She knew he was in his office because she'd returned his phone call there; she'd quickly memorised the number when it had become apparent to her that returning telephonic visitations from on high was going to be part of her new job. 'That's really brilliant, Barlow,' he continued. 'May I ask how long you think it will be before he takes his people to the streets again?'

'If you'd give me more manpower, we wouldn't have to worry about the streets or anything else.'

'You've got all you're getting. Unless you want Presley.'

Another DCI? Not on your life, she thought. 'I don't need Presley. I need a visible police presence on the street. I need more constables.'

'What you need is to knock a few heads together. If you can't do that –'

'My job's not crowd control,' Emily countered. 'We're trying to investigate a murder over here, and the family of the dead man –'

'May I remind you that the Maliks are *not* Querashi's family, despite the fact that these people seem to live inside each other's pyjamas?'

Emily blotted the sweat from her forehead. She'd always suspected that Donald Ferguson was in reality an ass in pig's clothing, and virtually every remark he made served to corroborate that suspicion. He wanted to replace her. He couldn't wait to replace her. The slightest excuse and her career was history. Emily dug for patience in her reply. 'They're the family he was marrying into, Don.'

'And you told them the truth. They caused a bloody riot this afternoon and in response you told them the flaming truth! Do you have *any* idea what that does to your authority, Inspector?'

'There's no point in keeping the truth from them since they're the first group of people I'm intending to interview. Enlighten me, please. How did you expect me to conduct an investigation into a murder without telling anyone it's a murder we're dealing with?'

'Don't take that tone with me, Inspector Barlow. What's Malik done so far? Besides instigate a riot. And why the hell isn't he under arrest?'

Emily didn't point out the obvious to Ferguson: the crowd had dispersed once the television filming had ceased, and no one had been able to nab a brick thrower. She said, 'He's done exactly what he said he'd do. Muhannad Malik's never made an idle threat, and I don't imagine we can expect him to start doing so just to accommodate us.'

'Thank you for the character sketch. Now answer my question.'

'He's brought in someone from London as he said he would. An expert in what he's calling "the politics of immigration".'

'Save us,' Ferguson muttered. 'And what did you tell him?'

'Do you want my exact words or their content?'

'Stuff the innuendo, Inspector. If there's something you want to say, I suggest you say it outright and have done.'

There was plenty to say, but now was not the time. 'Don, it's late. I'm bloody tired. It feels about thirty degrees in here, and I'd like to get home sometime before dawn.'

'That can be arranged,' Ferguson said.

Jesus. What a miserable little tyrant. How he loved to pull rank. How he *needed* to do it. Had the superintendent been in her office, Emily could imagine him unzipping his trousers to demonstrate which one of them was really the man. 'I told Malik that we've called in a Home Office pathologist who'll perform the post-mortem tomorrow morning,' she replied. 'I told him Mr Querashi's death appears to be what he himself thought it was from the first: a murder. I told him the *Standard*'s got the story, and they'll run it tomorrow. Okay?'

'I like the sound of *appears*,' Ferguson said. 'It gives us elbow room to keep the lid on things. See that you start doing just that.' He rang off in his usual fashion, by dropping the receiver into its cradle. Emily held the phone away from her ear, gave it two fingers, and did the same at her end.

In the airless room that was her office, she grabbed a tissue and pressed it fully against her face. It came away greasily blotted. She would have given her big toe for a fan. She would have given her entire foot for air conditioning. As it was, she had only a lousy tin of warm tomato juice, which was better than nothing to ameliorate the effects of the day's blistering heat. She reached for this and used a pencil to prise open its pop-top. She took a swig and began to massage the back of her neck. I need a workout, she thought, and once again she acknowledged that one of the disadvantages of her line of employment – in addition to having to deal with pigs like Ferguson – was having to forego physical activity more often than was her natural inclination. If she'd had her way, she'd have been outdoors rowing hours ago, instead of doing what duty called upon her to do: return the day's phone calls.

She tossed the last of her returned telephone messages into the rubbish bin and followed them with the tomato juice tin. She was cramming a stack of file folders into her canvas hold-all when one of the WPCs assigned to the Querashi investigation came to the doorway, trailing several pages of an uncut fax.

'Here's the background on Muhannad Malik you were asking for,'

Belinda Warner announced. 'Clacton's Intelligence Unit's just sent it over. You want it now or in the morning?'

Emily held out her hand. 'Anything more than we already know?'

Belinda shrugged. ''F you ask me, he's nobody's blue-eyed boy. But there's nothing here to confirm it.'

This was what Emily had expected. She nodded her thanks and the WPC disappeared down the hall. A moment later her footsteps clattered on the stairway of the ill-ventilated building that served as the police station in Balford-le-Nez.

As was her habit, Emily glanced through the entire report quickly before making a more detailed study. One important issue stood out in her mind: her superintendent's implicit threats and career ambitions aside, the last thing the town needed was a major racial incident, which was what this death on the Nez was fast becoming. June was the beginning of the tourist season proper, and with the hot weather calling city dwellers to the sea, hopes in the community had begun to run high that the long recession was at last coming to a profitable end. But how could Balford expect an influx of visitors if racial tensions took its inhabitants into the streets for confrontations with one another? The town couldn't, and every businessman in Balford knew it. Investigating a murder while simultaneously avoiding an outbreak of ethnic conflict was the delicate prospect before her. And the fact that Balford was teetering precariously on the edge of an Asian/English clash had been made more than evident to Emily Barlow that day.

Muhannad Malik – along with his cronies in the street – had conveyed this information. Emily had known the young Pakistani since her days in uniform when, as a teenager, Muhannad Malik had first come to her attention. Having grown up on the streets of South London, Emily had early learned to handle herself in conflicts that were often multi-racial, consequently developing the hide of an elephant when it came to taunts that were directed at the colour of her skin. So as a young police constable, she'd had little patience with those who used race as the wild card in each deck from which a hand was dealt them. And Muhannad Malik was someone who, even at sixteen, had waved the race card at every opportunity.

She had learned to give little credence to his words. She simply had not allowed herself to believe that all of life's difficulties could be put down to issues of race. But now there was a death to consider, and not only a death but a bona fide murder, with its victim an Asian who had been the intended bridegroom of Muhannad Malik's own sister. It was inconceivable that, when faced with this murder, Malik would not attempt to make a connection between its occurrence and the racism he claimed to see everywhere round him.

And if a connection could be established, the result would be the very thing that Donald Ferguson feared: a seaside summer of conflict, aggression, and bloodshed, all of which had been promised by that afternoon's chaos.

In response to what had occurred both inside and outside the town council meeting, phones at the police station had begun ringing in panic as the minds of Balford's citizens made the leap from placards and bricks to the acts of extremism which had been carried out globally in the past few years. And among those phone calls had come one from the Lady Mayor, the result of which was a formal request for information made to those officers whose job it was to assemble profiles of those most likely to cross the criminal line. The pages that Emily now held represented the material that the divisional headquarters' intelligence unit had been gathering on Muhannad Malik for the past ten years.

There wasn't much, and most of it seemed innocuous, suggesting that Muhannad at twenty-six, despite his behaviour that afternoon, had mellowed from the hot-headed teenager who'd first come to the attention of the police. Emily had in her possession his school records, his GCSEs and A-level results, details of his university career, and his employment history. He was the respectful son of a member of the town's council, the devoted husband of a wife of three years, the committed father of two small children, and a competent manager in the family business. All in all, save for one blemish, he had grown into a model citizen.

But Emily knew that small blemishes frequently hid larger flaws. So she read on. Malik was the acknowledged and admitted founder of *Jum'a*, an organisation for young male Pakistanis. The association's stated purpose was to strengthen the ties between Muslims in the community and to emphasise and celebrate the myriad differences between these same Muslims and the westerners among whom they lived. Twice in the past year, *Jum'a*'s involvement had been suspected in altercations that had erupted between young Asians and their English counterparts. One was a traffic dispute that had turned into an ugly fistfight; one was an incident where bottles of cow's blood had been thrown at an Asian schoolgirl by three members of her form. Assaults had occurred in the aftermath of both these incidents, but afterwards no one had been willing to implicate *Jum'a*.

This wasn't enough to put the man out of commission. It wasn't enough even to view him somewhat askance. Still Muhannad Malik's brand of activism – put on display that day – didn't sit well with Emily Barlow. And after completing her examination of the report, she had read nothing that set her mind at rest.

She'd met him and the man he'd called his expert in the 'politics of immigration' several hours after the demonstration. Muhannad had let his companion do most of the talking, but his own presence had been impossible to ignore, as he'd no doubt intended.

He radiated antipathy. He wouldn't sit down. Rather, he stood against the wall with his arms folded across his chest, and he never took his eyes from her face. His expression of contemptuous distrust challenged Emily to try to get away with lying about Querashi's death. She hadn't considered doing so . . . at least not about the essentials.

Both to forestall any outbursts from him and subtly to under-score the unstated fact that there was no connection between the demonstration and her agreeing to see them, Emily had directed her comments to Muhannad's companion, whom he'd introduced as his cousin Taymullah Azhar. Unlike Muhannad, this man had an air of serenity about him, although as a member of Muhannad's *khāndān*, Azhar would doubtless be governed by an agenda identical to whatever the family's was. So Emily had been careful with her choice of words.

'We began with the knowledge that Mr Querashi's death appeared suspicious,' she'd told him. 'Once we'd determined that, we asked for a pathologist from the Home Office. He'll arrive tomorrow to perform the P.M.'

'Is this an English pathologist?' Muhannad asked. The implication was obvious: an English pathologist would serve the interests of the English community; an English pathologist would hardly take seriously the death of an Asian.

'I have no idea what his ethnic background is. We aren't allowed to put in requests.'

'And where does the investigation stand?' Taymullah Azhar had a curious way of speaking, courteous without being at all deferential. Emily wondered how he managed it.

'The moment the death was deemed suspicious, the site was secured,' Emily replied.

'Which site is this?'

'The pillbox at the foot of the Nez.'

'Has it been determined that he died in the pillbox?'

Azhar was very quick. Emily had to admire that. 'Nothing's been determined yet, aside from the fact that he's dead and –'

'And it took them six hours to determine that much,' Muhannad put in. 'Imagine the fire that would have been lit under the bobbies' pink bums had the body been white.'

'– and, as the Asian community suspected, it appears to be a murder,' Emily finished.

She waited for Malik's reaction. He'd been howling 'Murder' since the corpse had been discovered thirty-four hours before. She didn't wish to deny him his moment of triumph.

He took it quickly. 'As I *said*,' he asserted. 'And if I hadn't been dogging you since yesterday morning, I expect you'd be calling this an unfortunate accident.'

Emily steadied herself inwardly. Argument was what the Asian wanted. A verbal brawl with the investigating officer would be useful as a rallying cry for his people. A meticulous conversation reporting the facts would be far less so. She ignored his jibe. Instead, she said to his cousin, 'The forensic team spent approximately eight hours going over the site yesterday. They bagged evidence, and they've taken it to the lab for analysis.'

'When can you expect the results?'

'We've let them know this is a top priority.'

'How did Haytham die?' Muhannad interjected.

'Mr Malik, twice I've tried to explain to you over the phone that –'

'You don't expect me to believe that you still don't know *how* Haytham Querashi was murdered, do you? Your medical examiner has seen the body. You admitted on the phone that you saw it yourself.'

'Looking at a body doesn't reveal anything,' Emily explained. 'Your own father can tell you that much. He made the formal identification, and I dare say he's as much in the dark as we are.'

'Are we correct in assuming there was no gun involved?' Azhar asked quietly. 'No knife either? No garrotte? No rope? Because, of course, the use of these would have left marks upon the body.'

'My father said he saw only one side of Haytham's face,' Muhannad said. Then he enhanced the implication behind his comment by continuing with 'My father said he was *allowed* to see only one side of his face. The body was covered with sheeting which was rolled down to the chin for less than fifteen seconds. And that was that. What are you hiding about this murder, Inspector?'

Emily poured herself water from a jug on the table behind her desk. She offered some to the men. They both declined, which was just as well since she'd taken the last of it and she didn't much feel like sending for more. She drank thirstily, but the water tasted vaguely metallic and it left an unpleasant flavour on her tongue.

She explained to the Asians that she was hiding nothing because there was nothing this early in the investigation to hide. The time of death, she told them, had been set between half-past ten and half-past midnight on Friday night. Prior to concluding that they were dealing with a homicide, the pathologist had determined that Mr Querashi's death was not a suicide and not the result of natural causes. But that was the extent –

'Bullshit!' Muhannad offered the expletive as the only logical conclusion to her remarks. 'If you can tell it wasn't a suicide or natural and you still say it *appears* to be a murder, do you really expect us to believe that you can't tell how he was killed?'

To clarify matters further, Emily told Taymullah Azhar as if Muhannad hadn't spoken that everyone living in the vicinity of the Nez was being questioned by a team of detective constables to determine what might have been seen or heard on the night of Mr Querashi's death. Additionally, appropriate measurements had been made at the site, clothing had been bagged, tissues would be taken from the body for microscopic analysis, blood and urine samples would go to the toxicologist, background information –

'She's stalling, Azhar.' Emily had to give Muhannad credit for the observation. He was very nearly as quick as his cousin. 'She doesn't want us to know what happened. Because if we know, we'll take to the streets again and this time we won't clear out till we have the answers and justice. Which, believe me, is exactly what they do *not* want at the beginning of their tourist season.'

Azhar raised a hand to silence his cousin. 'And photographs?' he asked Emily quietly. 'You took them, of course.'

'That's always done first. The entire site is photographed, not only the body.'

'May we see these, please?'

'I'm afraid not.'

'Why?'

'Because as we've determined the death is a homicide, no element of the formal investigation can be shared with the public. It just isn't done.'

'And yet information is leaked to the media quite frequently in the midst of an investigation of this kind,' Azhar pointed out.

'Perhaps it is,' Emily said, 'but not by the officer in charge.'

Azhar observed her with large, intelligent brown eyes. If the room hadn't been insufferably hot already, Emily knew she would have flushed under his scrutiny. As it was, the heat was her alibi. Everyone in the building – save the Asians – was crimson with discomfort, so her own colouring was indication of nothing.

'In what direction do you go from here?' he finally asked.

'We wait for all the reports to come in. And we place everyone who knew Mr Querashi under suspicion. We'll begin interviewing –'

'– everyone brown who knew him,' Muhannad concluded.

'I didn't say that, Mr Malik.'

'You didn't have to, Inspector.' He made her rank sound too polite to indicate anything other than his scorn for it. 'You have no intention of pursuing this murder into the white community. If you had your way, you probably wouldn't bother to pursue it as the murder it is. And don't bother to deny the accusation. I've a bit of experience in how the police treat crimes committed against my people.'

Emily didn't rise to this additional baiting, and Taymullah Azhar gave no indication he'd even heard his cousin. He merely said, 'Since I didn't know Mr Querashi, may I have access to the photographs of his body? It would set my family's mind at rest to know the police are hiding nothing from us.'

'I'm sorry,' Emily said in reply.

Muhannad shook his head, as if he'd expected this answer all along. He said to his cousin, 'Let's get out of here. We're wasting our time.'

'Perhaps not.'

'Come on. This is bullshit. She's not going to help us.'

Azhar looked thoughtful. 'Are you willing to meet our needs, Inspector?'

'In what way?' Emily was immediately wary.

'Through compromise.'

'Compromise?' Muhannad echoed. 'No. No way, Azhar. If we compromise, we'll end up watching the carpet being lifted and Haytham's murder being swept –'

'Cousin.' Azhar glanced his way. It was the first time he'd even looked at him. 'Inspector?' he repeated, turning back to Emily.

'There can be no compromise in a police investigation, Mr Azhar. So I don't understand what you're suggesting.'

'What I'm suggesting is a way to assuage the community's most pressing concerns.'

She decided to read the implication at its most potentially efficacious: he could be suggesting a way to keep the Asians in line. That would certainly serve her interests. She replied carefully. 'I won't deny that the community's foremost in my thoughts,' she said, and waited to see where he was heading.

'Then I would propose regular meetings between you and the family. This will allay all of our concerns – not only among the family but also among the larger community – as to how you're proceeding with your enquiry into Mr Querashi's death. Will you agree to that?'

He waited patiently for her answer. His expression was as bland as it had been from the first. He was acting as if nothing – least of all peace in Balford-le-Nez – depended upon her willingness to cooperate. Watching him, Emily suddenly realised he'd anticipated every one of her previous answers, having planned to end up with this suggestion as the logical outcome of everything she'd said. She'd just been outmanoeuvred by the two of them. They'd played a mild variation of good cop/bad cop, and she'd fallen for it like a schoolgirl arrested for pinching sweets.

'I'd like to cooperate as fully as possible,' she said, choosing words with care to avoid committing herself. 'But in the midst of an investigation, it's difficult to guarantee that I'll be available when you want me.'

'A convenient response,' Muhannad said. 'I suggest we end this charade, Azhar.'

'I suspect you're drawing an inference I don't intend,' Emily told him.

'I know bloody well what you intend: letting anyone who raises a hand against us get away with it. And with murder as well.'

'Muhannad,' Taymullah Azhar said quietly. 'Let's give the inspector an opportunity to compromise.'

But Emily didn't want to compromise. In an investigation, she didn't want to find herself obliged to have meetings at which she would have to watch her every step, guard her every word, and maintain her temper. She didn't have the inclination for the game.

More important, she didn't have the time. She was already twenty-four hours behind where she should have been. But Taymullah Azhar had just given her a way out, even if he did not realise the fact. 'Will the family accept a substitute for me?'

'What sort of substitute?'

'Someone to liaise between you – the family and the community – and the investigating officers. Will you accept that?' And go on your bloody way, she added silently. And keep your fellows in line, at home, present at their jobs, and off the damn streets.

Azhar exchanged a look with his cousin. Muhannad shrugged abruptly. 'We accept,' Azhar said, getting to his feet. 'With the proviso that this individual will be replaced by you should we find it necessary to reject him as biased, ignorant, or deceiving.'

Emily had agreed to the condition, after which the two men had left her. She'd blotted her face with a tissue and rubbed it to bits against the sweat on the back of her neck. Picking the tissue fragments off her damp skin, she'd returned her phone calls. She'd talked to her superintendent.

Now, having read the intelligence report on Muhannad Malik, she jotted down the name 'Taymullah Azhar' and requested a similar report on him. Then she looped the strap of her hold-all over her shoulder and switched out the lights in her office. Having dealt with the Muslims, she'd bought a little time. And time counted for everything when dealing with murder.

Barbara Havers found the Balford police station on Martello Road, a lane of shambling red-brick structures that marked yet another route to the sea. The station was housed in one of these. It was a gabled and many-chimneyed Victorian building that had doubtless once housed one of the town's more prominent families. An antique blue light whose glass shade was embellished with the white word *Police* identified the building's current use.

As Barbara pulled to a halt in front of it, evening floodlights came on, arcing shells of incandescence against the station's façade. A female figure was coming out of the front door, and she paused to adjust the strap of a bulky shoulder bag. Barbara hadn't seen Emily Barlow in eighteen months, but she recognised her instantly. Tall, wearing a white tank top and dark trousers, the DCI had the broad shoulders and the well-defined biceps of the dedicated triathlete that she was. She may have been approaching forty, but her body was timelocked at twenty. In her presence – even at a distance and in the growing darkness – Barbara felt as she had done when they'd taken their courses together: a candidate for liposuction, a wardrobe makeover, and six intensive months with a personal trainer.

'Em?' Barbara called quietly. 'Hullo. Something told me I'd find you still hard at it.'

At the initial sound of Barbara's voice, Emily's head rose sharply. But by the end of the other woman's greeting, she'd stepped away from the station door and approached the pavement. She said, 'Good God. Is that Barb Havers? What the devil are you doing in Balford?'

How exactly would it play? Barbara wondered. *I'm trailing an exotic Pakistani and his kid in the hope of keeping them out of the nick.* Oh, yes, DCI Emily Barlow was certain to go for that strange tale in a major way. 'I'm on holiday,' Barbara settled upon saying. 'I've just got in. I read about the case in the local rag. I saw your name and thought I'd come along to suss out the situation.'

'That sounds like a busman's holiday.'

'Can't keep my fingers out of the pie. You know how it is.' Barbara fished in her bag for her cigarettes but remembered at the last moment not only that Emily didn't smoke but also that she was always willing to go one or two rounds with anyone who did. Barbara relinquished the Players and fumbled for the Juicy Fruit instead. 'Congratulations on the promotion,' she added. 'Bloody hell, Em. You're climbing fast.' She folded the stick of gum into her mouth as the DCI joined her.

'Congratulations may be premature. If my Super has his way, I'm back to constable.' Emily frowned. 'What happened to your face, Barb? You look like hell.'

Barbara made a mental note to remove the bandages as soon as she was within spitting distance of a mirror. 'I forgot to duck. On my last case.'

'I hope he looks worse. Was it a *he*?'

Barbara nodded. 'He's in the nick for murder.'

Emily smiled. 'Now that's excellent news.'

'Where are you heading?'

The DCI shifted her weight and that of her hold-all and ran a hand through her hair in the habitual manner that Barbara remembered. It was jet black hair, dyed punk and cut punk, and on any other woman her age it would have looked absurd. But not on Emily Barlow. Emily Barlow didn't do absurd, in appearance or in anything else. 'Well,' she said frankly, 'I was supposed to meet a gentleman friend for a few discreet hours of moonlight, romance, and what usually follows moonlight and romance. But to tell you the truth, his charms have just about run their course, so I cancelled. Somewhere along the line I knew he'd start whingeing about the wife and kids, and I just wasn't up to holding his hand through another attack of the galloping guilts.'

The reply was vintage Emily. She'd long ago relegated sex to just another aerobic activity. Barbara said, 'Have you time for a chat, then? About what's going on?'

The DCI hesitated. Barbara knew she would be considering the propriety of the request. She waited, understanding that Emily was unlikely to agree to any action that would jeopardise either the case itself or her newly acquired position. She finally glanced back at the building and seemed to come to a decision of some sort. She said, 'Have you eaten, Barb?'

'At the Breakwater.'

'That was courageous. I can imagine your arteries hardening even as we speak. Well, I haven't had a bite since breakfast and I'm heading home. Come along. We can talk while I have my dinner.'

They wouldn't need the car, she added as Barbara fished her keys from her lumpy shoulder bag. Emily lived just at the top of the street, where Martello Road became the Crescent.

It took them less than five minutes to walk there, at a brisk pace that Emily Barlow set. Her house stood at the near end of the Crescent. It was the last in a row of nine terraced dwellings that appeared to be in various stages of either renaissance or decay. Emily's belonged to the former group: three storeys of scaffolding fronted it.

'You'll have to pardon the mess.' Emily led Barbara up the eight cracked front steps and on to a shallow porch that was walled with chipped Edwardian tiles. 'It'll be a real showpiece when I've got it done, but right now finding the time to work on it is the biggest problem.' She shouldered open a paint-stripped front door. 'Back here,' she said, heading down a steamy corridor that was redolent of sawdust and turpentine. 'It's the only part that I've managed to get into remotely livable condition.'

If Barbara had had any thoughts of dossing down with Emily Barlow, she gave them a decent burial when she saw what *back here* was like. Emily appeared to be living entirely in the airless kitchen. Not much more than a cupboard-sized room, it contained a refrigerator, a spirit stove, and the requisite sink and work tops. But in addition to these features typical of a kitchen, crammed into the room with them were a camp bed, a card table, two folding metal chairs, and an antique bathtub of the sort once used before the days of indoor plumbing. Barbara didn't want to ask where the toilet was.

A single bare bulb from the ceiling served as illumination, although a torch and a copy of *A Brief History of Time* by the camp bed indicated that Emily did some recreational reading – if one could actually call astro-physics recreational reading – by additional light while in bed. And bed consisted of a sleeping bag and plump pillow with a case decorated with Snoopy and Woodstock flying the World War I doghouse above the fields of France.

It was as odd a living environment as any Barbara could have imagined for the Emily Barlow she'd known at Maidstone. If she'd taken the time to picture anything in the way of digs for the DCI, it would have been something spare and modern with an emphasis on glass, metal, and stone.

Emily seemed to read her thoughts because she dumped her hold-all on the work top and leaned against it with her hands in her pockets, saying, 'It takes my mind off the job. When I finish renovating this place, I'll get another. That and having a regular bonk with a willing bloke are what keep me sane.' She cocked her head. 'I haven't yet asked. How's your mother, Barb?'

'Speaking of sane . . . or otherwise?'

'Sorry. I didn't mean the connection.'

'Don't apologise. I didn't take offence.'

'Do you still have her with you?'

'I couldn't cope.' Barbara sketched the details for the other woman, feeling as she always felt when reluctantly revealing that she'd confined her mother to a private home: guilty, ungrateful, selfish, unkind. It made no difference that her mother was in better hands than she'd ever been living with Barbara. She was still her mother. The debt of birth would always hang between them, no matter that no child ever seeks to incur it.

'That must have been rough,' Emily said when Barbara concluded. 'You can't have made the decision easily.'

'I didn't. But it still feels like payback.'

'What for?'

'I don't know. For life, I suppose.'

Emily nodded slowly. She seemed to be examining Barbara and under her scrutiny, Barbara felt her skin begin itching beneath the bandages. It was miserably hot in the room and although the single window was open – *and* painted black for some reason – not even the faint promise of a breeze came into the kitchen.

Emily roused herself. 'Dinner,' she said. She went to the fridge and squatted in front of it, bringing out a container of yoghurt. She took a large bowl from a cupboard and spooned yoghurt into it in three huge globs. She reached for a packet of dried fruit and nuts. 'This heat,' she said, pausing to rake her fingers through her hair. 'God almighty. This bloody *heat*.' She ripped the packet open with her teeth.

'The worst kind of weather for a CID investigation,' Barbara said. 'No one has the patience for anything. Tempers go fast.'

'Tell me about it,' Emily agreed. 'I haven't done much more in the last two days than try to keep the local Asians from burning down the town and my guv from assigning his golfing mate to take over the case.'

Barbara was gratified that her fellow officer had given her an opening. 'Today's demonstration made ITV. Did you know?'

'Oh, yes.' Emily dumped half the packet of nuts and fruit on top of the yoghurt and patted everything in place with her spoon before reaching for a banana from a bowl of fruit on the work top. 'We had a score of Asians at a town council meeting, howling like werewolves about their civil liberties. One of them alerted the media and when a camera crew showed up, they started lobbing chunks of concrete. They've imported outsiders to help in the cause. And Ferguson – that's my guv – has taken to getting on the blower once or twice an hour to tell me how to do my job.'

'What's the Asians' main concern?'

'It depends on who you talk to. They're intent on exposing whatever they can: a cover-up, a spate of footdragging by the local coppers, a CID conspiracy, or the start of ethnic cleansing. Take your pick.'

Barbara sat on one of the two metal chairs. 'Which comes closest?'

The DCI shot her a look. 'Brilliant, Barb. You sound just like them.'

'Sorry. I didn't mean to suggest –'

'Forget it. The whole bloody world's on my back. Why not you as well?' From a drawer, Emily took a small knife which she wielded against the banana, adding slices to the yoghurt, nuts, and fruit. 'Here's the situation. I'm trying to keep the leaks to a minimum. Things are dicey as hell in the community, and if I'm not careful about who knows what and when, there's a loose cannon in town who'll start firing away.'

'Who is it?'

'A Muslim. Muhannad Malik.' Emily explained his relationship to the deceased man and described the importance of the Malik family – and hence Muhannad himself – in Balford-le-Nez. His father, Akram, had brought the family to the town eleven years ago with the dream of starting their own business. Unlike many Asian newcomers who confined themselves to restaurants, markets, dry cleaners, or petrol stations, when Akram Malik dreamed, he dreamed big. He saw that in a depressed part of the country, he might not only be welcomed as a source of future employment but he might also make his mark. He'd started small, making mustard in the back room of a tiny bakery on Old Pier Street. He'd ended up with a complete factory in the north of the town. There he manufactured everything from savoury jellies to vinaigrettes.

'Malik's Mustards & Assorted Accompaniments,' Emily finished. 'Other Asians followed him here. Some of them relatives, others not. We've a growing community of them now. With all the interracial headaches.'

'Muhannad's one of them?'

'A migraine. I'm up to my neck in political bullshit because of that prick.' She reached for a peach and began to slice it, tucking wedges of fruit along the rim of the yoghurt bowl. Barbara watched her, considered her own healthless dinner, and managed to subdue her guilt.

Muhannad, Emily informed her, was a political activist in Balford-le-Nez, fiercely dedicated to equal rights and fair treatment for all his people. He'd formed an organisation whose putative purpose was support, brotherhood, and solidarity among youthful Asians, but he was a real hot head when it came to anything remotely suggestive of a racial incident. Anyone who harassed an Asian found himself in short order going eyeball-to-eyeball with one or more relentless Nemeses whose identity victims were always conveniently unable to recall. 'No one can mobilise the Asian community like Malik,' Emily said. 'He's been dogging my heels since Querashi's body was found, and he'll be dogging them till I make an arrest. Between seeing to him and seeing to Ferguson, I've had to manufacture time to conduct the investigation.'

'That's rough,' Barbara said.

'What it is is a pisser.' Emily tossed the knife into the kitchen sink and carried her meal to the table.

'I had a talk with a local girl at the Breakwater,' Barbara said as

Emily went to the fridge and brought out two cans of Heineken. She passed one to Barbara and popped the top on her own. She sat with natural and unconscious athleticism, lifting one leg over the seat of the chair rather than easing her way into it with studied feminine grace. 'There's some talk that Querashi had a mishap with drugs. You know what I mean: ingested heroin prior to leaving Pakistan.'

Emily spooned up some of her yoghurt concoction. She rolled her beer can across her forehead where the perspiration was glistening on her skin. She said, 'We haven't yet got the final word from toxicology about Querashi. There may be a drug tie. With the harbours nearby, we've got to keep it in mind. But drugs didn't kill him, if that's what you're thinking.'

'D'you know what did?'

'Oh, yeah. I know.'

'Then why're you playing your cards so close? I saw there's been no cause of death given, so it's still not clear if you've even got a murder. Is that where things stand?'

Emily swallowed some beer and eyed Barbara carefully. 'How much of a holiday are you on, Barb?'

'I can hold my tongue, if that's what you're asking.'

'What if I'm asking more?'

'D'you need my help?'

Emily had scooped up more yoghurt, but she set her spoon back in the bowl and meditated on it before answering slowly. 'I may do.'

This was far better than greasing her way in, Barbara realised. She jumped at the opportunity the DCI was unknowingly offering. 'Then you've got it. Why're you holding the press off? If it isn't drugs, is it sex related? Suicide? Accident? What's going on?'

'Murder,' she said.

'Ah. And when the word gets out, the Asians're going to hit the streets again.'

'The word *is* out. I told the Pakistanis this afternoon.'

'And?'

'And they'll be breathing, peeing, and sleeping for us from this moment on.'

'Is it a racist killing, then?'

'We don't know yet.'

'But you do know how he died?'

'We knew that the moment we got a clear look at him. But it's something I'd like to keep from the Asians as long as I can.'

'Why? If they know it's a murder –'

'Because this kind of murder suggests the very thing they're claiming.'

'A racial incident?' And when Emily nodded, Barbara asked, 'How? I mean, how could you tell by looking at the body that it's a race killing? Were there marks on it? Swastikas or something?'

'No.'

'Some sort of National Front calling card left at the scene?'

'Not that either.'

'Then how can you conclude –'

'He was seriously bruised. And his neck was broken, Barb.'

'Whoa. Bloody hell.' Barbara's tone was hushed. She recalled what she'd read. Querashi's body had been found inside a pillbox on the beach. This suggested a lying in wait and an ambush. Taken in conjunction with a beating, the death could indeed be interpreted as having been racially motivated. Because premeditated killings – unless they were preceded by the sort of tortures favoured by serial killers – were generally swift since the object was death. Additionally, a broken neck suggested another man as the killer. No average woman would have the strength even to begin to break a man's neck.

As Barbara considered these points, Emily went to the work top and fetched her canvas hold-all. At the table, she shoved her plate to the edge and pulled out three manila folders. She opened the first, placed it to one side, and opened the second. It contained a set of glossy photographs. She flipped through these for several she wanted and handed them to Barbara.

The photographs depicted the corpse as he appeared on the morning of his discovery in the pillbox. The first picture concentrated on his face, and Barbara saw that he was nearly as banged-up as she herself was. His right cheek was especially contused, and a gash bisected one of his eyebrows. Two other photographs displayed his hands. Both were scored and abraded as if they'd been raised protectively.

Barbara thought about the implication behind the pictures. The right cheek's condition suggested a left-handed assailant. But the wound on the forehead was on the left, which itself suggested either ambidexterity on the part of the killer or an accomplice.

Emily handed her another photograph, saying, 'Are you familiar with the Nez?'

'I haven't been there in years,' Barbara replied. 'But I remember the cliffs. A caff of some sort. An old watch tower.' The additional picture was an aerial shot. It included the pillbox, the cliff looming above it, the columnar watch tower, the L-shaped café. A car park to the southwest of the café contained police vehicles that surrounded a hatchback. But it was what was missing from the picture that Barbara took note of, what otherwise might have loomed above the car park, washing it with illumination after dark. 'Em,' she said, 'are there any lights out there? On the Nez? On the clifftop? Are there lights?' She looked up and found Emily watching her, an eyebrow raised to acknowledge the direction in which she was heading. 'Hell. There aren't, are there? And if there aren't any lights . . . ?' Barbara went back to studying the picture and she directed her next question to it. 'Then what the dickens was Haytham Querashi doing out on the Nez in the dark?'

She raised her head once more to see Emily saluting her with her Heineken. 'That's certainly the question, Sergeant Havers,' she said and upended the beer into her mouth.

Chapter Four

———◆———

'**Sh**'ll I help you up to bed, Mrs Shaw? It's gone past ten, and the doctor said I was to mind that you got your rest.'

Mary Ellis's voice was pitched at precisely that diffident tone which made Agatha Shaw want to claw the girl's eyes out. She restrained herself, however, turning slowly from the three large noticeboards on easels that Theo had assembled for her in the library. On them were representations of Balford-le-Nez in the past, the present, and the future. She'd been studying them for the last thirty minutes, using them as a means of harnessing the rage she'd been feeling ever since her grandson had informed her of the means by which her carefully planned and 'specially called town council meeting had been derailed. So far it had been quite a fine evening of rage, with her anger escalating over dinner as Theo went through the council meeting and its aftermath for her step by step.

'Mary,' she said, 'do I look as if I need to be treated like an advertisement for terminal senility?'

Mary considered the question with a concentration that puckered her spotty face. Irony had always been lost on her. 'Pardon?' she said and she wiped her hands against the sides of her skirt. The skirt was cotton, a pale and hideously anaemic blue. Her palms left splodges of damp against it.

'I'm aware of the time,' Agatha clarified. 'And when I'm ready to retire for the evening, I shall call for you.'

'But as it's gone near half-ten, Mrs Shaw . . .' Mary's voice drifted off, and the way her teeth pulled at the centre of her lower lip was supposed to convey the rest of her remark.

Agatha knew this. She hated being manipulated. She realised the girl wanted to be on her way – no doubt with the intention of allowing some equally spotty-faced hooligan access to her questionable charms – but the very fact that she wouldn't come out and say what was on her mind provoked Agatha into baiting her. It was the girl's own fault. She was nineteen years old, which was quite old enough to be able to say what she meant. At her age, Agatha had already been a Wren for a year and had lost the only man she'd ever loved in a bombing raid on Berlin. In those days, if a woman wasn't able to say what she meant, chances were very good that she wouldn't have the opportunity to say anything to anyone next time round. Because chances were excellent that there wouldn't be a next time round at all.

'Yes?' Agatha encouraged her pleasantly. 'As it's gone near half-past ten, Mary . . . ?'

'I thought . . . Don't you want . . . It's just that my hours're supposed to be just till nine. We agreed on that, you and me, right?'

Agatha waited for more. Mary squirmed, looking as if a centipede were crawling up her thigh.

'It's just that . . . As it's getting late . . .'

Agatha raised an eyebrow.

Mary looked defeated. 'Give me a call when you're ready, ma'm.'

Agatha smiled. 'Thank you, Mary. I shall do so.'

She turned back to her contemplation of the pictures as Mary Ellis took herself off into the bowels of the house. On the first easel Balford-le-Nez in the past was represented by seven neatly arranged photographs taken during its fifty-year heyday as a holiday hotspot between 1880 and 1930. Central to the pictures was a large depiction of Agatha's first love, the pleasure pier, and petalling out from this carpel, were additional pictures of the locations that had once attracted visitors. Bathing machines lined the seafront at Princes Beach; parasol-shaded women strolled along a crowded High Street; waders gathered at the outer end of a longshore net being landed on the beach by a lobster boat. Here was the famous Pier End Hotel, and there the distinguished Edwardian terrace overlooking the Balford Promenade.

Damn the coloureds, Agatha thought. If not for them and their surly demands that everyone in Balford lick their backsides because one of their kind had probably got a comeuppance he'd richly deserved . . .

if not for them, Balford-le-Nez would be one step closer to becoming the seaside resort it had once been and was meant to be. And *what* had the Pakis been shrieking about? What had they destroyed *her* meeting of the town council to beat their skinny chests about?

'It's a civil liberties question to them,' Theo had said at dinner, and blast the idiot if he didn't look as though he agreed with the bloody barrel of them.

'Perhaps you wouldn't mind explaining that to me?' Agatha had requested of her grandson. Her words were icy. She noted the look of instant discomfiture they seemed to arouse in Theo. His heart bled too readily for Agatha's liking. His belief in fair play, the equality of man, and justice given to all on demand, were certainly not attributes he'd inherited from her. She knew what he meant by the phrase 'a civil liberties question', but she wanted to coerce him into saying it. She wanted this because she wanted a fight. She was looking for an all-out, hands-down, pitched battle, and if she couldn't manage one as she was now – trapped inside a body that threatened to fail her at any moment – then she'd settle for verbal fisticuffs. A good row was better than nothing.

Theo wouldn't rise to the challenge, though. And upon reflection Agatha had to admit that this refusal to take her on could actually be interpreted as a positive sign. He needed to toughen up if he was to man the helm of Shaw Enterprises after her death. Perhaps his skin was already thickening.

'The Asians don't trust the police,' he said. 'They don't believe they're getting equal treatment. They want to keep the town focused on the investigation in order to put pressure on the CID.'

'It seems to me that if they desire to be treated equally – which I can only assume means that they wish to be treated like their English counterparts – then they might consider acting for once like their English counterparts.'

'There've been plenty of demonstrations that the whites have organised over the years,' Theo said. 'The poll tax riots, the blood sports protests, the movement against –'

'I'm not speaking about demonstrations,' she cut in. 'I'm speaking about being treated English when they decide to start acting English. And dressing English. And worshipping English. And bringing up their children English. If an individual decides to emigrate to another country, he should not expect that country to cater to his whims, Theodore. And if I'd been in your place at the council meeting, you may depend upon it: I'd have said just that.'

Her grandson folded his napkin precisely and laid it perpendicular to the table edge as Agatha had taught him. 'I've little doubt of that, Gran,' he said wryly. 'And you would've waded right into the riot afterwards and beaten in a few heads with your stick.' He pushed back his chair and came to hers. He laid his hand on her shoulder and kissed her forehead.

Agatha gruffly pushed him away. 'Stop your nonsense. And Mary Ellis has yet to bring in the cheese.'

'None for me tonight.' Theo headed towards the doorway. 'I'll fetch the display from the car.'

Which he had done, and she stood before it now. Balford-le-Nez of the present was depicted in all its decrepitude on the centre easel: the abandoned buildings along the seafront with boarded windows and wooden architraves shedding their paint like sunburned skin; the moribund High Street where every year another shop closed its doors a final time; the grubby indoor swimming pool whose stink of mildew and woodrot couldn't possibly be captured by a camera's lens. And like the easel displaying Balford of the past, among these pictures of Balford now was a photo of the pier, which Agatha had purchased, which Agatha had renovated, which Agatha Shaw had restored and rejuvenated, breathing life like a god into her personal Adam, making the pleasure pier an unspoken promise to the sea town where Agatha had spent her life.

That life and its impending close would have been given some meaning by Balford of the future: hotels refurbished, businesses lured to the sea by the guarantee of low ground rents and landlords committed to redevelopment and restoration, buildings gentrified, parks replanted – and *big* parks, not plots of grass the size of an envelope which *some* people dedicated to Asian mothers with utterly unpronounceable names – and attractions added along the seafront. There were plans for a leisure centre, for a renovated indoor swimming pool, for tennis and squash courts, for a new cricket pitch. This was what Balford-le-Nez could be, and it was to this end that Agatha Shaw was striving, seeking her own slice of immortality.

She'd lost her parents during the Blitz. She'd lost her husband at thirty-eight. She'd lost three of her children to careers round the globe and the fourth in a car crash at the hands of his limp-willed Scandinavian wife. Early on she'd come to know that the wise woman kept her expectations humble and her dreams to herself, but in these final years of her life she'd found herself growing as weary of submission to the will of the Almighty as she would have grown weary of fighting that will. So she'd taken up her final cause like a warrior, and she was fully determined to see this battle through to the end.

Nothing was going to stop this project, least of all the death of some foreigner she didn't know. But she needed Theo to be her right hand. She needed Theo quick-witted and strong. She wanted him impenetrable and invincible, and the last thing her plans for Balford had required of him was his tacit agreement to their derailment.

She clutched her three-pronged stick in a grip so tight that it made her arm tremble. She concentrated the way her physiotherapist had told her that she would now have to concentrate in order to walk. It was an unspeakable cruelty to have to tell each leg what to do before it would do it. She who once had ridden, played tennis, golfed, fished, and boated was reduced to saying, 'First left, then right. Now left, then right,' just to get to the library door. Her teeth ground on the words. If she'd had the temperament to be a dog owner, had possessed a faithful and affectionate Corgi, and had been equal to the effort required, she would have kicked the animal in sheer frustration.

She found Theo in the old morning room. He'd long ago converted it to his lair, equipping it with television, stereo, books, comfortable old furniture, and a personal computer on which he communicated with the world's social misfits who happened to share his particular passion: amateur palaeontology. Agatha thought of it as an adult's excuse to grub round in the mud. But to Theo it was an avocation that he pursued with a dedication that most men used when pursuing pudenda. Day or night mattered little to Theo: when he had a free hour, off he would stride in the direction of the Nez, where the eroding cliffs had been disgorging dubious treasures for as long as the sea had been gnawing at the land.

He wasn't at the computer tonight. Nor was he using his magnifying glass to study a misshapen bit of stone – 'This is actually a rhino tooth, Gran,' he'd say patiently – culled from the cliffs. Rather, he was speaking into the telephone in a low hushed voice, rushing sentences that Agatha couldn't distinguish into the ear of someone who clearly didn't want to hear.

She caught the words, 'Please. *Please.* Listen to me,' before he looked towards the door and, seeing her, replaced the receiver in its cradle as if no one were on the other end of the line.

She studied him. The night was nearly as torrid as the day had been and since this room was on the west side of the house, it had taken the worst of the day's heat the longest. So there was at least one reason why Theo's face was flushed and why his fair skin was damp and oily-looking. But the other reason, she supposed, was sitting somewhere holding a dead telephone receiver in a damp palm, doubtless wondering why 'Listen to me' had ended rather than extended a conversation.

The windows were open, but the heat in the room was insufferable. Even the walls looked as if they wanted to sweat right through their old William Morris paper. The clutter of magazines, newspapers, books, and most of all the clutter of stones – 'No, Gran, they only *look* like stones. They're actually bones and teeth, and here, look for yourself, this's part of a mammoth tusk,' Theo would say – made the room even more unbearable, as if they raised its temperature another ten degrees. And, despite her grandson's care to clean them, they imbued the air with a disturbingly fecund smell of earth.

Theo moved from the telephone to the broad oak table. This was finely sheened with dust because he wouldn't allow Mary Ellis to apply a rag to its surface and disarrange the fossils he'd assembled there in compartmentalised wooden trays. There was an old balloon-backed chair in front of the table, and he took this and swung it round to face her.

She understood that he was making a place for her, well within her reach. This realisation made her feel like pinching the lobes of his ears until he wailed. She wasn't ready for the grave despite its having been dug, and she could do without the tender gestures revealing that others anticipated her imminent demise. She chose to stand.

'And the end result?' she demanded as if there had been no break in their conversation.

His eyebrows drew together. He used the back of his curled index finger to wipe the perspiration from his forehead. His glance went to the telephone, then back to her.

'I'm not the least interested in your love life, Theodore. You'll learn soon enough that it's an oxymoron. I pray nightly that you develop the presence of mind not to be led by either your nose or your penis. Otherwise, what you do in your free time is between you and whoever shares the momentary joy of experiencing the mingling of your bodily fluids. Although in this heat, why anyone would even think of intercourse –'

'Gran!' Theo's face was flaming.

My God, Agatha thought. He's twenty-six years old with the sexual maturity of a teenager. She could only imagine with a shudder what it was like to be on the receiving end of his earnest grappling. At least his grandfather – for all his faults, one of which happened to be dropping dead at the age of forty-two – had known how to take a woman and be done with it. A quarter of an hour was all Lewis had ever needed, and on the nights when she was extremely lucky, he managed the act in less than ten minutes. She considered sexual intercourse a medicinal requirement of marriage: one kept the juices flowing in every part of the body if one wished for health.

'What did they promise us, Theo?' she asked. 'You pressed for another special council meeting, of course.'

'Actually, I . . .' He remained standing as she did. But he reached for one of his precious fossils and turned it over in his hand.

'You did have the presence of mind to demand another meeting, didn't you, Theo? You didn't let those darkies take command and do nothing about it, did you?'

His expression was the answer.

She said, 'My God.' He was so like his brainless mother.

Despite herself, Agatha needed to sit. She lowered her body on to the seat of the balloon-backed chair and sat as she had been taught to sit in girlhood, ramrod straight. She said, 'What on earth is the matter with you, Theodore Michael? And sit down, please. I don't want a stiff neck to mark this encounter.'

He pulled an old armchair round to face her. It was covered in faded corduroy, upon its seat a frog-shaped stain the origin of which Agatha didn't care to speculate on. 'It wasn't the time,' he said.

'It wasn't . . . what?' She'd heard him perfectly, but she'd found long ago that the key to bending others to her will was to force them to examine their own with such diligence that they ended up rejecting whatever idea they'd begun with, in favour of hers.

'It wasn't the time, Gran.' Theo sat. He leaned towards her, bare arms resting on his fawn, linen-draped legs. He had a way of making wrinkles look like *haute couture*. She didn't think such a sense of fashion was seemly in a man. 'The council had their hands full with keeping a lid on Muhannad Malik. Which they failed to do, as things turned out.'

'It wasn't his meeting.'

'And with the issue being a man's death and the Asians' concerns about how it was being handled by the police –'

'Their concerns. Their *concerns*,' Agatha mocked.

'Gran, it wasn't the time. I couldn't make demands in the middle of chaos. Especially demands about redevelopment.'

She thumped her stick on the carpet. 'Why not?'

'Because it seemed to me that getting to the bottom of the Nez killing was more pressing an issue than the funding of the renovation of the Pier End Hotel.' He help up his hand. 'No, wait a moment, Gran. Don't interrupt. I know this project is important to you. It's important to me as well. And it's important to the community. But you've got to see that there's hardly any point in channelling money into Balford if there isn't going to be a community left.'

'You certainly can't be suggesting that the Asians have the power or even the temerity to destroy this town? They'd be cutting their own throats.'

'I'm suggesting that unless the community is a place where future visitors don't have to be afraid of being accosted by someone with a grudge against the colour of their skin, any money we pour into redevelopment is money we might as well send up in flames.'

He was surprising her. For a moment Agatha saw the shadow of his grandfather in him. Lewis would have thought exactly the same way.

'Hmph,' she sniffed.

'You see I'm right, don't you.' He phrased it not as a question, she noted, but as a statement, which was like Lewis as well. 'I'll give it a few days, let the tension pass, and organise another meeting then. It's for the best. You'll see.' He glanced at a carriage clock on the mantelpiece and got to his feet. 'And now it's time you were in bed. I'll fetch Mary Ellis.'

'I shall ask for Mary Ellis when I'm ready, Theodore. Stop treating me like –'

'No arguments.' He went to the door.

She spoke before he could open it. 'You're going out, then?'

'I said I'd fetch –'

'I don't mean out of the room. I mean out. *Out.* Out of the house. Are you going out again tonight, Theo?' His expression told her she'd pushed too far. Even Theo – malleable as he was – had his limits. Too much delving into his personal life was one of them. 'I ask because I wonder about the wisdom of these nocturnal wanderings of yours. If the situation in the town is as you suggest – tense – I dare say no one should be out and about after dark. And you've not been taking the boat out again, have you? You know how I feel about sailing at night.'

Theo regarded her from the doorway. There it was once again, that look of Lewis's: the features settling into a pleasant mask beneath which she could read absolutely nothing. When had he learned to dissemble so? she wondered. And why had he learned it?

'I'll fetch Mary Ellis,' he said. And he left her with her questions unanswered.

Sahlah was allowed to be part of the discussion because, after all, it was her fiancé whose life had been taken. Otherwise, she'd not have been included and she knew it. It wasn't the way of the Muslim men of her acquaintance to pay attention to what a woman had to say, and although her father was a gentle man whose tenderness often showed itself in the soft pressure of his knuckles against her cheek as he was passing by, when it came to convention, he was Muslim to the core. He devoutly prayed five times each day; he was on his third reading of the Holy Qur'aan; he made certain that a portion of the profits from his business went to the poor; and twice already he'd paced in the footsteps of millions of Muslims who had walked the perimeter of the *Ka'bā*.

Thus on this night, while Sahlah herself was permitted to listen to the men's discussion, her mother merely served the purpose of bringing food and drink from the kitchen to the front room, while Sahlah's sister-in-law made herself scarce. Yumn did this for two reasons, naturally. One was a bow to *haya*: Muhannad insisted upon the traditional interpretation of feminine modesty, so he would allow no man save his father ever to look upon his wife. And one was her nature: had she remained downstairs, her mother-in-law might have ordered her to help with the cooking, and Yumn was the laziest cow on earth. So she'd greeted Muhannad in her usual fashion, fawning over him as if her dearest desire were that he might wipe his boots on the seat of her drawstring trousers, and then she'd disappeared upstairs. Her excuse was the need to be vigilant should Anas have another one of his terrible nightmares. The truth was that she'd be entertaining herself by flipping through magazines which displayed the western fashions that Muhannad never allowed her to wear.

Sahlah sat well away from the men, and in deference to their sex, she neither ate nor drank. She wasn't the least bit hungry anyway, although she felt a craving for the *lassi* that her mother served to the others. In the heat, the yoghurt drink would be a source of blessed refreshment.

As was his custom, Akram Malik thanked his wife courteously as she set plates and glasses before their guest and their son. She touched his shoulder briefly, saying, 'Be well, Akram,' and left the room. Sahlah often wondered how her mother could defer to her father in all things, as if she had no will of her own. But when asked, Wardah always replied simply, saying, 'I don't defer, Sahlah. There's no necessity. Your father is my life as I am his.'

There was a bond between her parents that Sahlah had always admired although she'd never completely understood it. It seemed to arise from an ineffable mutual sadness that neither of them spoke of, and it manifested itself in the sensitivity with which they treated and spoke to each other. Akram Malik never raised his voice. But then, he never had to. His word was law to his wife, and it was supposed to be law to his children as well.

But Muhannad, as a teenager, had sneeringly called Akram an 'old fart' behind his back. And in the pear orchard beyond their house, he would hurl stones at the wall and viciously kick the mosaic-barked trunks of the trees to vent himself of the fury he felt whenever his father thwarted his wishes. He was careful never to let Akram see his rage, however. To him, Muhannad was silent and obedient. Sahlah's brother had spent his adolescence biding his time, doing his father's bidding, and knowing that as long as he put his obligations to the family first, the family business and fortune would be his in the end. It was *his* word that would then be law. Sahlah knew that Muhannad longed for that day.

But at the moment he was faced with his father's unspoken outrage. In addition to the turmoil he'd roused in town that day, he had brought Taymullah Azhar not only to Balford but into their home. This constituted the gravest act of defiance against their family. For although he was the eldest son of Akram's brother, Sahlah knew that Taymullah Azhar had been cast out of his family, and to be cast out meant that he was dead to everyone. Including his uncle's family.

Akram had not been at home when Muhannad arrived with Taymullah Azhar, disregarding Wardah's quiet but urgent 'You must *not*, my son,' spoken with a warning hand on his arm. Muhannad had said, 'We need him. We need someone with his experience. If we don't start getting the message out that we won't let Haytham's murder be swept under the rug, we can expect business as usual from this town.'

Wardah had looked worried but said nothing more. After the first moment of startled recognition, she didn't even look at Taymullah Azhar. She merely nodded – the deference towards her husband translating automatically into deference towards her only son – and she retreated to the kitchen with Sahlah, awaiting the moment when Akram returned home from arranging for Haytham's replacement at the mustard factory.

'*Ammī,*' Sahlah had asked in a low voice as her mother began assembling a meal, 'who is that man?'

'He is no one,' Wardah had replied firmly. 'He does not exist.'

But clearly, Taymullah Azhar did exist, and Sahlah first heard his name – and immediately realised who he was from the past ten years of family gossip among the younger cousins – when her father came into the kitchen upon his return home and Wardah intercepted him, telling him about the visitor who had arrived with their son. They exchanged hushed words. Akram's eyes displayed his only reaction to the visitor's identity. Behind his glasses, they narrowed quickly.

He said, 'Why?'

His wife replied, 'Because of Haytham.' She glanced at Sahlah with compassion in her eyes, as if in the belief that her daughter had actually come to love the man she'd been told to marry. And why not? Sahlah realised. Under identical circumstances, Wardah had learned to love Akram Malik. 'Muhannad says that your brother's son has experience in these matters, Akram.'

Akram snorted. 'It all depends on what "these matters" are. You should not have let him into the house.'

'He came with Muhannad,' was her reply. 'What could I do?'

He was with Muhannad still, seated at one end of the sofa while Sahlah's brother took the other. Akram was in an easy chair, with one of Wardah's embroidered pillows cradling his back. The oversize television was playing another of Yumn's Asian films. She'd muted the sound instead of dousing the picture before scuttling upstairs. Now, over her father's shoulder, Sahlah could see two desperate young lovers meeting secretly like Romeo and Juliet. Except instead of upon a balcony, they met, embraced, and fell to the earth to do their business in a field where maize grew to their shoulders and hid them from view. Sahlah averted her eyes and felt her heart beating in her throat like a trapped bird's wings.

'I know you're not happy with everything that happened this afternoon,' Muhannad was saying, 'But we've got the police to agree to meet us daily. That'll keep us informed of what's going on.' Sahlah could tell by the clipped way her brother spoke that he chafed beneath their father's unuttered disapproval and disgust. 'We wouldn't have got that far in one interview had Azhar not been there, Father. He positioned the DCI so that she had no option but to agree. And he did it so smoothly that she wasn't aware of the direction he was leading her till she arrived there.' He shot Azhar a look of admiration. Azhar crossed his legs, pressed the crease of his trousers between his fingers, but said nothing at all. He kept his gaze fixed on his uncle. Sahlah had never seen anyone look so composed in a situation in which he was so unwelcome.

'And this was your purpose in causing a riot?'

'The point isn't who caused what. The point is that we got an agreement.'

'And you think this is something we could not have managed on our own, Muhannad? This agreement, as you call it.' Akram lifted his glass and drank some of the *lassi*. He hadn't glanced once at Taymullah Azhar.

'The cops know us, Father. They've known us for years. And familiarity makes people lax when it comes to fulfilling their responsibilities. Who shouts the loudest gets heard the soonest, and you know it.'

These last four words were a mistake, born of Muhannad's impatience and of his aversion to the English. Sahlah understood his feelings – having also been on the receiving end of childhood torment at the hands of schoolmates – but she knew that their father did not. Born in Pakistan and coming to England as a man in his twenties, he'd had only one experience of racism that he ever spoke of. Even that one episode of public humiliation in a London underground station had not soured him about the people he'd decided to adopt as his countrymen. In his eyes, Muhannad had disgraced their people that day. Akram Malik wasn't likely to forget that fact soon.

'Who shouts the loudest often has the least to say,' he responded.

Muhannad's face tightened. 'Azhar knows how to organise. The way we need to organise now.'

'What is now, Muni? Is Haytham less dead than he was at this time yesterday? Is your sister's future any less destroyed? How does one man's presence change what is?'

'Because,' Muhannad announced, and the tone of his voice told Sahlah that her brother had saved the best for last, 'they've now admitted it's murder.'

Akram's face grew grave. However irrationally, he'd been consoling himself, his family, and Sahlah especially with the belief that Haytham's death had been an unfortunate accident. Now that Muhannad had ferreted out the truth, Sahlah knew that her father would have to think in different terms. He would have to ask why, which might very well lead him in a direction in which he didn't wish to go.

'*Admitted*, Father. To us. Because of what happened at today's council meeting and in the street afterwards. Wait. Don't respond yet.' Muhannad pressed his point, rising to his feet and pacing to the fireplace where the mantelpiece held a score of framed family photographs. 'I know I angered you today. I admit that things got out of hand. But I ask you to look at the results I got. And it was Azhar who suggested the town council meeting as a place to start. Azhar, Father. When I phoned him in London. Can you tell me that when you spoke to the CID they admitted murder to you? Because they didn't to me. And God knows they didn't tell Sahlah anything.'

Sahlah lowered her eyes as the men looked her way. She didn't need to confirm her brother's words. Akram had been in the room for her brief conversation with the police constable who'd come to inform them of Haytham's death. He knew exactly what had been said: 'There's been a death on the Nez, I'm sorry to say. The deceased appears to be a Mr Haytham Querashi. We need someone to identify the body formally, however, and we understand you were to marry him.'

'Yes,' Sahlah had replied gravely, while inside she was screaming, No no no!

'This may be,' Akram said to his son. 'But you have gone too far. When one among us has died, it is not up to you to see to his resurrection, Muhannad.'

He was, Sahlah knew, not speaking of Haytham. He was speaking of Taymullah Azhar. Azhar was supposed to be dead to everyone in the family once his parents had proclaimed him so. If you saw him on the street, you were to look through him or avert your eyes. His name wasn't to be mentioned. His existence wasn't to be spoken of to anyone even in the most oblique terms. And if you thought of him, you quickly busied your mind with something else lest thinking of him turned to speaking of him turned to a willingness to consider allowing him entrance to the family once more. Sahlah had been too young to be told what crime Azhar had committed within the family to have been cast out, and once the casting out had been accomplished, she'd been forbidden to speak of him to anyone.

Ten years of solitude, she thought as she observed her cousin. Ten years of wandering in the world alone. What had it been like for him? How had he survived without his relations?

'What's more important, then?' Muhannad was attempting to sound reasonable. He didn't want to be any further at odds with their father than the day's proceedings had already made him. He couldn't risk being cast out himself. Not with a wife, two children, and the need to be gainfully employed. 'What's more important, Father? Tracking down the man who murdered one of our own, or making certain Azhar is cut off for life? Sahlah is a victim of this crime as much as Haytham. Don't we have an obligation to her?'

When Muhannad looked in her direction again, Sahlah lowered her eyes modestly a second time. But her insides shrivelled. She knew the truth. How could anyone not see her brother for what he was?

'Muhannad, I do not need your instruction in this or any other matter,' Akram said quietly.

'I'm not *trying* to instruct you. I'm only telling you that without Azhar –'

'Muhannad.' Akram reached for one of the *parāthās* that his wife had prepared. Sahlah could smell the minced beef that had been folded within the pastry. Her stomach lurched at the odour. 'This person you speak of is dead to us. You should not have brought him into our lives, much less into our home. I have no argument with you about the crime that has been committed against Haytham, your sister, and all of our family, if indeed it is a crime.'

'But I *told* you the DCI said it was murder. And I told you she was forced to admit it because of the pressure we've put on the CID.'

'The pressure you brought to bear this afternoon was not on the CID.'

'But that's how it works. Don't you see that?' The room was stifling. Muhannad's white T-shirt clung to his muscled frame. In contrast, Taymullah Azhar sat in a state of such cool calm that he appeared to have transported himself to another world. Muhannad changed gears. 'I'm sorry to have caused you pain, and maybe I should have warned you in advance that there would be a disruption in the meeting –'

'Maybe?' Akram asked. 'And what occurred at the meeting wasn't a simple disruption.'

'All right. All *right*. Maybe I approached it wrong.'

'Maybe?'

Sahlah saw her brother's muscles tense. But he was too old to throw stones at the wall and there were no tree trunks in the room to be kicked. His face was beaded with sweat, and for the first time Sahlah realised the importance of having someone like Taymullah Azhar acting as intermediary for the family in future discussions with the police. Tranquillity under duress wasn't Muhannad's strong suit. Intimidation was, but more than intimidation was going to be called for. 'Look where the demonstration got us, Father: an interview with the DCI heading the investigation. And an admission of murder.'

'I see that,' Akram acknowledged. 'So now you shall offer formal thanks to your cousin for his advice and send him on his way.'

'Bugger that shit!' Muhannad swept three framed pictures from the mantel on to the floor. 'What's the matter with you? What are you afraid of? Are you so tied to these bloody westerners that you can't even think that —'

'Enough.' Akram stepped out of character: he raised his voice.

'No! It's not enough. You're afraid that one of these English murdered Haytham. And if that's what happened, you're going to have to do something about it — like feel differently about them. And you can't bloody face that because you've been playing at being a sodding Englishman for twenty-seven years.'

Akram was up and across the room so quickly that Sahlah didn't realise what had happened until her father struck Muhannad across his face. It was then that she cried out.

'Stop it!' She heard the fear in her voice. It was fear for both of them, for what they were capable of doing to each other and how what they did had the potential to rip their family apart. 'Muni! *Abhy-jahn!* Stop!'

The two men squared up, Akram with a warning finger held stiffly in front of Muhannad's eyes. It was the posture he'd adopted throughout his son's childhood, but with a difference. Now he held his finger up to his son's face because Muhannad topped him by more than two inches.

'We all want the same thing,' Sahlah said to them. 'We want to know what happened to Haytham. And why. We want to know why.' She wasn't sure of the veracity of either of those statements. But she said them anyway because it was more important that her father and brother remain at peace with each other than it was that she speak the complete truth to them. 'Why are you arguing, then? Isn't it best to follow the path that'll lead us to the truth the quickest? Isn't that what we want?'

The men didn't answer. Upstairs, Anas began to cry, and in response Yumn's feet pattered down the corridor in her expensive sandals.

'It's what I want,' Sahlah said quietly. She didn't add the rest because she didn't have to: I am the injured party because he was to be my husband. '*Muni. Abhy-jahn.* It's what I want,' she repeated.

Taymullah Azhar rose from his place on the sofa. He was smaller than the two other men, slighter of build and shorter in height. But he seemed their equal in every way as he spoke, even though Akram didn't look at him. '*Chachā*,' he said.

Akram winced at the appellation. *Father's brother.* It claimed a tie of blood where he would not acknowledge one.

'I don't wish to bring trouble to your home,' Azhar said, and held Muhannad off with a gesture when he would have interrupted hotly. 'Let me serve the family. You won't see me unless it's necessary. I'll stay elsewhere so that you needn't break your vow to my father. I can help because, when necessary, I work with our people in London when they have troubles with the police or the government. I have experience with the English –'

'And we know where that experience took him,' Akram said bitterly.

Azhar didn't flinch. 'I have experience with the English that we all can use in this situation. I ask you to let me help. Because I have no direct connection with this man or his death, I have less emotion tied up in it. I can think more clearly and see more clearly. I offer myself to you.'

'He disgraced our name,' Akram said.

'Which is why I no longer use it,' Azhar replied. 'I can show my regret in no other way.'

'He could have done his duty.'

'I did my best.'

Instead of answering further, Akram studied Muhannad. He seemed to be taking the measure of his son. Then he turned heavily and looked at Sahlah where she still sat, perched this time on the edge of her seat.

He said, 'I would not have had this happen in your life, Sahlah. I see your sorrow. I want only to bring it to an end.'

'Then let Azhar –'

Akram silenced Muhannad by raising his hand between them. 'This is for your sister,' he told his son. 'Do not let me see him. Do not let him speak to me. And do not bring another moment of disgrace on this family's name.'

With that, he left them. His footsteps struck each stair heavily.

'Old fart.' Muhannad spat the words. 'Ignorant, grudge-bearing, bloody-minded old fart.'

Taymullah Azhar shook his head. 'He wants to do what's best for his family. It's a concept that I, of all people, understand.'

After Emily's meal, Barbara and she had moved to the back garden of the house. They'd been interrupted by a telephone call from Emily's paramour, who'd said, 'I can't believe you really wanted to cancel tonight, not after last week. When have you ever come so many –' before Emily snatched up the phone, cutting off the answer machine and saying, 'Hi. I'm here, Gary.' She'd swung round so that her back was to Barbara. The conversation had been brief, consisting of Emily saying, 'No ... It's got nothing to do with that. You said she had a migraine and I believed you ... You're imagining things ... It has *nothing* to do with ... Gary, you know how I hate it when you interrupt me ... Yes, well, I've someone here at the moment, so I can't go into it ... Oh, for God's sake, don't be ridiculous. Even if that were the case, what would it matter? We agreed at the start how things would be ... This isn't *about* control. I'm working tonight ... And that, my darling, is none of your business.'

She'd hung up smartly and said, 'Men. Jesus. If they didn't have the right equipment to amuse us, they'd hardly be worth the trouble.'

Barbara didn't attempt a clever riposte. Her experience with men's equipment was too limited to offer anything more than a roll of the eyes, which she hoped Emily would read as 'Ain't it the truth?'

The DCI had appeared satisfied with this response. She'd grabbed a bowl of fruit and a bottle of brandy from the work top, and saying 'Let's get some air,' she led Barbara to the garden.

The garden wasn't in much better condition than the house. But the worst of the weeds had been hacked away, and a flagstone path had been laid in a curve to a horse chestnut tree. Beneath this, Barbara and Emily now sat in low-slung canvas chairs, with the bowl of fruit between them, two glasses of brandy that Emily kept topped up, and a nightingale singing somewhere in the branches above them. Emily was eating her second plum. Barbara was munching a handful of grapes.

It was, at least, cooler in the garden than it had been in the kitchen, and there was even a bit of a view. Cars passed on the Balford Road below them, and beyond it the night-time lights of the distant summer cottages blinked through the trees. Barbara wondered why the DCI just didn't bring her camp bed, her sleeping bag, her torch, and *A Brief History of Time* out here.

Emily cut into her thoughts. 'Are you seeing anyone these days, Barb?'

'Me?' The question seemed ludicrous. Emily had no trouble with her vision, so surely she could deduce the answer without having to ask the question. Just look at me, Barbara wanted to say, I've the body of a chimpanzee. Who d'you think I'd be seeing? But what she said was, 'Who has the time?' and hoped it sounded casual enough for the subject to be dismissed.

Emily glanced her way. A streetlamp burned on the Crescent, and since Emily's was the last house in the row, some of its light made its way into her back garden. Barbara could feel Emily making a study of her.

'That sounds like an excuse,' she said.

'For what?'

'For maintaining the status quo.' Emily lobbed her plum stone over the wall, where it fell into the weeds of the untended soil next door. 'You're still alone, aren't you? Well, you can't want to be alone for ever.'

'Why not? You are. Being alone's not holding you back.'

'Right. It's not. But there's being alone, and there's being *alone*,' Emily said wryly. 'If you know what I mean.'

Barbara knew what she meant well enough. While she lived by herself, Emily Barlow had never been without a man on the string for more than one month. But that was because she had it all: good looks, a fine body, a singular mind. Why was it that women who slew men by virtue of simply existing always thought that other women had the same power?

She craved a cigarette. It was beginning to seem like days since she'd last had one. What the bloody hell did non-smokers do to buy time, to displace unwanted attention, to avoid discussion, or simply to quell nerves? They said, 'Sorry, but I don't want to discuss it,' which wouldn't exactly be the best response in a situation in which Barbara was hoping to work closely with the DCI heading up a murder investigation.

'You don't believe me, do you?' Emily asked when Barbara made no response.

'Let's just say that experience has encouraged my scepticism. And anyway –' She hoped the gust of air she expelled would give the impression of insouciance. 'I'm happy enough with things as they are.'

Emily reached for an apricot. She rolled it round her palm. 'Are you.' The words were a thoughtful statement.

Barbara chose to interpret this remark as a two-word termination of their discussion. She sought a clever transition into a new topic. Something along the lines of 'Speaking of murder' would have done, except that they hadn't spoken of murder since leaving the kitchen. Barbara was reluctant to press in that direction, her quasi-professional status in the case being more tenuous than she was used to, but she also wanted to get back to the real matter at hand. She'd come to Balford-le-Nez because of a police investigation, not to consider the ramifications of solitude.

She went for the direct approach, adopting the pretence that there had been no interruption to their discussion of the death on the Nez in the first place. 'It's the racial bit that I'm wondering about,' she said, and lest Emily think she was expressing concerns that her social life might become an arena for miscegenation, she went on with, 'If Haytham Querashi had only recently come to England – and that's what the telly reported, by the way – then that suggests he may not have known his killer. Which in turn suggests the sort of random racist violence one hears about in America. Or in any big city around the world, for that matter, times being what they are.'

'You're thinking like the Asians, Barb,' Emily said, taking a bite of her apricot. She washed the fruit down with swig of brandy. 'But the Nez is no place for a random act of violence. It's deserted at night. And you saw the pictures. There're no lights, either on the clifftop or on the beach. So if someone goes there alone – and let's assume for the moment that Querashi went there by himself – he goes for one of two reasons. To be alone for a walk –'

'Was it dark when he left his hotel?'

'It was. With no moon to speak of, by the way. So we cross out the walk unless he was planning to stumble along like a blind man, and we speculate that he was there to be alone for a think.'

'Perhaps he was getting cold feet about the forthcoming marriage? He wanted to call it off and was wondering how?'

'That's a good theory. Reasonable, as well. But there's another point we have to consider: his car was done over. Someone tore it to pieces. What does that suggest to you?'

There seemed only one possibility. 'That he'd gone there deliberately to meet someone. He'd taken something with him to deliver. He didn't hand it over as prearranged and he paid with his life. After which someone searched his car for whatever he was supposed to hand over.'

'None of which suggests a racist killing to me,' Emily said. 'Those killings are arbitrary. This killing wasn't.'

'But that doesn't mean someone English didn't kill him, Em. For a reason having nothing to do with race.'

'Don't remind me. But it also doesn't mean someone Asian didn't kill him.'

Barbara nodded but continued with her own line of thought. 'If you bring in someone English for the crime, the Asian community will see it as a racist killing because the death *looks* racist. And if that happens, everything'll explode. Right?'

'Right. So while it complicates the hell out of matters, I have to say I'm relieved that the car was done over. Even if the crime was racial in nature, I can interpret it otherwise till I know for sure. That'll buy me time, keep a lid on things, and give me a chance to strategise. For a while, at least. And only if I can keep Ferguson off the bloody phone for twenty-four hours.'

'*Could* a member of Querashi's community have killed him?' Barbara reached into the fruit bowl for another handful of grapes. Emily settled into her chair with her brandy glass balanced on her stomach and her head tilted up to examine the black webbing of chestnut leaves that hung above them. Somewhere safely hidden by these leaves, the nightingale continued his liquid song.

'It's not out of the question,' Emily said. 'I think it's even likely. Who else did he know well enough for murder other than Asians?'

'And he was supposed to marry the Malik daughter, wasn't he?'

'Yeah. One of those take-away marriages, all boxed up pretty by Mummy and Dad. You know what I mean.'

'So perhaps there were problems with that. She didn't ring his chimes. He didn't ring hers. She wanted out, but he wanted to immigrate, and she was his ticket. The whole situation ended up getting settled permanently.'

'Neck breaking's an extreme measure for ending an engagement,' Emily noted. 'Anyway, Akram Malik's been part of this community for years, and from everything I know about him, he treasures his daughter. If she hadn't wanted to marry Querashi, I can't think her father would have forced her.'

Barbara mulled this over and went in a new direction. 'They still use dowries, don't they? What was the daughter's? Could Querashi have been a little too ungrateful for what the family saw as generosity?'

'So they eliminated him?' Emily stretched out her long legs and cradled the brandy between her palms. 'I suppose that's a possibility. It's completely out of character for Akram Malik, but for Muhannad . . . ? I wouldn't put violence past that bloke. But that doesn't address the problem of the car.'

'Was there an indication that something had been taken?'

'It was completely torn apart.'

'And had the body been searched?'

'Definitely. We found the keys in a patch of samphire growing on the cliff. I doubt Querashi would have tossed them there.'

'Was anything left on the body when he was found?'

'Ten pounds and three condoms.'

'No identification?' And when Emily shook her head, 'Then how did you know who the victim was?'

Emily sighed and closed her eyes. Barbara had the impression that they'd finally come to the meaty part, the part she'd so far managed to withhold from everyone outside the investigation.

'He was found yesterday morning by a bloke called Ian Armstrong,' Emily said. 'And Ian Armstrong knew who he was by sight.'

'An Englishman,' Barbara said.

'*The* Englishman,' Emily said grimly.

Barbara immediately saw the direction in which Emily was heading. 'Armstrong has a motive?'

'Oh, yes.' Emily opened her eyes and turned her head to Barbara. 'Ian Armstrong worked for Malik's Mustards. He lost his job six weeks ago.'

'Did Haytham Querashi sack him, or something?'

'It's worse than that, although it's vastly better from Muhannad's point of view, considering what he'll probably do with the information if it leaks out that Armstrong found the body.'

'Why? What's the story?'

'Revenge. Manipulation. Necessity. Desperation. Whatever you like. Haytham Querashi replaced Ian Armstrong at the factory, Barb. And the minute that Haytham Querashi died, Ian Armstrong got his old job back. How's that for a motive from heaven?'

Chapter Five

===◆===

'That could be dicey,' Barbara admitted. 'But wouldn't Armstrong have had an even stronger motive to kill whoever gave him the sack?'

'In some circumstances, yes. If he was after revenge.'

'But in these circumstances?'

'Armstrong had apparently been doing a spot-on job. The only reason he was let go was to make room for Querashi in the family business.'

'Bloody hell,' Barbara said. 'Has Armstrong an alibi?'

'Claims he was home with the wife and a five year old. With a flaming ear ache – that's the kid, not Armstrong.'

'And the wife would corroborate that, right?'

'He's the main breadwinner and she knows what side her slice is buttered on.' Emily restlessly played her fingers along the curve of a peach in the fruit bowl. 'Armstrong said he'd gone to the Nez for an early-morning walk. He said he'd been taking early-morning walks on both days at the weekend for some time now, getting away from the missus for a few quiet hours. He doesn't know if anyone's seen him on these walks, but even if they have done, he could have used a normal weekend activity as a form of alibi.'

Barbara knew what she was thinking: it wasn't that rare an occurrence that a killer made a pretence of stumbling on to a corpse after the fact, the better to direct the spotlight of guilt on to someone else. Yet something Emily had earlier noted prodded Barbara to take a different tack. 'Forget the car for a moment. You said Querashi had three condoms and £10 on him. Could he have gone to the Nez to meet someone for sex? To meet a prostitute, perhaps? If he was about to marry, perhaps he wouldn't have wanted to risk being seen by someone who'd report his liaison back to his future father-in-law.'

'What prostitute do you know who'd give it a go for £10, Barb?'

'A young one. A desperate one. Perhaps a beginner.' When Emily shook her head, Barbara said, 'Then perhaps he was meeting a woman who'd otherwise be unavailable to him, a married woman. The husband caught on and did him in. Is there any indication that Querashi knew Armstrong's wife?'

'We're looking for connections,' Emily said, 'with everyone's wife.'

'This Muhannad bloke,' Barbara said. 'Is he married, Em?'

'Oh, yes,' Emily said quietly. 'Oh, yes indeed. He had his own boxed-up marriage some three years ago.'

'A happy marriage?'

'You tell me. Your parents inform you that they've matched you up with a mate for life. You meet this person and the next thing you know, you're locked into marriage. Does that sound like a recipe for happiness to you?'

'Not really. But they've been doing it for centuries, so it can't be all bad. Can it?'

Emily cast her a glance that was eloquent in its wordlessness. They sat in silence, listening to the nightingale's song. In her mind, Barbara rearranged the facts that Emily had been laying before her. The body, the car, the keys in the bushes, the pillbox on the beach, a broken neck.

She finally said, 'You know, if someone in Balford has an agenda for racial trouble, it doesn't really matter who you arrest, does it?'

'Why's that?'

'Because if they want to use an arrest to stir up trouble, they're going to use an arrest to stir up trouble. Put an Englishman in the nick, and they riot because the murder's an issue of racial violence. Arrest a Pakistani, and the arrest's an issue of police prejudice. The prism's just turned a bit. What they're examining through the prism remains the same.'

Emily stopped fingering the peach. She examined Barbara. When she next spoke, it seemed she'd reached a sudden and adroit conclusion. 'Of course,' she said. 'How are you on committees, Barb?'

'What?'

'You said earlier you were ready to help. Well, I've a need for an officer with a talent for committee work and I think you're that officer. How are you at dealing with Asians? I could use another pair of hands in all this, if only to swat my guv off my back.'

Before Barbara could riffle through her life history and produce an answer, Emily continued. She'd agreed to regular meetings with members of the Pakistani community during the course of the investigation. She needed an officer to serve that group. Barbara, if she agreed, would be that officer.

'You'll have to deal with Muhannad Malik,' Emily said, 'and he'll be hot to push you as hard and as far as he can, so keeping your wits about you is crucial. But there's another Asian, a bloke from London called Something Azhar, and he appears to be able to keep a collar on Muhannad, so you'll get some help from him whether he realises he's helping or not.'

Barbara could only imagine how Taymullah Azhar would react to seeing her bruised face at the first meeting between the Asians and the local rozzers. She said, 'I don't know. Committees aren't exactly my thing.'

'Nonsense.' Emily brushed her objections aside. 'You'll be brilliant. Most people see reason when the facts are laid in front of them in the proper order. I'll work with you to decide what the proper order is.'

'And it'll be my neck if things come to a crisis?' Barbara asked shrewdly.

'Things won't come to a crisis,' Emily countered. 'I know you can handle whatever comes up. And even if that weren't the case, who better than Scotland Yard to assure the Asians they're getting the red carpet treatment? Will you do it?'

That was the question, all right. But she *would* be of service, Barbara realised. Not only to Emily, but to Azhar. Who indeed could better navigate the waters of the Asians' hostility than someone acquainted with one of them? 'All right,' she said.

'Brilliant.' Emily held her wrist up to the dim light from the streetlamp. She said, 'Hell. It's late. Where're you staying, Barb?'

'I haven't booked anywhere yet,' Barbara said, and hurried on lest Emily think she was hinting for an invitation to share the dubious comforts of her gentrification project. 'I thought I'd try for a room along the seafront. If there's going to be a cool breeze within the next twenty-four hours, I'd like to be the first to know.'

'Even better,' Emily said. 'Inspired, in fact.' Before Barbara could question what was so inspired about longing for a breeze to cool the stifling air, Emily went on. The Burnt House Hotel would be perfect for Barbara's needs, she said. It had no immediate access to the strand, but it sat at the north end of the town above the sea, with nothing to impede a breeze should one decide to blow in its direction. Since it had no immediate access to sand and water, it was always the last hotel to get booked up once the tourist season – such as it was these days in Balford-le-Nez – began. And even if that weren't the case, there was one other point about the Burnt House that made it a desirable domicile for New Scotland Yard's Detective Sergeant Barbara Havers during her sojourn in Balford.

'What's that?' Barbara asked.

The murdered man had stayed there, Emily told her. 'So you can help me out with some nosing round.'

Rachel Winfield often wondered where normal girls went for advice when the larger moral questions in life loomed in front of them demanding answers. Her fantasy was that normal girls went to their normal mothers. What happened was this: the normal girls and their normal mothers sat together in the kitchen and they shared a pot of tea. What went with the tea was conversation, and the normal daughters and their normal mothers chatted companionably about whatever subject was near and dear to their hearts. That was the key: hearts in the plural. The communication between them was a two-way street, with mother listening to daughter's concerns and then giving daughter the benefit of her own experience.

In Rachel's case, had mother even considered giving daughter the benefit of her own experience, that experience would have been of little use in the present situation. What good was listening to the tales of a middle-aged – however successful – competitive dancer if competitive dancing was not what was on one's mind? If what was on one's mind was murder, then hearing a spirited account of an elimination competition, danced to the manic measures of 'The Boogie Woogie Bugle Boy' wouldn't be much of a help.

Rachel's mother, Connie, had on this very evening been deserted by her regular dancing partner – left at the metaphorical altar, which was disturbingly reminiscent of having been left at the real altar not once but twice by men too repugnant even to be named – and this desertion had taken place not twenty minutes before the competition. 'His *stomach*,' Connie had announced bitterly upon arriving home with a small but nonetheless shining third-place trophy on which two dancers contorted impossibly in bouffant skirt and form-fitting trousers. 'He spent the evening in the loo doing his business and screaming about his flaming bowels. I'd've had first place if I hadn't had to dance with Seamus O'Callahan. Thinks he's Rudolph bloody Valentino –'

Nureyev, Rachel corrected her silently.

'– and it's all I can do, isn't it, to keep him from squashing my feet to bits when he leaps about. Swing dancing is *not* about leaping, I keep telling him, don't I, Rache? But does that make a difference to Seamus O'C? Would that ever make a difference to a bloke who sweats like an overcooked turkey in the oven? Ha! Not bloody likely.'

Connie placed her trophy on one of the metal, designed-to-look-like-wood shelves of the unit fitted to the lounge wall. She fixed its position among the two dozen awards already displayed there. The smallest of them was a pewter shot glass engraved with a man and a woman at arm's length from each other and in full swing. The largest was a silver-plated bowl – with *First Place Southend Swingtime* scrolled on it – whose plating was wearing off from too much dedicated polishing.

Connie Winfield stepped back from the shelf and admired the latest addition to her collection. She looked a little the worse for wear after her hours on the dance floor. And the beginnings of the ruination that the exercise had wrought upon her fresh hair-do from Sea and Sun Unisex had been consolidated by the heat.

At the lounge door, Rachel watched her mother. She noted the love bite on her neck and wondered who had done the honours: Seamus O'Callahan or Connie's regular swing partner, a bloke called Jake Bottom, whom Rachel had found in the kitchen the morning after the night her mother had met him. 'Couldn't get his car started,' Connie had whispered confidentially to Rachel when her daughter had stopped short at the sight of Jake's hairless and heretofore unknown chest at the breakfast table. 'Slept on the sofa, Rache.' To which remark Jake had raised his head and winked lewdly.

Not that Rachel had needed that wink to put two and two together. Jake Bottom wasn't the first man who'd had engine trouble at their front door over the years.

'They're something, aren't they?' Connie asked with reference to her collection of trophies. 'Never thought your mum could trip the bright fantastic –'

The light fantastic, Rachel corrected her silently.

'– like she does, did you?' Connie eyed her closely. 'Why's your mug all pinched up, Rachel Lynn? You didn't forget to lock the shop, did you? Rache, if you've gone and caused us a break-in, I'll crack you a good one.'

'I locked up,' Rachel said. 'I double checked to make sure.'

'Then what's up? You look like you're sucking on sour plums. And why'n't you using that make-up I bought you? God knows, you can do something with what you've got if you'd only work at it, Rache.' Connie crossed to her and fussily rearranged her hair, doing what she always did with it: pulling it forward so that wings of black fell like a veil against a good part of her face. Stylish this way, Connie would tell her.

There was no point telling Connie that rearranging her hair would do little to improve her overall appearance. Her mother had gone twenty years pretending that there was nothing wrong with Rachel's face. She wasn't likely to change her tune now. Rachel knew that.

'Mum . . .'

'Connie,' her mother corrected her. She'd decided upon Rachel's twentieth birthday that she couldn't abide being the mother of a budding adult. 'We look more like sisters anyway,' she'd said when she'd first informed Rachel that they were to be Connie and Rache from that moment forward.

'Connie,' Rachel said.

Connie smiled and patted her cheek. 'Better,' she said. 'But put some colour on, Rache. You've got perfect cheekbones. Women die for cheekbones like you've got. Why'n't you use them, for God's sake?'

Rachel trailed Connie into the kitchen. She was squatting before the tiny refrigerator and brought out a Coke and an oversize rubber band that she kept inside a plastic bag. The rubber band – five inches wide and two feet long – she slapped on to the kitchen table. The Coke she poured into a glass, adding two sugar cubes as she always did and watching the bubbles rise from them in a froth. She carried this drink to the table as well and kicked off her shoes. She unzipped her dress, stepped out of it, stepped out of her petticoats, and sat on the floor in her underwear. She had the body of a woman half her forty-two years, and she liked to show it off it there was the slightest indication of a compliment – fulsome or otherwise, Connie wasn't picky – being tossed her way.

Rachel did her duty. 'Most women'd kill to have a stomach that flat.'

Connie reached for her rubber band and hooked it round her feet. She began alternately doing sit-ups and pulling the band – made more resistant by its time in the fridge – high above her head. 'Well, it's all about exercise, isn't it, Rache? *And* eating right. And thinking young. How're my thighs? Not going dimply, are they?' She paused to lift a leg in the air, toe pointed heavenward. She ran her hands from her ankles to her garters.

'They're fine,' Rachel said. 'In fact, they're perfect.'

Connie looked pleased. Rachel sat at the table as her mother continued to exercise.

Connie puffed. 'Isn't this heat the worst? I s'pose that's why you're up so late. Couldn't sleep? I'm not surprised. It's a wonder to me you *ever* sleep, all done up like a Victorian granny. Sleep in the nude, girl. Liberate yourself.'

'It's not the heat,' Rachel said.

'No? Then what? Some laddie got your knickers all in a twist?' She began her leg splits, grunting slightly. Her long-nailed fingers kept count of the repetitions, tapping against the linoleum floor. 'You're not putting out without protection, are you, Rache? I told you how you got to insist that the bloke wears a condom. If he won't wear a condom when you tell him to wear a condom, then you give him the shove. When I was your age –'

'Mum,' Rachel cut in. It was ridiculous to talk about insisting on condoms. Who did her mother think she was, anyway? The reincarnation of Connie herself? Connie had had to drive men off with a cricket bat from her fourteenth birthday, to hear her tell it. And nothing was dearer to her heart than the idea of having a daughter who was faced with the same 'inconvenience'.

'Connie,' Connie corrected her.

'Yeah. I meant Connie.'

'I'm sure you did, love-boodle.' Connie winked, changed her position to lie on her side, and began sideways lifts with her arms thrown over her head. One thing about Connie that Rachel admired was her single-minded dedication to an objective. It didn't really matter what the moment's objective was. Connie gave herself to it like a young girl becoming the bride of Christ: she was the picture of complete devotion. This was a fine attribute in competitive dancing, in exercising, even in business. At the moment, however, it was also an attribute that

Rachel could have done without. She needed her mother's undivided attention. She screwed up her courage in order to request it.

'Connie, c'n I ask you something? Something personal? Something about your insides?'

'My insides?' On the floor, Connie raised an eyebrow. A drop of perspiration trickled from it, glittering like a liquid jewel in the kitchen light. 'You wanting to know the facts of life?' She puffed and chortled, leg lifting and falling. Her cleavage was beginning to glisten with sweat. 'Bit late for that, i'n't it? Didn't I see you going between the beach huts with some bloke more 'n once at night?'

'Mum!'

'Connie.'

'Right. Connie.'

'Didn't know I knew about that, did you, Rache? Who was he, anyway? Did he do bad by you?' She sat, draped the band round her shoulders, began to pull it forward and release it, working on her arms. The patch of damp she'd left on the lino looked vaguely the shape of an upended pear. 'Men, Rache: you got to forget about trying to read their minds or control their doings. If you both want the same thing, then go ahead and have yourselves some fun. If one of you doesn't, forget it And always keep fun just that, Rache: fun. And use protection, because you don't want any little surprises after the fact, with legs or without them. The surprises, that is. That's how I've lived and it's served me fine.' She watched Rachel brightly, as if waiting for the next probing question or a girlish admission prompted by her own womanly candour.

'It's not about insides like that,' Rachel said. 'It's about your real insides. Your soul and your conscience.'

Connie's expression wasn't encouraging. She looked utterly baffled. 'You getting religion?' she asked. 'Did you talk to those Hare Krishnas last week? Don't look so innocent. You know the ones I mean. They were dancing round by Princes Breakwater beating on their tambourines. You must've ridden by on your bike. Don't tell me you didn't.' She went back to her arm pulls.

'It's not about religion. It's about right and wrong. That's what I want to ask you about.'

Clearly, these were deeper waters. Connie dropped the rubber band and pulled herself to her feet. She took a large gulp of Coke, and reached for a packet of Dunhills that lay in a plastic basket in the centre of the table. She eyed her daughter warily as she lit up and inhaled, holding the smoke in her lungs for a moment before exhaling a stream of it in Rachel's direction. 'What've you been up to, Rachel Lynn?' She'd become all mother in an instant.

Rachel was actually grateful for the change. She felt buoyed momentarily as she had been in childhood at those moments when Connie's maternal instincts battled their way past her natural indifference to the calls of motherhood.

'Nothing,' Rachel said. 'It's not about doing right or wrong. At least not really.'

'Then what?'

Rachel hesitated. Now that she had her mother's attention, she wondered how it was going to serve her. She couldn't tell her everything – she couldn't tell *anyone* everything – but she needed to tell someone just enough so that the someone might give her advice. 'Suppose,' Rachel said delicately, 'suppose something bad happened to a person.'

'Okay. I'm supposing.' Connie smoked, looking as thoughtful as one could hope to look in a black strapless bra, matching knickers cut high on the thigh, and a lace suspender belt.

'This is a seriously bad thing that happened. And suppose you know something that might help people understand why this bad thing happened in the first place.'

'Understand why?' Connie said. 'Why does anyone need to understand why? Bad things happen to people all the time.'

'But this is a really bad thing. This is the worst.'

Connie inhaled again, eyes on her daughter speculatively. 'The worst, eh? Now, what could that be? House burned down? Winning lottery ticket got tossed in the rubbish? Wife ran off with Ringo Starr?'

'I'm being serious,' Rachel said.

Connie must have seen the anxiety in her daughter's face because she pulled out a chair and lowered herself into it, joining Rachel at the table. 'Okay,' she said. 'Something bad happened to someone. And you know why. Is that right? Yes? So what's this something, then?'

'Death.'

Connie's cheeks puffed out. She took up her cigarette and drew on it deeply. 'Death, Rachel Lynn. What're you on about?'

'Someone died. And I –'

'You mixed up in something nasty?'

'No.'

'Then what?'

'Mum, I'm trying to explain. I mean, I'm trying to ask you –'

'What?'

'For help. For advice. I need to know if when a person knows something about a death, that person should tell the whole truth no matter what. If what a person knows may not have anything at all to *do* with that death, then should that person hold back on telling what she knows if she's asked what she knows in the first place? Because I know that the person doesn't need to say anything if no one asks her. But on the chance that she *is* asked, should she say something if she isn't sure it could be of help?'

Connie looked at her as if she'd just sprouted wings. Then her eyes narrowed. Despite Rachel's rambling presentation, when Connie next spoke, it was clear that she'd made some sophisticated leaps of comprehension. 'Is this a sudden death we're talking of, Rache? Is this death unexpected?'

'Well. Yeah.'

'Is it unexplained?'

'I s'pose so. Yeah.'

'Is it recent?'

'Yeah.'

'Is it local?'

Rachel nodded.

'Then is it . . .' Connie stowed her cigarette between her lips and rooted in a stack of newspapers, magazines, and post that lay beneath the plastic basket from which she'd taken her cigarettes. She looked at the front page of one *Tendring Standard*, discarded it in favour of another, discarded that in favour of a third. 'This?' She tossed the paper in front of Rachel. It was the one reporting the death on the Nez. 'D'you know something about this, my girl?'

'What makes you think that?'

'Come on, Rache. I've not gone blind. I know you're thick with the coloureds.'

'Don't say that.'

'Why? You never made a secret that you and Sally Malik –'

'Sahlah. Not Sally. And I didn't mean don't say I'm thick with them. I meant don't call them coloured. It's ignorant, Mum.'

'Well, *par*don me.' Connie tapped her cigarette against an ashtray. This was shaped like a high-heeled shoe, with the heel a resting spot for the fag. Connie didn't use this, since to use it meant to forego a few lungfuls of smoke, which was something she was clearly loath to do at the moment. She said, 'You best tell me direct what's got your knickers knotted, girl, because I'm not up to playing mind games tonight. Do you know something about this bloke's death?'

'No. Not exactly, that is.'

'So you know something unexactly. That it? You know this bloke personal?' The question, once asked, seemed to push a button of some sort, because Connie's eyes widened and she stubbed out her cigarette so quickly that she upended the ashtray on to the table. 'Is *this* the bloke you were going between the beach huts with? God Almighty, were you letting some coloured man do you? Where's your sense, Rachel? Where's your decency? Where's your value of yourself? D'you think a coloured man would ever give two figs if he put you in the club? *Not* bloody likely. And if he gave you one of those coloured diseases? What then, girl? And what about some virus? What's it called? Enola? Oncola?'

Ebola, Rachel corrected her silently. And it had nothing to do with getting poked by a man – white, brown, black, or purple – between the beach huts in Balford-le-Nez. 'Mum,' she said patiently.

'*Connie* to you. ConnieConnieConnie!'

'Yes. Right. No one's poking me, Connie. D'you actually think that anyone – no matter his colour – would want to poke me?'

'And whyever not?' Connie demanded. 'What's wrong with you? With a beautiful body and fabulous cheekbones and wonderful legs, why wouldn't some bloke want to have his way with Rachel Lynn Winfield every night of the week?'

Rachel could see the desperation in her mother's eyes. She knew it would be pointless – worse, it would be unnecessarily cruel – to wring an admission of the truth from Connie. She was, after all, the person who had given birth to the baby without a proper face. That would probably be as difficult a reality to live with as it was to live with the face itself. She said, 'You're right, Connie,' and felt a quiet despair settle over her, like a net whose webbing was composed of sorrows. 'But this bloke on the Nez? I didn't do it with him.'

'But it's his death you know something about.'

'Not exactly his death. But something related. And I wanted to know, should I say something if someone asks me.'

'What kind of someone?'

'Maybe a police kind of someone.'

'Police?' Connie managed to say the word with barely a movement of her lips. She plucked a pink paper napkin from the plastic seashell

holder, and she dabbed her mouth with it as daintily as if she'd
been having a cup of tea with the Queen. But beneath the fuchsia
blusher she wore, her skin had gone quite pale so that the streaks of
make-up on her cheeks stood out like sodden rose petals. She didn't
look at Rachel again as she spoke. 'We're businesswomen, Rachel Lynn
Winfield. We're businesswomen first and we're businesswomen last.
What we got – no matter how little it is – depends on the good will of
this town. And not just the tourists' good will, mind you, coming here
in the summer, but everyone else's good will as well. You got that?'

'Sure. I know.'

'So you get a name as someone who opens her gob too easy and
spills what she knows to every Tom, Dick, and Harry coming in off
the street, and the only people who lose out are us: Connie and Rache.
People shy away from us. They stop coming into the shop. They take
their business over to Clacton, and it's no inconvenience for them to
do that because they'd rather go somewhere they feel comfortable,
where they can say "I need something pretty for a very special lady",
and they can wink when they say it and know that wink isn't going
to get back to their wives. Am I being clear on this, Rache? We got
a business to run. And business comes first. Always.'

That said, she took up her Coke once again, and this time when she
took a gulp, she pulled a copy of *Woman's Own* from the pile of bills,
catalogues, and newpapers on the table. She opened it and began to
study the table of contents. Their conversation was at a close.

Rachel watched her running her long red fingernail down the list
of articles contained in the magazine. She watched as Connie flipped
to one entitled 'Seven Ways to Know if He's Cheating'. The title made
Rachel shiver despite the heat, so accurately did it hit the very nail on
the very head. She needed an article called 'What to Do When You
Know', but she had her answer, really. Do nothing and wait. Which
was what, she realised, everyone should do when it came to betrayals
petty or otherwise. Acting upon a knowledge of them led nowhere
else but to disaster. The past few days in Balford-le-Nez had proved
that to Rachel Winfield beyond a shadow of a doubt.

'For an indefinite stay?' The proprietor of the Burnt House Hotel fairly
salivated over the words. As it was, he rubbed his hands together as
if he were already massaging the money Barbara would have to part
with at the end of her stay. He had introduced himself as Basil Treves
and had added the information that he was a retired army lieutenant

– 'in Her Majesty's Armed Forces' as he put it – once he read upon her registration card that her place of employment was New Scotland Yard. This apparently made them compatriots of some sort.

Barbara supposed it was the idea of having to wear uniforms both in the army and in the Met. She herself hadn't worn a uniform in years, but she didn't share this bit of personal trivia. She needed Basil Treves on her side, and anything that served to put him there and keep him there was well worth preserving. Besides, she appreciated the fact that he'd tactfully made no mention of the condition of her face. She'd removed the remaining bandages in the car after leaving Emily, but her skin from eyes to lips was still a panorama of yellow, purple, and blue.

Treves led her up one flight of stairs and down a dim corridor. Nowhere was there much to indicate to Barbara that the Burnt House Hotel was a banner of delights just waiting to unfurl for her pleasure. A relic of long-ago Edwardian summers, it boasted faded carpets over creaking floor boards above which hung water-stained ceilings. It was possessed of a general atmosphere of genteel decay.

Treves seemed oblivious of all this, however. He chatted incessantly the entire way to Barbara's room, smoothing his sparse and oily hair up from a parting just above his left ear and across the gleaming dome of his skull. She would find the Burnt House had every possible convenience, he confided: a colour television in every room *with* a remote control device, and another large-screen telly in the residents' lounge should she decide to be sociable of an evening; tea-making facilities next to one's bed for a morning cuppa; bathrooms in nearly *every* room and additional toilets and baths on each floor; telephones with a direct line into the world upon the touch of a nine; and that most mystical, blessed, and cherished of mod cons – a fax machine in reception. He called it a facsimile sender, as if he and the machine were still on formal terms with each other, and he went on to add, 'But you won't be wanting that, I dare say. Here for a holiday, are you, Miss Havers?'

'Sergeant Havers,' Barbara corrected him and added, 'Detective Sergeant Havers.' There was no better time than the present, she decided, to position Basil Treves where she needed him. Something about the man's sharp little eyes and expectant posture told her he would be only too happy to assist the police with information if given a chance. The framed newspaper photo of himself in reception – celebrating his election to the town council – told her that he was the sort of man who didn't come by personal glory often or easily. So when the opportunity arose to garner a bit, he doubtless would be the first to jump at it. And what greater glory than to be an unofficial part of a murder investigation? He might prove to be quite useful, and with only a little effort on her part. 'I'm here on business, actually,' she told him, allowing herself a slight economy with the truth. 'CID business, to be more precise.'

Treves paused outside the door of her room, its key dangling from his palm by an enormous ivory tag that was shaped like a roller coaster. Each of the keys, Barbara had noted when registering, was identified in similar fun-fair fashion: other tags were shaped like everything from a dodgem car to a miniature Ferris wheel, and the rooms they gave access to were named accordingly.

'Criminal Investigations?' Treves said. 'Is this about ... But of course, you absolutely can*not* say, can you? Well, mum's the word at *this* end of things, I assure you of that, Detective Sergeant. No one will hear who you are from *these* lips. Here we are, then.'

Swinging open the narrow door, he switched on the overhead light and stood back to let her enter ahead of him. When she had done so, he bustled past her, humming tonelessly as he set down her haversack on a collapsible luggage rack. He pointed out the bathroom with the proud announcement that he'd especially given her 'the loo with a view'. He patted his hands against the bilious green chenille counterpanes of both twin beds, saying, 'Nice and firm, but not too much, I hope,' and he flicked the pink skirt of a kidney-shaped dressing table to rearrange it. He straightened both the prints on the walls – matching Victorian ice skaters who glided away from each other, looking none too happy about taking the exercise – and he fingered through the teabags that lay in a basket waiting for morning. He switched on the bedside lamp, then switched it off. Then switched it on again, as if sending signals.

'You'll have all that you require, Sergeant Havers, and if you need anything more, you shall find Mr Basil Treves at your service day and night. At any hour.' He beamed at her. He held his hands folded at chest height and stood at a modified kind of attention. 'As for this evening, any final requests? A nightcap? Cappuccino? Some fruit? Mineral water? Greek dancing boys?' He chortled happily. 'I'm here to serve your every whim, and don't you forget it.'

Barbara thought about asking him to brush the dandruff from his shoulders, but she didn't think it was the sort of request that he had in mind. She moved to open the windows. The room was so stifling that the air seemed to shimmer, and she wished that one of the hotel's mod cons had been air conditioning or even room fans. The air was still. It seemed as if the entire universe were holding its breath.

'Wonderful weather, isn't it?' Treves said jauntily. 'It'll bring the visitors here in droves. Lucky you've come when you have, Sergeant. In another week we'll be booked to the roof. Not that I wouldn't have made room for *you*. Police business takes precedence, doesn't it?'

Her fingers, Barbara noted, were black-tipped with grime from having opened the window. She rubbed them surreptitiously against her trousers. 'As to that, Mr Treves . . .'

Birdlike, he cocked his head. 'Yes? Is something . . . ?'

'A Mr Querashi was staying here, wasn't he? Haytham Querashi?'

It hardly seemed possible that Basil Treves could stand any more to attention, but he appeared to manage it. Barbara thought he might even salute. 'An unfortunate occurrence,' he said formally.

'That he was staying here?'

'Great Scot, no. He was welcome to stay here. He was more than welcome. The Burnt House doesn't discriminate against anyone. Never has done. And never will do.' He gave a glance over his shoulder towards the open door, saying, 'If I may . . . ?' When Barbara nodded, he closed it and continued in a lower voice. 'Although to be *perfectly* honest, I do keep the races separate as you'll probably note during your stay. This hasn't to do with my own inclinations, mind you. I haven't the *slightest* prejudice against coloured people. Not the slightest. But the other guests . . . To be frank, Sergeant, times have been difficult. It doesn't make good business sense to do anything that might engender ill will. If you know what I mean.'

'So Mr Querashi stayed in another part of the hotel? Is that what you're saying?'

'Not so much in another part, but just away from the others. Ever so slightly. I doubt he even noticed.' Treves raised his folded hands to his chest once again. 'I have several permanent residents, you see. These are ageing ladies, and they simply aren't used to the way times have changed. In fact, this is almost too embarrassing to mention, but one of them actually mistook Mr Querashi for a servant the first morning he came down to breakfast. Can you imagine it? Poor thing.'

Barbara wasn't sure whether he was referring to Haytham Querashi or the old woman, but she felt she could hazard a fairly accurate guess. 'I'd like to see the room he stayed in, if I may,' Barbara said.

'Then you *are* here because of his demise?'

'Not his demise. His murder.'

Treves said, '*Murder*? Good God,' and he reached behind him till his hand came into contact with one of the twin beds. He sank on to it, said, 'If you'll pardon me,' and lowered his head. He breathed deeply, and when he finally raised his head again, he said in a hushed voice, 'Does it have to be known that he was staying here? Here at the Burnt House? Will the newspapers mention it? Because with business *promising* to pick up at long last . . .'

So much for his reaction having to do with shock, guilt, or the milk of human kindness, Barbara thought. Not for the first time, she had validation for her long-held belief that *homo sapiens* was genetically linked to pond scum.

Treves must have seen this conclusion on her face, because he went on quickly. 'It's not that I don't *care* what happened to Mr Querashi. I do. Indeed I do care most deeply. He was quite a pleasant chap, for all his ways, and I regret his unfortunate passing. But with business about to pick up, and after all these years of recession, one can't take the chance of losing even one –'

'His ways?' Barbara headed off his discourse on the nation's economy.

Basil Treves blinked. 'Well, they are different, aren't they?'

'They?'

'These Asians. Why, surely you know? You'd have to, wouldn't you, working in London? Good grief. Don't deny it.'

'How was he different?'

Treves apparently inferred something more than she intended from the question. His eyes started to go opaque and he crossed his arms. *Defences are rising*, Barbara thought with interest, and she wondered why he was arming himself. Nonetheless, she knew it wouldn't do for them to be at odds, so she hastened to reassure him. 'What I meant is that since you saw him regularly, anything unusual that you can tell me about his behaviour will help. Culturally he would have been different from the rest of your guests –'

'He certainly isn't the *only* Asian in residence,' Treves interrupted, still driving home the point about his liberality. 'The Burnt House's doors will always be open to all.'

'Right. Of course. Then I take it he was different even from the other Asians. Whatever you tell me I'll keep in confidence, Mr Treves. Anything that you know, saw, or even suspected about Mr Querashi may be the fact we need to get to the root of what happened to him.'

Her words seemed to mollify the man, encouraging him to reflect upon his own importance to a police investigation. He said, 'I see. Yes. I do see,' and proceeded to look thoughtful. He stroked his scraggly, unclipped beard.

'May I see his room?'

'But of course. Yes. Yes.'

He led her back the way they had come, ascending one more flight of stairs and walking along a corridor towards the rear of the building. Three of the doors along the corridor stood open, awaiting tenants. A fourth was shut. Behind it television voices spoke at a considerate, low volume. Haytham Querashi's room was next to this one, the fifth room at the very end of the passage.

Treves had a master key. He said, 'I haven't touched it since his . . . well . . . the accident . . .' There was indeed no euphemism for *murder*. He gave up searching for one and said, 'The police came by to tell me about it – just that he was dead. They told me to keep his room locked up till I heard from them.'

'We don't like anything to be disturbed till we know what we're working with,' Barbara told him. 'Natural causes, a murder, accident, or suicide. You haven't disturbed anything, have you? No one else has?'

'No one,' he said. 'Akram Malik called in with his son. They wanted the personal effects to send back to Pakistan, and believe me, they weren't happy hikers when I wouldn't let them into the room to collect them. Muhannad acted as if I was part of a conspiracy to commit crimes against mankind.'

'And Akram Malik? What did he think?'

'Our Akram plays his cards ve-ry close, Sergeant. He wouldn't be fool enough to let me know what he was thinking.'

'Why's that?' Barbara asked as Treves swung open the door to Haytham Querashi's room.

'Because we loathe each other,' Treves explained pleasantly. 'I can't abide upstarts and he doesn't like to be considered one. It's a shame he emigrated to England, when you think of it. He'd have done much better in the US, where the first concern is whether you have money, and who your people are ranks down round your shoe size. Here we are.' He switched on the overhead light.

Haytham Querashi's room was a single with a small casement window overlooking the back garden of the hotel. It was decorated as haphazardly as Barbara's room. Yellow, red, and pink all battled to be the dominant colour.

'He seemed to be quite happy here,' Treves said as Barbara took in the depressingly narrow bed, the one armless and lumpy chair, the pseudo-wood of the clothes cupboard, and the gaps in the tassels on the shade of a wall sconce. There was a print above the bed, another Victorian scene, this one a young woman languishing on a chaise longue. The paper it was mounted on had long since gone dingy.

'Right.' Barbara grimaced at the odour in the room. It was the smell of burned onions and sprouts too long cooked. Querashi's room was located above the kitchen, doubtless a subtle reminder to the man of what his place was in the hotel hierarchy. 'Mr Treves, what can you tell me about Haytham Querashi? How long had he been staying with you? Had he any visitors? Any friends who called in? Any particular phone calls that he made or received?' She pressed the back of her hand against the hot dampness on her forehead and went to the chest of drawers to have a look at Querashi's belongings. She paused and rustled through her shoulder bag for the evidence bags that Emily had given to her before she'd left the Crescent.

Querashi, Basil Treves informed her, had been staying at the Burnt House for six weeks while waiting for his wedding. Akram Malik had arranged for the room. Apparently, a house had been purchased for the soon-to-be newlyweds as part of the Malik daughter's dowry, but as it was undergoing redecoration, Querashi's stay at the hotel had been extended several times. He went to work before eight in the morning and generally returned round half-past seven or eight at night, taking breakfast and dinner at the Burnt House on weekdays, dinner elsewhere at the weekend.

'With the Maliks?'

Treves shrugged. He ran one finger down a panel in the opened door and examined its tip which, even from where Barbara stood at the chest of drawers, she could see was furred with dust. He couldn't *swear* that Querashi was with the Maliks every weekend. While it would make sense were that the case – 'since in usual circumstances the lovebirds would want to be together as often as possible, wouldn't they?' – because these circumstances were rather abnormal, there was always a possibility that Querashi spent his weekend hours in other pursuits.

'Abnormal circumstances?' Barbara turned from the chest of drawers.

'An arranged marriage,' Treves explained, with delicate emphasis on the adjective. 'Rather medieval, wouldn't you say?'

'It's cultural, isn't it?'

'Whatever you call it, when you force fourteenth-century mores upon twentieth-century men and women, you can't be surprised what develops as a result, can you, Sergeant?'

'What developed in this case?' Barbara turned back to take note of the items on top of the chest: a passport, neatly arranged stacks of coins, a moneyclip clasping fifty pounds in notes, and a brochure for a place called the Castle Hotel and Restaurant which was – according to the map that accompanied it – on the main road to Harwich. Barbara opened this curiously. The tariff sheet fell out. She noted that listed last among the rooms was a honeymoon suite. For £80.00 per night, Querashi and his bride would have been set up with a four-poster, one half bottle of Asti Spumante, one red rose, and breakfast in bed. Romantic devil, she thought, and went on to a leather case that, upon inspection, she found locked.

She realised that Treves hadn't answered her question. She glanced his way. He was pulling thoughtfully at his beard, and she noticed for the first time a few disagreeable flakes of skin caught up in it, product of a mild case of eczema that mottled the lower part of his cheeks. He was wearing that sort of expression that powerless people seeking power often wear. Lofty, knowing, and undecided about the wisdom of sharing his knowledge. Bloody hell, Barbara thought with an inward sigh. It looked as if she was going to have to massage his ego every step of the way.

'I need your insight into him, Mr Treves. Aside from the Maliks, you're probably the best source of information we have.'

'I understand that.' Treves gave his beard a preening pat. 'But you must understand that a hotelier is not entirely unlike a confessor. To the successful hotelier, what one sees, hears, and concludes is of a confidential nature.'

Barbara wanted to point out to him that the state of the Burnt House hardly justified the adjective *successful* being applied to him. But she knew the rules of the game he was playing. 'Believe me,' she intoned, 'whatever information you supply will be treated in confidence, Mr Treves. But I've got to have it if we're to work together as equals.' She wanted to snarl when she said the final words. She covered this desire by sliding open the top drawer of the chest, searching through carefully folded socks and underwear for the key to the locked leather case.

'If you're sure of that . . .' Treves was apparently so eager to part with what he knew – despite his words – that he went on without waiting for her assurances. 'Then I must tell you. There was someone else in his life besides the Malik girl. It's the only explanation.'

'For what?' Barbara went on to the second drawer. A stack of perfectly folded shirts was arranged by colour: white giving way to ivory, to grey, and finally to black. Pyjamas were in the third drawer. Nothing was in the fourth. Querashi travelled light.

'For why he went out at night.'

'Haytham Querashi went out at night? How often?'

'At least twice a week. Sometimes more. And always after ten. I thought at first that he was going to see his fiancée. It seemed a reasonable enough conclusion, despite the odd hour. He'd want to get to know her, wouldn't he, before the wedding day? These people aren't complete heathens, after all. They may give their sons and daughters away to the highest bidder, but I dare say they don't give them away to total strangers without allowing them a chance to get acquainted. Do they?'

'I haven't a clue,' Barbara replied. 'Go on.' She went to the bedside table, a wobbly affair with a single drawer. She slid this open.

'Well, the point is that on *this* particular night, I saw him as he was leaving the hotel. We chatted a bit about the upcoming nuptials, and he told me he was going to the seafront for a run. Pre-wedding nerves and all. You know.'

'Right.'

'So when I heard he died on the Nez, of all places – which as you may or may not know, Sergeant, is in the opposite direction from the seafront if you leave from this hotel intending to have a run – I realised he hadn't wanted me to be privy to what he was up to. Which can only mean that he was up to something he hadn't ought to be up to. And, since he regularly left the hotel at the exact hour at which he left on Friday night, and since on Friday night he ended up dead, I think it's safe to deduce not only that he was meeting someone whom he met on the other nights but also that this someone was a person he ought not to have been meeting in the first place.' Treves folded his hands at chest height once again and looked as if he expected Barbara to shout, 'Holmes, you amaze me!'

But since Haytham Querashi had been murdered and since the conditions suggested the death was no random act, Barbara had already concluded that the man had gone to the Nez to meet someone. The only piece of information Treves had added was that Querashi may have made this a regular rendezvous. And, reluctant as she was to admit it, that was an extremely valuable titbit. She threw the hotelier a bone. 'Mr Treves, you're in the wrong profession.'

'Really?'

'Believe it.' And those two words weren't even a lie.

Thus buoyed, Treves came to inspect the contents of the bedside table with her: a yellow-bound book with a matching satin marker that, opened, displayed several lines bracketed off and an entire text that was written in Arabic; a box of two dozen condoms, half of which were gone; and a 5" x 7" manila envelope. Barbara placed the book into an evidence bag as Treves tut-tutted over the condoms and everything that possession of such sexual paraphernalia seemed to imply. As he clucked, Barbara upended the manila envelope into her palm. Two keys fell out, one not much larger than the length of her first knuckle to the tip of her thumb, the other quite tiny, fingernail size. This second had to be the key to the leather case on the chest of drawers. She closed her fingers round both of the keys and contemplated her next move. She wanted a look inside the case, but she preferred the look to be a private one. So before she took action, she had to take care of her bearded Sherlock.

She thought about how best to do this while still keeping the man's good will. He wouldn't take kindly to the dawning knowledge that, as he knew the victim, he was one of the suspects in Querashi's murder until an alibi or other evidence eliminated him.

She said, 'Mr Treves, these keys may be crucial to our investigation. Would you step into the corridor and keep watch, please? The last thing we want at a moment like this is eavesdroppers or spies. Give me the word if the coast is clear.'

He said, 'Of course, of *course*, Sergeant. I'm only too happy . . .' and hurried off to fulfil his commission.

Once he gave her the all clear, the heave ho, and the anchors aweigh, she took a closer look at the keys. They were both brass, the larger of them attached to a chain on which a metal tag also hung. This was stamped with the number 104. Locker key? Barbara wondered. And what sort of locker? Railway locker? Bus station locker? Personal locker somewhere on the seafront, the sort of metal cupboard in which people stowed their clothes while they were swimming in the sea? They were all possibilities.

The second key slid into the lock of the small leather case. The key turned smoothly. She flicked the catch on the case to the right. The lid unlatched. She eased the case open.

'Finding anything useful?' Treves' whisper came from the doorway, 007-like in its intensity. 'All clear on this side of things, Sergeant.'

'Keep guard, Mr Treves,' she whispered back.

'Will do,' he murmured. She could tell that he was beginning to feel he'd been born to live the cloak-and-dagger life.

'I'm depending on you,' she said and went for a between-the-teeth articulation, which she hoped would heighten the sense of intrigue apparently necessary to keep him in line. 'If anyone stirs . . . And I mean anyone at *all*, Mr Treves –'

'Absolutely,' he said. 'Carry on without fear, Detective Sergeant Havers.'

She smiled. What a goofball, she thought. She added the keys to the evidence bag. Then she turned to the leather case.

Its contents were neatly aranged: a pair of gold cuff links, a gold money clip with something engraved in Arabic on it, a small gold ring – perhaps intended for a woman – with a ruby in the centre, one gold coin, four gold bangles, a cheque book, and a yellow piece of paper that was folded in half. Barbara paused to consider Querashi's predilection for gold and what, if anything, such a predilection meant and how, if possible, such a predilection might fit into the overall scheme of what had happened to the man. Avarice? she wondered. Blackmail? Kleptomania? Foresight? Obsession? What?

The cheque book, she saw, was for a local branch of Barclays. It was the sort of book with a receipt stub running along the left side of the cheques. Only one had been written and documented on a receipt, £400 to an F. Kumhar. Barbara examined the date and did her maths: three weeks prior to Querashi's death.

Barbara slid the cheque book into the evidence bag and took up the folded bit of yellow paper. This turned out to be a receipt from a local shop. It was called Racon Original and Artistic Jewellery and beneath this name were the italicised words 'Balford's Finest'. Barbara thought at first that the receipt went with the small ruby ring. Perhaps a memento purchased by Querashi for his future bride? But upon inspection, she saw that the receipt wasn't made out to Querashi. Instead it was made out to Sahlah Malik.

The receipt did not make clear what had been purchased. Whatever it was, it had been identified only by two letters and a number: AK-162. And next to these was a phrase written in inverted commas: 'Life begins now'. At the bottom of the receipt was the price that Sahlah Malik had paid: £220.

Intriguing, Barbara thought. She wondered how Querashi had come to have the receipt in his possession. Obviously, it was the receipt for something purchased by the man's fiancée, and 'Life begins now' was probably what she intended to have engraved on it. Wedding ring? That was the most logical surmise. But did Pakistani husbands wear them? Barbara had never seen one on Taymullah Azhar, but that didn't mean much because not every man in her own culture wore one, so who was to say what the Asian custom was? But even if the receipt *was* for a wedding ring, having it in his possession indicated that Querashi planned to return whatever it was that Sahlah had purchased. And the act of returning a gift engraved with the hopeful and trusting words 'Life begins now' suggested a real fissure in the wedding plans.

Barbara glanced at the bedside table whose drawer was still open. From across the room she could see the half empty box of condoms, and she recalled that among the contents of the man's pockets had been three other condoms. In tandem with the receipt from the jewellery shop, the condoms served to underscore a single conclusion.

Not only had there been a fissure in the wedding plans, but there had likely been a third party involved, one who'd possibly encouraged Querashi to abandon his arranged marriage in favour of another relationship. And this had been done recently, since he still had in his possession the evidence that he was planning a honeymoon.

Barbara added the receipt to the other items she'd lifted from the bedside table. She locked the leather case and put it in the evidence bag as well. She wondered what sort of response would be given to the fiancé in an arranged marriage if he asked to call the arrangement to a halt. Would tempers flare? Would revenge be plotted? She didn't know. But she had an excellent idea of how to find out.

'Sergeant Havers?' From the corridor, it was not so much a whisper as a hiss. 007 was getting restless.

Barbara strode to the door and swung it open. She stepped into the corridor and took Treves' arm. 'We may be on to something,' she told him tersely.

'Really?' He was all agog and aquiver.

'Absolutely. D'you keep records of telephone calls? Yes? Good. I want those records,' she directed him. 'Every call he made. Every call he received.'

'Tonight?' Treves licked his lips enthusiastically. Doubtless, Barbara saw, if he were given his way, they'd be up to their elbows in hotel paperwork till dawn.

'Tomorrow's fine,' she told him. 'Get some sleep now. Be fresh for the fray.'

His whisper was excitement itself. 'Thank God I kept everyone out of that room.'

'Continue to do that, Mr Treves,' she said. 'Keep the door locked. Stand watch if you have to. Hire a guard. Set up a video camera. Wire the place for sound. Whatever it takes. But on no account let a single soul cross that threshold. I'm depending on you. Can I do that?'

'Sergeant,' Treves said, his hand at his heart, 'you can depend upon me to the absolute death.'

'Brilliant,' Barbara said. And she couldn't help wondering if those very same words had been recently said to Haytham Querashi.

Chapter Six

The morning sun awakened her. It was accompanied by the sound of gulls and the faint scent of brine in the air. As on the day before, this last was utterly still. Barbara could tell that by squinting out of the open window from her semi-foetal position in one of the room's two beds. Beyond the glass, a bay laurel tree stood, and not a dusty leaf on it so much as quivered. By midday, mercury was going to be bubbling in thermometers all over town.

Barbara ground her knuckles into the small of her back, which ached from its night's exposure to a mattress troughed by several generations of bodies. She swung her legs over the side of the bed and stumbled blearily into the loo with a view.

This bathroom continued the hotel's established theme of genteel decay: the tiles on the walls and the grout round the tub grew mildew in furry verdigris tufts, and the doors to the cupboards below the sink were held closed by means of an elastic band stretched between their knobs. One gained access to the view through a small window above the toilet, four grimy panes of glass behind a limp curtain on which appliquéd dolphins leaped out of a frothing sea that had long since gone the depressing colour of a winter sky.

Barbara assessed the environment with an 'ugh', and she gazed at her face in the age-spotted mirror above the sink, where perhaps two dozen gold cupid transfers shot amorous arrows at each other from clusters at the glass's four corners. She assessed her appearance with a second and more fervent 'ugh'. The combination of bruises going yellow at the edges from her eyes to her chin and the sleep creases across her left cheek created an unappealing vision to have to gaze upon directly before breakfast. The sight could definitely put one off one's bangers, Barbara decided, and turned from it to take in the view that the loo-with provided her.

The window was open to its fullest extent, affording a generous five inches of fresh morning air. She breathed this in and scrubbed her fingers through her thatch of hair as she looked across the slope of lawn to the sea.

On a bluff approximately one mile north of the town's centre, the Burnt House Hotel was positioned propitiously for travellers who came to Balford seeking only a view. To its south Princes Beach carved a crescent of sand punctuated by three stone breakwaters. To its east the lawn ended in a cliff beyond which endlessly stretched the sea, motionless this morning and edged by a roll of grey fog that hovered on the distant horizon, making a beguiling promise of cooler weather. To its north, the cranes of distant Harwich Harbour lifted their dinosaur necks far above the ferries that passed beneath them on their way to Europe. Barbara could see all of this from her window, small though it was, and all of this and more would be on display for anyone sitting in one of the drooping canvas chairs that were scattered across the hotel's lawn.

A landscape painter or a sketch artist might find that the Burnt House served his interests, Barbara decided, but for a traveller coming to Balford-le-Nez to sample more than just a pleasant vista, the hotel's location was a study in utter commercial folly. The distance between the hotel and the town proper – with its seafront esplanade, pleasure pier, and High Street – underscored this fact. These locations constituted the commercial heart of Balford-le-Nez, where tourists spent their money. While they were a convenient walking distance from the other hotels, the guest houses, and the summer cottages in the fading seaside town, they were not a convenient walking distance from the Burnt House Hotel. Parents with children in tow, young people eager for whatever questionable nightlife the town now afforded, travellers seeking everything from sand to souvenirs, would not find it here on the bluff north of Balford proper. They could walk into the town, of course. But there was no direct access along the seafront. Instead, pedestrians heading townward from the Burnt House would have to trudge inland first along Nez Park Road and then back out again to the Esplanade.

Basil Treves, Barbara concluded, was lucky to have anyone staying here at any time of year. Which meant he was lucky to have had Haytham Querashi staying as a long-term resident. Which in turn brought into question the part Treves may or may not have played in Querashi's marriage plans. It was an interesting speculation.

Barbara gazed in the direction of the pleasure pier. Construction was going on at its end, where the Jack 'awkins Cafeteria had once stood. And even at this distance she could see that the pier itself gleamed with clean new paint – white, green, blue, and orange – while bright motley flags flew from the poles that lined its sides. None of that had existed when she'd last been in Balford.

Barbara turned away. At the mirror once more, she examined her face and wondered if removing the bandages had been as inspired an idea as she'd originally thought. She'd brought no make-up with her. Her supply of cosmetics being limited to one tube of Blistex and a pot of rouge once belonging to her mother, tossing them into her haversack had hardly seemed worth the effort. She liked to consider herself a bird whose moral fibre wouldn't allow the rank dishonesty of doing anything more than pinching the cheeks to give a bit of colour in the face. But the truth was, given a choice between painting her flesh and sleeping for another fifteen minutes in the morning, she'd spent a lifetime selecting sleep. In her line of work, it seemed more practical. Thus, her preparation for the current day took less than ten minutes, and four of these she spent digging through her haversack, cursing, and looking for a pair of socks.

She gargled, ran a brush through her hair, shoved into her shoulder bag the goodies she'd removed from Querashi's room on the previous night, and headed out of the door. In the corridor, breakfast odours clung to the air like importunate children to their mother's skirt. Somewhere, eggs and bacon had been fried, bangers had been grilled, toast had been burned, tomatoes and mushrooms had been cooked. Barbara needed no map to find the dining room. She just followed the ever-intensifying smells down one flight of stairs and along a cramped ground-floor corridor towards the sound of cutlery being wielded against plates and voices murmuring about the day's plans. Which was when she heard it.

One voice stood out as she approached. A child was saying brightly, 'Did you know about the lobster boat ride? C'n we go, Dad? And the Ferris wheel? C'n we ride it today? I watched it and watched it from the lawn with Mrs Porter last night and she said that when *she* was my age, the Ferris wheel –'

A low murmur interrupted the hopeful chatter. As it usually did, Barbara realised grimly. What the hell was the matter with the man? He squelched every impulse the little girl had. Barbara advanced to the door, feeling unaccountably irritated and battle-ready where she knew she had no business feeling anything other than blandly disinterested.

Hadiyyah and her father sat in a dark corner of the old, heavily panelled dining room. They'd been placed well away from the other hotel residents: three elderly white couples whose tables lined up along the open french windows. These latter people attended to their breakfasts as if no one else were present, save for one old woman with a Zimmer frame resting next to her chair. She appeared to be the aforementioned Mrs Porter because she was nodding at Hadiyyah as if in encouragement from her end of the room.

Barbara wasn't completely surprised at the coincidence of being at the same hotel as Hadiyyah and Taymullah Azhar. She'd expected to find them staying with the Malik family, but as that apparently had not been possible, then the Burnt House Hotel was a logical choice. Haytham Querashi had stayed here, after all, and Azhar was in Balford because of Querashi.

'Ah. Sergeant Havers.' Barbara swung round to see Basil Treves behind her, two plates of breakfast in his hand. He beamed at her. 'If you'll allow me to show you to your table . . . ?'

As he attempted to shimmy past her to do the honours, Hadiyyah gave a happy shout. 'Barbara! You came!' And she dropped her spoon into her cereal, splashing milk across the pink tablecloth. She popped out of her chair and did her usual hop-and-skip across the room, singing, 'You came! You came! You came to the seaside!' with her yellow-ribboned plaits dancing round her shoulders. She was dressed like sunshine: yellow shorts and striped T-shirt, yellow-banded socks and sandals. She gripped Barbara's hand. 'Have you come to build a sandcastle with me? Have you come to pick cockles? I want to play the penny slide and ride the dodgem cars as well. Do you?'

Basil Treves was watching this interaction with some consternation. He said with more meaning, 'If I may show you to your table, Sergeant Havers?' and nodded pointedly at a table next to an open window and decidedly among the English residents.

'I'd rather be over there,' Barbara told him, jerking her thumb in the direction of the Pakistanis' dark corner. 'Too much fresh air in the morning puts me right off my kippers. D'you mind?'

Without waiting for him to reply, she sauntered over to Azhar. Hadiyyah skipped ahead. She cried out, 'She's here! Look, Dad! She's here! She's here!' and didn't appear to notice that her father was greeting Barbara's arrival with that special joy one generally reserves for embracing lepers.

Basil Treves, in the meantime, had deposited the two breakfast plates in front of Mrs Porter and her companion. He hurried over to usher Barbara into a seat at the table next to Azhar's. He was saying, 'Yes, oh yes. Of course. And will it be orange juice, Sergeant Havers? What about grapefruit segments?' He whipped the napkin out of its teepee folds with a flourish that suggested having the sergeant sit among the darkies had always been part of his master plan.

'No, with us! With us!' Hadiyyah crowed. She tugged Barbara to their table, saying, 'It's okay, Dad, isn't it? She *must* sit with us.'

Azhar observed Barbara evenly with his unreadable brown eyes. The only indication of feeling that he gave was the deliberate hesitation he employed before getting to his feet in greeting.

'We'd be very pleased, Barbara,' he said formally.

Bollocks, Barbara thought. But she said, 'If you've room . . . ?'

'Can make room. Can do,' Basil Treves said. And as he moved cutlery and crockery from her table to Azhar's, he hummed with the fierce determination employed by a man making the best of a bad situation.

'I'm so happy, happy, happy!' Hadiyyah sang. 'You've come for your holiday, haven't you? We can go to the beach. We can look for shells. We can go fishing. We can play on the pier.' She climbed back on to her chair and retrieved her spoon from the middle of her cereal where it lay like a silver exclamation mark, commenting on the morning's proceedings. Hadiyyah scooped it up, oblivious of the milk that dripped from it on to the front of her striped T-shirt. 'Yesterday Mrs Porter looked after me while Dad did some business,' she confided to Barbara. 'We read a book about fossils on the lawn. I mean,' she giggled, 'we *read* on the lawn. Today we were s'posed to take a walk along the Cliff Parade, but it's way too far to walk all the way to the pier. Too far for Mrs Porter, that is. But *I* c'n walk that far, can't I? And now that *you're* here, Dad will let me go to the arcade. Won't you, Dad? Won't you let me go if Barbara comes with me?' She squirmed in her chair so that she faced Barbara. 'We c'n ride the roller coaster and the

Ferris wheel, Barbara. We c'n shoot in the shooting gallery. We can play the crane grab. Are you good at the crane grab? Dad is brilliant. He grabbed me a koala bear once, and once he grabbed Mummy a pink –'

'Hadiyyah.' Her father's voice was firm. It silenced her with its usual proficiency.

Barbara studied her menu with religious devotion. She decided on her breakfast and gave her order to Treves who hovered nearby.

'Barbara is here to rest, Hadiyyah,' Azhar told his daughter as Treves took himself in the direction of the kitchen. 'You are not to force yourself into her holiday. She's been in an accident and will not be well enough to run about the town.'

Hadiyyah made no reply, but she cast a hopeful look in Barbara's direction. Her eager face had *Ferris wheel*, *arcade*, and *roller coaster* written all over it. She was swinging her legs and fairly bouncing in her seat, and Barbara wondered how her father managed to deny her anything.

'These creaking bones might be able to make a trip to the pier,' Barbara said. 'But we'll have to see how things develop.'

The marginal promise was apparently enough for the child. She said, 'Yea! Yea! Yea!' and before her father could discipline her once more, she tucked into the remains of her cornflakes.

Azhar, Barbara saw, had been eating boiled eggs. He'd finished one egg and had begun the second when she joined them. She said, 'Don't let me hold you up,' and gave a nod towards his plate. Again he used hesitation to communicate his reluctance, but whether it was a reluctance to eat or a reluctance to be in her company, she couldn't have said, although she suspected the latter.

He removed the top of the egg with his spoon and deftly separated the shimmering white from its shell. He held the spoon in his smooth brown fingers, but ate nothing from it until he'd spoken. 'How coincidental it is,' he remarked without irony, 'that you should come for your holiday to the same town that Hadiyyah and I have come to, Barbara. And even more coincidental that we should all find ourselves in the same hotel.'

'This way we can be together,' Hadiyyah announced happily. 'Barbara and I. And when you go off, Dad, Barbara can look after me instead of Mrs Porter. Mrs Porter's all right,' she informed Barbara in a lower voice. 'I like her. But she isn't able to walk very well because she's got some sort of palsy.'

'Hadiyyah,' her father said quietly. 'Your breakfast.'

Hadiyyah ducked her head, but not before she shot Barbara a radiant smile. Her feet kicked energetically against the legs of her chair.

Barbara knew that it was pointless to lie. The first time he came to a meeting between the police and the Asian community representatives, Azhar would discover the truth about what she was doing in Balford. Indeed, she realised that she was grateful she had a truth to tell him which was not the original truth that had brought her to Essex in the first place.

'Actually,' she said, 'I'm here on business. Well, quasi-business, I expect you'd call it.' She went on breezily to tell him that she'd come to town to help out an old friend in the local CID: the detective chief inspector heading up a murder investigation. She waited to gauge his response to this. It was quintessential Azhar: he barely flickered an eyelash. 'A man called Haytham Querashi was found murdered three days ago not far from here,' she went on, and added innocently, 'he was staying in this hotel, as a matter of fact. Have you heard about his death, Azhar?'

'And you're working on this case?' Azhar asked. 'How can this be? Your work is in London.'

Barbara walked a fine line with the truth. She'd received a phone call from her old mate Emily Barlow, she explained. Old Em had somehow got word – 'Police gossip and all, you know how it is' – that Barbara was free at the moment. She'd rung up and invited her to Essex. And that was that.

Barbara kneaded the dough of her friendship with Emily until it rose appropriately, sounding as if they were something between soul mates and twins once joined at the hip. When she was certain he got the I'd-do-anything-for-Em impression, she went on to say, 'Em's asked me to serve on a committee that's been set up to keep the Asian community informed on the progress of the case.' And again she waited for his reaction.

'Why you?' Azhar set his spoon beside his egg cup. Barbara noted that half the egg was uneaten. 'Have the local police inadequate manpower?'

'All of CID will be working the investigation itself,' Barbara told him, 'which is, I expect, what the Asian community wants. Wouldn't you think so?'

Azhar removed the napkin from his lap. He folded it neatly and placed it next to his plate. 'Then it seems we're here on similar missions, you and I.' Azhar looked at his daughter. 'Hadiyyah, are you finished with your cereal? Yes? Good. Mrs Porter looks as if she wishes to make plans with you for today.'

Hadiyyah looked stricken. 'But I thought that Barbara and I –'

'Barbara has just told us that she's here on business, Hadiyyah. Go to Mrs Porter. Help her out to the lawn.'

'But –'

'Hadiyyah, I believe my words were clear.'

She shoved back her chair and, droopy-shouldered, trudged across the room to Mrs Porter, who indeed was struggling with her aluminium Zimmer, attempting with trembling hands to square it in front of her chair. Azhar waited until Hadiyyah and the elderly woman had disappeared through the french windows that led to the lawn above the sea. Then he turned back to Barbara.

As he did so, Basil Treves whisked into the dining room with Barbara's breakfast and deposited it in front of her with a flourish. He said, 'If you need me, Sergeant . . .' and nodded meaningfully towards reception, which Barbara interpreted as indicating he'd been standing with telephone in hand, ready to punch the triple nines should Taymullah Azhar step out of line.

'Thanks,' Barbara said, and tucked into her eggs. She decided to wait for Azhar to speak. Better to see how much he was willing to reveal about his business in Balford than to play her cards of information before she had an idea of what his hand was.

He was the incarnation of laconism. As far as Barbara could tell, he hid nothing from her: the murdered man had been engaged to marry Azhar's cousin; Azhar had come to town at the request of the family; he was assisting them in a similar capacity to what Barbara would be doing for the local police.

Barbara didn't tell him that she'd already exceeded her designated job description of liaison officer. Liaison officers didn't prowl round victims' bedrooms, paw through their belongings, and bag items of interest. She said instead, 'This couldn't be better, then. I'm glad you're here. The police need to be put clearly into the picture about Querashi. You can help, Azhar.'

He looked immediately wary. 'I serve the family.'

'No question about that. But you're a step removed from the killing, so you've got more objectivity than the family have. Right?' She hastened on before he could answer. 'And at the same time, you're on the inside of the group closest to Querashi, so that gives you information as well.'

'The family's interests come first, Barbara.'

'I dare say the family are interested –' she put gentle and ironic emphasis on the word '– in getting to the bottom of who offed Querashi.'

'Of course they're interested. They're more than interested.'

'I'm glad to hear it.' Barbara slathered butter on a triangle of toast. She forked up a portion of fried egg. 'So here's how things work. When someone is murdered, the police are after the answers to three questions: Who had the motive? Who had the means? Who had the opportunity? You can help the police get at the answers.'

'By betraying my family, you mean,' Azhar said. 'So Muhannad is right after all. The police wish to find guilt among the Asian community, don't they? And as you are working with the police, you too –'

'The police,' Barbara interrupted with determination, and she pointed her knife at him to emphasise the fact that she wasn't about to submit to an attempt to manipulate her with charges of racism, 'want to get to the truth, no matter where it leads them. You'd do your family a good turn by making that clear to them.' She munched on the toast and watched him watching her. Inscrutable, she thought. He'd have made a fine cop. She said past a wad of toast in her cheek, 'Look, Azhar, we need to understand Querashi. We need to understand the family. We need to understand the community at large. We're going to be looking at everyone he came into contact with, and some of those people are going to be Asian. If you intend to get sweaty-collared every time we start treading on Pakistani turf, we'll get nowhere. Fast.'

He reached for his cup – he'd been drinking coffee – but he merely rested his thin fingers against its handle rather than picking it up. 'You're making it clear that the police don't wish to view this as a racially motivated incident.'

'And you, my man, are jumping to conclusions from here to hell and back again. Which is not a good habit for a liaison officer to get into, is it?'

Despite himself, a smile quirked one corner of his mouth. He said, 'Accepted, Sergeant Havers.'

'Good. So let's agree to something up front. If I ask you a question, that's what it is, okay? A question. It doesn't mean that I'm heading in any direction at all. I'm just trying to understand the culture so I can understand the community. Okay?'

'As you wish.'

Barbara decided to take this as his wholehearted agreement to lay bare any and all facts at his fingertips. There was no point forcing him into signing with his blood a contract of cooperation. Besides, he seemed to be accepting her somewhat broad interpretation of her role as police liaison, and while she had him in that state, she wanted to get as much information out of him as she could.

She tucked into her eggs and forked up a wedge of bacon to accompany them. 'Let's suppose, just for a moment, that this wasn't a racially motivated crime. Most people are murdered by someone they know, so let's suppose that was the case with Querashi. Are you with me?'

Azhar turned his cup in his saucer. He'd still not drunk from it. He was watching Barbara. He nodded slightly.

'He hadn't been in England long.'

'Six weeks,' Azhar said.

'And he'd been working at the mustard factory with the Maliks during that time.'

'Correct.'

'So can we agree that the majority of his acquaintances here in England – not all, but the majority, okay? – were probably Asians?'

His expression was sombre. 'For the moment, we can agree on that probability.'

'Good. And his marriage was to be an Asian marriage. Isn't that the case?'

'It is.'

Barbara sliced into more bacon and dipped it into the egg yolk. 'I need to understand one thing, then. What happens if an Asian engagement – an arranged engagement – is broken?'

'What do you mean, *broken*?'

'I mean, what happens if one of the parties calls off an arranged marriage?'

It seemed like a simple enough question, but when he didn't answer immediately, Barbara looked up from the triangle of toast to which she was administering a generous dollop of blackcurrant jam. His face was expressionless, but it seemed too controlled. Damn the man. He was jumping to conclusions despite what she'd said about needing to gather information.

Impatiently, she said, 'Azhar —'

'Do you mind?' He took out a packet of cigarettes. 'May I? Since you're eating . . . ?'

'Fire it up. If I could smoke and eat simultaneously, believe me, I'd be doing it.'

He used a small silver lighter against the tobacco. He turned in his chair to gaze in the direction of the french windows. Outside on the lawn, Hadiyyah was throwing a red and blue beach ball into the air. He seemed to be considering how best to answer the question and seeing this, Barbara felt the pinch of irritation. If their every conversation was going to be a round of the political correctness minuet, they'd still be sitting in Balford at Christmas.

'Azhar, do I need to rephrase this?' she asked him.

He turned back to her. 'Haytham and Sahlah had both acquiesced to the arrangement of their marriage,' he said, rolling the tip of his cigarette against the table's ashtray. 'If Haytham decided to reject the arrangement, he would in effect be rejecting Sahlah. This would be viewed as a grave insult to her family. To my family.'

'Because the family arranged the marriage in the first place?' Barbara poured herself a cup of tea. It was viscous and had the look of a brew that had been bubbling away like a hell broth for the better part of a week. She loaded it up with sugar and milk.

'Because Haytham's actions would cause my uncle to lose face and thus lose the respect of the community. Sahlah herself would be branded as discarded by her intended husband, which would do nothing to heighten her desirability to other men.'

'What about Haytham? What would he suffer?'

'In rejecting the marriage, he would be defying his own father. This could result in his being cast out from his family if the marriage had been considered an important liaison.' The act of inhaling and expelling smoke served to screen Azhar's face. But Barbara could see that he was observing her through the smoke as he went on. 'To be outcast is to have no contact with the family. No one communicates with the outcast for fear of being cast out as well. On the street, one turns away. At the home, doors are not opened. Telephone calls are not returned. Post is sent back unacknowledged.'

'Like being dead?'

'Completely unlike. The dead are remembered, mourned, and revered. The outcast never existed in the first place.'

'Rough,' Barbara acknowledged. 'But would this have been a problem for Querashi? Isn't his family in Pakistan? He wouldn't have been seeing them anyway, right?'

'It would have been Haytham's intention to bring his family to England as soon as he had the money to do so. Sahlah's dowry would have provided him with that money.' Azhar looked back to the french windows. Hadiyyah was hopping across the lawn, bouncing the beach ball on her head. He smiled at the sight and kept his gaze on her as he continued. 'Thus, Barbara, I think it unlikely that he was attempting to back out of marriage to Sahlah.'

'But what if he'd fallen in love with someone else? I can understand the whole arranged marriage business, and I can see how someone might agree to do his duty and all that — hell, look at the flaming monarchy and the mess they've made of their lives in the name of duty — but what if someone else came along and he fell in love with her before he really knew what was happening? People do that, you know.'

'Quite true,' he said.

'Right. So, what if he was set to meet a lover the night he died? And what if the family found out about it?' When Azhar frowned, looking doubtful, she said, 'He had three condoms in his pocket, Azhar. What does that suggest to you?'

'A preparation for intercourse.'

'Not a love affair? A love affair significant enough to cause Querashi to want to call off his wedding plans?'

'It might be that Haytham had fallen in love with someone else,' Azhar replied. 'But love and duty are often mutually exclusive ideas to my people, Barbara. Westerners think of marriage as the logical consequence of love. Most Asians do not. Thus Haytham may have fallen in love with another woman — and possession of the condoms suggests he went to the Nez for purposes of sex if not for purposes of love, I will agree — but it does not follow that he would wish to abrogate his agreement to marry my cousin.'

'Okay. I'll accept that for the moment.' Barbara dropped a square of toast on to her plate and forked it about in the remaining yolk of her egg. She knifed it up with some bacon and chewed thoughtfully, considering alternative scenarios. When she had one, she spoke, aware of the fact that Azhar was frowning. No doubt he was assessing her table manners, which at breakfast left something to be desired. She was used to eating on the run and had never got out of the habit of bolting down her breakfast as if pursued by Mafia hitmen. 'Then what if he'd got some woman pregnant? Condoms don't always work the way one would like. They leak, they break, they're not put on in time.'

'If she was pregnant, why did he have condoms with him that night? They'd hardly've been necessary.'

'Right. Closing the barn door too late,' Barbara agreed. 'But he might not have known she was in the club. He went prepared to do the dirty as usual, and she broke the news to him when he got there. So she's pregnant and he's engaged to someone else. What then?'

Azhar stubbed out his cigarette. He lit another before answering. 'That would be unfortunate.'

'Okay. Good. So let's imagine it happened. Wouldn't the Maliks –'

'But Haytham would still consider himself contracted to Sahlah,' he said patiently. 'And the family would consider the pregnancy to be the responsibility of the woman. Since she'd likely be English –'

'Hang on,' Barbara cut in, her dander up at this blithe assumption. 'Why would she *likely* be anything? How would he know any English women, anyway?'

'This is your conjecture, Barbara, not mine.' It was clear that he read her vexation. It was also clear that he wasn't bothered by it. 'She'd likely be English because young Asian women are careful about their virginity in ways that young English women are not. English girls are easy and available, and Asian men seeking sexual experience will seek it from them, not from another Asian.'

'How nice of them,' Barbara commented acidly.

Azhar shrugged. 'The community's values predominate when it comes to sex. The community values virginity in women prior to marriage and chastity in women after marriage. A young man seeking to sow wild oats will therefore sow them in an English girl's field, because English girls are seen as not considering virginity important. Thus, they are there for the taking.'

'And what if Querashi happened to run into an English girl who didn't share this charming attitude? What if he ran into an English girl who thought having it off with a bloke – whatever his colour, race, or religion – meant making a bloody commitment to him?'

'You're angry,' Azhar said. 'But I meant no offence with this explanation, Barbara. If you ask questions about our culture, you'll doubtless hear answers now and again that are in conflict with your own beliefs.'

Barbara shoved her plate to one side. 'And you'd do well to toss round the idea that my beliefs – as you call them – might bloody well reflect the beliefs of *my* culture. If Querashi put some English girl in the club and then came on like Rodney Righteous about how he had to do his duty to Sahlah Malik, and excuse me but it doesn't really matter that you're up the spout because you're flipping English, how do you think her father or brother would react to this news?'

'Perhaps badly,' Azhar said. 'Indeed, perhaps with murderous intentions. Wouldn't you agree?'

Barbara wasn't about to let him lead their conversation to an end of *his* choosing: the guilt of an Englishman. He was quick as a whip, but she was obdurate. 'And what if the Maliks discovered all of this: the affair, the pregnancy. What if the woman – whoever she is – informed them in advance of telling Querashi? Wouldn't they be just a little put out?'

'You're asking if they would have murderous intentions as a result,' Azhar clarified. 'But killing the bridegroom would hardly serve the purposes of the arranged marriage, would it?'

'Bugger the arranged marriage!' The crockery rattled when Barbara smacked her hand on the table. The remaining diners in the room glanced their way. Azhar had left his packet of cigarettes on the table, and she helped herself to one, saying in a lower voice, 'Come on, Azhar. This situation plays both ways, and you know it. Sure, these are Pakistanis we're talking about, but they're also humans with human feelings.'

'You wish to believe someone within Sahlah's family committed this crime, perhaps Sahlah herself or someone acting for Sahlah.'

'I hear Muhannad's got something of a temper.'

'But there were several reasons why Haytham Querashi was chosen for her, Barbara. And foremost among them is that the family needed him. Every member of the family. He had expertise that they wanted: a business degree from Pakistan and experience in running the production side of a large factory. This was a mutually beneficial relationship: the Maliks needed him and he needed the Maliks. No one would have been likely to forget that, no matter what Haytham planned upon doing with the condoms in his pocket.'

'And they couldn't have got that same expertise from an Englishman?'

'They could have done, naturally. But my uncle's desire is to maintain this as a family business. Muhannad already serves in an important position. He cannot do two jobs. There are no other sons.

Akram could bring in an Englishman, yes, but that would not be keeping the job within the family.'

'Unless Sahlah married him.'

Azhar shook his head. 'Which would never be allowed.' He extended his cigarette lighter, and Barbara realised she'd not lit the fag that she'd been in such a tearing hurry to enjoy. She leaned into the flame. 'So you see, Barbara,' Azhar concluded smoothly, 'the Pakistani community had every reason to keep Haytham Querashi alive. It is only among the English that you will find the motive to kill him.'

'Is that so?' Barbara asked. 'Well, let's not saddle our horses till we've put on our spurs, all right, Azhar?'

Azhar smiled. It looked as though he smiled in spite of an inner wisdom telling him not to. 'Do you always address yourself to your work with this degree of passion, Sergeant Barbara Havers?'

'It makes the day just fly by,' Barbara retorted.

He nodded and played his cigarette round the edge of the ashtray. Across the room, the last of the elderly couples were tottering towards the door. Basil Treves was hovering at the sideboard. He made busy noises as he filled six glass cruets from a plastic drum.

'Barbara, do you know how Haytham died?' Azhar asked quietly, eyes still on his cigarette's tip.

His question took her by surprise. What took her more by surprise was her instant inclination to tell him the truth. She pondered for a moment, asking herself where this inclination had come from. And she found her answer in that nanosecond of warmth she'd felt between them when he'd asked her about the passion she applied to her work. But she'd learned the hard way to discount any warmth she might feel for another human being, especially a man. Warmth led to weakness and irresolution. Those two qualities were dangerous in life. They could be fatal when it came to murder.

She temporised with, 'The post-mortem's scheduled for this morning.' She waited for him to say, 'And when they receive the report . . . ?' But he didn't say it. He merely read her face, which she attempted to keep clear of incriminating information.

'Dad! Barbara! Look!'

Saved by the bell, Barbara thought. She looked towards the french windows. Hadiyyah was standing just outside with her arms extended to the sides and the red and blue beach ball sitting on her head.

'I can't move,' she announced. 'I can't move a muscle. If I move, it'll fall. Can you do this, Dad? Can you do this, Barbara? Can you balance like this?'

That was the question, all right. Barbara scrubbed her napkin across her mouth and got to her feet. 'Thanks for the conversation,' she said to Azhar, and then to his daughter, 'the real pros can steady it on their noses. I expect you to have that mastered by dinner.' She took a final hit of her fag and stubbed it out in the ashtray. With a nod to Azhar, she left the room. Basil Treves followed her.

'Ah, Sergeant . . . ?' He appeared Dickensian, Uriah Heepish in tone and posture with his hands clasped high on his chest as usual. 'If I could have a moment . . . ? Just over here . . . ?'

Over here was reception, a cavelike cubicle built under the stairs. Treves padded behind the counter and bent to retrieve something contained within a drawer. It was a sheaf of pink chits. He handed them to Barbara and leaned over the counter to speak conspiratorially. 'Messages,' he breathed.

Barbara momentarily considered the disturbing implication behind the cloud of gin he exhaled. She glanced at the chits and saw that they were torn from a book, carbon copies of telephone messages received. For an instant she wondered how she could have come to amass such a collection in so short a time, especially since no one from London knew where she was. But then she saw that they were made out to *H. Querashi*.

'I was up before the birds,' Treves whispered. 'Went through the message book and pulled all of his. I'm still working on his outgoing phone calls. How much time do I have? And what about his post? We don't generally record letters received by residents, but if I put my thinking cap on, I might be able to recall something helpful to our needs.'

Barbara didn't miss the plural possessive pronoun. 'Everything and anything is helpful,' she said. 'Letters, bills, phone calls, visitors. Anything.'

Treves' face lit up. 'As to that, Sergeant . . .' He glanced about. No one was near. The television in the lounge was playing the BBC morning news at a volume that would have drowned out Pavarotti bellowing *Pagliacci*, but Treves still maintained his air of caution. 'Two weeks before he died, there *was* a visitor. I hadn't thought about it because they were engaged, after all, so why shouldn't she . . . ? Although it did seem unusual to see her all got up that way. I mean, she doesn't usually. Not that she goes about in public that much. The family wouldn't have that, would they? So how am I to say that it was unusual in this case?'

'Mr Treves, what the hell are you talking about?'

'The woman who came to see Haytham Querashi,' Treves said reasonably. He looked miffed that Barbara hadn't been following a train of thought that was chugging towards a perfectly obvious destination. 'Two weeks before he died, he was visited by a woman. She came in that get-up they wear. God knows she must have been *cooking* under it, what with this heat and all.'

'A woman in a *chādor*? Is that what you mean?'

'Whatever they call it. She was all done up from head to toe in black, with slits for the eyes. She came in and asked for Querashi. He was in the lounge having his coffee. They had a whisper over by the door, right next to that umbrella stand, mind you. Then they went upstairs.' He looked pious as he concluded with, 'I have no idea what they got up to in his room, by the way.'

'How long were they up there?'

'I didn't actually time them, Sergeant,' Treves answered archly. Then he added, as she was about to walk off, 'But I dare say it was quite long enough.'

Yumn stretched languidly and turned from her back on to her side. She studied the back of her husband's head. In the house beneath their bedroom, she could hear the morning sounds telling her both of them should be up and about, but she liked the fact that while the rest of the family were busying themselves with the day's concerns, she and Muhannad were cocooned together with no concerns except for each other.

She raised a lazy hand to her husband's long hair – freed from its ponytail – and she insinuated her fingers into it. '*Meri-jahn*,' she murmured.

She did not have to glance at the small calendar on the bedside table to know what day this morning heralded. She kept a scrupulous record of her female cycle, and she'd seen the notation on the previous night. Relations with her husband today could lead to another pregnancy. And this more than anything – indeed, more than keeping the puling Sahlah firmly and permanently in her place – was what Yumn wanted.

Two months after Bishr's birth, she had begun to feel the urge for another child. And she'd begun turning to her husband regularly, arousing him to plant the seed of another son in the fertile soil of her more than willing body. It *would* be another son, of course, once the pregnancy was achieved.

Yumn felt a physical stirring for him as she touched Muhannad. He was so lovely. What a change her marriage to such a man had brought to her life. The eldest sister, the least attractive, the most hopelessly unmarriageable in the eyes of her parents, and she – Yumn the cow and not one of her mild and doelike sisters – had proved herself an exceptional wife to an exceptional husband. Who would have thought it possible? A man like Muhannad could have had his pick of women, no matter the size of the dowry that her father had assembled to tempt him and his parents. As the only son of a father overly eager for grandchildren, Muhannad could have made certain that his every wish for a mate be embodied in the woman he ultimately took as his wife. He could have laid out his requirements in terms his father would not have dared to deny him. And having done so, he could have evaluated each potential bride presented by his parents and rejected anyone not meeting his specifications. But he had accepted his father's choice of her without question, and on the night they'd met, he had sealed their agreement to marry by taking her roughly in a dark corner of the orchard and making her pregnant with their first son.

'We make quite a pair, *meri-jahn*,' she murmured, easing closer to him. 'We're very good for each other.' She brought her mouth to his neck. The taste of him increased her desire. His skin was faintly salty, and his hair smelled of the cigarettes he smoked out of his father's presence.

She glided her hand down his bare arm, but lightly so that his coarse hairs tickled her palm. She clasped his hand then moved her fingers to the fur on his belly.

'You were up so late last night, Muni,' she whispered against his neck. 'I wanted you. What were you and your cousin talking about for so long?'

She'd heard their voices long into the night, long after her in-laws had trudged up to bed. She lay, impatient for her husband to join her, and she wondered what it might cost Muhannad to defy his father by bringing the outcast into their home. Muhannad had told her of his plan the night before he'd put it into action. She'd been bathing him. Afterwards, as she rubbed lotion into his skin, he spoke in a low voice of Taymullah Azhar.

He didn't care what the old fart said, he'd told her. He would bring his cousin to their assistance in this matter of Haytham's death. His cousin was an activist when it came to the rights of Pakistani immigrants. This much he knew from a member of *Jum'a* who'd heard him speak at a conference of their people in London. He'd been talking about the legal system, about the trap that immigrants – legal and otherwise – fall into by allowing their cultural traditions and predispositions to colour their interactions with police, with solicitors, and with courtrooms. Muhannad had remembered all of this. And when Haytham's death was not at once declared an accident, he moved quickly to obtain assistance from his cousin. Azhar can help, he'd told Yumn as she went from the lotion to brushing his hair. Azhar *will* help.

'But help do what, Muni?' she'd asked, feeling a pinch of worry at what the advent of this interloper might mean to her own plans. She didn't want Muhannad's time and his thoughts to be consumed with the death of Haytham Querashi.

'To see to it that these bloody police track down the killer,' Muhannad said. 'They'll try to pin it on an Asian, naturally. I don't intend to let that happen.'

The declaration pleased Yumn. She loved the defiant part of his nature. She herself shared it. She made the necessary sounds and gestures of obeisance to her mother-in-law, as required by custom, but she took great pleasure in rubbing Wardah's face in the ease with which the obedient daughter-in-law had so far been able to reproduce. She hadn't missed the brief expression of black envy that had passed across Wardah's features when Yumn proudly announced her second pregnancy twelve weeks after the birth of her first son. And she'd taken every opportunity that arose to flaunt her fecundity in front of her mother-in-law.

'But has your cousin your brains, *meri-jahn*?' she whispered. 'For he has nothing else of yours, I think. Such a puny man. Such a little man.'

She walked her fingers downward from her husband's belly, curling the ever-thickening hair round her fingers and pulling it gently. She felt the insistent aching of her own desire. It grew until there was only one way to ease it.

But she wanted him to want her first. Because if she could not arouse need in him this morning, Yumn knew that he would seek arousal elsewhere.

It would not be the first time. Yumn did not know the name of the woman – or women, for that matter – with whom she was forced to share her husband. She knew only that they existed. She always pretended sleep when Muhannad left their bed at night, but once he shut the bedroom door upon his exit, she crept to the window. She listened for the sound of his car starting at the bottom of the street, where he'd let it roll silently. Sometimes she heard it. Sometimes she didn't.

But always she lay awake on those nights that Muhannad left her, staring up into the darkness and counting slowly to mark the time. And when he returned to her just before dawn – easing his body into their bed – she tested the air for the thick scent of sex, despite knowing that the smell of his betrayal would be as tormenting as the actual sight of it. But Muhannad was careful not to carry to their bed the odour of sex with another woman. And he gave her no concrete evidence to work with. So she had to confront her unknown rival with the only weapon she had.

She ran her tongue along his shoulder. 'Such a man,' she whispered. Her fingers found his penis. It was erect. She began to work him. She grazed her breasts against his back. She moved her hips rhythmically. She whispered his name.

Finally, he moved. He reached for her hand and clasped his own round it. He tightened her grip. He increased the pace with which she worked him.

Outside the bedroom, the morning sounds of the household intensified. The younger of her two sons wailed. Sandals slapped against the floor in the upstairs corridor. Wardah's voice called out something from the direction of the kitchen. Sahlah and her father exchanged quiet words. Outside the house, birds were chirruping from the pear orchard and a dog barked somewhere.

Wardah would be angry that her son's wife had not risen early to see to Muhannad's breakfast. Old woman that she was, she would never understand the importance of seeing to other things.

Muhannad's hips were jerking unconsciously. Gently, Yumn urged him on to his back. She flung back the sheet under which they'd slept. She lifted her nightdress and began to straddle him. His eyes opened.

He grabbed her hands. She looked at him. She breathed, 'Muni, *meri-jahn*, how good you feel.'

She raised herself to take him inside her. But he slid quickly out from beneath her.

'But, Muni, don't you –'

His hand shot to her mouth and silenced her, fingers digging into her cheeks with such strength that she felt his nails like hot coals against her flesh. He moved behind her and pressed up against her, drawing her head back. His other hand felt for her breast, and between his thumb and his index finger, he pinched her nipple till she writhed. She felt his teeth on her neck and his hand, releasing her breast, travelled over her belly until it found her mound of hair. He grabbed this roughly. Then just as roughly he shoved her downward so that she was on her hands and knees. Still with his hand at her mouth, he found the spot he wanted and he began to thrust. He took his pleasure in less than twenty seconds.

He released her and she fell on to her side. He knelt above her for a moment, eyes closed, head raised to the ceiling, chest rising and falling rapidly. He shook back his hair and combed his fingers through it. Sweat gleamed on him.

He moved off the bed and reached for the T-shirt he'd discarded the previous night. It lay on the floor among his other clothes, and he wiped himself with it before he threw it back where he'd found it. He picked up his jeans and stepped into them, drawing them up over his naked buttocks. He zipped them and, bare-chested and bare-footed, he left the room.

Yumn watched his back, watched the door close. She felt the slick deposit from his body oozing out of hers. Hastily, she reached for a tissue and raised her hips to work a pillow beneath them. She began to relax as she pictured the frantic flight of his sperm, seeking the solitary egg that lay waiting. It would happen this very morning, she thought.

Such a man her Muni was.

Chapter Seven

Emily Barlow was plugging the flex of an oscillating fan into a socket in her office when Barbara arrived. The DCI was on her hands and knees beneath a table on which a computer terminal sat. The monitor of this terminal was glowing with a format that Barbara recognised even from the doorway: it was HOLMES, the program that systematised criminal investigations throughout the country.

The office was already like a steam bath, despite the fact that its single window had been opened to its widest capacity. And three empty Evian bottles told the tale of what Emily had been doing so far to beat the heat.

'The damn' building didn't even so much as cool off during the night,' she told Barbara as she crawled out from beneath the table and punched the button on the fan's highest setting. Nothing happened. 'What the ... Jesus!' Emily went to the door and shouted. 'Billy, I thought you said this damn' thing worked!'

A man's disembodied voice called back. 'I said, "Give it a try", Guv. I didn't make any promises.'

'Brilliant.' Emily stalked back to the machine. She punched the off button, then each of the settings in succession. She drove her fist on to the plastic housing of the motor. Finally, the fan blades began a listless rotation. They didn't so much create a breeze as lethargically massage what rank air was in the room.

Emily shook her head in disgust, slapped the dust from the knees

137

of her grey cotton trousers, and said, 'What've we got?' with a nod towards Barbara's hand.

'Telephone messages received by Querashi over the last six weeks. I had them off Basil Treves this morning.'

'Anything we can use?'

'There's quite a stack. I've gone through only the first third.'

'Christ. We could've got to them two days ago if Ferguson had been remotely cooperative and marginally less interested in sacking me. Give them here, then.' Emily took the collection of messages from her and shouted, 'Belinda Warner!' in the direction of the corridor. A WPC came running. Her uniform blouse was already damp from the heat and her hair hung limply across her forehead. Emily introduced her briskly. She told her to see to the messages – 'Organise, collate, log, and report back' – and then turned back to Barbara. She gave her fellow officer a closer scrutiny and said, 'Good God. Disaster. Come with me.'

She barrelled down the narrow stairway, pausing on the landing to shove a window open more fully. Barbara followed her. In the back of the rambling Victorian building, what had probably once been a dining or sitting room had been converted to a combination of workout and locker room. A fitness centre was set up in the middle – complete with exercise bicycle, rowing machine, and a sophisticated four-position weights module. Lockers lined one wall, with two showers, three wash basins, and a mirror standing opposite. A beefy red-head in a complete sweat suit worked the rowing machine, looking like a potential candidate for cardiac care. Otherwise the room was empty.

'Frank,' Emily barked, 'you're overdoing it.'

'Got to lose two stone before the wedding,' he panted.

'So? Have some discipline about you at mealtimes. Cut out the fish and chips.'

'Can't do that, guv.' He increased his pace. 'It's Marsha's cooking. I can't offend her.'

'She'll be more than offended if you drop dead before she gets you to the altar,' Emily shot back, and marched to one of the lockers. She spun through its combination lock, pulled out a small sponge bag, and led the way to the wash basin.

Barbara followed uneasily. She had an idea what was going to transpire, and she didn't much like it. She said, 'Em, I don't think –'

'*That's* clear enough,' Emily retorted. She unzipped the bag and she rummaged through it. On the edge of the basin she placed a bottle of liquid foundation, two thin palm-sized cases, and a set of brushes.

'You can't be wanting to –'

'Look. Just *look*.' Emily turned Barbara to the mirror. 'You look like hell on a January morning.'

'How d'you expect me to look? A bloke beat me up. My nose was smashed. I broke three ribs.'

'And I'm sorry about it,' Emily said. 'Getting beaten up couldn't have happened to anyone who deserved it less. But it's no excuse, Barb. If you're going to work for me, then you're going to have to appear at least halfway the part.'

'Em! Bloody hell. I never wear this goop.'

'Chalk it up to another life experience. Here. Face me.' And when Barbara hesitated, ready to protest again, 'You're not meeting the Asians looking like that. This is an order, Sergeant.'

Barbara felt like minced beef being made into meatballs, but she submitted herself to Emily's ministrations. The DCI made a quick job of it, purposefully wielding sponges and brushes, deftly applying colour. The entire procedure took less than ten minutes, and when she was finished, Emily stood back and studied her handiwork with a critical eye.

'You'll do,' she said. 'But that hair, Barb. It's beyond redemption. It looks like you cut it yourself in the shower.'

'Well . . . yeah,' Barbara said. 'I mean, it seemed like a good idea at the time.'

Emily raised her eyes heavenward but made no comment. She repacked her cosmetics. Barbara took the opportunity to examine her own appearance.

'Not bad,' she said. The bruises were still there, but they were greatly reduced in colour. And her eyes – which she generally thought of as pig-like – actually appeared an acceptable size. Emily was right: her hair was a disaster. But otherwise, she wouldn't terrify innocent maidens and toddlers. 'Where'd you get that stuff?' she said in reference to Emily's make-up.

'Boots,' the DCI replied. 'You *have* heard of Boots, I suppose? Come on. I'm expecting a report on the post-mortem from my man who stood in on it. And I'm hoping for something from forensic as well.'

The report was in. It lay in the centre of Emily's desk, its pages rustling in desultory fashion from the fan's efforts with the stifling air. Emily scooped it up and scanned the paperwork as she ran her fingers through her hair. The report had come in with another set of photographs. Barbara retrieved these.

They depicted the corpse, disrobed and prior to dissection. Barbara saw that the beating he'd taken was a thorough one. There was bruising evident on his chest and his shoulders as well as the bruising she'd seen in the earlier photographs of his face. The discolourations were of an uneven nature, however. And neither their sizes nor their shapes suggested contact from someone's fists.

As Emily continued to read, Barbara ruminated. A weapon must have been used on Querashi. But if so, what sort? While the bruising didn't appear consistent with marks made by flailing fists, it also didn't appear consistent, full stop. One mark might have been made by a tyre iron, another by a board, a third by the back of a shovel, a fourth by the heel of a boot. All of which suggested an ambush, more than one assailant, and mortal combat.

'Em,' she said contemplatively, 'for him to look this bad, there'd've been signs all over the pillbox – inside and out – that he'd been in a fight. What did your crime-scene team pick up in there? Were there blood splatters? Maybe something used to whack him?'

Emily looked up from the report. 'Nothing. Not a sprat.'

'What about something on the top of the Nez? Bushes tramped down? Ground stomped over?''

'Nothing there either.'

'Then on the beach?'

'There might have been something in the sand initially. But the tide took care of that.'

Was it really possible that mortal combat could occur without leaving its traces anywhere but on the body? And even if combat had occurred on the beach itself, how practical was it to assume that every indication of an ambush had been washed away by the tide? Barbara wondered about these questions as she looked at the condition of the corpse. It was certainly bruised, but the inconsistency of the bruises directed her thinking to another possibility.

She picked up a close shot of Querashi's bare leg and then an enlargement of one section of that leg. A ruler marked the area of flesh that the pathologist wished the police to note. Here, on the shin, was a hair'swidth cut.

In comparison with the contusions and scrapes on the upper part of his body, a two-inch cut on his leg seemed small potatoes. But taken in conjunction with what she and Emily already knew about the crime scene, the cut provided an intriguing detail for them to consider.

Emily slapped the report on to her desk. 'Not much that we didn't already know. The broken neck killed him. Preliminarily, there's nothing obvious in the blood. The pathologist says to give the clothes a going over, though. He recommends having a close look at the trousers.'

Emily went behind her desk and punched a number into the phone. She waited, rubbing the back of her neck with a limp face flannel that she dug from her pocket. She muttered, 'This *heat*,' and then after a moment, she said, 'DCI Barlow here. Is that Roger?' into the receiver. 'Hmm. Yes. Bloody miserable. But at least you've got air conditioning where you are. Try it over here for some real suffering.' She screwed up the flannel and shoved it away. 'Listen, have you got something for me? . . . On the Nez killing, Roger . . . You do recall it? . . . I know what you said, but we're being advised by the Home Office bone man to give his clothes a going over . . . What? Come on, Rog. Dig it out for me, won't you? . . . I understand, but I'd rather not wait for the report to be typed.' She rolled her eyes. 'Roger . . . Roger . . . Damn it! Would you just get the bleeding information for me?' She covered the mouthpiece and spoke to Barbara. 'Prima donnas, this lot. You'd think they'd been trained by Joseph Bell.'

She went back to listening, reaching for a notebook in which she began to scribble. She interrupted twice, once to ask how long, once to ask if there was a way to tell how recently the damage had been done. She rang off with a brusque 'Thanks, Rog,' telling Barbara, 'One of the trouser legs had a rip in it.'

'What sort of rip? Where?'

'Five inches from the bottom. A straightforward tear. It was fresh, he said, because the threads were broken but they weren't worn or smooth the way you'd expect if the trousers had gone through a wash.'

'The pathologist has given you a photo of his leg,' Barbara told her. 'There's a cut on the shin.'

'To match the tear in the trousers?'

'That's where my money is.' Barbara handed over the pictures. Those that had been taken on the Nez on Saturday morning were sitting on the edge of Emily's desk. As the DCI looked at the photos of the body itself, Barbara sorted out the pictures of Querashi in the pillbox and went on to those of the location. She saw where the victim had left his car – at the top of the cliff, abutting one of the white poles that bordered the car park. She noted the distance from the car to the café, and then from the car to the edge of the cliff. And then she noticed what she had seen without registering upon her first viewing of these same photographs on the previous night. She certainly should have remembered them from her own long-ago visit to the Nez with her brother: a set of steep concrete steps that carved a diagonal gash down the face of the cliff.

She could see that unlike the pleasure pier, the Nez steps had undergone no renovation. The handrails on either side of them were pitted and rusting, and the steps themselves were not faring well as the North Sea continued to erode the cliff. They bore deep-looking cracks. They bore dangerous gouges. They also bore the truth.

'The steps,' Barbara said quietly. 'Hell, Em. He must have fallen down the steps. That's got to be why the body's so bruised.'

Emily looked up from the pictures of the corpse. 'Look at his trousers, Barb. Look at his leg. Somebody used a trip wire on him.'

'Bloody hell. Was anything like that found at the scene?' Barbara asked.

'I'll have a go with the evidence officer and see,' Emily replied. 'But it's a public place. Even if a wire was left there – which I doubt – it'd be easy enough for a decent defence lawyer to explain away.'

'Unless it's got fibres from Querashi's trousers on it.'

'Unless,' Emily acknowledged. She made a note.

Barbara scanned the other photographs of the site. 'The killer must have moved the body to the pillbox after Querashi took the tumble. Were there signs, Em? Footprints in the sand? Any indication that the body had been dragged from the steps?' Then she realised the answer herself. 'There wouldn't have been. Because of the tide.'

'Right.' Emily rooted in one of her desk's drawers and brought out a magnifying glass. She studied the picture of Querashi's leg. She ran her finger down the autopsy report and said, 'Here it is. The cut's four centimetres long. Received some brief time prior to death.' She set the report to one side and looked at Barbara, but the expression on her face indicated that what she really saw was the Nez, the Nez in darkness without a light to guide the unsuspecting walker past, over, or round a wire that had been strung across the steps to cause a fatal fall. 'What size of wire are we looking for?' she asked rhetorically. She glanced at the oscillating fan that continued its anaemic efforts. 'An electrical wire?'

'That wouldn't have cut him,' Barbara pointed out.

'Unless it'd been stripped,' Emily said. 'Which it would have been, to be camouflaged by the dark.'

'Hmm. I s'pose. But what about fishing line? Something strong, but thin as well. And flexible.'

'There you go,' Emily agreed. 'There're piano strings as well. Or whatever it is they use for making sutures. Or wire used for binding up crates.'

'In other words, almost anything thin, strong, and flexible.' Barbara produced the evidence bag with its collection of goodies from Querashi's room. 'Have a go with this, then. It's from his room at the Burnt House. The Maliks wanted inside, by the way.'

'I'll bet they did,' Emily said cryptically. She pulled on a pair of latex gloves and opened the bag. 'Have you logged this in with the evidence officer?'

'On my way in. He says to tell you he wouldn't say no to a fan for the lock-up, by the way.'

'In his dreams,' Emily muttered. She flipped through the yellow-covered book from Querashi's bedside table. 'So it wasn't a crime of passion. And it wasn't a spur-of-the-moment fight. It was premeditated murder from the first, orchestrated by someone who knew where Querashi was going when he left the Burnt House Hotel on Friday night. Possibly the very person he was going to the Nez to meet. Or someone who knew that person.'

'A man,' Barbara said. 'Since the body was moved, it had to have been a man.'

'Or a man and a woman working together,' Emily pointed out. 'Or even a woman alone if the body was dragged from the steps to the pillbox. A woman could have managed that.'

'But then, why move him?' Barbara asked.

'To delay the discovery, I should think. Although,' Emily sounded reflective, 'if that was the object, why leave the car so obviously done over? It was a signpost indicating something was wrong. Anyone who came upon it would notice it, and having noticed it, would be hyperaware of everything else about the location.'

'Perhaps the car-thief was in a hurry and couldn't worry about someone noticing.' Barbara watched as Emily ran her finger down the page in the book that had been marked with the satin ribbon. The DCI tapped her nail against the bracketed section. 'Or perhaps investigating the damaged car was just an excuse for finding the body.'

Emily looked up. She blew an errant hair off her forehead. 'We're back to Armstrong again, right? Jesus, Barb, if he's involved in this, the Asians are going to tear up the town.'

'It works, though, doesn't it?' Barbara said. 'You know the sort of game I mean. He pretends to be out there for a stroll, and he comes upon the car. "Goodness me," he exclaims, "*what* have we here? It looks like someone made a real mess of this car. I wonder what else I might find on the beach?"'

'Okay, it plays,' Emily said. 'But only just. Look at how elaborate a set-up he would have been engineering: track Querashi from the day of his arrival, memorise his movements, choose the right evening, set the wire, hide till he fell, move the body, do over the car, and then return the next morning before anyone happens on the scene in order to pretend to find the body. Does that sound remotely reasonable to you?'

Barbara shrugged. 'How desperate was he to have his job back?'

'Accepted. Fine. But I've spoken to the man, and I'm willing to swear he isn't clever or sharp enough to plan something this detailed.'

'But he's back to being production manager of the factory, isn't he? You said yourself he was doing a decent job there before Querashi turned up. If that's the case, he's got to have some decent beans in his pot.'

'Damn!' Emily was flipping through the rest of the book. 'Great. Sanskrit. It's all the same.' She strode to the door. 'Belinda Warner!' she shouted. 'Find me someone who can decode Pakistani.'

'Arabic,' Barbara said.

'What?'

'The writing. It's Arabic.'

'Whatever.' Emily dug out the condoms, the two brass keys, and the leather case from the evidence bag. 'This one's a bank key, I expect,' she noted, indicating the larger key with the tagged number 104 on it. 'It looks to me like a key to safe-deposit box. We've got Barclays, Nat West, Lloyds, and Midland. Here and in Clacton.' She made a note regarding this.

'Were his fingerprints on the car?' Barbara asked as Emily wrote.

'Whose?'

'Armstrong's. You had the Nissan impounded, right? So you've got to know. Were his prints on it, Em?'

'He has an alibi, Barb.'

'They were on the car, right? And he has a motive. And —'

'I said, he has an alibi!' Emily snapped. She tossed the evidence bag on to her desk. She went to a small cooler that sat next to the door. She opened it, brought out a tin of juice. She tossed it to Barbara.

Barbara had never seen Emily frazzled, but she'd also never seen her under real pressure. She was suddenly aware for the first time — and acutely so — that she wasn't working with Inspector Lynley whose ease of manner had always encouraged his subordinates to argue their point of view freely and with as much passion as the subject warranted. The DCI was a different beast. Barbara knew it behoved her to remember that fact. 'Sorry,' she said. 'I tend to push.'

Emily sighed. 'Listen, Barb. I want you in on this. I need someone on my side. But you're chasing a wild goose if you go after Armstrong. And you're giving me aggro. Which I'm already getting in spades from Ferguson.' Emily opened her juice and downed a gulp. She said with studied patience, 'Armstrong claimed his prints were on the car because he had a look inside. He'd found it standing there with its door open, and he was worried someone might be in trouble.'

'Do you believe him?' Barbara made her next point delicately. Her position on this case was a tenuous one. She wanted to maintain it. 'Because he could have done over that car himself.'

'He could have done,' Emily said flatly, and she went back to the evidence bag.

'Guv?' a woman's voice shouted from somewhere in the building. 'Bloke called Kayr al Din Siddiqi at London University. You hear that, guv? He can do Arabic if you fax something over.'

'Belinda Warner,' Emily said drily. 'The girl can't type a bloody report, but give her a phone and she's magic. Right,' she shouted back and sent the yellow-bound book to the copier machine. She pulled Haytham Querashi's cheque book from the evidence bag.

Seeing it, Barbara realised there was another direction to head in besides the road signposted to Ian Armstrong's door. She said, 'Querashi wrote a cheque two weeks ago. He's entered it on the stub. Four hundred pounds to someone called F. Kumhar.'

Emily found the entry and frowned down at it. 'Not exactly a fortune, but not a paltry sum. We'll need to track him down. Or her.'

'The cheque book was locked inside that leather case, by the way, and there was a jewellery receipt locked with it. From Racon Jewellery here in town. The receipt has Sahlah Malik's name on it.'

'Odd to lock up a cheque book,' Emily said. 'It's not as if anyone but Querashi could have used it.' She tossed it to Barbara. 'Have a go with it. See to the jewellery receipt as well.'

It seemed a generous offer, considering the moment of friction between them over Ian Armstrong's potential guilt. And Emily increased the generosity of it with her next words. 'I'll have a second go with Mr Armstrong. Between the two of us, we should finally be able to make some decent headway today.'

'Right,' Barbara said, and she wanted to thank the other woman: for seeing to her battered face, for allowing her to work at her side, for even considering her view on the case. But instead she said, 'I mean, if you're sure?'

'I'm sure,' Emily said with the ease and the confidence Barbara remembered. 'As far as I'm concerned, you're one of us.' She slipped her sunglasses on and took up her key ring. 'Scotland Yard has a professional cachet that the Asians are going to respect and even my super might acknowledge. I need them off my back. I need him off my back. I want you to do what you can to make that happen.'

Calling out to her subordinates that she was heading off to put Mr Armstrong through his paces, Emily shouted, 'And I've got the mobile if you want me,' in the direction of the back of the building. She nodded at Barbara and shot down the stairs.

Alone in the DCI's office, Barbara fingered through the items from the evidence bag. She thought about what conclusions she could draw from those items when they were presented in conjunction with Emily's determination that a trip wire had been used to murder Haytham Querashi. A key potentially to a safe-deposit box, a passage in Arabic, a cheque book with an Asian name inscribed in it, and one very curious jewellery receipt.

This last seemed the best place to start. If there were details to be eliminated in the search for a killer, it was always wise to go with the most accessible of them first. It gave one the decided feeling of success, no matter how irrelevant to the case it was.

Barbara left the fan Rolfing the intemperate air. She descended the stairs and went out to the street where her Mini was soaking in the day's growing heat like a tin on the top of a barbecue.

The steering wheel was hot to the touch and the worn seats embraced her like the hug of an inebriated uncle. But the engine started with less mechanical coquetry than usual, and she drove down the hill and turned right in the direction of the High Street.

She hadn't far to go. Racon Original and Artistic Jewellery was situated on the corner of the High Street and Saville Lane, and it had the distinction of being one of only three businesses that were apparently still operational in a row of seven.

The shop was not yet open for the day, but Barbara knocked on the door in the hope that someone was in the back room, which she could see through a doorway just beyond the counter. She rattled the handle and knocked a second time, more aggressively. This effected the desired result. A woman with formidably styled hair of an equally formidable shade of red appeared in that doorway and gestured to the *Closed* sign in the front window. 'Not quite ready for the day yet,' she called with an air of determined good cheer. And doubtless because she'd come to realise the folly of turning away any potential customer in the current business climate of Balford, she added, 'Is it an emergency, love? D'you need a birthday gift or something?' and came forward to open the door anyway.

Barbara displayed her warrant card. The woman's eyes widened. She said, 'Scotland Yard?' and turned for some reason to glance at the room from which she'd emerged.

'I'm not after a gift,' Barbara told her. 'Just some information, Mrs . . . ?'

'Winfield,' she said. 'Connie Winfield. Connie of Racon.'

It took Barbara a moment to realise that the other woman wasn't identifying her place of genesis *à la* Catherine of Aragon. She was referring to the name of the shop. 'This is your business, then?'

'Quite.' Connie Winfield closed the door behind Barbara and patted it smartly. She returned to the counter and began arranging the display inside. This was covered with a maroon flannel cloth, which she folded back to reveal earrings, necklaces, bracelets, and other baubles. Not the standard stuff of jewellery stores, all were of unique design, leaning heavily towards coins, beads, feathers, polished stones, and leather. Where precious metal was used, it was the traditional gold or silver, but fashioned unusually.

Barbara thought of the ring she'd seen in the leather case in Querashi's room. A traditional design with a single ruby, the ring had definitely not been purchased here.

She fished out the receipt that had been in Querashi's possession. She said, 'Mrs Winfield, this receipt –'

'Connie,' the other woman replied. She'd gone on to a second display case and was uncovering the ornaments within it. 'Everyone calls me

Connie. Always have done. I've lived here all my life, and I never saw the point of becoming Mrs Winfield to people who used to see me running down the street in a dirty nappy.'

'Right,' Barbara said. 'Connie.'

'Even my artists call me Connie. That's who do my jewels, by the way. Artists from Brighton to Inverness. I sell their pieces on commission, which is why I've been able to ride out the recession when most of the shops – the luxury shops, that is, not the grocer's or the chemist or the necessary shops – have had to close their doors these last five years. I've got a good mind for business, always have done. And when I opened Racon ten years ago, I said, "Connie, don't you put all your money into stock, darling girl." That's as good as setting sail to Port Failure with all engines blasting, if you know what I mean.'

From beneath the counters she began taking display stands made of polished wood and artfully shaped like trees. These were devoted to earrings, and their beads and coins jangled together as Connie set them on the counter and deftly arranged them to their best advantage. She worked energetically, and Barbara couldn't help wondering if the attention she was giving to the products on sale was typical of a morning's activity or the nervous reaction to a visit from the police.

Barbara laid the receipt next to one of the earring trees. She said, 'Mrs . . . Connie, this receipt is from your shop, isn't it?'

Connie picked it up. 'Says *Racon* right on the top,' she agreed.

'Can you tell me what purchase went with it? And what does the phrase, "Life begins now" refer to?'

'Hang on.' Connie went to a corner of the shop where an oscillating floor fan stood. She switched this on and Barbara was relieved to note that, unlike the fan in Emily's office, it worked as one might hope an oscillating fan would work. Connie opted for the medium setting.

She carried the receipt over to the till, where a black notebook lay. This bore the words *Racon Jewellery* embossed in gold. Connie opened it. 'AK means the artist,' she explained to Barbara. 'That's how we identify the pieces. This is Aloysius Kennedy, a bloke from Northumberland. I don't sell many of his pieces because they get a bit pricey for the sort of trade we do in Balford. But this one . . .' She licked her middle finger and leafed through a few pages. She ran a long acrylic fingernail – painted, it seemed, to match her hair – down the page. 'The 162 refers to the stock number,' she said. 'And in this case . . . Yes. Here it is. It was one of his hinged wrist cuffs. Oooh. This was a lovely one. I haven't another exactly like it, but –' she switched to sales mode '– I can show you something close, if you'd like to have a look.'

'And "Life begins now"?' Barbara said. 'What would that refer to.'

'Common sense, I expect,' Connie said, and she laughed a little too forcefully at her own small joke, showing tiny childlike white teeth. 'We'll have to ask Rache, won't we? This's her writing.' She went to the doorway to the back room and called, 'Rache, love-boodle. We got Scotland Yard in the shop asking about a receipt of yours. Could you bring me a Kennedy?' She shot Barbara a smile. 'Rachel. My daughter.'

'*Ra* of Racon.'

'You're quick, aren't you?' Connie acknowledged.

From the back room, footsteps clacked on a wooden floor. In a moment, a young woman stood in the doorway. She kept to the shadows and held a box in her hand. She said, 'I was seeing to the shipment from Devon. She's doing shells this time. Did you know?'

'Is she? Cor, you can't tell that woman a thing about what sells, can you? This is Scotland Yard, Rache.'

Rachel moved forward only slightly but enough for Barbara to see that she was nothing like her mother. Despite her unnaturally flaming hair, Connie was a pretty-featured woman with flawless skin, long eyelashes, and a delicate mouth. In contrast, her daughter looked as if someone had put her together from the discarded pieces of five or six unattractive individuals.

Her eyes were abnormally wide-set, and one of them drooped as if she suffered from a form of palsy. What went for her chin was a small protuberance of flesh beneath her lower lip below which was her neck. And where her nose should have been, she'd obviously once had nothing at all. A cosmetically created projection served to take its place, and while shaped like a nose, it had insufficient bridge, so it dipped into her face as if a thumb had been pressed into a model made of clay.

Barbara didn't know where to look without seeming offensive to the young woman. She racked her brains to remember what people with deformities wanted from their fellow men: staring was crass, but gazing elsewhere while attempting to speak to the victim of such physical disfigurement seemed even more cruel.

'What c'n you tell Scotland Yard about this, sweet thing?' Connie said. 'It's a Kennedy piece with your writing on it, and you sold it to . . .' Her voice drifted off as she read the name at the top of the receipt for the first time. She raised her eyes to her daughter, and her daughter met her gaze. A subtle communication seemed to pass between them.

'The receipt indicates that it was sold to Sahlah Malik,' Barbara told Rachel Winfield.

Rachel finally came forward into the direct light of the shop. She stood some two feet from the counter on which the receipt lay. She looked at it tentatively as if it were an alien creature best not approached too quickly. Barbara could see that a vein in her temple was throbbing, and while she gave the receipt an arm's-length scrutiny, she hugged herself and, with the hand not holding the box she'd brought from the back room, she rubbed her thumb fiercely against her upper arm.

Her mother went to her side and, with a cluck, fussily rearranged the younger woman's hair. She pulled a bit of it forward and fluffed another bit of it outward. Rachel looked irritated, but didn't shake her mother off.

'Your mum says this is your handwriting,' Barbara told her. 'So you must have made the sale. Do you recall it?'

'Not a sale exactly,' Rachel said. She cleared her throat. 'More like a trade. She makes some of our jewellery, Sahlah does, so we sort of bartered. She doesn't . . . well, she doesn't have any money of her own.' She indicated a display of ethnic necklaces. They were heavy with foreign coins and carved beads.

'So you do know her,' Barbara said.

Rachel went at things from another angle. 'It would be an inscription, what I've written there. "Life begins now" would be an inscription for the inside of the bracelet. We don't do inscriptions here, though. We have the pieces sent out if someone wants one.' She placed the box on the counter and prised it open. Inside, an object was wrapped in soft purple cloth. Rachel removed this and laid a gold bracelet on the counter. Its style was in keeping with the overall fashion of the rest of the jewellery in the shop. While its purpose was obvious by its circular shape, its design was indefinite, as if it had been poured into a malleable mould that had been allowed to take whatever shape chance gave it. 'This is a Kennedy piece,' Rachel said. 'They're all different, but it'll give you the general idea of what AK-162's like.'

Barbara fingered the bracelet. It was unique. And had she seen one similar to it among Querashi's belongings, she would have remembered it. She wondered if he'd been wearing it the night he died. Although the bracelet could have been removed from his body after he'd fallen to his death, it hardly seemed likely that his killer had then turned over his car in order to find it. And had he died for a bracelet worth £220? It was a possibility, but a conjecture that Barbara was unwilling to bet her next pay rise on.

She took up the receipt again and gave it a second observation. Rachel and her mother said nothing, but another look passed between them and Barbara could feel a tension that she wanted to pursue.

The reaction of the women told her that in one way or another, they had a connection with the murdered man. But what sort of connection might it be? she wondered. She knew the risks inherent in drawing premature conclusions – especially drawing premature conclusions that were prompted by something as potentially baseless as personal appearance – but it was difficult to see Rachel Winfield in the guise of Querashi's putative lover. It was difficult to see Rachel Winfield in the guise of anyone's lover. No devastating beauty herself, Barbara knew the role that an appealing countenance played in attracting men. So it seemed logical to conclude that whatever the connection might be, it wasn't a romantic or sexual one. On the other hand, the young woman had a nice body, so there was that to consider as well. And under cover of darkness ... But Barbara realised that she was getting ahead of herself. The real question was Querashi's possession of the receipt and what it was doing among his belongings when the bracelet wasn't.

Thinking of the receipt, she glanced at the till. Next to this with its cover curled open lay a booklet of receipts heretofore unused. Barbara registered their colour. They were white. And the receipt from Querashi's room was yellow.

She saw upon this latter paper what she might have noted before had she not been concentrating on the name *Salah Malik*, the phrase 'Life begins now', and the cost of the item. Printed in minuscule letters at the bottom of the page were two more words: *Business Copy*.

'This is the shop's receipt, isn't it?' she asked Rachel Winfield and her mother. 'The customer gets the original white one from the book by the till. The shop keeps the yellow as a record of the sale.'

Connie Winfield interjected hastily, 'Oh, we're never as clever as that, are we, Rache? We just tear the receipt off and shove one of the two copies over. I don't expect we mind much which one they get, so long as we keep one for ourselves. Isn't that so, love-boodle?'

But Rachel, it seemed, had realised her mother's mistake. She blinked hard when Barbara reached for the receipt book. Those documenting previous sales were folded back along with the booklet's cover. Barbara leafed through them. Every copy left was yellow.

She saw they were numbered and she riffled through the pages to find the original of the copy she had in her possession. It was receipt number 2395. Numbers 2394 and 2396 were in the book in yellow; and 2395 wasn't there in either colour.

Barbara closed the book, saying, 'Is this always in the shop? What do you do with it when you lock up for the night?'

'It goes under the cash drawer in the till,' Connie said. 'Fits snug as a bug. Why? Have you found something wrong with it? God knows me and Rache are a bit loose when it comes to our bookkeeping, but we've never done something *illegal.*' She laughed. 'You can't cook the books when the chef's yourself, if you know what I mean. There's no one to cheat. 'Course, I suppose we could cheat the artists if we had a mind to, but that'd catch up with us in the end because we give them an accounting twice a year and they have the right to go over our books themselves. So if we have any sense at all – and I like to think that we do, mind you – we can –'

'This receipt was among a dead man's belongings,' Barbara cut in.

Connie gulped and raised a closed fist to her sternum. And she kept her eyes so fixed on Barbara that it seemed only too clear whose face she was determined not to glance at. Even when she spoke, she didn't look at her daughter. 'Fancy that, Rache. How d'you suppose it happened? Are you talking about that bloke from the Nez, Sergeant? I mean, you're the police and that bloke's the only dead man round here that the police are interested in. So it must be him. He must be the dead man. Yes?'

'The same,' Barbara said.

'Fancy that,' Connie breathed. 'I couldn't say for money how he came to have one of our receipts. What about you, love-boodle? D'you know anything about this, Rache?'

One of Rachel's hands closed over a fold in her skirt. It was one of those Asian skirts, Barbara noted for the first time, the translucent sort that were sold in open-air markets all over the country. The skirt didn't exactly tie the girl to the Asian community. But it also didn't extricate her from a situation in which her reluctance to speak was indicating that she was – however tangentially – involved.

'Don't know a thing,' Rachel said faintly. 'P'rhaps that bloke picked it up off the street or something. It has Sahlah Malik's name on it. He would have recognised that. P'rhaps he meant to give it back to her and he never had the chance.'

'How would he have known Sahlah Malik?' Barbara asked.

Rachel's hand jerked on the skirt. 'Didn't you say that him and Sahlah —'

'The story was in the local rag, Sergeant,' Connie put in. 'Rache and I c'n both read, and the paper said this bloke was here to marry Akram Malik's daughter.'

'And you know nothing more than what you read in the paper?' Barbara asked.

'Not a thing more,' Connie said. 'You, Rache?'

'Nothing,' Rachel said.

Barbara doubted that. Connie was too determinedly loquacious. Rachel was too taciturn. There was a fishing expedition to embark upon here, but she would have to return when she had better bait. She took out one of her cards. Scrawling the name of the Burnt House on it, she told the two women to phone her if anything jogged their memories. She gave the Kennedy bracelet a final scrutiny and tucked the receipt for AK-162 among her own belongings.

She ducked out of the shop, but glanced back quickly. Both women were watching her. Whatever they knew, they would talk about eventually. People did that when the conditions were right. Perhaps, Barbara thought, the sight of that gold bracelet would light a fire beneath the Winfields and defrost their tongues. She needed to find it.

Rachel locked herself in the loo. The moment the sergeant moved out of their range of vision, she bolted into the back room. She dashed down the passage created between the wall and a freestanding row of shelves. The loo was next to the shop's back door, and she made for this and bolted the door behind her.

She pressed her hands together to stop their shaking, and when she was unsuccessful at doing this, she used both of them to turn on the tap in the small, triangular basin. She was burning hot and icy cold at the same time, which didn't seem possible. She knew there was a procedure to follow when physical sensations like these came over one, but she couldn't have said for love or money what that procedure was. She settled on splashing her face with water, and she was splashing away when Connie banged on the door.

'You get out here, Rachel Lynn,' she ordered. 'We got some talking to do, you and me.'

Rachel gasped, 'Can't. I'm being sick.'

'Being sick, my little toe,' Connie snapped. 'You going to open this door for me, or am I going to break it in to get you?'

'I wanted to go the whole time she was here,' Rachel said, and she lifted her skirt to sit on the toilet for the complete effect.

'I thought you said you were being sick?' Connie's voice bore the sound of triumph associated with mothers who catch their daughters in a lie. 'Isn't that what you just said? So what is it, Rachel Lynn? You sick? You going? What?'

'Not *that* kind of sick,' Rachel said. 'The other. You know. So c'n I have a bit of privacy, please?'

There was a silence. Rachel could imagine her mother tapping her small and shapely foot against the floor. It was what she usually did when she was planning a course of action.

'Give me a minute, Mum,' Rachel pleaded. 'My stomach's all clenched up on itself. Listen. Is that the shop door ringing?'

'Don't play with me, girl. I'll be watching the clock. And I know how long it takes to do what in the loo. You got that, Rache?'

Rachel heard her mother's sharp footsteps fading as she headed to the front of the building. She knew that she'd bought herself a few minutes only, and she struggled to gather her fragmented thoughts together in order to form them into a plan. You're a fighter, Rache, she told herself in much the same mental voice she'd used in childhood when preparing every morning for another round of bullying from her merciless schoolmates. So think. *Think.* It doesn't matter two pins if everyone in the world goes and lets you down, Rache, because you've still got yourself and yourself is what counts.

But she hadn't believed that two months before when Sahlah Malik had revealed her decision to submit herself to her parents' wishes for an arranged marriage to an unknown man from Pakistan. Instead of remembering that she still had herself, she'd been horrified at the thought of losing Sahlah. After which she'd felt both lost and abandoned. And in the end she'd believed herself cruelly betrayed. The ground upon which she'd long had faith that her future was built had fractured suddenly and irreparably beneath her, and in that instant she'd forgotten life's most important lesson completely. For the ten years following her birth, she'd lived with the certain belief that success, failure, and happiness were available to her through the effort of a single individual on earth: Rachel Lynn Winfield. Thus, the taunts of her schoolmates had stung her but they'd never scarred her, and she'd grown adept at forging her own way. But meeting Sahlah had changed all that, and she'd allowed herself to see their friendship as central to what the future held.

Oh, it had been stupid – *stupid* – to think in such a fashion, and she knew that now. But in those first terrible moments when Sahlah had revealed her intentions in that calm and gentle way of hers – the way that had made her, too, the victim of bullies who wouldn't *dare* to raise a nasty hand against Sahlah Malik or to voice a slur about the hue of her skin whenever Rachel Winfield was in the vicinity – all that Rachel could think was What about me? What about us? What about our plans? We were saving up to put money on a flat, we were going to have pine furniture in it with big deep cushions, we were going to set up a workshop for you on one side of your bedroom so you could make your jewellery without your nephews getting into your trays, we were going to collect shells on the beach, we were going to have two cats, you were going to teach me to cook, and I was going to teach you . . . what? What on earth could I have taught you, Sahlah? What on earth had I ever to offer you?

But she hadn't said that. Instead, she'd said, 'Married? You? Married, Sahlah? Who? Not . . . But I thought you always said that you couldn't –'

'A man from Karachi. A man my parents have chosen for me,' Sahlah had said.

'You mean . . . ? You can't mean a stranger, Sahlah. You can't mean someone you don't even *know*.'

'It's the way my parents married. It's the way most of my people marry.'

'Your people, your *people*,' Rachel had scoffed. She'd been trying to laugh the idea off, to make Sahlah see how ludicrous it was. 'You're English,' she said. 'You were born in England. You're no more Asian than I am. What d'you know about him, anyway? Is he fat? Is he ugly? Does he have false teeth? Does he have hairs sprouting from his nose and his ears? And how old is he? Is he some bloke of sixty with varicose veins?'

'His name is Haytham Querashi. He's twenty-five years old. He's been to university –'

'As if that makes him a good candidate for a husband,' Rachel said bitterly. 'I suppose he's got lots of money as well. Your dad would go in big for that. Like he did with Yumn. Who cares what sort of monkey crawls into your bed just so long as Akram gets what he wants from the deal? And that's it, isn't it? Isn't your dad getting something as well? Tell the truth, Sahlah.'

'Haytham will work for the business, if that's what you're asking,' Sahlah said.

'Hah! See what they're doing? He's got something they want – Muhannad and your dad – and the only way they can get it is to hand you over to some oily bloke you don't even know. I can't believe you're doing it.'

'I have no choice.'

'What d'you mean? If you said you didn't want to marry this bloke, you can't tell me your dad would make you do it. He dotes on you. So all you have to do is tell him that you and me, we've got plans. And none of them have to do with marrying some twit from Pakistan you've never even met.'

'I want to marry him,' Sahlah said.

Rachel had gaped at her. 'You want . . .' The immensity of the betrayal cleft her. She hadn't ever thought five simple words could cause such pain, and she had no armour to protect herself from it. 'You *want* to marry him? But you don't know him and you don't love him and how can you begin to live such a lie?'

'We'll learn to love,' Sahlah replied. 'That's what happened for my parents.'

'And is that what happened for Muhannad? What a joke! Yumn's not his beloved. She's his doormat. You've said so yourself. Do you want that to happen to you? Well, do you?'

'My brother and I are different people.' Sahlah had averted her head when she said this, and a length of her *dupattā* shielded her from view. She was withdrawing, an action that made Rachel want to cling to her even harder.

'Who cares about that? It's how different your brother and this Haybram –'

'Haytham.'

'Whatever he's called. It's how different your brother and he are from each other. And you don't know if they're different at all. And you won't know that, will you, till the first time he smacks you a good one, Sahlah. Just like Muhannad. I've seen Yumn's face after she's had a good one from your wonderful brother. What's to prevent Haykem –'

'Haytham, Rachel.'

'*Whatever*. What's to prevent him from treating you the same way?'

'I can't answer that. I don't know the answer yet. When I meet him, I'll see.'

'Just like that?' Rachel asked.

They'd been in the pear orchard beneath the trees, canopied in mid-spring by fragrant blossoms. They'd been sitting on the same teetering bench that they'd sat upon so many times as children when they'd swung their legs and made plans for a future that now would never come. It wasn't fair to be denied what was rightfully hers, Rachel thought, to have snatched from her the one person she had learned to depend upon. Not only was it not fair, though, it also wasn't right. Sahlah had lied to her. She had played along with a game that she'd never intended to complete.

Rachel's sense of loss and betrayal had shifted slightly, like ground growing used to a new position once an earthquake has done its work. A bud of anger began to grow within her. And with anger came its companion: revenge.

'My father's told me that I can decide against Haytham when we meet,' Sahlah said. 'He won't force me into a marriage if he sees I'm unhappy about it.'

Rachel read her friend's meaning behind the words, however Sahlah sought to make them appear. 'But you won't be unhappy about it, will you? No matter what, you're going to marry him. I can see that in you. I know you, Sahlah.'

The bench upon which they sat was old. It rested unevenly on the ground beneath the tree. Sahlah picked at a splinter on the edge of the seat, raising it slowly with the smooth crescent edge of her thumbnail.

Rachel felt a rising sense of desperation accompanying her need to strike out and wound. It was inconceivable to her that her friend had changed to such a marked degree. They'd seen each other only two days prior to this conversation. Their plans for the future had still been in place then. So what had happened to alter her so? This wasn't the Sahlah she'd shared hours and days of companionship with, the Sahlah she'd played with, the Sahlah she'd defended before the bullies of Balford-le-Nez Junior School and Wickham-Standish Comprehensive. This wasn't a Sahlah she'd ever met.

'You talked to me about love,' Rachel said. 'We talked to each other about it. We talked about honesty too. We said that in love, honesty comes first. Didn't we?'

'We did. Yes. We did.' Sahlah had been watching her parents' house as if she were worried about someone observing their conversation and the passion of Rachel's reaction to her news. She turned to Rachel now, though. She said, 'But sometimes complete – absolute – honesty isn't possible. It isn't possible with friends. It isn't possible with lovers. It isn't possible between parents and children. It isn't possible between husbands and wives. And not only isn't it always possible, Rachel, it's not always practical. And it's not always wise.'

'But you and I've been honest,' Rachel protested, the fear of Sahlah's meaning fast and hard upon her. 'Or at least I've been honest with you. Always. About everything. And you've been honest with me. About everything. Haven't you? About everything?'

In the Asian girl's silence, Rachel heard the truth. 'But I know all about ... You told me ...' But suddenly everything was open to question. What, indeed, had Sahlah told her? Girlish confidences about dreams, hopes, and love. The kind of secrets, Rachel had believed, that sealed a friendship. The kind of secrets she had sworn – and had meant – to reveal to no one.

But she hadn't expected such pain. She had never once thought that she'd encounter in her friend such a calm and steely resolve to smash her world to ruins. Such determination, and everything that arose from such determination, called for an action in response.

Rachel had chosen the only course open to her. And now she was living with the consequences.

She had to think what to do. She'd never have believed that one simple decision could have been such a significant domino, toppling a structure of other pieces until nothing was left.

Rachel knew that the police sergeant had not believed either her or her mother. Once she picked up the receipt book and fingered through it, she'd seen the truth. The logical move for her to make was to speak to Sahlah now. And once she did that, every possibility for a new beginning with the Asian girl would be destroyed.

So actually, there was little to consider as a course of action. It lay before her like a road without a single diversion upon it.

Rachel rose from the toilet and tiptoed to the door. She drew back the bolt in near silence and created a crack through which she could see the back room and hear what was going on in the shop. Her mother had turned on the radio and tuned into a station that doubtless reminded her of her youth. The choice of music was ironic, as if the DJ were a mocking god who knew the secrets of Rachel Winfield's soul. The Beatles were singing 'Can't Buy Me Love'. Rachel would have laughed had she felt less like weeping.

She slithered out of the loo. Casting a hurried glance towards the shop, she slipped to the back door. It stood open, in the hope of creating cross ventilation from the steamy alley behind the shop through to the equally steamy High Street. No breeze stirred, but the open door provided Rachel with the exit route she needed. She stole into the alley and hurried to her bicycle. She mounted it, and began to pedal energetically in the direction of the sea.

She'd caused the dominoes to topple, it was true. But perhaps there was a chance to right a few before the lot of them were swept from the table.

Chapter Eight

———◆———

Malik's Mustards & Assorted Accompaniments was in a small industrial estate at the north end of Balford-le-Nez. It was, in fact, on the route to the Nez itself, situated at a dog-leg created where Hall Lane, having veered northwest away from the sea, became Nez Park Road. Here, a ramshackle collection of buildings housed what went for industry in the town: a sailmaker, a seller of mattresses, a joinery, an auto repair business, a fencemaker, a dealer in junk cars, and a maker of custom jigsaw puzzles whose naughty choice of subjects generally kept him only one step ahead of public censure from the pulpits of every church in the town.

The buildings that housed these establishments were mostly prefabricated metal. They were utilitarian and suited to the environment in which they sat: a pebble-strewn lane cratered with potholes curved among them; orange skips bearing the oxymoronic name *Gold Coast Dumping* in purple letters listed on the uneven ground, spilling out everything from chunks of canvas to rusty bedsprings; several abandoned bicycle frames served as latticework for a gardener's nightmare of nettles and sorrel; sheets of corrugated metal, rotting wooden pallets, empty plastic jugs, and unwieldy, corroded sawhorses of iron made negotiating the industrial estate an ambitious undertaking.

In the midst of all this, Malik's Mustards & Assorted Accompaniments was both an anomaly and a reproach to its companion businesses. It comprised one-third of the estate, a long, many-chimneyed Victorian building that had in the town's heyday been the Balford

Timber Mill. The mill had fallen into disrepair with the rest of the town in the years following World War II. But now it stood restored with its bricks scoured of one hundred years of grime and its woodwork replaced and yearly repainted. It served as a wordless example of what the other businesses could do with themselves had their owners half the energy and one quarter the determination of Sayyid Akram Malik.

Akram Malik had purchased the derelict mill on the fifth anniversary of his family's arrival in Balford-le-Nez, and a plaque with words commemorating that occasion was the most impressive object that Emily Barlow took note of inside the building after she parked her Peugeot in a space that was relatively clear of debris along the lane.

She was fighting off a headache. There had been a disturbing undercurrent to her morning's meeting with Barbara Havers. This weighed on her mind. She didn't need a member of the Political Correctness Police on her team, and Barbara's willingness to saddle guilt exactly where the bloody Asians wanted guilt assigned – on the back of an Englishman – bothered her, causing her to wonder exactly how clear the other detective's vision was. Additionally, the presence of Donald Ferguson in her life – hovering on its periphery like a stalking cat – gave an added twist to her misery.

She'd begun her day with yet another phone call from the superintendent. He'd barked without so much as a good morning or a pleasant comment of commiseration about the weather, 'Barlow. Where do we stand?'

She'd groaned. At eight in the morning her office had been like Alec Guinness's sweat box on the River Kwai, and a quarter of an hour's search for a fan in the choking, dust-filled air of the old station's attic had done nothing to improve her disposition. Stirring Ferguson into the mix of heat and aggravation was almost too much to bear.

'Don, are you going to give me a free hand in this?' she'd asked. 'Or will you and I be playing report-to-the-teacher every morning and afternoon?'

'Watch your mouth,' Ferguson warned. 'You'd do well to keep in mind who's sitting at the other end of this telephone line.'

'I'm not likely to forget it. You don't give me the chance. Do you keep this sort of short rein on the others? Powell? Honeyman? What about our lad Presley?'

'They've more than fifty years' experience between them. They don't need watching over. Least of all Presley.'

'Because they're male.'

'Don't let's turn this into a gender issue. If you've a chip on your shoulder, I suggest you knock it off before someone else with more clout does it for you. Now, where are we, Inspector?'

Emily cursed him soundly under her breath. Then she'd brought him up to date without reminding him how remote was the possibility of there having been a major break in the case between his last call on the previous evening and this one in the morning.

He said thoughtfully, 'And you say this woman's from Scotland Yard? I like that, Barlow. I like it very much. It has just the right ring of sincerity, doesn't it?' Emily could hear the sound of him swallowing and the clink of a glass against the telephone receiver. Donald Ferguson was passionate about Fanta Orange. He drank it steadily all day, always with an odd, paper-thin slice of lemon and always with a single cube of ice. This was probably his fourth of the morning. 'Right. Then what about Malik? What about this screamer from London? Are you riding their shirt tails? I want you on them, Barlow. If they sneezed last week, I want you to know the colour of the handkerchief that collected the snot. Is that clear?'

'Intelligence have already given me a report on Muhannad Malik.' Emily took pleasure in having managed to be one step ahead of him. She recited the salient details on the young Asian. 'And I put a request in yesterday to gather what we can on the other: Taymullah Azhar. As he's from London, we'll have to liaise with SO11, but I expect having Sergeant Havers on our team will help with that.'

Ferguson's glass clinked again. Doubtless, he was taking the opportunity to manhandle his surprise into submission. He'd always been the sort of man who claimed women's hands had been shaped by God to curve perfectly over the handle of a Hoover. The fact that a female had actually been capable of thinking ahead and anticipating the investigation's needs was no doubt wreaking havoc with the preconceived notions that the superintendent held dear.

'Is there anything else?' she asked amiably. 'I've got the day's activities briefing in five minutes. I don't like to be late for it. But if you've a message for the team . . . ?'

'No message,' Ferguson said brusquely. 'Get on with it, then.' He slammed down the phone.

Now at the mustard factory, Emily smiled at the memory. Ferguson had supported her promotion to DCI because circumstances – in the form of a negative Home Office evaluation of Essex Constabulary's commitment to equal opportunities – had forced his hand. He'd let her know privately that every decision she made would undergo examination beneath the lens of his personal microscope. It was j-o-y in its purest form to better the little worm in at least one round of the game he'd determined they'd be playing with each other.

Emily shoved open the door to Malik's Mustards, where the reception desk was occupied by a young Asian woman in a creamy linen tunic and matching trousers. Despite the day's temperature, which was not appreciably lowered by the thick walls of the factory building, she wore an amber shawl over her head. Perhaps in a bow to couture, however, she'd arranged it fashionably in folds round her shoulders. When she looked up from the computer terminal at which she was working, her earrings of bone and brass clinked softly. They matched an intricate necklace she wore. A name plate on her desk identified her: *S. Malik.* This would be the daughter, Emily thought, the fiancée of the murdered man. She was a pretty girl.

Emily introduced herself and flipped open her identification. She said, 'You're Sahlah, aren't you?'

A strawberry birthmark high on the girl's cheek deepened in hue as she nodded. Her hands had been hovering over her terminal's keyboard, but she quickly lowered them to the wrist rest in front of the keys and kept them there, her thumbs and her knuckles pressed together.

She certainly looked the picture of guilt. Her hands were saying, Shackle me now. Her expression was crying, Oh no, please, no. 'I'm sorry about your loss,' Emily said. 'This can't be an easy time for you.'

'Thank you,' Sahlah said quietly. She looked at her hands, seemed to realise how odd their position was, and eased them apart. It was a surreptitious movement, but Emily didn't miss it. 'May I help you with something, Inspector? My father's working in the experimental kitchen this morning, and my brother hasn't yet arrived.'

'I don't need them, actually, but you can help me with Ian Armstrong.'

The girl's gaze went to one of two doorways that led off the reception area. Its upper half comprised bevelled glass through which Emily could see several desks and what appeared to be an advertising campaign spread out on an easel.

'He's here, isn't he?' Emily said. 'I was told he'd be stepping into the position that Mr Querashi's death left vacant.'

The girl agreed that Armstrong was working at the factory that morning. When Emily asked to see him, she pressed a few keys to exit whatever she'd been doing at her terminal. She excused herself and slipped silently through the other of the two doors, this one plain and leading into a corridor that ran the width of the factory.

Emily noticed the plaque then. It was bronze, and it hung on a wall that was given to a photographic mural of a harvester working in a vast yellow field of what were undoubtedly mustard plants. Emily read the plaque's inscription: *'Lo! He produceth creation, then reproduceth it, that He may reward those who believe and do good works with equity.'* This was followed by an additional inscription in Arabic beneath which were the words, *'We were blessed with a vision that brought us to this place on the 15th of June'*, and thereafter the year.

'He has been good to us,' a voice said behind Emily. She turned and saw that Sahlah hadn't produced Ian Armstrong as requested, but rather her father. She hovered behind him.

'Who?' Emily asked.

'Allah.' The name was spoken with a simple dignity that Emily couldn't help admiring. After saying it, Akram Malik came across the room to greet her. He was dressed for cooking, in medical-looking whites with a stained apron tied round his waist and a paper cap moulded to his head. The lenses of his glasses were speckled with something from the kitchen and he took a moment to wipe them on his apron as he nodded his daughter back to her work.

'Sahlah tells me you've come to see Mr Armstrong,' Akram said, dabbing his wrist against both his cheeks and his forehead in what Emily at first thought was some sort of Muslim greeting, until she realised he was simply removing the perspiration from his face.

'She said he's here today. I doubt our interview will take much more than a quarter of an hour. There was no real need to disturb you, Mr Malik.'

'Sahlah did the appropriate thing in fetching me,' her father said in a tone that indicated Sahlah Malik did the appropriate thing by knee-jerk reflex. 'I'll take you to Mr Armstrong, Inspector.'

He indicated the bevelled glass door with a nod, and he led Emily through it to the office beyond. This contained four desks, numerous filing cabinets, and two drafting tables in addition to the easels Emily had seen from reception. At one of the tables, an Asian man was working at some sort of design with calligraphy pens, but he ceased his work and rose respectfully as Akram led Emily through the office. At the other table, one middle-aged woman in black and two younger men – all of them Pakistani like the Maliks – were considering a set of glossy colour photographs in which the company's products were displayed in a variety of vignettes from picnic lunches to New Year's Eve dinners. They too set their work aside. No one spoke.

Emily wondered if the word had gone out that the police had come calling. Certainly, they'd have had to be expecting a visit from Balford CID. One would think they might have prepared themselves for it. But, like Sahlah in reception, everyone managed to look as if the next stop in his life's itinerary was destined to be the gallows.

Akram guided her into a small corridor off which three offices opened. Before he had a chance to leave her with Armstrong, however, Emily seized the opportunity with which Sahlah had presented her.

'If you've a moment, Mr Malik, I'd like a word with you as well.'

'Of course.' He gestured to an open doorway at the end of the corridor. Emily could see a conference table and an antique dresser whose shelves held not crockery but, rather, a display of the company's products. It was an impressive arrangement of jars and bottles containing sauces, jellies, mustards, chutneys, butters, and vinaigrettes. The Maliks had come a long way from their first efforts at simple mustard production in the erstwhile bakery on Old Pier Street.

Malik shut the door behind them, but not completely. He left two inches open, perhaps in deference to being alone in the conference room with a woman. He waited until Emily had sat at the table before he did likewise, removing his paper cap and folding it twice into a neat triangle.

'How may I be of help to you, Inspector Barlow?' he asked. 'My family and I are anxious to get to the bottom of this tragedy. Please be assured that we have every intention of assisting you in whatever way we can.'

His English was remarkable for a man who'd spent the first twenty-two years of his life in a remote Pakistani village with a single well and neither electricity, indoor plumbing, nor telephones. But Emily knew from the literature he'd provided during his campaign for town council as well as from the door-to-door canvassing he'd done that Akram Malik had studied the language for four years with a private tutor when he'd arrived in England. 'The good Mr Geoffrey Talbert,' he'd called him. 'From him I learned to love my adopted country, the richness of its heritage, and its magnificent language.' The claim had played well with a public disinclined to trust foreigners, and it had served Akram's purposes even better: he'd won his seat easily, and there was little doubt that his political aspirations didn't end in the stuffy council room of Balford-le-Nez.

'Your son told you that we've determined Mr Querashi was murdered?' Emily said. When Akram nodded gravely, she went on. 'Then anything you can tell me about him will be of help.'

'There are those who believe this to be a random racial crime,' Malik said. It was a clever way of addressing the issue, not accusing so much as contemplating.

'Your son among them,' Emily said. 'But we've evidence that shows the crime was premeditated, Mr Malik. And premeditated in such a way as to suggest that Mr Querashi – and not just any Asian – was the target. This doesn't mean that an English killer isn't involved. And it doesn't mean that race isn't an issue at some level either. But it does mean that it's a personal crime.'

'That doesn't seem possible.' Malik made another careful fold in his paper cap and smoothed his dark fingers along the crease he'd created. 'Haytham had been here so brief a time. He knew so few people. How can you be certain that he knew his killer?'

Emily explained to him that there were some details of the investigation that procedure required she keep to herself, things that only the killer and the police knew, and thus things that ultimately could be used to construct a trap if a trap became necessary. 'But we do know that someone studied his movements to be assured that he'd be on the Nez that night, and if we learn what his regular movements were, we may be able to trace them to that person.'

'I hardly know where to begin,' Malik said.

'Perhaps with his engagement to your daughter,' she suggested.

Malik's jaw tightened slightly. 'Surely, you don't mean to suggest that Sahlah is involved in Haytham's death?'

'I understand that this was an arranged marriage. Was she agreeable to it?'

'More than agreeable. And she knew that neither her mother nor I would force her to marry against her will. She met Haytham, she was allowed to spend some time with him alone, and she decided favourably. Quite favourably, in fact. She was eager to marry. Had she felt otherwise, Haytham would have returned to his family in Karachi. That was the arrangement we made with his parents, and both sides agreed to it before he came to England.'

'You didn't think a Pakistani boy born in England would be more suitable for your daughter? Sahlah was born here, wasn't she? She'd be more used to others born here as well.'

'Asian boys born in England are sometimes at odds with their origins, Inspector Barlow. They're often at odds with Islam, with the importance of family, with our culture, with our beliefs.'

'Like your son, perhaps?'

Malik sidestepped. 'Haytham lived by the tenets of Islam. He was a fine man. He wished to be a *haji*. This was an attribute I valued highly in a husband for my daughter. Sahlah felt likewise.'

'And how did your son feel about Mr Querashi's becoming part of your family? He holds a position here at the factory, doesn't he?'

'Muhannad is our director of sales. Haytham was our director of production.'

'Positions of equality?'

'Essentially. And, as I know you will next ask: there was no conflict between them. Their jobs were unrelated to each other.'

'Both of them would want to perform well, I expect,' Emily noted.

'I should hope so. But their individual performances would not change the future. Upon my death, my son will rise to become managing director of the company. Haytham knew this. Indeed, he would have fully expected that to be the case. Thus, Muhannad had no need to fear Haytham's advent among us, if that's what you're suggesting. In fact, the situation was very much the contrary. Haytham took a burden off Muhannad's shoulders.'

'What sort of burden?'

Malik unfastened the top button of his shirt and once again pressed his wrist against his face to dab off the perspiration. The room was airless, and Emily wondered why he didn't open one of the two windows. 'Before Haytham's arrival, Muhannad had the extra job of overseeing Mr Armstrong's work. Mr Armstrong was only a temporary employee and as he isn't a member of the family, he required more supervision. As director of production, he was responsible for the workings of the entire factory, and while he did a fine job, he knew his employment was temporary and thus did not have reason to be as meticulous as someone with a permanent interest here.' He raised a finger to stop Emily from speaking when she would have asked another question. 'I do not mean to imply that Mr Armstrong's work was unacceptable to us. I wouldn't have asked him back upon Haytham's death had it been so.'

This, of course, was very much the point as well as the detail which

Barbara Havers had stressed. Armstrong *had* been asked back to Malik's Mustards. 'How long do you expect to have Mr Armstrong working here this time round?'

'As long as it takes to find my daughter another suitable husband who can also work in the factory.'

Which, Emily thought, could mean quite some time, cementing Ian Armstrong's position in the business. 'And did Mr Armstrong know Mr Querashi? Had they ever met?'

'Oh, yes indeed. Ian trained Haytham for five days prior to leaving us.'

'And their relationship?'

'It appeared quite cordial. But then, Haytham was an easy man to like. And he had no enemies here at Malik's Mustards.'

'He knew everyone in the factory?'

'He had to. He was the factory director.'

Which meant interviews with everyone, Emily thought, because everyone had enemies, no matter what Akram Malik believed. The trick was to smoke them out. Mentally, she assigned two DCs to the task. They could use this conference room. They would be discreet. She said, 'And outside the factory? Who else did Mr Querashi know?'

Akram considered this. 'So few. But there was the Gentlemen's Cooperative. I suggested he join, and he did so at once.'

Emily knew about the Gentlemen's Cooperative. It had featured prominently in the portrait that Akram Malik's campaign literature had painted of him. It was a social club of the town's businessmen, which Akram Malik had organised shortly after opening his factory. They met weekly for lunch and monthly for dinner, and their purpose was to foster good will, cooperation in commerce, and commitment to the growth of the town and the well-being of its citizens. The point was to discover and encourage commonalities among members, its founder having the philosophy that men at work on a mutual goal are men who live in harmony together. It was interesting, Emily realised, to note the difference between the Gentlemen's Cooperative, which Akram Malik had founded, and *Jum'a*, which had been founded by his son. She wondered how much at odds the two men were and if this condition extended to the future son-in-law.

'Is your son a member of this group as well?' she asked curiously.

'Muhannad's attendance is not what I would wish,' Malik said. 'But he is indeed a member.'

'Less devoted to the cause than Mr Querashi?'

Malik's face was grave. 'You're seeking to connect my son to Mr Querashi's death, aren't you?'

'How did your son feel about this arranged marriage?' she countered.

For a moment, Akram Malik's face registered a look that suggested he would answer no further questions about his son unless and until he was told what Emily had in mind when she asked them. But he relented. 'As Muhannad's own marriage was arranged, he had no difficulty with his sister's being likewise.' He stirred in his chair. 'My son, Inspector, has not been the easiest child to rear. He has, I believe, been too much influenced by western culture. And perhaps one sees this in his behaviour in a way that makes him difficult to understand. But he respects his roots and takes great pride in his blood. He is a man of his people.'

Emily had heard that phrase invoked often enough about IRA hooligans and other wild-eyed political extremists. While it was true that Muhannad's political activism in the town supported his father's contention, the existence of *Jum'a* suggested that what could be identified as the younger man's pride in his blood could also be seen as an inclination to cross the line and an ability to manipulate people by playing upon their ignorance and fear. Still, the thought of *Jum'a* prompted her to ask, 'Did Mr Querashi also belong to your son's fraternity, Mr Malik?'

'Fraternity?'

'You know about *Jum'a*, don't you? Was Haytham Querashi part of it?'

'That I would not know.' He unfolded his cap with the same care he'd used to fold it, and he gave all his attention to his fingers' movement on the thin paper. 'Muhannad will be able to tell you that.' He frowned, then, and finally looked up. 'But I must confess that the direction you've taken with these questions troubles me. It makes me wonder if my son – who is admittedly quick to make allegations when it comes to matters of race – is correct in assuming you will turn a blind eye to the possibility of hate and ignorance being the sole motives behind this crime.'

'I'm not blind to that at all,' Emily said. 'Racial crime is a global problem, and I'd be a fool to deny it. But if hatred and ignorance are behind Querashi's murder, they were directed at a specific target and not merely any Asian whom the killer came across on the street. We need to know Mr Querashi's contacts in both communities. It's the only way we'll track down his killer. The Gentlemen's Cooperative represents one view of life in Balford-le-Nez. *Jum'a*, you'll agree, represents another.' She stood. 'If you'll take me to Mr Armstrong . . . ?'

Akram Malik gazed upon her thoughtfully. Under his scrutiny Emily became conscious of the differences between them, not just the standard male-female differences, but the cultural differences that would always define them. They were present in her manner of dress: thin tank-top, grey trousers, no covering on her head. They were present in the freedom afforded her: a woman on her own in a vast world that was hers for the taking. They were present in the position she held: the dominant figure in a team comprised mostly of men. She and Akram Malik – despite his professed love of the country he'd adopted – may as well have been from different universes.

He got to his feet. 'This way,' he said.

Barbara bounced along the cratered lane and found a place to park her Mini at the far side of a prefabricated building with a sign that announced its business ambiguously as Hegarty's Adult Distractions. She noted the air conditioner set into one of its front windows, and she gave some moments' consideration to the idea of staggering inside and planting herself in front of it. That would be an adult distraction well worth the effort, she thought.

The heat on the coast was beginning to feel worse than the heat in London, which was borderline inconceivable. If England was going to turn into a tropical environment as part of the global warming that scientists had been predicting for years, Barbara decided that it would be nice to have some of the accoutrements of the tropics as well. A white-jacketed waiter carrying a tray of Singapore Slings wouldn't have gone down badly at all.

She looked in her rear-view mirror to see how Emily's make-up job on her face was holding up to its exposure to sweat. She expected to see her countenance dissolving like one of Dr Jekyll's transmogrifications. But both foundation and blusher were where they were supposed to be. Perhaps, after all, there was something to be said for playing about with pots of colour each morning in the quest for devastating beauty.

Barbara made her way back over the uneven lane to Malik's Mustards & Assorted Accompaniments. A stop at the Malik residence had allowed her to glean that Sahlah worked at the factory with her father and brother. This information had been passed on by a dowdy, plump woman with one child on her hip, another held by the hand, a wandering eye, and a feathery but nonetheless noticeable growth of black hair on her upper lip. She'd looked at Barbara's warrant card and said, 'It's Sahlah you want, then? Our little Sahlah? Oh, my goodness, whatever has she done that someone from the police should want to talk to her?' But there was a certain delight to her questions, the sort of excitement evidenced by a woman who had either little diversion in her life or an axe to grind with her sister-in-law. She'd informed Barbara of their relationship up front, via the announcement that she was the wife of Muhannad, the elder child and the only son of the household. And *these* – she indicated the children with pride – were the sons of Muhannad. And soon – and here she'd nodded meaningfully in the direction of her stomach – there would be a third son, a third in three years. A third son for Muhannad Malik.

Yadda, yadda, yadda, Barbara thought. She decided that the woman needed a hobby if this was the extent of her conversation. She'd said, 'I need a word with Sahlah, if you'll fetch her for me.'

But that wasn't possible. Sahlah was at the factory. 'It's always best to keep busy when one's heart is broken, don't you agree?' the woman pronounced. But once again, there was an enjoyment in her expression that was at odds with the statement. She gave Barbara the creeps.

So Barbara took herself off to Malik's Mustards, and as she approached the brick structure now, she removed the jewellery receipt from her bag and slipped it into the pocket of her trousers.

She swung inside the factory, where the air was stale and a potted fern next to the reception desk appeared to be about to give up the ghost. A young woman sat at a computer terminal, looking remarkably cool despite the fact that she was fully clothed from head to foot, her arms covered to the wrists and her dark hair mostly hidden beneath a traditional shawl. This was long hair, though, and a thick braid of it hung down the woman's back to her waist.

There was a name plate on her desk, so Barbara knew she had to look no further for Sahlah Malik. She produced her warrant card and introduced herself. 'Could I have a word?'

The girl looked towards a door whose half-glass construction revealed some sort of interior office. 'With me?'

'You're Sahlah Malik, aren't you?'

'Yes, but I've spoken to the police already if this is about Haytham. I spoke to them the very first day.' On her desk there was a long computer print-out which appeared to list names. She took a yellow felt pen from the desk's centre drawer and began highlighting some names and crossing others out with a pencil.

'Did you tell them about the bracelet, then?' Barbara asked her.

She didn't look up from the print-out although Barbara saw her eyebrows tighten momentarily. It could have been an expression of concentration had the common activity of highlighting names required concentration. On the other hand, it could have been confusion. 'Bracelet?' she asked.

'A piece by a bloke called Aloysius Kennedy. Gold. Engraved with the words "Life begins now". Is this sounding familiar?'

'I don't understand the nature of your question,' the girl said. 'What has a gold bracelet to do with Haytham's death?'

'I don't know,' Barbara said. 'P'rhaps nothing. I thought you might be able to tell me. This –' she set the receipt on the desk '– was among his things. Locked up among his things, by the way. Can you think why? Or what it was doing in his possession in the first place?'

Sahlah capped the yellow pen and set the pencil to one side before she took the receipt. She had lovely hands, Barbara noted, with fingers that were slender and nails that were clipped to the tips of her fingers but smooth and buffed-looking. She wore no rings.

Barbara waited for her to respond. In her peripheral vision she saw movement in the inner office and looked that way. In a corridor at the far end, Emily Barlow was speaking to a middle-aged Pakistani man wearing what looked like a chef's outfit. Akram Malik? Barbara wondered. He looked old enough and grave enough for the part. She gave her attention back to Sahlah.

'I don't know,' Sahlah said. 'I don't know why he had it.' She spoke to the receipt rather than to Barbara. 'Perhaps he was seeking a way to reciprocate and this seemed best to him. Haytham was a very good man. A very kind man. It wouldn't have been unlike him to attempt to discover the cost of something so that he could make an equal offering in return.'

'Sorry?'

'*Lenā-denā*,' Sahlah said. 'The giving of gifts. It's part of the way we establish our relationships.'

'The gold bracelet was a gift for him? From you? For Mr Querashi?'

'As his fiancée I would present him with a token. He would do likewise to me.'

But again there remained the question of where the bracelet was now. Barbara hadn't seen it among Querashi's belongings. She hadn't read in the police report about its being found upon the body. Would someone really stalk a victim and carefully arrange his death for possession of a gold bracelet? People had died for less, to be sure, but in this case . . . Why was it that the thought seemed so unlikely?

'He didn't have the bracelet,' Barbara said. 'It wasn't on his body and it wasn't in his room at the Burnt House. Can you explain why?'

Sahlah used the yellow pen against another name. 'I hadn't yet given it to him,' she said. 'I would have done on the day of the *nikāh*.'

'Which is what?'

'When our marriage contract would have been formally signed.'

'So you have the bracelet?'

'No. There was no point to keeping it. When he was killed, I took it . . .' Here she paused. Her fingers touched the edges of the computer print-out, straightening them perfectly. 'This will sound absurd and melodramatic, like something out of a nineteenth-century novel. When Haytham was killed, I took the bracelet and threw it from the pier. From the end of the pier. I suppose it was a way of saying goodbye.'

'When was this?'

'On Saturday. The day the police told me what had happened to him.'

This begged the question of the receipt, however. 'So he didn't know you had a bracelet to give him?'

'He didn't know.'

'Then what was he doing with the receipt?'

'I can't say exactly. But he would have known I was going to give him something. It's traditional.'

'Because of . . . What did you call it?'

'*Lenā-denā*. Yes. Because of that. And he wouldn't have wanted his gift to me to be out of balance with my gift to him. That would have been an insult to my family and Haytham was careful about that sort of thing. I imagine –' and here she looked at Barbara for the first time since their discussion had begun 'I imagine that he did some minor detective work on his own to discover what I'd purchased for him and where. It wouldn't have been that difficult. Balford's a small town. The shops that carry items worthy of an occasion like a *nikāh* are easy enough to unearth.'

Her explanation was reasonable, Barbara thought. It made perfect sense. The only problem was that neither Rachel Winfield nor her mother had said anything that could come close to supporting this conjecture.

'From the end of the pier,' Barbara said. 'What time of day was this?'

'I have no idea. I didn't look at a watch.'

'I don't mean the exact time. But was it morning? Afternoon? Night?'

'Afternoon. The police came to us in the morning.'

'Not at night, then?'

Perhaps she saw too late where Barbara was heading, because her gaze faltered. But she seemed to realise the difficulty she'd be causing herself if she changed her story. She said, 'It was the afternoon.'

And a woman dressed as Sahlah dressed would doubtless have been noticed ... by someone. The pier was being renovated. That very morning Barbara had herself seen the workmen perched on a building being constructed at the very place Sahlah had claimed she'd disposed of the gold bracelet. So there had to be someone on the pier who could corroborate her story.

Movement in the inner office caught her attention again. It wasn't Emily this time, but two Asian men who'd come into Barbara's line of vision. They walked to a drafting table where they engaged in an earnest discussion with a third Asian man who was working there. The sight of them reminded Barbara of the name.

'F. Kumhar,' she said to Sahlah. 'Does someone of that name work here?'

'Not in the office,' Sahlah said.

'The office?'

'It wouldn't be someone in either accounting or sales. Those are the office positions.' She indicated the windowed door. 'But as to the factory itself ... That's production. I know the regular employees in production, but not those we bring in for extra work like labelling when a big order goes out.'

'These are part-time people?'

'Yes. I don't always know them.' She gestured to the print-out on her desk. 'I've never seen the name among these, but as we don't pay the part-time people by computer, I wouldn't have done.'

'Who knows the part-timers, then?'

'The director of production.'

'Haytham Querashi,' Barbara said.

'Yes. And Mr Armstrong before him.'

*   *   *

Which was how Barbara and Emily crossed paths at Malik's Mustards, with Sahlah leading Barbara back to meet Mr Armstrong.

If size of office was anything to go by – as it was in New Scotland Yard where importance of position was measured by the number of windows one had – then Ian Armstrong was occupying a position of some prominence, however impermanently. When Sahlah tapped on the door and a voice called out for her to enter, Barbara saw a room large enough to accommodate a desk, a round conference table, and six chairs. As it was an interior office, there were no windows. Either the heat or Emily Barlow's questions were making Ian Armstrong's face drip.

Armstrong was saying, '. . . no real necessity for taking Mikey to the doctor last Friday. That's my son's name, by the way. Mikey.'

'Was he running a temperature?' Emily nodded as Barbara slipped into the room. Sahlah pulled the door shut and departed.

'Yes, but children often run high temperatures, don't they?' Armstrong's eyes flicked to Barbara before returning to Emily. He didn't seem to notice the perspiration that was dribbling from his forehead, down one cheek.

For her part, Emily looked as if Freon rather than blood were coursing through her veins. Coolly, she sat at the conference table with a small tape player before her, recording Ian Armstrong's answers.

'One can't rush a child to the casualty ward simply because his forehead's hot,' Armstrong explained. 'Besides, the boy's had so many ear aches that we know what to do at this point. We have drops. We use heat. He soon settles after that.'

'Can anyone other than your wife confirm this? Did you phone your in-laws looking for advice on Friday? What about your own parents? A neighbour? Or a friend?'

His expression clouded. 'If . . . If you'll give me a moment to think . . .'

'Take your time, Mr Armstrong,' Emily said. 'We want to be accurate.'

'It's just that I've never been involved in anything like this, and I'm feeling a bit jittery. If you know what I mean.'

'Indeed,' Emily said.

As the DCI waited for the man's reply to her question, Barbara took note of the office. It was functional enough. Product posters hung framed on the walls. The desk was serviceable steel as were the filing cabinets and the shelves. The table and chairs were relatively new but inexpensive-looking. The only items of note were on Armstrong's desk. These were framed photographs, and there were three of them. Barbara sidled round to have a look. A sour-looking woman with blonde hair curled in a retro fashion from the early-sixties was depicted in one, a child speaking earnestly to Father Christmas was in another, and the third displayed the happy family together in a stair-step arrangement with child on mother's lap and father standing behind them with hands on mother's shoulders. Armstrong looked rather startled in this photograph, as if he'd come to his position of paterfamilias quite by accident and much to his surprise.

He was certainly settling in at the factory, for a temporary employee. Barbara could imagine him bustling in that very morning with his photos stowed inside a briefcase, dusting them off with a handkerchief and humming happily as he set them in position prior to getting down to work.

It seemed a fantasy at odds with his current behaviour, however. He kept glancing anxiously at Barbara as if with the concern that she was about to go through his desk. Emily finally introduced them. Armstrong said, 'Oh. Another . . . ?' and then hastily swallowed whatever else he had in mind. Finally he said, 'My in-laws.' And then he went on with growing conviction. 'I can't be completely accurate about the time, but I'm certain I spoke to them on Friday night. They knew Mikey was ailing, and they phoned us.' He smiled. 'I'd forgotten, because you asked if I'd phoned them and it was just the opposite.'

'The approximate time?' Emily asked.

'When they phoned? It would have been sometime after the news. On ITV.'

Which came on at ten o'clock, Barbara thought. She watched the man through narrowed eyes and wondered how much of this he was manufacturing on the spot and how quickly he'd pick up the phone to get his in-laws' cooperation with the tale once she and Emily left his office.

While Barbara considered this proposition, Emily switched gears. She moved on to Haytham Querashi and Armstrong's relationship with the murdered man. It was, according to the temporary production manager, a fine relationship, an excellent relationship; they were practically blood brothers to hear Armstrong describe it.

'And he didn't have any enemies here at the factory, as far as I could tell,' Armstrong concluded. 'Indeed, if the truth be told, the factory workers were delighted to have him.'

'And not sorry to see you leave?' Emily asked.

'I suppose that would be the case,' Armstrong admitted. 'The majority of our workers are Asian, and they'd prefer one of their own overseeing them, far more than an Englishman. This isn't unnatural when you think of it, is it?'

He looked from Emily to Barbara, as if waiting for one of them to reassure him. When neither woman did, he went back to his previous thought. 'So there was no one, really. If you're looking for a motive among the workers here, I can't say how you'll be able to find one. I've been back only a few hours, and from what I've been able to tell, there's been nothing but a true sense of mourning among his people.'

'What about someone called Kumhar?' Barbara asked. She joined Emily and Armstrong at the table.

'Kumhar?' Armstrong frowned.

'F. Kumhar. Are you familiar with the name?'

'Not at all. Is it someone who works here? Because I know everyone in the factory . . . Well, one has to because of the job. And unless it's someone hired during Mr Querashi's tenure, someone whom I've yet to meet . . .'

'Miss Malik seems to feel it would be someone brought in part-time when work gets heavy. She mentioned special labelling needs.'

'A part-time employee?' Armstrong looked towards Emily. He said, 'If I may . . . ?' as if he believed he was under her supervision. He went to one of the shelves and pulled down a ledger, which he carried to the table. He said, 'We've always been careful about our records. In Mr Malik's position, employing illegals could be disastrous.'

'Is that a problem round here?' Barbara asked. 'As far as I know, illegals generally head for a city. London, Birmingham, places where there's a large Asian community.'

'Hmm, yes. I expect they do,' Armstrong said as he flipped through a few pages of the ledger, examining the dates at the top. 'But we're not that far from the harbours, are we? Illegals can always slip through the net at the port, so Mr Malik insists upon vigilance, lest any of them end up here.'

'If Mr Malik were employing aliens, could Haytham Querashi have uncovered that fact?' Barbara asked.

Ian Armstrong looked up. He clearly saw the direction in which the questions were heading, and he appeared frankly relieved to have the spotlight removed from him. Nonetheless, he didn't seem to attempt to skew his answer. 'He might have suspected. But if someone presented him with well-forged papers, I don't see how he would have sussed them out. He wasn't English after all. How would he have known what to look for?'

Barbara wondered what being English had to do with it.

Armstrong looked over a page he'd selected. Then he went through two others. 'These are the most recent part-timers,' he told them. 'But there's no Kumhar among them. Sorry.'

Then Querashi would have known him in another context, Barbara concluded. She wondered what it was. The Pakistani organisation that Emily told her had been founded by Muhannad Malik? It was a possibility.

Emily was saying, 'What about someone given the sack by Querashi, part-time or otherwise? Would he be listed there?'

'The terminated employees have personnel files, naturally,' Armstrong said, indicating the filing cabinets along one wall. But as he spoke, his voice drifted off and he sat back in his chair, looking thoughtful. Whatever he was thinking apparently served to ease his mind because he finally took out a handkerchief and blotted his face with it.

'You've thought of something else?' Emily asked him.

'A terminated employee?' Barbara said.

'It may be nothing. I know about it, actually, only because I had the word from one of his fellow employees in shipping after it happened. There was quite a to-do, evidently.'

'About what?'

'Trevor Ruddock, a boy from the town. Haytham gave him the sack about three weeks ago.' Armstrong went to one of the filing cabinets and fingered through a drawer. He brought out a folder and carried it to the table, reading a document contained inside. 'Yes, here it is . . . oh, dear. Well, it's not very nice.' He looked up and smiled. He'd obviously read good tidings for himself in Trevor Ruddock's file, and apparently he wasn't above celebrating the fact. 'Trevor was sacked for stealing, it says here. The report's in Haytham's writing. It seems he caught Trevor red-handed with a shipping crate of goods. He sacked him on the spot.'

'You said a boy,' Barbara noted. 'How old is he?'

Armstrong referred to the file. 'Twenty-one.'

Emily was with her. 'Has he a wife? Children?'

And Armstrong wasn't far behind them. 'No,' he said. 'But he lives at home, according to his employment application. And I do know that five children live there, along with Trevor, his mum, and his dad.

And from the address he's given . . .' Armstrong looked up at the two police officers. 'Well, it isn't exactly an upmarket area. I should guess his family needed whatever money he made. That's the way it is in that part of town.'

Having said this, he seemed to realise that any attempt to direct their suspicions on to another could serve to heighten their suspicions about him. He continued hastily. 'But Mr Malik intervened for the boy. There's a copy here of a letter he wrote, asking another businessman in town to give Trevor a chance to redeem himself through a job.'

'Where?' Barbara asked.

'At the pleasure pier. And doubtless that's where you can find him. I mean, if you want to speak to him about his relationship with Mr Querashi.'

Emily reached forward and shut off her tape recorder. Armstrong looked relieved, off the hook at last. But when Emily spoke, she put him back on. 'You won't be leaving town within the next few days, will you?' she asked pleasantly.

'I have no plans to go –'

'Good,' Emily Barlow said. 'We'll no doubt need to speak with you again. With your in-laws as well.'

'Of course. But as to this other matter . . . to Trevor . . . to Mr Ruddock . . . ? Surely you'll be wanting to . . .' Still, he wouldn't complete the sentence. He didn't dare. *Ruddock's got a motive* were the words that Ian Armstrong couldn't afford to speak. Because although Haytham Querashi had cost both men their jobs, only one of them had immediately benefited from the Pakistani's death. And all of them round the table knew that the chief beneficiary of the Tendring Peninsula's first act of deadly violence in five years was sitting in Querashi's erstwhile office, having resumed the job that Querashi's arrival in England had cost him.

Chapter Nine

————◆————

Cliff Hegarty saw them come out of the mustard factory together. He hadn't seen them go in together. Instead, he'd seen only the short, dumpy bird with the pudding basin haircut who'd climbed out of a dilapidated Austin Mini carrying a shoulder bag the size of a pillar box. He hadn't given her much thought, other than wondering why a woman with her body was wearing drawstring trousers that served only to emphasise the absence of a waist. He'd seen her, evaluated her personal appearance, absently registered her as someone unlikely to browse through Hegarty's Adult Distractions, and consequently dismissed her. It was only upon his second sight of her that he realised who – or rather what – she was. And then he knew that the day, which had already started out bad, had the distinct potential for becoming worse.

The second time the bird came into view, she was with another woman. This one was taller, so physically fit that she looked like she could wrestle a polar bear to the ground, and so commanding in the way she carried herself that there could be only one explanation for what she was doing at Malik's Mustards in the aftermath of the death on the Nez. She was the fuzz, Cliff realised. She had to be. And the other – with whom she stood in the kind of conversation that suggested professional if not personal intimacy – therefore had to be a copper as well.

Shit, he thought. The last thing he needed was to have the cops prowling round the industrial estate. The town council was bad enough. They loved to harass him, and despite the lip-service they paid to bringing Balford back from the dead economically, they'd equally love to drive him out of business. And those two cops – two *female* cops – would probably be only too delighted to weigh in with the opposition once they got a look at his jigsaws. And there was no doubt that they'd see them. If they popped in for a chat, which they were bound to do given enough time to pin down everyone who might have laid eyes on the corpse before he was a corpse, they'd end up getting an eyeful of their own. That visit itself, beyond the questions they'd be asking which he'd be doing his best to avoid answering, was one of several upcoming events that Cliff didn't anticipate with boundless joy.

His business was almost entirely mail-order, so Cliff could never understand what the fuss was about when it came to his puzzles. It wasn't as if he advertised them in the *Tendring Standard* or stuck up posters in the shops on the High Street. He was more discreet than that. Hell, he was always discreet.

But discretion didn't count for much once the coppers decided to start causing a bloke aggro. Cliff knew that from his Earl's Court days. When cops took that route, they began popping up on one's doorstep daily. Just a question, Mr Hegarty. Could you help us out with a problem, Mr Hegarty? Would you step down to the nick for a chat, Mr Hegarty? There's been a burglary (or mugging or purse snatching or assault, it never mattered which), and we're wondering where you were on the night in question? Can we have a bit of a go with your dabs? Just to clear you of suspicion, of course. And on and on until the only way to get them to give it a rest was to move out, move on, and start over somewhere else.

Cliff knew he could do that. He'd done it before. But that was in the days when he was alone. Now that he had someone – and not just some hanger-on this time but someone with a job, a future, and a decent place to live on the strand in Jaywick Sands – he wasn't about to be forced out again. Because while Cliff Hegarty could set up business anywhere, Gerry DeVitt couldn't so easily get employment in the building trade. And with the promise of Balford's future redevelopment so close to coming true, Gerry's own future was looking rosy. He wouldn't up stakes at this point, when at long last there was the prospect of making some decent money.

Not that money was Gerry's preoccupation, Cliff thought. Life would be a hell of a lot easier if only that were the case. If Gerry just trundled off to the job each morning and worked himself to exhaustion blow torching away at that restaurant on the pier, life would be grand. He'd come home hot, sweaty, and tired, with nothing more on his mind than dinner and sleep. He'd keep thinking about the bonus that the Shaws had promised him should he have the building up and running by the next bank holiday. And he wouldn't turn his concerns anywhere else.

As he'd obviously been doing that very morning, much to Cliff's rising anxiety.

Cliff had come into the kitchen at six a.m., having been awakened from a fitful sleep by the sudden knowledge that Gerry was no longer in bed at his side. He'd wrapped himself in a towelling bathrobe and found Gerry where he'd apparently been for some time, standing fully clothed at the open window. This looked out upon five feet of concrete promenade beyond which was the strand, beyond which was the sea. Gerry had been standing there, holding a mug of coffee, thinking the sort of private thoughts that always made Cliff begin to worry.

Gerry wasn't a bloke who generally kept his thoughts private at all: to him, being lovers meant living in each other's socks, which in its turn meant engaging in soulful conversations, frequent breast barings, and endless evaluations of 'the state of the relationship'. Cliff couldn't really abide this way of being involved with a bloke, but he'd learned to put up with it. These were Gerry's digs, after all, and even if that hadn't been the case, he *liked* Gerry well enough. So he'd schooled himself to cooperate in the conversation game with a fair amount of grudging good grace.

But recently, the situation had altered subtly between them. Gerry's concern for the state of their union seemed to have faded. He'd stopped talking so much about it and, more ominously, he'd stopped clinging quite so tightly to Cliff. This made Cliff want to start clinging to him. Which was ludicrous, daft, and just plain idiotic. Which pissed Cliff off because most of the time it was Cliff who needed space and Gerry who never wanted him to have it.

Cliff had joined him at the kitchen window. Over his lover's shoulder he'd seen that bright snakes of early-morning light were beginning to crawl across the sea. Backlit against them, a fishing boat chugged north. Gulls were silhouetted against the sky. While Cliff was no lover of natural beauty, he knew when a vista offered the opportunity for contemplation.

And that's what Gerry had appeared to be doing when Cliff came upon him. He seemed to be thinking.

Cliff had put his hand on Gerry's neck, knowing that in the past, their roles would have been reversed. Gerry would have offered the caress, a gentle touch but one that demanded in spite of itself, saying: Acknowledge me, please, touch me in turn, tell me you love me as well, as much, as blindly, as selflessly as I love you.

Before, Cliff would have wanted to shrug Gerry's hand away. No, truth be told, his first reaction would have been wanting to *slap* Gerry's hand away. In fact, he would have wanted to swat Gerry right across the room, because that touch of his – so solicitous and tender – would have made demands upon Cliff that he hadn't the energy or the ability to meet. But this morning he'd found himself playing Gerry's rôle, wanting a sign from Gerry that their relationship was still intact and foremost in the other man's thoughts.

Gerry had stirred beneath his hand, as if roused from sleep. His fingers made an effort at contact, but their graze felt to Cliff like a duty done, similar to one of those dry, stiff-lipped kisses exchanged by people who've been together too long.

Cliff had let his hand drop from Gerry's neck. Shit, he thought, and wondered what to say. He started with the obvious. 'Couldn't sleep? How long've you been up?'

'A while.' Gerry raised his coffee mug.

Cliff had observed the other man's reflection in the window and tried to read it. But because it was a morning rather than a night-time image, it showed little more than the shape of him, a beefy man who was bulky and solid with a body hard and strong from labour.

'What's wrong?' Cliff had asked him.

'Nothing. I couldn't sleep. It's too hot for me. This weather's unbelievable. You'd think we were living in Acapulco.'

Cliff had tested the water in a way that Gerry himself might have done had their positions been reversed. He said, 'You *wish* we were living in Acapulco. You and all those nice young Mexican boys . . .'

And he'd waited for the kind of reassurance that Gerry himself once would have wanted from him: me and nice young Mexican boys? You daft, mate? Who gives a flying one for a greasy kid when I can have *you*?

But it hadn't come. Cliff drove his fists into the pockets of his bathrobe. Hell, he thought with self-directed disgust. Who would've thought that *he'd* be wearing the sodding shoes of insecurity? He –

Cliff Hegarty and not Gerry DeVitt – was the one who'd always said that permanent fidelity was nothing but a pit stop on the road to the grave. He was the one who'd preached about the dangers of seeing the same tired face at breakfast every morning, of finding the same tired body in bed every night. He'd always said that after a few years of that, only the knowledge of having had a secret encounter with someone new on the side – someone who liked the thrill of the chase, the pleasures afforded by anonymity, or the excitement of deception – would stimulate a bloke's body into performing for a long-term lover. That's just the way it was, he'd always said. That was life.

But Gerry wasn't supposed to *believe* that Cliff had actually meant what he said. Flaming hell, no. Gerry was supposed to say with sardonic resignation, 'Right, mate. You keep on talking, 'cause that's what you're good at, and talk is just talk.' The last thing Cliff had ever expected was that Gerry might take his words to heart. Yet with a stomach quickly turning sour, Cliff forced himself to admit that Gerry must have done exactly that.

He wanted to say belligerently, Look, you want to end it, Ger? But he was too frightened of what his lover's answer might be. He realised in a flash of clarity that no matter how much he talked about roads to the grave, he didn't really want to split from Gerry. Not just because of these digs in Jaywick Sands, a few feet from the beach where Cliff liked to roam, nor because of the old speedboat that Gerry had lovingly restored and in which the two of them roared across the sea in the summer, and not because Gerry had been talking about an Australian holiday during the months when wind rattled the house like a Siberian cyclone. Cliff didn't want to split with Gerry because . . . well, there was something bloody comforting in being hooked up with a bloke who said he believed in permanent fidelity . . . even if one never got round to mentioning that particular point to him.

Which was why Cliff said with far more indifference than he actually felt, 'You looking for a Mexican boy these days, Ger? Got a taste for dark meat instead of white?'

Gerry turned from the window at that. He set his cup on the table. 'You been keeping count? Want to tell me why?'

Cliff grinned as he raised his hands in mock defence. 'No way. Hey, this i'n't about me. We been together long enough for me to know when somethin's on your mind. All's I'm asking is, do you want to talk about it?'

Gerry side-stepped and crossed the kitchen to the fridge. He opened it. He began to gather the ingredients for his usual breakfast, placing four eggs into a bowl and sliding four bangers out of their wrapper.

'You cheesed off about something?' Cliff reached for the tie of his bathrobe nervously. He retied it and returned his hands to his pockets. 'Okay, I know I mouthed off nasty when you cancelled our Costa Rica holiday, but I thought we'd set ourselfs straight about that. I know the pier job's a big one for you, and along with that house renovation . . . What I'm saying's that I know there hasn't been enough work in the past and now there is and you want to take the pickin's and you can't take time off. I understand. So if you've been cheesed off about what I said –'

'I haven't been cheesed off,' Gerry said. He cracked the eggs and whipped them in the bowl while the bangers began to hiss on the cooker.

'Okay. Well, good.'

But was it good, really? Cliff didn't think so. Lately, he had begun to notice changes in Gerry: the uncharacteristic, lengthy silences, the frequent weekend retreats to the small garage where he played his drums; the long nights he spent working on that private renovation job in Balford; the intense evaluative looks he'd taken to giving to Cliff when he thought Cliff wouldn't notice. So sure, maybe Ger wasn't cheesed off at the moment. But he was definitely something.

Cliff knew that he ought to say more, but what he realised was that he very much wanted to leave the room. He reckoned that it would be wiser, anyway, just to pretend everything was fine despite all indications to the contrary. That made more sense than running the risk of finding out something he didn't want to know.

Still, he remained in the kitchen. He watched the way his lover was moving, and he tried to suss out what it meant that Gerry was seeing to his breakfast with such a combination of assurance and concentration. It wasn't that assurance and concentration were out of character in Gerry. To be a success in his line of work, he needed both qualities. But neither was a quality that Gerry usually demonstrated when he was with Cliff.

Now, though . . . This was a different Gerry. This wasn't a bloke whose main concern had always been that problems between them got solved, questions got answered, and irritations got smoothed away without either of them raising their voices. This was a Gerry who sounded and acted like a bloke who'd put his oars in the water and knew exactly how far he had to row to get to the shore.

Cliff hadn't wanted to think about what this meant. He'd wished like hell he had stayed in bed. He heard the kitchen clock ticking loudly on the wall behind him, and it sounded just like the steady drumbeat that led the condemned to the chopping block. Shit, he thought. Fuck, hell, shit.

Gerry had taken his breakfast to the table. It was a hearty meal to see him through till lunch: eggs, bangers, two pieces of fruit, toast and jam. But when he had it laid out with cutlery in position, a glass of juice poured, and a napkin tucked into the top of his T-shirt, he didn't eat. He just stared at the food, curled his hand round the juice glass, and swallowed so loudly that Cliff had to think he was choking on a stone.

Then he looked up. 'I think,' Gerry said, 'we both need to have blood tests.'

The kitchen walls swam. The floor felt unsteady. And their shared history came back at Cliff in a sickening rush.

Who they'd been would always haunt them, two blokes who'd lied to their respective families about how and when and where they'd met: in a public loo at a period of time when 'taking precautions' wasn't as important as buggering the first bloke willing to have it. He and Ger knew the truth about each other, about who they'd been and, more important, who they could easily go back to being if the time was right and the temptation was there and the market square loo was empty save for just one other accommodating bloke.

Cliff had wanted to laugh, to pretend he'd misheard. He'd thought about saying, 'You daft? What the hell're you on about, mate?' But instead, he said nothing. Because long ago he'd learned the value of waiting for panic and terror to subside before saying the first thing that came into his head.

'Hey, I love you, Gerry DeVitt,' he'd finally declared.

Gerry bowed his head and began to weep.

Now Cliff watched the two cops yakking outside Hegarty's Adult Distractions, just like two old biddies over their tea. He knew they'd soon be going to every business in the industrial estate. They'd have to do it. The Paki'd been murdered, and they'd want to talk to anyone who might have seen the bloke, talked to him, or observed him talking to anyone else. Next to his digs, the industrial estate was the logical place to begin. So it was only a matter of time before they got themselves over to Hegarty's Adult Distractions.

'Shit,' Cliff whispered. He was sweating despite the air conditioner in the window that blew a frigid breeze in his direction. What he didn't need right now was a run-in with the rozzers. He had to keep them away from Gerry. And he had to avoid telling anyone the truth.

An impressive turquoise cruisemobile swung into the industrial estate just as Emily was saying, 'We can be sure of one thing, based on the fact that Sahlah didn't know who F. Kumhar was. He's a man, as I've thought from the first.'

'How d'you reckon that?'

Emily put up a hand to hold Barbara's question at bay for a moment as the car rumbled into the lane. An American convertible, it was all sleek lines and leather interior with chrome that glittered like polished platinum. Thunderbird sports car, Barbara thought, at least forty years old and perfectly restored. Someone wasn't hurting for lolly.

The driver was a tea-skinned male somewhere in his twenties, with long hair tied back in a ponytail. He wore wrap-around sunglasses of a style that Barbara had always associated with pimps, gigolos, and card sharks. She recognised him from the demonstration that she'd witnessed on television the previous day. Muhannad Malik.

Taymullah Azhar was with him. To his credit, he didn't look particularly comfortable arriving at the factory like a fugitive from *Miami Vice*.

The men got out. Azhar remained by the car, arms folded across his chest, while Muhannad sauntered to join the two police officers. He removed his sunglasses and tucked them into the pocket of his white shirt. This was perfectly ironed and fresh-looking, and he wore it with jeans and snake-skin boots.

Emily made the introductions. Barbara felt her palms getting damp. Now was the moment for her to tell the DCI that no introduction to Taymullah Azhar was going to be necessary. But she held her tongue. She waited for Azhar to clarify matters on his part for his cousin. Azhar glanced Muhannad's way but held his tongue as well. This was an unexpected turn of events. Barbara decided to see where it led them.

Muhannad's gaze passed over her in the sort of scornful, evaluative look that made Barbara itch to sink her thumbs into his eyeballs. He didn't stop walking towards them until – she was certain – he knew he'd come too close for comfortable conversation.

'And this is your liaison officer?' He gave ironic emphasis to the adjective.

'Sergeant Havers will meet you this afternoon,' Emily told him. 'Five o'clock at the station.'

'Four o'clock suits us better,' Muhannad countered. He didn't try to disguise the statement's purpose: an attempt at dominance.

Emily didn't play along. 'Unfortunately, I can't guarantee that my officer will be there at four,' she said, unruffled. 'But you're welcome to come then. If Sergeant Havers isn't in when you arrive, one of the constables will see that you're settled comfortably.' She smiled pleasantly.

The Asian favoured first Emily then Barbara with an expression that suggested he was in the presence of a substance whose odour he was at pains to identify. When he'd made his point, he turned to Azhar. 'Cousin,' he said, and headed towards the factory door.

'Kumhar, Mr Malik,' Emily called out as his hand touched the handle. 'First initial *F*.'

Muhannad halted, turned back their way. 'Are you asking me something, Inspector Barlow?'

'Is that name familiar?'

'Why do you ask?'

'It's come up. Neither your sister nor Mr Armstrong recognised it. I thought you might.'

'Why?'

'Because of *Jum'a*. Is Kumhar a member?'

'*Jum'a*.' Muhannad's face, Barbara noted, betrayed nothing.

'Yes. *Jum'a*. Your club, your organisation, your brotherhood. Whatever it is. You can't think the police don't know about it.'

He gave a low chuckle, said 'What the police don't know could fill volumes,' and pushed the door inward.

'Do you know Kumhar?' Emily persisted. 'It's an Asian name, isn't it?'

He paused, half in light, half in shadow. 'Your racism's showing, Inspector. Just because a name's Asian, it doesn't follow I'm acquainted with the man.'

'I didn't say Kumhar was a man, did I?'

'Don't overstep yourself. You asked if Kumhar belonged to *Jum'a*. If you know about *Jum'a*, I assume you know it's a society of men only. Now is there anything else? Because if there isn't, my cousin and I have work to do inside.'

'Yes, there is something else,' Emily said. 'Where were you on the night Mr Querashi died?'

Muhannad let go his hold on the door. He came back into the light and returned his sunglasses to his nose. 'What?' he asked quietly, certainly more for effect than because he'd not heard the question.

'Where were you the night Mr Querashi died?' Emily repeated.

He snorted. 'And this is where your investigation has taken you? Right where I expected you to go. A Paki's dead, so a Paki did it. And what better place to pin your hopes than on me, the most obvious Paki of choice.'

'That's certainly an intriguing observation,' Emily noted. 'Perhaps you'd care to explain it?'

He removed his sunglasses once again. His eyes were full of contempt. Behind him, Taymullah Azhar's expression was guarded. 'I get in your way,' Malik said. 'I take care of my people. I want to make them proud of who they are. I want them to hold their heads up high. I want them to know that they don't need to be white in order to be worthy. And all of that is the last thing you want, Inspector Barlow. So what better way to oppress my people – to humiliate them into a subservience you can live with – than to shine the light of your pathetic investigation upon me?'

The man was no intellectual sluggard, Barbara realised. What could be more successful in disarming dissent in the community than attempting to present the dissenters' leader to them as a shrill, tin god? Except ... maybe he was. Barbara ventured a quick look at Azhar, to see how he was reacting to the exchange between the DCI and his cousin. She found him watching not Emily but herself. See? his expression seemed to be saying. Our conversation at breakfast was prescient, wasn't it?

'That's a fine analysis of my motives,' Emily told Muhannad. 'And we'll be certain to discuss it at a later date.'

'In front of your superiors.'

'Whatever you wish. As for now, please answer the question or come with me to the nick to have a think about it.'

'You'd like me there, wouldn't you?' Malik said. 'I'm sorry to have to deprive you of the pleasure.' He went back to the door and shoved it open. 'Rakin Khan. You'll find him in Colchester, which I trust isn't too difficult a task for someone of your admirable investigative powers.'

'You were with somone called Rakin Khan on Friday night?'

'Sorry to disappoint your hopes.' Not waiting for an answer, he disappeared into the building. Azhar nodded at Emily, then followed him.

'He's quick,' Barbara noted grudgingly. 'But he ought to deep-six those sunglasses.' She repeated the question she'd asked a moment before Muhannad's arrival. 'So how do you reckon Kumhar's a man?'

'Because Sahlah didn't know him.'

'So? Like Muhannad just said –'

'That was bullshit, Barbara. The Asian community in Balford is small and it's tight. If there's an F. Kumhar among them, believe me, Muhannad Malik of all people knows him.'

'So why wouldn't his sister?'

'Because she's a woman. The family's traditional – witness the marriage bit. Sahlah would know the community of Asian women, and she'd know the men who work here at the factory. But it doesn't follow that she'd know other men unless they're married to her acquaintances or boys from her schooldays. How would she? Look at her life. She probably doesn't date. She doesn't go to pubs. She doesn't move freely round Balford. She hasn't been away to school. She's as good as a prisoner. So if she's not lying about not recognising the name – which of course she could be –'

'Right. She could be,' Barbara cut in. 'Because F. Kumhar could well be a woman and she could know that. F. Kumhar could be *the* woman, in fact. And Sahlah may have sussed that out.'

Emily rummaged in her bag and brought out her sunglasses. Absently, she rubbed them against the front of her tank top before she replied. 'The cheque stub tells us that Querashi paid Kumhar £400. A single cheque, a single payment. If the cheque's been written to a woman, what was Querashi paying her for?'

'Blackmail,' Barbara offered.

'Then why kill Querashi? If he was being blackmailed by F. Kumhar and he'd made a payment, why break his neck? That's killing the goose.'

Barbara considered the DCI's questions. 'He was going out at night. He was meeting someone. He was carrying condoms. Couldn't F. Kumhar be the woman he was bonking? And couldn't F. Kumhar have come up pregnant?'

'Then why take the condoms if she was already pregnant?'

'Because he wasn't meeting *her* any longer. He'd already moved on to someone else. And F. Kumhar knew it.'

'And the £400? What was that for? An abortion?'

'A very private abortion. Perhaps, even, a botched abortion.'

'With someone seeking revenge afterwards?'

'Why not? Querashi had been here six weeks. That's long enough to put someone in the club. If word got out that he'd done it – to an Asian woman, no less, for whom virginity or chastity is a big deal in capitals – maybe her father, brother, husband, or other assorted relations were looking to set things right. So. Have any Asian women died recently? Have any been admitted to hospital with suspicious haemorrhaging? It's something we need to look into, Em.'

Emily shot her a wry look. 'Have you gone off Armstrong so soon, then? We've still got his dabs on the Nissan, you know. *And* he's still sitting inside that building, happily doing Querashi's job.'

Barbara looked at the building, once again seeing the copiously sweating Mr Ian Armstrong being put through his paces by DCI Barlow. 'His sweat glands were giving a power performance,' she admitted. 'So I wouldn't cross him off the list.'

'What if the in-laws corroborate his Friday night phone call story?'

'Then I think I'd start sifting through BT's records.'

Emily chuckled. 'You're a real pit bull, Sergeant Havers. If you ever decide to leave the Yard for the seaside, I'll have you on my team in a flash.'

Barbara felt a rush of pleasure at the DCI's praise. But she was never one to take a compliment and run with it, so she shifted her weight and fished her car keys out of her bag. 'Right. Well. I want to check out Sahlah's story about the bracelet. If she tossed it from the pier on Saturday afternoon, then somebody probably saw her. It's not like she isn't noticeable, what with the gear she wears. So shall I track down this bloke Trevor Ruddock as well? If he's working on the pier, I can kill two birds.'

Emily nodded. 'Sort him out. In the meantime, I'll see about this Rakin Khan that Muhannad's so hot to have me talk to. Although I've little doubt he'll confirm the alibi. He'll be wanting his brother Muslim to – how did our Muhannad phrase it exactly? – be able to hold his head up high. Now there's a delicious image for you to dwell on.' She gave a short laugh and headed towards her car.

With a wave, she was on the road, pointed towards Colchester and another alibi.

Being on the Balford pleasure pier for the first time since her sixteenth summer wasn't the trip down memory lane that Barbara had expected it might be. The pier was greatly changed, with a rainbow sign over its entrance that spelled *Shaw Attractions* in colourful neon. Still, the bright fresh paint, new planking, crisp-looking deck chairs, refurbished rides and games of chance, and a modern arcade offering everything from old-fashioned penny slides to video games, didn't alter the never-to-be-forgotten smells of her annual visits to Balford. The scent of fish and chips, hamburgers, popcorn, and candy floss mingled sharply with the brine of the sea. And the sounds were the same as well: children laughing and shouting, arcade games ringing cacophonously, the calliope playing as the roundabout horses rose and fell on their shiny brass poles. Ahead of her, the pier shot straight out into the sea, widening at its end in spatulate fashion. Barbara walked to this point, where the old Jack 'awkins Cafeteria was being renovated and from which location Sahlah Malik had allegedly thrown the bracelet she'd bought for her fiancé.

From the shell of the old cafeteria rose the sound of voices shouting above the pounding of tools against metal and the loud hiss of a blow torch welding reinforcements on to the original infrastructure. Heat seemed to throb from the building, and when Barbara peered inside, she felt it pulsating against her face.

The workers were scantily dressed. Jeans cut off at the thigh, heavy-soled boots, and grimy T-shirts – or none at all – appeared to be the uniform of choice. These were big-muscled men, intent on their jobs. But when one caught sight of Barbara, he set down his tools and shouted, 'No visitors! Can't you read? Clear out of here before you get hurt.'

Barbara pulled out her warrant card, more for effect than anything else, since he couldn't have seen what it was at that distance. She shouted back, 'Police.'

'Gerry!' The man directed his attention to the welder whose protective headgear and concentration on the flame he was shooting towards the metal seemed to make him oblivious of everything else.

'Gerry! Hey! DeVitt!'

Barbara stepped over three steel girders that were lying on the floor, awaiting placement. She dodged several huge coils of electrical wire and a stack of unopened wooden crates.

Someone yelled, 'Keep back! You want to get hurt?'

This apparently got Gerry's attention. He looked up, saw Barbara, and doused the flame on his blow torch. He removed his headgear to reveal a bandana. He whipped this off and dried first his face with it, then his shining and hairless skull. Like the others, he wore cut-off jeans and a sleeveless T-shirt, and he had the sort of body that would quickly go to seed if exposed to the wrong kind of food or a period of inactivity. Neither appeared to be the case. He was extremely fit-looking and brown from the sun.

Before he, too, had a chance to warn her off, Barbara lifted her warrant card again, saying, 'Police. Can I have a word with you blokes?'

He frowned, returning the bandana to his head. He tied it at the back and with the single hoop earring he wore, the overall effect was piratical. He spat on to the floor – to the side, at least – and dug into his pocket for a roll of Polos. He thumbed one out and popped it into his mouth. 'Gerry DeVitt,' he said. 'I'm the guv here. What d'you need?'

He came no closer, so Barbara knew he couldn't read her identification. She introduced herself, and although his eyebrows made a quick furrowing movement when she said *New Scotland Yard*, he didn't evince any other reaction.

He glanced at his watch and said, 'We don't have much time to spare.'

'Five minutes,' Barbara said, 'perhaps less. No one's in trouble, by the way.'

He evaluated this, then nodded. Much of the work had ceased in the building anyway, so he waved the men over. There were seven of them, sweat-streaked, smelly, and patched with grease.

'Thanks,' Barbara said to DeVitt. She explained what she was seeking: verification that a young woman – probably dressed in traditional Asian garb – had come to the end of the pier on Saturday and had thrown something from it. 'This would have been in the afternoon,' Barbara said. 'Do you work on Saturdays?'

'We do,' DeVitt said. 'What time?'

Since Sahlah had claimed not to know the exact time, Barbara speculated that if her story was accurate and if she had gone into work that day as an excuse to be out of the house alone, it would probably have been late in the afternoon, a possible detour she'd taken on her way home. 'I'd say round five o'clock.'

Gerry shook his head. 'We're out of here by half-past four.' He turned to his men. 'Any of you lot see this bird? Any of you still here after five?'

One man said, 'You joking, mate?' and others laughed at the thought, it seemed, of hanging about any longer than necessary after a day's work. No one was able to corroborate Sahlah Malik's story.

'We would've noticed her if we were still here,' DeVitt said. He jerked his thumb at the other workers. 'This lot? Let a good-looking bird come by and they're hanging by their knees trying to get her attention.' The men guffawed. DeVitt grinned at them and then said to Barbara, 'This one you're speaking of: is she a looker?'

She was very pretty, Barbara confirmed. She was the sort of woman that men looked at twice. And with the costume she was wearing – here at the seaside, where women dressed like Sahlah were rarely seen on their own – she would hardly have gone unnoticed.

'Must've been after we'd cleared out, then,' DeVitt said. 'Anything else we can do for you?'

There was not. But Barbara handed the man one of her cards anyway, scrawling the name of the Burnt House Hotel on the back of it. If he remembered anything, if any of them remembered anything at all . . .

'Is this important information or something?' DeVitt asked curiously. 'Does this have to do with . . . Since it's an Asian you're talking about, does this have to do with that bloke who died?'

She was just checking out some facts, Barbara said. That's all she could tell them at the moment. But if anything relating to that incident came to any of their minds . . .

'Doubt it will,' DeVitt said as he shoved the card into the back pocket of his jeans. 'We steer clear of the Pakistanis. It keeps things simpler.'

'How's that?'

He shrugged. 'They've got their ways and we've got ours. Mix the two and what you've got is trouble. Blokes like us –' and he indicated his workers with a wave of his arm '– don't have time for trouble. We work hard, have a pint or two afterwards, and then go home so we can work hard tomorrow.' He scooped up his headgear and his blow torch once again, saying, 'If this bird you're asking about's an important part of things, you'd best have a word with the rest of the pier. One of them might've seen her pass by.'

She would do that, Barbara told them. She nodded her thanks and picked her way out of the building. A bust, she thought. But DeVitt was right. The attractions on the pier were open from morning until late at night. Unless Sahlah had swum or boated out to the end of the pier and climbed up to it in order to toss the bracelet dramatically into the sea from on high, she would have had to walk past all of them.

It was strictly plod work, the sort of questioning that Barbara had always loathed. But she began doggedly working her way from attraction to attraction, beginning with a tea cup ride called the Waltzer and ending with a take-away snack stall. The land end of the pier was covered, a roof of Plexiglas arching over the arcade, the roundabout, and the kiddie rides. Here the noise was intense, and Barbara had to shout to make herself heard. But no one was able to confirm Sahlah's story, not even Rosalie the Romany Palm Reader who sat on a three-legged stool in front of her den, dressed in swathes of colourful shawls, sweating, smoking, fanning herself with a paper plate, and watching every passerby for their potential to cross her palm with a five-pound note. If anyone had seen Sahlah Malik, Rosalie was the most likely candidate. But she hadn't seen her. She did, however, offer Barbara a reading: palm, tarot cards, or general aura. 'You could do with a reading, luv,' she said sympathetically. 'Believe you me. Rosalie can tell.'

Barbara begged off, saying that if the future was going to be as charming as the past, she'd much rather be in the dark about it.

She stopped at Jack Willies Wet Fish and Seafood, and bought a basket of deep fried whitebait, a snack she hadn't eaten in years. They were served with a suitable sheen of grease and a small pot of tartar sauce for dipping. Barbara took them back to the open-air section of the pier and lounged on one of the bright orange benches. She munched away and thought about the situation.

Since no one had been able to report seeing the Pakistani girl on the pier, there were three possibilities. The first had the most potential to muddy the waters: Sahlah Malik was lying. If this was the case, Barbara's next step was to ascertain why. The second possibility was the least plausible: Sahlah was telling the truth, even though not a single person on the pier remembered having seen the girl. Barbara had noted from her sojourn on the pier so far that the typical garb among visitors seemed to run heavily to black leather – despite the heat – and body rings. So unless Sahlah had come to the pier incognito – which was possibility number three – then what Barbara was left with was possibility number one: Sahlah was lying.

She finished her whitebait and wiped her fingers on a paper napkin. Leaning against the bench, she lifted her face to the sun and thought further, in another direction, back to F. Kumhar.

The only female Muslim name beginning with *F* that she could think of was Fatimah, although there had to be others. But assuming that the F. Kumhar to whom Querashi had written a cheque for £400 *was* a woman, and assuming that the cheque was somehow tied into

Querashi's murder, what could one reasonably deduce the cheque had been written for? Certainly an abortion was a possibility: he'd been meeting someone illicitly; he was carrying condoms; he had more prophylactics in his bedside table. But what else was possible? A purchase of some sort, perhaps the *lenā-denā* gift that Sahlah was expecting to receive from him, a gift that he himself had not yet picked up. A loan of money to someone in need, a fellow Asian who could not turn to other members of her family for help. A down payment on an object to be delivered after Querashi's marriage: a bed, a sofa, a table, a fridge.

Even if F. Kumhar was a man, the possibilities weren't much different. What did people purchase? Barbara wondered. Naturally, they purchased concrete items like objects, property, food, and clothing. But they also purchased abstract items like loyalty, betrayal, and sedition. And they purchased the absence of items as well, by securing silence, temporising, or departure.

In any case, there was only one way to know what Querashi had purchased. She and Emily were going to have to track Kumhar down. Which reminded Barbara of the secondary purpose she'd had in coming to the Balford pier: tracking down Trevor Ruddock.

She blew out a breath and swallowed, tasting the lingering flavour of the whitebait and feeling the greasy deposit they'd left on the roof of her mouth. She realised that she should have bought a drink with which to wash the lard-laden mess down her gullet, preferably something scalding hot that would have thoroughly melted it and sent it on its havoc-wreaking way through her digestive system. In half an hour, she'd doubtless begin paying the price for her impulsive purchase at Jack Willies Wet Fish and Seafood. Perhaps a Coke would appease her stomach, which was already beginning to grumble in an ominous fashion.

She rose, watching the flight of two gulls who soared above her and alighted on the roof that covered the land end of the pier. She noted for the first time a set of windows and an upper storey above the arcade. They appeared to be for offices. They were one last place for her to seek someone who had witnessed an Asian girl walking on the pier and the first place she needed to head to seek Trevor Ruddock before someone on the pier put the word out to him that a tubby detective was on his tail.

The stairs to the upper storey were inside the arcade, tucked between Rosalie's palm-reading establishment and a hologram exhibition. They led up to a single door upon which a black sign was printed with the single word: *Management.*

Inside, a corridor was lined with windows, which were open to catch whatever faint breeze might finally stir the torrid air. Offices opened off this passage, and from them emanated the sounds of telephones ringing, conversations developing, office machinery running, and fans oscillating. Someone had designed the office space well, because the horrific noise of the arcade directly below was almost entirely muffled.

Barbara could see, however, how unlikely it would be that anyone up here might have observed Sahlah Malik on the pier. Glancing into one of the offices to her right, she noted that its windows offered a view of the sea, south Balford, and the colourful tiers of beach huts on the shore. Unless someone had happened along the corridor at the precise moment that Sahlah had been walking past the Red Baron airplane ride below, the only hope of her having been observed came from the office at the far end, the windows of which seemed to overlook both the pier immediately below it and the sea to its side.

'May I help you with something?' Barbara turned to see a toothy girl at the door of the first office. 'Are you looking for someone? These are the management offices.'

When she spoke, Barbara saw that she'd had the centre of her tongue pierced and she wore a glittering stud in the hole. The sight gave Barbara the shivers – which was rather gratifying, considering the heat – and she sent a thankful prayer heavenward that she'd grown to adulthood at a period of time when harpooning one's body parts hadn't been in vogue.

Barbara presented her identification and ran Tongue-stud through the routine by rote. But the answer was as Barbara had expected. Tongue-stud had seen no one like Sahlah Malik on the pier. Never had done, in fact. An Asian girl alone? she repeated. Lord, she couldn't recall ever having seen an Asian girl alone. Leastways, not done up like the detective was describing.

But done up another way? Barbara wanted to know.

Tongue-stud played her teeth against her tongue's decoration, tap-tapping it thoughtfully. Barbara's stomach curdled.

No, she said. Which wasn't to say that some Asian girl hadn't been on the pier dressed like a *normal* person, mind. It's just that if she *had* been dressed like a *normal* person, well . . . she wouldn't have been very noticeable, would she?

That, naturally, was the rub.

Barbara asked who occupied the office at the end of the corridor. Tongue-stud told her that was Mr Shaw's office. Of Shaw Attractions, she added meaningfully. Did the detective sergeant wish to see him?

Why not? Barbara thought. If he couldn't add anything to what she'd already learned about Sahlah Malik's alleged visit to the pier – which was sod bloody all – then as the pier's owner, at least he'd be able to tell her where to find Trevor Ruddock.

'I'll just check, then,' Tongue-stud said. She went to the far door and stuck her head inside. 'Theo? The fuzz. Wanting a word.'

Barbara couldn't hear a reply, but in a moment a man came to the doorway of the office. He was younger than Barbara – somewhere in his mid-twenties – wearing fashionable, loose-fitting linen clothes. His fists were sunk into his pockets casually, but his expression was one of concern.

'There isn't trouble again, is there?' He directed a glance out of the windows, towards the amusements below. 'Is something out of order?'

He didn't mean with the equipment, she knew. He meant with his customers. A businessman in his position would know the value of a trouble-free environment. And when the police came calling, there was usually trouble in the air.

'Can I have a word?' she asked.

'Thanks, Dominique,' Theo said to Tongue-stud.

Dominique? Barbara thought. She'd expected a name like Slam or Punch.

Dominque took herself off to the office nearest the stairs. Barbara followed Theo Shaw into his. She saw at once that his windows gave him the view she'd suspected he'd have: overlooking the sea on one side, overlooking the pier at the office's far end. So if anyone at all had seen Sahlah Malik, Barbara knew she was down to her last possibility.

She turned to him, the question on her lips. It died in place.

He'd removed his hands from his pockets while she was taking in the view. And thus removed, they presented her with the object she'd been seeking all along.

Theo Shaw was wearing an Aloysius Kennedy golden bracelet.

Chapter Ten

When she'd first made her escape from the jewellery shop, Rachel had only one destination in mind. She knew that she had to do something to mitigate the uneasy situation in which her actions had placed Sahlah, not to mention herself. The problem was that she wasn't sure what that something might be. She knew only that she had to act at once. So she'd begun pedalling her bicycle furiously in the direction of the mustard factory. But when she'd realised the factory was the most logical place for the detective sergeant to head next, she decreased her speed, coasting until the bike glided to a stop on the seafront.

Her face was dripping. She blew a breath upward to cool her steamy forehead. Her throat was parched, and she wished she'd thought to bring a bottle of water with her. But she'd thought of nothing, really, other than the desperate need to get to Sahlah.

By the seafront, however, Rachel had realised that she couldn't possibly outrace the police. And if the detective went to Sahlah's house first, matters could even turn out worse. Sahlah's mum or that slimy Yumn would tell the detective the truth – that Sahlah had gone to work with her father (*despite* the untimely death of her intended, which was what Yumn would no doubt add) – so the sergeant would take herself off to the mustard factory next. And if she showed up while Rachel was there, trying to rationalise what Sahlah would surely believe was an unforgivable betrayal – not to mention trying to warn her friend of an impending police visit that would be rife with questions to take her by surprise ... How would it look? It would look like someone was bloody well guilty of something, all right. And while it was true that Rachel *was* guilty, she wasn't guilty of the Big Thing. She hadn't harmed Haytham Querashi at all. Only . . . Well, perhaps that wasn't quite true when one thought about it, was it?

She'd lifted her bicycle on to the pavement and rolled it to the seawall. She'd leaned it against the barrier and sat for a good quarter of an hour, feeling the sun's heat rise from the concrete like blistering bubbles against her bum. She wasn't ready to go back to the shop and face her mother's probing questions. She couldn't get to Sahlah before the police. So she'd realised that she had to come up with a place to go until the coast was clear, allowing her to bike back to the mustard factory and have a word with her friend.

Which was how she finally ended up where she was at the moment: at the Clifftop Snuggeries. It had been the only place she could think of.

She'd had to retrace her route to get here, bypassing the High Street and Racon Original and Artistic Jewellery by pedalling along the Marine Parade instead. This was a rougher go because she had to wend her way up the steep acclivity of the shoreline's Upper Parade, an activity that was sheer torture in the heat, but she had no real choice in the matter. Trying to get to the Snuggeries via Church Road's gentler slope would have meant pedalling up the High Street, directly in front of Racon Jewellery. One glimpse of Rachel darting by on her bike and Connie would have been out of the shop in a fury, screeching like the victim of a shotgun hold-up.

As a result, Rachel had arrived at the Snuggeries in a virtual lather. She'd dropped her bicycle next to a dusty bed of begonias, and she'd staggered round to the back of the flats. Here there was a garden comprising a strip of sunbrowned lawn, three narrow flower beds planted with drooping cornflowers, tickseed, and daisies, two stone birdbaths, and a wooden bench. Rachel sank on to this last. It faced not the sea but the flats themselves, and they looked at her in a silent reproach that she could barely tolerate. They displayed what she'd loved best about them: the balconies above and the terraces below, both of which looked out not only on the garden but on the winding path of Southcliff Promenade, which curved above the sea.

We're lost to you, lost to you, the Clifftop Snuggeries seemed to be saying. Your well-laid plans went awry, Rachel Winfield, and where are you now?

Rachel turned from the sight of them, her throat tight and sore.

She rubbed the back of her arm against her forehead and wished for a Twister, imagining how soothing the lemon and lime ice cream would have felt as it slid down her throat. She pivoted on the bench and looked out at the sea. The sun blazed above without a hint of pity, while far out on the horizon, a thin bank of fog lay as it had for days.

Rachel balanced her chin on her fist, her fist on the back of the bench. Her eyes stung as if a fierce salty wind were blowing, and she blinked hard and fast to make the tears disappear. She wished herself anywhere but where she was, facing the lonely place that anger, resentment, and jealousy had taken her.

What did it really mean to pledge yourself to another person? At one time she would have been able to answer the question with ease. Pledging yourself meant extending your hand and holding within it another's heart, the secrets of her soul, and the dearest of her dreams. It meant offering safety, a haven where anything was possible and everything between two kindred souls was perfectly understood. Pledging yourself meant saying 'We're equals' and 'Whatever trouble comes, we'll face it together'. That's what she'd thought about pledging at one time. How artless her promise of loyalty had been.

But they *had* begun as equals, she and Sahlah, two schoolgirls who were chosen last for teams, who weren't allowed, invited – or who just didn't dare – to attend their schoolmates' parties or dances, whose coyly decorated Valentine shoeboxes at the back of their classroom in junior school would have gone empty had each of them not remembered the other and what it felt like to be out in the cold. She and Sahlah had indeed begun as equals. It was where they'd finished that upset the scales.

Rachel swallowed against the tight soreness in her throat. She hadn't meant harm to anyone, really. She'd only meant the truth to come out. It was all for the best when people learned the truth. Wasn't it better than living a lie?

But Rachel knew that the real lie was the one she was telling herself right now. And the evidence of this was right behind her, played out in brick with ruched curtains at the windows and a red *For Sale* sticker pasted across its door.

She didn't want to think of the flat. 'Our very last one,' the salesman had called it, twinkling at her meaningfully and doing his best to ignore the freak-show nature of her face. 'Just the thing for a starter home. That's what you're looking for, I'll wager, isn't it? Who's the lucky bloke?'

But Rachel hadn't thought of marriage and children when she'd walked through the flat, examining cupboards, looking out at the view, swinging open windows. She'd thought of Sahlah. She'd thought of cooking dinner together, of sitting in front of the grate that held that glowing hopelessly artificial fire, of drinking tea on the minuscule terrace in the spring, of talking and dreaming and being to each other what they'd been for a decade: a very best friend.

She hadn't been looking for a flat when she'd stumbled across Clifftop Snuggeries' final unit. She'd been bicycling back from Sahlah's. It had been a visit like many other visits they'd had together over the years: talk, laughter, music, and tea, but this time interrupted by Yumn's bursting into the room with one of her imperious demands. She wanted Sahlah to give her a pedicure. At once. Now. It had made no difference that Sahlah was entertaining a guest. Yumn had given an order, and she expected it to be obeyed. Rachel had noticed how Sahlah changed when her sister-in-law spoke. The joyous girl she was became a submissive servant: obedient, docile, and once again the frightened child at the junior school who'd been teased and bullied.

So when Rachel came to the red billboard with the announcement '*Final Phase! All Mod Cons!*' emblazoned on it, she'd turned her bicycle off Westberry Way and coasted up the drive to the flats. What she'd encountered in the salesman was not an overweight and overeager middle-aged failure with a stain on his tie, but a purveyor of dreams.

But dreams, she'd learned, had a way of fracturing and leading one to disappointment. Perhaps, therefore, it was better never to dream at all. Because when one learned to harbour hopes, one also –

'Rachel.'

Rachel started. She swung round from her view of the endless level sheet of North Sea. Sahlah was standing before her. Her *dupattā* had fallen round her shoulders, and her face was grave. The strawberry birthmark on her cheek had deepened in colour, signalling as it always did the depth of feeling that she couldn't hide.

'Sahlah! How did you . . . ? What're you . . . ?' Rachel didn't know how to begin what they had to say to each other.

'I went to the shop first. Your mum said you'd run off, after the woman from Scotland Yard came round. I thought you might come here.'

''Cause you know me,' Rachel said miserably. She plucked at a gold thread in her skirt. It wove brightly through the red and blue swirls of the material's pattern. 'You know me better than anyone, Sahlah. And I know you.'

'I thought we knew each other,' Sahlah said. 'But I'm not sure now. I'm not even sure we're friends any longer.'

Rachel didn't know what hurt worse: the knowledge that she'd dealt Sahlah a terrible blow or the blow that Sahlah was dealing in return. She couldn't look at her because at the moment it felt like looking at her friend would be opening herself up for a more grievous injury than she could bear.

'Why did you give the receipt to Haytham? I know he had it because of you, Rachel. Your mum wouldn't have been likely to pass it on. But I don't understand why you gave it to him.'

'You told me you loved Theo.' Rachel's tongue felt thick and her mind searched desperately for an answer that could explain what was inexplicable even to herself. 'You *said* you loved him.'

'I can't be with Theo. I told you that as well. I said my family would never allow it.'

'And it broke your heart. You said that, Sahlah. You said, "I love him. He's like the other half of myself." That's what you said.'

'I also said that we couldn't marry, despite what I wanted, despite everything we shared and hoped and . . .' Sahlah's voice faltered. Rachel looked up. Her friend's eyes were liquid, and she turned her head away abruptly, looking north towards the pier where Theo Shaw was. After a moment she went on. 'I said that when the time came, I would have to marry the man chosen by my parents. We'd talked about that, you and I, and you can't deny it. I said, "Theo's lost to me, Rachel." You remember that. You knew I could never be with him. So what did you hope to accomplish by giving the receipt to Haytham?'

'You didn't love Haytham.'

'Yes. All right. I didn't love Haytham. And he didn't love me.'

'It's not right to marry when you don't love each other. You can't be happy when you don't love each other. It's like starting out life in the middle of a lie.'

Sahlah came to the bench and sat. Rachel lowered her head. She could see the edge of her friend's linen trousers, her slender foot, and the strap of her sandal. The sight of these parts of the whole that was Sahlah struck Rachel with sadness. Never in years had she felt so alone.

'You knew my parents wouldn't allow a marriage to Theo. They would've cast me out of my family. But you told Haytham about Theo anyway –'

Rachel's head flew up in swift reaction. 'Not his name. I swear. I didn't tell Haytham his name.'

'Because,' Sahlah continued and she spoke more to herself than to Rachel, as if she were in the process of deducing Rachel's motivation as she went along, 'you hoped Haytham would end his engagement to me. And then what?' Sahlah gestured towards the row of flats, and for the first time Rachel saw them as Sahlah doubtless saw them: cheaply built, without character or distinction. 'I would have been free to live here with you? Did you expect my father would really have allowed that?'

'You love Theo,' Rachel said weakly. 'You said.'

'Are you trying to tell me that you were acting in *my* interests?' Sahlah asked. 'Are you saying that you would've been pleased had Theo and I married? I don't believe you. Because there's another truth that you're not admitting: had I tried to marry Theo – which I wouldn't, of course – but had I tried, you would have done something to stop that as well.'

'I wouldn't!'

'We would have planned to run off because that's the only way I could have managed it. I would have told you: my best friend. And you would have made certain it didn't happen. Probably by telling my father in advance. Or by telling Munhannad or even by –'

'No! I never! I *never!*' Rachel couldn't prevent the tears, and she hated herself for a weakness which she knew that her friend would never show. She swung round again, her face to the sea. The sun beat on her, heating her tears as soon as she shed them, heating them so quickly that they dried on her skin and she felt the pulling tightness of their salt.

Sahlah said nothing at first. The only answer to Rachel's sobbing was the cry of gulls and the sound of a distant speedboat hurtling madly along in the sea.

'Rachel.' Sahlah touched her shoulder.

'I'm sorry,' Rachel wept. 'I didn't mean . . . I didn't want . . . I only thought . . .' Her sobs broke the words like finely blown glass. 'You can marry Theo. I won't stop you. And then you'll see.'

'What?'

'That all I wanted was for you to be happy. And if being happy means being with Theo, then that's exactly what I want you to do.'

'I can't marry Theo.'

'You can! You can! Why d'you always say that you can't and you won't?'

'Because my family won't accept it. It isn't our way. And even if it was –'

'You can tell your dad that the next bloke he brings over from Pakistan won't do. You can say the same about the bloke after that, and the next one as well. He won't *make* you marry anyone. You've said that yourself. So after a time, when he knows you're unhappy with the blokes he's chosen –'

'That's just the point, Rachel. I don't have the time. Can't you see that? I don't have the time.'

Rachel scoffed. 'You're just twenty years old. And no one thinks twenty is old these days. Not even the Asians. Girls your age go to university every day. They take jobs as bank clerks. They study law. They learn to be doctors. They don't all get married. What's wrong with you, Sahlah? You used to want more. You used to have dreams.'

Rachel felt all the hopelessness of her situation, made worse by the fact that she couldn't force her friend to understand her meaning or accept her truths. She wrestled for words and finally gave up, saying, 'D'you want to be like Yumn? Is that what you want?'

'I am like Yumn.'

'Oh, right,' Rachel noted sardonically. 'Just exactly like. With your body going completely to seed and nothing to look forward to 'cept a spreading bum and a baby every year.'

'That's right,' Sahlah said, and her voice was desolate. 'Rachel, that's just exactly right.'

'It isn't! You don't have to *be* that way. You're clever. You're pretty. You can be more.'

'You aren't listening to me,' Sahlah said. 'You haven't heard, so you don't understand. I don't have time. I don't have options. Not any longer, if I ever did. I *am* like Yumn. Just exactly like Yumn.'

Rachel felt one final reflex protest rise to her lips. But this time Sahlah's expression stopped it. She was watching her so intently, her dark eyes so pained, that Rachel's remark was quashed. She breathed in to say bitterly, 'You've gone half-cracked if you think you're like Yumn,' but the words were a fire thoroughly doused by what Sahlah's face was telling her.

'Yumn,' Rachel said on the breath she'd taken to excoriate her friend. 'Oh m'God, Sahlah. *Yumn.* D'you mean . . . You and Theo . . . ? You never said!' Involuntarily, her gaze went over her friend's body, so carefully concealed beneath her loose clothing.

'Yes,' Sahlah said. 'Which is why Haytham agreed to move the marriage forward.'

'He *knew*?'

'I couldn't have pretended the baby was his. Even if I'd thought I could do it, I had to tell him. He'd come here to marry me but he was content to wait a bit – perhaps for six months – to give both of us time to get to know each other. I had to tell him there was no time. What could I say? Truth was my only option.'

Rachel felt staggered by the immensity of what her friend was telling her, taken in the context of her background, her religion, and her culture. And then she saw – even as she hated herself for seeing it – the possibility of salvation. Because if Haytham Querashi already knew that Theo Shaw was Sahlah's lover, then giving him that receipt, saying mysteriously, 'Ask Sahlah about this,' and waiting for the desired result was behaviour for which she could forgive herself. She would only have been telling him something he already knew, accepted, and had come to terms with . . . if Sahlah had spoken the entire truth to him. 'Did he know about Theo?' Rachel asked, trying not to sound as anxious as she felt for affirmation. 'Did you tell him about *Theo*?'

'That's what you did for me,' Sahlah said.

Rachel's hope died again, and this time completely. 'Who else knows?'

'No one. Yumn suspects. She would do, wouldn't she? She knows the signs well enough. But I've said nothing to her, and no one else knows.'

'Not Theo?'

Sahlah lowered her gaze, and Rachel followed this to her hands, which were clasped in her lap. The knuckles were whitened and they grew whiter. As if Theo Shaw's name had not come up, Sahlah said, 'Haytham knew how little time we had to do the normal things couples do before they marry. Once I told him about my . . . about the baby, he didn't want me to be humiliated. He agreed to marriage as soon as possible.' She blinked slowly, as if to erase a memory. 'Rachel, Haytham Querashi was a very good man.'

Rachel wanted to tell her that in addition to being a very good man, it was also likely that Haytham Querashi was a man who didn't want to bear the scorn of people within their community who would despise him for marrying an unchaste woman. It had been to his advantage as well that they marry as quickly as possible so as to pass the child off as his, no matter how light the colour of the baby's skin. But instead, Rachel thought about Theo Shaw, Sahlah's professed love for him, the knowledge she herself now possessed, and what she could do with it to make things right. But she had to know for certain first. She didn't want to take another misstep.

'Does Theo know about the baby?'

Sahlah gave a dispirited laugh. 'You still don't understand, do you? Once you gave that receipt to Haytham, once Haytham knew it was for a gold bracelet, once he ran into Theo at that idiotic Gentlemen's Cooperative that's supposed to bring this pathetic little town back to life . . .' Sahlah stopped herself, as if suddenly aware of the uncharacteristic bitterness of her words and how they revealed the chaotic state of her mind. 'What difference does it make to anything now if Theo knows or doesn't know?'

'What are you saying?' Rachel heard her fear and tried to quell it for the other girl's sake.

'Haytham's dead, Rachel. Don't you see? Haytham's *dead*. And he'd gone to the Nez. At night. In the dark. Which is less than half a mile from the Old Hall, where Theo lives. And which is also the place that Theo's been collecting fossils for the last twenty years. Do you understand now?' Sahlah asked sharply. 'Rachel Winfield, do you understand?'

Rachel gaped at her. 'Theo?' she said. 'No. Sahlah, you can't think Theo Shaw . . .'

'Haytham would have wanted to know who it was,' Sahlah told her. 'He was prepared to marry me, yes, but still he would have wanted to know who'd made me pregnant. What man wouldn't, no matter what he said to me about living in ignorance? He would have wanted to know.'

'But even if he knew, even if he actually *talked* to Theo, you can't think that Theo . . .' Rachel couldn't finish the sentence, so horrified was she at the pure logic behind Sahlah's words. She could even picture how everything had happened: a meeting in the dark on the Nez, Haytham Querashi's conversation with Theo Shaw in which he spoke of Sahlah's pregnancy, Theo Shaw's subsequent desperation to rid the world of the man who stood between himself and his one true love and what he knew – *had* to know – to be his moral duty . . . Because he'd want to do his duty by Sahlah, Theo Shaw would. He loved Sahlah and if he knew he'd made her pregnant, he'd want to stand by her side. And because Sahlah was so reluctant – indeed, so afraid – to be cast out from her family for marrying an Englishman, he would also have known that there was only one way to bind her to him.

Rachel swallowed. She sucked in her lip and bit it, hard.

'So look what you've done in passing along the receipt for that bracelet, Rachel,' Sahlah said. 'You've given the police a connection – which they might otherwise have never known about – between Haytham Querashi and Theo Shaw. And when a murder's been done, that's the first thing they look for: a connection.'

Rachel began to babble, so acute was her guilt and so horrifying the knowledge of the part she'd played in the tragedy on the Nez. 'I'll phone him straightaway. I'll go to the pier.'

'No!' Sahlah sounded horrified.

'I'll tell him to throw the bracelet in the rubbish. I'll make sure he doesn't wear it again. The police have no reason to talk to him anyway. They don't know he knew Haytham. Even if they talk to all the blokes in the Gentlemen's Cooperative, it'll take them days to talk to everyone, won't it?'

'Rachel –'

'And that's the only way they'll know to talk to Theo Shaw. There's no other connection between him and Haytham. Just the Cooperative. So I'll get to him first. And they won't see the bracelet. They won't know about anything. I swear they won't know.'

Sahlah's head was shaking, her expression a mixture of disbelief and despair. 'But don't you see, Rachel? That doesn't address the real problem, does it? No matter what you tell Theo, Haytham's still dead.'

'But the police'll rest the case or close it or whatever they do. And then you and Theo –'

'Then Theo and I what?'

'You can get married,' Rachel said. And when Sahlah didn't answer at once, she added weakly, 'You and Theo. Married. You know.'

Sahlah rose. She pulled her *dupattā* back over her head. She looked towards the pier. The calliope music of the roundabout floated towards them on the air, even at this distance. The Ferris wheel glittered in the sunlight, and the Wild Mouse frantically tossed its shrieking passengers from side to side. 'Do you actually think it's as easy as that? You tell Theo to throw the bracelet in the rubbish, the police go away, and he and I marry?'

'It could happen that way, if we make it happen.'

Sahlah shook her head, then turned back to Rachel. 'You don't even begin to understand,' she said. Her voice was resigned, a decision made. 'I must have an abortion. As soon as possible. And I need you to help me make all the arrangements.'

The bracelet was unmistakably an Aloysius Kennedy piece: thick, heavy, amorphous swirls similar to the bracelet Barbara had seen in Racon Jewellery. She was willing to admit that Theo Shaw's possession of such a unique item might be pure coincidence, but she hadn't been involved in Criminal Investigations for eleven years for nothing: she knew how unlikely coincidences were when it came to murder.

'Can I get you something to drink?' Theo Shaw's tone was so friendly that Barbara wondered if, against all reason, he thought her visit was a social call. 'Coffee? Tea? A Coke? I was about to grab a drink myself. Bloody hot weather, isn't it?'

Barbara said that a Coke would be fine, and when he left his office in search of one, she took the opportunity to have a look round. She wasn't sure what she was looking for, although she wouldn't have said no to the sight of a nice coil of incriminating wire – suitable for tripping someone in the darkness – lying squarely in the middle of his desk.

But there wasn't much to take note of. A set of book shelves held one row of green plastic binders and a second row of account books with successive years stamped on the spine of each in flaking gold numerals. A metal in-and-out tray on top of a filing cabinet contained a batch of invoices that appeared to be for foodstuffs, for electrical work, for plumbing, and for business supplies. A bulletin board on one of the walls had posted upon it four architectural blueprints: two for a structure identified as the Pier End Hotel and two for a leisure centre called Agatha Shaw Recreational Village. Barbara took note of this latter name. Mother of Theo? she wondered. Aunt? Sister? Wife?

Idly she picked up a large paperweight that was holding down a pile of correspondence, all of which appeared devoted to a plan to redevelop the town. When she heard Theo's approaching footsteps in the corridor, she removed her attention from the letters to the paperweight, which appeared to be a large blob of pocked stone.

'*Raphidonema*,' Theo Shaw said. He carried two Coke cans with a paper cup fitted over one of them. He handed this one over to Barbara.

'Raphi-who?' she said.

'*Raphidonema. Porifera calcarea pharetronida lelapiidae raphidonema* to be more exact.' He smiled. He had a most appealing smile, Barbara thought, and she hardened automatically at the sight of it. She knew well enough what degree of complicity an appealing smile was able to hide. 'I'm showing off,' he said ingenuously. 'It's a fossil sponge. Lower Cretaceous period. I found it.'

Barbara turned the rock in her hands. 'Really? It looks like . . . hell, I don't know . . . sandstone? How'd you know what it was?'

'Experience. I've been playing palaeontologist for years.'

'Where did it come from?'

'Along the coast, just north of town.'

'On the Nez?' Barbara asked.

Theo's eyes narrowed, but so fractionally that Barbara would have missed the movement had she not been watching for some indication that he knew, at heart, what she was doing in his office. 'Right,' he said. 'The red crag traps them and the London clay releases them. All you have to do is wait for the sea to erode the cliffs.'

'That's your primary spot for fossil-hunting, then? Out on the Nez?'

'Not on the Nez,' he corrected her. 'On the beach below it, at the base of the cliffs. But yes, that's the best spot for fossils along this stretch of coastline.'

She nodded and placed the fossilised sponge back on top of the papers it had been weighing down. She popped open her Coke and drank straight from the can. The paper cup she crumpled slowly into her hand. A tiny elevation of Theo Shaw's eyebrows told her that he didn't misunderstand the gesture.

First things first, she thought. The Nez and the bracelet made Theo himself a subject that she wished to pursue, but there were other fish to fry before she got to him. She said, 'What can you tell me about a bloke called Trevor Ruddock?'

'Trevor Ruddock?'

Did he sound relieved? Barbara wondered. 'He works somewhere on the pier. D'you know him?'

'I do. He's been here for three weeks.'

'He came to you via Malik's Mustards, I understand.'

'He did.'

'Where he was given the sack for pilfering goods.'

'I know,' Theo said. 'Akram wrote to me about it. Phoned as well. He asked me to give the chap a chance because he believed there were extenuating circumstances behind the pilfering. The family's poor. Six kids. And Trevor's dad has been out of work with a bad back for the last eighteen months. Akram said he couldn't in conscience keep Ruddock on, but he wanted to give him a second chance somewhere else. So I took him on. It's not much of a job, and it doesn't pay nearly what he was making with Akram, but it's something to tide him over.'

'What's he do?'

'Clean the pier right now. After hours.'

'So he's not here at the moment?'

'He starts work at half-past eleven at night. There'd be no point in coming to the pier before that, unless he was doing it for his own amusement.'

Mentally, Barbara added another tick to Trevor Ruddock's name in the list of suspects. The motive was there and now the opportunity. He could easily have done away with Haytham Querashi on the Nez and still clocked in at the pier on time.

But that begged the question of what Theo Shaw was doing with the Aloysisus Kennedy bracelet. If indeed it was *the* Kennedy bracelet. And there was only one way to find out.

Enter Thespian Havers, Barbara thought. She said, 'I'll need a current address for him if you've got it.'

'No problem at all.' Theo went to his desk and sat in the wheeled oak chair behind it. He turned the spool of an old Rolodex and flipped through its cards until he came to the one he wanted. He wrote the address on a Post-it and handed this over. Which gave Thespian Havers the opportunity she wanted.

'Whoa,' she said. 'Is that an Aloysius Kennedy you've got on? It's gorgeous.'

'What?' Theo said.

Score a point, Barbara thought. He hadn't bought the bracelet himself, because if he had done, there was little doubt that one of the Winfields would have waxed eloquent on its origins. 'That bracelet,' Barbara said. 'It looks like one I've been drooling over in London. A bloke called Aloysius Kennedy designs them. Can I have a look?' She added with what she hoped was her best display of girlish artlessness, 'This is probably as close as I'm ever going to get to owning one, if you know what I mean.'

For a moment she thought she hadn't been able to hook him, but as the bait of her interest floated in front of him, Theo Shaw made the decision to bite. He handed over the gold wrist cuff, unfastening it with his thumbnail and slipping it off.

'It's great,' Barbara said. 'May I . . . ?' She gestured towards the window, and when he nodded, she carried it over. She turned it this way and that in her hand. She said, 'The man's a genius, isn't he? I like these swirls. And the metal's perfect. He's the Rembrandt of goldsmiths, if you ask me.' She hoped the artistic allusion was right. What she knew about Rembrandt – not to mention what she knew about gold and jewellery – could easily fit into a teaspoon. She went on to remark on the weight of it, she ran her fingers over the shape of it, she examined its cleverly hidden clasp. And when the time was right, she looked at its inside and saw what she had believed she would see. Three words were engraved in a fluid scroll: *Life begins now*.

Ah. Time to apply the thumbscrews. Barbara returned to the desk and set the bracelet next to the fossilised sponge. Theo Shaw didn't put it on at once. His colour was slightly higher than it had been when Barbara had taken the bracelet from him. He'd seen her read the inscription inside and she had little doubt that she and the young man were about to dance the careful *pas de deux* of How-to-find-out-what-the-rozzers-know. She realised that, when the music began, she was going to need to outstep him.

'Makes a nice statement, that,' she said, indicating the bracelet with a nod. 'I wouldn't mind finding one on my doorstep some morning. Just the sort of thing one hopes to have passed one's way by a nameless admirer.'

Theo reached for the bracelet and snapped it back on. 'It was my dad's,' he said. *Voilà*, Barbara thought. He should have kept his mug plugged but in her experience, the guilty parties so rarely did, feeling compelled to demonstrate their spurious innocence for one and all.

'Your dad's dead, then?'

'My mother as well.'

'Then all of this –' Here she indicated the pier itself followed by the blueprints on the bulletin board. 'Is all of this commemorating your parents?'

He looked nonplussed. She went on. 'When I came here as a kid, this was Balford Pier. Now it's Shaw Attractions. And the leisure centre – Agatha Shaw Recreational Village. Is that your mum's name?'

His expression cleared. 'Agatha Shaw's my grandmother, although she's done duty as my mother since I was six. My parents were killed in a car crash.'

'That must have been rough,' Barbara said.

'Yeah. But . . . well, Gran was great.'

'She's all you've got left?'

'All that's here. The rest of the family scattered years ago. Gran took us in – I've an elder brother trying his luck in Hollywood – and raised us as her second set of kids.'

'Nice to have something to remember your dad by,' Barbara noted, with another nod at the bracelet. She wasn't about to let him slither away from the topic at hand with Dickensian recollections of being orphaned and passed along to an ageing relative. She gazed at him fixedly. 'Sort of modern to be a family heirloom, though. It looks like it was made last week.'

Theo returned her gaze just as fixedly, although he couldn't prevent the rush of colour on his neck, which gave him away. 'I'd never thought of that. But I suppose it does.'

'Yes. Well. It's interesting to run across it like this, because, oddly enough, we're on the trail of a Kennedy piece that's very much like it.'

Theo frowned. 'On the trail . . . ? Why?'

Barbara avoided a direct answer and went back to the window overlooking the pier. Outside, the Ferris wheel had begun to revolve, lifting a score of happy riders into the air. She said, 'How do you know Akram Malik, Mr Shaw?'

'What?' Clearly, he expected something else.

'You mentioned he phoned you about hiring Trevor Ruddock. That suggests you know each other. I was wondering how.'

'From the Gentlemen's Cooperative.' Theo went on to explain what it was. 'We try to help each other out. This was an instance when I could do him favour. He'll do me one in return one day.'

'Is that your only connection with the Maliks?'

He looked from her to the window. Outside, a gull had come to sit on an extractor fan on the roof of the arcade below them. The bird looked expectant. Barbara did likewise. She knew Theo Shaw was walking a delicate line at the moment. Not knowing what she had already been told about him from other sources, he would have to choose carefully between truth and lie. 'Actually, I helped Akram set up his factory's computer system,' he settled on saying. 'And I went to junior school here in town with Muhannad. To the comprehensive as well, but that was in Clacton.'

'Ah.' Barbara mentally waved away the geography of his relationship with the family. Clacton or Balford hardly mattered. What was important was the connection itself. 'You've known them for years, then.'

'In a manner of speaking.'

'What manner of speaking is that?' Barbara lifted her Coke for another swig. It was doing wonders to settle the earlier consumed whitebait into her digestive system.

Theo followed her lead and took a swallow of Coke himself. 'I knew Muhannad from school, but we weren't friends, so I never knew the family until I did their computers at the factory. This was a year ago, perhaps a bit more.'

'So I assume that you know Sahlah Malik as well?'

'I've met Sahlah, yes.' He did what, in Barbara's experience, so many people did when trying to look nonchalant about a piece of information that was causing their insides to shimmy: he continued to look her straight in the eye.

'So you'd recognise her. On the street, say. Or perhaps on the pier. Dressed Muslim or otherwise.'

'I suppose. But I don't see what Sahlah Malik has to do with anything. What's this all about?'

'Have you seen her on the pier in the last few days?'

'No. No, I haven't.'

'When did you last see her?'

'I can't recall. From what I could tell when I was doing their computers, Akram keeps her on a rather short tether. She's the only daughter, and it's their way. What makes you think she was on the pier?'

'She told me she was. She told me she threw a bracelet something like this one –' with a flip of her thumb at his Kennedy gold '– off the end of the pier once she was told that Haytham Querashi was dead. She said it'd been a gift for him and she gave it the toss on Saturday afternoon. But here's what's odd: as far as I've been able to tell, not a soul saw her. What d'you make of that?'

As if of their own volition, his fingers reached for his wrist and closed over the bracelet. 'I don't know,' he said.

'Hmm.' Barbara nodded gravely. 'It's intriguing, though, isn't it? That no one saw her.'

'It's getting on for high summer. There're scores of people on the pier every day. It's not very likely that one of them would stick in the memory.'

'Perhaps,' Barbara said, 'but I've been the length of it and here's what I noticed: no one's out there in Muslim garb.' Barbara rooted casually through her bag to find her cigarettes. She said, 'Mind?' And when he waved her onward with a flick of his fingers, she lit up and said, 'Sahlah wears the traditional get-up at work. She came here directly from work, according to what she told me. Taken with the fact that she'd have had no reason to come on to the pier incognito, we've got her here wearing Muslim garb. Wouldn't you agree? I mean, it's not like she was doing something illegal that required a disguise: she was just tossing an expensive piece of jewellery into the drink.'

'I suppose that makes sense.'

'So if she said she was here and if no one saw her and if she came here wearing her usual togs, then there's only one conclusion to draw. Isn't there?'

'Drawing conclusions is your job, not mine,' Theo Shaw said, and Barbara gave him credit for saying it evenly. 'But if you're suggesting that Sahlah Malik's somehow involved in what happened to her fiancé ... That's just not on.'

'How'd we get on to this business at the Nez?' Barbara asked. 'That's rather a jump.'

He refused to be baited or trapped this time. He said, 'You're the police, and I'm not stupid. If you're asking whether I knew the Maliks, you're involved in investigating the death on the Nez. Right?'

'And you knew she was to marry Querashi?'

'I'd been introduced to him at the Gentlemen's Cooperative. Akram called him his future son-in-law. I didn't think he was here to marry Muhannad, so it seemed reasonable to conclude he was here to marry Sahlah.'

Touché, Barbara saluted him mentally. She'd thought she had him, but he'd dodged adroitly.

'So you knew Querashi yourself?'

'I'd met him. I wouldn't call it knowing him.'

'Yes. Right. But you knew who he was. You'd have recognised him on the street.' When Theo Shaw acknowledged this to be the case, Barbara went on with, 'Just for clarity's sake, then, where were you on Friday night?'

'I was at home. And since you're going to inquire anyway, if not of me then of someone else, home is at the end of Old Hall Lane which is itself a ten-minute walk from the Nez.'

'Were you alone?'

His thumb created a small dent in the Coke can. 'Why the hell are you asking me this?'

'Because Mr Querashi's death on the Nez was a murder, Mr Shaw. But I expect you know that already, don't you?'

His thumb relaxed. The Coke can *pinged*. 'You're trying to mix me up in this, aren't you? I'll tell you that Gran was upstairs in bed while I was down in my workroom. You'll note that I therefore had opportunity to dash off to the Nez and do away with Querashi. Of course, I had no reason to kill him, but that detail is of no consequence, apparently.'

'No reason?' Barbara said. She flicked cigarette ash into the waste-paper basket.

'No reason.' Theo Shaw's words were firm, but his gaze skittered to the telephone. It hadn't rung, so Barbara wondered who it was he was going to phone the second she left his office. He wouldn't be stupid enough to make the call while she was skulking in the corridor, though. Whatever else he might have been, Theo Shaw wasn't an idiot.

'Right,' Barbara said. Cigarette dangling between her lips, she scribbled the number of the Burnt House Hotel on the back of one of her cards. She handed it over, telling Theo to phone should he recall anything pertinent to the case – like the truth about his possession of the gold bracelet, she added mentally.

Outside with the cacophony of the arcade swirling round her, Barbara thought of the implications behind both Theo Shaw's possession of the gold piece and his lies about its origin. While it was possible that two Aloysius Kennedy golds could exist harmoniously in the same town, it was unlikely that they'd be inscribed identically. This being the case, the reasonable conclusion to draw was that Sahlah Malik had been lying about throwing the bracelet from the pier and the bracelet she claimed to have thrown from the pier was resting round Theo Shaw's wrist. And there were only two ways that the bracelet had come into Theo Shaw's possession: either Sahlah Malik had given it to him directly or she'd given it to Haytham Querashi and Theo Shaw had seen it and taken it from Querashi's body. In either case, Theo Shaw was standing squarely in suspicion's doorway.

Another Englishman, Barbara thought. She wondered what would actually happen to the community's tenuous peace if it turned out that Querashi had met his death at the hands of a Westerner. Because at this moment it seemed to her that they had two solid suspects, Armstrong and Shaw, both of whom were English. And next on her list was Trevor Ruddock, in line to be Englishman Number Three. Unless F. Kumhar came up smelling like three-day-old cod or one of the Maliks began to sweat more than one expected in this heat – except for Sahlah who appeared to have been born without pores – then an Englishman was likely the perp they were seeking.

However, at the thought of Sahlah, Barbara hesitated, her car keys dangling from her fingers and Trevor Ruddock's address crumpled into her hand. What did that previous conclusion imply? What did it mean if Sahlah had given the bracelet to Shaw and not to Querashi? It meant the obvious, didn't it? Since 'Life begins now' wasn't exactly the sort of comment one made to a casual acquaintance, then Theo Shaw wasn't a casual acquaintance. Which meant he and Sahlah knew each other rather more intimately than Theo had suggested. Which in turn meant that not only Theo Shaw had a motive to off Querashi. Sahlah Malik may very well have had a motive to kill her fiancé as well.

An Asian was finally firmly on the list of suspects, Barbara thought. So the case was still anybody's game.

Chapter Eleven

===≫◦◦◦≪===

Barbara grabbed a bag of popcorn and a second bag of rainbow rock from a free-standing stall at the land end of the pier. The stall was called Sweet Sensations, and its emanating odours of dough frying, candy floss spinning, and corn popping were too tempting to disregard. So she made her purchase and with barely a twinge of guilt. After all, she told herself, it stood to reason that she might be taking her next meal with the calorifically abstemious Emily Barlow. If that was the case, she wanted to bulk up on her daily junk food quota.

She went for the small packet of old-fashioned rainbow rock first, popping a piece of it into her mouth and beginning the hike back to her car. She'd left the Mini parked on The Parade, a strip of seafront road that climbed towards the higher section of the town. Here, a row of Edwardian villas not unlike Emily's overlooked the sea. They were Italianate in design, with balconies and arched windows and doorways, and in 1900 they would have been regal. Now, much like Emily's house, they needed renovation. Bed and breakfast signs hung in every front window, but curtains sagging with grime and woodwork shedding paint on to the pavement doubtless put off the less hardy adventurer. They looked completely unoccupied and more than half ready for the wrecking ball.

At her car, Barbara paused. This was her first real opportunity to survey the town from the vantage point of the seafront, and what she saw wasn't very appealing. The road along the shore rose prettily enough, but the buildings that fronted it were like the villas: in disrepair. Years of sea air had eaten away paint and had rusted through metal. Years of isolation from the tourist trade – as inexpensive package holidays to Spain became more alluring than a drive to Essex – had leeched the lifeblood from the local economy. The result lay before her like an urban Miss Havisham, jilted and frozen in a fragment of time.

The town was in desperate need of exactly what Akram Malik was providing: a source of employment. It was also in need of what the Shaw family apparently had in mind: redevelopment. Looking it over, Barbara wondered if there was a point of conflict between the two that Balford CID ought to be exploring.

As she thought of this and meditated on the picture that the seafront provided, she saw two little dark-skinned boys – perhaps ten years old – come out of Stan's Hot and Cold Snacks. They were eating Cornettos, and they wandered in the direction of the pier. Like children who've been instructed well, they paused for traffic at the edge of the pavement. A dusty van braked to let them cross.

Partially hidden behind a filthy windscreen, the driver waved them towards the other side of the street. The boys nodded their thanks and stepped off the kerb. Which was what, it seemed, the van's occupants wished.

With a blare of its horn, the van shot forward. The roar of its engine echoed against the buildings. Starled, the children jumped back. One dropped his ice cream and in a reflex movement, bent to retrieve it. The other, a hand on his collar, quickly jerked him out of harm's way. 'Fuckin' Pakis!' someone shouted from the van and a bottle flew out. It hadn't been sealed, so its contents arced into the air as it sailed. The boys dodged but didn't quite make it. Yellow liquid splashed into their faces and across their clothes before the bottle broke at their feet.

'Bloody hell,' Barbara muttered. She dashed across the street.

'My ice cream!' the smaller boy cried. 'Ghassan, my ice cream!'

Ghassan's face was a study in disgust, but he was directing it towards the fleeing vehicle. The van was tearing up the shore road, which curved out of sight beneath the shade of a cypress tree. Barbara tried and failed to make out its number plates.

'You all right?' she asked the boys. The smaller child had begun to cry.

The blistering street and pavement quickly heated the liquid that had been tossed. The sharp odour of urine seeped upward. The boys had it on their clothes and their skin, nasty yellow stains against their white shorts and yellow droplets speckling their brown legs and their cheeks.

'I lost my ice cream,' the smaller boy wailed.

'Shut up, Muhsin,' Ghassan scowled. 'They want you to cry. So shut up!' He shook him roughly, one hand on his shoulder. 'Here, take mine. I don't want it.'

'But –'

'Take it!' He shoved the Cornetto at the other boy.

'You all right?' Barbara repeated. 'That was a rotten thing to do.'

Ghassan finally looked her way. She could have tasted the scorn in his expression, had it had a flavour. 'English cunt.' He said the words so distinctly that she couldn't have mistaken them for anything else. 'Get away from us. Come on, Muhsin.'

Barbara felt her mouth drop open, and she snapped it shut as the boys walked off. They went in the direction they'd intended from the first, towards the pier. No one, it seemed, was going to stop them from doing what they had planned to do.

Barbara would have admired them had she not seen how the entire episode – as brief as it had been – served to underscore all the racial tensions in Balford, tensions that only a few nights previously might have led to murder. She watched the boys descend the path to the pier before she returned to her car.

She didn't have far to drive to Trevor Ruddock's house. She didn't, in fact, have to drive there at all. A quick purchase of a town map at Balford Books and Crannies revealed that Alfred Terrace was less than a five-minute walk from the High Street and the bookshop itself. It was also a five-minute walk from Racon Jewellery, a detail that Barbara took note of with interest.

Alfred Terrace comprised a single line of seven salt cellar-sized dwellings that ran along one side of a little square. Each house was decorated with derelict window boxes, and each possessed a front door so narrow that inhabitants of the terrace doubtless had to consider their daily food intake and how it might affect their ability to gain access to their sitting rooms. The houses were uniformly dirty white, their faded doors the only distinguishing feature about them. These were each painted differently, in colours that ran from yellow to puce. The paint had faded over time, however, for the terrace faced west and it took the very worst of the day's sun and heat.

Which was what it was doing at the moment. The air was still and the temperature seemed ten degrees higher than it had been on the pier. Egg-frying on the pavement was called for. Barbara could feel her skin cooking where it was bare.

The Ruddock family lived along the terrace at number 6. Their door colour had at one time been red, but the sun had reduced it to the shade of raw salmon. Barbara rapped sharply and gave a quick glance towards the single front window. She could see nothing through its net curtains, although she could hear rap music playing somewhere in the house and the loud chatter of a television accompanying it. When no one answered her first knock on the door, she gave it a more meaningful assault.

This got results. Footsteps clattered against an uncarpeted floor, and the door swung open.

Barbara found herself looking at a child playing dressing-up. She couldn't tell if the creature was male or female, but whatever the case, Dad's clothes had apparently been appropriated for the game. The shoes were clown-sized and, no matter the day's heat, an old tweed jacket hung down to the knees.

'Yeah?' the child asked.

'Wha' is it, Brucie?' a woman's voice shouted from the back of the house. 'You at the door? Someone here? Don't you go outside in your dad's gear. You hear me, Brucie?'

Brucie observed Barbara. The corners of his eyes, she noted, could have done with a thorough cleaning.

She gave the child her happiest hello, to which he responded by wiping his nose on his father's jacket sleeve. Underneath it he wore only underpants with the elastic stretched beyond redemption. The pants hung perilously on his bony frame. 'I'm looking for Trevor Ruddock,' she explained. 'Does he live here? Are you his brother?'

The child turned in his clown shoes and shouted into the house. 'Mum! It's some fat bird asking for Trev!' Barbara's hands itched to become acquainted with the circumference of his neck.

'For Trev? It's not that grotty thing from the jewellery shop again, is it?' The woman came from the back towards the door, trailed by two more children. These were girls from the look of them. They wore blue shorts, pink halter tops, and white cowboy boots with rhinestone decoration, and one of them carried a sequined baton. She used this to bop her little brother on the head. Brucie screamed. He flew to the attack, hurtling past his mother and catching his sister in the midriff. His jaws locked over her arm.

'Wha' is it?' Mrs Ruddock appeared not to notice the shrieking and scuffling that was going on behind her as the other sister endeavoured to disengage Brucie's teeth from her sibling's arm. The two girls began yelling, 'Mum! Make him stop!' Mrs Ruddock continued to ignore them. 'You looking for my Trevor?' She looked old and tired, with washed-out blue eyes and lank bottle-blonde hair that she'd tied away from her face with a purple shoe lace.

Barbara introduced herself and dangled her warrant card before the woman's face. 'Scotland Yard CID. I'd like a word with Trevor. Is he home?'

Mrs Ruddock seemed to stiffen even as she reached for a feathering of loosened hair and tucked it behind her ear. 'What d'you want with my Trevor? He i'n't in trouble. He's a good boy.'

The three wrangling children behind her lurched into the wall. A picture above them crashed to the floor. A man's voice yelled from upstairs, 'Jesus! Can't a bloke sleep round here? Shirl! Jesus! What're they on to?'

'You! That's enough!' Mrs Ruddock grabbed Brucie by the collar of the jacket he wore. She grabbed his sister by a handful of hair. All three children howled. 'Enough!' she shouted.

'She hit me!'

'He bit me!'

'Shirl! SHUT THEM UP!'

'Now you've gone and waked your dad up, haven't you?' Mrs Ruddock said, giving the warring parties a good shake. 'You get into the kitchen, all three of you. Stella, there's ice lollies in the fridge. See everyone gets one.'

The promise of a treat seemed to mollify the three children. They trotted as one in the direction from which their mother had come. Above their heads, someone's feet thudded across the floor boards. A man cleared his throat violently and hawked with enough force to make Barbara wonder if he was engaging in a do-it-yourself tonsillectomy. She couldn't understand how he'd possibly been asleep in the first place prior to her arrival. At a committed volume, a rap group was chanting about Gettin it, doin it, havin it, WOE-man. And in competition with this, two blowsy females were having a heads together on *Coronation Street*, and at a roar that left nothing to the imagination.

'Not exactly trouble,' Barbara said. 'I just have a few questions to ask him.'

'About what? Trev gave back them jars of whatever-it-was. Okay, so we sold a few 'fore the coloureds caught on, but it's not like they really missed the money. He's rolling in beans, that Akram Malik. You seen where they live, the lot 'f them?'

'Is Trevor here?' Barbara was striving for patience but with the sun bearing down on her, what little she had was evaporating quickly.

Mrs Ruddock favoured her with a marginally hostile look, apparently realising that her words were making little impression. She shouted, 'Stella!' over her shoulder and when the elder of the two girls returned from the kitchen with an ice lolly plugged into the centre of her mouth, she went on with, 'Take her up to Trev. And tell Charlie to turn down that racket while you're at it.'

'Mum ...' Stella's whine made the appellation two syllables, a difficult feat to manage round the ice lolly, but she looked like a girl who was up to any challenge.

'Do it!' Mrs Ruddock barked.

Stella removed the ice lolly from her mouth and blew out a breath that flapped her lips together noisily. 'Come on, then,' she said, and began to trudge up the stairs.

Barbara felt Mrs Ruddock's inimical gaze following her as she walked in the trail of Stella's clomping white cowboy boots. It was clear that no matter what offence had caused Trevor to lose his job at the mustard factory, it was no offence to his mum.

The guilty party himself was in one of the two bedrooms on the first floor of the house. The raucous chanting of rap music throbbed right through the door. Stella opened this unceremoniously, but six inches only because something hanging above it seemed to prevent its further movement. She shouted, 'Charlie! Mum says you're s'posed to turn that the fuck down!' She said to Barbara over her shoulder, 'He's in here if you want him,' as Mr Ruddock shouted from behind the other door, 'Can't a man bloody SLEEP in his own bloody HOUSE?'

Barbara nodded her thanks to Stella and ducked into the bedroom. Duck was an action of necessity because the object that prevented the door's complete mobility drooped downward like a fishing net. The curtains were drawn over the windows, so the lighting was dim. The heat throbbed within like a beating heart.

The noise was deafening. It reverberated between the walls against one of which was a set of bunk beds. The upper of these was occupied by a teenaged boy armed with a set of wooden chopsticks which he was using against the bed's footboard to accompany the music. The lower was empty. The room's other occupant was seated at a table on which a fluorescent lamp was shedding a shaft of bright light on balls of black yarn, various spools of coloured cotton, a pile of black pipe-cleaners, and a plastic box filled with round sponges of differing sizes.

'Trevor Ruddock?' Barbara shouted over the din. 'Could I have a word with you? CID. Police.' She managed to emphasise her identity in such a way as to get the attention of the boy on the bed. He saw her extended warrant card and, perhaps reading either her lips or the expression on her face, he reached for a knob on the boom box at the foot of his bed and lowered the volume.

'Hey, Trev!' he shouted despite the sudden quelling of the boom box's noise. 'Trev! The cops!'

The boy at the table stirred, turned in his chair, and saw Barbara. His glance dropped to her warrant card. Slowly, he raised his hands to his ears and began to unscrew from them a pair of wax earplugs.

As he did so, Barbara studied him in the dim light. He had *National Front* written all over him: from his bare scalp where the faintest shadow of dark hair merely stubbled the skin, to his heavy and unmistakably military boots. He was clean-shaven: utterly, in fact. He was devoid of facial hair, even of eyebrows.

His movement had revealed what he'd been working on at the table. It appeared to be the model of a spider, from what Barbara could surmise from three spindly pipe-cleaner legs that had been affixed to a black-and-white-striped sponge body. It had two sets of eyes fashioned from black beads: two large and two small semi-circling the head like an ocular tiara.

Trevor flicked a look at his brother, who'd squirmed to the edge of the upper bunk and was swinging his legs and watching Barbara uneasily. 'Clear out,' he said to Charlie.

'I won't say nothing.'

'Bugger off,' Trevor said.

'Trev.' Charlie offered what appeared to be the family's signature whine: he turned the first syllable of his brother's name into two.

'I said.' Trevor shot him a look. Charlie said, 'Shit,' managing it monosyllabically, and hopped from the bed. Boom box under his arm, he passed Barbara and left the room. He shut the door behind him.

This gave Barbara the opportunity to see what had been pressing against the top of the door when she entered. It *was* indeed an old fishing net, but it had been crafted into an enormous web upon which a collection of arachnids cavorted. Like the spider being assembled on the table, these were not garden variety bugs: brown, black, multi-legged, and suitable for devouring flies, ticks, and centipedes.

They were exotic in both colour and shape, featuring bodies of red, yellow, and green, prickly legs with speckles, and ferocious eyes.

'Nice work,' Barbara said. 'Studying entomology, are you?'

Trevor made no reply. Barbara crossed the room to the table. There was a second chair to one side of it, stacked with books, newspapers, and magazines. She set these on the floor and sat. She said, 'Mind?' and casting a glance at the cigarettes in her hand, he shook his head. She offered the pack, and he took one. He lit it with a match from a book. He left her to see to her own.

With the absence of rap music, the other sounds in the house gained amplification. *Coronation Street*'s nymphs continued their gossip at a pitch that would have served for calling the score at a football match, and Stella began shrieking about the theft of a necklace, apparently perpetrated by Charlie, whose name she was managing to wail in three syllables.

'I understand you got the sack from Malik's Mustards three weeks ago,' Barbara said.

Trevor inhaled, eyes narrowed and fastened on Barbara. His fingers, she noted, bore angry-looking hangnails.

'So what?'

'Want to tell me about it?'

He exhaled a snort of smoke. 'Like I got the option, you mean?'

'What's your side of the story? I've heard theirs. You couldn't deny pilfering the goods, I understand. You were caught with them. Redhanded, as it were.'

He reached for one of the pipe cleaners and wound it round his index finger, the cigarette between his lips and his glance directed at the half-assembled spider on the table. He reached for a pair of wire cutters and snipped a second pipe cleaner in half. Each half became a leg of the spider. Glue served to hold the leg to the body, and he meticulously applied this from a tube.

'Maliks make it sound like grand larceny or something? Shit, it was less than two boxes of the stuff. Thirty-six jars in a box. It's not like I broke the bank. And anyways, I didn't take straight mustard or jelly or sauce, did I, which might've cocked up some major punter's big order. I mixed it all up.'

'Creating a variety pack. I get it.'

He shot Barbara a black look before giving his attention back to the spider. It had an authentic-looking segmented body created out of differing sizes of sponge. Glancing at it, Barbara wondered idly how the body segments were attached to one another. With glue? With staples? Or had young Mr Ruddock used wire? She looked for a spool of it on the table, but in addition to the spider paraphernalia, the surface was a jumble of insect books, unfolded newspapers, half-melted candles, and tool boxes. She couldn't see how he managed to locate anything on it.

'I was told that Mr Querashi sacked you. Is that the story?'

'I suppose it is if that's what you've heard.'

'D'you have a different version, then?' Barbara looked for an ashtray but didn't see one. Trevor shoved an empty custard carton in her direction. Its insides were gritty with ash. She added to this.

'Whatever,' he said.

'Were you sacked unfairly? Did Querashi act too quickly?'

Trevor looked up from the spider. Barbara noticed for the first time that he had a tattoo beneath his left ear. It was a spider's web with an unpleasantly realistic-looking crawlie picking its way towards the centre. 'Did I kill him because he gave me the sack? That what you're asking?' Trevor worked his fingers over the spider's pipe-cleaner legs, plucking at the covering until it resembled hairs. 'I'm not stupid, you know. I seen the *Standard* today. I know the police are calling this a murder. I figured you'd be round to poke at me, or someone like you. And here you are. I got a motive, don't I?'

'Why don't you tell me about your relationship with Mr Querashi, Trevor?'

'I nicked some jars from the labelling and packing room. I worked in shipping, so it was dead easy. Querashi caught me and sacked me, he did. And that's the story of our relationship.' Trevor gave a sarcastic emphasis to the final word.

'Wasn't that risky, pinching jars from the packing room when you didn't work in the packing room?'

'I didn't nick them when anyone was there, did I? Just a jar here and a jar there during breaks and lunch. And just enough to have something to flog in Clacton.'

'You were selling them? Why? Did you need extra money? What for?'

Trevor pushed himself away from the table. He went to the window and thrust back the curtains. Lit by the day's pitiless sun, the room displayed cracked walls and hopelessly shabby furnishings. In spots, the rug on the floor was worn through to its backing. For some reason, a black line had been painted on to it, dividing the sleeping from the working areas.

'My dad can't work. And I got this stupid wish to keep the family off the streets. Charlie helps by doing odd jobs round the neighbourhood, and sometimes Stella gets hired to baby sit. But there's eight of us here and we get hungry. So Mum and I sell what we can at the market square in Clacton.'

'And the jars from Malik's became part of what you could sell.'

'Tha's right. Just part of the lot and at a cut-rate price. I don't see that it did any harm anyways. It's not like Mr Malik sells his jellies and stuff round here. Just to posh shops and snooty hotels and restaurants.'

'So you were actually doing the consumer a favour?'

'Maybe I was.' He leaned his bum against the window sill and played with the cigarette in his mouth, turning it with his thumb and index finger. The window was wide open, but they may as well have been having their conversation inside an oven. 'It seemed safe enough to flog them in Clacton anyways. I didn't expect Querashi to turn up there.'

'So you were caught trying to sell the jars in the market square? Querashi caught you there?'

'Right. Large as life, he was. 'Course, he didn't expect to see me in Clacton any more'n I expected to see him there. And considering what he was up to, I figured he'd turn a blind eye to my little character lapse and forget all about it. 'Specially since he was having a little character lapse of his own.'

Barbara's fingertips tingled at this remark, the way they always tingled when a new direction was unpredictably unveiled. But she also felt wary. Trevor was watching her closely to gauge her reaction to the titbit he'd just dropped. And the very closeness of his scrutiny suggested he'd had more than this single run-in with the police. Most people were at least discomposed when answering official questions. But Trevor seemed completely at ease, as if he'd known in advance what she'd ask and what he'd say in reply.

'Where were you on the night that Mr Querashi died, Trevor?'

A flicker in his eye told her she'd disappointed him in not nosing after the scent of Querashi's 'little lapse of character'. That was good, she thought. Suspects weren't supposed to be the ones directing the investigation.

'At work,' Trevor said. 'Cleaning the pier. You c'n ask Mr Shaw if you don't believe me.'

'I have done. Mr Shaw says you report for work at half-past eleven.

Is that what you did on Friday night? D'you have a time card there, by the way?'

'I punched it when I always punch in.'

'At half-past eleven?'

'Somewheres thereabouts, yeah. And I didn't leave, if you want to know. I work with a crew of blokes and they'll tell you that I didn't leave once all night.'

'What about before half-past eleven?' Barbara asked him.

'What about it?'

'Where were you then?'

'When?'

'Before half-past eleven, Trevor.'

'What time?'

'Just account for your movements, please.'

He took a final draw on his cigarette before he flipped it out of the window and into the street below. His forefinger took the cigarette's place. He gnawed at it thoughtfully before he replied. 'I was home till nine. Then I went out.'

'Out where?'

'Nowheres special.' He spat a sliver of fingernail to the floor. He examined his handiwork as he continued. 'I got this girl I sort of see off and on. I was with her.'

'She'll corroborate?'

'Huh?'

'She'll confirm that you were with her on Friday night?'

'Sure. But it's not like she was a date or anything. She's not my girlfriend. We just get together now and again. We talk. Have a smoke. See what's what with the world.'

Too right, Barbara thought. Why was it that she had trouble picturing Trevor Ruddock embroiled in deep philosophical colloquy with a female?

She wondered about the explanation he was giving, about why he found it necessary to give one in the first place. He'd either been with a woman or he hadn't been with a woman. She would either confirm his alibi or she wouldn't. Whether the two of them had been snogging, discussing politics, playing snap, or boffing each other like two hot monkeys made no difference to Barbara. She reached for her bag and brought out her notebook. 'What's her name, then?'

'You mean this girl?'

'Right. This girl. I'll need to have a word with her. Who is she?'

He shuffled from one foot to the other. 'Just a friend. We talk. It's no big –'

'Give me her name, okay?'

He sighed. 'She's called Rachel Winfield. She works at the jewellery shop on the High Street.'

'Ah, Rachel. We've already met.'

He clasped his left hand round his right elbow. He said, 'Yeah. Well, I was with her on Friday night. We're friends. She'll confirm.'

Barbara observed his discomfiture and mentally toyed with the nature of it. Either he was embarrassed to have it known that he associated with the Winfield girl or he was lying and hoping to get to her before Barbara checked his story out. 'Where were the two of you?' she asked, seeing the need to establish a second source of corroboration. 'A caff? A pub? The arcade? Where?'

'Uh . . . None of those, actually. We just went for a walk.'

'On the Nez maybe?'

'Hey, no way. We were on the beach all right, but nowheres near the Nez. We were off by the pier.'

'Anyone see you?'

'I don't think so.'

'But at night the pier's crowded. How could someone not have seen you?'

'Because . . . Look, we weren't *on* the pier. I never said we were on it. We were at the beach huts. We were –' He raised his forefinger and gnawed again viciously. 'We were *in* a beach hut. Got it? Okay?'

'In a beach hut?'

'Yeah. Like I said.' He dropped his hand from his mouth. His look was defiant. There was little doubt what he'd been up to with Rachel, and Barbara knew it probably had little to do with discussing what was what with the world.

'Tell me about Mr Querashi and the market square,' she said. 'Clacton's not that far from here. What are we talking about: twenty minutes in the car? It's not exactly a trip to the moon. So what was unusual about Haytham Querashi's being in the market square?'

'It's not him being there,' Trevor corrected. 'It's a free country. He can go where he likes. It's what he was up to there. And with who.'

'All right. I'll go for it. What was he up to?'

Trevor returned to his seat at the table. He pulled an illustrated book from beneath a disorganised array of newspapers. It was open at a colour photograph. Barbara saw that the picture was of the spider that

Trevor was in the process of creating. 'Jumping spider,' he informed her. 'It don't use a web like the others do, which is what makes it different from them. It hunts its prey. It goes out on the prowl, it finds a likely meal, and *fumph –*' His hand shot out and alighted on her arm. 'He eats.' The young man grinned. He had odd eyeteeth, one long and one short. They made him look dangerous, and Barbara could tell that he knew and enjoyed this fact.

She disengaged her arm from his hand. 'This is a metaphor, right? Querashi the spider? What was he hunting?'

'What a randy bloke generally hunts when he goes someplace he doesn't think he'll be known. Only, I saw him. And he knew I saw him.'

'He was with someone?'

'Oh, they didn't make it look that way, but I saw them talking and I watched them afterwards. And sure enough, they trotted off to the toilets one at a time – real casual, you know – looking like cats with feathers in their teeth.'

Barbara observed the young man, and he observed her. She said carefully, 'Trevor, are you telling me that Haytham Querashi was doing some cottaging in Clacton market square?'

'Looked that way to me,' Trevor said. 'He's standing there giving some scarves the finger at a stall across the square from the toilets. Some bloke comes up and does his own bit with the scarves 'bout five feet from him. They look at each other. They look away. This other bloke walks past and drops a line in his ear. Haytham heads for the gents straightaway. I watch. Two minutes later this bloke slides in there as well. Ten minutes after that, Haytham comes out. Alone. Looking the look. And that's when he sees me.'

'Who was this other bloke? Someone from Balford? Do you know him?'

Trevor shook his head. 'He was just some poofter wanting to score. Some poofter with a fancy for a poke of a different colour.'

Barbara jumped on this. 'He was white? The homosexual? He was English?'

'Could've been. But he could've been German, Danish, Swedish. Maybe even Norwegian. I don't know. But he wasn't a coloured, that's for sure.'

'And Querashi knew you'd seen him?'

'Yes and no. He saw me but he didn't know I'd watched him pull this other bloke. It was only when he wanted to give me the sack that

I told him I seen the whole thing.' Trevor shoved the spider book back where he'd taken it from. 'I thought I'd have something to hold over him, see? Like he wouldn't sack me if he knew I might give the word to old Akram that his future son-in-law was buggering white boys in a public convenience. But he denied the whole thing, Querashi did. All he said was that I'd better not hope to keep my job at the factory by spreading the nasties about him. Akram wouldn't believe them, he said, and I'd end up without my job at Malik's and without the new spot at the pier either. I needed the pier job, so I shut my gob. End of story.'

'You told no one else? Not Mr Malik? Not Muhannad? Not Sahlah?' Who would, Barbara believed, doubtless be horrified to know that her intended husband was betraying her and threatening the family's sense of honour. And it *would* be an honour issue for the Asians, wouldn't it? She needed to explore this issue with Azhar.

'It was my word against his, wasn't it?' Trevor said. 'It's not like he was caught in the act by the rozzers or anything.'

'So even you don't know for sure what he was doing in the toilets that day.'

'I didn't go in to check it out personally, if that's what you're saying. But I'm not daft, am I? Those toilets are used for cottaging all the time, and everyone knows it. So if two blokes go in there and don't come out in the time it takes to pee . . . Well, you figure it out.'

'What about Mr Shaw at the pier. Did you tell him?'

'Like I said. I didn't tell no one.'

'What'd this other bloke look like, then?' Barbara asked.

'Dunno. Just a bloke. Real tanned. Wearing a black baseball cap backwards. Not a big bloke, y'know, but not exactly a poofter-type either. I mean, not to look at. Oh, yeah, one other thing. He had a ring through his lip. A little gold hoop.' Trevor shuddered. 'Jesus,' he said without a trace of irony, fingertips resting against the spider on his neck, 'what some blokes'll do to their appearance.'

'Homosexuality?' Emily Barlow said. Her voice heightened sharply with interest.

Barbara had found her in the incident room of the old police station, where she held her daily meetings with the investigation's team of detective constables. She'd been penning names and activities on to a Chinagraph board.

Barbara saw that since Emily's visit to the factory, two DCs had been assigned to Malik's Mustards and were already in the process of conducting interviews there with all the employees. They would be seeking information that could lead them to an enemy of Haytham Querashi.

This new detail about the dead man would be invaluable to them, and the DCI didn't waste any time before striding to the door and giving the order to pass the information along to the constables post haste. 'Page them first,' she directed WPC Belinda Warner, who was working at the computer in the next room. 'When they phone in, give them the word, but for Christ's sake tell them to play their cards close.'

Then she turned back to the conference room, recapping her felt tip pen smartly and setting it on the Chinagraph board's tray. Barbara had reported on her entire day's activities: from her conversation with Connie and Rachel Winfield to her failed attempts to corroborate Sahlah Malik's story about tossing the gold bracelet from the pier. Emily had nodded and continued to make her entries on the board. It was only when the issue of Querashi's putative homosexuality came up that she'd reacted.

'How the Muslims feel about homosexuality.' She made the phrase sound like a category that she was setting up mentally in the investigation.

'I haven't a clue how they feel about it,' Barbara replied. 'But on my drive back here, the more I thought about the question of homosexuality the less I could attach it to Querashi's murder.'

'Why's that?' Emily went to one of the notice boards which lined the walls. Copies of photographs of the victim had been posted there, and she studied them earnestly, as if by this she could somehow get verification of Querashi's sexual proclivities.

'Because it seemed more likely that if one of the Maliks found out that Querashi was cottaging, they'd just call off the marriage and give him the boot back to Karachi. They sure as hell wouldn't kill him, would they? Why go to the bother?'

'They're Asians. They wouldn't want to lose face,' Emily stated. 'And they wouldn't be able to – how did Muhannad put it? – hold their heads up with pride if the word got out that Querashi was playing them for fools.'

Barbara thought about what Emily was suggesting. Something seemed slightly out of joint. She said, 'So one of them killed him? Hell, Em, that's taking ethnic pride to the extreme. It seems to me that Querashi'd be likely to go after anyone who knew his secret, rather than someone going after Querashi because he *had* a secret. If homosexuality's at the root of this, doesn't it make more sense to see Querashi as the killer and not as the victim?'

'Not if an Asian, outraged by the knowledge that a man was planning to use Sahlah Malik as a cover for his homosexual lifestyle, went after Querashi.'

'If that's what Querashi was planning,' Barbara said.

Emily picked up a small plastic bag that was lying on top of one of the room's computer terminals. She untwisted its wire tie and dug out four carrot sticks. Seeing this, Barbara tried not to look guilty about her previously consumed whitebait and rock – not to mention her cigarettes – as the DCI began to munch virtuously. 'Which Asian comes to mind when you think of someone being driven to murder in order to revenge that sort of arrangement?'

'I know where you're heading,' Barbara said. 'But I thought Muhannad was supposed to be a man of his people. If he isn't and if he offed Querashi, then why's he raising hell about the murder?'

'To paint himself in a saintly light. *Jihad*: the holy war against the infidels. He shouts for justice and directs the spotlight of guilt on to an English killer. And, coincidentally, off himself.'

'But, Em, that's no different to what Armstrong may be doing with the vandalised car. A different approach, but the same intent.'

'Armstrong has an alibi.'

'What about Muhannad's? Did you find this Rakin Khan in Colchester?'

'Oh, I found him all right. He was holding court in a private room of his father's restaurant, with half a dozen others of his ilk. In a suit by Armani, slip-ons by Bally, wristwatch by Rolex, and a diamond signet ring from Burlington Arcade. He was an old friend of Malik's, he claimed, from their days at university.'

'What did he say?'

'He confirmed everything, chapter and verse. He said the two of them had dinner that evening. They began at eight and went on till midnight.'

'A four-hour dinner? Where? A restaurant? That restaurant?'

'Wouldn't that be lovely for our side? But no, this dinner took place, he said, at his own home. *And* he cooked the entire meal himself, which was what took so long. He likes to cook, loves to cook, cooked all the time for Muhannad at university, he said, because they neither of them have ever been able to abide English food. He even recited the menu for me.'

'Can anyone confirm the story?'

'Oh, yes. Because, conveniently, they weren't alone. Another foreign bloke – and intriguing, isn't it, that everyone's foreign? – was there as well. Also a mate from their university days. Khan said it was a little reunion.'

'Well,' Barbara said, 'if they both confirm . . .'

'Bullshit.' Emily crossed her arms. 'Muhannad Malik had plenty of time before I got to Colchester to phone Rakin Khan and tell him to corroborate his story.'

'For that matter,' Barbara said, 'Ian Armstrong's had plenty of time to ask his in-laws to do the same. Have you spoken to them?'

Emily made no response.

Barbara went on. 'He's got a solid motive, Ian Armstrong. What's Muhannad got that's holding your interest?'

'He protests too much,' Emily said.

'P'rhaps he's got something to protest about,' Barbara pointed out. 'Look, I agree he comes off like a lag in the making. And this Rakin Khan may be just as bad. But you're leaving out some details that you can't tie to Muhannad. Think of just three of them: you said Querashi's car was done over. His body was moved. His car keys were thrown into the undergrowth. If Muhannad killed Querashi for the honour of his family, then why do over the car and why move the body? Why put neon lights round what otherwise might have been taken for an accident?'

'Because he didn't want it to be taken for an accident,' Emily said. 'Because he wanted just what he's got: an incident that he can rally his people round. He meets two ends at once this way: he evens the score with Querashi for blackening the family name and he cements his position in the Asian community.'

'Okay. Perhaps,' Barbara said. 'But on the other hand, why should we believe Trevor Ruddock about this homosexuality thing in the first place? He's got a motive as well. Okay, he didn't get his job back like Armstrong did, but he didn't seem the type to say no to a decent spot of revenge if he had the chance to get it.'

'You said he has an alibi as well.'

'Bloody hell! They *all* have flaming alibis, Em! Someone's got to be lying somewhere.'

'Which, Sergeant Havers, is *exactly* my point.' Emily's voice was quite even. But there was a steely quality to it that reminded Barbara once again of two facts: that not only was Emily her superior officer by reasons of talent, intelligence, intuition, and skill, but also that she herself had been admitted to work on this case on DCI Barlow's generous sufferance.

Back off, she told herself. This is not your patch, Barb. She was suddenly aware of how bloody hot the incident room was. It was worse than an oven. The harsh light of late afternoon poured in like an armed invasion. When, she wondered, had the country ever had a summer this beastly and miserable at the seaside?

'I checked on Trevor's alibi,' she said. 'I stopped by Racon Jewellery on my way back here. According to her mum, Rachel did a runner right after I left them. Her mum couldn't say where Rachel was on the murder night because she herself was dancing in some ballroom competition in Chelmsford. She did say something interesting, though.'

'What's that?' Emily asked.

'She said, "My Rachel only goes with white boys, and mind you remember that, Sergeant." What d'you think that means?'

'That she's worried about something.'

'We know that Querashi was probably meeting someone that night. We have only Trevor Ruddock's word that Querashi was cottaging in the first place. And even if Querashi *was* cottaging, that doesn't mean he didn't swing both ways.'

'You're putting Querashi with Rachel Winfield now?' Emily asked.

'She gave him that jewellery receipt, Em. She had to have a reason.' Barbara considered one other element of the puzzle that they'd not yet tried to place. 'But that doesn't really take care of the question of the bracelet: what Theo Shaw's doing with it. I've assumed that Sahlah gave it to him. But he could always have taken it from Querashi's body. If he did that, though, it means that Sahlah's lie about having tossed the bracelet from the pier was prompted by the fact that she knows that whoever has the bracelet is involved in all this. Why else lie?'

Behind her, Emily said with some passion, 'Jesus. This is just like going down the bloody rabbit hole.'

The tone of Emily's comment prompted Barbara to study the DCI more closely. Emily was leaning her bum against the edge of the table. For the first time, Barbara noticed the smudged skin under her eyes.

'Em?' she said.

'If it's one of them, Barb, this town's going to blow.'

Barbara knew what she was implying: if the killer was English and the town caved in to more racial unrest because of that fact, heads would roll. And the first would be Emily Barlow's.

In the silence that hung between them, Barbara heard voices in the entry downstairs. Terse words were spoken by a man and answered by a woman sounding calm and professional. Barbara recognised the man, at least. Muhannad Malik was in reception, arrived for his afternoon meeting with the police.

Azhar would be with him. So the moment had arrived when Barbara knew she ought to tell Emily Barlow the truth.

She opened her mouth to do so but found that she couldn't. If she fully explained – at least as fully as she was able, considering how little she had bothered to examine her motives before setting forth to Balford – Emily would have to dismiss her from the case. She could hardly view Barbara as an objective party in the investigation when at the side of at least one of the suspects moved a man who lived a bare fifty yards from her own shacklike dwelling in London. And Barbara wanted to stay on the case for more than one reason now. While it was true that she'd initially come to Balford-le-Nez for the sake of her Pakistani neighbours, she realised that she wished to remain for the sake of her colleague.

Barbara was well aware of the myriad prices women had to pay to succeed in policework. Men in the profession didn't have to persuade a single soul that their competence was unaffected by their sex. Women lived with having to do that daily. So if she could help Emily maintain her position and prove herself as a DCI, she was determined to do it.

'I'm on your side, Em,' she said quietly.

'Are you.' Once again Emily said the two words; she didn't ask them. Which reminded Barbara of another fact: the higher one climbed in authority and power, the fewer true friends one actually had. But a moment later, Emily roused herself from whatever black thoughts of the future were troubling her. She said, 'So where was Theo Shaw on Friday night?'

'He says he was at home. His grandmother was there, but she won't be able to confirm anything, as she'd gone to bed.'

'That part of his story is probably true,' Emily said. 'Agatha Shaw – that's the grandmother – had a stroke some time ago. She'd need her rest.'

'Which gives Theo plenty of opportunity to have taken himself over to the Nez on foot,' Barbara pointed out.

'Which would explain why no one in the vicinity claims to have heard another car.' Emily frowned thoughtfully. She directed her attention to a second Chinagraph board. On it she had scrawled surnames of suspects and first initials, followed by their alleged whereabouts for the time in question. She said, 'The Malik girl seems docile enough, but if she was secretly involved with Theo, she may have had a reason to send her fiancé tumbling down the Nez stairs. It would sure as hell end her obligation to Querashi. Permanently.'

'But you said her dad claimed that he wouldn't have forced her to marry the man.'

'He says that now. But he could be covering up for her. Perhaps she and Theo are in this together.'

'Romeo and Juliet killing off Count Paris instead of themselves? Okay. I see that it works. But aside from the car which we'll forget about for the moment, here's something else we're not considering: let's say Querashi got tricked into going to the Nez to meet Theo Shaw for a confab about Theo's relationship with Sahlah. Then how do we explain the condoms in his pocket?'

'Shit. The condoms,' Emily said. 'Okay, so he may not have been going to meet Theo Shaw at all. But even if he didn't know about Theo, one thing is certain: Theo knew about him. There'd been an announcement of the engagement in the *Standard*. If Sahlah hadn't broken the news to him yet, he may have read about it there. Or heard about it in the Gentlemen's Cooperative. I can't imagine Akram introducing Haytham Querashi as anything but his prospective son-in-law.'

Barbara had to admit that the scales of culpability were beginning to tip in the direction of one of the Englishmen. She wondered what the hell she was going to report to the Pakistanis when they had their meeting. She could only imagine what Muhannad Malik would do with any information that supported his belief in the crime's racial nature.

'Okay,' she said, 'but we can't forget that we've caught out Sahlah Malik in a lie. And since Haytham Querashi had the receipt, I think we can conclude that someone must have wanted him to know that Sahlah had another relationship.'

'Rachel Winfield,' Emily said. 'She's still the enigma in all this for me.'

'A woman went to see Querashi at the hotel. A woman wearing a *chādor*.'

'And if that woman was Rachel Winfield, and if Rachel Winfield wanted Querashi for herself –'

'Guv?' Emily and Barbara turned to the door, where Belinda Warner stood with a stack of chits in her hand. These were neatly clipped together in several different piles. Barbara recognised them as the copies of the telephone messages from the Burnt House Hotel that she'd handed over to Emily that morning.

'What is it?' Emily said.

'I've sorted through this lot, arranged them in categories, and tracked everyone down. Or at least nearly everyone.' She entered and placed each small stack down as she identified it. 'Calls from the Maliks: Sahlah, Akram, and Muhannad. Calls from a contractor: a bloke called Gerry DeVitt from Jaywick Sands. He was doing some work on the house that Akram'd bought for the newlyweds.'

'DeVitt?' Barbara asked. 'Em, he works on the pier. I spoke to him this afternoon.'

Emily made an entry into her notebook, which she scooped from a table in the incident room. 'What else?' she asked Belinda.

'Calls from a decorator in Colchester, also working on the house. And this last, miscellaneous calls: from friends, I expect, by their names: Mr Zaidi, Mr Faruqi, Mr Kumhar, Mr Kat—'

'Kumhar?' Emily and Barbara said simultaneously.

Belinda looked up. 'Kumhar,' she confirmed. 'He phoned the most. There're eleven messages from him.' She licked her index finger and flicked through the final stack of chits. She pulled from them the one she wanted. 'Here it is. Fahd Kumhar,' she said.

'Bloody hell. There you are,' Barbara put in reverently.

'It's a Clacton number,' Belinda went on. 'I phoned it, but I only got a newsagent on Carnarvon Road.'

'Carnarvon Road?' Emily said quickly. 'Are you absolutely sure it was Carnarvon Road?'

'I've got the address right here.'

'Now there's a development from the gods, Barb.'

'Why?' Barbara asked. There was a map of the area on one of the notice boards and she went to this and looked it over, seeking the location of Carnarvon Road. She found it, rising perpendicular from the sea and Clacton's Marine Parade. It passed the railway station and ultimately led to the A133, which was the road to London. 'Is there something important about Carnarvon Road?'

'There's something too coincidental for coincidence,' Emily said.

'Carnarvon Road runs along the east side of the market square. *Clacton* market square, that is, of recent cottaging fame.'

'Now that's a tasty detail,' Barbara said. She turned from the map and saw the DCI watching her. Emily's eyes were bright.

'I think we may be looking at a whole new cricket match, Sergeant Havers,' she announced. And her voice was full of the vigour that Barbara had always encountered in Barlow the Beast. 'Whoever Kumhar is, let's track this bloke down.'

Chapter Twelve

$\Longrightarrow\!\!\blacklozenge\!\!\Longleftarrow$

Sahlah used great care to set out the tools of her craft. She lifted the transparent plastic trays from their green metal workbox and lined them up neatly. She took the narrow-nosed pliers, the drill, and the wire cutter from their protective sheaths and she laid them on either side of the row of cords, cables, and lengths of gold chain that she used to assemble the intricate necklaces and earrings which Rachel and her mother had kindly undertaken to sell among the jewellery in their shop. 'This's every bit as good as anything we got at Racon,' Rachel had declared loyally. 'Mum'll *want* to show it, Sahlah. You'll see. Anyway, what c'n it hurt to try? If it sells, you got some money for yourself. If it doesn't, you got some new jewellery, right?'

There was a degree of truth to Rachel's words. But beyond the money – three-quarters of which she turned over to her parents once she'd earned enough to pay off Theo's bracelet – it had been the idea of doing something on her own and something that was purely an expression of herself that had motivated Sahlah to design and create for eyes and purses outside her family's.

Had this been the first step? she wondered as she reached for the tray of African beads and trickled them slowly into her palm like winter raindrops, cool and smooth. Was it when she decided to engage in this solitary creative act that she'd first awakened to the possibilities offered by a world beyond the realm of her family? And had this act of creating something as simple as jewellery in the isolation of her bedroom produced the first fissure in her contentment?

No, she realised. Nothing was ever as simple as that. There was no primary cause-and-effect that she could point a finger at, explaining not only the restlessness of her spirit but also the soreness of an insular heart. What there was instead was the entire duality of a life lived with her feet attempting to march in two conflicting worlds.

'You're my English girl,' her father had said to her nearly every day as she scooped up her schoolbooks in the morning. And she'd heard the pride in his voice. She was born in England; she went to the junior school right there in town with English children; she spoke the language by virtue of both birth and exposure and not from having had to learn it as an adult. Therefore, in her father's mind she was English, and as verifiably English as any child with porcelain cheeks that flushed like peach skin after play. She was, in fact, as English as Akram secretly longed to be.

Muhannad was right in this, Sahlah realised. Although their father attempted to wear two different suits of cultural clothing, his true love was with the three-piece suits and brollies of his adopted country despite his duty's entanglement with the *shalwār-qamīs* of his heritage. And from the moment of his children's births, he'd expected them to share and understand this perplexing dichotomy. At home they were to be dutiful: Sahlah subdued and obedient, honing skills in homemaking to please a future husband; Muhannad respectful and industrious, preparing himself to shoulder the burdens of the family business and eventually producing sons who would shoulder those burdens in their turn. Beyond the home, though, the two Malik children were to be quintessentially English. Counselled by their father to mix with their schoolmates, they were supposed to establish friendships in order to garner respect and affection for the family name and consequently for the family business. And to this latter end, Akram monitored their schooldays, looking for signs of social progress where he could not possibly hope to find them.

Sahlah had tried to humour him. Unable to face being the cause of her father's disappointment, she'd made Valentines and birthday cards addressed to herself, and she'd brought them home, signed in the names of fellow pupils. She'd written herself chatty, gossipy notes ostensibly passed her way during science and maths. She'd found discarded pictures of classmates and autographed them to herself, with love. And when her father got wind of birthday parties, off she went in mock attendance to a celebration in which she was never included, jubilating instead in a tree at the bottom of the orchard where she was hidden from the house and from the prospect of her father's disillusion.

But Muhannad made no similar attempt to fulfil their father's fantasies. He had no conflicts about being dark-skinned in a white-faced world, and he didn't seek to mitigate any consternation he encountered, consternation aroused at the sight of a foreigner living among a populace largely unused to dark faces. Born in England like herself, he no more considered himself an Englishman than he considered cows capable of flight. Indeed, the last thing on earth Muhannad would have wanted to be was an Englishman. He scorned what passed for the English culture. He had only contempt for the ceremonies and traditions that formed the foundation of English life. He ridiculed the stiff upper lips that propriety required of men who dubbed themselves gentlemen. And the masks that westerners wore to hide their biases and prejudices he eschewed entirely. He displayed his own biases, prejudices, and animosities like the family escutcheon. And the demons that haunted him were not and had never been the demons of race, no matter how he tried to convince himself and others that this was the case.

But she wouldn't think of Muhannad now, Sahlah decided. And she took up her long-nosed pliers as if making a pretence of work would somehow assist her in driving from her mind any consideration of her brother. She pulled paper towards her to sketch a necklace design, hoping that putting pencil to paper and carved beads in position would obliterate from memory that glitter in her brother's eye when he was determined to have his way, that streak of cruelty which he always managed to keep diligently hidden from both of their parents, and most of all that anger of his and how it whipped through his arms and burst from the tips of his fingers when she least expected.

Somewhere in the house below her, Sahlah heard Yumn calling to one of her boys. 'Baby, precious baby,' she was cooing. 'Lovely boy. Come to your *ammī-gee*, little man.'

Sahlah's throat closed, her head grew light, and the African beads melded one into the other on the table before her. She released her grip on the long-nosed pliers, crossed her arms on the tabletop, and sank her head into their cradle. How could she think of her brother's sins, Sahlah wondered, when her own were as grievous and just as capable of rending the family irreparably?

'I've seen you with him,' Muhannad had hissed in her ear. 'You slut. I've seen you with him. Do you hear me? I've *seen*. And you're going to pay. Because all whores pay. Especially white men's filthy slags.'

But she hadn't intended anything harmful. Least of all had she intended love.

She'd been allowed to work with Theo Shaw because her father knew him from the Gentlemen's Cooperative and because accepting Theo Shaw's offer of his computer expertise was yet another way that Akram Malik could demonstrate solidarity with the English community. The mustard factory had recently moved to its new location in the industrial estate on Old Hall Lane, and this expansion had necessitated an updating of business procedures.

'It's time we entered the twentieth century,' Akram had told his family. 'Business is good. Sales are increasing. Orders are up by eighteen per cent. I've spoken to the good gentlemen of the Cooperative about this, and among them is a decent young man willing to assist us in computerising each of our departments.'

The fact that Akram had perceived Theo as decent was what made his interaction with Sahlah acceptable. Despite his own affection for them, Akram would have preferred that his daughter had no contact with western men. Everything about a daughter of Asia was to be safeguarded and kept in trust for a future husband: from the moulding of her mind to the protection of her chastity. Indeed, her chastity was nearly as important as her dowry, and no step was too great to take if it could ensure that a woman went to her husband a virgin. Since western men did not hold these same values, it was from them that Akram had to guard his daughter from the onset of puberty. But he put aside any and all worries when it had come to Theo Shaw.

'He's from a good family, an old town family,' Akram had explained, as if this fact made a difference in his level of acceptability. 'He'll work with us to set up a system that will modernise every aspect of the company. We'll have computerised word processing for correspondence, spread sheets for accounting, programs for marketing, and desktop design for advertising and labelling. He's done this already for the pier, he tells me, and he says that within six months we'll see the results in accumulated man hours as well as in increased sales.'

No one had argued against the wisdom of accepting Theo Shaw's help, not even Muhannad, who was least likely to welcome an Englishman into their midst if that Englishman were to be in any position of superiority, even one as arcane as computer expertise. So Theo Shaw had come to Malik's Mustards, setting up the computer programs that would revolutionise the manner in which the factory did business. He'd trained the staff to operate these same programs. And among the staff had been Sahlah herself.

She hadn't intended to love him. She knew what was expected of her as an Asian daughter, despite her English birth. She would marry a man carefully chosen by her parents because, having her interests at heart and knowing her better than she knew herself, her parents would be able to identify the qualities in a prospective husband most complementary to her own.

'Marriage,' Wardah Malik had often told her, 'is like the joining of two hands. Palms meet –' she demonstrated by holding her own hands up in an attitude of prayer '– and fingers intertwine. Similarity of size, shape, and texture make this joining both smooth and lasting.'

Sahlah couldn't have this joining with Theo Shaw. Asian parents did not choose western men for their daughters to marry. Such a choice would only serve to adulterate the mother culture from which the daughter sprang. And that was unthinkable.

So she hadn't considered Theo as anything other than the young man – affable, attractive, and casual in a way that only western men were casual with a woman – who was doing a friendly service for Malik's Mustards. She hadn't really thought of him at all until he placed the stone on her desk.

He'd earlier admired her jewellery, the necklaces and earrings fabricated from antique coins and Victorian buttons, from African and Tibetan beads intricately carved by hand, even from feathers and copperas that she and Rachel collected on the Nez. He'd said, 'That's nice, that necklace you're wearing. It's quite different, isn't it?' And when she'd told him she made it, he'd been openly impressed.

Had she been trained in jewellery making? he'd wanted to know.

Hardly, she'd thought. She'd have had to go off somewhere to school to be educated in her craft, perhaps to Colchester or regions beyond. That would have taken her away from her family, away from the business where she was needed. *It's not allowed* was what she wanted to say. But she'd told him instead a version of the truth. I like to teach myself things, she'd informed him. It's more fun that way.

The next day when she'd come into work, the stone had been on her desk. But it wasn't a stone, Theo explained to her. It was a fossil, the fin of a holostean fish from the Upper Triassic period. 'I like its shape, the way the edges look feathered.' He coloured slightly. 'I thought you might be able to use it for a necklace. As a centrepiece or something . . . ? I mean, whatever you call it.'

'It would make a fine pendant.' Sahlah turned the stone in her hand. 'But I'd have to drill a hole through it. You wouldn't mind that?'

Oh, the jewellery wasn't for him, he told her hastily. He meant her to use the fossil in a necklace for herself. He collected fossils out on the Nez where the cliffs were collapsing, you see. He'd been looking through his display trays last night. He'd realised this particular fossil had a look and a shape that might lend it to being used artistically. So if she thought she could make something of it and with it, well . . . she was quite welcome to keep it.

Sahlah had known that to accept the stone – no matter how innocently it had been offered – would be to cross an invisible line with Theo Shaw. And she saw the part of herself that was Asian lowering her head and quietly sliding the serrated bit of prehistoric fish across the desk in polite refusal of the gift. But the part of herself that was English took action first, fingers closing round the fossil and voice saying, 'Thank you. I know I can use it. I'll show you the necklace when I've finished it, if you'd like.'

'I'd like that very much indeed,' he said. Then he'd smiled and an unspoken bargain had been struck between them. Her jewellery making would be their excuse for conversation. His fossil collecting would justify their continuing to meet.

But one did not fall in love because a single stone or a thousand stones passed from a man's hand into a woman's. And Sahlah Malik hadn't fallen in love with Theo Shaw because of a stone. Indeed, until she was in the midst of loving him, she hadn't even realised that there was a simple word of four letters that explained the softness she felt round her heart, the yearning she experienced in the palms of her hands, the warmth that rose from her throat, and the lightness in her body as if she had no real body when Theo was present or when she heard his voice.

'White man's slag,' Muhannad had cursed her, and she'd heard the hiss – like a snake's – in his words. 'You're going to pay. The way all whores pay.'

But she wouldn't think of it, she wouldn't, she *wouldn't*.

Sahlah raised her head from her arms and looked down at the paper, the pencil, the beads, the beginning of a sketch that was no sketch because nothing within her could create a design or put objects together in a pattern that was balanced and pleasing to the eye. She was lost, now. She was paying the price. She'd been awakened to a longing that couldn't be met within the narrow definition of the life she was expected to lead, and she'd begun to pay the price for this longing months before Haytham's advent among them.

Haytham would have saved her. He possessed an earnest concern for others that set the self aside, and because he was capable of acts of generosity beyond her ken, he'd greeted the news of her pregnancy with a question that swept aside both her guilt and her fear. 'And have you carried this dreadful burden these months all alone, my Sahlah?'

She hadn't wept until that moment. They'd been sitting in the orchard, side by side on the wooden bench whose back legs slid too far into the soil. Their shoulders had been touching but nothing else touching, until she confided in him. She hadn't been able to look at him as she spoke, knowing how much depended upon the next few minutes of conversation. She couldn't believe he would take her as his wife once he knew that she carried another man's child. But by the same token, she couldn't bring herself to marry him and then to attempt to pass off the birth of a healthy baby as the birth of an infant that would have to be taken as at least three months premature. Besides, he'd been in no immediate hurry to marry, and her parents had seen in his suggestion that they wait not a reluctance to fulfil his part of the marital agreement but a wise man's decision to learn to know the woman who would his wife . . . before she became his wife. But Sahlah had no leisure to pursue an acquaintance with Haytham Querashi.

So she'd had to speak. And then she'd had to wait, her future and her family's honour held in the palm of a man she'd known less than one week. 'And have you carried this dreadful burden these months all alone, my Sahlah?' And when his arm went round her shoulders, Sahlah realised that she'd been saved.

She'd wanted to ask him how he could take her as she was: defiled by another, pregnant with that other's child, tainted by the touch of a man who could never be her husband. I've sinned and I've paid the price of sinning, she wanted to say. But she said nothing, merely weeping in near silence and waiting for him to decide her fate.

'So we'll marry sooner than I had expected,' he'd said meditatively. 'Unless . . . Sahlah, you don't wish to marry your child's father?'

She'd clenched her hands together between her thighs. Her words were fierce. 'I don't. I can't.'

'Because your parents . . . ?'

'I can't. If they knew, it would destroy them. I'd be cast out . . .' She could say nothing else as the grief and fear within her – so long held in check – were finally given release.

And Haytham required no other explanation from her. He'd repeated his initial question: Had she carried the burden alone? Once he understood that she had, he sought only to share it and to comfort her.

Or so she had concluded, Sahlah thought now. But Haytham was a Muslim. Traditional and religious at heart, he would have been deeply offended at the notion that some other man had touched the woman meant to be his wife. He would have sought a confrontation with that man, and once Rachel had alerted him to the existence of a gold bracelet, a very special gold bracelet, a gift of love . . .

All too clearly, Sahlah could picture the meeting between them: Haytham asking for it and Theo eager to comply. 'Give me time,' he'd begged her when she'd told him she would marry a man from Pakistan chosen by her parents. 'For God's sake, Sahlah. Give me more time.' And he would have struck out to buy himself that time, eliminating the man who stood between them in order to prevent what he saw he couldn't stop: her marriage.

Now she had a surfeit of time and no time at all. A surfeit of time because there was no man waiting in the wings to rescue her from disgrace in such a way that she would not lose her family as a result. No time at all because a new life grew in her body and promised the destruction of all that she knew, held dear, and depended upon. If she did not act decisively and as soon as possible.

Behind her, the bedroom door opened. Sahlah turned as her mother entered the room. Wardah's head was covered modestly. Despite the unabating heat of the day, her entire body was clothed so that only her hands and her face were bare. Her choice of dress was dark, as was her custom, as if she were permanently in mourning over a death that she never acknowledged in words.

She came across the room and touched her daughter's shoulder. Silently, she removed Sahlah's *dupattā* and loosened her hair from its single plait. She took a hairbrush from the chest of drawers. She began to brush her daughter's hair. Sahlah couldn't see her mother's face, but she could feel the love in her fingers, and she could sense the tenderness in every stroke of the brush.

'You didn't come into the kitchen,' Wardah said. 'I missed you.

I thought at first that you weren't home yet. But Yumn heard you come in.'

And Yumn would have reported, Sahlah thought. She'd be maliciously eager for her mother-in-law to know Sahlah's every lapse in duty. 'I wanted a few minutes,' Sahlah said. 'I'm sorry, *Ammī*. Have you started dinner?'

'The lentils only.'

'Then shall I –'

Wardah pressed her daughter's shoulders gently when Sahlah would have risen. 'I can cook the dinner with my eyes closed, Sahlah. I missed your company. That's all.' She curled a long lock of Sahlah's hair round her hand as she brushed it. She laid the lock against Sahlah's back and chose another, saying, 'Shall we speak to each other?'

Sahlah felt the pain of her mother's question like a fist that was gripping her heart. How many times since her childhood had Wardah said those same six words to her daughter? A thousand times? A hundred thousand? They were an invitation to share confidences: secrets, dreams, puzzling questions, ruffled feelings, private hopes. And the invitation was always extended with the implicit promise that what was said between mother and daughter was to be held in trust.

Tell me what happens with a man and a woman. And Sahlah had listened – both frightened and awestruck – as Wardah explained what occurred when a man and a woman bound themselves to each other in marriage.

But how do parents know what person is good for a marriage to one of their children? And Wardah quietly delineated all the ways in which fathers and mothers are fully capable of knowing their children's hearts and minds.

And you, Ammī? Were you ever frightened to marry someone you didn't know? More frightened to come to England, Wardah told her. But she'd trusted Akram to do what was best for her, just as she'd trusted her father to choose a man who would care for her throughout life.

But weren't you ever afraid in your life? Even to meet Abhy-jahn? Naturally, her mother said. But she'd known her duty, and when Akram Malik had been presented to her, she'd thought him a good man, a man with whom she could make a life.

This is what we aspire to as women, Wardah told her in those quiet moments when she and her daughter lay side by side on Sahlah's bed in the darkness before Sahlah fell asleep. We achieve fulfilment as women by meeting the needs of our husbands and our children, and by sending our children into marriages of their own with suitable mates.

True contentment grows from tradition, Sahlah. And tradition binds us together as a people.

In these night-time conversations with her mother, the room's shadows hid their faces from each other and freed them to speak their hearts. But now ... Sahlah wondered how she could possibly speak to her mother. She wanted to do so. She yearned to open her heart to Wardah, to receive the comfort and to feel the safety that her mother's quiet presence had always provided her. Yet to seek that comfort and safety now meant to speak a truth that would destroy the very possibility of comfort and safety for ever.

So she said in a low voice the only thing she could say, 'The police were at the factory today, *Ammī.*'

'Your father phoned me,' Wardah replied.

'They've sent two detective constables. The constables are talking to everyone, and they're recording the interviews. They're in the conference room and one by one they call in someone to question. From the kitchen, from shipping, from storage, from production.'

'And you, Sahlah? Have these constables spoken to you as well?'

'No. Not yet. But they will. Soon.'

Wardah seemed to hear something in her voice, because for a moment she stopped brushing Sahlah's hair. 'You fear an interview with the detective constables? Do you know something about Haytham's death? Something you haven't spoken of yet?'

'No.' Sahlah told herself it wasn't a lie. She didn't know anything. She merely suspected. She waited to see if her mother would hear a hesitation in her words that gave her away or an uncharacteristic inflection that revealed the roiling of a soul in which guilt, sorrow, fear, and anxiety all warred. 'But I'm frightened,' she said. And this, at least, was a truth she could part with.

Wardah put the hairbrush on the chest of drawers. She returned to her daughter and placed her fingers beneath Sahlah's chin. She tilted her face and gazed into it. Sahlah felt her heart beating rapidly, and she knew the birthmark on her cheek had suffused with colour.

'You have no reason to fear,' Wardah told her. 'Your father and your brother will protect you, Sahlah. As will I. No harm can possibly come to you from the harm that came to Haytham. Before that ever could happen, your father would lay down his own life. As would Muhannad. You know this, don't you?'

'Harm has already come to us all,' Sahlah whispered.

'What happened to Haytham touches all our lives,' Wardah agreed. 'But it needn't contaminate us if we choose not to let it. And we make that choice by speaking the truth. Only lies and denials have the power to taint us.'

These words were nothing that Wardah had not said in the past. But now their power to wound astonished her daughter. She couldn't blink the tears away before her mother saw them.

Wardah's face softened and she drew her close, holding Sahlah's head against her breast. 'You're quite safe, dearest,' her mother said. 'I promise you that.'

But Sahlah knew that the safety of which her mother spoke was as insubstantial as a piece of gauze.

Barbara suffered through Emily's ministrations to her face a second time that day. Before allowing her to meet the Pakistanis in her first official appearance as police liaison officer, Emily took her to the locker room and stood her in front of the basin and mirror for another go with the foundation, powder, mascara, and blusher. She even dotted Barbara's mouth with lipstick, saying, 'Stuff it, Sergeant,' when Barbara protested. 'I want you looking fresh for the fray,' she instructed. 'Don't underestimate the power of personal appearance, especially in our line of work. You'd be a fool to think it doesn't count.'

As she repaired what the heat had damaged, she gave her directions for the forthcoming meeting. She listed what details Barbara was to share with the Asians, and she reiterated the dangers of the minefield they were walking through.

She concluded by saying, 'The last thing I want is for Muhannad Malik to use anything from this meeting to fire up his people, all right? And watch them both while you're at it. Watch them like a hawk. Watch everyone like a hawk. I'll be meeting the rest of the team in the conference room, if you need me.'

Barbara was determined not to need her, as well as to do justice to the DCI's faith in her. And as she faced Muhannad Malik and Taymullah Azhar across the table in what had once been the Victorian house's dining room, she recommitted herself to those ends.

The two men had been kept waiting a quarter of an hour. During that time, someone had provided them with a jug of water, four glasses, and a blue paper plate of Oreos. But they appeared to have touched nothing. When Barbara entered, both men were sitting. Azhar rose. Muhannad did not.

'Sorry to keep you waiting,' she told them. 'Some last-minute details we had to clear up.'

Muhannad didn't look as if he believed that remark. Obviously, he was experienced enough to know when power-jockeying was being attempted by an adversary. For his part, Azhar made a study of Barbara as if trying to gaze beneath her skin for the truth of the matter. When she returned his scrutiny, he lowered his eyes.

'Details we wait to hear,' Muhannad said. Barbara had to credit him with opening the meeting with an attempt to sound polite.

'Yes. Well.' On to the table she slapped the folders she was carrying. There were three of them, and she'd brought them along more for effect than for any other reason. She topped them with the yellow-bound book she'd taken from Querashi's hotel room. Then she drew out a chair, sat, and gestured Azhar to do likewise. She'd brought along her cigarettes, and she took a moment to light up.

The room was only a degree or two less stifling than Emily Barlow's office had been, but unlike Emily's office, there was no fan circulating the tepid air. Muhannad's forehead glistened. Azhar, as usual, could have stepped from an icy shower a moment prior to Barbara's entrance.

Barbara indicated the yellow-bound book with her cigarette. 'I'd like to begin with this. Can you tell me what it is?'

Azhar reached across the table. He turned the book with the back cover face up and read what Barbara would have thought to be the final page. He said, 'This is the Holy Qur'aan, Sergeant. Where did you get it?'

'In Querashi's room.'

'As he was a Muslim, that can't come as a surprise.' Muhannad pointed out.

Barbara extended her hand for the book, and Azhar complied. She opened it to the page she'd noted on the previous night, marked with a satin ribbon. She directed Azhar's attention to the passage on the page, where brackets had been drawn in blue ink. 'As you obviously read Arabic,' she said, 'would you translate this for me? We've sent a fax of it to a bloke at the University of London for deciphering, but we'll be that much ahead of the game if you're willing to do the honours right now.'

Barbara saw a small flicker of irritation cross Azhar's face. In revealing that he read Arabic, he'd inadvertently given her an advantage over him that she'd otherwise not have had. In telling him that she'd already sent the page to London, she'd made it impossible for him to manufacture a translation that might meet ends other than the truth. Love-fifteen, she thought with no little pleasure. It was important, after all, that Taymullah Azhar understand their acquaintance wasn't going to stand in the way of Sergeant Havers getting her job done. It was equally important that both men knew they weren't dealing with a fool.

Azhar read the passage. He was silent for a minute, during which time Barbara could hear voices coming from the first-floor conference room as the door opened and shut upon Emily's afternoon meeting with her team. She shot a glance at Muhannad but couldn't decide whether he looked bored, eager, hostile, overheated, or tense. His eyes were on his cousin. His fingers held a pencil and tapped its rubber end against the top of the table.

Finally, Azhar said, 'A direct translation isn't always possible. English terms aren't always adequate or comparable to those in Arabic.'

'Right,' Barbara said. 'The point's duly noted. Just do your best.'

'The passage refers to one's duty to go to the aid of those who are in need of help,' Azhar said. 'Roughly, it reads, "How should you not fight for the cause of Allah and of the feeble among men and of the women and the children who are crying: Our Lord! Bring us forth from out this town of which the people are oppressors! Oh, give us from thy Presence some protecting friend!"'

'Ah,' Barbara said wryly. 'Roughly, as you say. Is there more?'

'Naturally,' Azhar said with delicate irony. 'But only this passage is marked in pencil.'

'I think it's clear enough why Haytham marked it,' Muhannad noted.

'Is it?' Barbara drew in on her cigarette and examined him. He'd pushed his chair back as his cousin was reading. His face wore the look of a person who'd had his suspicions confirmed.

'Sergeant, if you'd ever sat on this side of the table, you'd know that it is,' Muhannad said. '"Bring us forth from out this town of which the people are oppressors!" There you have it.'

'I did hear the translation.'

'Did you? Then let me ask you this: What more do you need? A message written in Haytham's blood?' He dropped his pencil on the table. He got to his feet and went to the window. When he next spoke, he gestured to the street and – metaphorically, it seemed – to the town beyond it. 'Haytham had been here long enough to experience what he'd never had to experience before: the smart of racism. How d'you think he felt?'

'We haven't the slightest indication that Mr Querashi –'

'Wear my skin for a day if you want an indication. Haytham was brown. And being brown means being unwelcome in this country. Haytham would have liked to catch the first flight back to Karachi, but he couldn't because he'd made a commitment to my family that he intended to honour. So he read the Qur'aan looking for an answer, and he saw it written that he could fight in the cause of his own protection. And that's what he did. And that's how he died.'

'Not exactly,' Barbara said. 'Mr Querashi's neck was broken. That's how he died. There's no indication that he was doing any fighting at all, I'm afraid.'

Muhanned turned to his cousin and gestured with his fist. 'I *told* you, Azhar. They were holding back on us all along.'

Azhar's hands were on the table. He pressed the tips of his fingers together. 'Why weren't we informed at once?' he asked.

'Because the post-mortem hadn't yet been performed,' Barbara answered. 'And no information's ever released in advance of the p.-m. That's how it's done.'

Muhannad looked incredulous. 'You can't sit there and tell us that you didn't know the moment you saw the body –'

'How exactly did the death occur?' Azhar asked with a quieting glance at his cousin. 'One's neck can break in a number of ways.'

'We're not clear on that point.' Barbara adhered to the police line that Emily Barlow had already drawn. 'But we're able to say with a fair degree of certainty that we're looking at a murder. Premeditated murder.'

Muhannad dropped into his seat. He said, 'A broken neck is an act of violence: the result of a brawl, a product of anger and rage and hated. A broken neck isn't something that someone can plan in advance.'

'I wouldn't actually disagree with that under normal circumstances,' Barbara said.

'Then –'

'But in this case, the circumstances indicate that someone knew Querashi would be on the Nez, and this someone got there before him and set events into motion that culminated in his death. That's premeditated murder, Mr Malik. No matter how you might like to think otherwise of Haytham Querashi's death, it wasn't a random killing arising from a racial brawl or incident.'

'What d'you know of racial incidents? What can you tell us of how they start? Do you know the look on a western face that tells a man to change direction when he's walking down the street, to lower his eyes when he pushes a handful of coins across the counter to pay for his newspaper, to ignore the stares of other patrons when he walks into a restaurant and finds himself the only brown face in the room?'

'Cousin,' Azhar said. 'This takes us nowhere productive.'

'Oh, yes it does,' Muhannad insisted. 'How can a white-skinned CID investigate the death of a man whose experience they can't even begin to understand? These people's minds are closed, Azhar. We'll only get justice if we open them.'

'Is that the purpose of *Jum'a*?' Barbara asked.

'The purpose of *Jum'a* isn't under discussion. Haytham's death is.'

'Was he a member of *Jum'a*?'

'You won't rest till you pin this on an Asian. That's where you're heading.'

'Just answer the question.'

'No, he wasn't a member of *Jum'a*. If you suspect that I murdered him over that fact, then arrest me.'

The expression on his face – so taut, so filled with anger and loathing – caused Barbara to reflect briefly on the child Ghassan whom she'd seen on the street, with the bottle-tossed urine dripping down his legs. Was it incidents like that, repeated throughout childhood and adolescence, that effected the sort of animosity she felt rolling off Muhannad Malik? He was right in so many ways, she thought. But he was wrong in so many others.

'Mr Malik,' she finally said, setting her cigarette on the edge of an ashtray at her elbow, 'I'd like to make something clear to you before we go on: just because a person's born with white skin, it doesn't follow that she spends the rest of her life attempting to prise a silver spoon from her mouth.' She didn't wait for a response. She went on to delineate the course that the investigation was taking at the moment: a safe-deposit box key found among the dead man's belongings was in the process of being traced to one of the banks in Balford or in surrounding towns; the Friday night whereabouts of everyone connected with Querashi were being sought and corroborated; paperwork found among Querashi's belongings was being sorted out; and Fahd Kumhar was being tracked down.

'You have his first name, then,' Azhar noted. 'May we know how you obtained it?'

'A piece of luck,' Barbara said.

'Because you have the name or because it's Asian?' Muhannad asked.

Jesus. Give it a rest, Barbara wanted to say. But what she did say was, 'Give us some credit, Mr Malik. We don't have time to waste tracking down some bloke just to satisfy our need to cause him aggro. We need to talk to him about his relationship to Mr Querashi.'

'Is he a suspect?' Azhar asked.

'Everyone who knew Querashi is under scrutiny. If this bloke knew him, consider him a suspect.'

'Haytham knew English people as well,' Azhar said, and he added in so bland a manner that Barbara knew he was already well aware of the answer, 'did anyone English benefit from his death?'

Barbara wasn't about to start walking on that wafer-like patch of ice with Azhar or anyone else. She said, 'Guys, can we lift our meetings out of the realm of Asian/English questions? What we're dealing with in this investigation isn't an Asian/English question at all. It's a straightforward guilt/innocence question. We're looking for a killer no matter the skin colour: a man or woman with a reason to do away with someone.'

'A woman?' Azhar asked. 'You aren't saying a woman could have broken his neck, are you?'

'I'm saying a woman may be involved.'

'Are you trying to implicate my sister?' Muhannad asked.

'I didn't say that.'

'But what other women are there? Those at the factory?'

'We're not sure, so we aren't closing any doors. If Mr Querashi knew Fahd Kumhar – a man clearly not from the factory, right? – it stands to reason he may well have known a woman not connected to the factory as well.'

'What are you doing to find this woman?' Azhar asked.

'Asking questions, following leads, looking for connections, digging out any altercations Querashi may have had with anyone in the weeks leading up to his murder. It's legwork, it's plodwork, and it has to be done.' She gathered her folders and placed the copy of the Qur'aan on top of them. Her cigarette had burned out in the ashtray, but she squashed its remains anyway as unspoken communication that their meeting was at an end. She stood, saying with deliberate politeness to Muhannad Malik, 'I expect you'll communicate all of this to your people. We don't want any misinformation to stir them up when it isn't necessary.'

It was clear that he read her meaning: if any sort of misinformation was leaked into the Asian community, it would only be coming from a single source. Muhannad stood also, and it appeared to Barbara that he used his height – at least eight inches over hers – to illustrate the fact that if intimidation was going to be a feature of their meetings, he would be doing the intimidating.

He said, 'If you're seeking Asian suspects, Sergeant, know that we intend to get to them first. Male or female, child or adult. We don't mean to allow you to interview any Pakistani without legal representation – Asian legal representation – present.'

Barbara regarded him long and hard before she replied. He needed to end their meeting in the one-up position, and she half wanted to let him get away with it. But that was the half of her that was tired and hot, eager to have a shower and a decent meal. The half of her that knew the importance of winning the first round of a pissing contest was the half that spoke. 'I can't tie your hands at the moment, Mr Malik. But if you muddy our waters by meddling where you don't belong, I must tell you that you're going to find yourself in the nick for obstructing a police investigation.' She nodded at the doorway and added, 'Can you find your way out?'

Muhannad's eyes narrowed fractionally. 'A good question,' he replied. 'You might want to answer it yourself, Sergeant.'

Emily was standing to one side of the Chinagraph board when Barbara joined the afternoon meeting of the CID team in the incident room. This was her first glimpse of the detectives manning the investigation, and she ran her gaze over them curiously. Fourteen men and three women, they were jammed into what had probably once been the first-floor drawing room of the old house. Some rested their bums on the edges of tables, arms crossed and ties loosened. Others sat on plastic chairs. Some of them gave their attention to Barbara as she entered, but the rest kept their focus on the DCI.

Emily stood with her weight on one leg, the Chinagraph marking pen in one hand and a bottle of Evian in the other. Like everyone else in the stifling room, she was glistening with perspiration.

'Ah,' she said, with a nod at Barbara. 'This is DS Havers joining us now. We'll have her and Scotland Yard to thank if the Pakistanis start toeing the line. Which finally lets the rest of us get going on a decent investigation.'

All eyes shifted towards Barbara. She tried to read them. At least four of the men looked like the sort of longtime detectives who had a fondness for bouts of harassment whenever joined by a female colleague. They stared. She felt lumpy. Emily spoke.

'Have a problem with this, mates?'

Point taken, they turned back to her.

The DCI said with a glance at the board, 'Right. To continue. Who's got the hospital run?'

'Nothing we can use,' came a response from a crane-like bloke near the window. 'An Asian woman died in Clacton last week, but she was seventy-five and it was heart failure. No one's been admitted to casualty with anything looking like a botched abortion. I've checked every local hospital, clinic, and doctor's surgery as well. Nothing.'

'If he's a ginger like you said, that's a blind alley anyway, i'n't it, Guv?' The question came from an older bloke who needed a shave and a new anti-perspirant. Rings of damp descended from his armpits nearly to his waist.

'It's too early to label anything useless,' Emily said. 'Until we have solid facts, we check out everything as if it's the gospel. Phil, what more do you have on the Nez?'

Phil removed a toothpick from his mouth. 'I had a second go at the houses backing on to it.' He gave a glance to a small blackbound notebook. 'Couple called the Sampsons were having themselves a night out, with a babysitter looking after their kids. Babysitter – girl called Lucy Angus – had her boyfriend there for a bit of a snog, but when I tracked her down and gave her memory a jangle, she recalled hearing a motor on Friday night round half-ten.'

There were some positive murmurs at this. Over them, Emily said, 'How legitimate is this? What sort of memory jangling are we talking about?'

'Didn't hypnotise her, if that's what you mean,' Phil said with a grin. 'She'd gone to the kitchen for a drink of water –'

'Guess we know how she worked up a thirst,' someone called out.

'Shut it.' Emily's order was brusque. 'Phil? Go on.'

'She heard a motor. She remembers the time because whoever was out there gunned the hell out of it and she looked outside but didn't see anything. Someone was running without lights, she said.'

'A boat?' Emily asked.

'From the direction of the noise, yeah. She says it was probably a boat.'

'Get on this, then,' Emily said. 'Check the marina, check every harbour from Harwich to Clacton, check the boat hires, and get inside the garage, the shed, the lock-up, and the back garden of everyone even remotely connected to Querashi. If someone took a boat out that night, someone else had to have seen it, heard it, or documented it. Frank, what've you got on that key from Querashi's room?'

'It was Barclays,' he said. 'All the way over in Clacton. The time lock was already running when I got there, so I'll have the goods in the morning directly they open.'

'Right,' Emily said. 'So here's where we head,' and she went on without pause, assigning the detectives to their activities for the next day. Foremost among the tasks was the effort to locate Fahd Kumhar. 'I want this bloke found,' Emily told them, 'and I want him found bloody fast before he has a chance to do a runner. Understand?'

Second among the tasks was the effort to break Muhannad's alibi, and there were several murmurs of surprise when Emily introduced the idea. But she was unmoved by them. She assigned a DC called Doug Trotter the task of sorting through Rakin Khan's neighbours for anyone who could swear to the fact that the Asian man was with someone other than Muhannad Malik on Friday night.

Barbara watched her. Directing a team like this was clearly nothing to Emily. She had an unflappable confidence that spoke volumes as to how she'd attained her position while so young. Barbara thought of her own performance on her last case; she cringed at the contrast between herself and the DCI.

After fielding questions and listening to suggestions, Emily ended the meeting. As the detectives dispersed, she took a hefty swig of her water and came to join Barbara.

'Well?' she said. 'The Asians. How did it go?'

'Muhannad's not threatening anything at the moment, but he's not backing off the racial bit.'

'He's been singing that song as long as I've known him.'

'I'm wondering, though,' Barbara said. 'Could he be right?' She told Emily of the incident with the two children which she'd witnessed near the pier that afternoon.

'Not bloody likely,' Emily said when she'd finished. 'Not with a trip wire, Barb.'

'I don't mean that it's an arbitrary killing based on race,' Barbara said. 'I mean, couldn't race actually be behind it, even if the killing was premeditated? Couldn't culture be behind it? Cultural differences and all the misunderstandings that come from cultural differences?'

Emily appeared to consider this, her attention on the Chinagraph board but her eyes not actually focused on its lists and data. 'Who're you looking at, then?'

'Theo Shaw can't be wearing that gold bracelet for nothing. He had to have a relationship with the Malik girl. If that's the case, how would he feel about her marrying? It's a cultural deal, the arranged marriage bit. But would he be likely to back out of the picture just because he's told to exit stage left? And what about Armstrong? His job went to another bloke. Why? Because it's the done thing: keeping positions in the family. But if he didn't deserve to be given the sack, wouldn't he want to do something to put things right?'

'Armstrong's alibi checks out solidly. The in-laws confirm. I spoke to them myself.'

'Okay, but aren't they likely to confirm, no matter what the truth? He's married to their daughter. He's the breadwinner. Are they going to say something that might put their own kid out on the streets?'

'A confirmation is a confirmation,' Emily said.

'But it isn't in the case of Muhannad,' Barbara protested. 'He's got an alibi as well, and you aren't buying it. Right?'

'So am I supposed to put Armstrong's in-laws on the rack?' Emily sounded impatient.

'They're relatives. That makes their confirmation weak. Muhannad's not related to this bloke Rakin Khan, is he? So why are you supposing that Khan would lie? What's his motive?'

'They stick together. It's part of who they are.'

But there was a patent lack of logic to that. 'If they stick together, then why would one of them kill another?'

Emily drained her bottle of water. She shot the empty towards a wastepaper basket.

'Em?' Barbara said when she didn't respond. 'That doesn't really follow. Either they stick together – which means it's unlikely that a fellow Asian offed Querashi – or they don't stick together – in which case, it doesn't make sense that Khan would lie for Muhannad Malik. You can't have it both ways. It seems to me –'

'This is gut,' Emily interrupted. 'This is instinct. This is a basic feeling that something stinks and I've got to track it down. If the trail goes into the Asian community, I can't help that, all right?'

There was no question of its being all right. Emily was, after all, directing the entire investigation. But Barbara felt a sense of disquiet with the entire idea of instinct. She'd been on cases before where *instinct* turned out to be just another word for something else.

'I s'pose,' she said uneasily. 'You're the guv.'

Emily glanced her way. 'That's right,' she said.

Chapter Thirteen

Rachel Winfield didn't walk directly on to the pleasure pier. Instead, she paused at its land end. She stood between the Pier End Hotel, whose windows and doors were boarded against the sea, and the row of kiddie-car rides that flagged each side of the pier's entrance. It was dinner time, so a lull had come in the day's activities. Rides still ran and the beeps and blasts of noise from the arcade games still drowned out the cries of gulls, but the time of day had reduced the number of pleasure seekers and the ringing of bells and the bleeping of horns from fruit machines, pinball machines, and other games of chance were intermittent now.

Thus, it was the perfect time to talk to Theo Shaw.

He was still on the pier. Rachel knew that from the sight of his BMW, parked in its usual spot just beyond the Lobster Hut, a tiny yellow-and-green striped cabin beyond the abandoned hotel that had never sold lobster and probably never would. She stared at the cabin's handpainted sign – *Burgers, Hot Dogs, Popcorn, Doughnuts* – and while she watched an elderly couple make a purchase of popcorn, she chewed on her lip and tried to consider all the ramifications of what she was about to do.

She had to talk to him. Theo may have made his mistakes in life – and certainly not leaping immediately to Sahlah's rescue upon the death of Haytham Querashi was one of them – but he was not a bad person at heart. Rachel knew that he would make things right in the end. After all, that's what people did when they were in love.

True, it hadn't been wise of Sahlah to keep the news of her pregnancy from Theo. And it had been even less wise to agree to a marriage to one man while she was carrying another man's baby. Theo could do his maths as well as anyone, and if Sahlah *had* married Haytham Querashi and produced a child – supposedly by that marriage – in less than eight or nine months . . . Well, Theo would have known the child wasn't Haytham's, and what would he have done then?

Of course, the real question was what had he done three days ago, on Friday night, out on the Nez? But this was a question that Rachel didn't want to answer and could only pray the police didn't ask.

This is all about love, she told herself stoutly. This isn't about hate and killing. If Theo had done something to hurt Haytham – which she didn't for a moment actually *believe* – then doubtless Haytham had provoked him to do it. Accusations might have been hurled. Nasty comments might have been made. And then all in a terrible instant, a blow might have been struck in anger, a blow from which this terrible situation that Sahlah was in had grown.

Rachel couldn't bear the thought of Sahlah submitting herself to an abortion. She knew it was the anguish of the moment that was propelling her friend in this direction anyway. Because Haytham was dead and it appeared to Sahlah that no other immediate solution to her troubles was available, she wanted to take a course of action that Rachel knew quite well she would live to regret.

Girls like Sahlah – sensitive, creative, protected from life, completely gentle and without guile – didn't get over abortions as easily as they thought they would. And they especially didn't get over abortions of babies whose fathers they obviously adored. So Sahlah was mad to think that ending the pregnancy was the only option she had. And Rachel was set upon proving that to her.

What harm could really come from Sahlah's ending up in a marriage with Theo Shaw? It was true that her parents might be peeved for a while when they discovered she'd run off with an Englishman. They might not want to speak to her for a few months, even. But when the baby was born – their own grandchild, the son or daughter of their own beloved child – then all would be forgiven; the family would reunite.

But the only way that any of this could happen was if Rachel warned Theo that the police might try to tie him to Haytham Querashi's murder. The only way that this could happen was if he got rid of that damning bracelet before the police connected it to him.

So her path was clear. She had to warn him. And she had to nudge him, however delicately, towards doing what was right by her friend and doing it before another day passed. Not that Theo Shaw would *need* nudging, of course. He may have been hesitating over the last few days because of what had happened to Haytham, but he'd be determined to do his duty once he learned that the clock was ticking on an upcoming abortion.

But still Rachel hesitated. What if Theo failed Sahlah? What if he didn't do what was right? Men often ran the other way when responsibilities cluttered their paths, and who was honestly and absolutely able to say that Theo Shaw wouldn't do the same? Clearly, Sahlah believed he'd abandon her, or she would have told him about the baby in the first place. Wouldn't she?

Well, Rachel thought stoutly, if Theodore Shaw didn't take up the burden of his obligations to Sahlah, Rachel Winfield would step in. That last flat of the Clifftop Snuggeries still remained to be sold, and Rachel's savings account still contained the money to put down towards a purchase. So if Theo didn't behave the way he ought to behave, if Sahlah's parents disowned her as a result, Rachel herself would provide a home for her friend. And together they would raise Theo's child.

But that probably wouldn't happen, would it? Once he learned about Sahlah's intention to be rid of their child, Theo Shaw would act decisively.

With all the ramifications explored, Rachel turned from the Lobster Hut and set off down the pier. She didn't have far to go, however. Just inside the arcade, she saw Theo Shaw talking to Rosalie the Romany Palm Reader.

This was definitely a positive sign, Rachel decided. Despite the fact that their conversation didn't actually look like a psychic consultation – since instead of his palm, the tarot cards, or a crystal ball, Rosalie appeared to be doing her reading from a piece of pizza in a plate on her lap – there was still the chance that between bites of pepperoni, Rosalie was giving Theo the benefit of her experience in dealing with the problems of her fellow men.

So Rachel waited until their discussion was at an end. When Theo nodded, rose, touched Rosalie's shoulder, and began to come in her direction, Rachel drew a breath and straightened her shoulders. She adjusted her hair to cover as much of her face as she could do, and she walked to meet him. He was wearing that gold bracelet, she saw with some concern. Well, he wouldn't be wearing it for much longer.

'I got to talk to you,' she said without preamble. 'It's real important, Theo.'

Theo looked at the colourful clown-face clock that was mounted above the arcade's doors. Rachel was afraid that he was going to say he had to be somewhere, so she went hurriedly on.

'It's about Sahlah.'

'Sahlah?' His voice was careful, non-committal.

'I know about the two of you. Sahlah and I don't have any secrets. We're best friends, you know. Been best friends since we were little.'

'Did she send you to me?'

Rachel was glad to hear that he sounded eager, and she interpreted this as another positive sign. Clearly, he wanted to be with her friend. And if that was so, Rachel knew her job was going to be easier than she'd anticipated.

'Not exactly.' Rachel looked around. It wouldn't do for them to be seen together, especially if the police were lurking nearby. She was already in enough trouble as it was, what with lying to the woman detective that morning and then doing a bunk from the shop. Her position would only worsen if she was caught talking to Theo while he had that gold bracelet on his wrist. 'C'n we talk somewhere? I mean, somewheres not so out in the open? It's real important.'

Theo's eyebrows drew together, but he cooperated well enough, gesturing towards the side of the Lobster Hut and the BMW parked near it. Rachel trailed him to the car, keeping a nervous eye towards the Marine Parade, half in the expectation that – her luck being what it was: rotten – she stood a fair to even chance of being seen by someone before they got to safety.

But that didn't happen. Theo disarmed the car's security system and slipped inside, unlocking the passenger door for her. She glanced about and then slid in, wincing as the hot upholstery singed her flesh.

Theo lowered the windows. He turned in his seat. 'What is it?'

'You got to get rid of that bracelet,' Rachel blurted out. 'The police know Sahlah bought it for you.'

He kept his eyes on her, but his right hand reached for his left wrist and, as if unconsciously, encircled the gold band. 'What do you have to do with all this?'

It was the one question she'd have preferred not to hear. She'd rather have had him say, 'Bloody hell. Absolutely,' and remove the bracelet without asking anything at all. It wouldn't have been at all disagreeable had he tossed the bracelet into the nearest rubbish bin, which was ten feet away and buzzing with flies.

'Rachel?' he prompted when she didn't reply. 'What do you have to do with this? Did Sahlah send you?'

'That's the second time you asked me that.' Even to her own ears, Rachel's voice sounded weak. 'You're thinking of her all the time, aren't you?'

'What's going on? The police have already been here, by the way, some heavyset woman with a roughed-up face. She had the bracelet off me for a look.'

'You didn't give it to her, Theo!'

'What else could I do? I didn't know why she wanted it till she'd already had a good look at it and told me she was searching for a similar one that Sahlah claimed to have thrown from the pier.'

'Oh, no,' Rachel whispered.

'But the way I see it, she can't know they're one and the same,' Theo went on. 'Anyone can own a gold bracelet. She can't prove anything by the fact that I have one.'

'But she knows,' Rachel said miserably. 'What's written inside it. She knows. And if she saw the engraving inside yours . . .' She saw that there was still a margin of hope, and she went on eagerly, 'Except maybe she didn't look inside the band?'

But Theo's expression told her that the Scotland Yard detective had done just that, reading those incriminating words and adding them to the information she'd already gleaned, first from Rachel and then from Sahlah. 'I should've phoned,' Rachel moaned. 'You and Sahlah. I should've phoned. Only I couldn't because Mum was there and she wanted to know what was going on and I had to get out of the shop directly the policewoman left.'

Theo had half turned in his seat to face her, but now he looked away to the Pier Approach: that concrete promenade that ran along the strand and separated it from the three rows of beach huts that climbed the hill. He didn't appear as panicked as Rachel had suspected he might be, all things considered. He looked confused.

He said, 'I don't understand how they traced it so quickly to me. Sahlah wouldn't have . . .' Then he turned back to her and his voice sounded eager once again, as if he'd drawn a conclusion that painted a picture he'd long hoped to see. 'Did Sahlah tell them she gave it to me? But no, she couldn't have if she told them she threw it off the pier. So how . . . ?'

There was only one way, of course, and he appeared to work that out soon enough, because he said, 'That police detective talked to you? How did she end up talking to you?'

'Because . . .' How could she describe her actions in a way that he would understand when she didn't really understand them herself? Oh, Sahlah had her own interpretation of what Rachel had meant in giving the jewellery receipt to Haytham, but Sahlah wasn't right. Rachel had meant no harm. She'd meant only the best: Haytham questioning his fiancée the way any man might and the truth about Sahlah's love for Theo coming out as a result; Sahlah being saved from a marriage that she didn't want; and Sahlah being free to marry where she chose, whom she chose, when she chose. Or if that was her choice, Sahlah not marrying at all. 'Haytham had the receipt,' Rachel said. 'The police found it with his belongings. They're tracking down everything connected with him. So they came to the shop and asked about it.'

If anything, Theo looked more confused than ever. 'But why would Sahlah have given him the receipt? That doesn't make sense unless she'd changed her mind about marrying him. Because no one else knew . . .' But then he saw and she could see that he saw. He sharpened his gaze on her.

Sweat trickled from Rachel's temples, following her hairline and the curve of her jaw. 'What does it matter how he got it?' she said quickly. 'She may have lost it on the street. She may have left it lying round somewheres at home. Yumn may have picked it up. Yumn hates Sahlah. You got to know that. And if she found that receipt, you c'n be sure she'd have gave it to Haytham straightaway. She likes to cause trouble, Yumn does. She's a real witch.' And the more Rachel thought about it, the more she was able to convince herself that this fabrication was well suited to her purpose. Yumn wanted to keep Sahlah as her personal slave. She'd have done just about anything to make sure her sister-in-law had no chance of marriage so she'd remain at home, under Yumn's thumb. Had she actually got her hands on that receipt, she would have turned it over to Haytham at once. There was no doubt in the world about that. 'Theo, what matters is what happens now.'

'So Haytham *knew* that Sahlah and I . . .' Theo had moved his gaze off Rachel, so there was nothing she could read in his eyes to explain why he sounded so thoughtful. But she could imagine well enough. If Haytham knew that Sahlah and Theo were lovers, then Haytham hadn't been on an information-fishing expedition on that fateful night at the Nez. Haytham knew. And that's why he'd asked Theo for a meeting and that's why he was so quick to accuse because it wasn't an accusation at all, it was the truth.

'Forget about Haytham,' Rachel said, words tumbling out to direct him where she wanted him to go. 'Okay, it's done. It happened. What's important now is Sahlah. Theo, listen to me. Sahlah's in a bad way. I know you probably think that she didn't do right by you in agreeing to marry Haytham, but maybe she agreed so fast because she thought you didn't mean to do right by her. This sort of stuff happens when people love each other. One person says one thing and it gets misunderstood and the other person says another thing and *it* gets misunderstood, and before you know it, no one knows what anyone else really means or thinks or feels any longer. People get themselves in a real twist. They make decisions they might not otherwise make. You see that, don't you?'

'What's going on with Sahlah?' he asked. 'I phoned her last night but she wouldn't listen to anything. I tried to explain –'

'She wants an abortion,' Rachel cut in. 'Theo, she's asked me to help her: to find out where she can have it and get her away from her family long enough for it to be done. She wants it as soon as possible, because she knows it'll take her father months to find her someone else to marry, and by that time it'll be too late.'

Rachel saw that she'd cleared from his mind all thought of the gold bracelet and its pernicious receipt. His hand shot out and grabbed her wrist. 'What?' he asked. The question was hoarse.

Thank God, Rachel thought, and she told herself that she meant it, truly. Theo Shaw did care. 'She thinks her mum and dad will disown her if they find out about the baby, Theo. And Sahlah doesn't think that you'll marry her. And she knows there's no hope of finding someone else fast. And she can't hide the truth forever. So she asked me to find a doctor or a clinic or whatever. And it's no trouble to do that, but I don't want to because if she goes through with it . . . Theo, can you imagine what it'll do to Sahlah? She loves you. So how can she kill your baby?'

He released her wrist. He turned his head and stared before them, into the rock wall that retained the hillside above which rose the town where Sahlah waited for Theo Shaw to decide her fate.

'You got to go to her,' Rachel said. 'You got to talk to her. You got to make her see that it's not the end of the world if you and she go off somewhere and get married. Sure, her mum and dad won't like it at first. But this isn't the middle ages. In modern times, people marry for love, they don't marry for duty or for anything else. I mean, they *do*, but the real marriages and the lasting marriages are the ones that grow out of love.'

He nodded, but she couldn't tell if he actually heard. He'd placed his hands on the BMW's steering wheel and they'd circled the wheel so tightly that his knuckles looked like they'd pop through his lightly freckled skin. A muscle worked spasmodically in his jaw.

'You got to do something,' Rachel told him. 'You're the only one who can.'

Theo made no reply. Instead, he moved his arm to curve it round his stomach, and before Rachel had a chance to tell him that he had only to claim Sahlah's hand in order to save the life of their child, he was out of the car. He stumbled over to the rubbish bin. There he vomited violently and for so long that Rachel thought he was close to losing his entire insides.

When the fetching passed, he drew a fist across his mouth. His gold bracelet caught the bright hot afternoon light. He didn't return to the car, however. Rather, he stood at the rubbish bin, chest heaving like a runner and head bent low.

Heaving wasn't an unreasonable reaction, Rachel decided. In fact, it was rather an admirable response to a piece of horrific news. Theo no more wanted Sahlah to submit herself to the surgeon's scalpel – or whatever it was they used to prise unwanted foetuses out of their mothers' bodies – than Rachel did.

Relief came over her like the cool water she'd been longing for since she'd left the shop. True, she'd done wrong by giving Haytham Querashi that receipt for the bracelet, but it had all come out right in the end: Theo and Sahlah would be together.

She began to plan her next encounter with Sahlah. She thought of the words she'd use to relate what had just passed between herself and Theo. She'd even got as far as imagining the look on her best friend's face as she heard the news that Theo would be coming for her, when Theo himself turned round from the rubbish bin and Rachel had a better look at his expression. Her bones felt liquid at the sight of him and what that sight meant.

His pinched features radiated the misery of a man who saw himself irrevocably trapped. And as he walked heavily back to the car, Rachel understood that he'd never intended to marry her friend. He was exactly like so many of the men Connie Winfield had dragged home over the years, men who spent the night in her bed, the morning at her breakfast table, and the afternoon or evening in their cars, fleeing the previously amorous scene like hooligans on the run from a petty crime.

'Oh, no.' Rachel's lips formed the words, but she emitted no sound. She saw it all: how he'd used her friend like a typical man as a casual and easy mark for sex, seducing her with a kind of attention and admiration that she couldn't hope to get from an Asian man, biding his time until she was ready for a physical approach. And that approach would have been subtle, no move made until he was certain that Sahlah was completely in love with him. She had to be ready. More, she had to be willing. If she was both, then the responsibility for anything untoward that happened as a result of the pleasure Theo Shaw took from Sahlah Malik would be Sahlah's alone.

And Sahlah herself had known this all along.

Rachel felt the animosity rising like a stream of bubbles escaping from her chest to her throat. What had happened to her friend was so bloody unjust. Sahlah was good, and she deserved someone equally good. That person obviously wasn't Theo Shaw.

Theo slid inside the car once more. Rachel opened her door.

'Well, Theo,' she said, making no attempt to hide the contempt in her voice, 'is there any message you want me to pass along to Sahlah?'

His answer came as no surprise but she'd wanted to hear it, just to make certain he was as low as she'd decided he was.

'No,' he said.

Barbara stepped back from the mirror in her 'loo with a view', and admired her handiwork. She'd stopped at Boots on her way back to the Burnt House and twenty minutes in the single aisle that went for a make-up department had been enough for her to purchase a bagful of cosmetics. She'd been aided by a youthful shop assistant whose face was a living, breathing testimony to her enthusiasm for painting her features. 'Super!' she'd cried when Barbara had asked for some guidance on the appropriate brands and colours. 'You're spring, aren't you?' she'd added obscurely as she'd begun piling a variety of mysterious bottles, cases, jars, and brushes into a basket.

The shop assistant had offered to 'do' Barbara right there in Boots, giving her the benefit of talents that appeared questionable at best. Evaluating the girl's yellow eye shadow and magenta cheeks, Barbara had demurred. She needed the practice anyway, she explained. There was no time like the present to get her toes damp by dipping them into the waters of cosmetic improvement.

Well, she thought as she observed her face now. She wouldn't exactly be finding herself on the cover of *Vogue* in the foreseeable future. Nor would she be selected as a sterling example of a woman's triumph over a broken nose, a bruised face, and an unfortunate set of features that could most mercifully be described as snubby. But for the moment, she would do. Especially in dim lighting or among people whose vision had recently begun to fail them.

She took a moment to shove her supplies into the medicine cabinet. Then she scooped up her shoulder bag and left the room.

She was hungry, but dinner was going to have to wait indefinitely. Through the windows of the hotel bar upon her arrival, she'd seen Taymullah Azhar and his daughter on the lawn, and she wanted to talk to them – or at least to one of them – before they got away.

She descended the stairs and crossed the passage to cut through the bar. Since he was well occupied with seeing to the needs of his resident diners, Basil Treves would not be able to waylay her. He'd waved at her meaningfully upon seeing her enter the hotel earlier. He'd gone so far as to mouth, 'We must talk,' and to waggle his eyebrows in a fashion that related he had something of a momentous nature to impart. But he'd been in the process of ferrying dishes to the dining room, and when he'd mouthed 'Later' and tilted his shoulders to indicate he was asking a question, she'd made much of giving him a vigorous thumbs-up to keep lubricated the machinery of his fragile ego. The man was unsavoury, beyond a doubt. But he had his uses. After all, he'd been responsible for unknowingly handing them Fahd Kumhar. God alone knew what other jewels he would manage to mine, given half a chance and equal encouragement. But at the moment she wanted to talk to Azhar, so she was just as happy to see that Treves was unavailable.

She ducked into the bar and crossed to the french windows, which were wide open to the dusk. There she hesitated for a moment.

Azhar and his daughter were sitting just outside on the flagstone terrace, the child hunched over a spotty wrought-iron table on which a chess board was set up, the father leaning back in his chair with a cigarette dangling from his fingers. A smile played round the corners of his mouth as he watched Hadiyyah. Obviously unaware that he was being observed, he allowed his features to take on a softness that Barbara had never seen in them before.

'How much time do you want, *khushi*?' he asked. 'I believe that

I have you trapped, and you're only prolonging your king's death throes.'

'I'm *thinking*, Dad.' Hadiyyah squirmed to a new position on her seat, rising on her knees with her elbows on the table and her bottom in the air. She made a closer scrutiny of the battlefield. Her fingers drifted first towards a knight, then towards the single remaining castle. Her queen had already been taken, Barbara noted, and she was attempting to mount an attack against far superior forces. She began to slide the castle forward.

Her father said, 'Ah,' in anticipation.

She withdrew her fingers. 'Changed my mind,' she announced hastily. 'Changed my mind, changed my mind.'

'Hadiyyah.' Her father drew her name out in affectionate impatience. 'When you make a decision, you must adhere to it.'

'Sounds just like life,' Barbara said. She stepped out of the bar to join them.

'Barbara!' Hadiyyah's little body rose on her chair till she was kneeling upright. 'You're here! I kept watching and watching for you at dinner. I had to eat with Mrs Porter 'cause Dad wasn't here, and I wished and wished that she was you. What've you done to your face?' Her own face screwed up then brightened as she realised. 'You've painted it! You've covered your bruises. You look quite nice. Doesn't Barbara look quite nice, Dad?'

Azhar had risen, and he nodded politely. When Hadiyyah chanted, 'Sit, sit, please sit,' he fetched a third chair so that Barbara could join them. He offered his cigarettes and lit hers wordlessly when she took one.

'Mummy uses make-up as well,' Hadiyyah confided chattily as Barbara settled in. 'She's going to teach me how to do it properly when I'm old enough. She makes her eyes the prettiest of prettiest that you've ever seen. They're big as anything when she's done. 'Course, they're big anyway, Mummy's eyes. She's got the loveliest eyes, hasn't she, Dad?'

'She has,' Azhar said, his own eyes on his daughter.

Barbara wondered what he saw when he gazed upon her. Her mother? Himself? A living declaration of their love for each other? She couldn't know and she doubted he'd say. So she gave her attention to the chess board.

'Dire straits,' she said as she studied the meagre collection of pieces with which Hadiyyah was attempting to wage war on her father. 'Looks like white flag time to me, kiddo.'

'Oh, pooh,' Hadiyyah said happily. 'We don't want to finish now anyway. We'd rather talk to you.' She adjusted her position so that she was sitting, and she swung her sandal-shod feet against the legs of the chair. 'I did a puzzle today with Mrs Porter. A jigsaw of Snow White. She was asleep and the prince was kissing her and the dwarfs were crying 'cause they thought she was dead. 'Course she didn't *look* dead and if they only thought about why her cheeks were so rosy, they could've worked it out for themselves that she was only sleeping. But they didn't and they didn't know that all she needed was a kiss to wake up. But since they *didn't* know, she met a real prince and they lived happily ever after.'

'A conclusion to which we all fervently aspire,' Barbara said.

'And we painted as well. Mrs Porter used to do watercolours and she's teaching me how. I did one of the sea and one of the pier and one of –'

'Hadiyyah,' her father said quietly.

Hadiyyah ducked her head and was silent.

'You know, I've got a real thing for watercolours,' Barbara told the little girl. 'I'd love to see them if you're up for that. Where've you got them stowed?'

Hadiyyah brightened. 'In our room. Shall I fetch them? I c'n fetch them easier than anything, Barbara.'

Barbara nodded and Azhar handed over the room key. Hadiyyah squirmed off her chair and dashed into the hotel, ribboned plaits flying. In a moment, they could hear her sandals clattering against the wooden stairs.

'Out for dinner this evening?' Barbara asked Azhar when they were alone.

'There were things to see to after our conference,' he replied. He dislodged ash from his cigarette and took a drink from a glass on the table. It held ice, lime, and something fizzy. Mineral water, she guessed. She couldn't see Azhar blithely swilling down gin and tonic, despite the heat. He replaced the glass exactly on the same ring of damp from which he'd taken it. Then he looked at her and with such intent scrutiny that she was certain she'd smeared her mascara. 'You acquitted yourself well,' he finally said. 'We gained something from the meeting, but not, I imagine, all that you know.'

And that's why he'd not returned directly to the hotel in time for dinner with his daughter, Barbara decided. He and his cousin had no doubt put their heads together for a discussion on their next move.

She wondered what that move would be: a meeting of the Asian community, another march in the streets, a request for intervention from their MP, an event designed to heighten media interest in the killing and the investigation once again? She didn't know and couldn't have said. But she had little doubt that he and Muhannad Malik had decided upon a course of action they'd take in the next few days.

'I need to pick your brains about Islam,' she told him.

'In exchange for . . . ?' he replied.

'Azhar, that can't be how we play the game. I can only tell you what DCI Barlow authorises me to tell you.'

'That's convenient for you.'

'No. That's how I stay involved in this case.' Barbara took a drag of her cigarette and considered how best to garner his cooperation. She said, 'And as I see the situation, it's to everyone's advantage that I stay involved. I don't live here. I have no axe to grind and no vested interest in proving or disproving anyone's guilt. If you blokes think that there's prejudice behind the investigation, then frankly, I'm your best bet of weeding it out.'

'And is there?' he asked.

'Bloody hell, I don't know. I've been here twenty-four hours, Azhar. I'd like to think I'm good, but I doubt I'm that good. So can we get on with it, you and I?'

He took time to think things over, and he seemed to be trying to read her face for the truth of what she'd said. 'You know how his neck was broken, though,' he finally said.

'Yeah. We know. But when you think about it, how else would we really be able to determine it was clear-cut murder?'

'And was it?'

'Know it.' She flicked ash on to the flagstones and drew in on her cigarette. She said, 'Homosexuality, Azhar. How does it sit with Islam?'

She could see that she'd taken him by surprise. When she'd told him she wanted to ask him about Islam, he'd no doubt concluded that whatever questions she had would be about arranged marriages, more of the same as she'd asked that morning. This was an entirely new direction, and he was clever enough to know how the question related to the investigation.

'Haytham Querashi?' he asked.

She shrugged. 'We have a statement that makes it possible, but only that. And the person who gave it has a good enough reason to want us heading off on a wild goose chase, so it may be nothing. But I need to know what sort of deal homosexuality is to Muslims, and I'd rather not have to send to London to find out.'

'One of the suspects made this statement,' Azhar said thoughtfully. 'Is this an English suspect?'

Barbara sighed, expelling a lungful of smoke. 'Azhar, can we give this symphony more than one note? What difference does it make if he's English or Asian? Do you lot want this murder solved no matter what? Or only if an Englishman did it? And the suspect *is* English, by the way. And he was turned over to us by someone else English. If the truth be told, we've got at least three possibilities, and all of them are English. Now, will you give it a rest and answer my flaming question?'

He smiled and crushed out his cigarette. 'Had you displayed this level of passion in our meeting today, Barbara, most of my cousin's trepidations would have been resolved. Why didn't you?'

'Because, frankly, I care sod bloody all about your cousin's trepidations. Even if I'd told him we had thirty English suspects, he'd hardly have believed me unless I'd given him their names. Am I right?'

'Admitted.' Azhar sipped his drink. Another time he managed to replace the glass on the same ring of condensation from which he'd taken it.

'So?' she said.

He waited a moment before answering. In the silence, Barbara heard Basil Treves ho-ho-hoing it at someone's joke. Azhar grimaced at the obviously false nature of the laughter. 'Homosexuality is expressly forbidden,' he said.

'So what happens if a bloke is homosexual?'

'It would be something that he would keep to himself.'

'Because?'

Azhar toyed with the queen he'd captured from his daughter, his dark fingers rolling the piece to the base of his thumb and back again. 'In openly practising homosexuality, he would be indicating that he no longer believed in Muslim ways. This is sacrilege. And for that – as well as for the homosexuality itself – he would be cut off from his family, from other Muslims as well.'

'So it follows,' Barbara said thoughtfully, 'that he'd want to keep this business quiet. Maybe he'd even want to get married and have a reasonable front, to deflect suspicion.'

'These are serious charges, Barbara. You must guard against denigrating the memory of a man like Haytham. In insulting him, you insult the family to which he was bound by contracted marriage.'

'I haven't "charged" anyone with anything,' Barbara said. 'But if someone opens up a field of enquiry, the police are bound to walk across it. That's our job. So what about the insult to the family if he *was* homosexual? He'd have been contracting himself to a marriage under false pretences, wouldn't he? And if a man does that to a family like the Maliks, what's the penalty?'

'Marriage is a contract between two families, not just between two individuals.'

'Jesus Christ, Azhar. You can't be telling me that Querashi's family would simply send over a different brother for Sahlah Malik to marry, like she was some fresh hot roll just waiting for a suitable sausage.'

Azhar smiled, it seemed, in spite of himself. 'Your defence of your sex is admirable, Sergeant.'

'Great. Thanks. So –'

He interrupted. 'But what I meant is this: Haytham's dissembling would have caused an irreparable breach between the two families. This breach – and the cause of it – would be known to the greater community as well.'

'So in addition to being cut off from his family, he would have done a job on their chances of emigrating, right? Because I expect that no one else would be hot to strike a marriage bargain with them, not after they'd palmed off spurious goods as the real thing. In a manner of speaking.'

'Correct,' Azhar said.

Finally, Barbara felt, they were making progress. 'So, he had a bucketful of reasons to keep the lid on if he was queer.'

'*If* he was,' Azhar acknowledged.

She stubbed out her cigarette, placing this new bit of knowledge into various positions in the puzzle of Querashi's murder, attempting to see where it best fitted. When she had a potential picture in her mind, she went on slowly. 'And if someone knew what he was hiding, knew it for certain because he'd seen Querashi in a situation where there was absolutely no mistaking what was going on ... and if that person got in contact with him and told him what he knew ... and if that same person made certain demands ...'

He said, 'Are you speaking of the person who suggested Haytham's homosexuality in the first place?'

Barbara noted his tone: simultaneously anxious and vindicated. She realised that her speculations were leading them both where he and his cousin ardently wished them to go. She burst his bubble. 'It's a rare Englishman who would know all the ramifications of a Muslim's homosexuality, Azhar. Especially all the ramifications of this particular Muslim's homosexuality.'

'Then you're saying an Asian knew.'

'I'm not *saying* anything.'

But by the way his eyes moved to and stayed on his glass, she saw that he was thinking. And his thoughts led him to the only Asian, aside from members of his own family, whom the police had mentioned in connection with Haytham Querashi. 'Kumhar,' he said. 'You think this man Fahd Kumhar played a part in Haytham's death.'

'You didn't hear that from me,' Barbara said.

'And you wouldn't have pulled that idea from nowhere,' he continued. 'Someone has told you of a relationship between Haytham and this man, yes?'

'Azhar –'

'Or something. Some*thing* has told you. And if you speak of demands being made under these circumstances, demands that Fahd Kumhar made of Haytham Querashi, you must be speaking of blackmail as well.'

'You're really getting ahead of yourself,' Barbara said. 'All I'm saying is that if one person saw Querashi doing a job where he wasn't employed, another person might have done the same. End of story.'

'And you think that other person is Fahd Kumhar,' Azhar concluded again.

'Look.' Barbara was feeling exasperated, partly because he'd read her so well and partly because his reading of her could lead to his muddying up the case by involving his cousin where his cousin wasn't wanted. 'What bloody difference does it make if it's Fahd Kumhar or the Queen of –'

'Here, here, here!' The sing-song cry came from Hadiyyah, who stood at the door. She waved her watercolours in one hand. In the other, she held a white-lidded jam jar. 'I only brought two 'cause the one of the sea's awfully bad, Barbara. And look, see what I caught as well? He was in the roses outside the dining room and after lunch I got a jar from the kitchen and he flew right in.'

She presented her jam jar for Barbara's inspection. In the fading light, Barbara saw a rather unhappy bee flinging itself hopelessly against the glass.

'I put some food in for him. Look. D'you see it? And I poked some holes through the top. D'you think he'll like London? I expect he will 'cause there's lot of flowers, so he can eat them up and then make honey.'

Barbara set the jar by the chess board on the table and gave it a close inspection. The food Hadiyyah had provided consisted of a wilting pile of rose petals and a few sad leaves with their edges curled inward. A Nobel-calibre entomologist in the making she clearly wasn't. But she was positively inspired when it came to the art of providing distraction.

'Well,' Barbara said, 'here's the problem with that, kiddo. Bees have families, and they all live together in hives. They don't like strangers, so if you take this bee back to London with you, he won't have any family to live with. I expect that's why he's in such a state at the moment. It's getting dark, and while it's been a nice visit, he'd like to go home.'

Hadiyyah came to stand between Barbara's legs. She crouched so that her chin was level with the table and her nose pressed up to the side of the jar. 'You think?' she asked. 'Should I let him go? Is he missing his family?'

'Sure,' Barbara said, picking up the child's watercolours for inspection. 'Besides, bees don't belong inside jars. It's not a good idea, and it isn't safe.'

'Why?' Hadiyyah asked.

Barbara looked past the paintings to the artist's father. 'Because when you ask a creature to live in a way that's against his nature, someone always ends up getting hurt.'

Theo wasn't listening, Agatha Shaw concluded. He wasn't listening any more than he'd listened during drinks, during dinner, during coffee, or during the nine o'clock news. His body had been present and he'd even managed to respond in such a way that a less perspicacious woman might have taken for holding up his end of the conversation. But the truth of the matter was that his mind was no more on the redevelopment of Balford-le-Nez than hers was on the current price of bread in Moscow.

'Theodore!' she snapped and wielded her stick at his legs. He was passing her sofa yet again, treading from his chair to the open window as if he'd decided to wear a path straight through the Persian carpet before the end of the evening. His grandmother couldn't decide which activity drove her more to distraction: his charade of conversing with her or his newly found interest in the state of the garden. Not that he could see much of the garden in the fast-dying light. But there was little doubt that if she demanded to know what was so enthralling outside the window, he would claim to be mourning the death of the lawn.

Her stick failed to stop him, missed him entirely. But when she said, 'Theodore Michael Shaw, traipse across this drawing room another time and I'll give you six of the best that you'll never forget. And I'll use this stick to do it. D'you hear me?' that did the trick.

Theo stopped, turned, and looked at her wryly. 'Think you're up to that, Gran?' The question was fondly asked, yet he seemed to feel the fondness in spite of himself. He walked no farther towards the window, but his gaze went to it nonetheless.

'What the devil is it?' she demanded. 'You haven't heard a word I've said all evening. I want this to stop and I want it to stop right now. Tonight.'

'What?' he asked, and to give him credit, he looked sufficiently nonplussed nearly to convince her.

But she was nobody's fool. She hadn't brought up four difficult children – six, if one counted Theo and his pig-headed brother – for nothing. She knew when something was going on, and she knew even better when that something was a something which someone was trying to hide from her.

'Don't be obtuse,' she replied tartly. 'You were late . . . again. You didn't eat more than ten mouthfuls at dinner. You ignored the cheese, let your coffee get cold, and for the past twenty minutes when you haven't been wearing a trail through my carpet, you've been watching the clock like a prisoner waiting for visiting hours.'

'I had a late lunch, Gran,' Theo said reasonably. 'And this heat's pure hell. How could anyone tuck into salmon pie in this kind of weather?'

'I managed,' she said. 'And hot food is appropriate when the weather's beastly. It cools the blood.'

'That sounds like an old wives' tale to me.'

'Piffle,' she said. 'And food isn't the point. You're the point. Your behaviour's the point. You haven't been yourself since . . .' She paused for thought. How long had it been since Theo hadn't been the Theo she'd known and loved – loved against her wishes, her wisdom, and her inclination – for the last twenty years? A month? Two? He'd started at first with long silences, he'd gone on to longer observations of her when he probably thought she wasn't looking, and he'd mixed these up with nocturnal disappearances, hushed telephone calls, and a disturbing weight loss. 'What in the name of Medusa is going on?' she settled on demanding.

He flashed her a smile, but she didn't miss the fact that this expression did nothing to alter the bleakness in his eyes. 'Gran, believe me. Nothing's going on.' He answered in that soothing tone that doctors always use when attempting to win the cooperation of a recalcitrant patient.

'Are you up to something?' she asked directly. 'Because if you are, I'd like to point out that you've little to gain from obfuscation.'

'I'm not up to anything. I've been thinking about business: how the pier's shaping up and how much money we're going to lose if Gerry DeVitt doesn't have that restaurant opened before the August bank holiday.' He returned to his chair, as if this action would prove his words. He clasped his hands loosely between his knees and gave her what went for his full attention these days.

She continued as if he hadn't spoken. 'Obfuscation destroys. And if you wish to argue about that, perhaps three names will emphasise my point: Stephen, Lawrence, Ulrika. All practitioners of the fine art of deception.'

She saw his eyes tighten in a wince that pleased her. She'd meant to hit him below the belt, and she was glad to know that he'd felt the blow. His brother, his father, and his pea-brained mother, those three were. All of them dissemblers, all of them consequently disinherited, all of them sent into the world to fend for themselves. Two of them were already dead, and the third . . . Who knew what insalubrious end Stephen Shaw would meet in that snake pit that went for a society in Hollywood?

Since Stephen's departure at nineteen years of age, she'd been telling herself that Theo was different. He was sane, reasonable, and enlightened in a way that his immediate family had never been. Upon him she'd learned to place her hopes and to him would go her fortune. If she didn't live to see the complete renaissance of Balford-le-Nez, it didn't matter because Theo would carry forward her dream. Through him and his efforts, she would live on.

Or so she had thought. But the past few weeks – or was it a month or two? – had seen the waning of his interest in her affairs. The past few days had shown her that his mind was deeply engaged elsewhere. And the past few hours had indisputably illustrated that she had to act soon to bring him back on track if she wasn't to lose him altogether.

'I'm sorry,' he said. 'I don't mean to ignore you. But I'm juggling the pier, the work on the restaurant, the plans for the hotel, this town council business . . .' As his voice drifted off, his gaze began to travel to that blasted open window, but he seemed to realise what he was doing because he quickly brought himself back to her. 'And this heat,' he said. 'I'm never my best in this sort of heat.'

She observed him through narrowed eyes. Truth or lie? she wondered. He went on.

'I've put a call in about another special town council meeting, by the way. I did that this morning. They'll get back to us, but we can't expect anything soon because of this business with the Asians and the dead man on the Nez.'

This was progress, she admitted, and felt the first stirrings of encouragement that she'd experienced since her stroke. It was snail-like and maddening to be sure, but it was progress all the same. Perhaps, after all, Theo was as fully ingenuous as he claimed to be. For the moment, she decided to believe that he was.

'Excellent,' she said. 'Excellent, *excellent*. So by the time we meet the council again, we'll have the necessary votes in our pockets. I dare say, Theo, I've come to see that disruption of yesterday's meeting as a stroke of divine intervention. This gives us an opportunity to court each council member personally.'

Theo's attention appeared to be on her, and while she had him interested, she intended to make the most of their conversation. She said, 'I've already seen to Treves, by the way. He's ours.'

'Is he?' Theo said politely.

'He is indeed. I spoke to the insufferable man myself this afternoon. Surprised? Well, whyever not speak to him? Whyever not set our ducks in position before we pick up our guns?' She could feel her excitement rising as she spoke. It came upon her like a sexual arousal, heating her up between the legs the way Lewis used to do when he kissed the back of her neck. She suddenly realised that it mattered to her very little whether Theo was listening or not. She'd been holding back her enthusiasm all day – there was absolutely no point in sharing her plans with Mary Ellis – and now she needed and intended to vent it. 'It took practically nothing to get him on our side,' she said happily. 'He loathes the Pakis as much as we do and he's willing to do anything to help our cause. "Shaw Redevelopment serves the interests of the community at large," he told me. What he meant was that he'd cut his own throat if that would keep the Pakis in their place. He wants an English name wherever a name's going to be seen: on the pier, on the park, on the hotels, on the leisure centre. He doesn't want Balford to be a stronghold for coloureds. He hates Akram Malik especially,' she added with great satisfaction, and she felt the same frisson of pleasure she'd experienced on the phone when it had first become clear to her that she and the loathsome hotelier had at least one characteristic in common.

Theo looked down at his hands, and she noted that he'd pressed his thumbs together tightly. He said, 'Gran, what does it really matter that Akram Malik named a patch of lawn, a fountain, one wooden bench, and a laburnum tree in memory of his mother-in-law? Why's that put you into such an uproar?'

'I am *not* in an uproar. And I'm certainly not in an uproar about that rodent-filled green of Akram Malik's.'

'Aren't you?' Theo raised his head. 'As I recall it, you didn't have any dreams of redevelopment until the *Standard* ran that article about the park's dedication.'

'Then your recollection is incorrect,' Agatha countered. 'We worked on the pier for ten long months before Akram Malik opened that park.'

'The pier, yes. But the rest of it – the hotel, the leisure centre, the buildings along the Marine Parade, the pedestrian walkways, the restoration of the High Street – none of that was even part of the picture until Akram's park. But once you read the story in the *Standard*, you couldn't rest till we'd hired architects, picked the brains of city planners from here to hell and back, and made sure everyone within hearing distance knew that long-range plans for Balford-le-Nez were in your hands.'

'Well, what of it?' Agatha demanded. 'This is my town. I've been here all my life. Who has more right to invest in its future than I?'

'If that's all this was about – investing in Balford's future – I'd agree,' Theo said. 'But Balford's future plays a minor role when it comes to your hidden agenda, Gran.'

'Does it?' she asked. 'And what, exactly, is my hidden agenda supposed to be?'

'Getting rid of the Pakistanis,' he said. 'Making Balford-le-Nez too expensive for them to buy property here, freezing them out economically, socially, and culturally by ensuring that there's no land available for them to build a mosque, no shop open in which they can buy *halal* meats, no employment available where they can find work –'

'I'm providing them with work,' Agatha cut in. 'I'm providing everyone in this town with work. Who do you expect to work in the hotels, the restaurants, or the shops if not Balford's inhabitants?'

'Oh, I'm certain you've spots allocated for the remaining Pakistanis that you can't drive out. Manual labour, washing dishes, making beds, scrubbing floors. Jobs that'll keep them in their places, ensuring they don't get above themselves.'

'And why should they get above themselves?' Agatha demanded. 'They owe their very lives to this country, and it damn well behoves them to keep that in mind.'

'Come on, Gran,' Theo said. 'Let's not pretend we're living out the last days of the Raj.'

She bridled at this, but more at the weary tone in which it was said than at the words themselves. All at once, he sounded so much like his father that she wanted to hurl herself at him. She could hear Lawrence in him. At this very moment, she could even *see* Lawrence. He'd sat in that same chair, solemnly telling her that he meant to leave his studies and marry a Swedish volleyball player twelve years his senior with nothing more to recommend her than enormous bosoms and a leathery tan.

'I'll cut you off without a shilling,' she'd shouted, 'without a farthing, without a bloody half-crown!' And it hadn't mattered to her in the least that the old money had gone out of use. All that had mattered was stopping him, and to this end she'd directed all of her resources. She'd manoeuvred, manipulated, and ultimately managed to do nothing but drive her son from the house and into his grave.

But old habits didn't so much die hard as they refused to die at all without being extirpated through determined effort. And Agatha had never been one to demand of herself the same dedication to expunging one's defects of character that she demanded of others. So she said, 'You listen to me, Theo Shaw. If you've a problem with my redevelopment plans and a wish to seek employment elsewhere as a result, just speak up now. You're easily enough replaced, and I'm happy to do it if you find me so repugnant to deal with.'

'Gran.' He sounded dispirited, but she didn't want that. She wanted surrender.

'I'm quite serious. I speak my mind. Always have done. Always will do. So if that's causing you to lose sleep at night, perhaps it's time we each went our own way. We've had a good run of it: twenty years together. That's longer than most marriages last these days. But if you need to go your own way like your brother, go. I'm not holding you back.'

The mention of his brother would serve to remind him of the manner in which his brother had left: with ten pounds and fifty-nine pence in his pocket, to which sum she'd added not one penny in the ten years he'd been gone. Theo rose, and for a terrible moment she thought she'd misjudged him, seeing a need for a maternal bond where he'd long outgrown it. But then he spoke, and she knew she'd won.

'I'll start phoning the council members in the morning,' he said.

She felt her face's rigidity loosen into a smile. 'You see, don't you, how we can use that disturbance in the council meeting to our own advantage? We'll win this, Theo. And before we're through, we'll have *Shaw* in lights all round this town. Think what life will be like for you then. Think of the man you'll be.'

He looked away from her, but not at the window. To the door this time, and to whatever lay beyond it. Despite the heat that seemed to throb in the air, he shuddered. Then he headed towards the door.

'What?' she asked him. 'It's nearly ten. Where're you going?'

'To cool off,' he said.

'Where do you expect to do that? It's no cooler outside than it is in this house.'

'I know,' he said. 'But the air's fresher, Gran.'

And the tone of his voice gave her an inkling of the cost that was attached to winning.

Chapter Fourteen

Since she had been the last diner that night, it was easy for Basil Treves to waylay Barbara. He did so as she passed the residents' lounge, having decided to forego postprandial coffee in favour of a prowl along the clifftop, where she hoped to encounter an errant sea breeze.

'Sergeant?' Snakelike, Treves sibilated when he whispered her title. The hotelier was in 007 mode. 'I didn't want to intrude on your meal.' A screwdriver in Treves' hand indicated that he'd been in the process of making some sort of adjustment to the large-screen television on which Daniel Day-Lewis was in the process of swearing eternal fidelity to a bosom-heaving woman prior to jumping through a waterfall. 'But now that you're finished . . . If you've a moment . . . ?'

Rather than wait for a response, he took Barbara's elbow between his thumb and index finger and firmly guided her down the passage to reception. He slid behind the desk and removed a computer print-out from its bottom drawer. 'More information,' he said conspiratorially. 'And I thought it best not to share it with you while you were engaged with . . . well, with others, if you know what I mean. But as you're free at the moment . . . You *are* free, aren't you?' He peered past her shoulder as if expecting Daniel Day-Lewis to dash out of the lounge and come to her rescue, flintlock rifle at the ready.

'Free's my middle name.' Barbara wondered why the odious man didn't do something about the condition of his skin. It was flaking off into his beard in significant clumps this evening. He looked as if he'd dipped his face into a plate of pastry crumbs.

'Excellent,' he said. He gave a glance round for eavesdroppers, and apparently finding none but still deciding to proceed with caution, he leaned over the counter to speak confidentially and to share the gin on his breath. 'Phone records,' he exhaled gustily. 'I had a new system put in last year, thank God, so I've a record of everyone's trunk calls. Before, all calls went through the switchboard and we had to keep records by hand and time them, the calls not the records, that is. An utterly Byzantine method and hardly accurate. Let me tell you, Sergeant, it led to the most unpleasant rows at check-out time.'

'You've tracked down Mr Querashi's outgoing calls?' Barbara said encouragingly. She found herself marginally impressed. Eczema or not, the man was actually proving himself to be a bit of a gold mine. 'Brilliant, Mr Treves. What have we got?'

As usual, he preened himself at her use of the plural pronoun. He turned the computer print-out round on top of the desk so that it faced her. She could see that he'd circled perhaps two dozen phone calls. They all began with the same double noughts. It was a list of foreign calls, Barbara realised.

'I did take the liberty of carrying our investigation a *leetle* further, Sergeant. I do hope I wasn't overstepping the mark.' Treves took up a pencil from a holder fashioned out of seashells glued to an erstwhile soup tin. He used it as a pointer as he went on. 'These numbers are in Pakistan: three in Karachi and another in Lahore. That's in the Punjab, by the way. And these two are Germany, both of them Hamburg. I didn't phone any of them, mind you. Once I saw the international code, I found that all I needed was the telephone directory. The country and city codes are listed there.' He sounded slightly chagrined by this final admission. Like so many people, he had doubtless assumed that policework comprised cloak-and-daggering when it didn't comprise stake-outs, shoot-outs, and lengthy car chases in which lorries and buses crashed into each other as the bad guys manoeuvred wildly through urban traffic.

'These are all his calls?' Barbara asked. 'For his entire stay?'

'Every trunk call,' Treves corrected her. 'For the local calls he made, of course, there is no record.'

Barbara hunched over the desk and began to examine the print-out page by page. She saw that the long-distance phone calls had been few and far between in the earliest days of Querashi's stay, and at that time they'd been made to a single number in Karachi. In the last three weeks of his stay, however, the international calls had increased, tripling in the final five days. The vast majority had been made to Karachi. Only four times had he phoned Hamburg.

She reflected on this. Among the telephone messages that callers had left for Haytham Querashi during his absence from the Burnt House, there had been none from any foreign country, because surely the competent WPC Belinda Warner would have made that point to her superior officer when reporting earlier that afternoon on the telephone chits she'd been given to research. So either he always got through to his intended party, or he didn't leave a message for a return call when he didn't get through. Barbara looked at the length of each of the calls and saw confirmation for this latter interpretation of the print-out: the longest call he'd made was forty-two minutes, the shortest thirteen seconds, surely not enough time to leave anyone a message.

But the pile-up of calls so close to his death was what Barbara found intriguing, and it was clear to her that she needed to track down whoever was at the other end of the telephone line. She glanced at her watch and idly wondered what time it was in Pakistan.

'Mr Treves,' she said, preparatory to disengaging herself from the man, 'you're an absolute marvel.'

He put a hand to his breast, humility incarnate. 'I'm only too glad to help you, Sergeant. Ask anything of me – anything at all – and I'll comply to the best of my ability. *And* with complete discretion, of course. Upon that you may rely. Should it be information, evidence, recollections, eye-witness accounts –'

'As to that . . .' Barbara decided that there was no time like the present to weasel from the man the truth about his own whereabouts on the night that Querashi died. She considered how best to ease it out of him without his awareness. 'Last Friday evening, Mr Treves . . .'

He was immediatiely all attention, eyebrows raised and hands clasped beneath the third button of his shirt. 'Yes, yes? Last Friday evening?'

'You saw Mr Querashi leave, didn't you?'

He did indeed, Treves told her. He was in the bar doing his bit with the brandy and the port. He saw Querashi coming down the stairs, reflected in the mirror. But hadn't he already imparted this information to the sergeant?

Of course he had, she reassured him hastily. What she was leading up to were the *others* in the bar. If Mr Treves was pouring brandy and port, it seemed logical to conclude that he was pouring it for other guests in the bar. Was that the case? And if so, did any of the others leave at the same time Querashi did, perhaps following him?

'Ah.' Treves lifted an index finger heavenward as he ascertained her point. He went on to tell her that the only people to leave the bar when Querashi left the Burnt House were poor old Mrs Porter with her Zimmer, clearly not fleet enough of foot to be in hot pursuit of anyone, and the Reeds, an ageing couple from Cambridge who'd come to the Burnt House to celebrate their forty-fifth wedding anniversay. 'We do a special for birthdays, weddings, and anniversaries,' he confided. 'I dare say they wanted to have at their champagne and choccies.'

As for the rest of the hotel residents, they had hung about the bar and the lounge till half-past eleven. He could vouch for each and every one of them, he told her. He was with them all evening.

Fine, Barbara thought. And she was pleased to see that he was none the wiser about having just provided her with an alibi for his own whereabouts. She thanked him, said goodnight, and with the computer print-out tucked beneath her arm, she took herself up the stairs.

In her room, she went straight to the phone. It stood on one of the two wobbly bedside tables, next to a dusty lamp that was shaped like a pineapple. With the print-out in her lap, Barbara punched for an outside line and then tapped in the first number in Germany. Several clicks and the connection was made. A phone began ringing somewhere across the North Sea.

When the ringing stopped, she drew in a breath to identify herself. But instead of a human being, she found she was listening to an answer machine. A male voice spoke in machine-gun German. She caught the number seven and two nines, but other than that and the word *Tschüs* at the end – which she took for a German form of 'cheerio bye-bye' – she gleaned nothing whatsoever from the message. The beep sounded, and she left her name, her phone number, and a request for a return call, all with the hope that whoever listened to her message spoke English.

She went on to the second number in Hamburg and found herself on the line with a woman saying something as unintelligible as had the male voice on the answer machine. But at least this was a real human being, and Barbara wasn't about to let her slip through her grasp.

God, how she wished she'd studied a foreign language at the comprehensive! All she knew how to say in German was *'Bitte zwei Bier'* which didn't seem applicable in the situation. She thought, Bloody hell, but gathered her wits enough to say, *'Ich spreche . . . I* mean . . . *Sprechen vous* . . . No, that's not right . . . *Ich bin ein* calling from England . . . Hell! Damn!'

This was apparently sufficient stimulus because the response came in English, and the words were surprising. 'Here is Ingrid Eck,' the woman said curtly and with an accent so heavy that Barbara half expected to hear *Das Deutschlandlied* playing in the background. 'Here is Hamburg Police. *Wer ist das, bitte?* How may I help you?'

Police? Barbara thought. Hamburg police? *German* police? What in hell was a Pakistani in England doing phoning the German police?

She said, 'Sorry. Detective Sergeant Barbara Havers here. New Scotland Yard.'

'New Scotland Yard?' the woman repeated. '*Ja?* To who will you wish –' *vill* and *vish*, she said '– to speak at this location?'

'I'm not sure,' Barbara said. 'We're looking into a murder and the victim –'

'You have a German victim?' Ingrid Eck asked at once. Except she said *haff* and *wictim* and went on to clarify with, 'Has a German national been involved' – *inwolved* – 'in a homicide, please?'

'No. Our victim is Asian. Pakistani, in fact. A bloke called Haytham Querashi. And he phoned this number two days before he was killed. I'm trying to trace the call. I'd like to speak to whoever he phoned. Can you help me?'

'Oh. *Ja.* I see.' And then she spoke past the receiver, rapid German of which Barbara caught the words *England* and *Mord.* Several voices answered, many gutturals like the clearing throats of a half dozen men afflicted with serious post-nasal drip. Barbara's hopes lifted at the passion of their conversation, only to be dashed when Ingrid's voice came back over the line.

'Here is Ingrid another time,' she said. 'I feel terror that we can be of no help.'

Terror? Barbara thought before she made the correction to *I'm afraid.* 'Let me spell out the name for you,' she said helpfully. 'Foreign names are odd when you hear them, aren't they, and if you see it written down, you might recognise it. Or someone else might if you pass it round.'

With stops and starts and at least five pauses to make corrections in the spelling, Ingrid took Haytham Querashi's name. She said in her creative and broken English that she would display it and circulate it round the station, but New Scotland Yard weren't to get their hopes up about receiving a helpful answer. Many hundred people worked at

Polizeihochhaus in Hamburg in one division or another, and there was no telling if the right person would see the circulated and displayed name any time soon. People were beginning to take their summer holidays, people were overworked, people's focus was on German rather than English problems . . .

So much for European unity, Barbara thought. She asked Ingrid to do her best, left her own number, and rang off. She blotted her hot face on the hem of her T-shirt, thinking how unlikely it was that she'd find an English-speaking recipient at the other end of her next set of phone calls. It had to be well after midnight in Pakistan, and since she didn't know a word of Urdu in which to tell an Asian sleeper why his slumber had been shattered by the ringing of his phone, Barbara decided to rustle up someone who could do the job for her.

She went up the stairs and made her way down the corridor to the section of the hotel in which Querashi's room had been. She paused before the door behind which she'd heard television voices on the previous night. Azhar and Hadiyyah had to be within. It was unthinkable that Basil Treves might have deviated from his odious separate-but-equal philosophy by placing the Asians in part of the hotel where his English guests would have their delicate sensibilities disrupted by a foreign presence.

She knocked quietly and said Azhar's name, then knocked again. The key turned in the lock within, and he was standing before her in a maroon dressing gown with a cigarette in his hand. Behind him, the room was semi-dark. A bedside lamp was shaded by a large blue handkerchief, but enough light was apparently left for him to read by. A bound document of some sort lay next to his pillow.

'Is Hadiyyah asleep? Can you come to my room?' she asked him.

He looked so startled at the request that Barbara felt her face begin to flame at the implication behind her words. She said hurriedly, 'I need you to phone some numbers in Pakistan for me,' and went on to explain how she'd come by them.

'Ah.' He glanced at the gold watch on his thin wrist. 'Have you any idea what time it is in Pakistan, Barbara?'

'Late.'

'Early,' he corrected her. 'Extremely early. Would your purposes not be better served by waiting till a more reasonable hour?'

'Not when we're dealing with a murder,' she said. 'Will you make the calls for me, Azhar?'

He looked over his shoulder into the room. Beyond him, Barbara could see the small humped figure of Hadiyyah in the second bed. She was sleeping with a large stuffed Kermit tucked in beside her.

'Very well,' Azhar said and stepped back into the room. 'If you'll give me a moment to change . . .'

'Forget it. You don't need to get dressed. This'll probably take less than five minutes. Come on.'

She didn't give him chance to argue. She set off down the corridor in the direction of the stairs. Behind her, she heard the sound of his door closing, followed by the scrape of the key as he locked up. She waited for him at the top of the stairs.

'Querashi was phoning Pakistan at least once a day in the last three weeks. Whoever got those calls is bound to remember if they've heard he's dead.'

'The family has been informed,' Azhar told her. 'Aside from them, I can't think whom he might have been phoning.'

'That's what we're about to find out.'

She shoved open the door of her room and ushered him inside. From the floor, she scooped up the underclothes, the drawstring trousers, and the T-shirt that she'd worn earlier that day. She tossed them into the clothes cupboard with an 'Excuse the mess', and led him to the bedside table where the computer print-out lay on the dingy counterpane.

'Have at it,' she said. 'Make yourself comfortable.'

He sat and looked at the print-out for a long moment, cigarette in his mouth and a plume of smoke rising like a vaporous serpent above his head. He tapped his fingers beneath one of the circled numbers and finally glanced in her direction.

'Are you certain you wish me to place these calls?'

'Why wouldn't I be certain?'

'We sit among opposing forces, Barbara. Should the parties at the other end of these numbers only speak Urdu, how will you know I'm relating the truth of the conversation to you?'

He had a point. Prior to fetching him, she hadn't dwelt long upon Azhar's reliability as a conduit of information. She hadn't thought about the question at all. She wondered why. Nonetheless she said, 'Our objective's the same, isn't it? We both want to get to the bottom of who killed Querashi. I can't think you'd do something to bury the truth once you knew it was the truth. Frankly, you've never seemed that type.'

He gazed at her, his expression something between thoughtful, enlightened, and perplexed. He finally said, 'As you wish,' and picked up the phone.

Barbara dug her cigarettes out of her bag, lit up, and dropped on to the dressing table's lime-cushioned stool. She moved an ashtray within reach of both of them.

Azhar used his long fingers to shove back a wing of black hair that had fallen across his forehead. He placed his cigarette into the ashtray and said, 'It's ringing. Have you a pencil?' Then a moment later; 'It's a recording, Barbara.' He frowned, listening. He jotted notes on the print-out. He left no message, however, when the recording finished. He just rang off. 'This number –' And he ticked off one of them. 'This is a travel agency in Karachi. World Wide Tours. The message gave their hours of operation, none of which –' he smiled and reached for his cigarette '– happen to be between midnight and seven a.m.'

Barbara looked at the print-out. 'He phoned them four times last week. What d'you make of that? Honeymoon plans? The great escape from his marriage?'

'Doubtless he was merely arranging for his family's transport, Barbara. They would have wanted to be here to celebrate his marriage to my cousin. Shall I continue?'

She nodded. He went on to the next number. The connection was made, and within moments he was speaking Urdu. Barbara could hear the voice on the other end of the line. The words, at first hesitant, quickly became both urgent and passionate. The conversation went on some minutes, with English interspersed where there was no Urdu translation. Thus, she heard her own name mentioned as well as *New Scotland Yard*, *Balford-le-Nez*, *Burnt House Hotel*, and *Essex Constabulary*.

When he rang off, she said, 'Well? Who was it? What did they –' but he held up his hand to stop her question and went on to make the next call.

This time he spoke at greater length, and he made notes as a man's voice on the other end of the line imparted what appeared to be a small volume of information. Barbara itched to wrest the receiver away from Azhar and make demands of her own. But she schooled herself to patience.

Without comment, Azhar went on to the fourth call, and this time Barbara recognised what seemed to be his standard opening: an apology for having phoned at such an hour, followed by an explanation in which Haytham Querashi's name came up more than once. This final conversation was longest of all, and at its conclusion, Azhar kept his attention gravely on the computer print-out until Barbara spoke.

His expression was so sombre that Barbara felt the queasiness of trepidation come over her. She *had* handed him a potential item of crucial interest in the investigation. He was free to do with it what he would, including lie about its significance or relate it – with suitable incendiary comments – to his cousin.

She said, 'Azhar?'

He roused himself. He reached for his cigarette and took a hit. Then he looked her way.

'The second call was to his parents.'

'That's the number that appears earlier on the print-out?'

'Yes. They are –' He paused, ostensibly seeking a word or a phrase. 'They are understandably crushed by his death. They wished to know about the status of the investigation. And they would like the body. They feel they cannot grieve their eldest son properly without having his body, so they ask if they must pay the police to release it.'

'*Pay?*'

Azhar continued. 'Haytham's mother is under a doctor's care, having collapsed when informed of his murder. His sisters are confused, his brother hasn't spoken a word since Saturday afternoon, and his paternal grandmother is attempting to hold the family together. But her heart is weakened by angina, the strain is great, and a strong attack may kill her. The ringing telephone frightened them all.'

He fastened his eyes on her. She said, 'Murder's a nasty business, Azhar. I'm sorry, but there's no making it easier for anyone to bear. And I'd be lying if I told you that the horror ends when we make an arrest. It doesn't. Ever.'

He nodded. Absently, he rubbed the back of his neck. For the first time, she noticed he wore only pyjama bottoms under his dressing gown. His chest was bare, and his dark skin appeared burnished in the light.

Barbara rose and went to the window. She could hear music coming from somewhere, the hesitant notes of someone practising the clarinet in one of the houses on the clifftop some distance away.

'The next number is for a *mulla*,' Azhar said behind her. 'This is a religious leader, a holy man.'

'Like an *ayatollah?*'

'Lesser. He's a local religious leader and he serves the community in which Haytham grew up.'

He sounded so grave that Barbara turned from the window to face him. She saw that he looked grave as well. 'What did he want with the *mulla*? Did it have to do with the marriage?'

'With the Qur'aan,' Azhar said. 'He wanted to speak of the same passage that he'd marked in the book: the passage I translated for you during our conference this afternoon.'

'About being brought forth from the oppressors?'

Azhar nodded. 'But his interest did not lie with the "town from which the people are oppressors" as my cousin thought. He wished to understand how to define the word *feeble*.'

'He wanted to know what *feeble* means? And he phoned all the way to Pakistan to find out? That doesn't make sense.'

'Haytham knew what *feeble* means, Barbara. He wanted to know how to apply the definition. The Qur'aan instructs Muslims to fight for the cause of the feeble among men. He wished to discuss the manner in which one recognises when a fellow man is feeble and when he is not.'

'Because he wanted to fight someone?' Barbara returned to the dressing-table stool. She sank on to it, reached for the ashtray, and crushed out her cigarette. 'Bloody hell,' she said more to herself than to Azhar. 'What was he up to?'

'The other call was to a *mufti*,' Azhar continued. 'This is a specialist in Islamic law.'

'D'you mean a lawyer?'

'Somewhat analogous to a lawyer. A *mufti* is one who provides legal interpretations of Islamic law. He's schooled to deliver what is called a *fatwa*.'

'Which is?'

'Something akin to a legal brief.'

'What did he want from this bloke, then?'

Azhar hesitated and Barbara could see that they'd come to the heart of whatever had caused the solemnity of his earlier expression. Instead of answering at once, he reached for the ashtray and crushed out his cigarette. A second time, he brushed his fallen hair from his forehead. He studied his feet. Like his chest, they were bare. Like his hands, they were thin. High-arched and smooth, they might have belonged to a woman.

'Azhar,' Barbara said. 'Please don't do a bunk on me now, okay? I need you.'

'My family –'

'Needs you as well. Right. But we all want to get to the bottom of this. Asian killer or English killer, we don't want Querashi's death to go unpunished. Even Muhannad can't want that, no matter what he says about protecting his people.'

Azhar sighed. 'From the *mufti*, Haytham sought an answer about sin. He wished to know if a Muslim – guilty of a serious sin – would remain a Muslim and hence part of the greater community of Muslims.'

'You mean: would he remain a part of his family?'

'A part of his family and a part of the community as a whole.'

'And what did the *mufti* tell him?'

'He spoke of *usul al-fiqh*: the sources of law.'

'Which are?'

Azhar raised his head to meet her eyes. 'The Qur'aan, the *Sunna* of the Prophet—'

'*Sunna?*'

'The Prophet's example.'

'What else?'

'Consensus of the community and analogical reasoning – what you call deduction.'

Barbara reached for her cigarettes unseeing. She shook out one for herself and offered Azhar the pack. He took the book of matches from the dressing table, striking one for her and then applying it to his own cigarette. He returned to his place on the edge of the bed.

'So when he and the *mufti* were done with their confab, some conclusion must have been reached, right? They had an answer to his question. Can a Muslim guilty of a serious sin remain a Muslim?'

He answered with a question of his own. 'How can one live in defiance of any one of the tenets of Islam and still claim to be a Muslim, Barbara?'

The tenets of Islam. Barbara tossed this phrase round in her head, attaching it to everything she'd learned so far about Querashi and about the people with whom he'd come into contact. Doing this, she saw the inevitable connection between the question and Querashi's own life. And she felt the heady rush of excitement as the Asian's behaviour began to make sense. 'Earlier – when we were outside – you said that homosexuality is expressly forbidden by the Qur'aan.'

'I did.'

'But he intended to marry. In fact, he was committed to marry. He was so committed that his family was ready to attend the celebration and he had the wedding night all planned out.'

'It seems reasonable to conclude that,' Azhar said cautiously.

'So can we reckon that after his conversation with the *mufti*, Haytham Querashi decided to start living by the tenets of Islam, in effect to go straight?' She warmed to her topic. 'Can we reckon that he'd been at war with himself about doing this – about going straight – ever since coming to England? He was committed to getting married, after all, and yet still he was drawn to the men he'd sworn to give up. In being drawn to them, he was probably drawn to locations they frequent, more than one location. So he met some bloke in Clacton market square and took up with him. They carried on for a month or so but he didn't want to live a double life – too much was at risk – so he tried to end it. Only he ended instead.'

'Clacton market square?' Azhar asked. 'What has Clacton market square to do with anything, Barbara?'

And Barbara realised what she'd done. So caught up was she in her desire to piece together what facts and speculations they had been able to gather that she'd inadvertently given Azhar a piece of information which only Trevor Ruddock and the investigators had. In doing so, she'd crossed a line.

Shit, she thought. She wanted to rewind the tape, to whisk the words *Clacton market square* out of the air and back into her mouth. But she couldn't unsay them. All she could hope to do was temporise. Temporising, however, was among the very least of her talents. Oh, to be in the company of Detective Inspector Lynley, Barbara thought. With his gracefully adroit conversational footwork, he'd ease them out of this situation in a flash. Of course, he'd never have got them into this situation in the first place since he wasn't in the habit of thinking aloud unless he was in the presence of his colleagues. But that was another matter entirely.

She decided to ignore the question by saying in as reflective a manner as possible, 'Of course, he may have had another person in mind when he was speaking to the *mufti*,' and having said this, she realised how close to the truth she may have just come.

'Who?' Azhar asked.

'Sahlah. Perhaps he'd discovered something about her that made him reluctant to marry her. Perhaps he was seeking from the *mufti* a way to get out of the marriage contract. Wouldn't a woman's grave sin – something that, if revealed, could result in her being cut off from Islam – be reason enough to nullify the marriage contract?'

He looked sceptical, then shook his head. 'It would nullify the contract. But what grave sin could my cousin Sahlah possibly have on her soul, Barbara?'

Theo Shaw, Barbara thought. But this time wisely she said nothing.

The doorbell rang in the midst of their argument. Connie's voice had reached such a shrill pitch that had Rachel not been standing in the sitting-room doorway, she wouldn't have heard it. But the two-note chime – the second note strangled as always like a bird shot down in the middle of a chirp – came at the moment when her mother was taking a breath.

Connie ignored the chimes. 'You answer me, Rache!' she shouted. 'You answer me now and you answer me good. What d'you know about this business? You was lying to that police detective and you're lying to me now and I'm not going to stand for it, Rachel Lynn. I truly am not.'

'That was the door, Mum,' Rachel said.

'*Connie.* I'm Connie and don't you forget it. And bugger the door. It won't get itself opened till you answer me straight. How're you mixed up with that dead bloke from the Nez?'

'I already said,' Rachel told her. 'I gave him the receipt so he could see how much Sahlah loved him. She told me she was worried. She said she didn't think he believed her and *I* thought that if he saw the receipt –'

'Bollocks!' Connie shrieked. 'Bloody flaming bollocks! If that rot's the truth, then I'm Mother Goose. Why didn't you tell that police person when she asked you about it, eh? But we know the answer to that one, don't we? You didn't say 'cause you hadn't cooked up a good explanation till now. Well, if you expect me to believe a half-arsed story about proving some coloured girl's eternal love for her intended bloody sodding bridegroom, then –'

The doorbell rang again. Three times in succession. Connie herself stormed to answer it. She flung the door open. It smashed against the wall.

'What?' she barked. 'What bloody *what*? Who the hell are you? And do you know what time it is, by the way?'

A young voice, male. It was carefully deferential. 'Rachel in, Mrs Winfield?'

'*Rachel*? What d'you want with my Rache?'

Rachel went to the door, standing behind her mother. Connie attempted to block her with her hip.

'Who is this wanker?' Connie demanded of her. 'And what's his business showing up at . . . Piss on your face! Do you know what time it is, you?'

It was Trevor Ruddock, Rachel saw. He was standing well into the shadows so that neither the light from the house nor the light from the streetlamps touched him. But still, he couldn't do much to hide. And he looked worse than usual because his T-shirt was dirty, with holes round the neckline, and his jeans had gone so long unwashed that they probably could have stood up on their own.

Rachel attempted to step past her mother. Connie caught her arm. 'We aren't finished, you and me, Missy-miss.'

'What is it, Trev?' Rachel asked.

'You *know* this bloke?' Connie demanded incredulously.

'Obviously,' Rachel replied. 'Since he asked for me, I probably know him.'

'C'n you talk for a minute?' Trevor asked. He shifted his weight, and his boots – unlaced and unpolished – scraped against the concrete front step. 'I know it's late, but I was hoping . . . Rachel, I need to talk to you, okay? Private.'

'About what?' Connie demanded hotly. 'What've you got to say to Rachel Lynn that you can't say in front of her mum? And who are you anyways? Why've I never seen you before if you and Rachel know each other good enough for you to come calling at quarter-past eleven?'

Trevor looked from Rachel to her mother. He looked back to Rachel again. His expression said clearly, *What d'you want her to know?* And Connie read it like a psychic.

She jerked Rachel's arm. '*This* is what you been messing with? This is what you snuck up round the beach huts for? You been lowering yourself to do the job with a wally no better than yesterday's rubbish?'

Trevor's lips jerked as if he were stopping himself from responding. Rachel did it for him.

'Shut up, Mum.' She twisted out of her mother's grasp and stepped on to the porch.

'You get back in this house,' her mother said.

'And you stop talking like I was a baby,' Rachel retorted. 'Trevor's my friend and if he wants to see me, I mean to know why. And Sahlah's my friend and if I want to help her, I'm going to do it. And no policeman – and not you neither, Mum – is going to make me do anything else.'

Connie gaped at her. 'Rachel Lynn Winfield!'

'Yeah, that's my name,' Rachel said. She heard her mother gasp at the sheer audacity of her reply. She took Trevor's arm and led him off the front step, in the direction of the street where he'd left his old motorscooter. 'We can finish our conversation once I talk to Trevor,' she called back to her mother.

A slammed door was the answer.

'Sorry,' she said to Trevor, stopping midway down the path. 'Mum's in a state. The cops came round to the shop this morning and I scarpered without telling her why.'

'They came to me, too,' he said. 'Some sergeant bird. Sort of fat with her face all . . .' He seemed to recall whose presence he was in and what a remark about a banged-up face might mean to her. 'Anyway,' he said, driving a hand into the pocket of his jeans. 'The cops came. Someone at Maliks told them I'd got the sack from Querashi.'

'That's rough,' Rachel said. 'But they don't think you did anything, right? I mean, what would've been the point? It's not like Mr Malik didn't know why Haytham sacked you.'

Trevor pulled out his keys. He played them through his fingers. To Rachel's eyes, he looked nervous, but until he went on, she didn't know why.

'Yeah, but why I got the sack's not really the point,' he said. 'The *fact* of getting the sack is. 'S far as they see it, I could've given him the chop to get revenge. That's what they're thinking. Besides, I'm white. He was coloured. A Paki. And with the rest of that lot making noise about hate crimes . . .' He lifted his arm and wiped it across his brow. 'Fucking hot,' he said. 'Whew. You'd think it'd cool off at night.'

Rachel watched him curiously. She'd never seen Trevor Ruddock nervous. He always acted like he knew what he wanted and getting it was only a matter of doing what it took. For sure, he'd been that way with her all right: smooth moving and easy talking. Definitely and positively easy talking. But now . . . This was a Trevor she'd not seen before, not even at school where he'd once stood out among the pupils as a hopeless yob with limited brainpower and a future to match. Even then he'd acted sure of himself. What he couldn't solve mentally, he'd solved with his fists.

'Yeah. It's hot,' she said carefully, waiting to see what would unfold between them. It couldn't be what usually unfolded between them. Not here with her mother steaming behind the lounge curtains and the nearby neighbours in the congested street only too willing to have a peep and a listen through their open windows. 'I can't remember when it's ever gone on like this, day after day, can you? I read a bit in the paper about global warming. Maybe this's it, huh?'

But it was evident that Trevor had not come to speak about science, atmospheric or otherwise. He shoved his keys back into his pocket, gnawed on his thumb, and cast a quick glance over his shoulder to the lounge window.

'Listen,' he said. He looked at the skin he'd bitten. He rubbed the thumb against the front of his T-shirt. 'Look 'ere, Rachel, c'n we talk for a sec?'

'We're talking.'

He jerked his head towards the street. 'I mean ... C'n we walk?' He headed to the pavement. He stopped at the rusty front gate and indicated – again with his head – that he wished her to follow.

She did so, saying, 'Aren't you s'posed to be at work, Trev?'

'Yeah. I'm going. But I got to talk to you first.' He waited for her to join him. But he walked no farther than his motorscooter, and he straddled it, planting his bum on the seat. He gave his attention to the handlebars, and his hands twisted round them as he continued. 'Look, you and me ... I mean ... Last Friday night. When Querashi got chopped. We was together. You remember that, right?'

'Sure,' she said, although the growing warmth of her chest and neck told her that she was going crimson.

'You remember what time we split, don't you? We went up to the huts round nine. We had that booze – bloody awful, it was – what was it called?'

'Calvados,' she said, and added uselessly, 'it's made from apples. It's for after dinner.'

'Well, we sort of had it before dinner, huh?' He grinned.

She didn't like it when he grinned. She didn't like his teeth. She didn't like to be reminded that he never saw a dentist. Nor did she like to be faced with the fact that he didn't bathe daily, that he never used a brush on his fingernails, and most of all that he was always careful that their meetings were private, beginning beneath the pier on the sea side of whatever pile was nearest the water and ending in that beach hut that smelled of mildew, where the rattan mats on the floor made a red lattice on her knees as she knelt before him.

Love me, love me, her actions had begged. *See how good I can make you feel?*

But that was before she knew that Sahlah needed her help. That was before she'd seen the expression on Theo Shaw's face that told her he intended to abandon Sahlah.

'Anyways,' Trevor said when she didn't chuckle at his lewd remark, 'we were still there at half-eleven, remember? I even had to make a dash for it to get to work on time.'

She shook her head, slowly. 'No, we weren't, Trev. I got home round ten.'

He grinned, still focused on the handlebars. When he raised his head with a nervous laugh, he still didn't look at her. 'Hey, Rache, that's not the way it was. 'Course, I don't expect you to get the time exactly straight 'cause we was sort of involved.'

'I was involved,' Rachel corrected him. 'I don't remember you doing much of anything after you pulled your prong from your trousers.'

He finally looked at her. For the first time ever in her recollection, his face was scared. 'Rachel,' he said miserably. 'Come on, Rache. You remember how it was.'

'I remember it being dark,' she said. 'I remember you telling me to wait ten minutes while you went up to the hut – third from the end in the top row, it was – to . . . What was it, Trev? To "air it out", you said. I was to wait underneath the pier and when ten minutes were up, I was supposed to follow.'

'You wouldn't've wanted to go inside when it was all smelly,' he protested.

'And you wouldn't've wanted to be seen with me.'

'That wasn't it,' he said, and for a moment he sounded so stiff with outrage that Rachel truly wanted to believe him. She wanted to believe that it really meant nothing that the single time they'd been in public together had been dinner at a Chinese restaurant conveniently located some fifteen miles from Balford-le-Nez. She wanted to believe that the fact that he'd never kissed her mouth meant he was only shy and working up his courage. And most of all, she wanted to believe that his letting her service him fifteen times without ever once wondering what she was getting out of the activity aside from the humiliation of yearning so openly for anything remotely resembling hope of a normal future, only meant that he'd not yet learned from her example how to give. But she couldn't believe. So she was stuck with the truth.

'I got home round ten, Trev. I know 'cause I felt all hollow inside, so I turned on the telly. And I even know what I watched, Trev. The middle and end of that old movie with Sandra Dee and Troy Donahue. I bet you know the one: they're kids and it's summer and they fall in love and mess around. And they sort of finally realise that love's more important than being scared and hiding who you really are.'

'Can't you just tell them?' he asked. 'Can't you say it was half-past eleven? Rache, the cops're going to ask you 'cause I said I was with you that night. And I was. If you tell them you got home round ten, don't you see what that means?'

'I expect it means you had time to give Haytham Querashi the business,' she answered.

'I *didn't* do it,' he said. 'Rache, I never saw the bloke that night. I swear. I *swear*. But if you don't back me up in what I said, then they'll know I'm lying. And if they know I'm lying about that, they'll think I'm lying about not having killed him. Can't you help me out? What's another hour?'

'Hour and a half,' she corrected him. 'You said half-eleven.'

'Okay. Hour and a half. What's another hour and a half?'

Plenty of time for you to show you had at least one thought in your mind about me, she told him silently. But she said, 'I won't lie for you, Trev. I might've once. But I won't do it now.'

'Why?' The word was a plea. He reached for her arm and ran his fingers up her bare skin. 'Rachel, I thought we had something special, you and me. Didn't you feel it? When we was together, it was like . . . Hey, it was like magic, didn't you think?' His fingers reached the sleeve of her blouse and insinuated themselves inside, up her shoulder, along the strap of her bra.

She wanted his touch so badly that she felt the damp answer to his question. It was between her legs, on the backs of her knees, and in the hollow of her throat where her heart was lodged.

'Rache . . . ?' The fingers grazed the front of her bra.

This was how it was supposed to be, she thought. A man touching a woman and the woman wanting, needing, melting –

'Please, Rache. You're the only one who c'n help me.'

But this was also the first and only time he'd touched her with tenderness and not as a hurried and impatient stimulation that would ultimately lead to his own pleasure.

That bird needs a bag on her head!

You look like a dog's arse, Rachel Winfield!

Blokes'll have to roger her wearing a blindfold.

She stiffened under his touch, remembering the voices and how she'd battled them throughout her childhood. She knocked Trevor Ruddock's hand away.

'Rache!' He even managed to look wounded.

Yes. Well. She knew how that felt.

'I got home round ten on Friday night,' she said. 'And if the cops ask, that's what I mean to tell them.'

Chapter Fifteen

On her bedroom ceiling, Sahlah studied the silhouettes of leaves illuminated by the moon. They didn't move. Despite the proximity of her family's house to the sea, there was no breeze. It would be another night of smothering heat when the thought of having bedclothes touch skin was akin to the idea of trying to sleep enshrouded in cling film.

Except that she knew she wouldn't sleep. She'd bade her family goodnight at half-past ten after suffering through an evening of tense conversation between her father and her brother. Akram had been first struck dumb by the news that Haytham's neck had been broken. Muhannad had seized what advantage their father's consternation gave him, announcing everything else that he'd learned in his meeting with the police – which was little enough, to Sahlah's ears – and outlining what he and Taymullah Azhar had planned as their next move. Akram had inserted, 'This is not a game, Muhannad,' and the dispute between them had grown from there.

Their words, spoken tersely by Akram and hotly by Muhannad, not only pitted father and son against each other but also threatened the peace of their household and the fabric of their family. Yumn sided with Muhannad, of course. Wardah reverted to a lifetime of acquiescing to males and said nothing at all, with her eyes cast down upon her embroidery. Sahlah tried to find a means of *rapprochement* between the two men. In the end, all of them sat in a silence so electric that the air itself seemed filled with sparks. Never one to deal with quiet in any of its forms, Yumn had jumped to her feet and seized the moment to slide a video into the machine. When the grainy picture appeared on the screen – an Asian boy following along behind a herd of goats, stick in his hand, as a sitar played and the credits rolled in Urdu – Sahlah said her goodnights. Only her mother responded.

Now it was half-past one. She'd been in bed since eleven. The house had been still since midnight, when she'd heard her brother moving round the bathroom, preparatory to finally retiring. The floors and walls had stopped their night-time creaking. And she waited fruitlessly for sleep.

But in order to sleep, she knew she would have to wipe her mind free from thoughts and concentrate on relaxing. While she might have managed the second activity, she knew she wouldn't be able to manage the first.

Rachel hadn't phoned, which meant that she hadn't gathered the necessary information for the abortion. Sahlah could only school herself to patience and hope that her friend would neither fail her nor betray her a second time.

Not for the first time since suspecting she was pregnant did Sahlah bitterly regret the lack of freedom imposed upon her by her parents. Not for the first time did she despise herself for having lived so docilely under the benign and loving but nonetheless implacable thumbs of her father and mother. She realised that the very womblike environment that had long kept her feeling so protected in an often unfriendly world was what stymied her now. The restrictions her parents had long placed upon her had sheltered her, indeed. But they'd also imprisoned her. And she'd never really known that till now, when more than anything she wished she had the coming-and-going lifestyle that English girls had, that carefree way of living in which parents seemed to be faraway planets orbiting only peripherally in the solar system of their daughters' lives.

Had she been a tearaway, Sahlah realised, she'd know what to do. In fact, had she been a tearaway she'd probably *announce* what she intended to do. She'd tell her story without a single face-saving digression and without regard for anyone's feelings. Because her family wouldn't mean anything to her if she were a tearaway, her parents' honour and pride – not to mention their natural, loving belief in their offspring – would be of no account.

But she'd never been a tearaway. Consequently, protecting the parents she loved was paramount to her, more important than her own personal happiness, dearer to her than life itself.

Dearer than this life certainly, she thought, automatically making a cradle of her hands to encircle her belly. But as quickly as she'd made the gesture, just as quickly did she force herself to reverse it. I can't give you life, she told the organism within her. I won't give life to something that would dishonour my parents and bring destruction upon my family.

And disgrace upon yourself, Sahlah dear? she heard the implacable voice of her conscience asking in that mocking tone she'd been listening to night after night and week after week. For who is to blame for the position in which you now find yourself if not yourself?

'Whore, slag,' her brother had cursed her in a whisper so violent that she shuddered from the simple memory of having heard it. 'You'll pay for this, Sahlah, the way all whores pay.'

She squeezed her eyes closed tightly, as if the complete darkness provided by doing so could somehow rid her mind of memory, her heart of anguish, and her conscience of the enormity of the act in which she had found herself a participant. But doing this only served to shoot flashes of light across the backs of her eyelids, as if an inner being over which she had no control were attempting to illuminate everything that she wished to keep hidden.

She opened her eyes once more. The flashing light continued. Perplexed, she watched it flicker and halt, flicker and halt at the point where the wall of her bedroom met the ceiling. It was a moment before she understood.

Short, short, long, pause. Short, short, long, pause. How many times had she seen that signal in the last year? It meant *Come to me, Sahlah.* It told her that Theo Shaw was outside, using a torch to announce that he was in the orchard.

She closed her eyes against it. Not so very long ago, she would have risen quickly, signalled with her own torch, and slipped quietly from her bedroom. Careful in slippers that muted the sound of her footsteps, she would have slid past her parents' room after hesitating at their closed door to listen for the reassuring sound of her father's thundering snore and her mother's accompanying, gentle one. She would have descended the stairs and made her way to the kitchen, and from there she would have flown into the night.

Short, short, long, pause. Short, short, long, pause. Even through her eyelids, she could see the light.

She sensed the urgency behind it. It was the same urgency she'd heard in his voice when he'd phoned her the previous evening.

'Sahlah, thank God,' he'd said. 'I've phoned you at least five times since I heard about Haytham, but you never answered, and the idea of leaving a message ... I didn't dare. For your sake. It was always Yumn who answered. Sahlah, I want to talk to you. We need to talk. We must talk.'

'We've talked,' she told him.

'No! Listen to me. You misunderstood. When I said I wanted to wait, it had nothing to do with how I feel about you.' His words were rapid, hushed. He sounded as if he believed she'd ring off before he had a chance to say everything he'd planned and probably rehearsed. But he also sounded as if he feared being overheard. And she knew by whom.

'My mother needs my help with dinner,' she said. 'I can't talk to you now.'

'You think it was because of you, don't you? I saw it in your face. I'm a coward in your eyes because I won't tell my grandmother I'm in love with an Asian. But the fact that I haven't told her has nothing to do with you. *Nothing.* All right? The time just isn't right.'

'I never believed it had anything to do with me,' she corrected him.

But she might not have spoken. She couldn't divert him from the course that he had apparently determined to take, because he hurried on. 'She isn't well. Her speech is getting bad. She practically can't walk. She's weak. She needs nursing. So I have to be here for her, Sahlah. And I can't ask you to come to this house – as my wife – only to burden you with taking care of a sick old lady who might die any minute.'

'Yes,' she said. 'You told me all of this, Theo.'

'So for God's sake, why won't you give me some time? Now that Haytham's dead, we can be together. We can make it happen. Sahlah, don't you see? Haytham's dying could be something that was meant to be. It could be a sign. It's as if the hand of God is telling us –'

'Haytham was murdered, Theo,' she said. 'And I don't think God had anything to do with it.'

He'd been silent at this. Was he shocked? she wondered. Was he horrified? Was he sifting through his thoughts to fabricate something with just the right ring of sincerity: tender words of compassion that offered a condolence which he did not feel? Or was something altogether different going on in his head, a fervid search for a subtle means to portray himself in the most positive light?

Say something, she'd thought. Ask a single question that will serve as a sign.

'How do you know . . . ? The newspaper . . . When it said the Nez . . . I don't know why, but I thought he had a heart attack or something, or maybe even a fall. But murdered? Murdered?'

Not, My God, how are you coping with this horror? Not, What can I do to help you? Not, I'm coming to you this instant, Sahlah. I'm taking my rightful place at your side, and we're putting an end to this bloody charade.

'The police told my brother this afternoon,' she'd said.

And another silence ensued. In it, she heard him breathing and she tried to interpret his respiration as she'd tried a moment earlier to gauge the meaning behind the delay between her revelation and his response.

He finally said, 'I'm sorry that he's dead. I'm sorry about the *fact* that he's dead. But I can't pretend to be sorry that you won't be marrying next weekend. Sahlah, I'm going to speak to Gran. I'm going to tell her everything, start to finish. I saw how close I came to losing you, and the moment we have this redevelopment project up and running, she'll be distracted, and I'll tell her.'

'And that's what you want her to be? Distracted? Because if she's distracted she might not notice when you introduce us that my skin is a colour she finds offensive?'

'I didn't say that.'

'Or is it that you don't intend to introduce us at all? Perhaps you hope that her project for the town will take enough out of her to finish her off. And then you'll have her money and your freedom as well.'

'No! Please! Listen to me.'

'I don't have the time,' she'd said, and she'd rung off just as Yumn came out of the sitting room and into the hall where the telephone sat on a stand at the foot of the stairs.

Her sister-in-law had smiled with such specious solicitude that Sahlah knew she'd heard her side of the conversation. 'Oh, my goodness, that phone hasn't stopped its ringing since word got out about our poor Haytham,' Yumn said. 'And how kind it is of all his closest friends, phoning to offer their sympathies to Haytham's pretty young bride. But she wasn't quite a bride, was our little Sahlah? Just a few days short of it. But never mind that. It must soothe her heart to know that so many people had a love for our Haytham that equalled her own.' Yumn's eyes laughed while the rest of her face formed an expression of funereal suitability.

Sahlah turned on her heel and went to her mother, but she heard Yumn's quiet laughter following her. She knows, Sahlah thought, but she doesn't know everything.

Now in her bed, she opened her eyes to see if the torch outside still flickered its message. Short, short, long, pause. Short, short, long, pause. He was waiting.

I'm asleep, Theo, she told him silently. Go home. Go to Gran. It doesn't matter anyway because even if you spoke – proud of our love and unafraid of your grandmother's reaction to it – I still wouldn't be free to come to you. You're like Rachel at heart, Theo. You see freedom as a simple act of will, a logical conclusion to recognising one's needs and desires and merely working to fulfil them. But I haven't that sort of freedom, and if I try to grasp it, we'll both be ruined. And when people who love find themselves and their fragile world in a shambles, love dies quickly and blame takes its place. So go home, Theo. Please. Go home.

She turned away so that her back was to the insistent, blinking message. But she still saw it, reflected in the mirror across the room. And it reminded her: of flying through the orchard to meet him, of hands reaching out for her, of lips and mouth on her neck and shoulders, of fingers sliding into her hair.

And of other things: the feverish anticipation of meeting, the secrecy, the exchange of clothing with Rachel so as to move camouflaged to the Balford Marina after dark, the hushed trip across the Wade when the tide was high – using not the Shaws' cabin cruiser but a small Zodiac raft pinched for a few hours from the marina boat hire, sitting in a shallow depression on Horsey Island by the fire he'd built and fed with driftwood, feeling the wind come up through the tall sea grasses and hearing it sough through the wild lavender and the sea purlane.

He'd brought his radio, and with the music as backdrop they'd begun by talking. They'd said all those things that time and the propriety of the workplace made forbidden to them, marvelling to discover how much there actually was to talk about in getting to know another person. But neither of them had been wise enough to see how easily talking to someone led to loving someone. And neither of them had realised how loving someone led to a longing the denial of which only made more intense.

Despite everything that had occurred in the last few months and the last few days, Sahlah felt that longing still. But she wouldn't go to him. She couldn't face him. She had no wish to see any expression upon his face that might – that doubtless would – communicate his fear, his pain, or his revulsion.

We all do what we must do, Theo, she told him silently. And, no matter our wishes otherwise, none of us can change the path that another chooses or has thrust upon him.

When Barbara arrived at the incident room the next morning, Emily Barlow was on the phone, completing a conversation with enough animosity attached to it that Barbara concluded she had to be speaking to her superintendent.

'No, Don,' she was saying. 'I'm not a mind-reader. So I won't know what the Pakistanis have planned until they do it . . . And where am I supposed to dig up an Asian for that sort of undercover work? . . . That's assuming that New Scotland Yard has nothing better to do than send us an officer to infiltrate an organisation which – as far as any of us have been able to ascertain – has never committed a single bloody crime . . . That's *what* I'm trying to dig up, for God's sake . . . Yes, I could do. If you'd be good enough to give me a chance to accomplish something other than yammering on the blower with you twice a day.'

Barbara could just make out a man's angry shouting on the other end of the line. Emily rolled her eyes and listened without comment until the superintendent abruptly ended their conversation by slamming the receiver into its cradle at his end. Barbara heard the *crack* of the two pieces meeting. Emily cursed as the sound struck her ear.

'He's had three town councillors in his office this morning,' Emily explained. 'They've got word of a protest set for midday on the High Street, and they're worried about the shops . . . what shops there are. Not that anyone has anything concrete to report to us, mind you.'

She went on with what she'd apparently been doing prior to Barbara's arrival and Ferguson's phone call: hanging a blue pillowcase over the uncurtained window of her office, perhaps with the intention of cutting down on the day's coming heat. She cast a look over her shoulder as she used the base of a stapler to pound drawing pins through the pillowcase and into the wall. She said, 'Decent job with the face paint, Barb. You finally look human.'

'Thanks. I don't know how long I can keep it up, but it does hide the bruises. I thought I could be quicker about it, though. Sorry to have missed the morning briefing.'

Emily waved the apology off. Barbara was, she told her, not on the time sheet. This was supposed to be her holiday. Her assistance with the Pakistanis was a bonus to Balford's CID. No one expected her to skin her nose on the grindstone doing anything else.

The DCI stepped down from her chair and continued with the drawing pins and the stapler base, lower down the pillowcase. She'd been to the newsagent's on Carnarvon Road in Clacton, she informed Barbara. She'd spent quarter of an hour there the previous night, having a chat with the owner. He himself ran the shop, and when she'd quizzed him about the Pakistani customer who used the phone to make calls to one Haytham Querashi, he'd responded at once with 'That'd be Mr Kumhar, that one. He i'n't in some sort of trouble, is he?'

Fahd Kumhar was a regular, he'd told her. Never caused a bit of trouble or worry, always paid cash. He came in at least three times a week for packets of Benson & Hedges. Sometimes he bought a newspaper as well. And lemon pastilles. He was tremendous fond of lemon pastilles.

'He's never asked Kumhar where he lives,' Emily said. 'But the bloke's evidently there often enough for us to make contact with him without much trouble. I've a man in the launderette across the street, watching the place. When Kumhar shows his face, our boy'll trail him and give us the word.'

'How far is the newsagent's from Clacton market square?'

Emily smiled grimly. 'Less than fifty yards.'

Barbara nodded. That location placed one more person in the proximity of the gentlemen's toilets, which gave them the first possibility of corroborating Trevor Ruddock's story. She told Emily about her phone calls to Pakistan the previous night. She didn't add that Azhar had placed them, and when Emily didn't ask her for clarification that would have led to that detail, she concluded that the information itself was more important than the manner in which she'd come by it.

Like Barbara, Emily homed in on the discussions that Querashi had had with the *mufti*. She said, 'So if homosexuality is considered a grave sin by the Muslims –'

'It is,' Barbara said. 'I've unearthed that much.'

'Then there's a decent chance that our boy Trevor is telling the truth. And that Kumhar – skulking about in the vicinity – knew about Querashi as well.'

'Perhaps,' Barbara said. 'But Querashi could have been phoning the *mufti* about someone else's sin, couldn't he? Sahlah's, for example. If she'd sinned by having it off with Theo Shaw – and fornication's as big a sin as any of them, I reckon – then she'd be cast out. And that, I reckon, would get Querashi off the hook of having to marry her. Maybe that's what he was looking for: a way out.'

'That would certainly set the Maliks off.' Emily nodded her thanks to Belinda Warner as the WPC carried a fax into the room and handed it over. 'Anything from London on those prints we lifted from the Nissan?' Emily asked her.

'I've put a call in to SO4,' Belinda said. 'I was asked did I realise that the print officers get the dabs of twenty-six hundred people every day and is there any special reason why *our* prints ought to have top priority?'

'I'll phone them,' Barbara told Emily. 'I can't promise anything, but I'll try to shake the tree.'

'That's from London, that fax,' Belinda went on. 'Professor Siddiqi's done the translation on the page from that book from Querashi's room. And Phil rang in from the marina. The Shaws have a boat there, a big cabin cruiser.'

'What about the Asians?' Emily asked.

'Only the Shaws.'

Emily dismissed the young woman and stared thoughtfully at the fax before she read it.

'Sahlah gave Theo Shaw that bracelet,' Barbara said to her. '"Life begins now". And his alibi's about as firm as jelly.'

But the DCI was still studying the fax from London. She read aloud. '"How should ye not fight for the cause of Allah and of the feeble among men and of the women and the children who are crying: Our Lord! Bring us forth from out of this town of which the people are oppressors! Oh, give us from thy Presence some protecting friend! Oh, give us from thy Presence some protector!" Well.' She flipped the fax on to her desk. 'That makes things as clear as mud.'

'It sounds like we can trust Azhar,' Barbara said. 'That's practically a word-for-word duplicate of his translation from yesterday. As to what it might mean, Muhannad argued it's a sign that someone was causing Querashi aggro. He homed in on the "bring us forth from out this town" part.'

'He's claiming Querashi was being continually persecuted?' Emily clarified. 'We've not a scrap of evidence of that.'

'Then Querashi might have wanted to be delivered from his marriage,' Barbara offered. She warmed to this idea, supporting – as it did – her earlier hypothesis. 'After all, he can't have been chuffed if he discovered that his fiancée had messed about with Shaw. It's logical that he'd try to call things off. And maybe he'd phoned Pakistan to talk to the *mufti* about that, using veiled terms to do it.'

'I'd say it's more likely that he'd realised he couldn't pretend to be straight for the next forty-odd years and was trying to get out of the marriage because of that, regardless of what he discussed with this *mufti* character. Then someone here got word of his reluctance about marrying Sahlah and –' She made a gun from her thumb and index finger, pointed it at Barbara, and released the trigger. 'You fill in the blanks, Barb.'

'But where does that put Kumhar? And what about the £400 changing hands from Querashi to him?'

'Wouldn't £400 make a nice start on a dowry? Perhaps Querashi was in the process of setting Kumhar up for one of his sisters. He has sisters, hasn't he? Surely I read it in one of these blasted reports.' She indicated the mess on her desk.

Emily's reasoning made sense, but her certainty roused an unease in Barbara. This unease wasn't mitigated when Emily went on.

'The killing was planned to the last detail, Barb. And the last detail had to be an ironclad alibi. No one who took the time to dog Querashi's night-time movements, to string a trip wire, and to make sure there was no evidence left behind, would fail to make certain that he also had an alibi for his whereabouts on Friday night.'

'Okay,' Barbara said. 'I'll go with that. But since everyone but Theo Shaw has an alibi – and more than one person also had a motive to off Querashi – don't we need to look for something else?' She went on to tell Emily of the other phone calls that Querashi had made. But she'd got only as far as the unintelligible message on the answer machine in Hamburg, when Emily interrupted her.

'Hamburg?' she asked quickly. 'Querashi phoned Hamburg?'

'The Hamburg numbers were on the computer print-out. The other call was to the central police station, by the way, although I didn't get far in trying to suss out who received the call. Why? Does Hamburg mean something special?'

Rather than reply, Emily pulled a plastic bag of trail mix from her drawer. Barbara tried not to look guilty about the breakfast she'd consumed earlier: a hefty plate of eggs, potatoes, sausages, mushrooms, and bacon, all swimming in cholesterol and fat. But it wouldn't have mattered had she been wearing the face of Judas.

Emily was so deep in thought that Barbara quickly realised that she wouldn't have noticed.

'Em?' she said. 'What is it?'

'Klaus Reuchlein.'

'Who?'

'He made a third at that dinner in Colchester on Friday night.'

'A *German*? But when you said a foreigner, I thought you meant . . .' How easily her own natural predispositions and unconscious prejudices influenced her thinking. Barbara had assumed the word *foreigner* meant an Asian when 'assume nothing' was one of the first rules of policework.

'He comes from Hamburg,' Emily said. 'Rakin Khan gave me his number. "If you don't believe me, and obviously you don't," he said, "confirm Muhannad's alibi with this." And he handed it over. Where did I . . .' She sifted through papers and folders on her desk and brought forth her notebook. She flipped through the pages until she found the one she wanted. She read the number out.

Barbara wrestled the print-out from her shoulder bag and found the first of the Hamburg telephone numbers. She said, 'Bloody hell.'

'Which I take to mean that you found yourself phoning Mr Reuchlein last night?' Emily smiled, then threw back her head and clenched a fist in the air. 'We've got him, Barb.'

'We've got a connection,' Barbara agreed cautiously. 'But this could just be a coincidence, Em.'

'Coincidence?' Emily's voice was incredulous. 'Querashi happens to have phoned the very same person whose name is produced as one half of Muhannad Malik's alibi? Come on, Barb. This is no coincidence.'

'Then what about Kumhar?' Barbara asked.

'What about him?'

'How does he fit in? He's obviously living in the vicinity of Clacton market square, in the very same area where Trevor claims he saw Querashi doing some cottaging. Is that a coincidence? And if it is, how can we say one fact in the case constitutes a coincidence and the other points to Querashi's killer? And if the Kumhar business isn't a coincidence, what have we got? A major conspiracy to murder Querashi, orchestrated by members of his community? And if so, why?'

'We don't need to know why. *Why* is the job of the prosecution. We just need to hand them a who and a how.'

'Fine,' Barbara said. 'Okay. Accepted. But we know a boat was heard offshore that night. And the Shaws have a boat. We know Ian Armstrong benefited directly from Querashi's death. And his alibi's a hell of a lot weaker than anyone else's. We also have a claim that Querashi was a real bent twig. And we know he was going to the Nez to meet someone, a person he met regularly. I don't see how we can dismiss all this in favour of pursuing one line of enquiry. I don't think that's decent policework, Em, and I don't believe you think it's decent work either.'

She knew at once that she'd gone too far. Her tendency to blab, argue, accuse, and confront – never a problem in working with the affable DI Lynley in London – had completely undermined her self-control. The DCI reacted by straightening her spine while her pupils contracted to the size of pinheads.

'Sorry,' Barbara said hastily. 'Bloody hell. I'm sorry. I get caught up in things and I just don't think. If you'll give me a moment, I'll try to pull my foot out of my mouth.'

Emily was silent. She was also unmoving, save for the index and middle finger of her right hand. These she tapped rapidly and alternately against the top of her desk.

The phone rang. She didn't pick it up. Barbara looked nervously from her to it.

The ringing ceased after fifteen seconds. Belinda Warner came to the door. 'Frank on the phone, Guv,' she said. 'He's got into Querashi's safe-deposit box at Barclay's in Clacton. He says he's got a bill of lading from a business called Eastern Imports –' Here she glanced at a piece of paper on which she'd apparently jotted down the information relayed to her by the DC at Barclay's. '"Purveyors of furniture, rugs, and other goods for the home," it says. An import company from Pakistan. He's also got an envelope with part of an address on it. *Oskarstraße 15*, but nothing else. And a page from a glossy magazine that he can't make anything of. There's also paperwork on a house on First Avenue and Querashi's immigration documents. And that's it on the safe-deposit box. Frank wants to know do you want him to bring this stuff in?'

'Tell him to use his bloody head for once,' Emily snapped. 'Of course I want him to bring the stuff in.'

Belinda gulped and exited hurriedly. Emily turned to Barbara.

'*Oskarstraße 15*,' she said meditatively but with a meaning Barbara couldn't avoid. 'Now, where d'you expect we'd find that address?'

'I was out of line,' Barbara said. 'I get the bit between my teeth sometimes and I just run with it. Can we forget what I said?'

'No,' Emily returned. 'We can't forget it.'

Shit, Barbara thought. There went her plans to work at the DCI's side, to learn something from her, and to keep Taymullah Azhar out of trouble. All defeated by her own flapping lips. 'Hell, Em,' she said.

'Go on.'

'I'm sorry. I'm really sorry. I never mean . . . Oh, *hell.*' Barbara sank her head into the palm of one hand.

'I didn't mean go on with your grovelling,' Emily said. 'Appropriate though it may be. I meant go on with what you were saying.'

Confused, Barbara looked up, trying to read her friend for irony and an intent to humiliate. But what she saw was only interest. And once again she was forced to recognise those qualities that were so essential in their line of work: the ability to back off, the willingness to listen, and the facility for altering one course of action if another presented itself.

Barbara licked her lips, tasting the thin film of lipstick that she'd applied earlier. 'Okay,' she said, but she proceeded gingerly, determined to control her ungovernable tongue. 'Forget Sahlah and Theo Shaw for a minute. What if we suppose that Querashi's intention in calling the *mufti* was actually to talk about his homosexuality, as you suggested. He phoned and asked if a Muslim who commits a grave sin is still a Muslim and he was talking about himself.'

'I'll go along with that.' Emily reached for a handful of trail mix and held it cupped in her palm as Barbara continued.

'He heard that a grave sin would cut him off, so he decided to end his affair and he told the other bloke at an earlier meeting. But this other bloke – his lover – didn't want to break it off. He asked for another meeting. Querashi took his condoms, figuring the last meeting might well end up with a farewell buggering. Better safe than sorry. Only this time, the lover arranged for Querashi's death, along the lines of "If I can't have you, no one can."'

'Querashi became his obsession,' Emily clarified, sounding as if she did so more for herself than for Barbara. She shifted her gaze to the oscillating fan that she'd unearthed from the attic the previous day. She hadn't yet turned it on. Stilled, the blades were tufted with dust. 'I can see how that works, Barb, but you're forgetting one thing: your own argument from yesterday. Why would the lover have killed Querashi and then moved the body? What might have been taken for an accident immediately became suspicious because of that. And because the Nissan was done over.'

'That bloody Nissan,' was Barbara's response, an admission that Emily had just shot down her theory. But when she thought of the events of that past Friday night – a secret rendezvous, a fatal fall, a body out of place, a car done over – she began to see another possibility. 'Em, what if there's a third party involved?'

'A *ménage à trois*? What d'you mean?'

'What if Querashi's supposed lover isn't his killer? D'you have the crime-scene pictures?'

The DCI again rooted through the files and papers on the top of her desk. She found the file and set the photos of the body to one side. She laid out the pictures of the scene itself. Barbara went to stand behind the DCI's chair, studying the photographs over her shoulder.

'Okay,' Emily said. 'Let's go with it. Let's see how it plays with the lover *not* Querashi's killer. On Friday if Querashi's intention was to meet someone, then that person was either already at the Nez waiting for him when Querashi got there or on his way to the rendezvous. Agreed?'

'Agreed.' Barbara continued with the scenario. 'So if that person either saw or heard Querashi fall or if he found him dead at the bottom of those steps –'

'Then he would have logically assumed it was an accident. He would have chosen one of two courses of action at that point: leaving the body there for someone else to find or reporting the accident himself.'

'Right. If he wants to keep their liaison secret, he leaves the body. If he doesn't care who knows –'

'He reports it,' Emily finished.

'But the entire picture changes if Querashi's lover actually *saw* something suspicious that night.'

Slowly, Emily's head turned from the photographs until she was meeting Barbara's eyes. She said, 'If the lover saw ... Christ, Barb! Whoever Querashi was going there to meet must have known it was murder when he fell.'

'So Querashi's lover is out of sight, waiting. He sees the killer string the trip wire, a shadow on the steps moving about. He doesn't know what he's watching, but when Querashi takes the tumble, he figures it out directly. He even sees the killer remove the wire afterwards.'

'But he can't come forward because he can't let it be known that he's been having a fling,' Emily went on.

'Because he's married,' Barbara said.

'Or involved with someone else.'

'In either case, he can't come forward, but he wants to do something to signal to the police that this is a murder and not an accident.'

'So he moves the body,' Emily finished. 'And he does over the car. Jesus Christ, Barb. D'you know what this means?'

Barbara smiled. 'We've got ourselves a flaming witness, Guv.'

'And if the killer knows that,' Emily added grimly, 'we also have someone who could be in danger.'

Yumn was standing at the window, changing the baby's nappy, when she heard the front door close and the sandalled footsteps head down the path towards the street. She looked out to see Sahlah pulling her amber *dupattā* over her thick hair as she hurried to her Micra, parked at the kerb. She was late for work again, but doubtless Akram's wondrous little precious would be forgiven this unfortunate lapse.

She'd spent half an hour in the bathroom with the water running into the bath to cover the sound of her morning retching. But no one else knew that, did they? They thought she was washing herself, an unusual rite for her in the morning – Sahlah was a night-time bather – but one that was understandable given the mind-numbing heat. Only Yumn knew the truth, Yumn who'd stood outside the door listening carefully, gathering information to store like kernels of corn against the potential famine of Sahlah's failure to please the sister-in-law to whom she owed respect, allegiance, and cooperation.

Such a little whore, Yumn thought as she watched Sahlah climb into the car and crank down both of the windows. Sneak out to meet him in the night, Sahlah, invite him into your room when the house is sleeping, spread your legs for him, join your bodies, rotate your hips, and still the next morning manage to look so pure so innocent so fragile so lovely so precious so . . . Little *whore*. Like a rotten egg that's perfect on the outside but, once cracked, reveals the corruption within.

The baby whimpered. Yumn looked down to see that instead of removing the soiled nappy from him, she'd inadvertently wrapped it tightly round his leg.

'Beloved,' she said, quickly removing it. 'Forgive your thoughtless *ammī-gee*, Bishr.'

He cooed in response, waving arms and legs. She gazed down at him. Naked, he was magnificent.

She used the washing flannel to clean him, drawing it through his legs and carefully wiping his tiny penis. She eased the foreskin back and smoothed the flannel round it. She sang, '*Ammī-gee's* little love, Bishr. Yes. Yes. You are. You're *Ammī-gee*'s one true love.'

When he was clean, she didn't reach for a fresh nappy at once. Instead, she admired him. From the shape of him, the strength, and the size, she could tell that he would be just like his father.

His masculinity affirmed her place as a woman. It was her duty to give her husband sons, and she'd done that duty and would continue to do it as long as her body allowed her the privilege. As a consequence, she would not only be cared for in her old age, she would be treasured. And that was more glory than loathsome little Sahlah would ever attain in a thousand lifetimes. She could not hope to be as fertile as Yumn, and she'd already transgressed the tenets of their religion so seriously that she could never redeem herself. She was damaged goods, soiled beyond redemption and ruined beyond the hope of reclamation. She was, indeed, good for nothing more than a life of servitude.

It was such a lovely thought.

'Yes,' Yumn crooned at the baby. 'Yes, yes, what a lovely thought indeed.'

She caressed the insignificant appendage between his legs. How incredible it was that such a small scrap of flesh could determine the role this child would play in life. But that was how the Prophet decreed it.

'Men are in charge of us,' Yumn crooned to the baby, 'because Allah made one to excel the other. Little Bishr, listen to *Ammī-gee*. Do your duty: shelter, protect, and guide. And seek a woman who knows how to do hers.'

Certainly Sahlah did not. She acted the part of obedient daughter, dutiful younger sister and sister-in-law, subservient and docile as required. But that was only a rôle she played. The real girl was the one who lay in a bed whose springs creaked rhythmically in the dead of night.

Yumn knew this. And she'd been intent upon holding her tongue about it. True, she'd not *completely* held her tongue. Some types of hypocrisy were not to be born. When Sahlah's morning vomiting had been followed so closely by her agreement to marry the first young man presented to her as a potential husband, Yumn had made the decision to act. She would not be party to so great a deception as the family's flowerlike Sahlah had obviously intended to perpetrate upon her fiancé.

So she'd gone to Haytham Querashi privately, slipping out of the house on one of the many evenings that Muhannad spent elsewhere. She'd buttonholed the intended bridegroom in his hotel and, sitting knee-to-knee in his garret of a room, she'd done her duty as any religious woman might have done, revealing the one ineradicable impediment to his forthcoming marriage to her sister-in-law. The brat Sahlah carried could be got rid of, of course. But her virginity once lost could not be regained.

Haytham, however, had not reacted as Yumn had expected. The announcement, *She's soiled, she's carrying another man's child*, had not led where tradition and logic dictated it should lead. In fact, Haytham had been so tranquil at Yumn's revelation that she had experienced a moment of dread in which she'd thought she'd somehow got events confused, with Sahlah's morning retching beginning *after* Haytham's advent instead of before it, making Haytham the father of Sahlah's child.

But she *knew* that this was not the case. She *knew* that Sahlah had been pregnant already when Haytham arrived. Thus his acquiescence to a marriage – taken in conjunction with his utter placidity once informed of Sahlah's sin – could only mean one thing. He'd known about her condition and he'd agreed to marry her anyway. The little bitch was saved, Yumn had realised. She was saved from disgrace and saved from dishonour because Haytham was eager, ready, and willing to take her away from the family home as soon as she wished to leave it.

The situation could not have been one iota more unfair. Having been forced to endure her mother-in-law's extolling of Sahlah's virtues for nearly three years, Yumn had been taking great pleasure in every opportunity she had to torment the girl. She'd heard quite enough about Sahlah's beauty, her artistry with those pitiful baubles she made, her intellectual gifts, her religious piety, her physical perfection, and especially her adherence to duty. Upon that last characteristic of her beloved child, Wardah Malik was fully capable of waxing utterly intolerable. And she had no compunction about invoking the image of Sahlah's earnest docility every time Yumn displeased her. If she overcooked the *sevian*, Wardah was good for twenty minutes on the subject of Sahlah's expertise in the kitchen. If she dared to omit one of the five daily prayers – and she was very likely to forego the *namāz* of sunrise – she was regaled with a ten-minute discourse about Sahlah's devotion to Islam. If she failed to dust well enough, to scour the bath completely, or to search out every cobweb in the house, her slovenly habits were compared to Sahlah's which were, of course, immaculate. So it had been a source of great enjoyment to Yumn, having a nasty little piece of knowledge to hold over her sister-in-law's head. And it had been a source of even greater enjoyment, knowing how she was going to be able to put that knowledge to use for her own benefit. Yumn had almost had to relinquish all of her dreams about indefinitely holding little Sahlah hostage to her wishes and commands once Haytham declared his intention of marrying her despite her sins. But now Yumn held the girl's future in her palm once again. And in Yumn's palm was where Sahlah Malik so richly deserved to be.

Yumn smiled down at her son. She began to enfold him in the fresh, soft nappy.

'How lovely life is, little god,' she whispered.

And she made a mental list of the duties she would have Sahlah perform when she arrived home that evening.

Chapter Sixteen

———◆———

The possibility of having a witness to Querashi's death invigorated and refocused the investigation. DCI Barlow began phoning her men on their mobiles, saying, 'Everyone who came in contact with Querashi is a potential witness to his murder as of now. I want everyone's alibi and I want it corroborated. Whoever was on the Nez that night, track him down.'

For Barbara's part, she went on her way to phone the fingerprint office in London, using what little influence she had to get SO4 to move on the prints that had been lifted from the Nissan. She knew that a match wasn't guaranteed. They would have a match only if the prints on the Nissan had been left by someone once arrested and run through a booking procedure somewhere in the country. But if that was the case, they'd have the best break they could get: an identity, something concrete that was beyond the realm of speculation.

Barbara made the call. Like most support services, the fingerprint people didn't warm to anything suggesting interference from another branch of the legal family, so she used the racial unrest in the town to promote her cause. She finished by saying, 'We're sitting on a powder keg out here, and we need your help to defuse it.'

SO4 understood. Everyone wanted their dabs given identities before the sun set on the first day of the investigation. But the sergeant needed to understand that a highly specialised work force such as SO4 could be expected to deal only with a limited number of evidential particulars on a given day. 'We cannot afford an error,' the department head intoned, 'not when guilt or innocence may well ride on a conclusion reached by this organisation.'

Right, right, right, Barbara thought. She told him to do his best and returned to Emily.

'I'm a bird with a lot less clout that I would like to be,' Barbara told her frankly. 'They'll do what they can. What's up?'

Emily was in the process of flipping through the contents of a file. She said, 'Querashi's picture,' and pulled it out. It was, Barbara saw, the same photograph of the murdered man that had run on the front page of the *Tendring Standard*: Querashi looked simultaneously solemn and harmless. 'If Trevor Ruddock's telling the truth about Querashi and his cottaging, there's a chance that someone else saw him in the market square in Clacton. And if someone else saw him, someone may have seen our potential witness with him. I want that witness, Barb. If Ruddock's telling the truth.'

'If,' Barbara said. 'He's got motive enough to kill Querashi himself, and I haven't checked on his alibi yet. I want to have a look at his time card for last week. And I want a talk with Rachel as well. A lot of roads seem to be leading to her. It's curious, if you ask me.'

Emily gave her approval to the plan. For her own part, she'd work the homosexual aspect of the case. With the market square angle to be explored and Fahd Kumhar to be located, other roads appeared to be leading to Clacton. She didn't want to ignore them. 'If he exists, that witness is our key,' she said.

They parted company in the patch of Tarmac that served as the old police station's car park. At one side, a corrugated metal lock-up acted as the digs of the evidence officer. In his shirt sleeves and with a blue handkerchief tied round his head to soak up the perspiration, he sat on a stool. He appeared to be in the process of checking evidence bags against a logbook. The temperature was beginning to reach heights that felt suitable for grilling bacon. That poor bloke, Barbara thought, had the worst job of all.

In the time that she'd been in the station, Barbara found that the Mini – even with its windows wide open – had soaked up enough heat to make breathing difficult once she was inside it. The steering wheel was fiery to the touch, and the car's seats sizzled through the thin material of her trousers. She looked at her watch and wondered at the fact that it wasn't yet midday. She had little doubt that by two o'clock she'd feel like an overcooked Sunday joint.

Racon Original and Artistic Jewellery was open for business when she arrived. Beyond the gaping front door, both Connie Winfield and her daughter were at work. They appeared to be in the process of arranging a new shipment of necklaces and earrings for display, because they were removing baubles from a cardboard box and using straight pins to mount them on an antique folding screen whose panels had been fashioned from cream-coloured velvet.

Barbara watched them for a moment without making her presence known. Idly, she noted two details. Between them they had the artistry to make the arrangement of jewellery enticing and attractive. And they worked in what seemed to be an inimical silence. The mother cast baleful looks upon the daughter. The daughter countered with haughty expressions indicative of her indifference to her mother's displeasure.

Both women started when Barbara said good morning. Only Connie spoke.

'I got my doubts that you're here to make a purchase.' She stopped what she was doing and went to the counter, where a cigarette burned in a quarter-moon ashtray. She tapped off ash and brought the cigarette to her mouth. She watched Barbara over it, eyes hostile.

'I'd like a word with Rachel,' Barbara said.

'Have it, then. And good luck to you. I'd like a word with the slag myself, but I'm getting nothing out of her. You may as well have a go. I can't hardly wait to hear what she's got to say for herself.'

Barbara didn't intend the mother to be in on the questioning, however. She said, 'Rachel, can you step outside? Can we have a walk?'

'What's this, then?' Connie demanded. 'I di'n't say she was free to go off somewheres. We got work to do. What you got to say to her, you c'n say here. While we do our unpacking.'

Over one of the folding screen's six finials, Rachel draped the necklace she'd been holding. Connie seemed to realise what this action implied. She went on. 'Rachel Lynn, don't you dare even think –'

'We c'n walk up to the park,' Rachel said to Barbara. 'It's not far, and I could do with a break.'

'Rachel Lynn!'

Rachel pointedly ignored her. She led the way out of the shop and on to the pavement. Barbara heard Connie bark her daughter's name once more – and then cry it out pleadingly – as they headed in the direction of the Balford Road.

The park in question was a square of sun-parched lawn a short distance beyond St John's Church. A freshly painted black wrought-iron fence surrounded it, but its gate stood open. A sign on this bade everyone welcome and named the place *Falak Dedar Park.* A Muslim name, Barbara noted. She wondered if it was indicative of the inroad that the Asian community was making into Balford-le-Nez.

A gravel path that edged the lawn took them to a bench, partially shaded by a laburnum tree heavy with cascades of yellow flowers. A fountain trickled in the centre of the park, a veiled girl rendered in cloud-coloured marble, who poured water from a tipped urn into a shallow pool that formed a shell at her feet. After arranging her filmy skirt, Rachel gave her attention to this fountain, not to Barbara.

Barbara told the girl why she was there: to ascertain her whereabouts on the previous Friday night. 'Four nights ago,' she reminded Rachel, lest the girl feign an inability to recall. Four nights hardly comprised a substantial enough leap in time to dim one's recollection, she was implying.

Rachel was obviously skilled in inference. She said, 'You want to know where I was when Haytham Querashi died.'

Barbara agreed that this was her purpose. She added, 'Your name's come up more than once in relation to this case, Rachel. I didn't want to say as much in front of your mum –'

'Ta,' Rachel said.

'– but it never looks good when one's name pops up in any way during a murder investigation. Smoke?'

Rachel shook her head and returned her gaze to the fountain. She said, 'I was out with a boy called Trevor Ruddock. He's a bloke from the pier. But I expect you know that already. He told me last night that you talked to him.' She smoothed her hand along a design in her skirt, a peacock's head that was cleverly camouflaged in the material's swirls of colour.

Barbara altered her position to pull her notebook from her shoulder bag. She flipped through the pages to find her notes of the earlier interview with Trevor Ruddock. As she did this, she saw Rachel's eyes catch the movement in her peripheral vision. The girl's hand stopped smoothing her skirt, as if she'd suddenly realised that any motion was liable to betray her.

Barbara refreshed her own memory on the subject of Trevor's evening with Rachel, then she turned to the girl. She said, 'Trevor Ruddock claims you were with him. He gets a bit vague with the details, though. And details are what I'm trying to suss out. So perhaps you can fill in his blanks for me.'

'I don't see how.'

'It's easy enough.' Barbara held her pencil in an attitude of expectancy. She said, 'What did you two do?'

'Do?'

'On Friday night. Where'd you go? Out for a meal? For coffee? To a film? Perhaps you went to a caff somewhere?'

Two of Rachel's fingers pinched the peacock's crested head. 'You're making a joke, aren't you?' Her tone was bitter. 'I expect Trev told you where we went.'

'He might have done,' Barbara admitted. 'But I'd like to have your version, if you don't mind.'

'And if I mind?'

'Then you mind. But minding's not such a good idea when someone's been murdered. When someone's been murdered, the best thing to do is to tell the truth. Because if you lie, the rozzers always want to know the reason. And they generally keep chipping away at you till they get it.'

The girl's fingers pinched her skirt more tightly. If the camouflaged peacock had been real, Barbara thought, he'd be gasping his final breath.

'Rachel?' Barbara prompted. 'Have we got a problem? Because I can always let you go back to the shop if you need to have a think before we talk. You can ask your mum what you ought to do. Your mum seemed real concerned about you yesterday, and I'm sure if she knew that the cops're asking about your whereabouts on the murder night, she'd give you all the advice you want. Didn't your mum mention to me yesterday that you –'

'All *right*.' Apparently, Rachel didn't need Barbara to offer more clarification on the subject of her mother. 'What he said is true. What he told you is true. All right? Is that what you want to hear?'

'What I want to hear are the facts, Rachel. Where were you and Trevor on Friday night?'

'Where he said we were. Up in one of the beach huts. Which is where we are most Friday nights. 'Cause no one's around up there after dark, so no one sees who Trevor Ruddock's decided to let blow him. There. Is that what you wanted to know?'

The girl's head turned. She was red to her hair. And the harsh and unforgiving daylight emphasised each of her facial deformities with a brutal precision. Seeing her fully, neither hidden by shadows nor in profile any longer, Barbara couldn't help thinking of a documentary film she'd once watched on the BBC, an exploration of what constitutes beauty to the human eye. Symmetry, the film concluded. *Homo sapiens* is genetically programmed to admire symmetry. If that was the case, Barbara thought, Rachel Winfield didn't stand a chance.

Barbara sighed. She wanted to tell the girl that life didn't need to be lived the way she was living it. But the only alternative she herself had to offer was the life she was leading, and she was leading it alone.

'Actually,' she said, 'what you and Trevor were up to doesn't much interest me, Rachel. It's your call who you want to do and why. If you're chuffed at the end of an evening with him, more power to you. If you're not, move on.'

'I'm chuffed,' Rachel said defiantly. 'I'm properly chuffed.'

'Right,' Barbara said. 'So what time did you find yourself so chuffed that you staggered home? Trevor tells me it was half-past eleven. What d'you say?'

Rachel stared at her. Barbara took note of the fact that she was biting her lower lip.

'What's it going to be?' Barbara asked her. 'Either you were with him till half-past eleven, or you weren't.' She didn't add the rest because she knew the girl understood it. If Trevor Ruddock had spoken to her, he'd have made it clear that her failure to corroborate his story in every detail would shine suspicion's spotlight on him.

Rachel looked away, back to the fountain. The girl pouring water was lithe and graceful, with perfect features and downcast eyes. Her hands were small and her feet – just visible at the bottom of the drapery that she wore to cover her body – were shapely and delicate like the rest of her. Gazing upon the statue, Rachel Winfield seemed to make up her mind. She said, 'Ten o'clock,' with her eyes fixed on the fountain. 'I got home round ten.'

'You're sure of that? You looked at a clock? You couldn't have misread the time somehow?'

Rachel gave a weary one-note laugh. 'You know how long it takes to blow some bloke? When that's all he wants and that's all you're likely ever to get? From him or anyone? Let me tell you. It doesn't take long.'

Barbara felt all the wretchedness of the girl's painful questions. She flipped her notebook closed and considered how best to reply. Part of her said that it wasn't her job to hand out advice, to salve psychic wounds, or to pour oil generously where soul waters roiled. The other part of her felt a kinship with the girl. For Barbara, one of life's most difficult and most bitter lessons had been the slow recognition of what constitutes love: both giving it and receiving it in turn. She still hadn't learned the lesson completely. And in her line of work, there were times when she wondered if she ever would.

'Don't put such a give-away price on yourself,' she finally settled on saying to the girl. She dropped her cigarette to the ground as she spoke, extinguishing it with the toe of her high top trainer. Her throat was dry, from the heat, the smoke, and the tautness of muscles fighting to hold back what she didn't particularly want to feel and even less want to remember about her own low prices and when she'd offered them. 'Someone's going to pay that price, sure, because it's a bargain. But the price you pay is bloody well higher.'

She rose, without giving the girl a chance to reply. She nodded her thanks for Rachel's cooperation and began to head out of the small park. As she followed the path to the gate, she saw a young Asian man affixing on to one of the wrought-iron railings a yellow paper that he took from a stack which he carried. By the time she reached the gate, he'd moved on and she saw him farther down the street, fixing another notice to a telegraph pole.

Curiously, she read the poster. The large black letters on yellow were hard to miss, and they spelled out a man's name across the top: FAHD KUMHAR. Beneath this was a boldly rendered message in both English and Urdu. 'Balford CID want to interrogate you. Do not speak to them without legal representation. *Jum'a* will provide this. Please phone.' These four sentences were followed by a local telephone number, which was repeated across the bottom of the page vertically so that it could be torn off by a passer-by.

At least they now knew what Muhannad Malik's latest move was, Barbara thought. And she felt a mixture of satisfaction and relief at what the yellow notice inadvertently revealed to her. Despite having good reason for doing so, Azhar hadn't betrayed to his cousin her slip of the tongue of the previous night. Had he done so, the only town in which the notices would have gone up was Clacton, and they'd have been concentrated round the market square.

She owed him one now. And as she walked back in the direction of the High Street, Barbara couldn't help wondering when and how Taymullah Azhar would call in the debt.

*　　*　　*

Cliff Hegarty couldn't concentrate. Not that concentration was really required in applying the jigsaw to the coupling men who would form the latest puzzle on offer from Hegarty's Adult Distractions. The machinery was programmed to run on its own. All he had to do was set the prospective puzzle in the correct position, choose which one of fifty designs he wanted the jigsaw to work in, turn a dial, flip a switch, and wait for the results. All of which he was used to doing as part of his daily routine when he wasn't taking telephone orders, preparing his next catalogue for the printer, or packing off one or another innocently wrapped item to some randy bloke in the Hebrides with an appetite for tasty diversions that he'd rather his postman not know about.

But today was different and for more than one reason.

He'd seen the cops. He'd even talked to them. Two detectives wearing plain clothes and lugging a tape recorder, clipboards and notebooks had gone into the mustard factory right at opening time. Two others had arrived twenty-one minutes later, also in plain clothes. These two started making visits to the other businesses on the industrial estate. So Cliff had known it was only a matter of time – and not very much of it – till they got to him.

He could have left, but that would not only have postponed the inevitable, it would also have encouraged the cops to make a run south to Jaywick Sands in order to track him down at home. And he didn't want that. Holy shit, he couldn't have that, and he was willing to do just about anything to prevent it.

So when they came in his direction after having a go at the sailmakers and the mattress works, Cliff girded himself for the coming interview by removing his jewellery and rolling down the sleeves of his T-shirt so the tattoo on his bicep was hidden. Cops' hatred of queers was notorious. The way Cliff saw it, there was no sense in announcing himself as a poofter while there was a chance they might think otherwise.

They'd shown their identification and introduced themselves as DCs Grey and Waters. Grey did the talking while Waters took notes. And both of them gave the eye to a display case featuring two-headed dildos, leather masks, and penis rings of ivory and stainless steel.

It's a living, mates, he wanted to say. But wisdom suggested that he hold his tongue.

He was glad of the air conditioner. Had it not been blasting away, he would have been sweating. And while the sweat would have been due in large part to working inside a structure fabricated from corrugated steel, in smaller part it would have come from nerves. And the less he displayed any symptoms of anxiety in front of the fuzz, the better he liked it.

They brought out a photograph and asked him if he knew the subject. He told them sure, it was the dead bloke from the Nez, Haytham Querashi. He worked at the mustard factory.

How well did he know Querashi? they asked next.

He knew who Querashi was, if that's what they meant. He knew him well enough to nod and say Good morning or Bloody hot day, i'n't it, mate?

Cliff was careful to appear as casual as possible. He came round the counter to answer their questions and he stood with his arms crossed beneath his chest, with one leg taking most of his weight. This posture emphasised the muscles in his arms, which he thought was a good idea. A muscular body equalled masculinity in the eyes of most straights. Masculinity equalled heterosexuality as well, especially in the view of the ignorant. And in Cliff's experience, most cops were about as pig-ignorant as you could get.

Did he know Querashi outside the industrial estate? was their next question.

Cliff asked them what they meant. He said that sure, he knew Querashi outside the industrial estate. If he knew him here, he'd know him elsewhere. He wouldn't exactly have a memory loss when it was after hours, would he?

They weren't amused by this remark. They asked him to explain how he knew Querashi.

He told them he knew Querashi outside work the same way he knew Querashi inside work. If he saw him in Balford or anywhere else, he said hello, he said, Bloody hot day, he nodded in recognition. That was the extent of it.

Where might he have seen Querashi outside work? they asked him.

And Cliff saw once again how cops twist everything to suit themselves. He hated the bastards in that instant. If he didn't mind his every syllable, they'd have him strolling with Querashi in the same jockskrap before they were finished.

He kept his temper and told them that he hadn't seen the bloke outside the industrial estate. He was merely telling them that *if* he'd seen him, he'd have known who he was and he would have acknowledged him the way he acknowledged anyone he recognised. He was that sort of chap.

Friendly, the cop called Grey remarked. He let his gaze wander over to the display case of goodies to make his point.

Cliff didn't challenge them with a belligerent: What's that supposed to mean? He knew that cops liked to cause aggro because feeling aggro put you off-guard with them. He'd played this game more than once with the rozzers. It had taken him only one night in lock-up to work out the importance of staying cool.

They changed gears on him, then, asking if he was familiar with someone called Fahd Kumhar.

He told him he wasn't. He admitted that he might recognise Fahd Kumhar on sight because by sight he knew most of the Asians who worked in the mustard factory. But he didn't know their names. Those names they have just sound like a slew of letters put together to make up noises and I can never remember them, he explained. Why don't those people give their kids proper names? What about William, Charlie, or Steve?

The cops didn't pick up on this friendly aside. Instead, they went back to Querashi again. Had he ever seen Querashi with anyone? Talking to anyone in the grounds of the industrial estate?

Cliff couldn't recall, he told them. He said he might have done, but it wouldn't have registered. There were people in the grounds all the time, lots of coming and going, lorries arriving, deliveries being made, goods being shipped.

This might well have been a man Querashi would have been talking to, Waters told him. And with a nod towards the display case, he asked Cliff if he and Querashi had ever done business.

Querashi was a ginger, Grey added. Did Cliff know that?

This question cut a little too close for comfort, the way a knife blade can nearly slice into one's skin. Cliff closed his mind to the memory of his conversation with Gerry in the kitchen on the previous morning. He shut his inner ears to their words: accusations on one part and angry denials and defences on the other.

What about fidelity? Where did that go?

What about fidelity? All I know about it is what you say about it. And there's a hell of a lot of difference between what blokes feel and what they say.

Was it the market square? Is that where it happened? Did you meet him there?

Oh, right, too right. Have it your way.

And the crash of the door put the full stop at the end of what went for their conversation.

But he couldn't betray any of that to the cops. No way could he let these blokes near Gerry.

No, he told them steadily. He'd never done business with Haytham Querashi, and it was news to him that the bloke was queer. He thought Querashi was supposed to be marrying Akram Malik's daughter. So were the cops sure they had their facts sorted out?

Nothing's ever sure in an investigation till a suspect's in the nick, Grey informed him.

And Waters added that if he remembered anything that he thought the police needed to know . . .

Cliff assured them that he'd have a proper think. He'd phone if anything popped into his head.

You do that, Grey told him. He gave a final look round the shop. When he and Waters stepped outside, he said 'Flaming dung-puncher', just loud enough to be certain that Cliff overheard it.

Cliff watched them walk off. When they disappeared into the joinery across the pitted lane, he allowed himself to move. He went behind the counter where his order desk was, and he thunked down on to the wooden chair.

His heart was racing, but he hadn't noticed while the cops were there. Once they left, though, he could feel it pounding so hard and so fast that it felt like it might leap straight through his chest to lie throbbing on the blue lino floor. He had to get a grip, he told himself. There was Gerry to think of. He had to keep his mind on Gerry.

His lover hadn't slept at home on the previous night. Cliff had awakened in the morning to find his side of the bed unruffled and he'd known at once that Gerry had never returned from Balford. His guts greeted this knowledge with a sickening twist. And despite the early heat of the day, his hands and feet had gone cold as dead fish at the thought of what Gerry's absence might mean.

He'd tried at first to tell himself that the other man had simply decided to work through the night and into the next day. After all, he was trying to complete the pier-end restaurant before the next bank holiday. And at the same time, he was working after hours on that house renovation in Balford. So Gerry had a good enough reason to be away from home. He might have gone directly from the first job to the second one, which was something he did quite often, in fact, sometimes working till three in the morning if he was anywhere close to completing a stage of the second project. But he'd never worked round the clock before. And in the past whenever he'd planned to work late into the night, he'd always phoned.

He hadn't phoned this time. He hadn't come home. And as Cliff had sat on the edge of the bed that morning, he sought clues within his last conversation with Gerry, details that might tell him of Gerry's whereabouts and of the condition of his heart and his mind. Except he had to admit that they hadn't had so much a conversation as an argument, one of those verbal brawls in which past behaviour suddenly becomes a bench mark for measuring present doubts.

Everything about their shared and individual pasts had been dragged out, aired, and laid down for a lengthy and intimate examination. The market square in Clacton. The gentlemen's toilet. Leather and Lace at the Castle. Gerry's endless work in that pishposh Balford house. Cliff's infuriating walks and his drives and his pints of Foster's at Never Say Die. Who used the motorcycle had been brought up, as well as who took the boat out and when and why. And when they'd run out of accusations to hurl, they went on to shout about whose family accepted that one of their sons was a poofter and whose dad would try to beat the living shit out of his son if he knew the truth.

Gerry usually backed down from a fight, but he hadn't backed down from this one. And Cliff was left wondering what it meant that his lover – usually so mild and so earnest – had altered into a yobbo ready to take him on if taking him on was necessary.

So the day had started out badly and had only got worse: waking up to find that Gerry had done a bunk and looking out of the shop window to see the coppers putting the cosh on everyone in sight.

Now, at the jigsaw, Cliff tried to give his mind to the work. There were orders to fill and puzzles to be cut, dodgy pictures to assess for their potential as future puzzles and decisions to be made about ordering in an array of novelty condoms from Amsterdam. He had at least sixteen videos to preview and reviews to write for *Crossdressers' Quarterly*. But he found that he could think of nothing but the questions the cops had wanted him to answer and whether he'd managed to be so convincing that they wouldn't show up in Jaywick Sands to ask Gerry DeVitt's assistance in their enquiry.

Theo Shaw's appearance didn't suggest a man who'd slept the sleep of the guileless, Barbara thought. Shaw was carrying luggage under his eyes and these were nearly bloodshot enough to give him the look of an albino rabbit. When Dominique the Tongue-stud had announced Barbara's arrival at the pier offices for a second visit, Theo had started to say brusquely, 'No way. Tell her –' but had choked off whatever else he'd intended to communicate when he saw Barbara standing directly behind the girl.

Dominique said, 'She's asking to see the time cards, Mr Shaw, last week's time cards. Sh'll I fetch them or what? I didn't want to do nothing till I talked to you first.'

'I'll handle this,' Theo Shaw said, and made no other comment until Dominique went swinging back towards reception in her orange platform shoes. Then he looked at Barbara, who'd entered his office without an invitation, installing herself in one of two rattan chairs that sat facing his desk. 'Time cards?'

'In the singular,' Barbara said. 'Trevor Ruddock's from last week, to be specific. Have you got it?'

He had. The card was with the accounting department, where the payroll was done. If the sergeant didn't mind waiting a minute . . .

Barbara didn't mind. Another opportunity to recce Theo Shaw's office was just fine by her. But he seemed to read her intention, because instead of heading off to fetch the requested time card himself, he picked up the phone, punched in three numbers, and asked that the card be brought to them.

'I hope Trevor's not in trouble,' he said.

The devil you do, Barbara thought. She said, 'Just confirming a few details.' She gestured towards the window. 'The pier looks more crowded today. Business must be picking up.'

'Yes.'

'Good for the cause, that.'

'What cause?'

'Redevelopment. Are the Asians part of it? Redevelopment, I mean.'

'That's an odd question. Why do you ask?'

'I was in a place called Falak Dedar Park. It looks new. There's a fountain in the centre: a girl in Arab garb pouring water. And the name sounds Asian. So I was wondering if the Asians are involved in your redevelopment plans. Or do they have their own?'

'Anyone's free to become involved,' Theo said. 'The town needs investors. We don't intend to hold anyone back if they want to be part of the project.'

'And if someone wants to go his own way? Have his own project?

With a different idea from yours about redevelopment? What happens then?'

'It makes more sense for Balford to accept an overall plan,' Theo replied. 'Otherwise, what you end up with is an architectural hotchpotch, like the south bank of the Thames. I've lived here most of my life and, frankly, I'd rather like to avoid that happening.'

Barbara nodded. His reasoning made sense. But it also suggested yet another area in which the Asian community might be in conflict with the longtime residents of Balford-le-Nez. She left her chair and approached the redevelopment plans, which she'd noticed on the previous day. She wanted to see how the plans affected such areas as the industrial estate where Akram Malik had obviously invested so much money in his mustard factory. But she was distracted by a town map that hung on the wall next to the blueprints and the artist's renderings of Balford-to-be.

This map indicated in which sections of the town the most money would be invested. But that wasn't what interested Barbara. Instead, she took note of the location of the Balford Marina. It was west of the Nez at the base of the peninsula. With advantageous tidal conditions, someone sailing from the marina up the Balford Channel into Pennyhole Bay would have easy access to the east side of the Nez, where Haytham Querashi had met his death.

She said, 'You have a boat, haven't you, Mr Shaw? Berthed at the marina?'

His expression was guarded. 'It's the family's, not mine.'

'Cabin cruiser, isn't it? Do any night sailing?'

'I have done.' He saw where she was heading. 'But not on Friday night.'

They would see about that, Barbara thought.

Trevor's time card was delivered by an antique gentleman who looked as if he'd worked on the pier since the day it was built. He doddered into the room, dressed in a linen suit, starched shirt, and tie despite the heat, and he handed the card over with a respectful, 'Mr Shaw, sir. Glorious day, isn't it? Like a gift from the Almighty.'

Theo thanked him, asked after his dog, his wife, and his grandchildren – in that order – and sent him on his way. He gave Barbara the time card.

She saw on it what she expected to see. Trevor Ruddock had been telling half-truth and half-lie during her interview with him: his time card indicated that he'd appeared for work at eleven-thirty-six. But if Rachel could be depended upon to be speaking the truth, then he hadn't been with her after ten that evening, and he had an hour and a half still to account for. Motive and opportunity were now his. Barbara wondered if the means lay among the clutter of his spider-making worktable.

She told Theo Shaw that she would need the time card. He made no protest, although he added, 'Trevor's a good sort, Sergeant. He looks like a lout, but that's the extent of it. He might engage in petty theft, but he'd never take it on to murder.'

'People can surprise you,' Barbara said. 'Just when you think you know what you're dealing with, they can do something that makes you wonder if you ever really knew them at all.'

She'd struck something with that: the right note, the wrong chord, a jangled nerve. She could see it in his eyes. She waited for him to make a comment that might betray himself in some way, but he didn't do it. He merely made the appropriate noises about being glad to be helpful in her investigation. Then he saw her on her way.

On the pier once more, Barbara slipped the time card into her shoulder bag. She managed to avoid Rosalie the Romany Palm Reader a second time, and she wended her way through the clumps of small children waiting with their parents to charge on to the kiddie rides. As was the case yesterday, the noise in this covered section of the pier reverberated from the walls and the ceiling. Clanging bells, shrilling whistles, a tooting calliope, and shouting voices all contributed to a din that made Barbara feel as if she were shooting round inside a gigantic pinball machine. She extricated herself from the cacophony by making her way to the uncovered section of the pier.

To her left the Ferris wheel was spinning. To her right, barkers were trying to seduce passersby into taking a chance at tossing coins, upending milk bottles, and firing air guns. Beyond, a roller-coaster car was hurtling downward with a load of screaming passengers. And a miniature steam train was chugging towards the end of the pier.

Barbara followed the train. The unfinished restaurant loomed over the sea, and the workers on its roof reminded her that there was a point she wished to clarify with the head of the project, Gerry DeVitt.

As on the previous day, DeVitt was welding. But this time he happened to look up as Barbara stepped past a mound of copper tubing and dodged a stack of timber. He doused the flame on his blow torch and pushed his protective mask to the top of his kerchief-bound head.

'What d'you need this time round?' He didn't sound either rude or impatient, but there was still an edge to his words. She wasn't welcome. Nor, Barbara thought, were her questions. 'Make it fast, all right? We've a load of work to get through today and not a lot of time to spend yammering with visitors.'

'Can I have a word with you, Mr DeVitt?'

'Looks to me like you're having it.'

'Right. Outside, though. Away from the noise.' In order to be heard, she had to raise her voice. The hammering, pounding, and sawing hadn't ceased with her entrance on this occasion.

DeVitt made a mysterious adjustment to the tanks that were connected to his equipment. Then he led the way to the front of the restaurant, which overlooked the end of the pier. Sidling past a serried arrangement of prefabricated windows that leaned against the doorway, he stepped outside. At the pier railing, he dug in the pocket of his cut-off jeans and brought out a roll of Polos. He popped one in his mouth, turned to Barbara, and said, 'So?'

'So why didn't you mention yesterday that you knew Haytham Querashi?' she said.

He squinted in the bright light. He didn't pretend to misunderstand her. He said, 'The way I recall it, you didn't ask. You wanted to know if we'd seen an Arab bird on the pier. We hadn't. End of story.'

'You said you didn't mix with the Asians, though,' Barbara said. 'You said something about Asians having their ways and English having theirs. "Put them together and you've got trouble," was your conclusion.'

'That's still my conclusion.'

'But you knew Querashi, didn't you? He had telephone messages from you at the Burnt House Hotel. That does something to suggest that you mixed with him.'

DeVitt changed position to lean against the pier railing, his elbows taking most of his weight. He was facing her, not the North Sea, but he was looking at the town. Perhaps in meditation, perhaps in the hope of avoiding her eyes. 'I didn't mix with him. I was doing some work for him in a house in First Avenue. It's where he was going to live after his marriage.'

'So you did know him.'

'I'd spoken to him a dozen times, maybe more. But that's the extent of it. If you want to call that knowing him, I knew him.'

'Where did you first meet him?'

'There. At the house.'

'The First Avenue house? You're certain of that?'

He shot her a glance. 'Yeah. That's right.'

'How did he know to contact you to work on it?'

'He didn't contact me,' DeVitt said. 'Akram Malik did. He said he had a rush renovation about two months ago and asked me if I'd take it on. I gave it a look and thought I could manage it. I could always do with the money. I met Querashi there – at the house – after I'd already begun the work.'

'But you're working here at the pier full-time, aren't you? So when do you work in First Avenue? At the weekend?'

'Nights as well.'

'Nights?' Barbara's voice rose instinctively.

He gave her a glance, this one more guarded than the last. 'That's what I said.'

She took stock of DeVitt. A long time had passed since she'd first concluded that one of the most foolish mistakes an investigator could make was drawing an inference based on appearance. With his powerful build and the kind of work he did, DeVitt had the look of a man who ended his blow torch days with a pint of bitter and a shag with the wife or the girlfriend. True, he was wearing an earring – the same gold hoop that he'd had on yesterday – but Barbara knew that earrings, toe rings, navel rings, or nipple rings meant sod bloody all in the current decade.

'We think that Mr Querashi was homosexual,' Barbara told him. 'We think he may have been intending to meet his lover on the Nez on the night he was killed. He was due to marry in the next few days, so we have an idea that he may have gone to the Nez to end that relationship once and for all. If he tried to live a double life while married to Sahlah Malik, someone was bound to find out eventually, and he had a lot to lose.'

DeVitt raised his hand to his mouth. The movement was studied, slow and steady, as if he wished to demonstrate that his nerves were unjangled in the face of this new information. He spat the Polo into his hand, then flicked it from his palm into the sea. 'I don't know anything about how the bloke got his rocks off,' DeVitt said. 'Men, women, or animals. We didn't discuss it.'

'He left the hotel at the same time several nights each week. And we're fairly certain he was meeting someone. He had three condoms in his pocket when his body was found, so I think we can safely conclude they were meeting for more than a casual after-dinner brandy at one of the pubs. Tell me this, Mr DeVitt. How often did Querashi come to First Avenue to check on the work you were doing there?'

She saw the reaction this time: a sharp movement of muscle in his jaw. He didn't reply.

'Did you work there alone, or did some of these blokes help you out?' Here, she indicated the restaurant by jutting her chin at it. Inside, someone had turned on a portable radio. Above the noise of the construction, a voice began chanting about having life to live and love to give as the accompanying music crescendoed. 'Mr DeVitt?' Barbara prompted.

'Alone,' he said.

'Ah,' she replied.

'What's that supposed to mean?'

'Did Querashi stop by often to check your work?'

'Once or twice. But so did Akram. And the wife, Mrs Malik.' He looked her way. His face was damp, but that could easily have been due to the heat. The sun was climbing and it throbbed down upon both of them, sucking the moisture through their pores. Her own face would have been damp as well, Barbara knew, had she not thoroughly brushed it with powder in step two of her facial beautification project. 'I never knew when any of them would drop in,' he added. 'I did the work, and if they decided to stop by and check it, that was fine by me.' He scrubbed his face on the sleeve of his T-shirt, adding, 'So if that's all you want from me, I'd like to get on with it.'

Barbara nodded him back to work, but as he approached the restaurant door, she spoke once more. 'Jaywick Sands, Mr DeVitt. Is that where you live? That's where your calls to Querashi came from.'

'I live there, yeah.'

'I've not been there in years, but as I recall, it's not far from Clacton. Just a few minutes by car, in fact. That's the case, isn't it?'

His eyes narrowed to a squint. But again the sun could have been his reason. 'What exactly are you on about, Sergeant?'

Barbara smiled. 'Just trying to keep my geography straight. There're a thousand details in a case like this. You never know which one is going to lead you to a killer.'

Chapter Seventeen

Emily's mobile rang the moment she hit Marine Parade East, which edged the waterfront on the approach to the pleasure pier in Clacton-on-Sea. She'd just braked for a group of pensioners who were crossing the street from the Cedars Nursing Home – three of them using Zimmer frames and two with walking sticks – when the trill of the phone cut into her thoughts of what a witness to the crime could mean to their case.

The caller was DC Billy Honigman, who'd spent the day in an unmarked Escort some thirty yards from Jackson & Son, the newsagent's shop in Carnarvon Road.

His message was terse enough: 'Got him, Guv.'

Kumhar, she thought. Where? she wanted to know.

He'd tailed the Pakistani to a house in Chapman Road, Honigman told her, not much more than round the corner from Jackson & Son. It looked like a boarding house. A sign in the window advertised rooms to let.

'I'm on my way,' Emily informed him. 'Sit tight. Don't approach.'

She rang off. When the pensioners were clear of her car, she surged forward and in less than a mile made the turn up Carnarvon Road. Chapman Road shot left off the High Street. It was lined with terraced Victorian houses, all identically constructed of umber brick with bay windows whose frames provided the only means of distinguishing among them. These were edged in a variety of colours, and when Emily joined DC Honigman, he indicated a house whose chosen window-frame colour was yellow. It sat twenty yards from where Honigman had parked his Escort.

'Lives over there,' he said. 'He made some purchases at the newsagent's – newspaper, cigarettes, and a chocolate bar – and walked back here directly. Nervous, though. Walked fast and kept his eyes straight ahead, but when he got to the house, he walked on past it. He went halfway to the end of the street and had a good look round before heading back.'

'Did he see you, Billy?'

'Might've. But what's to see? Bloke looking for a parking space for a day at the sea.'

He had a point. With his usual attention to detail, Honigman had strapped a collapsible plastic lounger to the roof of the car. In a bow to both continuity and incognito, he was wearing khaki shorts and an open-necked shirt of a decidedly tropical print. He didn't look the part of a policeman.

'Let's see what we have, then,' Emily said with a nod at the house.

The door was answered by a woman with a poodle in her arms. She and the dog looked amazingly similar: white-haired, long-snouted, and recently coiffed. She said, 'Sorry. The sign's still up, but all the rooms're let. I need to pull it down, I know. But my lumbago stops me taking it out the window.'

'It' was the *Vacancy* notice that hung between the diaphanous white curtains and the glass of the ground-floor bay window. Emily told the woman that they weren't there in search of accommodation. She produced her warrant card.

The woman gave a sheeplike bleat. Offering her name as 'Gladys Kersey, that's Mrs, by the way, although Mr Kersey's gone to Jesus', she went on to assure them that everything was in perfect order in her establishment, always had been, always was, and certainly always would be. She clutched the poodle beneath her arm as she spoke and the dog gave a yip not unlike the owner's bleat.

'Fahd Kumhar,' Emily said. 'If we might have a word with him, Mrs Kersey?'

'Mr Kumhar? He's not in some sort of trouble, is he? He seems a nice enough young man. Very clean, he is, bleaches those shirts of his by hand and what that's doing to his skin, by the way, isn't a very pretty sight. His English isn't much to speak of, but he watches the morning news in the lounge and I can tell he's trying hard to learn. He's not in trouble, is he?'

'Can you show us to his room?' Emily aimed her voice for polite but firm.

Mrs Kersey excavated for substance beneath the question. 'This i'n't about that business in Balford, is it?'

'Why do you ask that?'

'No reason.' Mrs Kersey hiked the poodle higher. 'Just what with him being one of them. You know . . .' She let the phrase dangle as if hoping Emily would complete it for her. When Emily did not do so, Mrs Kersey buried her fingers in the poodle's curly fur and told both of the police visitors to 'come along with you, then'.

Fahd Kumhar's room was on the first floor at the back of the house. It was one of three bedrooms, all of which opened off a square little hall. Mrs Kersey rapped softly on the door, gave a glance over her shoulder at her companions, and called, 'Mr Kumhar? You've visitors asking to have a word with you.'

This was greeted with silence.

Mrs Kersey looked puzzled. She said, 'I saw him come in not ten minutes ago. We even spoke, we did. He's always polite, that way. And he never goes out without saying goodbye.' She knocked again, this time more forcefully. 'Mr Kumhar? I say, did you hear me?'

A muted sound of wood sliding on wood came from within the room. Emily said, 'Step aside, please,' and when Mrs Kersey did so, she reached for the knob. She said, 'Police, Mr Kumhar.'

A shriek of wood followed. Emily quickly turned the doorknob. DC Honigman slid past her like a cat. He caught Fahd Kumhar by the arm as the other man was attempting to climb out of the window.

Mrs Kersey just had time to exclaim, 'Why, Mr Kumhar!' before Emily closed the door on her and the dog.

Honigman had managed to grab on to a leg as well as an arm, and he yanked the Pakistani back into the room. 'Not so hasty there, mate,' he said as he dropped the man on to the floor. Kumhar cowered where he fell.

Emily went to the window. Below was the back garden of the house, but it was a considerable drop from the first-floor window. There was nothing beneath to break the fall. Nor was there a drainpipe fastened to the house, allowing someone to do an easy runner. Kumhar could just as easily have broken a leg as he could have scarpered from the cops.

She turned to him. 'Balford Criminal Investigations Department,' she told him. She kept her words slow. 'I'm Detective Chief Inspector

Barlow. This is Detective Constable Honigman. Can you understand my English, Mr Kumhar?'

He scrambled to his feet. DC Honigman made a move towards him. Kumhar held up his hands as if he wanted to show them that he had no weapons.

'Papers,' he said. 'I have papers.'

'What's this, then?' Honigman directed the question to Emily.

'You please wait, yes?' Kumhar said, again with hands up, but now moved to his chest in a defensive posture. 'I show you papers. Yes. Okay? You watch papers.'

He moved to a wicker chest of drawers. As he reached for the handles of the top drawer, Honigman said, 'You hold it there, mate! Step back. Do it quick. Here. Back.'

Kumhar's hands went up again. He cried, 'Not hurt. Please. Papers. I have papers.'

Emily understood. They were the police. He was a foreigner. 'He wants to show us his legal documents, Billy. They must be in the drawer.' She shook her head at the Pakistani. 'We're not here to inspect your papers, Mr Kumhar.'

'Papers, yes.' Kumhar nodded frantically. He began to pull open one of the wicker drawers.

Honigman shouted, 'Hang on right there, mate!'

The Pakistani jumped away. He fled to the wash basin in the corner of the room. Beneath was a toppled stack of magazines. They looked heavily thumbed-through, with dog-eared pages and covers that were stained with coffee and tea rings. From her position by the open window, Emily could see the titles: *Country Life*, *Hello!*, *Woman's Own*, *Vanity Fair*. A paperback *Collier's Dictionary* lay among them. It looked as well used as the magazines.

DC Honigman riffled through the drawer that Kumhar had begun to open. He said, 'No weapons in here,' and slammed it shut.

For his part, Kumhar watched their every move. His entire concentration seemed to be given to keeping himself from hurling his body out of the open window. Emily considered exactly how his patent desire to escape fitted into the case in hand.

She said, 'Sit down, Mr Kumhar,' and she indicated the room's only chair. This stood before a small newspaper-covered table on which a partially completed dolls' house was being constructed. It appeared that Kumhar had interrupted work on the dolls' house to go to Jackson & Son. It also appeared that the arrival of the police had disrupted further work on this same project. A tube of glue was uncapped on the table and five miniature roofing tiles were speckled with it. The house itself was of a decidedly English design: a wattle and daub miniature of the sort of dwelling one could find in nearly every corner of the country.

Cautiously, Kumhar crossed the room to the chair. He crab-walked, as if in the belief that a false move would cause the heavy arm of the law to crash down upon him. Emily maintained her position at the window. Honigman moved to the door. Behind it, faintly, the poodle whined. Obviously, Mrs Kersey hadn't made the connection between a door slamming in her face and the desire for privacy.

Emily jerked her head at the door. Honigman nodded. He opened it and had a few quiet words with the house's owner. He allowed her a moment to poke her head inside the room to reassure herself that her tenant was unharmed. Apparently having watched many episodes of American police dramas, she expected to find Fahd Kumhar on the floor, bloodied and handcuffed. Seeing him sitting unmolested on the chair, she gulped, hiked the poodle beneath her chin, and retreated. Honigman closed the door.

Emily said, 'Haytham Querashi, Mr Kumhar. Please explain your relationship with him.'

Kumhar stuffed his hands between his knees. He was painfully thin, with a concave chest and sloping shoulders. These were covered by a neatly pressed white shirt that, despite the heat, was buttoned both at the neck and at the cuffs. He wore black trousers, belted with a strip of brown leather that was too long for his waist and dangled limply like the tail of a reprimanded canine. He made no reply. He merely swallowed, and his teeth vigorously worked his lips.

'Mr Querashi wrote you a cheque for £400. Your name was on more than one telephone message for him at the Burnt House Hotel. If you read any of these –' she indicated the newspapers that served as protection between the dolls' house and the table beneath it '– then you know that Mr Querashi is dead.'

'Papers,' Fahd Kumhar said, his head turning from her to the chest of drawers to Honigman.

'I'm not here about your papers.' Emily spoke more slowly and in a louder voice, although her real wish was to shake him into comprehension. Why on earth, she wondered, did people emigrate to a country whose language was a mystery to them? 'We're here to talk about Haytham Querashi. You knew him, didn't you? Haytham Querashi?'

343

'Mr Querashi, yes.' Kumhar's hands tightened on his knees. He was trembling so badly that the material of his shirt shimmered as if a breeze were blowing it.

'He was murdered, Mr Kumhar. We're investigating that murder. The fact that he gave you £400 makes you a suspect. What was that money for?'

The Asian could have been having a mild seizure, so much did his tremors increase. It seemed to Emily that he *had* to be able to understand her. But when he replied, he did so in his own tongue. A babble of indistinguishable words spewed out of him.

Emily cut into what she knew had to be a stream of rising protestations of innocence. She said impatiently, 'English please, Mr Kumhar. You heard his name well enough. And you understand what I'm asking. How did you know Mr Querashi?'

Kumhar continued his babble.

'Where did you meet him?' Emily asked. 'Why did he give you money? What did you do with it?'

More babble, louder this time. Kumhar moved his hands to his chest and began to wail.

'Answer me, Mr Kumhar. You live not far from the market square. We've heard that Mr Querashi went there. Did you ever see him? Is that how you two met?'

It sounded as if the Asian was repeating the word *Allah* over and over again. It was contained within a ritualised chant. Brilliant, Emily thought, it was bow-to-Mecca time.

'Answer the questions,' she said, matching her volume to his.

Against the door, Honigman stirred. 'I don't think he's following you, Guv.'

'Oh, he's bloody well following,' Emily said. 'I dare say his English's as good as ours when the humour takes him.'

'Mrs Kersey did say he's not got much of it,' Honigman noted.

Emily ignored this. Sitting before her was a veritable fountain of information about the murdered man, and she bloody well intended to tap the source while she had him alone and at her mercy.

'Did you know Mr Querashi in Pakistan? Did you know his family?'

'"*Ulaaa-'ika 'alaa Hudammir-Rabbihim wa 'ulaaaa-ika humul-Muf-lihuun,*"' he chanted.

Emily raised her voice above his gibberish. 'Where do you work, Mr Kumhar? How do you support yourself? Who pays for this room? Who buys your cigarettes, your magazines, your newspapers, your sweets? Do you have a car? What are you doing here in Clacton?'

'Guv,' Honigman said uneasily.

'*"Innallaziina 'aamanuu wa 'amilus-saalihaati lanhum –"*'

'Goddamn it!' Emily slammed her hand on to the table top. The Asian immediately shrank back and fell silent.

'Take him,' Emily said to her detective constable.

Honigman said, 'What?'

'You heard me, Constable. Take him. I want him in Balford. I want him in custody. I want him to have a chance to decide how much English he really understands.'

'Got it,' Honigman said.

He approached the Asian and took him by the arm, lifting him to his feet. Kumhar's babbling began again, but this time it quickly dissolved to tears.

'Jesus,' Honigman said to Emily. 'What's wrong with this bloke?'

'That's exactly what I intend to find out,' Emily stated.

The door of number 6 Alfred Terrace was gaping open when Barbara arrived. From within the cramped house, music blared and the television chattered as loudly as on the previous day. She knocked on the side of the faded architrave, but there was no way anything less than a jack-hammer in full operation was going to make a dent in the din.

She stepped out of the blazing sun and into the entry. The stairway directly in front of her was littered with discarded clothing and plates of half-eaten food. The corridor towards the kitchen was strewn with flat bicycle tyres, a tattered canvas push chair, two trugs, three brooms, and a Hoover bag with a rip up its side. And to her left, the sitting room seemed to be serving as a stopping-off point for articles about to be moved from one location to another. Surrounding the television, on which roared an Act Three chase scene from yet another American action film, cardboard boxes bulged with what appeared to be clothing, towels, and household goods.

Curious, Barbara investigated. The boxes, she saw, contained everything from a small and rusting Calor gas stove to a faded needlepoint sampler stitched with the words 'I must down to the seas again'. Considering this in conjunction with the state of the house, Barbara couldn't help wondering if the Ruddocks were planning a quick departure from Balford, one stimulated by her previous visit.

'Hey! You keep your mitts away from that lot, hear?'

Barbara swung around. Trevor's brother Charlie had come to the sitting-room door, and he was followed in quick succession by his elder brother and their mother. All three of them had apparently just come into the house. Barbara wondered how she'd missed seeing them on the street. Perhaps they'd trotted along from somewhere in Balford Square, of which Alfred Terrace served as one of the four sides.

'What's this, then?' Shirl Ruddock demanded. 'And who're you to go busting into people's houses uninvited?'

She pushed Charlie to one side and strode into the sitting room. She was fragrant with sweat and with the strong fishy scent of a woman in need of a bath. Her face was blotched with grime, and her shorts and skimpy halter top were banded with perspiration.

'You got no right to walk into people's gaff. I know what's what when it comes to the law.'

'Moving house?' Barbara said, taking herself from one box to the next for a closer inspection despite Shirl Ruddock's words. 'Are the Ruddocks on their way out of Balford?'

Shirl's fists punched her own hips. 'What business is it of yours? If we want to move house, we move house. We got no duty to let the cops know where we're hanging our hats every night.'

'Mum.' Behind her, Trevor spoke. Like his mother, he was shiny with sweat and grimy of body, but not flaring of temper. He too entered the sitting room.

Three people among the boxes and the furniture were two people too many. Charlie trailed his brother and swelled their numbers.

'What d'you want?' Shirl demanded. 'You had your say with my Trevor. And a fine disruption you caused in this house going about it, by the way. You got his dad in an uproar, and he needs his rest. He isn't well, Trevor's dad, and you didn't help matters one little bit.'

Barbara wondered how anyone could manage to rest in a household in which earsplitting noise was the dominant feature. As it was, they were all virtually shouting at one another simply to be heard over the vehicular crashes on the television. Rap music added another element to the auditory chaos of the household. As on the previous day, it was booming from upstairs at a volume so high that Barbara could feel the vibrations of the sound in the air.

'I want a word with Trevor,' Barbara said to his mother.

'We're busy,' she replied. 'You c'n see that for yourself. You aren't blind as well as dim, are you?'

'Mum,' Trevor said again cautiously.

'Don't you "Mum" me. I know my rights. And nothing in them says a cop can come here and prowl through my belongings like they were her own. Come back later, you. We got work to do.'

'What sort of work?' Barbara asked.

'None of your business.' Shirl grabbed a box and heaved it to waist height. 'Charlie,' she barked, 'get on with it.'

'Do you know what it looks like, moving house while the police are investigating a murder?' Barbara asked.

'I bloody well don't care what anything looks like,' Shirl replied. 'Charlie! Get off that bleeding couch. Turn off that telly. Your dad'll tan you good if you wake him again.' She turned on her heel and left the room. Barbara watched through the window as she crossed the street and entered the square where a row of cars were parked. Charlie bellowed a sigh, picked up another box, and followed his mother.

'We aren't moving house,' Trevor said when he and Barbara were alone. He crossed to the television set and doused its volume. The picture remained: a helicopter in pursuit of a flame-engulfed pantechnicon. They were on a bridge. Disaster loomed for someone.

'What's up, then?' Barbara asked.

'We got the market square in Clacton. This lumber's for the stall.'

'Ah,' she said. 'How d'you come by it?'

His neck turned red. 'Isn't nicked, if that's what you're thinking, okay?'

'Okay. So how'd you get these goods, Trevor?'

'Me and Mum go to car boot sales at the weekends. We buy what we can, fix it up, then flog it for a higher price in Clacton. Isn't much, this clutter, but it helps us get by.' He touched one of the boxes with the toe of his boot.

Barbara observed him closely, trying to evaluate him for his level of guile. He'd already lied to her once, so his stock was low. But this, at least, was a reasonable tale. She said, 'Rachel didn't corroborate your story, Trevor. We need to talk.'

'I didn't chop that bloke. I was nowheres near the Nez on Friday.'

'So she wasn't lying.'

'I didn't have no reason to do nothing to him. Sure, I di'n't like that he sacked me, but I took my chances when I nicked those jars from the factory. So I know I got to pay the price.'

'Where were you on Friday night?'

He raised a fist to his mouth and tapped it against his lips. It looked to Barbara like a nervous movement. 'Trevor?' she prompted.

'Yeah. Okay. But it's not much good if I tell you 'cause there's no one who can say it's the truth. So you won't believe me. So what's the point?'

'The point is trying to clear your name, which is something I'd think you'd be fairly hot to do. Since you're not, it makes me wonder why. And wondering why leads me straight to the Nez. Your time card tells me you clocked in at work at half-past eleven. Rachel tells me you left her before ten. That's ninety minutes to account for, Trevor, and it doesn't take a genius to figure out that ninety minutes is plenty of time for a bloke to get from the beach huts to the Nez and from there to the pier.'

Trevor's glance went to the sitting-room door, perhaps in anticipation of his mother's return for another box to load into their car for the trip to the market square. He said stubbornly, 'I told you what I'm going to tell you. I wasn't on the Nez that night. And I didn't give that bloke the chop.'

'And that's all you have to tell me?'

'That's all.'

'Then let's go upstairs.'

He looked immediately alarmed, the very picture of a bloke with something to hide. With his mother not there to tell him what his rights were in the situation, it was clear to Barbara that she had the upper hand. She made for the stairs. He was hot on her heels.

'There's nothing up there,' he said. 'And you got no call to be –'

She swung to face him. 'Did I say I was looking for something, Trevor?'

He stuttered, 'Y . . . you said . . .'

'I said, let's go upstairs. I have an itch to make this conversation more private.'

She continued to climb. The rap music came from behind one of the doors, but it wasn't the door to Trevor's room this time. Since it was accompanied by the sound of water roaring out of a large tap, Barbara assumed that one other member of the family was using the unintelligible chanting as an accompaniment to a bath.

She entered Trevor's room, holding the door open for him and shutting it behind them. Once inside, she sauntered to the table where his spider paraphernalia was spread out. She began to sift through it.

'What're you doing?' he demanded. 'You said you wanted to talk in private.'

'I lied,' she replied. 'What's this about anyway, all this junk? And how'd you get into spiders, a nice lad like you?'

'Hang on!' he cried as she shifted a collection of half-assembled arachnids to see what was in the box beneath them. 'Those'll fall apart.'

'I *was* wondering how you held them together when I was here yesterday,' Barbara admitted.

She rooted through various sizes of sponges, through tubes of paint, through pipe cleaners, black plastic beads, straight pins, and glue. She moved aside reels of cotton in black, yellow, and red.

Trevor said angrily, 'You got no bleeding business with that.'

But Barbara saw otherwise when she moved two old encyclopaedias to one side. Crammed between the volumes and the wall was another reel. But this one didn't have cotton wound round it. It was wound with wire.

'I think I have business with this, though.' She straightened and held the reel up for him to see. 'Want to tell me about it?'

'About what? About that? It's just some old wire. You c'n see as much yourself.'

'That I can.' She slipped the reel into her shoulder bag.

'What d'you want with it? Why're you taking it? You can't take something from my room like that. And it's nothing anyway. It's just some old wire.'

'Used for what?'

'Used for anything. Used for fixing that net –' He jerked his head at the fishing net above his door, where the model spiders still cavorted. 'Used for keeping the spider bodies together. Used for . . .' He struggled for another use. Words failed him, though, and he advanced on her. 'You give me that bloody wire!' He said the six words through his teeth. 'I didn't do nothing and you can't make it like I did. And you can't take nothing without my permission because –'

'Oh, but I can,' Barbara said pleasantly. 'I can take you.'

He gawped at her. His eyes bulged and his mouth fell open and then snapped shut.

'D'you want to come quietly for a chat at the nick, or do I need to phone and have some assistance sent over?'

'But . . . No . . . Why . . . I didn't do –'

'So you've said,' she told him. 'So I expect you won't mind giving us your dabs, will you? Someone as innocent as you doesn't need to worry about where he's left his fingerprints.'

Aware of the difference in their sizes and strength, Barbara didn't give Trevor a chance to resist. She had him by the arm, out of the room, and on the stairs before he had the opportunity to protest. She wasn't so lucky, however, in the case of his mother.

Shirl was hoisting another box – this one to her shoulder – while Charlie made himself less than useful by playing with the television. She caught sight of Barbara and her eldest son as they were halfway down the stairs. She dropped the box.

'Now, you hang on!' She made a dash for the stairway and blocked their path.

'You don't want to interfere, Mrs Ruddock,' Barbara told her.

'I bloody well mean to know what you're doing,' Shirl replied. 'I know my rights. No one let you into this house, and no one agreed to talk to you. So if you think you can waltz in here and expect my Trevor –'

'Your Trevor's a suspect in a murder,' Barbara said, overheated and patience worn to gossamer. 'So step to one side and do it nicely before more than one Ruddock gets run into the nick.'

She advanced anyway. Trevor said, 'Mum! We don't need no trouble. Mum! D'you hear?'

Charlie had come to the sitting-room door. Upstairs, Mr Ruddock had begun to yell. At that moment the youngest boy ran towards them from the kitchen, a jar of honey in one hand, a bag of flour in the other.

'Mum?' Charlie said.

'Shirl!' Mr Ruddock shouted.

'See!' Brucie cried and poured the honey and the flour together on to the floor.

Barbara watched and listened and silently clarified Trevor's statement. The Ruddocks didn't need any *more* trouble. But what was often the case was that those not in need were blessed with more of what they already had.

'Take care of the kids,' Trevor said to his mother. He cast a sideways look towards the stairs. 'Don't let him get at them while I'm gone.'

Muhannad showed up for mid-afternoon prayers. Sahlah hadn't expected him to do so. The argument with their father on the previous night had bled into the morning's breakfast. There had been no further exchange of words about Muhannad's activities with respect to the police investigation, but still the animosity that lingered between them had charged the air.

'Be concerned about offending these bloody westerners if that's what you have to do,' Muhannad had snapped, standing rigidly, one finger punching the air. 'Just don't ask me to do the same. I won't allow the police to question even one of our people without representation, and if that makes your position on the town council difficult, then that's just the way it's going to be. You can trust what parades as the good will and noble intentions of this filthy community as much as you like, Father. You're free to do so because as we both know, the world has plenty of room for fools.'

Sahlah had shuddered, waiting for her father to strike him. Instead, although a vein throbbed in his temple when he replied, Akram's words were calm.

'In front of your wife, whose duty is to obey and respect you, I will not do as I ought, Muni. But there will come a day when you are forced to realise that promoting enmity gains one nothing.'

'Haytham is dead!' was Muhannad's response and he made it slamming his fist into his palm with every syllable. 'Wasn't that the first blow struck in the cause of enmity? And who struck that blow?'

Sahlah had left before Akram replied, but not before she'd seen her mother's hands fumble at the mess she was making of her embroidery, and not before she'd seen Yumn avidly absorbing the altercation as if the hot words between father and son were feeding her blood. Sahlah knew why. Any antagonism between Akram and Muhannad had the potential to push the son away from the father and closer to his wife. And that's what Yumn had wanted from the first: Muhannad entirely and solely to herself. In the traditional way of things, she could never have him solely. He had duties to his parents that precluded this. But tradition had flown out of the window with Haytham's death.

Now, in the courtyard of the mustard factory, Sahlah saw that her brother had come to stand in the shadows – behind the factory's three Muslim women – while the other workers faced the *mihrab* that Akram had fashioned into the wall, so that they might direct their prayers eastward towards Mecca. But Muhannad didn't engage in any of the bows or prostrations, and when *shahada* was recited, his lips didn't move in the profession of faith: 'There is no God but Allah and Muhammad is His Prophet.'

These words weren't in English, but everyone knew their meaning. As they knew the meaning of the *Fatihah* that followed.

'*Allahu Akbar*,' Sahlah heard her father murmur. And her heart was sore with the need to believe. But if God *was* most great, why had He brought their family to this: one member pitted against another, each engagement between them an attempt to illustrate which person had power and which was forced by age, by birth, or by temperament to submit?

The prayers continued. Inside the factory, the few westerners whom her father employed took time from their own work like their Asian counterparts. Akram had long ago told them that they might use the periods each day during which the Muslims prayed as a group to pray formally on their own or to meditate. Instead, Sahlah knew, they hurried out to smoke in the lane, as happy to take advantage of her father's generosity as they were willing to remain in ignorance about the tenets of his religion and his way of life.

But Akram Malik didn't see that. Nor did he notice the way their lips curved slightly behind his back, offering smug smiles of superiority in the face of his foreign ways. Nor did he observe the glances they exchanged – eyes moving subtly skyward and shoulders shrugging – each time he shepherded his Muslim employees to the courtyard in which they said their prayers.

As they were doing now, and with a devotion that Sahlah herself couldn't pretend to feel. She stood as they stood, she moved as they moved, her lips formed the appropriate words. But in her case, it was all performance.

A movement out of the ordinary caught her attention. She turned. The outcast cousin – Taymullah Azhar – had come into the courtyard. He was speaking in a whisper to Muhannad. In response to whatever Azhar was telling him, Muhannad's face went rigid. In a moment, he gave a single sharp nod and indicated the door with a canting motion of his head. The two men left together.

Akram rose from his final prostration at the front of their small congregation of believers. He concluded their prayers with a recitation of the *taslim*, asking for peace, mercy, and the blessings of God. As Sahlah watched him and listened to his words, she wondered when any of those three requests would be granted to her and to her family.

As was always the case, the Malik employees returned to work quietly. Sahlah waited for her father just inside the door.

She watched him, momentarily unobserved. He was getting older, and she'd hardly noticed until this moment. His hair was combed and spread carefully across the top of his head but thinner than she'd ever remembered. His jaw was no longer firm, and his body – which she'd always seen as ironlike in strength – was soft in appearance, as if some sort of resistance had gone out of him. The skin beneath his eyes was dark, charcoal-smudged beneath his lower lashes. And his gait that had been swift and firm of purpose seemed hesitant now.

She wanted to tell him that nothing mattered so much as the future he'd so long held dear, a future in which he planted roots and a family in a small Essex town and built a life there for children and grandchildren and for other Asians like himself who'd left behind their country in pursuit of a dream. But she'd been a party to obliterating that future. Any reference that she made to it now would be born of a need to maintain a pretence which, at the moment, she hadn't the heart to attempt.

Akram came inside the building. He paused to close and lock the door behind him. He saw her waiting by the water cooler and he came to her, taking the paper cup that she extended for him.

'You look tired, *Abhy*,' she said. 'You don't need to stay at the factory. Mr Armstrong can keep things going for the rest of the afternoon. Why don't you go home?' She had more than one reason for making this suggestion, of course. If she left the factory herself while her father was there, he would know soon enough and he'd want to know why. *Rachel's phoned and there's an emergency* had served her purposes on the previous day when she'd left to confront her friend at the Clifftop Snuggeries. She couldn't use that excuse again.

He touched her shoulder. 'Sahlah. You bear the weight of our trouble with a strength I can't quite comprehend.'

Sahlah didn't want the praise, so sorely did it abrade her conscience. She looked for something to use as a response, something that was at least close to the truth because she couldn't bear to continue the process in which she'd been engaged these many months: constructing a careful maze of lies, projecting a purity of heart, mind, and soul that she didn't possess. '*Abhy*, I wasn't in love with him. I hoped to love him eventually, as you and *Ammī* love. But I hadn't learned to love him yet, so I don't feel the grief that you think I feel.'

His fingers tightened on her shoulder, then moved to graze her cheek. 'I want you to know in your own life the devotion that I feel for your mother. That's what I hoped for you and for Haytham.'

'He was a good man,' she said, and she inwardly acknowledged the truth of this statement. 'You made a good choice of husband for me.'

'A good choice or a selfish one?' he asked meditatively.

Slowly, they moved along the back corridor of the factory, past the locker room and the employees' lounge. 'He had much to offer the family, Sahlah. That's why I chose him. And every hour since his death I've asked myself if I still would have chosen him had he been hunchbacked, evil, or ridden with disease. Would I have chosen him anyway, just because I needed his talents here?' Akram's gesture encompassed the factory wall. 'We persuade ourselves to believe all manner of falsehood when our self-interest guides us. Then, when the worst befalls us, we're left to gaze back over our actions. We wonder whether one of them might have been the cause of disaster. We question whether an alternative action might have averted the worst from happening.'

'You aren't blaming yourself for Haytham's death?' she said, aghast at the thought of her father carrying this burden.

'Who else is to blame? Who else brought him to this country? And to meet *my* need of him, Sahlah. Not yours.'

'I needed Haytham as well, *Abhy-jahn.*'

Her father hesitated before passing through the doorway to his own office. His smile was infinitely sad. 'Your spirit's as generous as it's pure,' he said.

No compliment could have grieved her more. She wanted in that instant to pour the truth before her father. But she recognised the selfishness of that desire. While it was true that she would experience the relief of finally dropping the guise of a goodness that she didn't possess, she would be dropping it at the expense of crushing the spirit of a man who had long been incapable of seeing that evil could exist under an exterior that was otherwise righteous.

It was her desperation to preserve her father's image of her that now caused her to say, 'Go home, *Abhy-jahn.* Please. Go home to rest.'

His answer was to kiss his fingers and press them to her cheeks. Saying nothing further, he entered his office.

She returned to reception, where her own duties awaited, her brain working anxiously to create an excuse to take her away from the factory for the time she needed to do what had to be done. If she claimed to be ill, her father would insist that someone accompany her home. If she claimed an emergency on Second Avenue – one of the children having disappeared and Yumn in a panic, for instance – he would himself charge into action. If she simply disappeared . . . But how could she do that? How could she cause her father more worry and trouble?

She sat behind the reception desk and watched the fish and bubbles float across the screen of her computer's monitor. There was work to be done, but she couldn't at the moment think what it was. She could only turn over the possibilities in her mind: what she could do to preserve her family and simultaneously to save herself. There was only one option.

The outside door opened, and Sahlah looked up. God *is* great, she exulted silently when she saw who was entering the factory. It was Rachel Winfield.

She'd come on her bicycle. It leaned just beyond the entrance, rusted from years in the town's salty air. She wore a long filmy skirt, and round her neck and dangling from her ears were a necklace and earrings of Sahlah's own creation, fashioned from polished rupees and beads.

Sahlah tried to take comfort from Rachel's attire, especially in the jewellery. Surely it meant that her need of help was foremost in Rachel's mind?

Sahlah didn't offer her a greeting. Nor did she let the gravity of her friend's face dismay her. The matter before them *was* a grave one. Becoming a party to ridding oneself of a burgeoning life – no matter how critical was the need to do so – wasn't an endeavour that Rachel would ever take lightly.

'Hot,' Rachel said by way of greeting. 'Hotter than I can remember. It's like the sun killed the wind and is getting ready to suck up the sea as well.'

Sahlah waited. There was only one reason for her friend to appear at the factory. Rachel was her route to the means by which she would begin to put her life back in order, and her arrival suggested that the means was at hand. It wouldn't be easy to arrange to be gone for the length of time necessary to take care of her problem – her parents had long ago made it their practice to hold her accountable for every moment of her day – but with Rachel's help, surely she'd be able to create a plausible excuse for an absence whose length would guarantee a successful visit to a doctor or a clinic or a casualty ward where someone skilled in the process could end the nightmare that she'd been living for the last –

Sahlah schooled herself to draw past the desperation. Rachel was here, she said silently. Rachel had come.

'Can you talk?' Rachel asked. 'I mean –' with a glance towards the door leading into the administration offices '– maybe outside is better than here. You know.'

Sahlah rose and followed her friend out into the sunlight. Despite the heat, she felt unaccountably cool, but the coolness ran beneath her skin as if her veins argued with what her senses perceived.

Rachel found a shady spot where the factory wall cast a shadow in the afternoon light. She faced Sahlah, looking beyond her shoulder to the sprawl of the industrial estate, as if the mattress factory held a fascination that she had to experience immediately.

Just when Sahlah was beginning to wonder if her friend would ever speak, Rachel finally did so. 'I can't,' she said.

The coolness beneath Sahlah's skin seemed to spread into her lungs. 'Can't what?'

'You know.'

'I don't. Tell me.'

Rachel moved her eyes from the mattress factory to Sahlah's face. Sahlah wondered that she'd never noticed before how misshapen those eyes were, one slightly lower than the other and too widely set – even after surgery – to be deemed natural. It was one of the features of Rachel that Sahlah had disciplined herself to overlook. Rachel couldn't help the way she'd been born. No one could.

'I've thought and thought,' Rachel said. 'All last night. I didn't even sleep. I can't help you with . . . you know . . . with what you asked.'

At first Sahlah didn't want to believe that Rachel was talking about the abortion. But there was no avoiding the implacable resolve that settled the odd, uneven features on her friend's face.

All Sahlah could manage to say was, 'You can't.'

'Sahlah, I talked to Theo,' Rachel said in a rush. 'I know, I know. You didn't want me to, but your thinking's wrong 'cause you're in a state. It's only fair for Theo to have some say in this. You got to see that.'

'This isn't Theo's concern.' Sahlah could hear the stiffness in her voice.

'Tell that to Theo,' Rachel said. 'He sicked up in a rubbish bin when I told him what you were planning to do. Now, don't *look* like that, Sahlah. I know what you're thinking. Like his being sick meant he didn't mean to do anything to help you. That's what I decided at first as well. But I thought and thought about this all last night, and I just know that if you wait and give things a chance to settle down and give Theo a chance to do right –'

'You didn't listen,' Sahlah finally cut in. Her body was tense with the need to take some sort of action and take it at once. She recognised the panic for what it was, but recognition did nothing to quell it. 'Did you hear anything I said to you yesterday, Rachel? I can't marry Theo, I can't be with Theo, I can't even talk to Theo publicly. Why won't you see that?'

'Okay, I see it,' Rachel said. 'And maybe you won't be able to talk to him for a while. Maybe you won't even be able to talk to him till the baby comes. But once the baby does come ... I mean, he's a human being, Sahlah. He's not a monster. He's a decent man who knows what's right. Some other bloke might look the other way for ever, but not Theo Shaw. Theo's not going to reject his own baby for long. You'll see.'

Sahlah felt as if she were sinking into the lumpy, hot ground beneath her feet. 'And how do you propose that I keep my family from knowing about all this? About being pregnant? About having a baby?'

'You can't,' Rachel said with perfect reason, in the voice of a girl who hadn't the slightest idea what kind of encumbrances went with being born female into a traditional Asian family. 'You'll have to tell your mum and dad.'

'Rachel.' Sahlah's mind careened from one possibility to the next, each of them presenting an unacceptable alternative of what to do and how to do it. 'You've got to listen to me. You've got to try to understand.'

'But it's more than just what's right for you and the baby and Theo,' Rachel said, still reason incarnate. 'I thought and thought last night about what's right for me as well.'

'How does this have anything to do with you? All I need from you is information. And a little help to get me away from here – or from my parents' house – for enough time to see a doctor.'

'But it's not like going to the market, Sahlah. You can't just pop in and say to some bloke, "I got a kid inside me I want to get rid of." We'd have to go more than once – you and me – and –'

'I wasn't asking you to go at all,' Sahlah said. 'I was just asking you to be willing to help me with information. But I can get that myself. And I *will* get that myself. And when I have it, all I'll need from you is the willingness to phone me and ask me to do something – it can be anything – that would serve as an excuse for me to be away from my parents' house for enough time to go to the clinic – or wherever it is that I can have it done.'

'Look at you,' Rachel said. 'You don't even want to say the word.

You call it *it*. And that should tell you pretty much how you'll feel if you get rid of the baby.'

'I know how I'll feel. I'll feel relieved. I'll feel as if I have my life back. I'll know I haven't destroyed my parents' belief in their children, split my family into pieces, struck a death-blow to my father, caused my world –'

'That won't happen,' Rachel said. 'And even if it happens for a day or a week or a month, they'll come round. They'll all come round. Theo, your mum and your dad. Even Muhannad.'

'Muhannad,' Sahlah said, 'will kill me. Once I can no longer hide my condition, my brother will kill me, Rachel.'

'That's rubbish,' Rachel said. 'You know that's rubbish. He'll be in a twist and he might even pick a fight with Theo, but he'll never lay a hand on you. You're his sister, for God's sake.'

'Please, Rachel. You don't know him. You don't know my family. You see their exterior – what everyone sees – but you don't know how it really is. You don't know what they're capable of doing. They'll see the disgrace –'

'And they'll get over it,' Rachel said with an air of finality to her voice that washed a wave of despair over Sahlah. 'And until they do, I'll take care of you. You know I'll always take care of you.'

Sahlah saw it then: how they'd come full circle. They were back where they'd been on Sunday afternoon, back where they'd met on the previous day. They were at the Clifftop Snuggeries, if only in mind rather than in body.

'Besides,' Rachel said in a tone that indicated she'd reached the conclusion of her remarks, 'I have my own conscience to think of, Sahlah. And how d'you expect I'd feel, knowing I'd made myself part of something I didn't think was right? I got to consider that.'

'Of course.' Sahlah's lips formed the words, but she couldn't hear herself say them. Instead, she felt as if she were being sucked out of Rachel's presence, out of the industrial estate altogether. An unseen force had her in its grip and was casting her away, away, away. She couldn't feel the ground beneath her, and the once hot sun had burnt itself to nothing, leaving cold in its place, and endless frost.

And from the distance she had left behind, Sahlah could heard Rachel's parting words. 'You don't need to worry, Sahlah. Really. It'll all work out for the best. You'll see.'

Chapter Eighteen

———◆———

Barbara handed Trevor Ruddock over to be fingerprinted, after which she escorted him to an interview room in the police station. She gave him the packet of cigarettes he requested, along with a Coke, an ashtray and matches. She told him to have a nice quiet think about what he'd been doing on Friday night and who — among his doubtless lengthy list of friends and acquaintances — was likely to corroborate whatever alibi he produced for the police. By locking the door upon her exit, she made certain he would have no access to a telephone in order to arrange this alibi. She went on her way.

Emily, she learned from WPC Warner, had brought in a suspect as well. 'The coloured bloke from Clacton' was how Belinda described him. 'The one on the phone chits from the hotel.'

Kumhar, Barbara thought. Emily's placement of the surveillance officer in Clacton had paid off more quickly than she would have expected.

She found Emily making arrangements to have Kumhar's fingerprints sent off to London. In the meantime, these prints would also go to the pathology lab in Peterborough, where officers would attempt to match them with those found on Querashi's Nissan. Barbara saw to it that Trevor Ruddock's dabs were added to Kumhar's. One way or another, it seemed that they were getting closer to the truth.

'His English is shit,' Emily told her laconically as they returned to her office. She blotted her face with a paper kitchen towel that she'd dug out of her pocket. She wadded it up and lobbed it into the wastepaper basket. 'Either that or he's pretending that his English is shit. We didn't get anywhere with him in Clacton. Just a lot of gabbling about his papers, as if we'd come to escort him to the nearest port of departure.'

'Is he denying that he knew Querashi?'

'I don't know what he's doing. He might be admitting, denying, outright lying, or reciting poetry. It's impossible to tell because he's doing it all in gibberish.'

'We'll need to get someone to translate,' Barbara said. 'That shouldn't be too rough a go, should it? I mean, what with the local Asian community and everything.'

Emily laughed shortly. 'You can imagine how well we'll be able to depend on the accuracy of a translation coming from that quarter. Damn it.'

Barbara couldn't argue with the DCI's perspective. How could they depend upon anyone from the Asian community to translate explicitly and objectively, given the racial climate in Balford-le-Nez?

'We could bring someone in from London. One of the DCs could bring out that bloke from the university, the one who did the translation of that page from the Qur'aan. What was his name?'

'Siddiqi.'

'Right. Professor Siddiqi. In fact, I could phone the Yard and ask one of our lads to round him up and drive him out here.'

'That may be our only option,' Emily said. They entered her office, where it seemed even hotter than it was in the rest of the building. The afternoon sun was blazing against the pillowcase that Emily had pinned over the window casting the room into an aqua glow which simultaneously suggested life in an aquarium while also doing nothing to enhance one's personal appearance.

'Want me to make the call?' Barbara asked.

Emily sank into the chair behind her desk. 'Not quite yet. I've got Kumhar locked up, and I'd like to give him time to feel what it's like to be in custody. Something tells me that all he really needs is a generous application of oil on the machinery of his ability to cooperate. And he's new enough in England not to be able to quote PACE to me, chapter and verse. I've the whip hand in this situation, and I'd bloody well like to use it.'

'But if he doesn't speak English, Em . . .' Barbara offered hesitantly.

Emily appeared to ignore the implication behind the words: weren't they wasting time by keeping him in a custody without making at least a desultory attempt to bring in a trustworthy agent who spoke his language? 'We'll find that out in a few hours, I dare say.' She directed her attention to WPC Warner, who entered the office with a sealed evidence bag in her hand.

'This's been logged in,' Belinda Warner said. 'And logged out to you. It's the contents of Querashi's safe-deposit box. From Barclays,' she added.

Emily extended her hand. Belinda made the delivery. As if wishing to assuage Barbara's unspoken concerns, Emily told the WPC to phone Professor Siddiqi in London, to ask him about his availability to translate for a Pakistani suspect should that be necessary. 'Have him standing by,' Emily said. 'If we need him, we'll want him out here fast.'

She gave her attention to the contents of the bag, most of which consisted of paperwork. There were a sheaf of documents relating to the house on First Avenue, a second sheaf that contained his immigration paperwork, a contract for renovation and construction signed by Gerry DeVitt as well as by Querashi and Akram Malik, and several loose papers. One of these had been torn from a spiral notebook, and as Emily picked this one up, Barbara took a second one.

'Here's *Oskarstraße 15* again,' Emily said, looking up from what she'd apparently read on her paper. She turned it over and gave it a closer scrutiny. 'No city, though. But my money's still on Hamburg. What've you got?'

It was a bill of lading, Barbara told her. It came from a place of business called Eastern Imports. '"Fine furniture, fittings, and accessories for the home,"' she read to Emily. '"Imports from India, Pakistan, and Bangladesh."'

'God only knows what anyone would be importing from Bangladesh,' Emily commented in a dry aside. 'It looks like the lovebirds were getting ready to furnish their house on First Avenue.'

Barbara wasn't so sure. 'But there's nothing listed on the bill, Em. If he and the Malik girl had been out buying the bridal bed and all the etceteras, wouldn't this be a receipt for their purchases? But it isn't. It's just a blank bill of lading for the company itself.'

Emily frowned. 'Where is this place, then? Hounslow? Oxford? The Midlands?' Which were all locations, they both knew, of substantial Indian and Pakistani communities.

Barbara shook her head as she took note of the address. 'Parkeston,' she said.

'Parkeston?' Emily sounded incredulous. 'Hand it over, Barb.'

Barbara did so. As Emily studied the bill of lading, she also pushed her chair back from her desk and went to examine the wall map of the Tendring Peninsula and, next to it, a larger map of the coastline. For her part, Barbara gave her attention to the three sheaves of documents.

The immigration papers all appeared to be in order, as far as she could tell. The documentation on the First Avenue house seemed likewise. Akram Malik's signature was neatly rendered on most of these latter papers, but that made sense if the house was part of Sahlah Malik's dowry. Barbara was leafing through the contract for renovations signed by Gerry DeVitt when yet another paper slid out from between the pages.

It was, she saw, a page from a glossy magazine. It had been carefully torn out and folded to pocket size. Barbara unfolded it and spread it on her lap.

Both sides of the page comprised advertisements from a section of the magazine that was called *At Your Service*. They ranged from International Company Services Limited on the Isle of Man, which appeared to arrange offshore corporations for the protection of one's assets and the avoidance of taxes, to Lorraine Electronics Discreet Surveillance for employers who doubted the loyalty of their workers, to Spycatcher of Knightsbridge, which offered the latest in bug-detecting devices for 'the serious businessman's total protection'. There were ads for car-hire companies, for serviced apartments in London, and for security services. Barbara read each of them. She was growing more and more nonplussed about Querashi's having stowed this particular paper among his other documents, thinking it surely had to be some sort of mistake, when a familiar name leapt out at her. *World Wide Tours*, she read, *Travel and Specialists in Immigration*.

Yet another very strange coincidence, she realised. One of the calls that Querashi had made from the Burnt House had been to this same agency, with one difference. Querashi had phoned World Wide Tours in Karachi, while this World Wide Tours was on the High Street in Harwich.

Barbara joined Emily at the coastal map, where the DCI was contemplating the peninsula north of Pennyhole Bay. Never an enthusiastic student of geography, until Barbara herself had a decent look at the map, she had no idea that Harwich was due north of the Nez and virtually identical to it longitudinally. It sat at the mouth of the River

Stour, directly connected to the rest of the country by a railway line. Without conscious intention, Barbara followed the barbed and black indication of this line as it headed west. The first stop it made – indeed, barely far enough out of Harwich to be considered a separate entity – was Parkeston.

'Em,' Barbara said, aware of a rising sense of connection being made and pieces falling into place, 'he's got an ad here for a travel agency in Harwich, but it's got the same name as the one he phoned in Karachi.'

But Emily, she saw, didn't make the jump between Karachi and Harwich, between Harwich and Parkeston. Instead, she appeared to be contemplating a small boxed list of information that was superimposed on the blue of the sea, to the east of Harwich. Barbara leaned forward to read it.

Vehicle Ferry from Harwich (Parkeston Quay) to:

Hook of Holland	6 to 8 hours
Esbjerg	20 hours
Hamburg	18 hours
Gothenburg	24 hours

'Well, well, well,' Barbara said.

'Interesting, isn't it?' Emily turned from the map. At her desk, she shifted papers, folders, and reports until she came up with the photograph of Haytham Querashi. She extended it to Barbara, saying, 'What d'you think of a drive this afternoon?'

'Harwich and Parkeston?' Barbara said.

'If he was there, someone saw him,' Emily replied. 'And if someone saw him, someone may be able to tell us –'

'Guv?' Belinda Warner was at the door again. She looked back over her shoulder as if expecting to be followed.

'What is it?' Emily asked.

'The Asian blokes. Mr Malik and Mr Azhar. They're here.'

'Shit.' Emily glanced at her watch. 'I'm not about to put up with this. If they think that they can show up whenever they please for another one of their bloody meetings –'

'Not that, guv,' Belinda cut in. 'They've heard about the bloke from Clacton.'

For a moment Emily stared at the WPC as if she didn't quite understand. She even said, 'Clacton.'

Belinda said, 'Right, Mr Kumhar. They know he's here. They're demanding to see him, and they won't be put off till you've given them a chance to have a word with him.'

'What bloody cheek!' Emily said.

But what she didn't say was what Barbara knew she had to be thinking: the Asians obviously knew the Police and Criminal Evidence Act better than the DCI had anticipated. And Barbara realised that intimate knowledge of PACE could have come from only one source.

Agatha Shaw replaced the telephone receiver into its cradle and allowed herself a crow of triumph. If she could have done, she would have danced a jig. She would have danced it straight across the library carpet, leaping and bouncing through its steps until she found herself in front of those three easels on which still stood – these two days after the failed council meeting – the artist's and architect's depictions of Balford-le-Nez as it could be. Then she would have swept each of those easels into her arms and kissed them soundly, like precious children worshipped by an adoring mother.

As it was, she shouted, 'Mary Ellis! Mary Ellis! You're wanted in the library and you're wanted now!' She planted her three-pronged stick between her legs and struggled to her feet.

The effort made her sweat like a suckling pig. Although it didn't seem possible, she found that she rose too quickly, despite the time it took her: dizziness blew against her like a gust of wind. 'Whoops,' she said. But she laughed as well. She had plenty to be dizzy about, hadn't she? She was dizzy with excitement, dizzy with possibility, dizzy with success, dizzy with joy. Damn it all, she had a *right* to be dizzy.

'Mary Ellis! Blast you, girl! Can't you hear me calling?'

The clatter of shoe soles on the stairs told her that the girl was finally coming. She arrived in the library red-faced and breathless, saying, 'Jesus God, Mrs Shaw. You gave me that much of a fright. Are you all right?'

'Of course I'm all right,' Agatha snapped. 'Where were you? Why don't you come when I call? What am I paying you for if I have to stand here and screech like one of the weird sisters whenever I need you?'

Mary came to her side. 'You wanted the drawing-room furniture switched round today, Mrs Shaw. Don't you remember? You didn't like the piano next to the fireplace and you said the sofas were fading 'cause they're too near the windows. You even wanted the pictures –'

'All right. All *right.*' Agatha attempted to shake Mary's clammy hand from her arm. 'Don't paw me like that, girl. I'm not an invalid. I can walk on my own, and you very well know it.'

Mary loosened her grip, saying, 'Yes, ma'am,' and waiting for further instructions.

Agatha eyed her. She wondered once again what on earth she was thinking of, keeping such a pathetic creature in her employ. Aside from her lack of intellectual gifts which rendered her useless for entertaining conversation, Mary Ellis was in the worst physical condition of anyone Agatha had ever known. Who else would be sweating, out of breath, and red in the face simply because of moving a piano and a few other paltry sticks of furniture?

'What are you good for, Mary, if you don't come at once when you're called?' Agatha demanded.

Mary dropped her gaze. 'I did hear you, ma'am. But I was on the ladder, wasn't I? I had that portrait of your granddad ready to move, and I couldn't put it down very easy.'

Agatha knew the picture she was talking about. Above the fireplace, nearly life size, in an ancient gilt frame ... At the thought of the girl successfully heaving that painting round the drawing room, Agatha eyed Mary Ellis with something akin to respect. It was, however, an emotion from which she quickly recovered.

Agatha *harrumphed.* 'Your obligation in this household is first and foremost to me,' she told the girl. 'See to it that you remember from now on.'

'Yes, ma'am.' Mary's voice was glum.

'Now don't sulk, girl. I appreciate your moving the furniture about. But let's just keep things in their proper perspective. Now give me your arm. I mean to go to the tennis court.'

'The tennis court?' Mary asked incredulously. 'What d'you want with the tennis court, Mrs Shaw?'

'I mean to see what condition it's in. I mean to start playing again.'

'But you can't –' Mary gulped the rest of her sentence back when Agatha cast a sharp look in her direction.

'I can't play?' Agatha said. 'Rubbish. I can do anything. If I can get on the phone and win every necessary vote on the town council without their even seeing the plans ...' Agatha chuckled. 'I can damn well do anything.'

Mary Ellis didn't ask for clarification on the topic of the town council as her employer would have liked her to do. Agatha was hungry – indeed she was ravenous – to tell someone of her triumph. Theo was the person she'd have liked to crow to, but these days Theo wasn't ever to be found where he was supposed to be, so she hadn't bothered to try him at the pier. She hoped her hint had been broad enough for someone even of Mary Ellis's limited mental powers to take and run with conversationally. But that was not to be. Mary stood mute.

'Damn it, girl,' Agatha said. 'Have you *got* a brain anywhere in your skull? Yes? No? Oh, bother you anyway. Give me your arm. Help me outside.'

They tottered together out of the library and towards the front door. Having a captive audience, Agatha explained herself.

She was talking of the redevelopment plans for Balford-le-Nez, she told her companion. When Mary made sufficient guttural noise to indicate comprehension, Agatha continued. The ease with which she'd got Basil Treves in her corner on the previous day had suggested that she might do the same if she invested equal telephone time with the rest of the council.

'Save Akram Malik,' she said. 'No point trying to get him in line. Besides,' and here again she chuckled, 'I want old Akram to face a *fait accompli.*'

'There's to be a fête?' Mary asked eagerly.

God, Agatha thought wearily. 'Not a fête, you idiot thing,' she said. 'A *fait.* A *fait accompli.* Don't you know what that means? Never mind.'

She didn't want a digression from the topic at hand. Treves had been the easiest of them all to get on board, she confided, what with the way he felt about the coloureds. She'd got him in her corner last night. But the others hadn't been as quick to haul themselves to her side. 'Still, I managed them all in the end,' she said. 'I mean, all of them that I need for the vote. If I've learned nothing else from business in all these years, Mary, I've learned that no man – or woman – turns away from the idea of investing money if the investment costs him next to nothing but still allows him to accrue a benefit. And that's the promise of our plans, you see. The town council invests, the town improves, the beach-goers arrive, and everyone benefits.'

Silent, Mary appeared to be mentally chewing on Agatha's scheme. She said, 'I've seen the plans. Those're them in the library on that artist stand.'

'And soon,' Agatha said, 'you shall see those plans taking concrete form. A leisure centre, a redeveloped High Street, renovated hotels, a reconstructed Marine Parade and Princes Esplanade. Just you wait, Mary Ellis. Balford-le-Nez is going to be the showplace of the coast.'

'I sort of like it like it is,' Mary said.

They were out of the front door and on the sweeping drive. The sun was baking it so thoroughly that Agatha could feel it. She looked down and realised that she wore her bedroom slippers rather than her walking shoes, and the heat from the gravel on the ground was seeping through the thin soles. She squinted, unable to recall the last time she'd been out of the house. The light was almost unbearably bright.

'Like it *is*?' Agatha dragged on Mary Ellis's arm, leading her towards the rose garden to the north of the house. The lawn dipped in a gentle slope beyond the plants, and at the base of this slope the tennis court lay. It was a clay court that Lewis had constructed for her as a gift for her thirty-fifth birthday. Prior to her stroke, she'd played three times a week, never very well but always with a stubborn determination to win. 'Have a bit of vision, girl. The town's gone to ruin. Shops are closing on the High Street, the restaurants are empty, hotels – such as they are, at this point – have more rooms to let than there are people on the street. If someone isn't willing to give Balford a transfusion, we'll be living inside a rotting corpse in another three years. There's *potential* in this town, Mary Ellis. All it takes is someone with the vision to see it.'

They worked their way into the rose garden. Agatha paused. She found that her breath was not coming easily – thanks to the bloody stroke, she fumed – and she used the excuse of examining the bushes to have a rest. Damn it all, when would she have her strength back?

'Blast it!' she snapped. 'Why haven't these roses been sprayed? Just look at this, Mary. D'you see these leaves? Aphids are dining at *my* expense and no one's doing a bloody thing about it! Do I have to tell the damn gardener how to do his job? I want these plants sprayed, Mary Ellis. Today.'

'Yes, ma'am,' Mary Ellis said. 'I'll phone Harry. It's not like him to overlook the roses, but his son had a burst appendix two weeks ago and I know it's worrying Harry 'cause they haven't been able to make him right.'

'He's going to have something more than a burst appendix to worry about if he lets the aphids ruin my roses.'

'His son's only ten years old, Mrs Shaw, and they haven't been able to get all the muck out of his blood. He's had three operations, Harry said, and he's still all swelled up. They think –'

'Mary, do I look as if I wish to engage in a discussion of paediatric medicine? We all have personal problems. But we continue to meet our responsibilities in spite of those problems. If Harry can't do that, then he'll be sacked.'

Agatha turned from the roses. Her stick had become embedded in the freshly turned earth at the edge of the flower bed. She attempted to free it, but found she lacked the strength.

'Damn and blast!' She jerked the handle and nearly lost her balance. Mary caught her by the arm. 'Stop babying me! I don't need your coddling. Christ in heaven, when will this heat abate?'

'Mrs Shaw, you're getting yourself in a state.' There was caution in Mary's voice, that eighteenth-century cringing tone of a servant who was afraid of being struck. Listening to it was worse than struggling with the miserable stick.

'I am not in a state,' Agatha said between clenched teeth. She gave a final yank to the stick and freed it, but the effort robbed her of breath again.

She wasn't about to let something as basic as respiration defeat her, however. She gestured towards the lawn beyond the flowers and resolutely began to move forward once again.

'Don't you think you'd like a rest?' Mary asked. 'You've gone a bit red in the face and –'

'What do you expect in this heat?' Agatha demanded. 'And I don't need a rest. I mean to see my tennis court and I mean to see it now.'

But the going on the lawn was worse than the going in the flower bed, where at least there had been a gravel path to follow. Here the ground was uneven, and the sun-browned grass masked its irregularity. Agatha stumbled and righted herself, stumbled and righted. She yanked herself away from Mary and snarled when the girl said her name solicitously. Damn the garden to hell, she cursed silently. And how had she forgotten the very nature of her own lawn? Had movement been so easy before that she'd never noticed the land's pernicious anomalies?

'We c'n rest if you want,' Mary Ellis said. 'I c'n fetch some water.'

Agatha lurched on. Her destination was in sight, no more than thirty yards away. It spread out like an umber blanket, with its net in place and its boundaries chalked freshly in anticipation of her next match. The court shimmered in the heat, and an illusion of light made it look as if steam were snaking up from it.

A trickle of perspiration worked its way from Agatha's forehead into her eye. Another followed. She found that her chest had grown quite tight and that her body felt as if a hot rubber shroud encased it. Every movement was a battle while next to her Mary Ellis simply glided along like a feather in the wind. Blast her youth. Damn her health. Curse her blithe assumption that both youth and health gave her some sort of hegemony in their small household.

Agatha could sense the girl's unspoken superiority, could even read her thoughts: *pathetic old woman, broken down cow*. Well, she would show her. She would stalk on to that tennis court and batter her opponent into fragments. She would serve her old serve of fire and wind. She would play the net and thunder returns down her victim's throat.

She would show Mary Ellis. She would show everyone. Agatha Shaw was not to be defeated. She'd bent the town council to her will. She'd breathed new life into Balford-le-Nez. She'd regained her strength and redesigned her life's purpose. And she would do the same to her contemptible body.

'Mrs Shaw ...' Mary's tone was chary. 'Don't you think that a rest ...? We can sit under that lime tree over there. I c'n get you a drink.'

'Rubbish!' Agatha found that she could only gasp the word. 'I want ... see ... tennis.'

'Please, Mrs Shaw. Your face's like a beetroot. I'm scared that –'

'Pish! Scared!' Agatha tried to laugh but it came out like a cough. How was it that the tennis court seemed just as distant as it had done when they'd first set out? It seemed they'd been walking for ages – for miles – and their destination wavered miragelike, no closer. How could this be? She was slogging forward, dragging her stick, dragging her leg, and she was feeling as if she were being pulled first backward then downward like a hundredweight sinking. 'You're ... holding me ... back,' she gasped. 'Damn' ... girl. Holding me, aren't you?'

'Mrs Shaw, I'm not,' Mary said, and her voice was higher and sounded scared. 'Mrs Shaw, I don't have my hand anywheres on you. Please, won't you stop? I c'n fetch a chair. And I'll get a brolly to keep the sun off you.'

'Nonsense ...' Weakly, Agatha waved her off. But she became aware that she'd ceased moving altogether. The landscape itself seemed to be moving instead. The tennis court receded into the distance and appeared to meld with the faraway Wade that lay in the shape of a green bucking horse beyond the Balford Channel.

Something told her that Mary Ellis was speaking, but she couldn't make out the words. She found that her head had begun to pound, that the dizziness she'd earlier felt upon rising in the library now swept against her like a current. And although she wanted to ask for help – or at least to say her companion's name – nothing emerged from her mouth but a groan. One arm and one leg became a drag upon her, numb anchors too heavy to heave along the ground.

She heard shouting coming from somewhere.

The sun beat down fiercely.

The sky became white.

Lewis cried, 'Aggie!'

Lawrence said, 'Mum?'

Her vision tunnelled to a pinprick before she fell.

Trevor Ruddock had managed to fill the interview room with enough cigarette smoke to make Barbara's lighting up nearly unnecessary. When she joined him, it was through a grey pall that she saw him seated at the black metal table, and an array of extinguished cigarette ends speckled the floor by his chair. She'd given him an ashtray to use, but apparently he'd needed to make a statement that only floor-stubbed cigarettes and flakes of ash could assist him in making.

'Had enough time for a think?' Barbara asked him.

'I get to make a phone call,' he said.

'Looking to have a solicitor sit with you? That's a curious request from someone who claims he had nothing to do with Querashi's murder.'

He said, 'I want my phone call.'

'Fine. You'll make it in my presence, of course.'

'I don't have to –'

'Wrong. You do.' There was no bloody way that she intended to give Trevor the slightest chance to cook up an alibi. And since he'd doubtless already attempted that with Rachel Winfield, his track record of honesty left something to be desired.

Trevor scowled. 'I admitted that I nicked stuff from the factory, didn't I? I told you Querashi gave me the sack. I told you *everything* I knew about the bloke. Why'd I do that if I also chopped him?'

'I've been considering that,' Barbara said agreeably. She joined him at the table. The room had no ventilation, so the air was close, saunalike in its weight as she took it into her lungs. The residual smoke from Trevor's habit didn't help much, and she real-ised there was little point in not joining him. So she took one of his remaining cigarettes and lit up. 'I had a chat with Rachel this morning.'

'I know that, don't I?' was his reply. 'If you came for me, it's 'cause you talked to her. She must've told you we split round ten. Okay. We did. We split round ten. Now you know it.'

'Right. I know it. But she told me something else that I really didn't put into proper perspective till you refused to tell me what you were up to on Friday night once you left her. And when I put together what she told me with what you've related about Querashi, and I blend those two facts with your secret activity on Friday night, I come up with only one possibility. And that's what we need to talk about, you and I.'

'What's this, then?' He sounded wary. He chewed on his index finger and spat away a flake of skin.

'Have you ever had sexual intercourse with Rachel?'

He lifted his chin, part defiance, part embarrassment. 'What if I have? She saying she didn't want it or something? 'Cause if she is, my memory tells me something different.'

'Just answer the question, Trevor. Have you ever had sexual intercourse with Rachel?'

'Lots of times.' He smirked. 'When I give her the call and tell her what day and what time, she comes round straightaway. 'N' if she has something else to do that night, she changes her plans. She's got a real itch for me.' Where his eyebrows would have been had he not shaved them off, the skin drew together. 'Is she telling you different?'

'Clothes-off sexual intercourse is what I'm talking about,' Barbara clarified, skimming past his other remarks. 'Or perhaps better stated, underclothes-off sexual intercourse.'

He chewed on his finger again and examined her. 'What're you on about, then?'

'I think you know. Have you ever had vaginal intercourse with Rachel?'

'There's lot of ways to shag. I don't need to give her a length like the pensioners do it.'

'Right. But you're not exactly answering me, are you? What I want to know is whether you've ever been inside Rachel Winfield's vagina. Standing, sitting, kneeling, or mounted on a pogo stick. I don't particularly care about specifics. Just the act itself.'

'We did it. Yeah. Just like you said. We did the act. She got hers and I got mine.'

'With your penis inside her?'

He grabbed the packet of cigarettes. 'Shit. What *is* this? I told you, we did it. Is she saying I raped her?'

'No. She's saying something a little more intriguing. She's saying sex between you was a one-way street. You didn't do anything but let Rachel Winfield play your flute, Trevor. Isn't that the case?'

'You just hang on there!' His ears had gone crimson. Barbara noticed that when the blood throbbed in his jugular, the spider that was tattooed on his neck seemed to come alive.

'You popped your cork every time the two of you got together,' Barbara went on. 'But Rachel didn't get anything out of it. Not even a passing greeting down under, if you get my meaning.'

He didn't deny it, but his fingers clutched the cigarette packet, partially crumpling it.

'So this is what I reckon,' she continued. 'Either you're a total dumbshit when it comes to women – thinking that having some bird give your prong the mouth business is the same as putting her on the path to heaven – or you don't much like females at all, which would explain why sex between you was limited to blow jobs. So which one is it, Trevor? Are you just a dumbshit or a bum boy in hiding?'

'I'm not!'

'Not which?'

'Not either! I like girls fine and they like me. And if Rachel tells you different –'

'I'm not so sure about any of that,' Barbara said.

'I c'n give you girls,' he declared hotly. 'I c'n give you dozens and dozens of girls. I c'n give you hundreds. I had my first when I was ten years old, and I c'n tell you right now, she liked it just fine. Yeah, I don't shag Rachel Winfield. I never did and I never will. So? What about it? She's an ugly cow and the only way she'll be rogered proper is if the bloke doing it to her is blind. Which I am not, 'n case you didn't notice.' He stabbed his index finger into the packet and brought out a cigarette. Apparently, it was the last one because he balled the packet into his palm and flung it into the corner of the room.

'Yes. Well,' Barbara said, 'I'm sure the motorway of your life is completely littered with sexual roadkill and all of the corpses are grinning ear to ear. At least in your dreams. But we aren't dealing with dreams, Trevor. We're dealing with reality, and reality is murder. I have only your word for it that you saw Haytham Querashi cottaging in Clacton market square, and I've come to realise that there's a very good chance he was cottaging with you.'

'That's a bloody lie!' He surged to his feet so quickly that his chair toppled over.

'Is it?' Barbara asked blandly. 'Sit down, please. Or I'll have a PC give you some assistance.' She waited till he'd righted the chair and planted himself in it. He'd thrown his cigarette to the table, and he retrieved it, lighting a match on the edge of a dirty thumbnail. 'You see how it looks, don't you?' Barbara asked him. 'You worked together at the factory. He gave you the sack and the excuse was that you'd nicked a few jars of mustard, some chutney and jelly. But perhaps that's not why he sacked you at all. Perhaps he sacked you because he was marrying Sahlah Malik and he didn't want you round the place any longer, reminding him of what he really was.'

'I want my phone call,' Trevor said. 'I got nothing more to talk to you about.'

'You do see how black things look, don't you?' Barbara crushed her own cigarette out, careful to use the ashtray and not the floor. 'A declaration of Querashi's homosexuality, consistent fellatio and nothing else with Rachel –'

'I already explained that!'

'– and Querashi dying at the very same time that you're without an alibi. So tell me, Trevor, does this make you any more inclined to reveal what you were up to on Friday night? If, of course, you weren't up to murdering Haytham Querashi.'

His mouth clamped shut. He stared at her defiantly.

'Right,' she said. 'Play it that way if you want. But just make sure you aren't also playing the fool.'

She left him to cool off and went in search of Emily. She heard the DCI before she saw her. Her voice – as well as a male voice taut with animosity – came from the lower floor. Barbara peered over the curved banister and saw Emily standing toe-to-toe with Muhannad Malik. Taymullah Azhar was directly behind his cousin.

'Don't explain PACE to me,' Emily was saying tersely as Barbara descended the stairs. 'I'm well aware of the law. Mr Kumhar is being held for an arrestable offence. I'm well within my rights to ensure that nothing interferes with potential evidence or puts anyone at risk.'

'Mr Kumhar is the one at risk.' Muhannad's face was hard. 'And if you're refusing to let us see him, there's only one possible reason why.'

'Would you care to explain?'

'I want to verify his physical condition. And don't let's pretend you've never used the term "resisting the police" to excuse some bloke's getting a beating while he's in the nick.'

'I think,' Emily said pointedly as Barbara reached her side, 'that you've been watching too much television, Mr Malik. It's not my habit to rough up suspects.'

'Then you'll have no objection to our seeing him.'

When Emily would have offered a rejoinder, Azhar interposed. 'The Police and Criminal Evidence Act also indicates that a suspect has the right to have a friend, relative, or other person who is known to him told without delay that he's in custody. May we have the name of whomever you informed, Inspector Barlow?'

He spoke without a glance in Barbara's direction, but even so she was certain he could feel her inward wince. PACE was all well and good, but when events began to outstrip the police's ability to keep up with them, more often than not even a good officer let slide exact compliance with the letter of the law. Azhar was betting on this having happened. Barbara waited to see if Emily was going to pull a friend or relative of Fahd Kumhar's out of a metaphorical hat.

She didn't bother. 'Mr Kumhar hasn't identified anyone he wishes to be notified.'

'Does he know he has that right?' Azhar asked astutely.

'Mr Azhar, we've hardly had the opportunity to speak to this man long enough to apprise him of his rights.'

'That's business as usual,' Muhannad pointed out. 'She's slapped him in isolation because it's the only way she can make sure he gets rattled enough to cooperate with her.'

Azhar didn't disagree with his cousin's assessment of the situation. He also didn't allow it to enflame him. Calmly, he asked, 'Is Mr Kumhar a native of this country, Inspector?'

Barbara knew that Emily was probably cursing the fact that she'd allowed Kumhar to jabber about his papers. She could hardly deny knowledge of the man's immigrant status, especially when the law was specific about what his rights were considering that status. If Emily prevaricated now – only to discover that Fahd Kumhar was involved in Haytham Querashi's death – she ran the risk of having her case tossed out of court later.

She said, 'At this point, we'd like to question Mr Kumhar about his relationship with Haytham Querashi. We've brought him to the station because he was reluctant to answer questions in his lodgings.'

'Stop avoiding the bloody issue,' Muhannad said. 'Is Kumhar an English national or not?'

'He doesn't appear to be,' Emily replied, but she spoke to Azhar and not to Muhannad.

'Ah.' Azhar sounded somehow comforted by this admission. Barbara saw why when he asked his next question. 'How good is his English?'

'I haven't given him a comprehension test.'

'But that's actually of no account, is it?'

'Azhar, bloody hell. If his English isn't —'

Azhar cut off his cousin's hot remark by the simple gesture of raising his hand. He said, 'Then I shall have to ask to be given access to Mr Kumhar immediately, Inspector. I won't insult either your intelligence or your knowledge of the law by pretending you don't know that the only suspects who have an unqualified right to visitors are those from abroad.'

Game, set, and match, Barbara thought with no little admiration for the Pakistani. Teaching microbiology to university students might have been Azhar's day job, but he was clearly no slouch when it came to moonlighting in the white knight arena for the protection of his people. She suddenly realised that she needn't have worried about the man's getting in over his head in this journey he'd made to Balford-le-Nez. It was fairly apparent that he had the situation — at least with respect to their dealings with the coppers — completely and satisfactorily in hand.

For his part, Muhannad was looking triumphant at this turn of events. With pointed courtesy he said, 'If you'll lead us to him, Inspector Barlow ...? We'd like to be able to report to our people upon Mr Kumhar's well-being. They're understandably anxious to know he's being treated well while he's in your hands.'

There wasn't much room for political manoeuvring. The message he sent was clear enough. Muhannad Malik could mobilise his people for yet another march, demonstration, and riot. He could just as easily mobilise them to keep the peace. The choice was DCI Emily Barlow's, as would be the responsibility.

Barbara saw the skin at the corners of the DCI's eyes tighten. It was the closest thing to a reaction that Emily was going to give the two men.

'Come with me,' she said.

She felt as if she were trapped in irons. Not irons that held her at the wrists and ankles, but irons that encased her from head to toe.

Lewis was talking inside her head. On and on he went about the children, his business, his infernal love for that antique Morgan that *never* ran properly no matter the money he poured into it. Then Lawrence took over. But all he said was, I love her, I love her, why can't you understand that I love her, Mum, and we want a life? And then that Swedish bitch herself chimed in, spouting psychobabble that she'd probably learned while swatting a volleyball on some beach in California: Lawrence's love for me cannot lessen his love for you, Mrs Shaw. You do see that, don't you? And you do want his happiness? And after that came Stephen, saying, It's my life, Gran. You can't live it for me. If you can't accept me as I am, then I agree with you: it's best that I leave.

All of them talking on and on. She needed something to erase her brain. There was no real pain to speak of at the moment. There were only the voices, endless and insistent.

She found she wanted to argue with them, order them about, bend their wills to hers. But all she could do was listen to them, held prisoner to their importuning, their irrationality, their constant noise.

She wanted to raise her fists to her skull. She wanted to beat them against her head. But the irons held her body fast in position, and every limb was a weight that she couldn't move.

She became aware of lights. With this awareness, the voices dimmed. They were replaced with other voices, however. Agatha strained to make out the words.

At first they all slurred together. 'Nottoomuchdifferentfromwhat-happenstotheheart,' someone was saying reasonably. 'Butthisisabrain-attackinstead.'

Butthisisabrainattackinstead? What did this mean? Agatha wondered. Where was she? And why was she lying so still? She might have thought she'd died and was having an out-of-body experience, but she was firmly and definitely *in* her body, all too aware of its presence, in fact.

'OhGodhowbadisit?' This was Theo's voice, and Agatha warmed to it. Theo, she thought. Theo was there. Theo was with her, in the room, nearby. Things couldn't be as bad as they seemed.

So relieved was she to have heard his voice that she caught only snatches of words for the next several minutes. *Thrombosis*, she heard. *Cholesterol deposits. Occlusion of artery.* And *right hemiparisis.*

Then she knew. And what she felt in the instant she knew was a despair so profound that it welled inside her like a fast-inflating balloon of a scream which she could not emit, which threatened to kill her. Would that it could, she thought brokenly. Oh, blessed Jesus, would that it could.

Lewis had called to her. Lawrence had called to her. But pig-headed as always, she hadn't joined them. She had things left to do, dreams to fulfil, and points left to make before she was done with living. So when the stroke had attacked and the blood clot had robbed her brain of oxygen for however long a time it had been, the substance and spirit of Agatha Shaw had fiercely fought back. And she had not died.

Now the words were becoming clearer. The light that filled the field of her vision began to transform itself into forms. From these forms, people emerged, indistinguishable from one another at first.

'It's the left middle cerebral artery that's been affected again.' A man's voice, and one she now recognised. Dr Fairclough, who'd seen her through her last stroke. 'You can see as much from the pull on her facial muscles. Nurse, use the needle again, please. See? There's no reaction. If we repeat the pricking on her arm as well, we'll have the same results.' He bent over the bed. Now Agatha could see him clearly. His nose was large, with pores that were the size of pinheads. He wore glasses whose lenses were oily and smudged. How could he possibly see anything through them? 'Agatha?' he called. 'Do you know me, Agatha? Do you know what's happened?'

Bloody stupid man, Agatha thought. How could she *not* know what had happened. With an effort, she blinked. The very act exhausted her.

'Yes. Good,' Dr Fairclough said. 'You've had another stroke, my dear. But you're all right now. And Theo's here.'

'Gran?' He sounded so tentative, as if she'd become an abandoned puppy that he was attempting to coax from a hiding place. He was standing too far away for her to see him clearly, but even seeing the shape of him was comforting to her, a sign that all might be well once again. 'Why the hell did you try to get to the tennis court?' Theo asked. 'Jesus, Gran, if Mary hadn't been with you ... She didn't even phone for an ambulance. She picked you up and rushed you here herself. Dr Fairclough thinks that saved your life.'

Who would have thought the silly cow had such presence of mind?

Agatha wondered. All *she* could ever recall Mary Ellis doing in an emergency situation was blubbering, blinking, and letting her nose dribble on to her upper lip.

'She isn't responding,' Theo said, and Agatha could see that he'd turned to the doctor. 'Can she even hear me?'

'Agatha?' the doctor said. 'Will you show Theo you can hear what he's saying?'

Slowly and once again with great effort, Agatha blinked. It seemed to take every ounce of her energy, and she felt the strain of the movement all the way to her throat.

'What we're seeing,' the doctor said in that blasted imparting-of-information voice that had always caused Agatha's hackles to rise, 'is called expressive aphasia. The clot denied blood – hence oxygen – to the left side of the brain. Since that's the region responsible for word-oriented rational reality, speech is affected.'

'But she's worse than last time. She had some words last time. So why doesn't she have them now? Gran, can you say my name? Can you say your own?'

Agatha forced her mouth to open. But the only sound she was able to make sounded to her like 'Ahg'. She tried a second time, then a third. And she felt that balloon scream trying to force its way out of her lungs again.

'It's a more serious stroke this time,' Dr Fairclough was saying. He put a hand on Agatha's left shoulder. She could feel him squeeze warmly. 'Agatha, don't strain yourself. Rest now. You're in excellent hands. And Theo's here if you need him.'

They stepped away from the bed and out of her range of vision, but she could still hear some of their hushed words.

'. . . no magic bullet unfortunately,' the doctor was saying. '. . . will need extensive rehabilitation.'

'. . . therapy?' this from Theo.

'Physical and speech.'

'. . . hospital?'

And Agatha strained to hear. Intuitively, she knew what her grandson was asking because it was what she herself felt desperate to know: What was the prognosis in a case like hers? And could she expect to remain in hospital, immobilised in a rail-sided bed like a blasted rag doll, until the day she died?

'Actually quite hopeful,' Dr Fairclough said, and he returned to her bedside to share the information with her. He patted her shoulder, then touched his fingertips to her forehead as if he were giving her a formal benediction.

Doctors, she thought. When they didn't think they were the Pope, they thought they were God.

'Agatha, the paralysis you're experiencing will improve over time with physical therapy. The aphasia ... Well, reacquisition of speech is more difficult to predict. But with care, with nursing, and most of all with a will to recover, you can live for any number of years.' The doctor turned then to Theo. 'She has to *want* to live, however. And she must have a reason to live.'

She had that, Agatha thought. Damn it to hell and back again, she had that. She *would* re-create this town to her image of what a sea side resort ought to be. She would do it from her bed, she would do it from her coffin, she would do it from her grave. The name Agatha Shaw would mean something beyond an abortive marriage brought to a meaningless early end, a failed motherhood with children either scattered to the globe or tucked into premature graves, and a life defined through the people she'd lost. So she had the will to live and endure. She had it in spades.

The doctor was continuing. 'She's enormously blessed in two respects, and we can hang our hopes of recovery on them. Overall, she's in excellent physical condition: heart, lungs, bone mass, muscles. She has the body of a woman in her fifties, and believe me, that's going to serve her well.'

'She was always active,' Theo said. 'Tennis, boating, riding. Until the first stroke, she did it all.'

'Hmm. Yes. And much to her benefit. But there's more to life than keeping the body fit. There's keeping the heart and soul fit as well. She does that through you. She isn't alone in the world. She has a family. And family give people a reason to go on.' The doctor chuckled as he asked his last questions, so apparently sure was he of the reply. 'Now, you aren't thinking of going off some-where, Theo? Not planning an expedition to Africa? No trips to Mars?'

There was a silence. In it, Agatha heard the bleeping of the monitors to which she was hooked up. They burbled and hissed just out of sight, beyond her head.

She wanted to tell Theo to stand within her view. She wished that she could tell him how she loved him. Love was balderdash and rubbish, she knew. It was nonsense and illusion that did nothing but wound one and wear one down. It was, in fact, a word she'd never used openly in her life. But she would have said it now.

She felt a longing for him, to touch him and hold him. She felt it down her arms and in her fingertips. She'd always thought touch was meant for discipline. How had she failed to see it was meant for forging bonds?

The doctor chuckled again, but this time it sounded forced. 'Good God, don't look like that, Theo. You're no expert in the field and you won't have to rehabilitate your grandmother on your own. It's your presence in her life that's important. It's continuity. You can give her that.'

Theo came close enough for her to see now. He gazed into her eyes and his own looked clouded. They looked, in fact, just the way they'd looked when she'd arrived at that urine-scented children's home where he and Stephen had been taken in the immediate aftermath of their parents' death. She'd said to them, 'Come along with you, then,' and when she didn't extend her hand to either of them, Stephen walked out ahead of her. But Theo reached up and grasped the waistband of her skirt.

'I'll be there for her,' Theo said. 'I'm not going anywhere.'

Chapter Nineteen

As liaison officer, Barbara came up with a compromise that all present declared themselves able to live with. Emily had stopped their procession outside the interrogation room, where she'd informed the two men that their access to Fahd Kumhar would be limited to visual access only. They could check for his physical condition, but they could ask him nothing. These ground rules caused an immediate argument between the DCI and the Pakistanis, with Muhannad manhandling the reins of the discussion away from his cousin. After listening to his threats of 'imminent community dissent', Barbara suggested that Taymullah Azhar – an outsider clearly not suspected of anything – act as an interpreter. Fahd Kumhar would hear his rights given to him in English, Azhar would translate anything that the man did not understand, and Emily would tape record their entire interaction for verification from Professor Siddiqi in London. This appeared to cover all possible permutations of what could happen in the room. Everyone agreed it was a viable alternative to squabbling indefinitely in the corridor. So the compromise was accepted as are most compromises: everyone accepted it; no one liked it.

Emily swung her shoulder against the old oak door and admitted them into a small room. Fahd Kumhar sat in a corner, as far as possible from the police detective – oddly clad in walking shorts and a Hawaiian shirt – who was attending him. He was cowering in his chair like a rabbit cornered by hounds, and when he saw the identity of the newcomers, his gaze skittered from Emily to Barbara and then beyond them to Azhar and Muhannad. It seemed that his body reacted without any intention on his part of doing so. His feet pushed against the wooden floor and forced the chair even farther into the corner. Fright or flight, Barbara thought.

She could smell his incipient panic. The acrid stench of male sweat made the air very nearly unbreathable. She could only wonder how the Asians would interpret the man's mental state.

She didn't have to wonder for long. Azhar crossed the room and squatted in front of his chair. As Emily switched on the tape recorder, he said, 'I'm going to introduce myself to him. My cousin as well.' He then spoke in Urdu. Kumhar's flash of a glance from Azhar to Muhannad and back to Azhar indicated that introductions had indeed been made.

When Kumhar whimpered, Azhar reached out and put his hand on one of the man's arms, which he still held up defensively against his chest. 'I've told him I've come from London to help him,' Azhar said. He went on quietly in his native tongue, repeating in English both his questions and Kumhar's answers. 'Have they hurt you?' he asked. 'Have the police treated you roughly, Mr Kumhar?'

Emily interposed at once. 'These weren't our parameters and you know it, Mr Azhar.'

Muhannad shot her a look. 'We can't tell him his rights till we know how many of them have already been violated,' he said. 'Look at him, Azhar. He's like melting jelly. Can you see any bruises? Check his wrists and his neck.'

The DC who'd been in the room upon their arrival stirred at this. He said, 'He was quiet enough till you lot got in here.'

'Consider what constitutes the *lot* of us, Constable,' was Muhannad's riposte. 'We didn't exactly walk in here without DCI Barlow, did we?'

At these remarks, Kumhar made an involuntary mewling. He said something rapidly, but it didn't appear to be directed at any of them.

'What's that?' Emily demanded.

Azhar coaxed one of the man's arms from his chest. He unbuttoned the cuffs of his white cotton shirt and examined each wrist in turn, saying, 'He said, "Protect me. I have no wish to die."'

'Tell him that I will see to it,' Muhannad said. 'Tell him –'

'Hang on,' Barbara broke in angrily. 'We had an agreement, Mr Malik.'

Simultaneously, DCI Barlow snapped, 'And that just bloody cuts it. Out of here. Both of you. Now.'

'Cousin,' Azhar said in a beleaguered fashion. He spoke to Kumhar, explaining to Emily and Barbara that he was reassuring the man that he had nothing to fear from the police, that the Asian community would see to his safety.

'That's gracious of you,' Emily said acidly. 'But you've already blown it. I want you out of here. Constable, if you can give us some assistance . . . ?'

By the door, the constable rose. He was enormous. Seeing him, Barbara wondered if half Kumhar's fear had to do with being enclosed with a man the size and shape of a mountain gorilla.

'Inspector,' Azhar said, 'I apologise. Both for myself and for my cousin. But you can see that Mr Kumhar's quite panic-stricken, and I suggest it's to everyone's advantage that we make his rights under the law quite clear to him. Even if he gives you a statement, I fear that in his present condition it's going to be disallowed as being made under extreme duress.'

'I'll take my chances,' Emily said, and let him know by her tone how little she believed in his expression of concern.

But Azhar had a point. Barbara sought a way out of the impasse that served the police interests of peace in the community at the same time as it allowed everyone to save face. She thought the best approach would be to squash the fly in the ointment by tossing Muhannad out on his ear. But she knew that suggestion would only serve to enflame Malik further.

She said, 'Inspector? If I could have a word . . . ?' When Emily joined her by the door – keeping a sharp eye on the Pakistanis – Barbara murmured, 'We won't get any sense out of that bloke in the state he's in anyway. We either send for Professor Siddiqi to settle him down and tell him how things stand for him legally, or we let Azhar – Mr Azhar – do it, with the proviso that Muhannad keeps his gob plugged. If we go for the first alternative, we end up cooling our heels till the professor gets here, which'll take at least two hours or more. In the meantime, Muhannad shoots his mouth off to his people about Mr Kumhar's state of mind. If we go for the second alternative, we mollify the Muslim community at the same time as we advance our own cause.'

Frowning, Emily crossed her arms. 'God, how I hate to give in to this bastard,' she said through her teeth.

'We're serving our own interests,' Barbara said. 'It only looks like we're giving in.'

Barbara knew she was right. But she also knew that the DCI's antipathy towards the Pakistani – in conjunction with everything Muhannad Malik did to encourage that antipathy – might prompt her to see otherwise. Emily was in a tenuous position. She couldn't afford to seem weak at the same time as she couldn't afford to risk igniting an already flammable situation.

The DCI finally drew a breath, and when she spoke, she sounded disgusted with the entire procedure. 'If you can guarantee your cousin's silence for the rest of this meeting, Mr Azhar, you may inform Mr Kumhar of his rights.'

Azhar nodded. He said to Muhannad, 'Cousin?'

Muhannad jerked his head in agreement. But he placed himself within full view of the quivering Asian man, standing with his denim-clad legs apart and his arms crossed, solid, like a guard.

For his part, Fahd Kumhar clearly had followed none of the heated exchange between the police and his brother Asians. He remained in his rabbitlike position, and he didn't seem to know where to look. So his eyes flicked from person to person with a speed suggesting that – soothing words from Azhar or not – he trusted absolutely no one.

With Muhannad adhering to his part of the bargain, despite the lack of grace with which he did the adhering, Azhar was able to communicate the essential information to Fahd Kumhar.

Did he understand that he was being held for questioning in the matter of the death of Haytham Querashi?

He did, he did. But he had nothing to do with that death, nothing, he didn't even know a Mr Querashi.

Did he understand that he had a right to have a solicitor with him when he was questioned by the police?

He didn't know a solicitor, he had his papers, they were all in order, he'd tried to show them to the police, he had never met a Mr Querashi.

Did he wish to arrange for a solicitor now?

He had a wife in Pakistan, he had two children, they needed him, they needed money to –

'Ask him why Haytham Querashi wrote him a cheque for £400 if the two of them had never met,' Emily said.

Barbara shot her a surprised look. She wouldn't have bet on the DCI's playing any one of her cards in the presence of the Pakistanis.

In reaction to Emily's words, she saw Muhannad's eyes narrow as he silently took in this piece of information before turning to assess the man in the chair.

But Kumhar's answer was much the same. He didn't know a Mr Querashi. There was some mistake, perhaps another Kumhar. It was a common enough name.

'Not round here' was Emily's reply. 'Finish it up, Mr Azhar. It's clear that Mr Kumhar needs some time to dwell upon his situation.'

But something in all of Kumhar's babble had struck a chord with Barbara. She said, 'He keeps talking about his papers. Ask him if he's had any dealings with an agency called World Wide Tours, either here or in Pakistan. They deal in immigration.'

If Azhar recognised the name from the calls he'd made to Karachi for her, he gave no indication. He merely acted as translator for the fact that Kumhar knew no more about World Wide Tours than he knew about Haytham Querashi.

Once Azhar had completed the process of informing Kumhar of his legal rights, he stood and moved away from the chair. But even this did not relax the young man. Kumhar had gone back to his original position with fists clenched tightly beneath his chin. His face dribbled sweat. His thin shirt clung to his skeletal frame. Barbara noted that he wore no socks beneath his black trousers, and where his foot met his cheap shoe, the flesh looked raw. Azhar studied him for a long moment before he turned to Barbara and Emily. He said, 'You'd do well to have a doctor examine him. At the moment, he's clearly incapable of making a rational decision about legal representation.'

'Thank you,' Emily said in a tone that was deadly polite. 'You've registered the fact that he's unbruised. You can see he's got an attendant here to keep him from harm. And now that you know he's fully aware of his rights –'

'We won't know that till he asserts them,' Muhannad put in.

'– Sergeant Havers can bring you up to date on the investigation and then you can leave.' Emily continued speaking steadily as if she hadn't heard Muhannad. She turned to the door, which the constable swung open for her.

'A moment, Inspector,' Azhar said quietly. 'If you have no charge to bring against this man, you can keep him in your custody for only twenty-four hours. I'd like him to know that.'

'Tell him,' Emily said.

Azhar did so. Kumhar didn't look relieved by the news. Indeed, he looked no different from the way that he'd looked when they'd walked into the room.

'Tell him also,' Muhannad said, 'that someone from *Jum'a* will come to the station to pick him up and escort him home at the end of those twenty-four hours. And –' this with an icy look at the police '– these officers had better have a damn good reason for holding him if he's not released at that time.'

Azhar glanced Emily's way, as if waiting either for her reaction or for her permission to pass this information on. Emily gave a single sharp nod. They heard the word *Jum'a* among the others as Azhar spoke.

Outside in the corridor, Emily directed her final comments to Muhannad Malik. She said, 'I trust you'll pass along the information about Mr Kumhar's well-being to all the relevant parties.'

The implication was obvious: she'd done her part, and she expected him to do his.

That said, she left them in Barbara's company.

When Emily stalked up to the first floor, blood on the boil at having had the two Pakistanis gain the upper hand in the meeting with Fahd Kumhar, she heard the news that Superintendent Ferguson was waiting for her on the other end of the telephone line. Belinda Warner called out the information just as Emily was about to dash into the loo.

'I'm unavailable,' she shot back.

'This is his fourth call since two o'clock, Inspector,' Belinda informed her with a rise in inflection that communicated a tentative, sisterly sympathy.

'Is it? Well, someone should remove the redial button from that idiot's phone. I'll talk to him when I talk to him, Constable.'

'What shall I tell him, then? He knows you're in the building. Reception told him.'

Reception's loyalty was a wonderful thing, Emily thought. 'Tell him we have a suspect and I can either spend time questioning him or waste time yammering with my naffing arsehole of a superintendent.'

That said, she shoved open the door of the loo and went in. At the wash basin, she turned on the water, pulled six paper towels from the holder, and dashed them under the tap. When they were thoroughly doused, she wrung them out and used them vigorously: against her neck and her chest, down her arms, pressed against her forehead and cheeks.

Christ, she thought, how she loathed that bloody Asian. She'd loathed him since she'd first come across him as a teenager, the pride of his parents with his future laid out, one into which he needed only to step in order to succeed. While the rest of the world had to fight their way through life, Muhannad Malik had life handed to him. But did he realise this fact? Did he give it the barest nod of acknowledgement? Of course not. Because people who had their lives presented to them on a platinum platter never had the sort of perspective that allowed them to recognise how bloody lucky they were.

There he was, with his Rolex watch and his signet ring, with his snake-skin God damn boots and the serpentine vein of a hosepipe gold chain just visible beneath his perfect, ironed T-shirt. There he was with his classic car and his Oakley sunglasses and a body that announced precisely how much leisure sodding time *he* possessed to see to its daily sculpted transcendence. Yet all he could talk about was how rotten he'd had it, how lousy life was, how rife with bias and hatred and prejudice his privileged little existence had been.

Christ, but she *hated* him and she had reason to hate him. For the last ten years, he'd been looking for racial bias under every pebble he found in his path, and she was sick to death, not only of him but of having to watch every word, every question, and every natural inclination when she was round him. When the police found themselves in a position of having to mollify the very people they suspected – and she'd suspected Muhannad of nearly every infraction of the law that had occurred on her patch in Balford since the day she'd met him – then they were playing the game at a disadvantage. As she was now.

She found the situation intolerable, and as she worked the wet paper towels against her steamy skin, she cursed Superintendent Ferguson, Muhannad Malik, the death on the Nez, and the entire Asian community for good measure. She couldn't believe she'd actually given in to Barbara's suggestion and allowed the Pakistanis to see Kumhar. She should have tossed them into the street on their ears. Better yet, she should have arrested Taymullah Azhar the moment she'd seen him loitering outside the station when she'd brought in Kumhar. He'd been quick enough to inform his bloody cousin that the cops had an Asian suspect in lock-up. Emily had no doubt that it was he who'd rushed off to give Muhannad and his cohorts the word. Who was he, anyway, this Azhar? What bloody right did he have to come into town and *challenge* the police like some pricey barrister, which he decidedly was not?

It was the question of who he was – and the annoyance of being bested by him – that sent Emily back to her office. Until that moment, she'd forgotten the request she'd made of the Intelligence Unit, seeking information about the unknown Pakistani who'd entered their midst on Sunday afternoon. Clacton Intelligence had been in possession of that request for more than forty-eight hours. While that wasn't a great deal of time in intelligence work, it was enough to gather whatever information had been amassed by SO11 in London, *if* Taymullah Azhar had ever attracted the attention of the silent service.

The plain of her desk had become hilled with files, documents, and reports. It took her a good ten minutes to sort through them all. Nothing had yet come in on Azhar.

Damn. She wanted something on the man, something to slide into their verbal sparring, even a minor fact or an insignificant secret whose revelation by either herself or Barbara Havers would tell him that he wasn't as secure in the police presence as he apparently felt himself to be. That kind of juicy detail about an adversary worked to wrest the upper hand away from him. And while she knew she still had the upper hand – indeed, information was hers to dole out or withhold as she saw fit – she wanted the Asians to realise that she had it.

She picked up the phone and rang Intelligence.

Emily was on the phone when Barbara joined her. The fact that she was engaged in a personal call was made evident by the timbre of her voice. She sat at her desk with her forehead cradled in one of her hands while the other held the receiver to her ear and she said, 'Believe me, I could do with *that* twice over, tonight. Three times even,' and then she laughed. It was a throaty laugh, punctuation within the sort of conversation that lovers had. Emily wouldn't, Barbara thought, be talking to her super. 'What time?' she was saying. 'Hmmm. I could manage that. But won't she wonder? ... Gary, no one walks a dog for three hours.' And to whatever remark Gary made in reply, she laughed once more. She shifted position in her chair.

Barbara side-stepped, ready to duck out of the office before the DCI raised her head. But that was movement enough. Emily looked up and lifted her hand to keep Barbara where she was, one finger indicating that she was bringing the conversation to a close.

'All right, yes,' she said. 'Half-past ten. And don't forget the condoms this time.'

Without embarrassment, she rang off. She said to Barbara, 'What did you give them?'

Barbara examined her, knowing full well that her face was flaming.

For her part, Emily was all business. Nothing in her expression even began to suggest that she'd just been arranging an assignation with a married man for later in the evening. Yet surely that was what she'd been doing: lining up for some energetic mattress activity the very same bloke to whom she'd given the brush-off on Sunday night. She might have been setting up a dental appointment.

Emily appeared to read Barbara with excruciating precision. She said, 'Fags, booze, ulcers, migraines, psychosomatic illness, or promiscuity. Choose your poison, Barb. I chose mine.'

'Yeah. Well,' Barbara said with a shrug, intending the movement of her shoulders to indicate her own membership in the sisterhood of women who casually crushed cobblers for stress reduction. The reality was that she was dying for a fag – not a man – and she could feel the need for nicotine building from her fingertips to the backs of her eyeballs, despite having sucked down three and a half cigarettes during her meeting with Azhar and his cousin. 'Whatever works.'

'This does for me.' Emily blew out a breath and raked her fingers back through her hair. A small curtain of sodden paper towels was draped over the unlit lamp on her desk, and she took one of them, rubbing it on the back of her neck. 'I swear to God, this weather feels like summer in New Delhi. Have you ever been there? No? Good. Don't waste your money. It's a real pit. What did you give them?'

Barbara made her report. She'd told the Asians that the police had tracked down and acquired the contents of Querashi's safe-deposit box at Barclays, that Siddiqi had confirmed Azhar's translation of the Qur'aan page from Querashi's hotel room, that they were working on his incoming and outgoing telephone calls, and that they had a suspect – beyond Kumhar – who was being held for questioning at the present time.

'Malik's reaction?' Emily said.

'He pressed.'

Which mildly understated the case. Muhannad Malik had demanded to know the race and identity of the second suspect. He'd asked for a list of the contents of Querashi's safe-deposit box. He'd demanded a complete definition of what it meant to be 'working' on incoming and outgoing telephone calls. He wanted to be put in touch with Professor Siddiqi in order to make certain that the man understood the nature of the crime that was being investigated in Balford-le-Nez.

'Christ. He's got such a bloody nerve,' Emily remarked upon Barbara's conclusion. 'What did you tell him?'

'I didn't have to tell him anything,' Barbara replied. 'Azhar did it for me.' And he'd done it in his usual fashion, with the aplomb that came from obviously having had on more than one occasion to deal with the police, with PACE, and with that law's ramifications. Which made Barbara wonder anew about her London neighbour. She'd labelled him *university professor* and *father of Hadiyyah* during the nearly two months of their acquaintance. But what else was he? she asked herself now. And what were the depth and the breadth of information that was missing from her knowledge of the man?

'You like this other bloke, this Azhar,' Emily said astutely. 'Why?'

Barbara knew she should say Because I know him from London, we're neighbours, and his daughter is special to me. But what she said instead was 'Just a gut feeling. He seems honest. He seems like he wants to get to the bottom of what happened to Querashi as much as we do.'

Emily gave out a sceptical bark of laughter. 'Don't put money on that, Barb. If he's thick with Muhannad, he's got an agenda that has nothing to do with getting to the bottom of what happened on the Nez. Or did you miss the subtext in our little rendezvous with Azhar, Malik, and Fahd Kumhar?'

'What subtext?'

'Kumhar's reaction when those two walked into the interrogation room. You saw it, didn't you? What do you think that meant?'

'Kumhar was bricking it,' Barbara admitted. 'I've never seen anyone so rattled in custody. But that's the real point, isn't it, Em? He's in custody. So where are you heading with this?'

'I'm heading to a connection between these blokes. Kumhar took one look at Azhar and Malik and nearly wore brown trousers.'

'You're saying he knew them?'

'Perhaps not Azhar. But I'm saying that he knew Muhannad Malik. I'm saying it's a dead cert that he knew him. He was shaking so badly, we could have used him to make martinis for James Bond. And believe me, that reaction had nothing to do with being locked up in the nick.'

Barbara sensed her certainty and met it with caution. 'But, Em, look at his situation. He's in custody – a suspect in a murder investigation – in a foreign country where his language skills wouldn't get him as far as the edge of town if he wanted to scarper. Isn't that reason enough for him to be –'

'Yes,' Emily said impatiently. 'Right. His English wouldn't serve him to call a dog to a bone. So what was he doing in Clacton? And, more to the point, how did he get there? We're not talking about a town teeming with Asians. We're talking about a town with so few of them that all we had to do was ask about a single Pakistani at Jackson & Son and the proprietor knew we were looking for Kumhar.'

'So?' Barbara asked.

'This isn't exactly a culture of free spirits. These people stick together. So what's Kumhar doing in Clacton by himself when the rest of his kind are here, in Balford?'

Barbara wanted to argue that Azhar was in London alone despite, as she had so recently learned, having a large family elsewhere in the country. She wanted to argue that the Asian community in London was centred mostly round Southall and Hounslow, while Azhar lived in Chalk Farm and worked in Bloomsbury. How typical is that? she wanted to ask. But she couldn't do that without jeopardising her position in the investigation.

Emily went on insistently. 'You heard DC Honigman. Kumhar was fine till those two blokes walked into the room. What do you suppose that means?'

It could mean anything, Barbara thought. It could also be twisted to mean what one wanted. She thought about reminding the DCI of what Muhannad had said: the Asians hadn't walked into the room alone. But arguing over a mere surmise seemed fruitless at the moment. Worse, it seemed inflammatory. So she backed away from Kumhar's state of mind. She said, 'If Kumhar already knows Malik, what's the connection between them?'

'Some sort of skulduggery, you can depend upon it. The same sort of thing Muhannad was up to as a teenager: something dodgy that can never quite be traced back to him. But his teenage offences – those minor infractions of the law – have given way to the big stuff now.'

'What sort of big stuff?'

'Who the hell knows? Burglary, car rings, pornography, prostitution, drugs, smuggling, running guns from the East, moving explosives, dabbling in terrorism. I don't know what it is, but I know one thing: there's money involved. How else do we explain that car of Muhannad's? That Rolex watch? The clothes? The jewellery?'

'Em, his father owns an entire flaming factory right here in town. The family's got to be rolling in lolly. And he'd have got a handsome dowry from his in-laws. Why wouldn't Muhannad put some of it on display?'

'Because that isn't their way. They may be rolling in lolly, but they're rolling it right back into Malik's Mustards. Or they're sending it to Pakistan. Or they're using it to bankroll other family members' entry into the country. Or they're saving it for dowries for their females. But, believe me, they are *not* using it for classic cars and personal baubles. Absolutely no way.' Emily tossed her damp paper towels into the wastepaper basket. 'Barb, I swear to you, Malik's dirty. He's been dirty since he was sixteen years old, and the only change from that time to now is that he's upped the stakes. He uses *Jum'a* as a front these days. He acts the part of Mr Man of his People. But the truth is that this is a bloke who'd slice his mother's jugular open if it would put another diamond in his signet ring.'

Classic cars, diamonds, a Rolex watch. Barbara would have given one lung to have had a cigarette at that moment in Emily's office, so taut did she feel her nerves being pulled. She wasn't so much disturbed by the DCI's words, as by the unacknowledged – and hence potentially dangerous – passion that ran beneath them. She had walked this road before. It was signposted Loss of Objectivity, and it didn't lead to a destination in which a decent cop wanted to head. And Emily Barlow was a decent cop. She was one of the best.

Barbara sought a way to keep the case in balance. She said, 'Wait. We've got Trevor Ruddock without an alibi and an hour and a half of free time on Friday night. We've got his dabs under scrutiny. I've sent his spider-making paraphernalia to the lab for some tests. So do we let him walk and go after Muhannad instead? Ruddock had wire in his bedroom, Em. He had a whole bleeding roll of it.'

Emily looked past her, at the wall of her office, at the Chinagraph board hanging there, at its scrawl of notations. She said nothing. Into her silence, telephones rang and someone hooted nearby, 'Jesus, mate. Stop kidding yourself.'

Right. How about it? Barbara thought. Come on, Em. Don't fail me now.

'We need to check the log.' Emily's words were decisive. 'Here and in Clacton. We need to see what's been reported and what's going unsolved.'

Barbara's spirits sank. 'The log? But if Muhannad's into something big, d'you think we're really going to find it sitting there unsolved on the police log?'

'We're going to find it somewhere,' Emily responded. 'Believe me. But we won't find it at all if we don't start looking.'

'And Trevor? What'll I do with him?'

'Let him go for now.'

'Let him . . . ?' Barbara dug her fingernails into the skin on the underside of her arm. 'But, Em, we can do with him what we're doing with Kumhar. We can let him stew till tomorrow afternoon. We can put him through his paces every quarter of an hour. I swear to God, he's hiding something, and until we know what that something is –'

'Let him go, Barbara,' the DCI said steadily.

'But we haven't heard about his fingerprints yet. And that wire of his has been sent to the lab and when I talked to Rachel . . .' Barbara didn't know what else to say.

'Barb, Trevor Ruddock isn't going to do a runner. He knows that all he has to do is keep his gob shut and our hands are tied. So we'll let him go till we've got the word from the lab. And in the meantime, we work the Asians.'

'Work them how?'

Emily ticked off items. The police log in Balford as well as the logs in surrounding communities would show if anything dodgy – connectable to Muhannad – was going on; the contents of Querashi's safe-deposit box had to be looked into; the offices of World Wide Tours in Harwich needed to be visited by someone with Querashi's picture in hand; a Polaroid of Kumhar had to be shown round the houses that backed on to the Nez; as a matter of fact, a Polaroid picture of Fahd Kumhar should be taken to World Wide Tours as well, just for good measure.

'I've a meeting with our team in less than five minutes,' Emily said. She rose and the inflection in her voice clearly indicated that their interview was over. 'I'll be making the assignments for tomorrow. Is there any of this that you want to take on, Barb?'

The implication was crystalline: Emily Barlow was directing the course of the investigation, not Barbara Havers. Trevor Ruddock would walk within the hour. They would begin to home in on the Pakistanis. On one particular Pakistani. On one Pakistani with one very good alibi.

There was nothing more that she could do, Barbara realised. 'I'll take World Wide Tours,' she said. 'I suppose I could do with a drive to Harwich.'

Barbara saw the classic turquoise Thunderbird the moment she turned into the car park at the Burnt House Hotel ninety minutes later. It was hard to miss, sleek, pristine, and exotic among the dusty Escorts, Volvos and Vauxhalls. The convertible looked as if someone spit-polished it every day. From its glittering hubcaps to the chromium curve of its windscreen's border, it could have been used as a mobile operating theatre, so unbesmirched was its every inch. It was sitting at the end of the row of cars, straddling two of the parking bays so as to keep anyone from scratching its paintjob when disembarking from a lesser machine. Barbara considered using her recently purchased lipstick to scrawl *selfish* across the car's windscreen as an unsubtle commentary on the driver's commandeering more than his share of the car park's spaces. But she settled for a suitable imprecation, and she squeezed her Mini into a slot at the rear of the hotel, fragrantly located near the kitchen rubbish.

Muhannad Malik was within, doubtlessly scheming with Azhar after having had his every request to examine evidence turned down flat with no court of appeal. He hadn't liked that. He'd liked it less when his cousin had informed him that the police were under no obligation to meet the Asians at all, let alone put evidence on display for them. Muhannad had gone all tight-lipped at that, but if he'd felt at cross-purposes with his cousin, he hadn't let on. Rather, he'd directed his antipathy and scorn towards Barbara. She could only guess with what joy he would now greet her arrival at the hotel should she run into him. Which she fervently hoped to avoid doing.

The combination of wisps of cigarette smoke and fragments of muted conversation told Barbara that the hotel residents were gathering in the bar for preprandial sherry and the ritual study of the daily menu. That the menu was as unvarying as the tide – pork, chicken, plaice, beef – seemed to have no impact on the residents' desire to peruse it with the intensity of devoted Bible scholars. Barbara could see them as she turned towards the stairs. A shower first, she decided. Then a pint of Bass with a whisky chaser.

'Barbara! Barbara!' A clatter of feet on the parquet floor accompanied the cry of her name. Hadiyyah, dressed to the nines in sunset silk, had caught sight of her from the bar's window seat and was leaping into immediate action.

Barbara hesitated, wincing inwardly. If she'd hoped to fumble her way through an evening's unexpected encounter with Muhannad Malik by pretending not to be acquainted with his cousin outside Balford-le-Nez, the gaff had just decidedly been blown. And Azhar was not quick enough to stop his daughter. He rose, but she was already dancing across the room. A limp white shoulder bag shaped like the moon dangled from her elbow to the floor.

Hadiyyah said, 'Come and see who's here. It's my cousin, Barbara. He's called Muhannad. He's twenty-six and he's married and he's got two little boys who're still in nappies. I forget their names, but I know I'll remember when I get to meet them.'

'I was just about to pop up to my room,' Barbara told her. She averted her eyes from the bar, irrationally hoping that by doing so, she would not be noticed in conversation with the girl.

'Pooh. It'll only take a minute. I want you to meet him. I asked him if he'd eat here with us, but he said his wife's waiting for him at home. And his mum and his dad. He's got a sister as well.' She sighed with pure pleasure. Her eyes were vivid. 'Imagine, Barbara. I didn't even know before tonight. I didn't know I even *had* a family besides Mummy and Dad. And he's ever so nice, my cousin Muhannad. Will you come and meet him?'

Azhar had come to the door of the bar. Behind him, Muhannad had risen from a cracked leather wing chair that faced the window. He held a drink, which he raised to his lips and finished off before setting the glass on a nearby table.

Barbara telegraphed her question to Taymullah Azhar. *What to say?*

But Hadiyyah had latched on to her hand, and any pretence of their having only two evenings' acquaintance predicated on a mutual love of the Burnt House Hotel's culinary masterpieces was quickly mooted by her words. '*You* thought the same, didn't you, Barbara? That's because we never much act like we have a family anywhere at all. I expect we'll see them in London now. They c'n come for weekends. And *we* c'n invite them to one of our barbecues, can't we?'

Sure, Barbara wanted to say. Muhannad Malik was no doubt chomping at the bit this very moment, desperate for an opportunity to tuck into Detective Sergeant Barbara Havers' grilled kebabs.

'Cousin Muhannad,' Hadiyyah was singing out. 'Come and meet my friend Barbara. She lives in London. We have the ground-floor flat, like I told you, and Barbara lives in the sweetest little cottage round the back of the house. We met her 'cause her refrigerator got delivered to our flat by mistake. Dad moved it for her. He got grease on his shirt. We got most of it out, but he doesn't like to wear it to the university any longer.'

Muhannad joined them. Hadiyyah caught his hand. Now she stood with her hands locked to both of them – Barbara and her cousin – and she couldn't have looked more pleased had she just successfully arranged their nuptials.

Muhannad's face was a study in active assessment, as if a computer in his brain were in the process of tallying information and placing it in appropriate categories. Barbara could well imagine what they were labelled: *betrayal, secrecy, deception.* He spoke to Hadiyyah, but he looked at her father.

'How very nice to meet your friend, little cousin. Have you known her long?'

'Oh, weeks and weeks and *weeks*,' Hadiyyah crowed. 'We go for ice creams on Chalk Farm Road and we've been to the cinema and she even came to my birthday party. Sometimes we go to see her mum in Greenford. We have ever so much fun, don't we, Barbara?'

'How coincidental it is, then, that you should find yourselves in the same hotel in Balford-le-Nez,' Muhannad said meaningfully.

'Hadiyyah,' Azhar said, 'Barbara has only just returned to the hotel, and it appears that you waylaid her on her way to her room. If you –'

'We told her we were going to Essex, you see.' Amiably, Hadiyyah offered the information to her cousin. 'We had to, because I left a message on her answer machine. I invited her for an ice cream, and I didn't want her to think I would forget. So I went to her cottage to tell her and then Dad came and then we said we were going to the sea. Only Dad didn't tell me *you* lived here, Cousin Muhannad. He made it a surprise. So now you can meet my friend Barbara and she can meet you.'

'That's been done,' Azhar said.

'But perhaps not as soon as it might have been,' Muhannad said.

'Listen, Mr Malik,' Barbara put in, but the appearance of Basil Treves supervened.

He was coming out of the bar in his usual bustle, the evening's dinner orders clutched in his hand. He hummed as always. The sight of Barbara with the Pakistanis, however, silenced him on what sounded like the fifth note of the title song to *The Sound of Music.*

'Ah! Sergeant Havers,' he said. 'You've had a phone call. Three, in fact, all from the same man.' He cast a speculative glance at Muhannad and then at Azhar before he added mysteriously but with an unmistakable air of importance that served to underscore his position as the compatriot, fellow investigator, and general soulmate of the Scotland Yard detective, 'You know, Sergeant. That little German concern of ours? He left two numbers: home and direct line into his office. I've put them both in your cubbyhole, and if you'll just wait a moment . . .'

As he scuttled away to fetch the telephone messages, Muhannad spoke again. 'Cousin, we'll speak later, I hope. Hadiyyah, good evening. It was –' His face softened with the truth of his words and his other hand cradled the back of her head in a tender gesture. He bent and kissed her crown. 'It was truly a pleasure to meet you at long last.'

'Will you come again? C'n I meet your wife and your little boys?'

'Everything,' he smiled, 'in good time.'

He took his leave of them, and Azhar – casting a quick look at Barbara – followed him out of the hotel. Barbara heard him say urgently, 'Muhannad, a moment,' as he got to the door. She wondered what on earth he was going to say to his cousin by way of explanation. No matter how one examined the situation, it didn't look good.

'*Here* we are.' Basil Treves was back with them, Barbara's messages fluttering from his fingers. 'He was most courteous over the phone. Quite surprising, for a German. Will you be joining us for dinner, Sergeant?'

She told him that she would be doing so, and Hadiyyah said, 'Sit with us, sit with us!'

Treves didn't look any happier at this turn of events than he'd looked at breakfast on Monday morning when Barbara had blithely crossed the invisible barrier that the hotelier erected between his white guests and his guests of colour. He patted Hadiyyah on the head. He looked at her with the special sort of superficial benignity one reserves for small animals to which one is violently allergic. 'Yes, yes. If she wishes,' he said heartily, past the aversion in his eyes. 'She can sit anywhere she wishes to sit, my dear.'

'Good, good, good!' Reassured, Hadiyyah scampered off. A moment later, Barbara heard her chatting with Mrs Porter in the hotel bar.

'It was the police,' Treves said confidentially. He nodded at the telephone messages in Barbara's hand. 'I didn't want to say as much in front of . . . those two. You know. One can't be too careful with foreigners.'

'Right,' Barbara said. She quelled the desire to smack Treves' face and trample on his feet. Instead, she went up the stairs to her room.

The heat inside had reached inferno intensity. The temperature seemed to have cooked the dust that clung to the curtains and embedded itself in the ancient furniture. Barbara felt her sweat glands moving into overdrive.

She tossed her shoulder bag on to one of the room's twin beds and went to the other. She slouched down on to it and examined her telephone messages. Each was made out to the same name: Helmut Kreuzhage. He'd phoned at three that afternoon, then again at five and at six-fifteen. She looked at her watch and decided to try him in his office first. She punched the German number into the phone and fanned herself with the plastic tray that she took from beneath the room's tin tea pot.

'*Hier ist Kriminalhauptkommissar Kreuzhage.*'

Bingo, she thought. She identified herself slowly in English, thinking of Ingrid and her modest command of Barbara's native tongue. The German switched languages immediately, saying, 'Yes, Sergeant Havers. I'm the man who took the telephone calls here in Hamburg from Mr Haytham Querashi.' He spoke with only the barest hint of an accent. His voice was pleasant and mellifluous. He must have driven Basil Treves half mad, Barbara thought, so little did he sound like a post-war cinema Nazi.

'Brilliant,' Barbara said fervently, and thanked him for returning her call. She quickly made clear to him all of the circumstances surrounding her having tracked him down.

He made a grave clucking sound on his end of the phone when she told him about the trip wire, the old concrete steps, and Haytham Querashi's fatal fall. 'When I had a look at his phone records from the hotel, the number for Hamburg police was among them. We're checking into every possible lead. I'm hoping you can help us out.'

'I fear I have little that would be of help,' Kreuzhage said.

'Do you remember your conversations with Querashi? He phoned Hamburg police more than once.'

'Oh, *ja*, I do remember quite well,' Kreuzhage answered. 'He wished to share some information about activities which he believed to be ongoing at an address in Wandsbek.'

'Wandsbek?'

'*Ja*. A community in the western sector of the city.'

'What sort of activities?'

'That, I fear, is where the gentleman became rather vague. He would describe them only as illegal activities involving both Hamburg and the port of Parkeston in England.'

Barbara felt her fingertips tingle. Bloody hell. Could it actually be possible that Emily Barlow was right? 'That sounds like a smuggling operation,' she said. Kreuzhage coughed phlegmily. He was a brother smoker, Barbara realised, but heavier on the fags than she. He held the phone away from his face and spat. She shuddered and vowed to ease up on the weed.

'I would be hesitant to limit my conclusions to smuggling,' the German said.

'Why?'

'Because when the gentleman mentioned the port of Parkeston, I arrived at the same conclusion. I suggested he phone *Davidwache an der Reeperbahn*. This is the harbour police here in Hamburg. They would be the ones to deal with smuggling, you see. But that, I am afraid, he was loath to do. He wouldn't even entertain the notion, which suggested to me that his concerns did not revolve around smuggling at all.'

'Then what *did* he tell you?'

'He would say only that he had information about a felonious activity that was ongoing, operating out of an address in Wandsbek, although he did not know that it was Wandsbek, of course. Just that it was in Hamburg.'

'*Oskarstraße 15*?' Barbara guessed.

'You've found the address among his things, I take it. *Ja*, that was the location. We looked into it, but found nothing at all.'

'He was on the wrong track? Did he have the wrong German city?'

'There is no real accurate way to know,' Kreuzhage replied. 'He may well have been correct about the illicit goings on, but *Oskarstraße 15* is a large apartment building with some eighty units inside, behind a locked front door. We have no cause to inspect those units and could not do so on the unfounded suspicions of a gentleman phoning from another country.'

'Unfounded suspicions?'

'Mr Querashi had no real evidence to speak of, Sergeant Havers. Or if he had it, he was not willing to share it with me. But on the strength of his passion and sincerity, I did place the building under surveillance for two days. It sits on the edge of *Eichtalpark*, so it was easy enough to place my men in an area where they could not be seen. But I have not the manpower to . . . how do you call it . . . sit out a building?'

'Stake out a building?'

'That American term, *ja*, this is it. I have not the manpower or the financial resources to stake out a building the size of *Oskarstraße 15* for the length of time it would take to ascertain if illegal activity is going on there. Not, I am afraid, with so little to go on.'

It was hardly an unreasonable position, Barbara thought. Doubtless, stormtrooping one's way into people's private homes and apartments had gone out of fashion in Germany after the war.

But then she remembered.

'Klaus Reuchlein,' she said.

'*Ja*? He is . . . ?' Kreuzhage waited politely.

'He's some bloke living in Hamburg,' Barbara said. 'I don't have his address, but I have his phone number. I'm wondering if there's any chance that he lives at *Oskarstraße 15*?'

'This,' Kreuzhage said, 'could indeed be ascertained. But beyond that . . .' He was good enough to sound regretful. He went on to tell her – in the sombre tone of a man with a thorough knowledge of the evils that other men do – that there were many arenas of misbehaviour which could possibly span the North Sea and tie England to Germany. Prostitution, counterfeiting, gun running, terrorism, extremism, industrial espionage, bank robbery, art theft . . . The wise policeman did not confine his suspicions to smuggling when two countries were connected in a criminal way. 'This I tried to point out to Mr Querashi,' he said, 'so that he might see how difficult was the task he wished me to perform. But he insisted that an investigation of *Oskarstraße 15* would provide us with the information we needed to make an arrest. Alas, Mr Querashi had never been to *Oskarstraße 15*.' Barbara could hear him sigh. 'An investigation? Sometimes people do not understand how the law regulates what we as policemen can and cannot do.'

How true. Barbara thought of the police dramas she'd seen on the telly, those programmes in which the rozzers regularly wrestled confessions from suspects who went from defiant to compliant within the convenient space of an hour. She made noises of agreement and asked Kreuzhage if he would check on Klaus Reuchlein's whereabouts. 'I have a phone call in to him as well,' she explained, 'but something tells me he's not going to return it.'

Kreuzhage assured her he would do what he could. She rang off. She spent a moment just sitting on the bed, letting its hideous counterpane soak a bit of the sweat from the backs of her legs. When she felt she had the energy to do so, she went to the shower and stood under it, too hot even to entertain herself with her usual medley of rock 'n' roll oldies.

Chapter Twenty

After dinner, Barbara ended up on the pleasure pier solely because Hadiyyah had extended the invitation. In her usual impulsive and generous manner, the little girl had announced, 'You must come with us, Barbara. We're going to the pier, Dad and I, and you must come as well. She must, Dad, mustn't she? It'll be ever so much more fun if she comes.' She'd craned her neck to see her father, who listened to the invitation soberly. The final diners of the evening, they were finishing their *sorbet-du-jour*. It was lemon tonight, and they'd had to consume it in a rush before the heat reduced it to slop. Hadiyyah had waved her spoon in the air as she spoke, sending lemon droplets across the table cloth.

Barbara would have preferred a quiet sit on the lawn above the sea. Mingling with the doubtlessly odoriferous pleasure seekers on the Balford pier and building up a new patina of sweat were activities she could have done without. But Azhar had been preoccupied throughout dinner, allowing his daughter to carry the conversation happily in whatever direction she chose, and at any length. This behaviour was so unlike him that Barbara knew it had to be connected with Muhannad Malik's departure from the Burnt House and whatever had been said between the two men in the car park prior to that departure. So she was willing to accompany Azhar and his daughter to the pleasure pier if for no other reason than to prise from the man an account of what had passed between him and his cousin.

Thus she found herself on the pier at ten o'clock, jostled by the sun-burned masses, her nostrils assailed by the mixed odours of lotions, sweat, frying whitebait, sizzling hamburgers, and popping corn. The noise was even more deafening at night than during the day, possibly because the stall-holders grew more desperate for custom as the closing hour approached. So they shouted for attention, attempting to beguile passers-by into tossing balls or spinning wheels or shooting ducks, and in order to be heard they had to match the volume of the calliope music from the roundabout and the whistles, bells, pops, and mechanical explosions of the games in the arcade.

It was to the arcade that Hadiyyah led them, having each of them by the hand. 'What fun, what fun!' she sang out, and she seemed oblivious of the fact that what passed between her father and her friend was mostly silence.

On every side of them, a glistening throng played video and pin ball machines in the din. Small children raced among the fruit machines, shouting and laughing. A crowd of adolescent boys drove virtual reality race cars to the accompaniment of admiring shrieks from teenaged girls. A line of elderly women sat at a counter playing Bingo, with the numbers being boomed out on a microphone that was wielded by a clown-suited man whose make-up had long since suffered the worst it could suffer from the relentless heat. No one in the arcade, Barbara noted, was Asian.

For her part, Hadiyyah seemed unmindful of everything: the noise, the smell, the temperature, the crowd, and being one of two parts of a distinct minority. She released her grip on her father and Barbara and whirled about, dancing from foot to foot. She crowed, 'The crane grab! Dad, the crane grab!' and dashed in the direction of that particular game.

When they caught up with her, she was pressed against the front of the machine, her nose to the glass as she studied its contents. It was filled with stuffed animals: pink pigs, spotted cows, giraffes, lions, and elephants. 'Giraffe, giraffe,' she sang out, poking her finger at the animal she wanted her father to try to win for her. 'Dad, c'n you do the giraffe for me? He's ever so good at the crane grab, Barbara. Just wait till you see.' She spun on one foot and grabbed her father's arm. She urged him forward to the machine. 'And when you win a giraffe for me, you must win something for Barbara next. An elephant, Dad. Remember the elephant you won for Mummy? Remember how I cut out its stuffing? I didn't mean to, Barbara. I was only five years old, and I was playing vets with it. It needed an operation, but it lost its stuffing when I cut it open. Mummy was in such a rage about that. She shouted and shouted. Didn't she, Dad?'

Azhar didn't answer. Instead, he applied his attention and his efforts to the crane grab. He did it as Barbara assumed he would do it: with the sort of solemn concentration that he gave to everything. He missed on the first try as well as the second. But neither he nor his daughter lost heart. 'He's just practising,' Hadiyyah informed Barbara confidently. 'He always practises first. Right, Dad?'

Azhar went about his business. On his third try, he positioned the crane quickly, dropped its hook efficiently, and secured the giraffe that his daughter wanted. Hadiyyah shouted with delight and swept the small stuffed animal into her arms as if she'd just been given the single gift she'd desired for the length of her eight short years.

'Thank you, thank you!' she cried and hugged her father round the waist. 'It'll be my souvenir from Balford. It'll be how I remember what a fine time we had on our holiday. Try for another. Please, Dad, won't you? Try for an elephant for Barbara's souvenir.'

'Another time, kiddo,' Barbara said hastily to the girl. The thought of being presented with a stuffed animal by Azhar was somehow disconcerting. 'We don't want to drop our lolly all in one place, do we? What about pin ball? Or the roundabout?'

Hadiyyah's face lit up. She darted ahead of them, squirming through the crowd on her way to the door. To get there, she had to pass the virtual reality race cars, and in her haste for fun, she elbowed her way into the group surrounding them.

It happened quickly, too quickly to see if what occurred was merely an accident or an intentional act. One moment Hadiyyah had disappeared into a mass of scantily clad adolescent bodies. The next moment she was sprawled on the floor.

Someone hooted with laughter, a sound barely discernible above the raucous noise of the arcade. But it was loud enough for Barbara to hear it, and she shot into the group without another thought.

'Shit. Pakis,' someone was saying.

'Just lookit that dress.'

'An Oxfam special.'

'Thinks she's going to meet the Queen.'

Barbara grabbed the limp, sweaty T-shirt of the boy nearest to her. She twisted it into her hand and jerked until he was less than two inches from her face.

'My little friend,' she said evenly, 'appears to have tripped somehow.

I'm sure one of you gentlemen would like to help her, wouldn't you?'

'Sod you, bitch,' was his succinct reply.

'Not even in your dreams,' she said.

'Barbara.' Azhar spoke somewhere behind her, sounding eminently reasonable as he always sounded.

In front of her, Hadiyyah was struggling to her knees among the Doc Martens, sandals, and trainers that surrounded her. Her silk dress had become soiled in her fall, and beneath her arm the seam had ripped. She didn't look so much hurt as surprised. She gazed round, her face bewildered at the sudden confusion.

Barbara gripped the boy's T-shirt more firmly. 'Think again, wanker-man,' she said quietly. 'I said that my little friend needs some help.'

'Fuck that, Sean. There's two of them and ten of us,' someone to Barbara's left advised.

'Right,' Barbara said pleasantly in answer, speaking to Sean and not to his counsellor. 'But I don't imagine that any of you have one of these.' With her free hand she felt in her shoulder bag until she had her police identification. She flipped this open and jammed it into Sean's face. She was too close for him to be able to read it, but reading it wasn't what she had in mind for him.

'Help her up,' she said.

'I di'n't do nothing to her.'

'Barbara.' Azhar spoke again.

She saw him out of the corner of her eye. He was going to Hadiyyah. 'Leave her,' Barbara said. 'One of these young louts –' another twist of the T-shirt '– is hot to prove what a gent he can be. Isn't that right, Sean? Because if one of these young louts –' another more savage twist of the shirt '– fails to prove what needs to be proved, the whole flaming lot of them are going to be phoning Mummy and Daddy from the nick tonight.'

Azhar, however, ignored Barbara's words. He went to his daughter and helped her to her feet. The adolescents gave him plenty of space to do so. 'You've not hurt yourself, Hadiyyah?' He reached for her giraffe, which had flown from her hands as she'd fallen.

'Oh, no!' she wailed. 'Dad, it's got all ruined.'

Sean still in her grasp, Barbara looked over. The giraffe had somehow become stained with ketchup. Its head had been flattened by someone's shoe.

A boy out of Barbara's range of vision sniggered. But before she could deal with him, Azhar said, 'This is something that can easily be repaired.' He spoke like a man who was aware of everything else in life that was well beyond mending. He worked his way out of the group, Hadiyyah walking in front of him, his hands on his daughter's shoulders.

Barbara saw the dejected angle at which the child held her head. She itched to head-butt Sean and drive her knee directly into his bollocks, but instead she released him and wiped her hand on her trousers. 'It takes real dreck to go after an eight-year-old girl,' she said. 'Why don't the lot of you celebrate the accomplishment by doing yourselves proud somewhere else?'

She shoved past them and followed Azhar and his daughter out of the arcade. For a moment she didn't see where they'd gone because the number of pleasure-seekers seemed to have grown. On her every side was a mass of black leather trousers, nose studs, nipple rings, dog collars, and chains. She felt as if she'd just burst into an S & M convention.

Then she saw her friends. They were to her right, Azhar leading his daughter out of the pavilion and on to the open section of the pier. She joined them.

'. . . manifestation of people's fear,' Azhar was saying to Hadiyyah's bowed head. 'People fear what they don't understand, Hadiyyah. Fear drives their actions.'

'I wouldn't've hurt them,' Hadiyyah said. 'I'm too little to hurt them anyway.'

'Ah, but they aren't afraid of being hurt, *khushi*. What they're afraid of is being known. Here is Barbara now. Shall we continue our evening? Allowing a group of strangers to determine whether we find joy in this outing seems ill advised.'

Hadiyyah raised her head. Barbara felt a tightness in her chest at the sight of her little friend's bleak face. 'I think those planes are calling to us, kiddo,' she said heartily, indicating a ride nearby: tiny aeroplanes soaring and falling round a central pole. 'What d'you say?'

Hadiyyah watched the planes for a moment. She'd been carrying her soiled and ruined giraffe, but now she handed it over to her father and straightened her shoulders. 'I especially love aeroplanes,' she said.

They watched her when they couldn't ride with her. Some of the amusements were child-sized: the miniature Army Jeeps, the train, the helicopters, and the planes. Others were made for larger occupants, and in these the three of them rode together, dashing from the teacups to the Ferris wheel to the roller coaster, always managing to stay at least one step ahead of disappointment and dejection. It wasn't until Hadiyyah insisted on three consecutive rides on the miniature sailing ships – 'They make my stomach go whoopee,' she explained – that Barbara had a chance to talk to Azhar alone.

'I'm sorry about what happened,' she said to him. He'd taken out his cigarettes and offered her one. She accepted. He lit them both. 'Rotten thing. On her holiday and everything.'

'I'd love to shield her from every pain.' Azhar watched his daughter and smiled at her laughter as her stomach whoopeed on the simulated wave which crested and fell beneath her tiny ship. 'But that's the desire of every loving parent, isn't it? It's a wish that's both reasonable to possess and completely impossible to fulfil.' He lifted his cigarette to his lips and kept his eyes fixed on Hadiyyah. He said, 'Thank you, however.'

'For?'

He canted his head in the direction of the arcade. 'Coming to her aid. It was good of you.'

'Bloody hell, Azhar. She's the best. I like her. I love her. What the hell else did you expect me to do? If I'd had my way, we wouldn't have walked out of that place like three of the meek with prospects of inheritance on our minds. Believe me.'

Azhar turned his head to Barbara. 'You're a pleasure to know, Sergeant Havers.'

Barbara felt her face get hot. She said, 'Yeah. Well,' and in some confusion she drew in on her cigarette and made a study of the beach huts on the shore, half lit by lamps that were shaped like old gaslights, half shadowed by the darkness. Despite the balminess of the night, most of the huts were closed up, their daytime occupants gone to the hotels and cottages where they spent their holiday nights.

She said, 'I'm sorry about the hotel, Azhar. About Muhannad. You know. I saw the Thunderbird when I pulled into the car park. I thought I could avoid him and duck upstairs. I was desperate for a shower, or I would have cooled my heels in a pub or something. Which, I realise, is probably what I should have done.'

'It was inevitable that my cousin should know we're acquainted,' he told her. 'I should have told him at once. That I didn't has caused him to question my commitment to our people. And rightfully so.'

'He looked pretty cheesed off when he left the hotel. How'd you explain things?'

'As you yourself explained them to me,' Azhar said. 'I told him your presence had been requested by DCI Barlow and that it was as much a surprise to you as it had been to me to find yourself involved in a situation in which a member of the opposition happens to be someone with whom you're acquainted.'

Barbara could feel him looking at her, and her face grew even hotter. She was glad of the shadow cast by the sailing ship ride. At least it kept her safe from the sort of scrutiny that was Azhar's stock in trade.

She was overcome by a strong compulsion to tell him the truth. Except she couldn't have said at the moment precisely what the real truth was. She seemed to have lost her grip upon it sometime during the last several days. And for the life of her, she couldn't identify when the facts had clothed themselves in such slippery garments. She wanted to offer him something in reparation for the lies she'd told. But as he himself had said, he and she represented opposing forces.

'How did Muhannad take that information?' she asked.

'My cousin has a temper,' Azhar replied. He flicked ash from his cigarette on to the pier. 'His is a nature that sees enemies everywhere. It was easy for him to conclude that the notes of caution I've attempted to strike during our conversations these last few days were evidence of my duplicity. He feels betrayed by one of his own, and that makes things difficult between us at the moment. This isn't unreasonable, however. Deception is the one sin in a relationship that people find nearly impossible to forgive.'

Barbara felt as if he was playing her conscience like a violin. To quell both her pangs of guilt and her desire for absolution, she kept the conversation anchored on his cousin. 'You didn't deceive him for malicious reasons, Azhar. Hell, you didn't deceive him at all. He didn't *ask* you if you knew me, right? Why should you have volunteered the information?'

'A point which Muhannad has difficulty accepting at the moment. Thus,' he shot her an apologetic glance, 'my usefulness to my cousin may be at an end. And yours to DCI Barlow as well.'

Barbara immediately saw where he was heading. 'Holy hell, are you saying Muhannad'll tell Emily about us?' She felt her face flame yet another time. 'I mean . . . not *us*. There isn't any us. But you know what –'

He smiled. 'I have no way of knowing what Muhannad may do,

Barbara. In many ways, he keeps his own counsel. Until this weekend, I hadn't seen him in nearly ten years, but as a teenager he was much the same.'

Barbara thought about this – about everything that keeping his own counsel could imply – especially in relation to the afternoon's interview with Fahd Kumhar. She said, 'Azhar, that meeting today, the one at the nick . . .'

He dropped his cigarette to the pier and ground it out. Over their shoulders, the ship ride was ending yet again. Hadiyyah called out for one last go. Her father nodded, gave a ticket to the operator, and watched his daughter sail the sea again. He said, 'The meeting?'

'With Fahd Kumhar. If Muhannad is someone who keeps his counsel like you're saying, is there any chance he already knew that bloke? Before he walked into the room, I mean.'

At once, Azhar looked cautious, guarded, and most importantly, unwilling to speak. Barbara wished that his cousin could have been with them that very second, so clearly did Azhar's expression show where his true loyalties lay.

She said, 'The reason I'm asking is that Kumhar's reaction was so extreme. You'd think the sight of you and Muhannad would have been a relief, but it didn't seem to be at all. He knotted himself up in a proper twist, didn't he?'

'Ah,' Azhar said. 'This is a class issue, Barbara. Mr Kumhar's reaction – consternation, subservience, anxiety – is born of our culture. When he heard my cousin's name pronounced, he recognised a member of a higher social and economic group than his own. His name – Kumhar – is what we call *Kami*, the artisan caste of labourers, carpenters, potters, and the like. My cousin's name – Malik – indicates membership in the landowning group of our society.'

'D'you mean he was gibbering like that because of someone's last *name*?' Barbara found that the explanation strained credulity. 'Bloody hell, Azhar. This is England, not Pakistan.'

'So I expect you understand my point. Mr Kumhar's reaction is hardly any different from an Englishman's discomfiture when in the presence of another Englishman whose pronunciation of the language or choice of vocabulary reveals his class.'

Damn the man. He was so insufferably and consistently astute.

'Excuse me?'

The voice came from behind them. Barbara and Azhar swung round to see a mini-skirted girl with waist-length blonde hair standing uneasily next to an overfull rubbish bin. She was carrying a giraffe identical to the one that Azhar had earlier scooped up for his daughter, and she shifted her weight from one sandalled foot to the other, her gaze moving uneasily from Azhar to Barbara to the sailing ship ride and back to Azhar.

'I've been looking for you everywhere,' she said. 'I was with them. I mean I was there. Inside. When the little girl . . .' She lowered her head and examined the giraffe before thrusting it in their direction. 'Would you give her this, please? I wouldn't want her to think . . . They act up, that lot. That's how it is. That's just how they are.'

She pressed the stuffed animal into Azhar's hand, smiled fleetingly, and hurried back to her companions. Azhar watched her go. He spoke some words quietly.

'What was that?' Barbara asked him.

'"Let not their conduct grieve thee,"' he said with a smile and a nod at the girl's retreating back. '"They injure Allah not at all."'

Hadiyyah couldn't have been more delighted with her new giraffe. She held it happily to her thin chest, tucking its head under her chin. The other giraffe, however, she refused to part with. She clutched it in her other hand, saying, 'It's not *his* fault he got smirched with ketchup,' as if the stuffed animal were a personal friend. 'We c'n wash him up, I expect. Can't we, Dad? 'N' if all the ketchup won't come out, we can just pretend he escaped from a lion when he was little.'

The buoyancy of children, Barbara thought.

They spent another hour enjoying the pleasure pier's attractions: losing themselves in the Hall of Mirrors, intrigued by the hologram exhibition, tossing balls at a basket, trying their luck at archery, deciding what they would have printed upon their souvenir T-shirts. Hadiyyah settled on a sunflower, Azhar chose a steam train – although Barbara found that she couldn't imagine him actually wearing anything less formal than one of his spotless linen shirts – and Barbara herself went for a cartoon egg that was shattered on rocky ground beneath a wall, with the words *Scramble Humpty-Dumpty* arching over the picture.

Hadiyyah sighed with pure pleasure as they made their way towards the exit. The attractions were beginning to shut down for the night, and as a result the noise had abated and the crowd had thinned out considerably. What remained were mostly couples now, boys and girls who sought the shadows as eagerly as they had earlier sought the games and amusements. Here and there, an entwined duo leaned against the pier railing. Some watched the lights of Balford fanned out on the shore, some listened to the sea as it slapped against the pilings beneath them, and some ignored everything but each other and the pleasure afforded by another's body pressed to one's own.

'This,' Hadiyyah announced dreamily, 'is the very best place in the whole wide world. When I grow up, I'm going to spend every one of my holidays here. And you'll come with me, won't you, Barbara? Because we'll know each other for ever and ever. Dad'll come with us, won't you, Dad? And Mummy as well. And this time when Dad wins Mummy an elephant, I won't cut it open on the kitchen floor.' She gave another sigh. Her eyelids were beginning to droop. 'We got to get postcards, Dad,' she added with a little stumble as she failed to lift her foot high enough when she took a step. 'We got to send a postcard to Mummy.'

Azhar stopped. He took the two giraffes from the little girl and handed them to Barbara. Then he lifted his daughter and settled her legs round his waist.

'I c'n walk,' she protested sleepily. 'I'm not tired. Not one little bit.'

Azhar kissed the side of her head. For a moment he stood motionless with his daughter in his arms, as if awash in an emotion that he wished to feel but not to exhibit.

Watching him, Barbara was overwhelmed for an instant with a longing that she didn't wish to identify, much less to experience. So she fumbled with the plastic bag in which their three T-shirts were folded, placing the two giraffes within it, finding it necessary to rearrange the bag's position on her arm. It was a moment in which her daily armour of derision and irony failed her entirely. There, on the pier in the company of a father and his child, circumstances suggested that she assess the elements comprising her personal life.

But she wasn't a woman who embraced such suggestions, so she looked about for other intellectual, emotional, and psychological employment. She found it without difficulty: Trevor Ruddock was heading in their direction, having just emerged from the brightly lit pavilion.

He was wearing sky blue overalls, attire so out of character in him that Barbara could only conclude it was a uniform worn by the maintenance and custodial crews who took care of the pier after it closed for the night. But it wasn't the overalls that caused her to take a second and closer look at young Mr Ruddock. He worked on the pier, after all. He'd been released from the nick some hours earlier. His presence at Shaw Attractions was hardly illogical, considering the hour. But the bulging backpack he was wearing slung over his shoulders was a less than reasonable accessory to his sartorial ensemble.

His eyes adjusting to the difference in lighting from the pavilion to the pier, Trevor didn't see Barbara and her companions. He went to a shed at the east side of the pavilion, where he unlocked its door and disappeared inside.

As Azhar started to move towards the exit again, Barbara put a hand on his arm. 'Hang on,' she said.

He followed the direction of her gaze, seemed to see nothing, and looked back at her, perplexed. 'Is there . . . ?'

'Just a little something I want to check out,' she said. The shed, after all, was a perfect place to store contraband. And Trevor Ruddock clearly had something other than his evening meal in his possession. With Balford's nearness to Harwich and Parkeston . . . It didn't make sense to let an opportunity like this one pass her by.

Trevor emerged – *sans* backpack, Barbara noted – pushing a large trolley. It was equipped with brooms and brushes, with buckets and dust pans, with a coiled hose pipe and an assortment of unidentifiable bottles, tins, and canisters. Cleansers and disinfectants, Barbara concluded. The upkeep of Shaw Attractions was a serious business. She wondered momentarily if Trevor's backpack had merely been a means of transporting all of his cleaning accoutrements. It was a possibility. She knew there was only one way to find out.

He took off towards the end of the pier, obviously with the intention of working his way towards and into the pavilion from the future site of the restaurant. Barbara seized the opportunity. She grabbed Azhar's elbow and hustled him across the pier to the shed. She tried the door, which Trevor had swung shut behind him. She found she was in luck. He hadn't relocked it.

She ducked inside. 'Just keep watch for me,' she requested of her friend.

'Watch?' Azhar shifted the bulk of Hadiyyah's weight from one arm to the other. 'For what? Barbara, what are you doing?'

'Just checking out a theory,' she said. 'I won't be a tick.'

He said nothing else and as she couldn't see him, she could only assume he was doing his bit and keeping an eye open for anyone approaching the shed with intent to enter. For her part, she considered what Helmut Kreuzhage had told her from Hamburg earlier in the evening: Haytham Querashi had suspected someone of an illegal activity involving both Hamburg and the nearby English harbours.

Drug smuggling was the obvious illegal activity of choice, despite what *Kriminalhauptkommisar* Kreuzhage had said to discourage this line of thought. It brought in big money, especially if the drug was heroin. But an illegal activity that involved smuggling didn't limit itself to narcotics. There was pornography to consider, as well as loose jewels like diamonds, explosives, and small arms, any of which could be carried on to the pleasure pier via backpack and hidden in a shed.

She looked round for the backpack, but it was nowhere in sight. She began a search. The only light inside came from that allowed by the partially open doorway, but it was sufficient for her to see by once her eyes became accustomed to the gloom. The shed was outfitted with a set of cupboards, and she went through these swiftly. She found nothing inside but five cans of paint, brushes, rollers, overalls, and tarpaulins, in addition to extra cleaning supplies.

Aside from the cupboards, there were two deep drawers and a chest. The drawers held tools for small repairs: spanners, screw drivers, pliers, a crow bar, nails, screws, and even a small saw. But nothing else.

Barbara went on to the chest. Its lid made a squeak that, she swore, probably could have been heard in Clacton. The backpack lay within, the sort of aluminium-framed rucksack that students use when they hitchhike during their holidays, determined to see the world.

Anticipation rising, feeling and believing that at last she was getting somewhere, Barbara lifted the pack out and laid it on the floor. But her hopes were dashed when she saw the contents. And confusion quickly took hope's place.

The backpack contained a hotchpotch of useless articles, at least articles that were useless to her present purposes. She emptied the pack of salt cellars fashioned like lighthouses, fishermen, anchors, and whales; pepper mills posing as Scotties and pirates; a plastic tea set; two dirty Barbie dolls; three unused and sealed decks of cards; a mug commemorating the short-lived marriage of the Duke and Duchess of York; a small London taxi missing a wheel; two pairs of child-sized sunglasses; an unopened box of Beehive nougat; two ping pong bats, a net for the game, and a box of balls.

Hell, Barbara thought. This was a total bust.

'Barbara,' she heard Azhar murmur from the other side of the door. 'A boy's walking in this direction from the pavilion. He's just come out.'

She stowed everything away again, trying to replace each article in the order in which she'd first found it. Azhar said her name again, more urgently this time.

'Right, right,' she whispered in response. She returned the backpack to the chest and rejoined Azhar outside on the pier.

They faded to the railing where the shadows were deep, just beyond the sailing ship ride. The newcomer rounded the corner of the shed, went to its doorway without hesitation, cast a surreptitious glance to the right and the left, and let himself inside.

Barbara knew him on sight, having had two occasions already to interact with the boy. It was Charlie Ruddock, Trevor's younger brother.

'Who is this, Barbara?' Azhar asked quietly. 'Do you know him?' Her head on his shoulder, Hadiyyah was fast asleep, and she murmured as if in answer to her father.

'He's called Charlie Ruddock,' Barbara said.

'Why do we watch him? And what were you looking for in that shed?'

'I don't exactly know,' she said, and when he looked sceptical, she went on. 'It's the truth, Azhar. I don't know. That's the hell of this case. It could be racial like you want it to be –'

'As *I* want it to be? No, Barbara. I am not –'

'All right. All right. Like *some* people want it to be. But it's starting to look like it could be something else as well.'

'What?' he asked. But he read her reluctance to part with information as clearly as if she'd communicated it to him. 'You won't explain yourself further, will you?'

She was saved from having to answer his question. Charlie Ruddock was exiting the shed. And on his back he wore the pack that Barbara had just examined. Curiouser and curiouser, she thought. Exactly what the hell was going on?

Charlie headed back towards the pavilion. Barbara said, 'Come on,' and began to follow.

The lights had been turned off now on the amusements, and the number of fun-goers had been reduced to the shadow-seeking couples and a few families still gathering up their straggling members prior to departure. The din had quieted. The smells had faded. In the attractions, on the rides, and within the numerous take-away food stalls, those whose livelihood was the pier readied it for another day.

With so few pleasure-seekers left and most of them wending their way towards the exit, it was easy enough to tail one young boy who was not only doing likewise, but doing it with a bulging pack on his back. As Barbara and her friends made their way through the pavilion and towards the seafront, she watched Charlie's progress and considered what she'd seen and heard that evening.

Haytham Querashi had been quite insistent that something illegal was taking place between Germany and England. Since he'd phoned Hamburg, it stood to reason that he believed the activity originated in that city. And German ferries leaving from Hamburg arrived in Parkeston harbour, near Harwich. But Barbara was no closer to learning what – if anything – was going on between the two countries and who – if anyone – was involved in the activity than she'd been when the condition of Querashi's abandoned Nissan had first suggested possession of contraband.

The fact that the Nissan had been torn apart brought everything about Querashi into question anyway, didn't it? And didn't the car's condition also emphasise the possibility of smuggling? And *if* it did, was Querashi involved? Or was he, a man of deep enough religious conviction that he'd phoned all the way to Pakistan merely to discuss a verse of the Qur'aan, attempting to blow the whistle on the illegal activity? And no matter what Querashi had been doing, how the hell did Trevor Ruddock fit into it? Or his brother Charlie?

Barbara knew how Muhannad Malik – and perhaps Azhar – would respond to those final two questions. The Ruddocks, after all, were white.

But she herself had seen this evening evidence of what she already knew about racial interactions. The adolescents who had harassed Hadiyyah and the one young girl who'd attempted to right the wrong were human microcosms of the population at large, and as such they gave testimony to Barbara's belief: some of her countrymen were xenophobic imbeciles; others most decidedly were not.

But where did that knowledge leave the investigation into Querashi's murder? she wondered. Especially in a situation in which the only suspects without alibis were white?

Ahead, Charlie Ruddock had gained the land side of the pavilion and stopped. Barbara and her friends did likewise, watching him. He was at the south railing of the pier, mounting an ancient, rust-corroded bicycle. Beyond him, the proprietors of the Lobster Hut were cranking down the metal shields over the establishment's ordering windows. A short distance away, Balford Balloons and Rock had already shut its doors for the night. The tiers of deserted beach huts that stretched along the promenade to the south of these two commercial concerns resembled an abandoned village. Both their doors and their windows were firmly barred, and the only noise emitted from their immediate vicinity was the echo of the sea as waves hit the shore.

'This boy is involved in something, isn't he?' Azhar asked. 'And it's something to do with Haytham's murder.'

'I don't know, Azhar,' Barbara said truthfully as they watched Charlie mount a dilapidated bike and begin to pedal in the general direction of the distant Nez. 'He's involved in something. That much seems obvious. But as to what it is, I swear to God, I just don't know.'

'Is this the sergeant or Barbara speaking?' Azhar asked quietly.

She looked away from the Ruddock boy to the man beside her. 'There's no difference between the two of them,' she said.

He nodded and shifted his daughter in his arms. 'I see. But perhaps there ought to be.'

Chapter Twenty-one

Barbara was on the road to Harwich by ten the next morning. She'd phoned Emily the moment her alarm had gone off, catching the DCI at home. She related what she'd heard from *Kriminalhauptkommissar* Kreuzhage in Hamburg and what she'd seen on the pier the previous night. She left out the fact that she'd been in the company of Taymullah Azhar and his daughter when she'd seen Trevor Ruddock, his brother, and the backpack, and she told herself that a lengthy explanation of her relationship with the Pakistanis would only fracture whatever fragile clarity they were finally beginning to bring to the investigation.

She soon learned that it wouldn't have made any difference had she mentioned her companions on the pier, however, because Emily appeared to have heard nothing else once Barbara mentioned the subject of her conversation with Helmut Kreuzhage. The DCI sounded brisk, rested, and completely awake. Whatever she and the faceless Gary had done to mitigate her stress after hours, it had obviously worked. 'An illegality of some sort?' she said. 'In Hamburg? Well done, Barb. I said Muhannad was into something dodgy, didn't I? At least now we're on the track of what it is.'

Barbara aimed for caution in her next remarks. 'But Querashi didn't give Inspector Kreuzhage any evidence about what sort of illegal activity was going on. And he didn't mention names – Muhannad's included. And when Kreuzhage staked out *Oskarstraße 15*, he came up cold, Em. His blokes didn't see a thing that didn't look strictly above board.'

'Muhannad's going to cover his tracks. He's been doing that for more than ten years. And we know that whoever killed Querashi covered up his tracks like a pro. The question is this: What the hell is Muhannad up to? Smuggling? Prostitution? International robbery? What?'

'Kreuzhage didn't have a clue. He didn't exactly launch an investigation, but what little he did wasn't enough to uncover anything. So here's what I think. If there's no real evidence of anything dodgy going down in Germany –'

'Then we'll have to find it at this end, won't we?' was Emily's riposte. 'And the Maliks' factory is set up to be the perfect stopping-point for any number of enterprises: from counterfeiting to terrorism. If there's evidence to be found, that's where we'll find it. They ship goods out of there at least once a week. Who knows what else goes into those boxes besides jars of mustards and jellies?'

'But, Em, the Maliks aren't the only people Querashi knew, so they can't be the only ones under suspicion in this Hamburg business, can they? Trevor Ruddock worked at that factory as well. And let's not forget that wire I found in his room. *And* there's Querashi's lover to consider, if we ever find him.'

'Barbara, whatever we find, it's going to lead to Muhannad.'

Barbara wondered about this as she drove to Harwich. She had to admit that there was a certain logic to Emily's conclusion about Muhannad and the mustard factory. But she felt a disturbing sense of unease at the speed with which the DCI had leaped to it. Emily had dismissed the strange behaviour of the Ruddocks with the simple declaration, 'Scavengers, that lot,' and she'd relayed information about Theo Shaw's grandmother having had a massive stroke on the previous afternoon as if that fact exonerated the young man from any part in Querashi's death. She'd said, 'I'm sending to London for this Professor Siddiqi character as well. He'll do the translating for Kumhar when I question him.'

'What about Azhar?' Barbara asked. 'Wouldn't it save time if you used him to translate? You could have him there without Muhannad.'

Emily scoffed at this idea. 'I've no intention of letting either Muhannad Malik or his slippery cousin anywhere near that bloke again. Kumhar's our pipeline to the truth, Barb, and I'm not going to risk plugging up the works by having anyone skulking round in the background when I question him. Kumhar's got to know something about that factory. Muhannad's the sales director at Malik's Mustards. And the sales director oversees the shipping department. Where do you think that tasty bit of information fits into the overall scheme of things?'

Inspector Lynley would have called Emily's deductions *intuitive policework*, something that came from long experience and a carefully honed awareness of what was going on in one's gut as suspects were questioned and evidence was accumulated. But Barbara had learned the hard way to be aware of what was going on within her *own* gut as a member of an investigative team, and the sensations that filled her after her conversation with Emily didn't please her.

She considered her uneasiness from every angle, probing it like a scientist confronted with an alien being. Certainly, if Muhannad Malik was the kingpin in some sort of malfeasance, he had a motive to kill Querashi if Querashi had made an attempt to play the whistle blower on him. But the existence of that possibility shouldn't have obviated the potential guilt of Theo Shaw and Trevor Ruddock, both of whom also had motives to be rid of Querashi and neither of whom had a decent alibi. Yet that was exactly what appeared to have happened, at least in Emily Barlow's mind. And as she thought about the peremptory dismissal of Trevor Ruddock and Theo Shaw as suspects, Barbara felt her uneasiness coalesce into a simple and potentially ugly question: Was Emily responding to gut-level intuition or to something else?

Inspector Kreuzhage had said it himself from Hamburg: there was no evidence of anything. So on what exactly was Emily basing her intuitive conclusions?

Barbara recalled her friend's easy success during the three courses they'd taken together in Maidstone, how she'd received the accolades of their instructors and the admiration of the other detectives. There had been no question in Barbara's mind then that Emily Barlow was a cut above the average cop. She wasn't merely good at what she did; she was superb. Her elevation to DCI at the age of thirty-seven underscored this fact. So, Barbara wondered, why was she entertaining even a single doubt about the DCI's capability now?

Her long partnership with DI Lynley had forced Barbara more than once to examine not only the facts in a case but also her motives in shining the spotlight of suspicion on one of those facts in preference to another. She engaged in much the same activity now as she spun between the summer wheat fields on the road to Harwich. Only this time she didn't scrutinise which facts she was spotlighting in the investigation and why she was spotlighting them. Instead, she studied the underpinning of her own discomfiture.

She didn't much like the result of her study because she concluded that she herself might well be the problem in the investigation into Querashi's death. Did finding guilt among the Pakistanis cut a little too close to the home of Detective Sergeant Barbara Havers? Perhaps she wouldn't have felt the smallest degree of uneasiness with seeing Muhannad Malik as everything from a street thug to a pimp had Taymullah Azhar and his appealing daughter not been hovering on the periphery of the investigation.

This final consideration gave her a jolt she could have done without. She found that she didn't want to speculate upon whose investigative mind was actually clear and whose was clouded. And she definitely didn't want to reflect upon her feelings for Azhar and Hadiyyah.

She pulled into Harwich determined to gather information objectively. She followed the High Street as it wound towards the sea, and she found World Wide Tours tucked between a take-away sandwich shop and an Oddbins that was advertising a cut-rate price on *amontillado*.

World Wide Tours comprised one large room with three desks at which two women and a man were working. It was sumptuously decorated, but oddly in the fashion of a by-gone era. The walls were papered in a *faux* William Morris print and hung with gilt-framed drawings of turn-of-the-century families on suitable holidays. The desks, chairs, and shelves were heavy mahogany. Five large palms stood in pots and seven enormous ferns hung from the ceiling where a fan circulated the air and rustled their fronds. Overall, there was an artificial Victorian fussiness to the whole set-up that made Barbara want to blast the office with a fire hose.

One of the two women asked if she required assistance. The other spoke into the telephone while their male colleague scanned a computer screen, murmuring, 'Lufthansa, come on.'

Barbara presented her warrant card. She saw by the presence of a name placard that she was speaking to someone called Edwina.

'Police?' Edwina said, pressing three fingers to the hollow of her throat as if she expected to be accused of something more untoward than accepting employment in a tastelessly reproduced office directly out of Charles Dickens. She glanced at her fellow workers. The man – his name placard identified him as Rudi – poked at the keyboard of his computer and swivelled his chair in their direction. He acted the part of Edwina's echo, and when he spoke the dread word again, the third employee brought her telephone conversation to an end. This person was called Jen, Barbara saw, and she gripped both sides of her chair seat as if thinking it might suddenly become airborne. The arrival of an officer of the law, Barbara thought not for the first time, always brought people's subconscious guilt to the surface.

'Right,' Barbara said. 'New Scotland Yard.'

'Scotland Yard?' This came from Rudi. 'You're here from London? I hope there's no trouble?'

There well might be, Barbara realised. The little sod spoke with a German accent.

She could almost hear Inspector Lynley's posh public school voice intoning his number one credo of policework: there is no such thing as coincidence in murder. Barbara examined the young bloke from head to toe. Tubby as a wine cask, cropped red hair receding from his forehead, he didn't look like a party to a recent murder. But then, no one usually did.

She fished her photographs from her shoulder bag and showed them Querashi's first, saying, 'This bloke look familiar to you lot?'

The other two gathered round Edwina's desk, shoulders hunched over the picture which Barbara placed dead centre. They examined it in silence, while above their heads the fern fronds susurrated and the ceiling fan spun. It was nearly a minute before anyone answered, and then it was Rudi, speaking to his colleagues and not to Barbara.

'This is the chap who inquired about air tickets, isn't it?'

'I don't know,' Edwina said doubtfully. Her fingers pulled at the skin just beneath the hollow of her throat.

Jen said, 'Yes. I remember him. I served him, Eddie. You were out of the office.' She met Barbara's eyes squarely. 'He came in – when was it, Rudi? – perhaps three weeks ago? I don't quite recall.'

'But you remember him,' Barbara said.

'Well, yes. I mean, there aren't actually many . . .'

'We see very few Asians in Harwich,' Rudolph said.

'And you yourself are from . . . ?' Barbara asked encouragingly, although she was fairly certain of the answer.

'Hamburg,' he said.

Well, well, well, she thought.

He said, 'Originally Hamburg, that is. I have been in this country for seven years.' *Haff*, he said.

She said, 'Right. Yes. Well. This bloke's called Haytham Querashi. I'm investigating his murder. He was killed last week in Balford-le-Nez. What sort of air tickets was he asking about?'

To their credit, they all seemed equally surprised or dismayed when the word *murder* was intoned. They dropped their heads as one to re-examine the photograph of Querashi as if it were a relic of a saint. Jen was the one to answer. He'd been inquiring about airline tickets for his family, she explained to Barbara. He wished to bring them to England from Pakistan. A whole party of people, it was: brothers and sisters, parents, the lot. He wanted them to join him in England permanently.

'You've a branch office in Pakistan,' Barbara noted. 'In Karachi, right?'

'In Hong Kong, Istanbul, New Delhi, Vancouver, New York, and Kingston as well,' Edwina said proudly. 'Our speciality is foreign travel and immigration. We've experts working in every office.'

Which was probably why Querashi had chosen World Wide Tours rather than an agency in Balford, Jen added, testimonial incarnate. He'd been asking about immigration for his family. Unlike most travel agencies solely eager to part customers from their cash, WWT had an international reputation – 'a proud international reputation' was how she put it – for its network of contacts with lawyers round the world who specialised in immigration. 'UK, EU, and US,' she said. 'We're travel agents for people on the move and we're here to help make that movement easier.'

Yadda, yadda, yadda, Barbara thought. The girl sounded like an advert. So much for any previous thoughts about Querashi's trying to skip town one step ahead of his wedding day. It sounded as if he'd been fully intending to uphold his end of the marriage agreement. Indeed, it sounded as if he'd been laying plans for the future of his family as well.

Barbara pulled the Polaroid of Fahd Kumhar from her shoulder bag next. This met with a different result. None of them knew this particular Asian. None of them had ever seen him. Barbara watched them closely, looking for an indication that one or all of them were lying. But no one quivered so much as an eyelash.

Bust, she thought. She thanked them for their help and stepped from the office into the High Street. It was eleven o'clock and she was already sweat-drenched. She was also thirsty, so she ducked into the Whip and Whistle across the street. There, she managed to talk the publican into parting with five ice cubes over which he poured lemonade. She carried this to a table by the window – along with a packet of salt and vinegar crisps – and she flung herself on to a stool, lit a cigarette, and prepared to enjoy her elevenses.

She'd consumed half of the crisps, three-quarters of the lemonade, and all of the cigarette when she saw Rudi step out of World Wide Tours across the street. He glanced right and left and right again, in a manner that Barbara decided could have been overly cautious – indicating the normal trepidation of a European unused to English traffic – or borderline stealthy. She cast her vote with the latter, and when Rudi took off up the street, she gulped down the rest of her lemonade and left the remaining crisps on the table.

Outside, she saw him unlocking a Renault on the street corner. Her own Mini was parked two cars away, so as the German fired up his vehicle and guided it into the traffic, she dashed to her own. In a moment, she was in pursuit.

Anything, of course, could have taken him from the travel office: a dental appointment, a sexual assignation, a visit to the chiropodist, an early lunch. But following so closely on the heels of her visit, Rudi's departure was too intriguing to let go uninvestigated.

She followed him at a distance. He took the A120 out of town. He drove with no interest in the speed limit, and he led her directly to Parkeston, just over two miles from the travel office. He didn't make the turn towards the harbour, however. Rather, he drove into an industrial estate just before the harbour road.

Barbara couldn't risk following him there. But she pulled into the lay-by that opened into the industrial estate, and she watched the Renault roll to a stop at a prefabricated metal warehouse at the farthest end. Barbara would have given her signed edition of *The Lusty Savage* for a pair of binoculars at that moment. She was too far from the building to read its sign.

Unlike the other warehouses in the estate, this one was closed up and looked unoccupied. But when Rudi rapped on the door, someone within admitted him.

Barbara watched from the Mini. She didn't know what she expected to see, and she was rewarded with seeing nothing. She sweated silently in the roasting car for a quarter of an hour that seemed like a century before Rudi emerged: no bags of heroin in his possession, no pockets bulging with counterfeit money, no video cassettes of children in compromising positions, no guns or explosives or even companions. He left the warehouse as he'd entered the warehouse, empty-handed and alone.

Barbara knew he'd see her if she remained on the edge of the industrial estate, so she pulled back on to the A120 with the intention of turning round and having a bit of recce among the warehouses once Rudi was gone. But as she looked for a suitable place to make a three-point turn, she saw a large stone building sitting back from the road on a horseshoe drive. *The Castle Hotel*, its roadside sign announced in mediaeval lettering. She recalled the brochure that she'd found in Haytham Querashi's room. She turned into the hotel's car park, making the decision to kill another bird with the stones she'd been fortuitously given.

Professor Siddiqi wasn't at all what Emily Barlow had expected him to be. She'd anticipated someone dark and middle-aged, with black hair sweeping back from an intelligent forehead, kohl-coloured eyes, and tobacco skin. But the man who presented himself to her in the company of DC Hesketh, who'd fetched him from London, was very nearly blond, his eyes were decidedly grey, and his skin was fair enough for him to be mistaken for a northern European instead of an Asian. Looking to be in his early-thirties, he was a compact man, not even her own height. He was toughly built like an amateur wrestler.

He smiled as she quickly adjusted her expression from surprise to indifference. He offered his hand in greeting and said, 'We don't all come out of the same mould, Inspector Barlow.'

She didn't like to be read that easily, especially by someone she didn't know. She ignored the remark, saying brusquely instead, 'Good of you to come. Would you like a drink or shall we get started with Mr Kumhar straightaway?'

He asked for grapefruit juice, and as Belinda Warner took herself off to fetch it, Emily explained the situation into which the London professor had been brought. 'I'll be tape recording the entire interview,' she said in conclusion. 'My questions in English, your translations, Mr Kumhar's answers, your translations.'

Siddiqi was astute enough to make the proper inference. 'You can rely upon my integrity,' he said. 'But as we've never met before now, I wouldn't expect you to depend upon it without a system of checks and balances.'

The major ground rules laid and the minor ones implied, Emily took him to meet his fellow Asian.

Kumhar hadn't benefited from his night in custody. If anything, he was more anxiety-ridden than on the previous afternoon. Worse, he was sodden with sweat and foul with the odour of faeces, as if he'd messed himself.

Siddiqi took one look at him and turned back to Emily. 'Where's this man been kept? And what the hell have you been doing to him?'

Another ardent viewer of pro-IRA films, Emily decided wearily. What Guildford and Birmingham had done to set back the cause of policework was inestimable. She said, 'He's been kept in a cell which you're more than welcome to inspect, Professor. And we've been doing nothing to him, unless serving him dinner and breakfast goes as torture these days. It's hot in the cells. But no more so than the rest of the building or the whole bloody town. He'll tell you as much if you care to ask him.'

'I'll do just that,' Siddiqi said. And he fired off a series of questions to Kumhar that he didn't bother to translate.

For the first time since being brought into the station, Kumhar lost the look of a terrified rabbit. He unclasped his hands and reached towards Siddiqi as if a life belt had been thrown him.

It was a gesture of supplication, and the professor apparently saw it as such. He used both of his hands to reach for the man, and having done so, he drew him to the table in the centre of the room. He spoke again, translating this time for Emily. 'I've introduced myself. I've told him that I'm to translate your questions and his answers. I've told him that you mean him no harm. I hope that's the truth, Inspector.'

What *was* it with these people? Emily wondered. They saw inequity, prejudice, and brutality under every lily pad. She didn't reply directly. Rather, she flipped on the tape recorder, gave the date, the time, and the individuals present. After which, she said, 'Mr Kumhar, your name was among the belongings of a murdered man, Mr Haytham Querashi. Can you explain to me how it got there?'

She expected a replay of yesterday's litany: a string of disavowals. She was surprised. Kumhar fastened his eyes on Siddiqi as the question was translated for him, and when he replied – which he did at great length – he kept his eyes on the professor. Siddiqi listened, nodded, and at one point halted the man's recital to ask a question. Then he turned to Emily.

'He met Mr Querashi outside Weeley on the A133. He – Mr Kumhar, that is – was hitchhiking and Mr Querashi offered him a ride. This took place nearly a month ago. Mr Kumhar had been working as a farm labourer, moving among the fields throughout the county. He'd become dissatisfied with the money he was making as well as with the working conditions, so he'd decided to look for other employment.'

Emily considered this, her brow furrowed. 'Why didn't he tell me this yesterday? Why did he deny knowing Mr Querashi?'

Siddiqi turned back to Kumhar, who watched him with the eagerness of a puppy determined to please. Before Siddiqi finished the question, Kumhar was answering, and this time he directed his response to Emily.

'"When you said that Mr Querashi was murdered,"' Siddiqi translated, '"I was afraid that you might come to believe that I was involved. I lied to protect myself from coming under suspicion. I'm new to this country, and I wish to do nothing to jeopardise my welcome here. Please understand how much I regret having lied to you. Mr Querashi was nothing but kindness to me and I betrayed that kindness by not speaking the truth at once."'

Emily noted the sweat that coated the man's skin like a film of cooking oil. That he'd lied to her on the previous day was a bona fide fact. What remained open to question was whether he was lying to her now. She said, 'Did Mr Querashi know that you were looking for employment?'

He did, Kumhar answered. He'd told Mr Querashi of his unhappiness with his farm employment. That had constituted the bulk of their conversation in the car.

'Did Mr Querashi offer you a job?'

At this Kumhar looked nonplussed. A job? he asked. No. There was no job offered. Mr Querashi merely picked him up and drove him to his lodgings.

'And wrote you a cheque for £400,' Emily added.

Siddiqi raised an eyebrow, but translated without comment.

It was true that Mr Querashi had given him money. The man was kindness itself, and Mr Kumhar would not lie and call this gift of £400 a loan. But the Qur'aan decreed and the Five Pillars of Islam required payment of the *zakat* to one in need. So in giving him £400 –

'What is *zakat*?' Emily interposed.

'Alms for the needy,' Siddiqi answered. Kumhar watched him anxiously whenever he switched to English and his expression suggested a man straining to understand and to absorb every word. 'Muslims are required to see to the economic welfare of members of their community. We give to support the poor and others like them.'

'So in giving Mr Kumhar £400 pounds, Haytham Querashi was simply doing his religious duty?'

'That's exactly the case,' Siddiqi said.

'He wasn't buying something?'

'Such as?' Siddiqi gestured to Kumhar. 'What on earth could this poor man have to sell him?'

'Silence comes to mind. Mr Kumhar spends time near Clacton market square. Ask him if he ever saw Mr Querashi there.'

Siddiqi gazed at her for a moment as if trying to read the meaning behind the question. Then he shrugged and turned to Kumhar, repeating the question in their own language.

Kumhar shook his head adamantly. Emily didn't require a translation for never, not once, not at any time, he himself had not been in the market square.

'Mr Querashi was the director of production at a local factory. He could have offered Mr Kumhar employment. Yet Mr Kumhar says the subject of a job never came up between them. Does he wish to change that claim?'

No, Kumhar told her through his interpreter. He did not wish to change that claim. He knew Mr Querashi only as a benefactor sent to him through the goodness of Allah. But there was a common thread that bound them to each other: they both had families in Pakistan whom they wished to bring to this country. Although in Querashi's case it was parents and siblings and in Kumhar's case it was a wife and two children, their intention was the same and thus there existed between them a greater understanding than might have otherwise existed between two strangers who meet on a public road.

'But wouldn't a permanent job have been far more of a benefit than £400 if you want to bring your family to this country?' Emily asked. 'How far could you have stretched that money in comparison to what you might have earned over time as an employee of Malik's Mustards?'

Kumhar shrugged. He had no way to explain why Mr Querashi hadn't offered him employment.

Siddiqi interjected a comment. 'Mr Kumhar was a wayfarer, Inspector. In giving him funds, Mr Querashi met his obligation to him. He wasn't required to do anything more.'

'It seems to me that a man who was "nothing but kindness" to Mr Kumhar is a man who would have seen to his future welfare as well as to his immediate needs.'

'We can't know what his ultimate intentions were towards Mr Kumhar,' Professor Siddiqi pointed out. 'We can only interpret his actions. His death, unfortunately, prevents anything more.'

And wasn't that convenient? Emily thought.

'Did Mr Querashi ever make a pass at you, Mr Kumhar?' she asked.

Siddiqi stared at her, absorbing the abrupt change in topic. 'Are you asking –'

'I think the question's clear enough. We've been given information that Querashi was homosexual. I'd like to know if Mr Kumhar was on the receiving end of anything besides Mr Querashi's money.'

Kumhar heard the question with some consternation. He declared his answer in a tone of strained horror: No, no, no. Mr Querashi was a good man. He was a righteous man. He could not have defiled his body, his mind, and his everlasting soul with such behaviour. It was an impossibility, a sin against everything Muslims believed.

'And where were you on Friday night?'

At his lodgings in Clacton. And Mrs Kersey – his most generous hostess – would be happy to tell Inspector Barlow as much.

That concluded their interview, which was what Emily recited into the tape recorder. When she switched it off, Kumhar spoke urgently to Siddiqi.

Emily said angrily, 'Hang on there.'

Siddiqi said, 'He only wants to know if he can return to Clacton now. He is, understandably, anxious to quit this place, Inspector.'

Emily meditated on the prospect of getting any more information out of the Pakistani if she held him longer and gave him time to sweat a little more in that sauna of a cell just off the weight room. If she grilled him another two or three times, she might wrest from him a detail that would take her one step closer to their killer. But in doing this, she also ran the risk of sending the Asian community back into the streets. Whichever member of *Jum'a* came to fetch Kumhar back to Clacton in the afternoon would be looking for anything useful to their cause that could be carried back and reported upon as a means of enflaming the people. She weighed this possibility against whatever potential information she could get from the Asian before her.

She finally went to the door and yanked it open. DC Honigman was waiting in the corridor. She said, 'Take Mr Kumhar to the weight room. See that he has a shower. Have someone get him lunch and some decent clothes. And tell DC Hesketh to take the professor back to London.'

She turned back to Siddiqi and his companion in the interrogation room. She said, 'Mr Kumhar, I've not finished with you, so don't even think about leaving the vicinity. If you do, I'll track you down and drag you back here by your bollocks. Is that clear?'

Siddiqi levelled an ironic gaze upon her. 'I expect he'll get your point,' he said.

She left them and returned to her office on the first floor. She'd long ago learned to trust her instincts in an investigation, and they were fairly screaming that Fahd Kumhar had more information than he was willing to part with.

Damn and blast the law and the proscription of torture and what both had done to the rights of the police, she fumed. A few minutes on the rack in the Middle Ages and that little worm would have been his inquisitor's pudding. As it was, he would walk away with his secrets intact while her head began to throb and her muscles went into extended spasm.

Christ. It was maddening. And what was worse was the fact that one brief interview with Fahd Kumhar had undone four hours of Gary's ardent ministrations the previous night.

Which made her want to snap someone's head off. Which made her want to yell at the first person who came within her line of vision. Which made her want to –

'Guv?'

'What?' Emily barked. 'What? *What*?'

Belinda Warner hesitated at the threshold of Emily's office. She was carrying a long fax in one hand and a pink telephone message in the other. Her expression was one of consternation, and she ventured a peek into Emily's office to see the source of the DCI's ill humour.

Emily sighed. 'Sorry. What is it?'

'Good news, Guv.'

'I could do with some.'

Reassured, the WPC joined her. 'We've heard from London,' she said. She gestured first with the telephone message and then with the fax. 'From SO4 and SO11. We've got a match on the fingerprints on the Nissan. And a report on that Asian bloke, Taymullah Azhar.'

The Castle Hotel didn't look much like a castle. Instead, it resembled a squat fortress, with balustrades rather than crenellations at the roofline. It was monochromatic on its exterior – constructed entirely of buff stone, buff bricks, and buff plaster – but that lack of colour had been more than compensated for in the hotel's interior.

The lobby was awash with colour and the predominant theme was pink: a fuchsia ceiling edged by a roseate dog-toothed cornice, walls papered in stripes of a candy-floss hue, maroon carpeting patterned with hyacinths. Just like walking into an enormous stick of rock, Barbara thought.

Behind the reception desk, a middle-aged man in tails watched her progress across the lobby with an expectant air. His nametag identified him as Curtis and his manner suggested a welcome rehearsed in the privacy of his home and in front of a mirror. First came the slow smile till he was assured of eye contact with her; then came the unveiling of teeth; afterwards the head was cocked with an air of helpful interest; one eyebrow raised; one hand picked up a pencil expectantly.

When with studied courtesy he offered her his assistance, she produced her warrant card. The eyebrow lowered. The pencil dropped. The head uncocked. He altered from Curtis-in-Reception to Curtis-Most-Definitely-on-Guard.

Barbara brought out her pictures again, laying Querashi's and Kumhar's side by side. 'This bloke was chopped at the Nez last week,' she explained laconically. 'This one's in the nick at the moment having a talk with the local DCI. Seen either of them?'

Curtis relaxed marginally. As he studied the pictures, Barbara noted that a brass container sitting on the reception desk held a collection of brochures. She picked one up and saw that it was a copy of the same brochure which she'd found in Querashi's hotel room. There were other brochures as well, and she fingered through these. The Castle Hotel, it seemed, boosted its business in these trying economic times by offering special weekend rates, dances, wine tastings, and holiday extravaganzas at Christmas, New Year, Valentine's Day, and Easter.

'Yes.' Curtis drew the word out thoughtfully on a breath. 'Oh, yes indeed.'

Barbara looked up from her study of the brochures. The picture of Kumhar he'd moved to one side. The picture of Querashi, however, he'd picked up and held between his thumb and his index finger. 'You've seen him?'

'Oh, yes indeed. I remember him quite well, in fact, because I've never before seen an Asian at Leather and Lace. They generally don't go in for it.'

'Pardon?' Barbara asked, nonplussed. 'Leather and Lace?'

Curtis riffled through the brass container and brought out a brochure that Barbara hadn't seen. Its cover was entirely black with a diagonal of white lace etched on to it. The word *Leather* was printed on the upper acute triangle, the word *Lace* on the lower. The inside comprised an invitation to a monthly dance held at the hotel. And the accompanying pictures of previous dances left no question at all as to the clientele being solicited.

Score a point for Trevor Ruddock, Barbara thought. 'This is a dance for homosexuals?' she asked Curtis. 'Not the usual sort of entertainment one finds in the countryside, is it?'

'Times are difficult,' he replied reasonably. 'A business that closes its door to potential profits finds that it's not a business very long.'

There was truth in that, Barbara thought. Basil Treves might well take a slice of this cake and chew upon it when considering his profits and losses at the end of the fiscal year. She said, 'And you saw Querashi at one of these dances?'

'Last month. Definitely. As I said, one sees very few Asians at this sort of gathering. One sees very few Asians in this part of the world altogether, as a matter of fact. So when he came in, I took note of him.'

'And you're certain he was here for the dance? Not for dinner? Not for a drink in the bar?'

'He was definitely here for the dance, Sergeant. Oh, not in drag, mind you. Not that he appeared to be the type to go in for that in the first place. No make-up. No ornaments. You know what I mean. But there was no question why he'd come to the Castle.'

'To pull another bloke?'

'Hardly. He wasn't alone. And his companion didn't look like someone who'd take lightly to being left out in the cold by a companion.'

'He had a date, then.'

'Very much so.'

Here, then, was the first corroboration they'd had of Trevor Ruddock's story about Querashi's sexuality. But simple corroboration didn't put Trevor in the clear.

'What did this bloke look like? Querashi's date, that is,' Barbara asked.

Curtis supplied her with a nonspecific and generally useless description in which everything about the man in question was medium: his height, his build, his weight. It wouldn't have served to locate a lightning bolt in a thunderstorm, save for one detail. When Barbara asked if Querashi's date had any visible tattoos, specifically a spider-on-its-web tattoo on his neck, Curtis was able to say he hadn't. *Definitely not* were his actual words, which he went on to clarify by explaining, 'When I see a tattoo, I never forget it because the thought of getting one makes me positively weak at the knees. Needle phobia,' he added. 'If someone ever wants me to give blood, I'll be completely done for.'

'Right,' Barbara said.

'How people can do what they do to their bodies in the name of fashion . . .' He shuddered. But afterwards he lifted a finger swiftly, as if his own statement had brought something to mind. He said, 'Wait. This bloke had a lip ring, Sergeant. Yes, indeed he had. He had earrings as well. And not just one, mind you. But at least four in each ear.'

Here, then, was what she'd been seeking. The lip ring matched with Trevor's claim. So they had at least one part of the truth at last: Querashi was bent.

She thanked Curtis for his help and went back to the car. She took a moment to rustle up her cigarettes and in the shade of a dust-coated hornbeam, she smoked and she thought about what corroboration for Trevor's story meant to the case.

Azhar had said that homosexuality was a grave sin to the Muslims, enough of a sin for a man to be cast out of his family as a permanent exile. Thus, it was an aberration serious enough to be held a closely guarded secret. But if someone had unearthed this secret, was it black enough – or deviant enough – to cause Querashi's life to be taken? Certainly, it would be an insult to the Malik family if Querashi had aligned himself with them as a cover for a clandestine life. But wouldn't a better revenge than death be to expose him to his own family and let them deal with him as they would?

And if his homosexuality was the key to what had happened to him on the Nez, where did that leave Kumhar? Or the phone calls to Germany and Pakistan? Or the discussions with the *mulla* and the *mufti*? Or the address in Hamburg? Or the papers in his safe-deposit box?

At the thought of these last items, Barbara took a final drag on her cigarette and returned to the Mini. She'd forgotten about Rudi's visit to the industrial estate. It made sense to recce it while she was in the area.

Less than five minutes took her back. She made certain that Rudi's Renault was nowhere in sight before driving through the entrance to the looming warehouses.

These were prefabricated and two-toned: green corrugated steel on the bottom, silver corrugated steel on the top. Attached to each was a reception office of dust-coloured brick. There wasn't a single tree in the entire estate; without the ameliorating effects of shade, the heat radiated from the structures with a mirage-producing intensity. Despite this fact, the warehouse into which Rudi had disappeared at the end of the lane was closed up completely, its huge door and high row of windows sealed off. This was in contrast to every other warehouse whose doors and windows gaped, hopeful of a breeze.

Barbara chose a spot for the Mini some distance from Rudi's warehouse. She parked next to a row of red and white rubbish bins against which clumps of dying pigweed drooped thirstily. She blotted her forehead on the back of her wrist, berated herself for having left the Burnt House without a bottle of water, admitted her stupidity at having smoked a cigarette and worsened her thirst, and shoved open the door of her car.

The industrial estate comprised two lanes, one shooting off perpendicular to the other. Both of them were lined with warehouses, and the proximity of the estate to Parkeston Harbour made them perfect for temporary storage for shipments both coming into and leaving the country. Sun-faded signs indicated the contents of each: electronics supplies, appliances, fine china and crystal, household goods, business machines.

The warehouse in question was more subtle in announcing its purpose and contents. Barbara had to trudge through the heat to within ten yards of the attached office before she was able to read the small white sign fixed above the building's door: *Eastern Imports* was lettered in black, and beneath it *Fine Furniture and Furnishings.*

Well, well, well, Barbara thought, and she tipped her hat mentally to Inspector Lynley. She could hear him saying, 'Well, there you are, Sergeant,' with quiet satisfaction. There is, after all, no real coincidence when it comes to murder. Either Rudi had scarpered from the office of World Wide Tours because he'd suddenly developed a passion for interior design and sought to fulfil it with the immediate redecoration of his bed-sit or he had known more than he'd been willing to let on. In either case, there was only one way to find out.

The office door was locked, so Barbara rapped on it smartly. When no one stirred, she squinted through the dusty window. Inside, there was evidence of recent occupation: a packed lunch of bread, cheese, apple, and sliced ham was spread out on a desk.

She thought at first that only a secret code knock would admit her to the building. But a second, sharper rap aroused the attention of someone within the warehouse. Through the window, she saw the door between the office and the larger building swing open. A thin bespectacled man – so skeletal that the ends of his trouser belt was looped round the buckle and tucked into his trousers – stepped through and carefully shut the door behind him.

He used his index finger to push his spectacles back into place as he crossed the office to the door. He was about six feet tall, Barbara noted, but his height was minimised by poor posture.

'I am so terribly sorry,' he said pleasantly when he had the door open. 'When I'm in the back, I generally lock up.'

Ven I'm in the back, Barbara thought. Another German. He was casually attired for a businessman. He wore cotton trousers and a white T-shirt. He had trainers – but no socks – on his feet. His tanned face was bristly with light brown whiskers the same colour as his hair. She said, 'Scotland Yard CID,' and presented him with her warrant card.

He frowned as he looked at it. But when he raised his face, his expression appeared to have the right balance of guilelessness and concern. He asked nothing and said nothing. He merely waited for her to continue, using the moment in which she said nothing to roll a slice of ham into a tube and to take a bite from it. He held it like a cigar.

In Barbara's experience, most people weren't able to let a silence hang between themselves and the police. But this German seemed like a bloke who could deal with silence indefinitely.

Barbara pulled out her photographs of Haytham Querashi and Fahd Kumhar for the third time. The German took another bite of ham and reached for a slice of cheese as he studied each picture in turn. He said, 'This one I've seen,' and indicated Querashi. 'This one, no. Him I have not.' *Have* he pronounced *haff*, but his English sounded marginally less practised than Rudi's.

Barbara said, 'Where'd you see this bloke, then?'

The German positioned his cheese on a slice of brown bread. 'In the newspaper. He was killed last week, yes? I saw his picture afterwards, perhaps Saturday or Sunday. I cannot recall which.' *Vas* and *vich*, he said. He bit into the bread and cheese and chewed slowly. There was nothing in his lunch to drink, but he didn't seem to be affected by this, despite the heat, the salt of the meat, and the gummy mixture of cheese and bread in his mouth. Just watching him chew and swallow Barbara longed even more strongly for a glass of water.

'Before the newspaper,' she said.

'Have I seen him before then?' he clarified. *Haff.* 'No. I have not. Why do you ask?'

'He had a bill of lading from Eastern Imports among his belongings. It was locked up in a safe-deposit box.'

The German stopped chewing for a moment. 'That is strange indeed,' he said. 'May I . . . ?' And he took up the picture in his fingers. Nice fingers, they were, with buffed nails and a fine gold signet ring.

'Stowing papers away in a safe-deposit box tends to indicate they've got some importance,' Barbara said. 'It doesn't make a lot of sense to lock them up for any other reason, wouldn't you say?'

'Indeed. Indeed. This is very true,' the man replied. 'But one would wish to keep a bill of lading among important papers if a purchase was recorded upon it. If this gentleman bought furniture that was not yet in our stock, he'd want to keep –'

'Nothing was written on the bill of lading. Aside from the name and address of this establishment, the paper was blank.'

The German shook his head in perfect perplexity. He said, 'Then I cannot say . . . This bill of lading was perhaps given to the gentleman by someone else? We import from the east and if he wished to make a purchase of furniture at some future date . . .' He shrugged and made a small moue with his mouth, that quintessential European male gesture that signified two words: Who knows?

Barbara considered the possibilities. True, what this bloke was saying made partial sense. But only as far as serving to explain the bill of lading's presence among Querashi's belongings. Explaining its presence inside his safe-deposit box was going to take another mental leap or two.

She said, 'Yeah. You're probably right. Mind if I have a look round while I'm here? I've a mind to do a bit of redecorating.'

The German nodded as he took another bite of bread and cheese. He reached into his desk and brought out a three-ring notebook, then a second, then a third. He flipped them open with one hand while the other rolled up another piece of ham.

Barbara saw that these were catalogues, and they contained everything from bedroom furniture to kitchenware to lamps. She said, 'You don't keep goods in the warehouse, then?' And she thought, If you don't, then why bloody have one?

'We do indeed,' he said. 'Our wholesale shipments. They are in the warehouse.'

'Perfect,' Barbara said. 'Could I have a look? I can't ever tell anything from a picture.'

'Our stock is low,' he said and sounded uneasy for the first time. 'If you could come back ... perhaps Saturday week?'

'Just a look is all,' Barbara said pleasantly. 'I'd like to get an idea of size and materials before I make up my mind.'

He didn't appear convinced, but he said, albeit reluctantly, 'If you don't mind the dust and a toilet that's gone down ...'

She assured him that she minded neither – what were dust and broken toilets when one was in search of the perfect three-piece suite? – and she followed him through the inner door.

She wasn't quite sure what she'd been expecting. But what she found within the cavernous guts of the warehouse wasn't a sound set for making snuff films, ongoing videotaping of hard core pornography, crates of explosives, or a factory for assembling Uzi sub-machine guns. What she found was a storehouse for furniture: three tiers of sofas, dining-room tables, armchairs, lamps, and bedframes. As her companion had said, the stock was low. It was also covered in plastic that was coated with dust. But as to thinking the furniture was anything else: it was impossible to stretch the imagination that far.

And he'd told the truth about the toilet. The warehouse was rank with the scent of sewage, as if two hundred people had used the facilities without flushing. Barbara saw the offending source through à half-open door at the end of the building: a toilet that had overflowed on to the concrete floor, pooling out into the warehouse for a good fifteen feet.

The German saw the direction of her gaze. 'I have called the plumbers three times these last two days. To no avail, as you see. I am so sorry. It is so unpleasant.' And he hastened forward to shut the door on the lavatory, stepping carefully round the pool of sewage. He clucked at a blanket and a sodden pillow that lay next to a row of dusty filing cabinets to one side of the lavatory. He picked up the former and folded it carefully, placing it on the nearest cabinet. The latter he threw in a rubbish bin next to a wall of cupboards.

He came to rejoin Barbara, taking a Swiss Army knife from his pocket. He said, 'Our sofas are the very best quality. The upholstery is all done by hand. Whether you choose wool or silk –'

'Yeah,' Barbara said. 'I get the idea. Nice stuff. You don't need to uncover it.'

'You do not wish to see?' *Vish*, he said.

'I've seen. Thanks.'

What she'd seen was that the warehouse was like the others in the industrial park. It had one large door that retracted into the metal rafters, allowing the entrance of large lorries. That lorries came and went was evident in the empty rectangle that extended from the door to the far side of the building. In that space, oil stains blotted the concrete floor, looking like continents floating on a grey map of sea.

She walked towards this, making a pretence of examining the furniture beneath the plastic shrouds. The building had no insulation, so it was like a boiler room inside. Barbara felt the sweat trickling down her back, between her breasts, from her neck to her waist.

'Hot,' she said. 'It's not bad for the furniture? Doesn't heat dry it out or something?'

'Our furniture comes from the East, where the weather is far less temperate than England's,' he responded. 'This heat is nothing in comparison.'

'Hmm. I s'pose you're right.' She stooped to examine the oil on the warehouse floor. Four of the stains were old, with small hillocks of dirt looking like depictions of mountains on the global map of the concrete. Three were more recent. In one of them, a single bare foot – man-sized – had left a perfect print.

When Barbara rose, she saw that the German was watching her. He looked perplexed, and his eyes travelled from her to the stains to the furniture. He said, 'Is there something out of order?'

She jerked her thumb at the oil stains. 'You ought to clean that up. Safety hazard. Someone could slip and break a leg, especially if he's running round without shoes on.'

'Yes, of course. Unquestionably,' he replied.

She had no reason to linger, aside from a feeling that she hadn't yet learned all there was to learn. She wished like hell that she knew what she was looking for, but if there was a sign of something dodgy going on in the warehouse, she failed to see it. All she had to go on was a hollow sensation in her gut, a drumlike feeling that she wanted to identify as incompletion. It was instinct and nothing else. Yet how could she act upon it when at the same time she continually questioned Emily Barlow for doing the same? Instinct was all well and good but, somewhere along the line, it needed to be supported by evidence.

But Rudi had left World Wide Tours within minutes of her own departure, she told herself. He'd driven directly here. He'd been admitted into this same building. And if those facts didn't mean something, what the hell did?

She sighed, wondering if the hollow feeling in her stomach was merely a desire for sustenance, vengeance taken for having left a third of her bag of crisps back in the Harwich pub. She rustled round in her shoulder bag and pulled out her notebook. She scrawled the number of the Burnt House Hotel on a spare sheet of paper and passed it over to the German, telling him to phone if he recalled anything pertinent, particularly how a bill of lading from Eastern Imports managed to end up among a dead man's belongings.

He examined the paper solemnly. He folded it precisely in half, then in quarters. He placed it in the pocket of his trousers. He said, 'Yes. If you have seen enough . . . ?' and without waiting for her reply, he made a courtly gesture in the direction of the office.

Once there, Barbara went through the routine: she thanked him for his help. She reminded him of the gravity of the situation. She emphasised the importance of full cooperation with the police.

He said, 'I understand, Sergeant. Already I'm going through my mind in an attempt to locate a connection between this man and Eastern Imports.'

Speaking of connections, she thought. And as she adjusted the strap of her bag so that it drew less heavily on her shoulder, she said, 'Yes. Well,' and went to the door, where she paused. She thought of what she knew of European history, and she drew her question from that. 'Your accent sounds Austrian. Vienna? Salzburg?'

'Please,' he said, a hand pressed to his chest in the offence that Barbara had hoped to rouse in him. 'I am German.'

'Ah. Sorry. It's difficult to tell. Where're you from?'

'Hamburg,' he replied.

Where else? she thought. 'And your name? I'll need it for my report to the DCI.'

'Naturally. It's Reuchlein,' he replied, and he spelled it helpfully. 'Klaus Reuchlein.'

Somewhere in the back of her mind, Barbara could hear Inspector Lynley chuckle.

Chapter Twenty-two

'Kreuzhage says that Reuchlein's paying rent on two flats at *Oskarstraße 15*,' Barbara concluded. 'But all of the flats in the building are small – bed-sits only, with individual kitchens and bathrooms – so if a bloke has money enough, Kreuzhage claims, he might use one flat as a bedroom and another as a sitting room. Especially if he entertains and doesn't much want his guests having to sit on his bed. So the *fact* of two flats shouldn't arouse our suspicions, he warns. Although they may well have aroused Querashi's suspicions, being from Pakistan where most people live – as Kreuzhage put it – more humbly.'

'And he's certain it's Klaus Reuchlein who's renting the flats? *Klaus* and not another first name?'

'It was Klaus, all right.' Barbara drank the last of the carrot juice that Emily had offered her upon their joining forces once again in the DCI's office. She did her best to hide a grimace when her tongue registered the flavour. No wonder people into health foods were so flaming skinny, she thought. Everything they ingested immediately obliterated any desire to ingest more. 'According to him, one of his blokes saw the rental agreement and the signature. Unless Klaus Reuchlein's German for John Smith and there's one under every rock, it's the same bloke.'

Emily nodded. She gazed across her office at the Chinagraph board where the CID team's activities were listed next to an officer's identification number. They'd begun five days ago with activity A1. Barbara saw that they were up to A320.

'We're closing in on him,' Emily said. 'I know it, Barb. This Reuchlein bit just about noose-ties Mr Hot Shot's neck. So much for saving his people from us. Someone ought to be saving his people from him.'

Barbara had stopped by the Burnt House prior to returning to the station. There, she'd picked up the message that *Kriminalhauptkommissar* Kreuzhage had phoned, leaving the cryptic message that 'information pertaining to the sergeant's interests in Hamburg had been obtained'. She'd phoned him at once, munching on a cheese and pickle sandwich provided by Basil Treves who'd had to be discouraged as subtly as possible from hanging about at the doorway of her room, the better to eavesdrop on her conversation. Kreuzhage first confirmed her suspicions that the Hamburg address matched the phone number that Querashi had rung from the Burnt House prior to his death, and when he did so she experienced the same sensation that the DCI was experiencing at the moment: a growing certainty that they were getting close to the truth. But when she combined that growing certainty with what she'd seen at Eastern Imports – which was absolutely nothing out of the ordinary except a broken toilet and a pillow on the floor – her mind filled with questions instead of with answers. Her intuition was telling her that everything she'd heard and seen today was connected in some way, if not to the murder of Querashi then at least to each other. But her brain refused to tell her how.

Belinda Warner entered the room, saying, 'Got the log checked, Guv. I've made a list of everything dodgy. Want it now or at the team meeting this afternoon?'

Emily answered by extending her hand. 'This may give us the rope to hang him,' she told Barbara grimly.

The document was pages long, a computer print-out of nuisances and crimes – petty and otherwise – that had been reported to the Balford police since the beginning of the year. WPC Warner had highlighted in yellow those activities which fell under the categorical description of being dodgy and hence worthy of the DCI's notice. It was these activities that Emily read aloud.

Six stolen cars since January – one per month and all of them accounted for, found in locations that spanned everywhere from the tidal track leading to Horsey Island to the golf course in Clacton-on-Sea. Dead rabbits placed on the front doorstep of the headmistress of the primary school. Four acts of arson: two in rubbish bins placed on the street for the dustbin men, one in a pillbox on the edge of the Wade, one in the graveyard of St John's Church where a crypt had been broken into and defiled with graffiti. Five beach lockers broken into. Twenty-seven burglaries among which were house-breakings, the prising open of a change machine at a launderette, break-ins to numerous beach huts on the sea front, and the theft of the till from a Chinese take-away. A handbag snatching on the pleasure pier. Three Zodiac inflatables taken from East Essex Boat Hire at the Balford Marina, one of them found abandoned at low tide on the south side of Skipper's Island and the other two with their electric motors dead in the middle of the Wade.

Emily shook her head with disgust at this last report. 'If Charlie Spencer gave half the attention to securing his Zodiacs that he gives to reading the racing form from Newmarket, he wouldn't be giving us aggro once a week.'

But Barbara was thinking of what she'd heard and seen on the previous afternoon, what she'd discovered on the previous night, and how both related to one of the reports Emily had just read out from the log. She wondered why she hadn't realised the truth before. Rachel Winfield had revealed it to her. She just hadn't seen its wider application. 'The break-ins in those beach huts, Em. What was nicked from them?'

Emily looked up. 'Come on, Barb. You can't be thinking that the beach hut break-ins are the connection we're looking for?'

'Perhaps not to Querashi's murder,' Barbara agreed, 'but they might fit somewhere. What was taken?'

Emily flipped through several of the print-out's pages. She appeared to read more closely than she had on her first run through the information, but she rejected its import by saying, 'Salt cellars. Pepper mills. Christ, it's nothing but rubbish. Who would want a sampler? Or a badminton set? I can understand lifting someone's Calor gas stove – you could use it or sell it, couldn't you? – but what about this: a framed photograph of Great-gran drooling under a beach umbrella?'

'That's it, then,' Barbara said urgently. 'That's the whole point: selling what's been nicked. That's just the sort of junk people flog at car boot sales, Em. It's the kind of rubbish the Ruddocks were moving from their sitting room to their car yesterday afternoon. *And* it's just like the junk that I found in Trevor Ruddock's backpack on the pier last night. That's what he was doing between the time he was with Rachel Winfield and when he showed up for work at the pier: nicking goodies from the beach huts to supplement the family's income.'

'Which, if you're right –'

'Bet on it.'

'– clears him off our slate.' Emily bent eagerly over the report. 'But what – Goddamn *what* – puts Malik back on it?'

Her telephone rang and she muttered a curse. She lifted the receiver and continued to study the report. She said, 'Barlow here . . . Ah. Well done, Frank. Take him into interrogation. We'll be with you directly.' She replaced the receiver and tossed the report on her desk. 'We finally had a match from SO4 on those fingerprints on Querashi's Nissan,' she told Barbara. 'DC Eyre's just brought our boy in.'

Their boy was locked into the same interrogation room that had previously been occupied by Fahd Kumhar. One look at him told Barbara that they'd managed to track down Querashi's putative lover. He fitted the description perfectly. He was a slight and wiry man, with close-cropped blond hair, a gold lip ring, and ears that displayed studs, hoops, and – hanging from one lobe – a plastic-topped safety pin generally used on an infant's nappy. A skimpy T-shirt with its arms ripped off revealed a bicep tattooed with what at first appeared to be a large lily with the words *gam me* spelled out beneath it. A closer look, however, revealed that the flower's stamen was actually a priapus. Charming, Barbara thought when she saw this. She liked the subtle touch.

'Mr Cliff Hegarty,' Emily said as she closed the door. 'Good of you to come in for some questions.'

'Didn't have much choice, far as I c'n see,' Hegarty said. When he spoke, he displayed the whitest and most perfect teeth Barbara had ever seen. 'Two blokes showed up and asked me if I *minded* coming down to the station. I always like the way cops make it sound like you got some choice when it comes to assisting with their inquiries.'

Emily wasted no time getting down to business. Hegarty's fingerprints, she told him, had been found on the car of a murdered man called Haytham Querashi. The car itself had been found at the crime scene. Would Mr Hegarty explain how they got there?

Hegarty crossed his arms. It was a movement that displayed his tattoo to greater effect. He said, 'I can phone a solicitor if I want.' His lip ring caught the overhead lighting as he spoke.

'You may,' Emily replied. 'But as I haven't even read you the caution, your need for a solicitor intrigues me.'

'I didn't say I need one. I didn't say I want one. I just said I could phone one if I want.'

'And your point is?'

His tongue slid from his mouth and darted, lizardlike in its speed, round his lips. 'I can tell you what you want to know, and I'm willing to do it. But you got to guarantee that my name gets kept away from the press.'

'I'm not in the habit of making anyone guarantees of anything.' Emily sat across the table from him. 'And considering the fact that your prints were found at the scene of a murder, you're in no position to be making deals.'

'Then I don't talk.'

'Mr Hegarty,' Barbara interposed, 'we had the ID on your dabs off SO4 in London. My guess is that you know the score: a London ID means you're sitting on a record of arrest. D'you need it pointed out that it looks a little dicey for a bloke if a felon's prints are associated with a murder and the bloke and the felon are one and the same?'

'I never hurt anyone,' Hegarty said defensively. 'In London or in anyplace else. And I'm not a felon. What I did was between two adults and just because one of the adults was paying, it wasn't like I ever had to force anyone into it. Besides, I was just a kid then. If you coppers paid more attention to stopping real crime and less attention to rousting blokes trying to make a few honest quid by using their bodies, just like a coal miner or a ditch digger uses his, then this country would be a better place to live.'

Emily didn't argue with the creative comparison between manual labourers and male prostitutes. 'Look. A solicitor can't keep your name out of the paper, if that's why you want one. And I can't guarantee that someone from the *Standard* won't be camped on your doorstep when you go home. But the quicker we get you in and out of here, the less likely that possibility is.'

He considered this, lizard-tonguing his lips once again. His biceps tightened and the phallus posing as the lily's stamen flexed suggestively. He finally said, 'It's like this, okay? There's another bloke. Him and me, we been together a while. Four years, to be specific. I don't want him to know about . . . well, about what I'm going to tell you. He already suspects but he doesn't know. And I want to keep it that way.'

Emily consulted a clipboard that she'd picked up from reception on her way downstairs. She said, 'You have a business, I see.'

'Shit. I *can't* tell Gerry you been after me about the Distractions. He already doesn't like me making them. He's always after me to be doing something legit – legit according to his definition of legit – and if he finds out that I've had some aggro from the cops –'

'And I see this business is in the Balford Industrial Estate,' Emily continued unperturbed. 'Which is where Malik's Mustards is. Which is where Mr Querashi was employed. We will, of course, be speaking to every businessman in the industrial estate in the course of our investigation. Does this meet your needs, Mr Hegarty?'

Hegarty blew out the breath he'd taken in order to voice further protest. Clearly, he'd received the implicit message. He said, 'Yeah. It does. Okay.'

'Right then.' Emily briskly switched on the cassette recorder. 'Begin with how you knew Mr Querashi. We *are* correct in assuming you knew him, I take it?'

'I knew him,' Hegarty said. 'Yeah. I knew the bloke all right.'

They'd met in Clacton market square. Cliff had taken to going there when he was caught up at work. He went for the shopping and for what he called: 'A bit of larking about, if you know what I mean. It just gets to be such a drag when you're with one bloke day in and day out. Larking about cuts the bordeom, see? And that's all it was. Just larking about.'

He'd seen Querashi checking out some counterfeit Hermès scarves. He hadn't thought much of him – 'dark meat not gen'rally being my preference' – until the Asian raised his head and gave him the eye. 'I'd seen him round Malik's before,' Hergarty said. 'But I never met him and I never gave him much of a thought. But when he looked at me, I knew what was what. It was a ginger look, and no mistaking. So I went to the toilets. He followed directly. And that's how it started.'

True love, Barbara thought.

He'd thought it would be a one-off, Hegarty explained, which was what he wanted and what he usually got when he went to the market square. But that's not how Querashi had wanted it. What Querashi had wanted was a permanent – if illicit – liaison, and the fact that Cliff was committed elsewhere served the Pakistani's essential needs. 'He told me he was engaged to Malik's daughter, but the deal between them was going to be on paper only. She needed him to be legit. He needed her for the same reason.'

'To be legit?' Barbara interjected. 'Is the Malik girl a lesbian?'

'She's in the club,' Hegarty answered. 'Least, that's what Hayth told me about her.'

Bloody hell, Barbara thought. 'Was Mr Querashi certain that she's pregnant?' she clarified.

'The bird told him herself, he said. She told him straightaway when they met. He figured it was fine because while he could've shagged her, he knew that shagging a woman was going to be a real chore. So if they could pass the kid off as his, all the better. He'd look like he'd done the husband business on his wedding night and if the kid was a boy, he'd be in clover and not have to bother with the wife any longer.'

'And all the time he'd have his assignations with you.'

'That was the plan, yeah. It suited me as well because like I said, having only one bloke day in and day out . . .' He lifted his fingers by way of a shrug. 'This gave me a bit on the side so it wasn't always Gerry, Gerry, Gerry.'

Emily continued taking Hegarty through his paces, but Barbara's mind was in overdrive. The word *pregnant* pulsed in her skull. If Sahlah Malik was pregnant and if Querashi wasn't the father, there could be only one person who was. *Life begins now* took on a whole new meaning. And so did the fact that Theodore Shaw had no alibi for the night of the murder. All he'd needed to do was sail his cabin cruiser from Balford Marina down the main channel so as to round the north point of the Nez and gain access to the area where Haytham Querashi fell to his death. The question was: Could he have taken the boat from the marina without being seen?

'We used the pillbox on the beach,' Hegarty was explaining to Emily. 'No place else was safe enough. Hayth had a place in the Avenues – where he was supposed to live once he and the girl got spliced – but we couldn't go there 'cause Gerry's working nights on it, fixing it up.'

'And on Gerry's work nights, you met Querashi?'

'That's how it was.'

They couldn't meet at the Burnt House for fear that Basil Treves – 'that limp-dick Treves' was how Hegarty identified him – would tell someone, specifically Akram Malik, his fellow town councillor. They couldn't meet in Jaywick Sands because the community was small and word could get back to Gerry, who wasn't about to put up with his lover doing the business with other blokes. 'AIDS and all,' Hegarty added as if he felt the need to explain Gerry's incomprehensible position to the police.

So they met in the pillbox on the beach. And that's where Cliff was, waiting for Querashi, on the night he died.

'I saw it happen,' he said, and his eyes grew cloudy as if he were reliving what he'd seen that night. 'It was dark, but I saw the lights of his car when he got there 'cause he parked near the edge of the cliff. He came to the steps and looked round, like he'd heard something. I could tell that, because I could see his silhouette.'

After a pause at the top of the steps, Querashi had begun his descent. His fall began not five steps from the top. He went down hard and toppled – head over heels over head over heels – all the way to the bottom of the cliff.

'I just froze.' Hegarty had begun to perspire. 'I didn't know what to do. I couldn't believe he'd fallen . . . I kept waiting for him to get up . . . dust himself off. Maybe laugh about it or something, like he was embarrassed. Anyway, that's when I saw the other one.'

'Someone else was there?' Emily said quickly.

'Tucked behind some gorse just at the cliff top.'

Hegarty described the movement he'd seen: a black-garbed figure slipping out of the shrubbery, descending a few steps, removing something from round an iron upright at either side of the concrete steps, then slipping away.

'That's when I figured someone'd done him in,' Hegarty concluded.

Rachel signed her name with a flourish on every line that Mr Dobson ticked off for her. It was so scorching in his office that her thighs were sticking to her chair and droplets of sweat plopped from her eyebrows on to the documents like tears. But she was far from crying. On this day of all days, crying was the last thing on her mind.

She had used her lunch hour to pedal over to the Clifftop Snuggeries. She had pedalled furiously without regard for heat, traffic, or pedestrians, working herself into a lather in order to get to the Snuggeries and Mr Dobson before someone else purchased that one remaining flat. Her spirits were so elevated that she didn't bother to duck her head from the stares of the curious as she usually did when out among strangers. What was their gawping when at last her future was being settled?

She had honestly believed her final words to Sahlah on the previous day. Theo Shaw, she had said, would come round. He wouldn't leave Sahlah to fend for herself. It wasn't in Theo Shaw's nature to desert someone he loved, especially not during a time of need.

But what she hadn't counted on was Agatha.

Rachel had heard the news about Mrs Shaw's stroke within ten minutes of opening the shop that morning. The old woman's condition was the talk of the High Street. Rachel and Connie had no more than uncovered the necklaces and bracelets in the main display case when Mr Unsworth from Balford Books and Crannies popped round with an oversized get well card for them to sign.

'What's this, then?' Connie wanted to know. The card was shaped like an enormous rabbit. It looked more suitable for wishing a child Happy Easter than for sending fond regards to a woman teetering on the edge of death.

Those three words were all Mr Unsworth needed to hold forth on the subject of 'apoplectic seizures', which was what he called Mrs Shaw's stroke. That was typical of Mr Unsworth. He read the dictionary between customers, and he always liked to puff himself up by using words that no one except him understood. But when Connie – not only unintimidated by his vocabulary but also unimpressed with anything that didn't directly relate to swing dancing or selling a bauble to a customer – said, 'Alfie, what'n hell're you squawking about? We got work to do,' Mr Unsworth dropped Mr Chips in favour of a more direct manner of communicating.

'Old Agatha Shaw blew a brain fuse, Con. It happened yesterday. Mary Ellis was with her. They got her in hospital, and she's hooked up to machines every which way to Sunday.'

A few minutes' conversation was enough to glean the details, the most important of which was Mrs Shaw's prognosis. Connie wanted to learn it because of what the elderly woman's continuing health meant to the redevelopment of Balford-le-Nez, a plan in which the owners of the High Street shops had a natural interest. Rachel wanted to learn it because of what Mrs Shaw's present condition could mean to her grandson's future behaviour. It was one thing to be certain that Theo would do his duty to Sahlah under normal circumstances. It was another to expect him to take up the burden of marriage and fatherhood in the midst of a family crisis.

And what Rachel had learned from Mr Unsworth – who'd had it from Mr Hodge at Granny's Bakery, who'd had it from Mrs Barrigan at Sketches, who was Mary Ellis's paternal aunt – was that Mrs Shaw's current situation constituted a family crisis of major proportions. True, she would live. And while this at first made it likely that Theo would indeed come round to accept his manly responsibilities to Sahlah Malik, when Mr Unsworth had expounded upon Mrs Shaw's condition at greater length, Rachel saw things differently.

He used words like *constant care* and *intensive rehabilitation*, words like *devotion of a loved one, thank her lucky stars* and *she's got that boy.* Hearing all this, it didn't take long for Rachel to understand that, whatever his responsibilities were to Sahlah, Theo Shaw faced greater responsibilities to his grandmother. Or at least that was how he was likely to see it.

So all morning long, Rachel had watched the clock. She'd been too much at odds with her mother recently to ask for time to go to the Snuggeries. But the moment the second hand swept past twelve, she was out of the shop and bent over her handlebars, pumping like a cyclist in the *Tour de France.*

'Brilliant,' Mr Dobson said as she affixed her signature to the final line of the purchase agreement. He removed it from the table and waved it in the air, as if drying the ink. He beamed at her and said, 'Brill-i-ant. Very nice indeed. You won't regret the purchase for a moment, Miss Winfield. A tidy investment, these flats are. 'Nother five years and your money will be doubled. Just see if it won't. Clever of you to snap up this last one before someone else got to it, 'f you ask me. But I expect you're a clever girl about most things, aren't you?'

He went on to chat about mortgage advice, building societies, and investment officers at the local Barclays, Lloyds, or NatWest. But she wasn't really listening. She nodded and smiled, wrote the down-payment cheque that would decimate her account at the Midland, and thought of nothing but the need to complete this piece of business as quickly as possible so that she could ride over to Malik's Mustards and be there to offer Sahlah her support when the news of Agatha Shaw's condition reached her ears.

Doubtless, Sahlah would interpret this news exactly as Rachel herself had done, seeing it as an immovable impediment to a life with Theo and their baby. There was no telling what sort of tailspin this piece of information would send Sahlah into. And since people in tailspins of worry and confusion were liable to make hasty decisions which they later regretted, it only made sense that she – Rachel Lynn Winfield – be in the immediate vicinty should Sahlah begin to think it necessary to do something rash.

Despite the need for haste, however, Rachel couldn't help taking just a minute to have a peek at the flat. She knew she'd be living in it soon enough – *they'd* be living in it soon enough – but still it seemed like such a dream actually to have the flat at last that she knew the only way to make the dream real would be to walk from room to room, to open cupboards, and to admire the view.

Mr Dobson parted with the key, saying, ''F course, 'f course,' and adding, '*Naturellement, chère mademoiselle,*' with a waggle of his eyebrows and a leer that, Rachel knew, were supposed to demonstrate that he wasn't the least put off by her face. She ordinarily would have responded curtly to a display of such spurious *bonhomie*, but this afternoon she felt only good will for her fellow man, so she shook back her hair to unveil the worst of her deformities, thanked Mr Dobson, clutched the key in her palm, and took herself off to number 22.

There wasn't much to it: two bedrooms, one bathroom, a sitting room, a kitchen. It was on the ground floor, so a tiny terrace directly off the sitting room overlooked the sea. Here, Rachel thought placidly, they would sit in the evenings, with the baby lying in its pram between them.

Looking out of the sitting-room window, Rachel drew in a happy breath and pictured the scene. Sahlah's *dupattā* rustled in the North Sea breeze. Rachel's skirt moved gracefully as she rose from her chair to adjust the blanket over the chest of the sleeping infant. She cooed at him – or her, possibly – and gently removed a miniature thumb from the cherub mouth. She caressed the softest little cheek she could ever remember touching, and she brushed her fingers lightly against hair that was . . . What colour? she wondered. Yes, indeed. What colour *was* his hair, or her hair, for that matter?

Theo was blond. Sahlah was deeply brunette. Their child's hair would be a combination of the two, as would his skin be a combination of Theo's fair complexion and Sahlah's olive tones.

Rachel was simultaneously enchanted by and utterly taken with the thought of this miracle of life that Sahlah Malik and Theo Shaw had created between them. In that moment, she realised that she could hardly wait the months that she knew she *had* to wait to see the form that this miracle would actually take.

Suddenly, she understood how very *good* she – Rachel Lynn Winfield – was and could continue to be for Sahlah Malik. She was more than a friend to her. She was a tonic. Exposed to her on a daily basis in the weeks and months until her delivery, Sahlah could only grow stronger, happier, and more optimistic about the future. And everything – *everything* – would work out in the end: Sahlah and Theo, Sahlah and her family, and most of all Sahlah and Rachel herself.

Rachel clasped this knowledge to herself with growing bliss. Oh, she had to dash to Sahlah at the mustard factory to share it all with her. She only wished she had wings so that she could fly there.

The ride across town was gruelling in the fiery sunlight, but Rachel hardly noticed. She pedalled along the sea route at a furious clip, swigging back tepid water from her bottle whenever the slope of the seaside esplanade allowed her to coast. She thought not at all of her discomfort. She thought only of Sahlah and of the future.

Which bedroom would Sahlah like to have? The front one was larger, but the back one faced the sea. The sound of the sea might lull the baby. It might lull Sahlah as well, in those moments when the responsibilities of motherhood weighed too heavily upon her shoulders.

Would Sahlah like to do the cooking for the three of them? Her religion placed restrictions on her diet, and Rachel herself was easier than easy when it came to adjusting to that sort of thing. So it made sense for Sahlah to cook for them. Besides, if Rachel were to be the breadwinner while Sahlah remained home with the baby, Sahlah would probably want to cook their meals as Rachel had seen Wardah Malik do for Sahlah's dad. Not, of course, that Rachel was going to act the part of anyone's dad, least of all the dad of Sahlah's baby! That would be Theo. And Theo *would* act that role eventually. He would do his duty and meet his obligations, in time and when his gran was recovered.

''Cording to the doctors, she could live for years,' Mr Unsworth had told them that morning. 'She's a real battleship, is Mrs Shaw. A bird like that is one'n a hunnerd. And all's the more better for us, right? She won't die till Balford's back on its feet. You wait and see, Con. Things're looking up.'

So they were. Every which way, things were looking up. And as Rachel made the final left turn into the old industrial estate at the north end of the town, she felt near to bursting with the need to pour her happiness like balm over Sahlah's worries.

She climbed off her bike and leaned it against a half-full skip that was open to the air. This was redolent with the smell of vinegar, apple juice, and rotting fruit, and it buzzed with flies. Rachel flailed her hands round her head to drive the pesky insects away. She took a last gulp of water, settled her shoulders, and made for the factory door.

Before she could get to it, however, it opened as if in anticipation of her arrival. Sahlah stepped outside. She was followed immediately by her father, not garbed all in white, which was usual for him during his working hours in the factory's experimental kitchen, but dressed in what Rachel thought of as mufti: a blue shirt and tie, grey trousers, and nicely polished shoes. A luncheon date between father and daughter, Rachel concluded. She hoped her news about Agatha Shaw didn't spoil Sahlah's appetite. But then again, no matter if it did. Rachel had other news that would revive it.

Sahlah saw her at once. She was wearing one of her fancier necklaces and at the sight of Rachel, her hand went up to grip it lightly as if it were a talisman. How often had she seen that gesture in the past? Rachel wondered. It was the primary sign of Sahlah's anxiety, and Rachel hurried forward to put this at rest.

'Hello, hello,' she called out gaily. 'Beastly hot again, isn't it? When d'you think the weather's going to break? That fog bank's been out there in the sea for ages, and all we need's some wind to blow it this way and we'll be cooled off. D'you have a minute, Sahlah? 'Lo, Mr Malik.'

Akram Malik said his good afternoon formally, the way he always said it, just like he was addressing the Queen. And he neither studied her face nor looked away from it hastily the way other people did, which was one of the reasons that Rachel liked him. He said to his daughter, 'It will take a moment to fetch the car, Sahlah. Speak to Rachel while I do so.'

When he had walked off, Rachel turned to Sahlah and impulsively hugged her. She said in a low voice, 'I've done it, Sahlah! Yes, indeed. I've done it. Everything's taken care of now.'

Beneath her hand, she felt the tension immediately drain out of Sahlah's stiff shoulders. Her friend's fingers dropped from the fawn stone pendant of the necklace, and she swung to face Rachel.

'Thank you,' she said earnestly. She reached for Rachel's hand and lifted it as if she meant to kiss her knuckles in gratitude. 'Oh, *thank* you. I couldn't believe you'd abandon me, Rachel.'

'I'd never do that, would I? I told you so a thousand times. We're friends till the end, you and me. The minute I heard about Mrs Shaw, I knew how you'd feel, so I went out and did it. Have you heard what happened?'

'The stroke? Yes. One of the town councillors phoned Dad about it. That's where we're going: to the hospital to pay our respects.'

Theo would doubtless be there, Rachel realised. She felt an interior niggle at this news, but she couldn't put a name to what it was. She said stoutly, 'That's real nice of your dad. But that's what he's like, isn't he? And that's why I'm sure –'

Sahlah went on as if Rachel hadn't spoken. 'I told Dad they'd probably not let us near her room, but he said that's not the point. We're going to the hospital to show our support to Theo, he said. He was generous with his help when we started using computers in the factory, and this is how we must respond to his present troubles: in friendship. The English form of *lenā-denā*. That's how Dad explains it.'

'Theo'll appreciate that,' Rachel said. 'And even if this stroke of his gran's means he can't do his duty by you now, Sahlah, he'll remember how good you acted in going to the hospital to visit. So when his gran's all better, you'll be together, you and Theo, and he'll do his duty like a proper dad. Just wait and see.'

Sahlah had still been holding on to Rachel's hand. But now she released it. 'Like a proper dad,' she repeated. Her fingers climbed to seek the pendant once more. It was the finishing piece on one of her least successful necklaces, an undefined mass of what looked like limestone but was – according to Sahlah's explanation – a fossil from the Nez. Rachel had never much liked it and had always been glad that Sahlah had never offered it for sale at Racon. The piece was far too heavy, she thought. People didn't want their jewellery to hang upon them like a guilty conscience.

'Sure,' she said. ''Course, things're bad at the moment, so he won't be seeing the future too clear. That's why I moved fast without talking to you. Once I heard about what happened to Mrs Shaw, I saw that Theo couldn't really do right by you while he was getting her back on her feet. But he *will* do right by you eventually, and until he does, you need someone to take care of you and the baby, and that someone's me. So I went to the Clifftops –'

'Rachel, stop,' Sahlah said quietly, and she'd taken to clutching her pendant so hard that Rachel could see that her hand was shaking. 'You said everything was taken care of. You said . . . Rachel, haven't you arranged . . . ? Got me the information . . . ?'

'I've got the flat, is what I've done,' Rachel said joyfully. 'I just signed the papers. I wanted you to be the first to know because of what's happened to Mrs Shaw. She's going to need someone to take care of her, see. *Constant care* is what they're saying. And you know Theo: he'll prob'ly dedicate himself to her till she's all recovered. Which means he won't be taking you away. He *could* do that, of course, but I sort of don't think he will, do you? She's his gran and she's raised him, right? And he'll see his first duty to her. So I got the flat so you have a place for you and the baby till Theo's got himself all clear on what his second duty is. Which is you. The two of you, that is.'

Sahlah closed her eyes as if the sun were suddenly too bright. At the end of the lane, Akram's BMW came rumbling towards them. Rachel considered whether she ought to announce her purchase of the flat to Sahlah's dad. But she rejected that plan in favour of letting her friend find the right time to break the news. She said, 'You'll have to hold out a month or six weeks till everything goes through, Sahlah: the building society, the loan, you know. But we c'n use the time to look at furniture and buy our linen and stuff like that. Theo c'n go with us if he wants. That way, the two of you c'n choose things that you c'n use later, when you're with him instead of with me. See how it'll all work out?'

Sahlah nodded. 'Yes,' she whispered. 'I do see.'

Rachel was delighted. 'Good. Oh, *good*. So when d'you want to start looking? There's some decent shops in Clacton, but I expect we might do better for ourselves if we went to Colchester. What d'you think?'

'Whatever's best,' Sahlah said. Her voice was still low and her eyes were on her approaching father. 'You decide, Rachel. I'll leave it to you.'

'You're seeing it my way now, and you won't regret it,' Rachel said confidently. She put her head nearer Sahlah's as Akram braked the car a few feet away and waited for his daughter to join him. 'You c'n tell Theo when you see him, now. The pressure's off everyone. So everyone can do what's completely right.'

Sahlah took a step towards the car. Rachel stopped her with a final remark. 'Ring me when you're ready to start looking, okay? For furniture and linen and dishes and things. You'll want to break the news to everyone, and I know that's likely to take a bit of time. But when you're ready, we'll start our shopping. For the three of us. Okay, Sahlah?'

Her friend finally looked away from her father, meeting Rachel's gaze with eyes that seemed somehow unfocused, as if her mind were a million miles away. Which, of course, it would be, Rachel realised. There were so many plans to make.

'Ring me?' Rachel repeated.

'Whatever's best,' Sahlah replied.

'I knew it'd look like an accident to everyone if I didn't do something to change the picture,' Hegarty continued.

'So you moved the body into the pillbox and you vandalised his car. That way, the police would know it was a murder,' Barbara concluded for him.

'I couldn't think of anything else,' he said frankly. 'And I couldn't come forward. Gerry'd know, then. And I'd've been cooked. It's not like I don't *love* Gerry, see. It's just that sometimes the thought of having one bloke for the rest of my life . . . Shit, it feels like a prison sentence, if you know what I mean.'

'And how d'you know that Gerry isn't already in the picture?' Barbara asked. Theo Shaw aside, here was yet another English suspect. She avoided Emily Barlow's eyes.

'What d'you . . . ?' Hegarty suddenly saw where the question was heading. He said quickly, 'No. It wasn't Ger on the clifftop. No way. He doesn't know about me and Hayth. He *suspects*, but he doesn't know. And if he did, he wouldn't've offed Hayth. He would've just sent me packing.'

Emily pushed past this diversion. 'Was the figure you saw on the clifftop a man or a woman?'

He couldn't tell, he said. It was dark, and the distance from the pillbox to the clifftop was too great. So as to age, as to sex, as to race or identity . . . he just didn't know.

'The figure didn't come down to the beach to check on Querashi?'

No, Hegarty said. Whoever it was, the person had hurried north along the top of the cliff, in the direction of Pennyhole Bay.

Which was, Barbara thought with triumph, more support for the theory of a killer arriving by cabin cruiser. 'Did you hear a boat's engine that night?'

He didn't hear anything but his own heart slamming against his eardrums, Hegarty said. He waited five minutes beside the pillbox, trying to collect himself and trying to think. He was in such a sweat that he wouldn't've noticed a nuclear explosion ten yards away.

Once he'd gathered his wits – three minutes, maybe five – he did what had to be done which took – maybe – quarter of an hour. Then he scarpered. 'Only boat engine I heard was my own,' he said.

'What?' Emily asked.

'The boat,' he said. 'That's how I got there. Gerry's got a motorboat that we use at the weekends. I always took that when I was meeting Hayth. I came up the coast from Jaywick Sands. It's more direct, that way, more exciting as well. And I like it to build. The excitement. You know.'

So here was the boat that had been heard in the water off the Nez that night. With a sinking heart, Barbara wondered if they were back at square one. She said, 'While you were waiting for Querashi, did you hear anything then? Another boat's motor? Large and running low?' He hadn't, he said. But the figure up on the top of the cliff would have been there before him anyway. The trap was set when Haytham got there, because Hegarty hadn't seen anyone near the steps until after he fell.

Emily said, 'We have an ID on you at the Castle Hotel with Mr Querashi, at an affair called . . . ?' She glanced at Barbara.

'Leather and Lace,' Barbara told her.

'Right. That ID doesn't square with your story, Mr Hegarty. Why did the two of you end up at a public dance in the Castle Hotel? That makes no sense if you were so intent upon keeping your relationship a secret from your lover.'

'Ger doesn't do the scene,' Hegarty said. 'He never did. How far's that hotel from here, anyway? Forty minutes' drive if you hit it good. More if you're going from Jaywick or Clacton. I didn't think anyone I know'd see me there and spill it to Gerry. And it was a work night in the Avenues for Ger, so I knew he'd never know I was gone. We were safe at the Castle, me and Hayth.' But having said that much, his eyebrows drew together and he frowned.

'Yes?' Emily asked him quickly.

'I thought for a moment . . . But it's nothing 'cause he didn't see us, so he never knew. And no way was Haytham going to tell *him*, of all people.'

'What are you talking about, Mr Hegarty?'

'Muhannad.'

'Muhannad Malik?'

'Yeah. Right. We saw him at the Castle as well.'

Jesus, Barbara thought. How much more convoluted could the case become? She said, 'Muhannad Malik's homosexual as well?'

Hegarty guffawed, fingering the nappy pin dangling from his earlobe. 'Not *at* the hotel like in *at* the hotel. We saw him afterwards, when we were leaving. He drove right in front of us, crossed over the road, and took a right towards Harwich. It was one in the morning and Haytham couldn't make out what Muhannad was doing in that part of the world in the middle of the night. So we followed him.'

Barbara saw Emily's hand tighten round the pencil she'd been holding. Her voice, however, betrayed nothing more of what she was feeling. 'Where did he go?'

He went, Hegarty said, to an industrial estate on the edge of Parkeston. He parked at one of the warehouses, disappeared inside for thirty minutes or so, and then left again.

'And you're sure it was Muhannad Malik?' Emily pressed.

There was no mistaking that fact, Hegarty told them. The bloke had been driving his turquoise Thunderbird, and it had to be the only car of its kind in Essex. 'Only that's right, isn't it?' Hegarty suddenly added. 'He wasn't driving that car when he left. He was driving a lorry. He pulled out of the warehouse in the lorry, in fact. And that's the last we saw of him.'

'You didn't follow him farther?'

'Hayth didn't want to risk it. It was one thing for us to see Muhannad. It was another if Muhannad spotted us.'

'And when was this exactly?'

'Last month.'

'Mr Querashi never mentioned it again?'

He shook his head.

Barbara could tell from the very intensity of her focus that the DCI was charged up to follow this bit of information. But treading along the Muhannad Trail ignored a signpost that Hegarty had already painted. For the moment, Barbara shoved to the back of her mind the three words that had set her thoughts roiling. *In the club* couldn't negate the presence of another suspect.

'This Ger,' she said. 'Gerry DeVitt.'

Hegarty, who'd even begun to relax in their presence, seeming to enjoy his moment of importance in the investigation, was at once wary. His eyes betrayed this, becoming watchful and alert. 'What about him? You're not thinking that Gerry ...? Look, I already said. He didn't know about me and Hayth. Which is why I didn't want to talk to you lot in the first place.'

'Why you *say* you didn't want to talk to us,' Barbara said.

'He was working on Hayth's house that night,' Hegarty insisted. 'Ask anyone on First Avenue. They would've seen the lights. They would've heard the banging. And I already told you what was what: if Ger found out about me and Hayth, he would've ended it with me. He wouldn't've gone after Hayth. That's not his way.'

'Murder,' Emily said, 'is generally not anyone's way, Mr Hegarty.'

She concluded the interview formally, giving the time and switching the tape recorder off. She stood, saying, 'We may be in touch again.'

'You won't ring me at home,' he said in request. 'You won't come to Jaywick.'

'Thank you for cooperating,' Emily said in reply. 'DC Eyre will take you back to work.'

Barbara followed Emily into the corridor, where the DCI spoke in a low terse voice, revealing that motive or not, Gerry DeVitt had not displaced her number one suspect. 'Whatever it is, Muhannad's taking it to the factory. He's boxing it there, and he's stowing those boxes with everything else being shipped out. He knows when orders are being assembled for shipment. Christ. That's part of his job. All he has to do is to time his own shipments with those going out from the factory. I want that place searched, top to bottom, inside and out.'

But in Barbara's mind, the interrogation of Hegarty could not be so easily dismissed. Thirty minutes with the bloke had raised at least half a dozen questions. And the answer to none of them was Muhannad Malik.

They passed reception on their way to the stairs. Barbara saw Azhar talking to the WPC on duty there. He looked up as she and Emily came within his field of vision. Emily saw him as well, saying obscurely to Barbara, 'Ah. Mr Devotion to his People. All the way from London to show us what a good Muslim can be.' She stopped behind the reception desk and spoke to Azhar. 'A little early for your meeting, aren't you? Sergeant Havers won't be available until late this afternoon.'

'I've come not for our meeting but to collect Mr Kumhar and return him to his home,' Azhar said. 'His twenty-four hours of custody are nearly at an end, as I'm certain you know.'

'What I know,' Emily replied tartly, 'is that Mr Kumhar hasn't requested your services as a chauffeur. And until he does, he'll be returned to his home in the same way he was taken from his home.'

Azhar's glance shifted to Barbara. He seemed aware of the sudden sea-change in the investigation as evidenced by the DCI's tone. She didn't sound like an officer who was worried any longer about the possibility of another community uprising. Which made her much less likely to compromise.

Emily didn't give Azhar a chance to reply. She turned away, caught sight of one of her team approaching, and said, 'Billy, if Mr Kumhar's had his lunch and his wash, take him home. Collect his work papers and his passport when you get there. I don't want that bloke disappearing on us till we can sort through everything he had to say.'

Her voice carried. Azhar clearly heard it. Barbara spoke with some care as they climbed the stairs. 'Even if Muhannad's at the bottom of all this, you don't think Azhar's – Mr Azhar's – involved, Em? He's come from London. He didn't even know about the killing before that.'

'We don't know a thing about what he knew or when he knew it. He came here posing as some sort of legal expert when, for all we know, he could be the brains behind Muhannad's game. Where was *he* on Friday night, Barb?'

Barbara knew the answer to that very well since, from behind the shelter of the curtains in her bungalow, she'd watched Azhar and his daughter grilling *halal* lamb kebabs on the lawn behind the Edwardian house in which they occupied the ground-floor flat. But she couldn't say this without betraying her friendship with them. So she said, 'Except . . . well, he's seemed a decent sort of bloke in our meetings.'

Emily gave a sardonic laugh. 'He's decent all right. He's got a wife and two kids that he ditched in Hounslow so he could set up house with some English tart. He gave her a brat, and then she walked out on him, this Angela Weston, whoever she is. God knows how many other women he's doing the business with in his spare time. He's probably planting half-breed bastards all over town.' She laughed again. 'Right, Barb. What a decent bloke our Mr Azhar is.'

Barbara's step faltered on the stairs. She said, 'What? How d'you –?'

Emily stopped above her. She glanced back and said, 'How did I what? Suss out the truth? I put a call out on him the first day he was here. I got the report when I got the ID on Hegarty's fingerprints.' Her look sharpened. Too perceptively, Barbara thought. 'Why, Barb? What's the truth about Azhar got to do with the price of petrol? Aside, of course, from confirming my belief that not one of these yobbos can be trusted half an inch.'

Barbara wondered about the question. She didn't much want to consider the true answer. She said, 'Nothing. Nothing really.'

'Good,' Emily replied. 'Let's take on Muhannad.'

Chapter Twenty-three

'**Y**ou have yourself a cuppa, Mr Shaw. I'll be right outside at the station, just where I am on every shift. If she takes a turn, I'll hear the machines start bleating.'

'Actually, I'm fine, Sister. I don't need –'

'No argument, young man. You look dead as a ghoul. You were here half the night, and you won't do anyone a bit of good if you don't start taking better care of yourself.'

It was the day nurse's voice. Agatha recognised it. She didn't have to open her eyes to know who was speaking to her grandson, which was just as well, because opening her eyes felt as if it would take too damned much effort. And besides, she didn't want to look at anyone. She didn't want to have to see the pity in their faces. She knew well enough what they'd be seeing to inspire that pity: a wreck of a woman, a virtual carcase, all shrivelled up on one side, her left leg useless, her left hand clawed into a dead bird's talon, her head tilted, her mouth and one eye following that tilt, and the disgusting drool following them both.

'All right, Mrs Jacobs,' Theo said to the nurse, and Agatha realised that he *did* sound tired. He sounded both exhausted and unwell. And at this thought she felt a moment of panic clutching at her lungs, making it suddenly difficult to breathe. What if something happened to Theo? she wondered feverishly. She hadn't once considered the possibility, but what if he didn't take care of himself? What if he fell ill? Or was in an accident? What, then, would become of her?

She felt his nearness from the scent of him: that clean odour of soap and the faint lime smell of the astringent he used. She felt the mattress of the hospital bed depress slightly as he leaned over her.

'Gran?' he whispered. 'I'm going down to the cafeteria, but don't you worry. I won't be long.'

'You'll be long enough to have yourself a decent meal,' Sister Jacobs said curtly. 'If you're back here in less than an hour, lad, I'm sending you off again. See if I don't.'

'What a task master she is, eh, Gran?' Theo said in some amusement. Agatha felt his dry lips press against her forehead. 'I'll be back in sixty-one minutes, then. You have a good rest.'

Rest? Agatha queried incredulously. How was she supposed to rest? When she closed her eyes, all she could see in her mind's vision was the hideous spectacle she herself presented: a misshapen shell of the vital woman she once had been, now helpless, immobile, catheterised, dependent. And when she tried to dismiss that vision in order to imagine the future instead, what she pictured in its place was what she had seen and scorned a thousand times, driving along the Esplanade below the Avenues in Balford, where that line of nursing homes overlooked the sea. There, the discarded ancients tottered, clinging to their Zimmer frames for support. Their backbones permanently curved like the mark of a question no one had the courage to ask, they shuffled along the pavement, an army of the forgotten and infirm. She'd been aware of these relics of humanity since her girlhood. And since her girlhood she'd sworn to herself that she'd end her own life before she was reduced to becoming one of their numbers.

Only now she didn't want to end her own life. She wanted to take her life back, and she knew that she needed Theo to do it.

'Now, now, sweetie, something tells me you're wide awake under those eyelids of yours.' Sister Jacobs was hanging over the bed. She wore a man's heavy deodorant, and when she perspired – which was copiously and often – the odour of spice wafted off her body like steam rolling off boiling water. Her hands smoothed back Agatha's hair. A comb went through it, caught on a tangle, pulled insistently, then gave up the effort. 'Lovely grandson you've got, Mrs Shaw. Such a love, he is. I've a daughter who'd like to meet your Theo. Available, is he? I ought to invite her round for a cuppa when I take my break. I think they'd get on, my Donna and your Theo. What d'you think of that? Would you like a nice granddaughter-in-law, Mrs Shaw? She could help you in your recovery, my Donna.'

Absolutely not, Agatha thought. Some peabrained tart with her claws into Theo was exactly what she did *not* need. What she needed was escape from this place, along with peace and quiet to gather her strength for the upcoming battle of convalescence. Peace and quiet were scarce commodities when one was lying in a hospital bed. In a hospital bed, what one received were probings, proddings, prickings, and pity. And she wanted none of that.

Pity was the worst. She hated pity. She herself felt it for no one, and she wanted no one to feel it for her. She'd rather experience others' aversion – which was what she'd felt for those doddering bits of human detritus on the Esplanade – than find herself a paralysed pilgarlic, the sort of person people spoke *about* rather than *to*, when they were in her presence. Aversion implied fear and horror, which could be used ultimately to one's own advantage. Pity implied the other's superiority, which Agatha had never had to face in her life. And she would not face it now, she swore.

If she allowed anyone to gain ascendancy over her, she would be defeated. Defeated, she would see her plans for Balford's future quashed. Nothing would remain of Agatha Shaw upon her death save whatever memories her grandson had and chose – when the time was right, of course – to pass on to future generations. But how could she rely upon Theo's devotion to her memory? He'd have other responsibilities then. So if her memory were to be established, if her life were to be given meaning before that life ended, she would have to do it herself. She would have to put the pieces and the players in position. Which was what she'd been in the course of doing when the damnable stroke supervened, knocking her plans awry.

Now, if she wasn't careful, that greasy, unwashed Malik monster would make his move. He'd done as much when her council seat had to be filled, sliding in to replace her, like a water moccasin slithering into a river. How much more he'd do once he got the word that she'd been laid out by another stroke.

Balford would be looking at more than Falak Dedar Park if Akram Malik had the opportunity to set his plans in motion. Before the town knew what was happening to it, he'd have a minaret in the market square, a gaudy mosque in place of their lovely St John's Church, and nasty-smelling tandoor cookeries on every street corner from the Balford Road right down to the sea. And then the real invasion would come: scores of Pakis with their scores of lice-ridden children, half of them on the dole, the other half illegal, and all of them polluting the culture and the traditions among which they'd chosen to live.

They want a better life, Gran, was how Theo would explain it to her. But she didn't need his soft-hearted and wrong-headed explication of what was so patently obvious. They wanted *her* life. They wanted the life of every English man, woman, and child. And they would not rest, desist, or retreat until they had it.

Especially Akram, Agatha thought. That bloody, nasty, miserable Akram. He spun a treacly line about friendship and brotherhood. He even acted the part of community conciliator with his ludicrous Gentlemen's Cooperative. But the talk and the actions didn't fool Agatha. They were subterfuges. They were ways to lull the sheeplike populace into a sense that the meadow was clear and safe for their grazing and not scrutinised every second by a pack of wolves.

But she would show him that she was wise to his ways. She would rise from this hospital bed like Lazarus, every inch of her an indomitable force that Akram Malik – with all his plans – could not hope to conquer.

Agatha realised that Sister Jacobs had gone. The odour of spice had dissipated, leaving in its place the scent of medicines, of plastic tubing, of her body's secretions, of the polish on the floor.

She opened her eyes. Her mattress was raised so that she lay at a modest angle rather than flat on her back. This was a marked improvement over the hours immediately following her stroke. Then, she'd had nothing but blurry acoustic ceiling tiles to look at. Now, at least, despite the fact that the sound had been muted and Sister Jacobs had forgotten to increase it upon her departure, she had the television to watch. A film was showing in which a frantic far-too-pretty-to-be-believable husband wheeled his hugely but still attractively pregnant even-prettier wife into a casualty ward for the delivery of their child. It was supposed to be a comedy, Agatha guessed, from their slapstick behaviour and the expressions on their faces. What a risible thought that was indeed. No woman *she* knew had ever found the act of childbirth a laughing matter.

With an effort, she managed to turn her head an inch, which was enough for her to see the window. Through it, a patch of sky the washed-out colour of a kestrel's tail told her that the heat was continuing unabated. She couldn't feel the effects of the outside temperature, however, as the hospital was one of the few buildings within twenty miles of Balford that was actually air conditioned. She would have celebrated that fact . . . had she only been at the hospital to visit someone – someone deserving of disaster, for instance. Indeed, she could have named twenty people more deserving of this disaster than she. She thought about this point. She began to name those twenty people. She entertained herself by assigning each one of them his own personal, private torment.

So she was unaware at first that someone had entered her room. A gentle cough told her that she had a visitor.

A quiet voice said, 'No, do not move, Mrs Shaw. Let me, please.' Footsteps came round the bed, and suddenly she was face to face with her soul's black adversary: Akram Malik.

She made an inarticulate noise, which was meant to be 'What do you want? Get out. Get *out*. I'll have none of your oleaginous gloating,' but which – strangled by the convoluted messages her damaged brain was sending to her vocal chords – came out only as a garbled mishmash of incomprehensible groans and howls.

Akram gazed at her intently. Doubtless, she thought, he was taking inventory of her condition, trying to assess how far he might have to push her so that she'd topple into her grave. That would clear the way for him to actuate his insidious plans for Balford-le-Nez. She said, 'I'm not about to die, Mr Wog. So wipe that hypocritical look of sympathy off your face. You have about as much sympathy for me as I'd have for you in similar circumstances.' But what she emitted from her mouth was the rising and falling of sounds alone, with nothing to separate them or give them definition.

Akram looked round the room and walked out of her line of sight for a moment. Panic-stricken, she thought he intended to switch off the machines that whirred and softly beeped just behind her head. But he returned with a chair, and he sat.

He was carrying, she saw, a bunch of flowers. He laid these on the table next to the bed. He removed from his pocket a small leather book. He set it upon his knee but didn't open it. He lowered his head and began to murmur a stream of words in his Pakistani mumbo-jumbo.

Where was Theo? Agatha thought desperately. Why wasn't he here to spare her from this? Akram Malik's voice was soft enough, but she wasn't about to be deceived by its tone. He was probably putting a hex on her. He was working black magic, engaging in voodoo, or doing whatever his sort did to defeat their enemies.

She wasn't about to put up with it. She said, 'Stop that muttering! Stop it at once! And get out of this room immediately!' But her form of language was as indecipherable to him as his was to her, and his only response was to lay a brown hand upon her bed, as if he were extending her a blessing that she did not need of him, much less want.

Finally, he raised his head again. He began to speak once more, only this time she understood him perfectly. And his voice was so compelling that she found she could do nothing but hold his gaze with her own. She thought dimly, Basilisks are just like this, they impale you with their steely eyes. But still she didn't look away.

He said, 'I heard only this morning of your trouble, Mrs Shaw. How deeply sorry I am. My daughter and I wished to pay our respects. She waits in the corridor – my Sahlah – because we were advised that only one of us at a time could come into your room.' He removed his hand from her bed and laid it on the leather book on his knee. He smiled and went on. 'I thought of reading from the holy book. Sometimes I find my own words inadequate for prayer. But when I saw you, the words came of themselves without any effort. At one time, I would have wondered about that and sought a greater meaning from it. But I've long since come to accept that the ways of Allah are most often beyond my comprehension.'

What *was* he on about? Agatha wondered. He'd come to gloat – there could be no mistake about *that* – so why didn't he get to the point and have done with it?

'Your grandson Theo has been a source of considerable help to me during this last year. Perhaps you know this? And for some time I've contemplated the best manner in which I could repay him for his kindness to my family.'

'Theo?' she said. 'Not Theo. My Theo. Don't hurt Theo, you nasty man.'

He interpreted this conglomeration of sounds, it seemed, as her expression of a need for clarification. He said, 'He brought Malik's Mustards into the present and into the future with his computers. And he was the first to stand by my side and involve himself in the Gentlemen's Cooperative. He has a vision not unlike my own, your grandson Theo. And I see in your current misfortune a way that I can finally reciprocate his acts of friendship.'

In your current misfortune, Agatha repeated in her mind. And she knew with certainty what he was about. Now was the moment he meant to sweep in like a raptor, making the kill. Just like a hawk, he'd chosen his time with an eye for the damage it could do to the victim. And she was without a single defence.

Damn his gloating, she thought. Damn his slimy, unctuous ways. Damn his pretence of saintliness. And damn most of all –

'I have long known your dream to redevelop our town and to restore it to its former beauty. Having been struck down a second time now, you must have great fears of your dream coming to nothing.' He put his hand back on the bed again. But this time it covered her own. Not her good hand, she noticed, which she could have flinched away from him. But her talon-hand that was incapable of movement. Clever of him, she thought bitterly. How wise to emphasise her infirmities before laying out his plans to destroy her.

He said, 'I intend to give Theo my full support, Mrs Shaw. The redevelopment of Balford-le-Nez shall proceed as you planned it. To the last detail and to your design, your grandson and I will make this town come to life once more. And that's what I've come to tell you. Rest easily now and concentrate your efforts on returning to health so that you may live many years among us.'

And then he bent and touched his lips to her deformed, ugly, crippled hand.

And, having no language in which to reply, she wondered how on earth she was going to be able to tell someone to wash it for her.

Barbara was trying like the devil to keep her mind where it belonged, which was on the investigation. But it kept drifting off insistently, bounding in the direction of London, specifically to Chalk Farm and Eton Villas, and even more specifically to the ground-floor flat of a yellow brick converted Edwardian house. At first she told herself that there had to be a mistake. Either there were two Taymullah Azhars in London or the information supplied by the Met's SO11 was inaccurate, incomplete, or out-and-out false. But the key facts on the Asian in question, supplied by London Intelligence, were among the facts that she already knew about Azhar. And when she read the report herself – which she managed to do upon her return to Emily's office with the DCI – she had to admit that the description being supplied by London was identical in many respects to the picture she already had. The home address of the subject was the same; the age of the child was correct; the fact that the child's mother was not in the picture also matched with what the report presented. Azhar was identified as a professor of microbiology, which Barbara knew he was, and his involvement with a London group called Asian Legal Awareness and Aid was certainly consistent with the depth of knowledge that he'd demonstrated over the past several days. So the Azhar in the London report had to be the Azhar she knew. Only the Azhar she knew didn't appear to be the Azhar she thought she knew. Which brought everything about him into question, especially his standing in the investigation.

Christ, she thought. She needed a fag. She was desperate for one. And while Emily groused about taking yet another tedious and time-consuming phone call from her superintendent, Barbara dashed into the lavatory and lit up hungrily, sucking on the tube of tobacco like a scuba diver running out of air.

Suddenly, a great deal about Taymullah Azhar and his daughter began to make sense to her. Among the puzzle pieces beginning to take on definition were Hadiyyah's eighth birthday party to which Barbara had been invited as the only guest; a mother ostensibly gone to Ontario but never revealing her whereabouts with so much as a postcard to her only child; a father who never spoke the word *wife* and never spoke at all of the mother of his child unless the subject was forced upon him; an absence of evidence in the ground-floor flat that an adult woman had lived there anytime recently. No emery board or nail polish left lying about, no discarded handbag, no sewing, no knitting, no *Vogue* or *Elle*, no remnants of a hobby like watercolour painting or flower arranging. Had Angela Weston – mother of Hadiyyah – ever lived in Eton Villas at all? Barbara wondered. And if she hadn't, exactly how long did Azhar expect to keep up the pretence of Mummy-on-holiday in place of the truth, which appeared to be Mummy-very-much-on-the-run?

Barbara wandered to the lavatory window and gazed at the small car park below. DC Billy Honigman was escorting a freshly washed, groomed, and dressed Fahd Kumhar to a panda car. As she watched, they were approached by Azhar. He spoke to Kumhar. Honigman warned him off. The detective constable stowed his passenger in the back seat of his vehicle. Azhar walked to his own car, and when Honigman took off, he followed, making no secret that he was doing so. He'd come to escort Fahd Kumhar home, as promised. Obviously, that's what he intended to do.

A man of his word, Barbara thought. A man of more than one word, in fact.

She considered the answers he'd given her in response to her questions about his culture. She saw now how they applied to him. He'd been cut off from his family just as he declared Querashi would have been had his homosexuality come into the open. He'd been so cut off from his family that his daughter's existence was not acknowledged.

They were – the two of them – an island unto themselves. No wonder he'd only too well understood and been able to expound upon the meaning of being an outcast.

Barbara processed all this with a fair degree of rational thinking. But she wasn't up to processing what this information about the Pakistani man meant to her personally. She told herself that it couldn't mean anything at all to her personally. She didn't, after all, have a personal relationship with Taymullah Azhar. True, she played the role of friend in his daughter's life, but when it came to defining a role in *his* life . . . She really didn't have one.

So she didn't understand why she felt somehow betrayed by the knowledge that he'd deserted a wife and two children. Perhaps, she concluded, she was feeling the betrayal that Hadiyyah would feel should she ever learn the truth.

Yes, Barbara thought. Doubtless that was it.

The lavatory door opened and Emily bounded inside, striding directly to one of the wash basins. Hastily, Barbara squashed her cigarette on the sole of her trainer and surreptitiously tossed the dog end out of the window.

Emily's nose twitched. She said, 'Jesus, Barb. Are you still on the weed after all these years?'

'I was never one to ignore my addictions,' Barbara confessed.

Emily turned on the tap and thoroughly soaked a paper towel beneath it. She applied this to the back of her neck, oblivious of or uncaring about the water that dribbled down her spine and dampened her tank top. She said, 'Ferguson,' as if the super's name were an execration. 'He has his interview for the assistant chief constable's job in just three days and he expects an arrest in the Querashi case before he faces the panel, thank you very much. Not that he's doing a single bloody thing to help move the investigation forward. Unless threatening me with Howard bloody Presley and dogging every step I take now constitute lending a helping hand. But he'll be happy enough to bow to the applause if we bring someone in without more public bloodshed. Fuck it. I despise that man.' She wet a hand and shoved it back through her hair. She turned to Barbara.

It was time to take on the mustard factory, she announced. She'd applied for a search warrant from the magistrate, and he'd come through in record time. Apparently, he was as anxious as Ferguson to bring the case to a close without another battle in the streets.

But there was a detail unrelated to the factory and to Emily's conviction about illegal activity going on within it, and Barbara wanted to pursue it. She couldn't ignore the fact that Sahlah Malik was pregnant, nor could she overlook the import this fact had in the case. 'Can we make a stop at the marina, Em?'

Emily glanced at her watch. 'Why? We know the Maliks don't have a boat, if you're hanging on to an arrival at the Nez by water.'

'But Theo Shaw has. And Sahlah's pregnant. And Theo got that bracelet off Sahlah. He's got a motive, Em. He's got it loud and clear, no matter what Muhannad and his mates are up to at Eastern Imports.'

Theo also didn't have an alibi, while Muhannad did have one, she wanted to add. But she held her tongue. Emily knew the score, no matter her determination to run Muhannad Malik to ground for one offence or another.

Emily frowned as she considered Barbara's request. She said, 'Right. Okay. We'll check it out.'

They set off in one of the unmarked Fords, making a turn into the High Street, where they saw Rachel Winfield teetering towards Racon Original and Artistic Jewellery from the direction of sea. The girl was red in the face. She looked as if she'd spent her morning in the bicycling third of an Iron Woman event. She paused to take a breather next to the signpost indicating that Balford Marina was just to the north. She waved happily as the Ford passed her. If she was guilty of something, she certainly didn't look it.

Balford Marina was perhaps a mile along the lane that ran perpendicular to the High Street. Its lower end comprised one-quarter of the little square whose opposite side was Alfred Terrace, where the Ruddock home stood in semi-squalor. It passed Tide Lake and a caravan park and, ultimately, the circular mass of a Martello tower that had once been used to defend the coast during the Napoleonic Wars. The lane ended at the marina itself.

This consisted of a series of eight pontoons at which sailing boats and cabin cruisers were tied in the placid water of a tidal bay. At the far north end, a small office abutted a brick building that housed lavatories and showers. Emily drove in this direction and parked next to a tier of kayaks above which hung a faded sign advertising *East Essex Boat Hire*.

The owner of that business also acted as harbour master, a limited line of employment considering the relatively small size of the harbour in question.

Emily and Barbara interrupted Charlie Spencer in the midst of a perusal of the racing form from Newmarket. 'You catch anyone yet?' were his first words when he looked up, saw Emily's identification, and shoved his gnawed pencil behind one ear. 'I can't sit here nights with a shotgun, you know. What's my taxes going for if I can't get service from the local constab. Eh? You tell me.'

'Improve your security, Mr Spencer,' Emily responded. 'I don't expect you leave your house unlocked when you aren't at home.'

'I got a dog takes care of the house,' he retorted.

'Then you need another to take care of your craft.'

'Which one of those is the Shaws'?' Barbara asked the man, indicating the lines of moored boats that lay motionless in the harbour. There were, she saw, very few people about, despite the hour of the day and the heat that encouraged travel on the sea.

'*Fighting Lady*,' he replied. 'The biggest one at the end of Pontoon Six. Shouldn't keep it here, the Shaws, you know. But it's convenient for them and they pay up regular and always have done, so who'm I to complain, eh?'

When they asked him why the *Fighting Lady* didn't belong in the Balford Marina, he said, 'Tide's the problem,' and went on to explain that anyone who wished to use a boat that large would be better served with a mooring that wasn't so dependent on the tide. At high water there wasn't a problem. Plenty of water to keep a large boat afloat. But when the tide went out, the bottom of the cruiser rested in the mud, which wasn't good for it since the cabin and the boat's machinery bore down on the infrastructure. 'Shortens the life of the craft,' he explained.

And the tide on Friday night? Barbara asked him. The tide between ten p.m. and midnight, for example?

Charlie set aside his racing paper to consult a booklet next to the till. Low, he told them. *Fighting Lady* – not to mention every other large pleasure craft in the marina – wasn't going anywhere on Friday night. 'Each one of them boats needs a good eight foot of water to manoeuvre in,' he explained. 'Now as to my complaint, Inspector . . .' And he turned to take issue with the DCI on the efficacy of training guard dogs.

Barbara left them in discussion. She went outside and wandered in the direction of Pontoon Six. *Fighting Lady* was easy enough to spot. It was the largest craft in the marina, gleaming with white paint, its woodwork and its chromium fixtures shrouded in protective blue canvas. When she saw the boat, Barbara realised that even if the tide had been high, there was no way that Theo Shaw or anyone else could have moored the craft anywhere close to shore. Mooring it off the Nez would have meant swimming to the beach, and it didn't seem likely that someone bent upon murder would begin his evening's task with a dip in the sea.

She headed back towards the office, studying the other craft in the harbour. Despite the marina's size, it served as a landing spot for a bit of everything: motor boats, diesel fishing boats, and even one snappy Hawk 31 – winched out of the water – that was called the *Sea Wizard* and looked as if it belonged somewhere along the coast of Florida or Monaco.

In the vicinity of the office, Barbara saw the craft that Charlie hired out. In addition to motor boats and kayaks resting on tiered racks, ten canoes and eight Zodiac inflatables sat on the pontoon. Two of these last were occupied by sea gulls. Other birds circled and called in the air.

Looking at the Zodiacs, Barbara recalled the list of dodgy activities that Belinda Warner had compiled from the police log. Previously, her interest had been directed towards the beach hut break-ins and how they applied to Trevor Ruddock and his alibi for the murder night. But now she saw that the dodgy activities had another point of interest as well.

She walked on to the narrow pontoon and examined the Zodiacs. Each, she saw, was equipped with a set of paddles, but each could also be fixed up with a outboard motor, a set of which were positioned on racks near the end of the pontoon. However, one of the inflatables was already in the water with a motor attached, and when Barbara turned the key to this, she discovered the motor was electric, not petrol, and virtually noiseless. She examined the blades hanging into the water. They extended downward less than two feet.

'Right,' she murmured when she made this assessment. 'Too bloody right.'

She looked up when the pontoon bobbed. Emily had joined her, one hand shading her eyes. From the expression on her face, Barbara could tell that the DCI had reached the same conclusion as her own.

'What did the police log say?' Barbara asked rhetorically.

Emily responded anyway. 'He's had three Zodiacs nicked without his knowledge. All three were later found round the Wade.'

'So how rough would it be, Em, pinching a Zodiac at night and manoeuvring it through the shallows? If whoever took it also returned it before morning, no one would be any the wiser. And it doesn't look like Charlie's security is much to speak of, does it?'

'Sure as hell doesn't.' Emily turned the direction of her gaze until she was looking northward. 'Balford Channel's just on the other side of that spit of land, Barb, just where you can see that fishing hut. Even at low tide there'd be water in the channel. And enough water here in the harbour to get to it as well. Not enough for one of the larger boats. But for an inflatable . . . ? No problem.'

'Where does the channel lead?' Barbara asked.

'Directly along the west side of the Nez.'

'So someone could have taken a Zodiac up the channel and round the north point of the Nez, beaching anywhere along the east side and walking south to the steps.' Barbara followed the direction of Emily's gaze. On the other side of the little bay which sheltered the marina, a series of cultivated fields rose to the back of an estate whose main building's chimneys were plainly visible. A well-used path etched the land from the estate along the northern perimeter of the fields. It ran eastward and ended at the bay, where it turned south and followed the coast. Seeing this walkway, Barbara asked, 'Who lives in that house, Em? The big one with all those chimneys.'

'It's called Balford Old Hall,' Emily said. 'It's where the Shaws live.'

'Bingo,' Barbara murmured.

But Emily resolutely turned from such a facile solution to the equation of motive-means-opportunity. She said, 'I'm not ready to tie a bow on that package. Let's get on to the mustard factory before someone gives Muhannad the word. If,' she added, 'Herr Reuchlein hasn't already done so.'

Sahlah spent her time in the hospital corridor watching the door to Mrs Shaw's room. The nurse had informed them that only one person at a time was allowed to see the patient, and she was relieved that this injunction prevented her from having to see Theo's grandmother. At the same time, she felt enormous guilt at her own relief. Mrs Shaw was ill – and desperately so if the glimpse Sahlah had had of the hospital machinery in her room was any indication – and the tenets of her religion directed her to minister in some way to the woman's need. Those who believed and did good works, the Holy Qur'aan instructed, would be brought into the gardens underneath which rivers flowed.

And what better work could be done than to visit the sick, especially when the sick took the form of one's enemy?

Theo, of course, had never directly stated the fact that his grandmother hated the Asian community as a whole and wished them ill individually. But her aversion to the immigrants who'd invaded Balford-le-Nez was always the unspoken reality between Sahlah and the man she loved. It had divided them as effectively as had Sahlah's own spoken revelations about her parents' plans for her future.

Sahlah knew at heart that the love between Theo and herself had been defeated long before its inception. Tradition, religion, and culture had acted in conjunction to vanquish it. But having someone to blame for the impossibility of a life with Theo was a temptation that had sought to beguile her from the first. And how easy it was to twist the words of the Holy Qur'aan now, moulding them into a justification of what had happened to Theo's grandmother.

Whatever good befalleth thee (O man) it is from Allah, and whatever of ill befalleth thee it is from thyself.

She could thus stoutly proclaim that Mrs Shaw's current state was the direct result of the loathing, bias, and prejudice that she fostered in herself and encouraged in others. But Sahlah knew that she could also apply those same words from the Qur'aan to herself. For ill had befallen her as surely as it had befallen Theo's grandmother. And just as surely, the ill was a direct result of her own selfish and misguided behaviour.

She didn't want to think about it: how the ill had happened and what she was going to do to bring it to an end. The reality was that she didn't know what she was going to do. She didn't even know where to begin, despite the fact that she was sitting in the corridor of a hospital where activities euphemistically labelled 'Necessary Procedures' were probably performed all the time.

Just for a moment with Rachel, she'd felt relief. When her friend had said, 'I've gone and done it,' such a weight had lifted from Sahlah's shoulders that she'd actually thought she might become airborne. But when it had become apparent that going and doing it had meant acquiring a flat into which Sahlah knew she would never move, despair had descended upon her forcefully. Rachel had been her only hope of ridding herself of the overt mark of her sin against her religion and her family, doing it in perfect secrecy and with minimum risk. Now, she knew, she was going to have to strike out on her own. And she couldn't even begin to determine the first move she had to make.

'Sahlah? *Sahlah?*'

She started at the sound of her name, said in the same hushed tone that he'd used in the pear orchard on those nights that they'd met. Theo stood to her right, stopped dead in his progress to his grandmother's room, one hand holding a can of Coke that was beaded with moisture.

She reached without thinking for the pendant she wore, as much to cover it up from him as to hold it in a form of taking sanctuary. But he'd seen the fossil, and he obviously drew a conclusion from the fact that she was wearing it because he came to the bench on which she was sitting, and he sat down next to her. He set his Coke on the floor. She watched him do it. Then she kept her eyes on the can's aluminium top.

'Rachel told me, Sahlah,' he said. 'She thinks –'

'I know what she thinks,' Sahlah whispered. She wanted to tell Theo to leave or at least to stand across the corridor and pretend their conversation was nothing save an expression of concern over his grandmother's condition on her part and a polite offering of gratitude for that concern on his. But the very nearness of him after the long weeks of not seeing him was like an intoxicant to her. Her heart wanted more and more of it even as her mind told her that the only way she could serve herself and ultimately survive was to accept less.

'How could you *do* it?' he asked. 'I've been asking myself that question over and over since I talked to her.'

'Please, Theo. It doesn't help to talk about it.'

'Doesn't help?' He asked the question bitterly. 'That's fine with me because I don't much care if it doesn't help. I loved you, Sahlah. You said you loved me.'

The top of the Coke can shimmered in her vision. She blinked quickly and kept her head lowered. Around them, the work of the hospital went on. Orderlies hurried by with trolleys in front of them, doctors made their rounds, nurses carried small trays of medication in to their patients. But she and Theo were divided from them as effectively as if they'd been encased in glass.

'What I've been wondering,' Theo said, 'is how long it took you to decide you loved Querashi instead of me? What was it – a day, a week, two? Or maybe it didn't happen at all because, like you kept telling me, your people's ways don't make love necessary when it comes to marriage. Isn't that how you put it?'

Sahlah could feel the blood beating fiercely behind the birthmark on her cheek. There was no way that she could make him understand when his understanding demanded a truth from her that she would not part with.

'I've also been wondering how it happened and where. You'll forgive me for that, I hope, because you'll understand that for the last six weeks I've thought of practically nothing else but how and where it *didn't* happen between the two of us. It could have, but it didn't. Oh, we came close enough, didn't we? On Horsey Island. Even that time in the orchard when your brother –'

'Theo,' Sahlah said. 'Please don't do this to us.'

'There isn't an us. I thought there was. Even when Querashi showed up – just like you said he was going to show up – I thought there still was. I wore that fucking bracelet –'

She flinched from the term. He wasn't, she saw, wearing the bracelet now.

'– and I kept thinking, She knows she doesn't have to marry him. She knows she can refuse to do it because there's no way in hell that her dad will make her marry anyone against her will. Her dad's Asian, yes. But he's English as well. Maybe more English than she is, really. But the days went by and turned into weeks and Querashi stayed. He *stayed* and your father brought him round to the Cooperative and introduced him as his son. "In a few weeks, he joins our family," he told me. "He takes our Sahlah as his bride." And I had to listen and offer best wishes and all the time I wanted to –'

'No!' She couldn't bear to hear the admission. And if he thought her refusal to listen meant her love for him was dead, that was just as well.

'Here's how it was at night,' Theo said. His words were terse. Their sound limned his bitterness. 'During the day, I could forget about everything and just work myself into a stupor. But at night I had nothing but the thought of you. And while I couldn't sleep and I couldn't much eat, I could deal with that because all along I thought you would be thinking of me as well. She'll tell her dad tonight, I kept thinking. Querashi will leave. And then we'll have time, Sahlah and I, time and a chance.'

'We never had either. I tried to tell you that. You didn't want to believe me.'

'And you? What did you want, Sahlah? Why did you come to me those nights in the orchard?'

'I can't explain it,' she whispered hopelessly.

'That's the thing about games. No one can ever bloody explain them.'

'I wasn't playing a game with you. What I felt was real. Who I was was real.'

'Right. Fine. And I'm sure that was true for you and Haytham Querashi as well.' He started to rise.

She stopped him, her hand reaching out and closing on the bare flesh of his arm. 'Help me,' she said, looking at him finally. She'd forgotten the exact blue-green of his eyes, the mole next to his mouth, the fall of his soft blond hair. She was startled by his sudden proximity and frightened by her body's response to the simple sensation of her hand's touching him. She knew she had to release him, but she couldn't. Not until he'd committed would she let him go. He was her only chance. 'Rachel won't, Theo. Please. Help me.'

'Get rid of Querashi's kid, you mean? Why?'

'Because my parents . . .' How could she possibly explain?

'What about them? Oh, your dad'll probably be bloody well cheesed off when he hears you're pregnant. But if the kid's a boy, he'll adjust quick enough. Just tell him you and Querashi were so hot for each other that you couldn't wait until after the ceremony.'

Beyond the rank injustice of his words – born however they were from his own suffering – their sheer brutality forced the truth from her. 'This isn't Haytham's baby,' she said. And then she dropped her hand from his arm. 'I was already two months pregnant when Haytham came to Balford.'

Theo stared at her, disbelieving. Then she could see him trying to bleed the full extent of the truth from an agonised study of her face. He said, 'What the hell . . . ?' But the question died before he finished it. He merely repeated the opening part, saying, 'Sahlah, what the *bloody* hell . . . ?'

'I need your help,' she said. 'I'm begging for your help.'

'Whose is it?' he asked. 'If it isn't Haytham's . . . Sahlah, whose is it?'

'Please help me do what I need to do. Who can I phone? Is there a clinic? It can't be in Balford. I can't take that chance. But in Clacton . . . ? There must be something in Clacton. Someone there who can help

475

me, Theo. Quietly and quickly so my parents don't know. Because if they find out, it will kill them. Believe me. It will kill them, Theo. And not only them.'

'Who else?'

'Please.'

'Sahlah.' His hand closed fiercely on her upper arm. It was as if he sensed in her tone everything that she could not bring herself to say. 'What happened? That night. Tell me. What happened?'

You're going to pay, he'd said, the way all whores pay.

'I brought it on myself,' she said brokenly, 'because I didn't care what he thought. Because I told him I loved you.'

'Oh, *God*,' he whispered, and his hand fell from her arm.

The door to Agatha Shaw's hospital room opened, and Sahlah's father stepped out. He closed it carefully behind him. He looked bewildered to see his daughter and Theo Shaw in earnest conversation. But his face warmed in an instant, perhaps with the certainty that Sahlah was doing her part to bring herself into the garden underneath which the rivers flowed.

He said, 'Ah. Theo. I'm so very happy that we won't have left the hospital without seeing you. I've just spoken to your grandmother, and I've given her my assurance – as a friend and town councillor – that her plans for Balford's renaissance will go forward unchanged and unimpeded in any way.'

Next to her, Theo rose. Sahlah did likewise. She ducked her head modestly, and in doing so, she hid from her father's vision the telltale sign of her birthmark's painful throbbing.

'Thank you, Mr Malik,' Theo said. 'That's good of you. Gran will more than appreciate your kindness.'

'Very good,' Akram said. 'And now, Sahlah my dear, shall we be on our way?'

Sahlah nodded. She cast Theo a fleeting look. The young man had gone pale beneath his light tan, and he was gazing from Akram to her and back to Akram as if he sought but failed to find something to say. He was her only hope, and like every other hope she'd once harboured about love and life, he was fading from her.

She said, 'It was lovely talking to you again, Theo. I hope your grandmother recovers quickly.'

He said, 'Thank you,' stiffly.

Sahlah felt her father take her arm, and she allowed herself to be led towards the lift at the end of the corridor. Each step seemed to take her away from safety. And then Theo spoke.

'Mr Malik,' he said.

Akram stopped, turned. He looked pleasantly attentive. Theo rejoined them.

'I was wondering,' Theo said. 'I mean, forgive me if I'm out of place because I don't pretend to know exactly what's right in this situation. But would you very much mind if I took Sahlah to lunch one day next week? There's a . . . well, there's a jewellery exhibition – it's at Green Lodge where they do the summer courses – and as Sahlah makes jewellery, I thought she might like to see it.'

Akram cocked his head and considered the request. He looked at his daughter as if gauging her readiness for such an adventure. He said, 'You are a good friend of the family, Theo. I can see no objection, if Sahlah wishes to go. Do you, Sahlah?'

She raised her head. 'Green Lodge,' she said. 'Where is that, Theo?'

His reply was as even as was his expression. 'It's in Clacton,' he told her.

Chapter Twenty-four

Yumn kneaded the small of her back and used her foot to kick the trug ahead of her in her assigned rows of her mother-in-law's loathsome vegetable garden. Sullenly, she watched Wardah cultivating two rows over – hovering over a vine of chillis with the devotion of a newlywed wife to her husband – and she wished upon the older woman everything foul that was humanly possible, from sun stroke to leprosy. It was approximately two million bloody degrees, working here among the plants. And to accompany the unbearable, deadly temperature, which that morning had been declared a record high by the BBC Breakfast News, the insect life in Wardah's garden was making a feast of more than the tomatoes, peppers, onions, and beans upon which they normally sated themselves. Gnats and flies buzzed round Yumn's head like malicious satellites. They landed on her perspiring face, while spiders worked their way beneath her *dupattā* and tiny green caterpillars dropped from vine leaves on to her shoulders. She flailed her hands and raged, attempting to drive the flies in her mother-in-law's direction.

This torment was yet another offence committed by Wardah against her. Any other mother-in-law, filled with what ought to have been gratitude at having been presented with two grandchildren in such rapid succession and so soon after her son's marriage – would have insisted that Yumn rest herself beneath the walnut tree at the edge of the garden where even at this moment her children – two *male* children – rolled their toy lorries along the miniature thoroughfare created by a space between the old tree's roots. Any other mother-in-law would have recognised that a woman on the verge of another pregnancy should not even be *relaxing* in the blazing sunlight, let alone should she be toiling in it. Hard manual labour wasn't good for a woman in her childbearing years, Yumn told herself. But try sharing that bit of information with Wardah, Wardah the Wonder who'd spent the entire day of her son Muhannad's birth washing every window of the house, cooking dinner for her husband, and scrubbing the dishes, the pots, and the kitchen floor before she squatted in the larder to deliver the baby. No. Wardah Malik was unlikely to see temperatures rising to thirty-five degrees as anything other than a minor inconvenience, just as she'd seen the hose pipe ban.

Every sensible person in the country had met the annual restriction on the use of hose pipes by limiting what was planted in his garden. But this, of course, was not Wardah's way. Wardah Malik had planted as usual, row upon row upon endless nasty row of fragile seedlings that she tended to every afternoon. The hose pipe banned because of the drought, she watered every loathsome plant by hand, hauling water by the bucketful from the outdoor tap near the kitchen.

She used two buckets for this exercise. While she was engaged in filling one bucket and carrying it to the edge of the vegetable patch, she expected Yumn to sling the other bucket round the plants. But prior to that daily exercise, there was cutting, pruning, picking, and weeding to be done. Which was what they were engaged in at the moment. And Wardah expected Yumn's help in this as well. Curse her to eternal, burning, scalding, skin-bubbling torment!

Yumn knew what truly lay behind Wardah's demands upon her: from cooking to cleaning to slaving in the garden. Wardah sought to punish her for doing so easily that which she herself had been nearly incapable of doing at all. It hadn't taken much investigation to discover that Wardah and Akram Malik had been married ten years before Wardah had been able to produce Muhannad. And another six years had passed before she'd been able to present her husband with Sahlah. That was sixteen years of effort resulting in only two children. Given the same amount of time, Yumn knew that she would be giving Muhannad more than a dozen babies and most of them males. So when Wardah Malik looked upon her son's wife, she saw her superior. And only by enslavement was she able to ensure that Yumn knew and remained in her place.

Curse her to everlasting, freezing, rat-infested, starvation-ridden torment, Yumn thought again as she hacked at the rock-hard earth that the sun had baked into a bricklike consistency, despite her daily ministrations of water. She aimed her hoe at a Gibraltar-shaped clod beneath one of the tomato plants, and as she drove it into the earth, she pretended the clod was Wardah's bum.

Whap went the hoe. The old witch rears back in surprise. *Whap. Whap.* The nasty crone howls in pain. Yumn smiled. *Whap. Whap. Whap.* Yumn draws first blood on the cow's backside. *Whap. Whap. Whap. WHAP.* Wardah falls to the ground. *WHAPWHAPWHAPWHAP.* She's at Yumn's mercy with her hands uplifted. She begs for a release that only Yumn can give her, but *WHAPWHAPWHAPWHAPWHAP*, Yumn knows that her time of triumph has come and with her mother-in-law at last defenceless, subdued, a slave to the killing whimsy of her own son's wife, a veritable –

'Yumn! Stop it at once! Stop!'

Wardah's cries broke into her thoughts as if disturbing a dream, and Yumn woke from them just as abruptly as a dreamer wakes. She found that her heart was pounding ferociously and the sweat was dripping from her chin on to the front of her *qamis*. The handle of the hoe had become slick from the wetness of her palms and her sandal-shod feet were buried in the earth she'd managed to rearrange in her attack. Dust was rising on every side of her and settling against her streaming face and her sweat-drenched clothes like a gauzy veil.

'What are you doing?' Wardah demanded. 'You stupid girl! Look what you've done!'

Through the haze of soil sent upwards by the flailing of her hoe, Yumn saw that she'd hacked down four of her mother-in-law's prized tomato plants. They lay like storm-felled trees. And their fruit was thoroughly pulped into crimson pellets, completely beyond redemption.

As, obviously, was Yumn herself. Wardah threw her secateurs into her trug and advanced upon her daughter-in-law angrily. 'Is there nothing you can do without destroying it?' she demanded. 'What do I ask of you that you don't ruin?'

Yumn stared at her, feeling her nostrils flare and her lips move into a sullen line.

'You're thoughtless, lazy, and completely selfish,' Wardah declared. 'Believe me, Yumn, had your father not paid us handsomely to take you off his hands, you'd still be at home tormenting your mother instead of exasperating me.'

This was the longest speech that Wardah had ever made in her presence, and Yumn was at first startled to hear her normally docile mother-in-law say so much. But her surprise quickly dissipated as her muscles coiled with a desire to strike the other woman across the face. *No one* was to speak to her like that. No one was *ever* to speak to the wife of Muhannad Malik without deference, subservience, and solicitousness in her voice. Yumn was gathering her wits to reply, when Wardah spoke again.

'Clean up this mess. Take those plants to the compost heap. Repair the row that you've ruined. And do it at once before I act in a way that I'll later regret.'

'I'm not your servant.' Yumn threw down her hoe.

'Indeed you're not. A servant with your talent for doing nothing would have been dismissed within a week. Pick up that hoe and do as I say.'

'I shall tend to my children.' Yumn began to stride towards the walnut tree, where her two boys – oblivious of the altercation between their mother and grandmother – zoomed their toy lorries along the old, exposed roots.

'You will *not*. You will do as I say. Get back to work at once.'

'My boys need me.' Yumn called to the children: 'Lovely ones, shall your *ammī-gee* play with you now?'

The boys looked up from their game. Wardah ordered, 'Anas. Bishr. Go into the house.'

Confused, the children hesitated.

Yumn said gaily, 'Here comes *Ammī-gee* to play with her boys. What shall we play? And where shall we play it? Or shall we walk to Mr Howard's for Twisters? Would you like that, darling boys?'

Their faces lit with the promise of ice cream. Again, Wardah intervened.

'Anas,' she said sternly, 'you heard what I said. Take your brother inside the house. Now.'

The elder boy grabbed his little brother by the hand. Together, they darted out from under the tree and made a dash for the kitchen door.

Yumn whirled back to her mother-in-law. 'Witch!' she cried. 'You filthy cow! How *dare* you take my children and –'

The slap came hard. And so unexpectedly that Yumn was rendered speechless. For an instant she forgot who she was and where she was. She was thrust back to her girlhood, hearing her father's shouting, and feeling the solid force of his knuckles as he railed against the impossibility of finding her a husband without paying a dowry ten times what she was worth. And in that instant of forgetting, she surged forward. She grabbed Wardah's *dupattā*, and as it slipped from her head to her neck, she jerked its two ends savagely, crying out and pulling until she had the older woman forced to her knees.

'Never,' she cried. 'You never, *never* . . . I who give your son his sons . . .' And once Wardah was on her knees, Yumn shoved her shoulders towards the earth.

She began to kick: at the neatly turned earth along the vegetable row, at the plants, at Wardah. The ruined tomatoes, she began to hurl. And as she did so, she shrieked, 'I am ten times the woman . . . Fertile . . . Willing . . . Desired by a man . . . While you . . . *You* . . . With your talk of talent for doing nothing . . . You . . .'

She was so intent upon finally venting her fury and rage that she didn't at first hear the shouting. She didn't know anyone had come into the garden until she felt her arms pinned behind her back and her body dragged away from the crumpled form of her husband's mother.

'Bitch! *Bitch*! Are you stark mad?'

The voice was so enraged that for an instant she didn't recognise it as Muhannad's. He shoved her roughly to one side and went to his mother, saying, '*Ammī*, are you all right? Has she hurt you?'

'I hurt *her*?' Yumn demanded. Her *dupattā* had fallen from her head and shoulders. Her hair had come unbraided. The arm of her *qamīs* was ripped out. 'She hit me. For nothing. That bloody cow –'

'Shut up!' Muhannad roared. 'Get in the house. I'll deal with you directly.'

'Muni! She struck your wife in the face. And for what? Because she's jealous. She –'

He shot to his feet. There was a burning intensity in his eyes that Yumn had never seen before. She retreated hastily.

She said in a quiet, more afflicted tone, 'Would you have your wife struck? By anyone?'

He cast her a look of such aversion that she recoiled. He turned back to his mother. He was helping her to her feet, murmuring and gently brushing at her clothes, when Yumn turned from them and hurried into the house.

Anas and Bishr were cowering in the kitchen, both of them in the far corner on the floor behind the table. But she didn't stop to soothe their fear. She went straight to the bathroom upstairs.

Her hands were trembling like a palsy victim's, and her legs felt as if they wouldn't continue to bear her weight. Her garments were plastered to her body by sweat, soil crusted in their every fold, the juice of ripe tomatoes staining the material like blood. The mirror showed her that her face was filthy and her hair – caught up with spider's webs, caterpillars, and leaves – looked worse than an unwashed gypsy's.

She didn't care. Right was on her side. No matter *what* she did, right was always on her side. And one look at the mark of Wardah's blow upon her face was going to confirm that.

Yumn washed the dirt from her cheeks and forehead. She bathed her hands and her arms. She patted her face upon a towel and examined herself once again in the mirror. She saw that the mark of Wardah's blow had faded. She renewed it by slapping herself repeatedly, stinging her flesh with the full force of her palm until her cheek was crimson.

Then she went to the bedroom that she shared with Muhannad. From the corridor she could hear the two of them downstairs: Muhannad and his mother. Wardah's voice was back to that patently false tone of subservient womanhood which she reserved for speaking to either her son or her husband. Muhannad's voice was . . . Yumn listened carefully. She frowned. She thought. He sounded unlike he'd ever sounded, even in their most intimate moments when they first looked upon their infant sons together.

She caught a few words. *Ammī-jahn . . . never to hurt . . . didn't intend . . . the heat . . . apologise and make reparation to you.*

Apologise? Make reparation? Yumn crossed the corridor and went into the bedroom. She slammed the door so hard that the windows shook in their frames. Let them try to make her apologise. She slapped her face again. She scored her cheeks until her nails drew blood. He would see how ill his beloved mother had used his wife.

When Muhannad entered the room, she had combed her hair and returned it to its braid. She'd done nothing else. She was sitting at her dressing table, where the light was the best for him to see the damage his mother had done to her.

'What would you have me do when your mother attacks me?' she demanded before he could speak. 'Am I to let her kill me?'

'Shut up,' he said. He walked to the chest of drawers and did what he never did in his father's house. He lit a cigarette. He stood facing the chest rather than her, and as he smoked, he leaned one arm against the wood and with the other he pressed his fingers to his temple. He'd returned home from the factory unexpectedly before noon. But rather than join the women and children for a midday meal, he'd spent the next few hours on the telephone, both making and receiving calls in a hushed and urgent voice. Obviously, he was still preoccupied with his business affairs. But he shouldn't be so preoccupied that he failed to note what his wife had suffered. While his back was turned, Yumn pinched her cheek so hard that tears came to her eyes. He *would* see how she had been abused.

'Look at me, Muni,' she demanded. 'Look at what your mother did and then tell me I'm not to defend myself.'

'I said, shut up. I meant it. Shut. Up.'

'I won't shut up till you look at me.' Her voice rose, changed key. 'I was disrespectful, but what would you have me do when she wants to harm me? Shouldn't I act to protect myself? To safeguard the child that – even at this moment – I might be carrying?'

This reminder of her most treasured capability roused Muhannad to take the action she wanted. He turned. A swift glance in the mirror told her that her cheek was mottled and blood-caked appropriately.

She said, 'I made a simple mistake among her tomatoes – an easy enough thing to do in this heat – and she began to beat me. In my condition –' Here, she rounded her hands beneath her stomach to encourage him to believe what he would. 'Am I to do nothing to protect the unborn? Do I let her vent all of her rage and her jealousy until –'

'Jealousy?' he snapped. 'My mother is no more jealous of you than –'

'Not of me, Muni. Of you. Of us. And of our children. And our future children. I do what she could never do. And she makes me pay for it by treating me worse than she would a servant.'

He observed her from across the room. Surely, she thought, he could see the truth of what she claimed. He could see the truth of it in her damaged face and upon her body, the body that gave him the sons he desired, quickly and effortlessly and repeatedly. No matter her unappealing looks and a figure best left hidden beneath the draperies that her culture required her to wear, Yumn had the single quality that all men prized in a wife. And Muhannad would want to safeguard it.

'What am I to do?' Yumn asked, casting her eyes downward with humility. 'Tell me, Muni. And I promise you: I'll do as you tell me.'

She knew she had won when he came to stand in front of the dressing-table's bench. He touched her hair, and she knew that afterwards – when they'd been to each other what they were meant to be – he would go to his mother and inform her that she was never again to make a single demand of the mother of his sons. He wrapped her braid round and round his wrist, and Yumn knew that he would pull her head back and find her mouth and take her even in the terrible heat of this terrible day. And after that –

He jerked her head back brutally.

'Muni!' she cried. 'You're hurting me.'

He bent and examined her cheek.

'See what she did to me.' Yumn squirmed under his grip.

He lifted her hand and examined it and examined her nails. He used one of his own to prise out from beneath hers a bit of the blood and the skin from her own face. His lip curled in disgust. He flung her hand to one side and released his grip on her braid so suddenly that she would have fallen backwards from the bench had she not grabbed on to his leg.

He disengaged her hands from him. 'You're useless,' he said. 'All that's required of you is to live with my family in peace, and you can't manage that much.'

'I?' she demanded. '*I* can't manage?'

'Go down and apologise to my mother. At once.'

'I will not. She struck me. She struck your wife.'

'My wife –' he sneered when he said the word '– deserved to be struck. You're lucky she hasn't struck you before.'

'What is this? Am I meant to be abused? Am I meant to be humiliated? Treated like a dog?'

'If you expect to be forgiven your duties to my mother because you've produced two children, think again. You'll do as she tells you. You'll do as I tell you. And you'll begin by taking your fat bum downstairs and apologising to her.'

'I will not!'

'And after that you'll go outside and clean up the mess you've made in her garden.'

'I'll leave you!' she said.

'Go ahead.' He laughed abruptly, not a friendly laugh at all. 'Why do women always assume that their ability to reproduce should give them rights reserved for others? It takes no brains to put yourself in the club, Yumn. You're expecting to be worshipped for something that takes as much talent as having a crap or a pee. Now get back to work. And don't bother me again.'

He strode to the door. She felt rigid, hot and cold at once. He was her husband. He had *no* right . . . She was going to give him yet another son . . . Even at this moment, that son might be growing within her . . . And he loved her, adored her, worshipped her for the children she bore him and the woman she was and he could not leave her. Not now, not like this. Not in an anger that might make him seek or want or turn to another or even think of . . . No. *No.* She would not allow it. She would not remain the focus of his anger.

The words came in a rush. 'I do my duty, to you and to your family. And my reward is the scorn of your parents and sister. They're spiteful and vicious to me. And why? Because I speak my mind. Because I am who I am. Because *I* don't hide behind a mask of sweetness and obedience. I don't lower my head and hold my tongue and pretend to be your father's perfect little virgin. Virgin? Her?' Yumn hooted. 'Well, in a few more weeks she won't be able to hide the truth underneath her *gharara*. And then we'll see who knows what real duty is and who lives precisely as she wishes.'

Muhannad turned from the door. His face was like stone. 'What are you saying?'

Yumn felt the relief. It was followed by triumph. She'd diverted a crisis between them. 'I'm saying just what you think I'm saying. Your sister's pregnant. Which is something everyone would have known if they weren't so intent on watching *me* all the time, just in case I make a move that they can give me a beating for.'

His eyes went opaque. She saw the ripple of muscles in his arm. She felt her lips want to draw back in a smile, but she maintained control. Precious Sahlah was in for it now. Four ruined tomato plants were hardly worthy of discussion in the face of this familial disgrace.

Muhannad jerked the door open. The force was so great that it crashed back against the wall and flew forward into his shoulder. He didn't flinch.

'Where are you going?' Yumn asked him.

He didn't reply. He strode from the room and clattered down the stairs. In a moment, she heard the roar of the Thunderbird followed by the noise from the driveway as the car's wheels spun wildly, flinging gravel against its sides. She went to the window and saw him tearing down the street.

Oh dear, she thought and allowed herself to experience the smile that she'd stifled in her husband's presence. Poor little Sahlah was in for it now.

Yumn went to the bedroom door and shut it.

How hot the day was, she thought, stretching her arms above her head. A woman in her childbearing years, she would be foolish to overexert herself in the sun. She would have a long, lovely rest before seeing to Wardah's tiresome plants.

'But, Em,' Barbara said, 'he's got it all, hasn't he? Motive, opportunity, and now the means. How long would it take him to walk from that house over to the marina? Fifteen minutes? Twenty? That's nothing, right? And the path from the house to the shore's so well marked that you can see it all the way from the boat hire. So he wouldn't even have needed a torch to show him the way. Which explains why we haven't been able to come up with a single witness who saw anyone on or near the Nez.'

'Except Cliff Hegarty.' Emily fired up the Ford.

'Right. And he's practically handed us Theo Shaw on a platter, what with the story about the Malik girl's pregnancy.'

Emily reversed out of the marina's car park. She didn't speak again until they were back on the lane leading into the town. Then she said, 'Theo Shaw's not the only person who could have come to the marina and nicked one of Charlie's Zodiacs, Barb. Are you ready to discount Eastern Imports, World Wide Tours, Klaus Reuchlein, and Hamburg? How many of the things that tie Querashi to Muhannad's dodgy business do you want to label coincidences? The phone calls to Reuchlein's flat in Hamburg? The bill of lading from Eastern Imports in the safe-deposit box? Muhannad's early-morning jaunt to that warehouse? What do we toss out, Barb?'

'*If* Muhannad's got a dodgy business going,' Barbara pointed out.

'Driving a lorry away from Eastern Imports at one in the morning?' Emily reminded her. 'What's that connected to if not something dodgy? Believe it, Barb. I know my man.'

They zoomed along the lane in the direction they'd come from, slowing as they re-entered the town. Emily braked at the corner of the High Street and waited for a family to cross in front of the car. Laden with canvas chairs, plastic buckets, shovels, and towels, they looked uniformly hot and unhappy as they straggled homeward from their day at the sea.

Barbara pulled on her lip, seeing the beachgoers trudging past but concentrating instead upon the case in hand. She knew that she couldn't rationally argue with Emily's logic. The DCI was perfectly right. There *were* too many flaming coincidences to be actual coincidences in the investigation. But she could not dismiss the fact that very nearly from the first, Theo Shaw had had a motive written above his head in neon, while – no matter his incendiary personality – Muhannad Malik had not.

Nonetheless, Barbara backed away from a full-scale debate over the efficacy of heading to the mustard factory in lieu of making a dash for the pleasure pier. Despite her inclination to follow up on the possibilities presented by the proximity of Balford Old Hall to the marina, she knew that neither she nor Emily had one piece of hard evidence to pin on anyone. Without an eyewitness to anything except a shadowy figure on the top of the Nez and with only a list of curious phone calls and a tangle of circumstantial bits and pieces to go on, their only hope for an arrest was going to be to dig up an incriminating detail that would implicate one of the men under suspicion or to trip someone up in an interview that would reveal guilt where innocence had been avowed.

With a search warrant in their hands, it did make more sense to pursue the factory end of the business. At least the factory presented the hope of digging up something that could lead to an arrest. A sojourn to the pier didn't promise much more than plodding through what they already knew and had already heard, hoping this time to listen with more discerning ears to whatever tale was told.

Still, she persisted. 'That bracelet did say "Life begins now". He could have meant to marry her, only to have Querashi get in the way.'

Emily gave her an incredulous glance. 'Theo Shaw marry the Malik girl? Not on your life. His grandmother would have cut him off without a penny. No, it was to Theo Shaw's advantage that Haytham Querashi came along. Querashi was Theo's best bet to be rid of Sahlah without a fuss. If anything, he had every reason to want Haytham Querashi to stay alive.'

They spun along the Esplanade. They left bicycle riders, pedestrians, and Rollerbladers behind them as they veered inland by the Coastguard station and cruised along Hall Lane towards the elbow that became Nez Park Road.

Emily pulled into the bedraggled industrial estate. She took the search warrant from the glove compartment and said, 'Ah. Here are the boys.'

The boys were the eight members of the squad whose pagers the DCI had instructed Belinda Warner to ring from the station. They'd been diverted from their current activities – everything from verifying Gerry DeVitt's alibi to contacting all of the owners of beach huts in an attempt to corroborate Trevor Ruddock's untold tale about petty burglary – in order to take part in the search of the factory. They were lounging about outside the old brick building, smoking, attempting to beat the heat with cans of Coke and bottles of water. They joined Emily and Barbara at the Ford, the smokers prudently crushing out their fags before they approached.

Emily instructed them to wait for her word, and she went into reception. Barbara followed. Sahlah Malik was not behind the desk. Instead, the reception area was occupied by a middle-aged woman – scarved and gowned – who was seeing to the day's post.

She greeted Emily's presentation of the search warrant by excusing herself hastily and disappearing into the administration office just beyond reception. In a moment, Ian Armstrong was hurrying towards them, with the temporary receptionist hanging behind at a safe distance to watch his confrontation with the police.

Armstrong came through the door, said, 'Detective Chief Inspector, Sergeant,' and nodded to both of them in turn. He dug into the breast pocket of his jacket. For a moment, Barbara thought he intended to present them with a legal document of his own, but he brought forth a crumpled handkerchief and blotted his forehead with it. 'Mr Malik isn't here. He's paying a call on Agatha Shaw. She's in hospital. A stroke, I'm told. How may I help you? Kawthar told me that you're requesting –'

Emily cut in with, 'It's not a request,' and she showed him the document.

He swallowed. 'Oh dear. With Mr Malik not here at the moment, I'm afraid I can't allow –'

'Allowing or not allowing isn't your option, Mr Armstrong,' Emily told him. 'Gather your people outside.'

'But we're mixing product at the moment.' He spoke weakly, as if he knew his protest was futile but felt compelled to make one anyway. 'This is a delicate stage of the operation, as we're working on a new sauce, and Mr Malik was quite firm in instructing our mixers . . .' He cleared his throat. 'If you can give us half an hour . . . ? Perhaps a bit more . . . ?'

For answer, Emily went to the door. She stuck her head out and said, 'Let's get on with it.'

'But ... but ...' Ian Armstrong wrung his hands and looked imploringly at Barbara, seeking an advocate. 'Surely, you have to tell me ... give me some indication of ... What is it exactly that you're looking for? As I'm the one in charge in the absence of the Maliks ...'

Emily said sharply, 'Muhannad's not here either?'

'Well, of course, he is ... I mean, he was earlier ... I had assumed ... He goes home for lunch.' Armstrong cast an agonised glance at the outer door as Emily's team came striding through it. She'd chosen the biggest and burliest men available, knowing that at least one-quarter of the power of search and seizure was intimidation. Ian Armstrong took one look at the assembling crowd of police officers, and obviously decided that discretion was the better part of whatever else he'd had in mind. He said, 'Oh dear.'

Emily said, 'Clear your people out of the building, Mr Armstrong.'

Emily's team spread throughout the factory. While the employees gathered on the cracked Tarmac fanning out from the front door, the detectives divided themselves among the administration offices, the shipping department, the production area, and the storage facility. They were seeking what could be shipped from the factory in the guise of product or tucked among the packed bottles and jars: drugs, hard core or child pornography, weapons, explosives, counterfeit money, jewels.

The team was elbow deep into the search when Emily's mobile sounded. She and Barbara were in the warehouse, searching through boxes that stood on the loading dock ready for shipment. The mobile phone was attached to the waistband of Emily's trousers, and when it rang, she snapped it off and, clearly annoyed at having so far found nothing within the factory, barked her name into the mouthpiece.

From her place on the other side of the loading dock, Barbara heard Emily's end of the conversation. It consisted of, 'Barlow here ... Yes. Goddamn it, Billy, I'm in the middle of something. What the hell is it? ... Right, that's what I ordered and that's what I want. That bloke's intent on doing a runner and the minute you let him out of your sight, he's going to do one ... He *what*? Have you had a good look? Everywhere? ... Yes, I can hear him babbling. What's he on about? ... *Stolen*? Since yesterday? Bullshit. I want him back at the nick. Directly ... I don't care if he pees in his pants. I want him under my thumb.'

She snapped the phone off and looked at Barbara. 'Kumhar,' she said.

'A problem?'

'What the fuck else?' Emily scowled, looking at the shipping boxes that they'd opened but obviously with her mind miles away from the factory. 'I told DC Honigman to collect Kumhar's papers when he returned him to Clacton. Passport, immigration documents, work permits, the lot.'

'So he wouldn't do a runner in case we need to talk to him again. I remember,' Barbara said. 'And?'

'And that was Honigman on the blower. It seems that our little Asian worm doesn't have any papers in Clacton at all. According to Honigman, he appears to be claiming that they were stolen while he was in the nick last night.' She shoved the mobile back on to the waistband of her trousers.

Barbara considered this information in the light of everything else they knew, what they had seen, and what they had heard. 'Querashi had immigration papers in the Barclays safe-deposit box, didn't he, Em? Is there a connection here? And even if there is, is there also a connection with something here?' She gestured round the shipping department.

'That,' Emily said, 'is exactly what I intend to find out.' She stepped off the dock. 'Keep with the search, Barb. And if Muhannad shows his mug, drag him over to the nick for a natter.'

'And if he doesn't show up?'

'Then check at his home. Run him to ground. Find him one way or the other. And bring him in.'

After the cops returned him to the industrial estate, Cliff Hegarty decided to declare himself officially on holiday for the rest of the afternoon. He used a sheet of polythene to cover his current Distraction – a jigsaw puzzle under construction, featuring a large and pendulously breasted woman together with a small elephant in a most fascinating if physiologically impossible pose – and he packed his tools away in their stainless steel chests. He swept up the fine sawdust, polished the surface of his display cabinets, emptied and washed the tea mugs, and locked his door. He hummed contentedly all the while.

He'd done his part to bring Haytham's killer to justice. True, he hadn't come forward at once like he might've done last Friday night when he'd seen poor Hayth go head over arse down the face of the Nez, but at least he knew he *would've* come forward had circumstances been different. Besides, he hadn't been thinking only of himself in hanging back from making a statement to the rozzers. There was Haytham to think of as well. Had Cliff made it known that the murder victim had gone to the Nez for a bit of brown, what would it have done to the bloke's reputation? No sense in tarring him once he was gone was Cliff's way of thinking about it.

And there had been Gerry to consider as well. What was the point in stirring up a hornet's nest of worry in Ger when it wasn't the least bit necessary? Ger talked about fidelity all the time, like he really believed in his heart of hearts that being true to one's lover was the number one topic on his mind. But the real truth was that Ger was scared shitless about HIV. He'd been getting himself tested three times a year since the scare began, and what he believed was that plugging only one bloke for the rest of his life was the key to survival. If he knew that Cliff had been doing the business with Haytham Querashi, he'd only worry himself into a state and probably bring on symptoms of some crazy disease that he didn't even have in the first place. Besides, Haytham always took precautions. Hell, there were times when taking it in the arse from Haytham was so antiseptic that Cliff had found himself tossing round the idea of setting up something with a third bucking bronco just to add a bit of salt to the mash.

Not that he would have done it, mind you. But there were times . . . Just now and then when Hayth would wrestle with that flaming Durex for about ten seconds too long for Cliff's liking . . .

However, those days were over now. Cliff made this decision as he strode to the car. Across the rutted lane, he could see six police cars sitting in front of the mustard factory, and he gave thanks that his part in the investigation was now at an end. He'd head for home and forget about it all, he decided. He'd had a close call, and he'd be a real boofhead if he didn't see what had happened in the past few days as a gilt-edged invitation from on high to turn over a new leaf.

He found himself whistling as he drove south through Balford, buzzing along the seafront, then cruising up the High Street. His life was definitely looking up. With the Haytham business completely behind him and his head finally straight on what he intended to do with the rest of his life, he knew he was ready to devote himself to Gerry. They'd been through a bad patch – him and Ger – but that's all it was, plain and simple.

He'd had to bring to bear all the fancy dancing he knew in order to convince Gerry that his suspicions were groundless. He'd begun his efforts at placation by using anger. When his lover had brought up the idea of being tested for HIV, Cliff's response had been outrage, finely tuned to illustrate that a grievous blow had been dealt him.

'Are we going to have this one again, Ger?' he'd demanded that morning in the kitchen. 'I'm not cheating on you, okay? Jesus Christ. How d'you think it feels —'

'You think HIV can't touch you.' Gerry was the maddening voice of reason as always. 'But it can and it will. Have you watched anyone die of AIDS, Cliff? Or do you leave the cinema when that scene comes on?'

'Is there something wrong with your hearing, mate? I said I'm not cheating. If you don't believe me, maybe you ought to tell me why.'

'I'm not stupid, okay? I work days at the pier. I work nights at that house. Want to tell me what you do while I'm gone?'

Cliff had felt ice running in his veins, so close was Gerry coming to the truth, but he'd rallied well enough. 'You want to tell *me* what you're on about? What's your point? Just spit it out, Ger.' This demand had been a calculated risk. But in Cliff's experience, the time to bluff was when he had absolutely no idea what cards his opponent was holding. In this case, he knew what Gerry's suspicions were, and the only way he could sway Gerry to see those suspicions as groundless was to force them into the open in order to beat them down with a convincing display of righteous rage. 'Go on, then. Spit it all out, Gerry.'

'Okay. All right. You go out when I'm working nights. And we haven't been doing it like we used to. I know the signs, Cliff. Something's going on.'

'Shit. I fucking do *not* believe this. You expect me to sit here and wait for you, right? But I can't sit here with nothing to do. I start climbing the walls. So I go out. I have a walk. I take a drive. I have a drink at Never Say Die. Or I work on a special order at the shop. D'you want some proof for all this? Should I get the barmaid to write me a note? How 'bout setting up a time clock at Distractions so I could punch in and out for you?'

This explosion achieved the desired result. Gerry's voice altered, a subtle gentling that told Cliff he was well on his way to having the upper hand. 'I'm saying that if we need to get tested, we need to get tested. Knowing the truth is better than living a death sentence without even knowing it.'

Gerry's alteration in tone told Cliff that an escalation of his own passion would douse even more of his lover's. 'Great. So get tested if you want to, but don't expect me to do the same because I don't need a test because I'm *not* bloody cheating. If you're going to start sifting through my business, though, I sure as hell c'n do the same to you. And just as easy. Believe me.' He raised his voice further. 'You're gone all day on the pier, aren't you, and half the bleeding night pounding away on some bloke's house – *if* by the way that's what you're really pounding on.'

'Hang on,' Gerry said. 'What's that supposed to mean? We need the money and as far as I know, there's only one legal way to get it.'

'Right. Fine. Work all you want, if that's what you're doing. But don't expect me to be like you. I've got to have breathing room, and if every time I need to have space you're going to think I'm fucking some bloke in a public loo –'

'You go to the square on market days, Cliff.'

'Christ! Jesus! That really cuts it. How else am I going to do the shopping if I don't go to the square on market days?'

'The temptation's there. And both of us know how you are round temptation.'

'Sure we know, and let's both get straight on *why* we know.' Gerry's face grew red. Cliff knew that he was inches away from scoring the definitive goal in this verbal football match they were engaged in. 'Remember me?' he taunted. 'I'm the poofter you met in the market square loo when "taking precautions" wasn't nearly as important as buggering any bloke willing to have you.'

'That's in the past,' Gerry responded defensively.

'Yeah. And let's have a look at the past. You liked your cottaging days as much as I did. Giving blokes the eye, slipping into the loo, doing the business on them without even finding out their names. Only I don't wave those days in front of your face when you don't act like I want you to do. And I don't take you through an inquisition if you stop in the market square for five minutes to pick up a lettuce. *If* that's what you're picking up, by the way.'

'Hang on, Cliff . . .'

'No. You hang on. Cheating works both ways, and you're out more nights than me.'

'I already said. I'm working.'

'Right. Working.'

'And you know how I feel about fidelity.'

'I know what you *say* about fidelity. And there's a hell of a lot of difference between what blokes say and what they feel. I figured you might understand that, Ger. I guess I was wrong.'

And that had been that. Deflated when his argument had been

turned against him, Gerry had backed off. He'd sulked for a while, but he wasn't a man who liked to be at odds with anyone, so he'd ended up apologising for his suspicions. Cliff hadn't accepted the apology initially. He'd said gloomily, 'I don't know, Gerry. How can we live in peace together – in harmony like you always said you wanted – when we get into rows like this?'

To which Gerry had said, 'Forget it. It's the heat. It's getting to me or something. I'm not thinking straight.'

Thinking straight was what everything was all about, in the end. And Cliff was finally doing that. He shot along the country road between Great Holland and Clacton – where the summer wheat languished under a sky that hadn't produced a drop of rain in four scorching weeks – and he realised that what was called for now was a rededication of the self to another. Everyone received a wake-up call sometime during his life. The key was to recognise that call for what it was and to know how to answer it.

His answer would be straightforward fidelity from this time on. Gerry DeVitt, after all, was a good enough bloke. He had a decent job. He had a house five steps from the sand in Jaywick. He had a boat and a motorcycle as well. Cliff could do a lot worse for a permanent situation than hooking up with Gerry. Hell, Cliff's past was a veritable study on that point. And if Gerry was a bit of a bore sometimes, if his compulsion for neatness and promptness began to wear against one's natural grain now and then, if he clung too closely so that one wanted to swat him into the next time zone every once in a while . . . weren't these in reality small inconveniences compared to what Gerry had to offer in return? Certainly. At least they seemed to be.

Cliff turned along the seafront in Clacton, spinning along Kings Parade. He always hated this stretch of going home: a line of seedy old buildings nudging the shore, a score of ancient hotels and decrepit nursing homes. He hated the sight of the doddering pensioners, clinging to their Zimmers with nothing to look forward to and only the past to talk about. Every time he saw them and the environment in which they lived, he renewed his vow never to be among them. He'd die first, he always told himself, before he ended his life this way. And always as he came in sight of the first of the nursing establishments, his foot pressed down on his old 2CV's accelerator and his eyes shifted to the undulating mass of the grey-green North Sea.

Today was no different. If anything, it was worse than usual. The heat had brought the pensioners out of their caves in herds. They were a bobbing, teetering, careening mass of shiny bald heads, blue hair, and bulging varicose veins. And traffic along the shore was halted, so Cliff was treated to a lingering look at what the happy golden years of old age had in store for the unfortunate.

Restlessly, he tapped the car's steering wheel as he watched them. Ahead, he could see the flashing lights of an ambulance. No two. Or was it three? Brilliant. A lorry had probably ploughed right into a group of them. And now he was going to be treated to a nice long sit as the paramedics sorted out the living from the dead. Not that they all weren't half-dead already. Why did people continue to live when it was so clear that their lives were useless?

Shit. Traffic was going nowhere. And he was parched with thirst. If he drove with two of his wheels on the pavement, he could make it up to Queensway and cut into the town from there. He went for it. He had to use the horn to clear the way and he was treated to a few raised fists, one tossed apple, and some shouts of protest. But he gave two fingers to anyone who hassled him, and he made it to Queensway and headed away from the shore.

This was definitely better, he thought. He'd crisscross through town. He'd drop back to the shore just beyond Clacton Pier, and then he'd have only a quick jaunt from there to Jaywick Sands.

Moving along again, he began to consider what he and Gerry could do to celebrate his conversion to monogamy and lifelong fidelity. Naturally, Gerry couldn't *know* that's what they were celebrating, since Cliff had been smiting the air – if that's what the word was – with major protestations of his fidelity for years. But a subtle celebration was certainly in order. And afterwards, with a little wine, a nice steak, a fresh green salad, some lovely veg, and a jacket potato oozing butter ... Well, Cliff knew that he could make Gerry forget any suspicions he might ever have entertained about his lover's roving eye. Cliff would have to dream up some phoney reason why they were having a celebration, of course, but there was time to think of that before Gerry came home.

Cliff zipped into the traffic on Holland Road, turning west in the direction of the railway line. He'd shoot beyond the tracks and make his next turn into Oxford Road, which would eventually take him back towards the sea. The scenery was grotty as hell going this way – nothing but dusty industrial estates and a couple of recreation grounds long gone the colour of straw in the deadly, continuing summer heat – but looking at filthy bricks and dying lawns was a

damn sight more appealing than watching the old farts down by
the shore.

Okay, he thought as he drove along, one arm out of the window and
the other hand resting easily on the steering wheel. What to tell Ger
about the celebration? A big new order come into Distractions? What
about a legacy left by old Aunt Mabel? Or perhaps an anniversary of
some sort? That last sounded nice. An anniversary. But was there
anything special or significant about today's date?

Cliff considered the question. When had he and Gerry met? He
couldn't remember the year without effort, much less the day or the
month. And since they'd first done it the day they'd met, he couldn't
exactly offer that momentous occasion as a point of celebration either.
They'd moved in together – or at least Cliff had moved into Gerry's
digs – in the month of March because the wind was blowing like a
bitch that day, so they must have met sometime in February. Except
that didn't seem right because it was cold as frozen shit in February
and he couldn't imagine having it off with anyone in the market square
toilet in the February cold. He *did* have some standards, after all, and
one of them was not freezing his jewels getting his rocks off with some
good-looking bugger who gave him the eye. And since he and Gerry
had indeed met in the market square, and since meeting had led directly
to doing the business, and since *that* had led to living together in fairly
short order . . . He knew that March as the moving-in date could not
be the right month at all. Shit. What was happening to his memory?
Cliff wondered. Ger's was like a steel trap and always had been.

Cliff sighed. That was the problem with Ger, wasn't it? He never
forgot a single flaming thing. If he only did have the occasional lapse
of memory – like who was where and at what time of night – Cliff
wouldn't be searching his brain at the moment, trying to come up
with something to celebrate. In fact, the whole idea of having to *have*
a celebration instead of just getting on with life left one feeling just a
bit aggrieved.

After all, if Gerry had one single milligram of trust in his body, Cliff
wouldn't be in the position of trying to placate him. He wouldn't be
trying to worm his way into Gerry's good graces because he'd never
have been out of his graces in the first place.

That was the other problem with Ger, wasn't it? You had to *try* so
bloody hard with the bloke. A single wrong word, a night or a morning
or an afternoon when you just didn't *feel* like doing it with him, and all
of a sudden the whole relationship was under the flipping microscope.

Cliff turned left into Oxford Road, feeling a bit more peeved with his lover. The road ran parallel to the railway, separated from it by another dingy industrial estate. Cliff glanced at the grimy soot-stained bricks, and he realised that that was exactly how a round of the guilts with Gerry made him feel: dirty, like he was something unclean and nasty while Ger was as pure as rainwater in Switzerland. Like that was really the case or something, Cliff thought scornfully. Everyone had weak spots, and Gerry had his. For all Cliff knew, his lover was shagging sheep on the side. He wouldn't really have put it past him.

At the bottom of Oxford Road, two other roads met in the apex of a triangle. These were Carnarvon and Wellesloey. The latter led to Pier Avenue, the former to the Marine Parade, and both of them led to the sea. Cliff paused here, his hand on the gear lever, not so much considering which direction he wanted to set off in as much as considering the manner in which the last few days had played out in his life.

Okay, so Gerry had gone a bit rough with him. It wasn't like he didn't deserve it. On the other hand, Gerry *always* went a bit rough when he got his teeth into a subject. He couldn't ever just let it go.

And when he didn't have his teeth into something – some short-coming of Cliff's that he felt needed an adjustment right NOW – he was all over him like a rash, looking for reassurance that he was loved and treasured and wanted and . . . Shit. Sometimes living with Gerry felt like living with a clinging woman. It was all long meaningful silences that had to be interpreted *just* so, soulful sighs that were supposed to signal God only knew what, nuzzles on the neck that were meant to be taken as foreplay, and – here was the worst and it made him crazy – that stiff dick poking against him in the morning, telling him what someone's expectations were.

And he *hated* anyone's expectations. He hated knowing that they were there, like unspoken questions he was supposed to answer immediately. When Gerry prodded him with his prong, there were times when Cliff just wanted to smash him in the face, wanted to shout, You want something, Ger? Then just fucking *say* it for once.

But he never said anything directly, did Gerry. Only when accused was he finally direct. And that – above all – really pissed Cliff off. It made him want to strike out, do things, break things, and hurt someone badly.

He saw that without thinking he'd taken the right side of that triangle whose apex was created by Carnarvon and Wellesloey Roads. Without realising where he was going, he'd driven to Clacton market square. He'd even pulled in to the kerb in much the same fugue state in which he'd made the turn.

Whoa, he told himself. Hang on here, son.

He grasped the steering wheel and stared beyond the windscreen. Someone had hung bunting above the market since his last visit, and the arrowhead banners of blue, red, and white all fanned out from a single small building at the square's far edge, as if with the intention of directing the gaze of every shopper to the public conveniences, a low brick building on which the sign *Gents* seemed to shimmer in the heat.

Cliff swallowed. Christ, he was thirsty. He could get a bottle of water in the market square, or a juice of some kind, or a Coke. And while he was here, he could also do most of the shopping as well. He'd have to pop round the butcher's for the steak, and although he'd previously been thinking that he could get the rest of the meal from the grocery in Jaywick, didn't it really make a hell of a lot more sense to buy everything here, where the food was fresh and the air one breathed was fresh as well? He could get salad and the veg and potatoes, and if he had the time – which he obviously had because he'd taken a half-day holiday, right? – he could browse through the stalls and see if there was something special to give as a peace offering to Ger. Not that he would *know* it was a peace offering, of course.

And anyway, he was so fucking thirsty that he had to get something to drink before he drove another mile. So even if he didn't do the shopping here, he could find something to cool the fire in his throat.

He shoved open the door, kicked it shut behind him, and strode confidently into the market square. He found the water he was looking for, and he drank down the bottle in one long go. God, he actually felt almost human again. He looked for a rubbish bin for the empty. That's when he noticed that Plucky the scarf seller was having a special sale of his phoney designer ties, scarves, and handkerchiefs. Now, that would do for a gift for Ger. Cliff wouldn't have to say where he bought it, would he?

He began to weave over to the stall where the brightly coloured bits hung on a line, fastened with plastic clothes pegs. There were scarves of every size and design, arranged with Plucky's usual attention to artistic detail. He did them in gradations of colour, did Plucky, working from a paint wheel that he'd nicked from the local ironmonger's.

Cliff fingered through them. He liked the feeling of their slickness against his skin. He wanted to bury his face in them because it seemed to him – in the godawful heat – as if they'd cool him like a mountain stream. And even then –

'Nice. Aren't they?' The voice came from his right, at the juncture of two of the stall's sides. A table there was laid out with boxes of handkerchiefs, and standing in front of them was a bloke in the sort of abbreviated muscle T-shirt that cut in from the shoulders and revealed his well-developed pectorals. The shirt revealed his nipples as well, Cliff noted, and one of them was pierced.

Christ, but he was a looker, Cliff thought. Awesome shoulders, just a nip of a waist, and wearing running shorts so short and so excruciatingly tight that it made Cliff shift his weight uncomfortably as his body registered its reaction to what his eyes were seeing in front of him.

All it would take was to give this bloke the look. All it would take was to lock eyes on to eyes and say something like, 'Dead nice, they are.' After that a smile – eyes still locked on eyes – and the willingness would be revealed.

But there were vegetables to be bought for dinner, he reminded himself. There was salad to be purchased, potatoes to take home and bake. There was dinner to concern himself with. The dinner for Gerry. Their celebration of unity, fidelity, and lifelong monogamy.

Only Cliff couldn't take his eyes off this bloke. He was tanned and fit and his muscles gleamed in the afternoon sun. He looked just like a sculpture come to life. Jesus, Cliff thought, why couldn't Gerry ever look like this?

Still the other man waited for a response. As if he could sense the conflict in Cliff, he offered a smile. He said, 'Bloody hot today, isn't it? But I love it hot. What about you?'

Christ, Cliff thought. Oh God. Oh God.

Damn that Gerry. He would always cling. He would always demand. He would always examine with his microscope and trot out his endless flaming questions. Why couldn't he ever just trust a bloke? Didn't he see what he could drive someone to?

Cliff flicked his glance to the toilets across the square. Then his gaze went back to the other.

'Can't get hot enough for me,' he said.

And then he sauntered – because he knew he sauntered better than anything – over to the Gents.

Chapter Twenty-five

The last thing Emily wanted to put up with was yet another in-your-face with one of the Asians, but when DC Honigman brought a quivering Fahd Kumhar back to the nick for another session in the interview room, Muhannad Malik's cousin was right on the DC's heels. Kumhar took one look at Emily and began spewing the same sort of mindless gibberish he'd engaged in on the previous day. Honigman gripped the bloke at the armpit, gave a little twist to the skin he had hold of, and growled at him to stow his mumbo-jumbo, which did absolutely nothing to quieten the man. Emily ordered the DC to toss the Asian into a cell until she could deal with him. And Taymullah Azhar confronted her.

She wasn't in the mood to be confronted. She'd arrived back at the station to yet another phone call from Ferguson, demanding chapter and verse on her search of the mustard factory. He was about as pleased with the news that she'd turned up nothing as she herself had been. His real concern, of course, was not so much the murder of Haytham Querashi as the outcome of his scheduled interview for the assistant chief constable's position. And what underlay his questions and comments was the fact that he faced the selection panel in less than forty-eight hours and he wanted to face it flush with triumph at having the Balford murder resolved.

He said, 'Barlow, good Christ. What's going on? I'm hearing sod bloody all from you to tell me that you lot aren't chasing your tails over there. You know the routine, don't you? Or do I have to recite it? If you can't guarantee me a suspect by tomorrow morning, I'm sending Presley over.'

Emily knew that she was supposed to quake with fear at the threat, after which she was supposed to produce a candidate for arrest – any bloody candidate, thank you very much – in order to give Ferguson the opportunity to paint himself in the most positive light for the muckety-mucks who held his promotion in the balance. But she was too incensed to play the game. Having to deal with yet another of Ferguson's obsessive attempts to have his professional feathers oiled made her want to crawl down the telephone line and kick the superintendent's arse black and blue.

So she said, 'Send Presley over, Don. Send half a dozen DCIs with him if you think that'll make you look good to the committee. But just get off my back, all right?' And having said that, she slammed down the phone.

Which was the moment when Belinda Warner passed along the unwelcome information that one of the Pakistanis was in reception, insisting upon having a word with her. Which was why she was facing Taymullah Azhar now.

He'd followed DC Honigman to Clacton when Emily had refused to allow him to escort Fahd Kumhar back to his digs himself. Distrusting the honour of the police in general and of Balford CID in particular, he'd intended to plant himself outside Kumhar's boarding house till Honigman departed, whereupon he meant to check on the Pakistani man's condition: mental, emotional, physical, and otherwise. So, waiting on the street for the detective constable's departure, he'd seen Honigman with Kumhar in tow once again. And he'd trailed them back to the nick.

'Mr Kumhar was weeping,' he told Emily. 'It's quite obvious that he's under considerable strain. You'll agree it's essential that once again he knows his –'

Emily cut into the song and dance about legalities. She said impatiently, 'Mr Azhar, Fahd Kumhar is in this country illegally. I expect you know what that does to his rights?'

Azhar looked alarmed at this sudden turn of events. He said, 'Are you saying that his current detention has nothing to do with the murder of Mr Querashi?'

'What I'm saying is what I've already said. He's not a visitor, he's not a working holidaymaker, he's not a domestic servant, a student, or somebody's spouse. He has no rights.'

'I see,' Azhar said. But he wasn't a man to admit defeat, as Emily quickly realised when he went on. 'And how do you plan to make this point clear to him?'

Blast the bloody man, Emily thought. He stood there in front of her – *sang-froid* incarnate, despite his nanosecond of alarm a moment earlier – and calmly waited for her to draw the only conclusion that she could draw from the fact that Fahd Kumhar spoke practically no English. She cursed herself for having sent Professor Siddiqi on his way back to London. Even if she got DC Hesketh on the mobile, by this time they'd probably be all the way to Wanstead. She'd lose at least another two hours that she could ill afford to lose if she ordered him to turn round and bring the professor back to Balford for another session with Kumhar. And this was exactly what Taymullah Azhar was betting that she didn't want to do.

She thought of what she'd learned about him in the report from London. SO11 had deemed him worth watching, but the intelligence gathered hadn't fingered him for anything more serious than adultery and abandonment. Neither act portrayed him in a flattering light, but neither was criminal. Had that been the case, everyone from the Prince of Wales to St Botolph's drunks would be shopped for a few years, deserving or not. Besides, as Barbara Havers had pointed out a day earlier, Taymullah Azhar wasn't involved in this business directly. And nothing Emily had read about him indicated a brotherhood with the Asian underworld represented by his cousin.

Even if that weren't the case, what bloody choice did she have between waiting for Siddiqi and attempting to get to the truth right now? None at all, as far as she could see. She lifted a monitory finger and held it inches away from the Asian man's face. She said, 'Come with me. But make one wrong move, Mr Azhar, and I'll have you charged as an accessory after the fact.'

'The fact of what?' he inquired blandly.

'Oh, I think you know the answer to that.'

The Avenues were on the other side of town from the mustard factory, backing on to the Balford Golf Course. There were several routes one could take to get there, but Barbara chose the way along the sea. She took with her one of the biggest detective constables who'd come to search the factory, a bloke called Reg Park, who did the driving and looked as if he'd happily go two or three rounds with anyone who didn't step lively should he make the suggestion that a jig was called for. Muhannad Malik, Barbara decided, was not going to be happy with her invitation to take a drive to the local constabulary for a confab with DCI Barlow. Despite the hours he'd been spending there in the past few days, she had little doubt that he clung to the Victorian bricks of the Balford nick only when it was his own idea. So DC Reg Park was her insurance policy, guaranteeing Malik's cooperation.

She kept an eye peeled for the Asian's turquoise Thunderbird as they drove. He'd not shown up during the search of the factory, nor had he phoned to check in or to give his whereabouts to anyone. Ian Armstrong hadn't found this curious behaviour, though. When Barbara queried him on the point, he'd explained that as director of sales, Muhannad Malik was often out of the factory for hours – if not days – at a time. There were conferences to attend, food shows to organise, advertising to arrange, and sales to stimulate. His job was not production-oriented, so his presence at the factory was less essential than were his efforts out on the road.

Which was where Barbara was searching for him as she and DC Park buzzed along the shorefront. He could have been out on company business, true. But a phone call from World Wide Tours or Klaus Reuchlein could have taken him out on other business as well.

She didn't see the turquoise car on their route, however. And when DC Park slowed in front of the Maliks' enormous half-timbered, many-gabled house on the other side of town, there was also no Thunderbird in its gravel driveway. Still, she instructed the DC to pull to the kerb. The absence of Muhannad Malik's car didn't necessarily equate with the absence of the man himself.

'Let's give it a go,' she told Park. 'But be ready to have to strong arm this bloke if he's here, okay?'

DC Park looked as if the idea of having to strong arm a suspect was just the ticket to make his afternoon complete. He grunted in a simian fashion that matched his overlong arms and pugilist's chest.

The detective constable lumbered up the front path behind her. This curved between two herbaceous borders which, despite the heat and the hose pipe ban, flourished with lavender, pinks, and phlox. To keep the flowers alive in the oppressive heat and sun, Barbara knew that someone had to be lovingly watering the plants by hand each day.

No one was stirring behind the diamond-paned windows on either of the house's two floors. But when Barbara rang the bell next to the heavy front door, someone inside opened what went for a peephole in the oak: a small square aperture that was covered with fancy grillework. It was a bit like visiting a religious order, Barbara thought, and the image was further cemented in her mind by the dim form she saw on the other side of the aperture. This was a veiled woman. She said, 'Yes?'

Barbara rustled up her warrant card and held it at the opening, introducing herself. She said, 'Muhannad Malik. We'd like a word with him, please.'

The aperture shut smartly. Inside the house, a bolt was drawn and the door swung open. They were face to face with a middle-aged woman, standing in the shadows. She wore a long skirt, a tunic buttoned to her throat and her wrists, and a headscarf that swathed everything from her forehead to her shoulders in yards of deep blue, so blue as to be nearly black in the muted light of the entry.

She said, 'What do you want with my son?'

'Mrs Malik, then?' Barbara didn't wait for a response. 'May we come in, please?'

The woman evaluated this request, perhaps for its propriety, because she looked from Barbara to her companion and she made the greater study of him. She said, 'Muhannad isn't here.'

'Mr Armstrong said he'd come home for lunch and not returned.'

'He *was* here, yes. But he left. An hour ago. Perhaps longer.' She inflected these last two phrases as if they were questions.

'You're not certain when he left? Do you know where he went? May we come in, please?'

Again, the woman looked at DC Park. She drew her scarf high and closer round her neck. At this, Barbara suddenly realised how unlikely it was that the Asian woman had ever entertained – if a visit from the police could qualify as entertaining – a western man in her home without her husband present. Thus, she added, 'DC Park will wait in the garden. He was admiring your flowers anyway, weren't you, Reg?'

The detective constable gave another grunt. He stepped off the porch and said, 'Give a shout, right?' to Barbara with a meaningful nod. He flexed his cigar-sized fingers and doubtless would have gone on to crack his knuckles had Barbara not said, 'Thanks, Constable,' with her own meaningful nod at the sun-drenched flower beds behind them.

DC Park safely out of the way, Mrs Malik took a step back from the door. Barbara interpreted this as her form of dusting off the welcome mat, and she ducked inside the house before the other woman had the opportunity to withdraw the invitation.

Mrs Malik made a gesture towards a room on their left which, by means of an archway, opened off the vestibule in which they stood. This was obviously the main sitting room. Barbara stopped in the centre and turned to face Mrs Malik across an expanse of brightly flowered fitted carpet. She noted with some surprise that there were no pictures on any of the walls. Rather, they were hung with samplers filled with Arabic writing, each of them embroidered and framed in gold. Above the fireplace hung a painting of a cube-shaped building backed with an azure cloud-filled sky. Beneath this painting sat the room's only photographs, and Barbara sauntered over to examine these.

One featured Muhannad and his hugely pregnant wife, arms round each other's waist and a picnic basket at their feet. Another showed Sahlah and Haytham Querashi posing on the front porch of yet another half-timbered house. The rest were of children, two little boys in a variety of poses, alone or with each other, dressed only in nappies or bundled up to their eyebrows against the cold.

'The grandkids?' Barbara asked, turning from the fireplace.

She saw that Mrs Malik hadn't yet entered the room. She was watching from the vestibule, keeping to the shadows in a way that suggested either secrecy, stealth, or an attack of nerves. Barbara realised that she had only the woman's word for it that Muhannad was no longer in the house.

Her senses went on the alert. She said, 'Where's your son, Mrs Malik? Is he still here?'

Mrs Malik said, 'No. As I said, no.' And as if a change in behaviour would underscore this answer, she joined Barbara, pulling her scarf closer to her head and throat again.

In the better light, Barbara could see that the hand which held the scarf at her throat was abraded and bruised. Noting this, she raised her eyes to the woman's face and saw much the same abrading and bruising there. She said, 'What's happened to you? Has someone roughed you up?'

'No, of course not. I fell in the garden. My skirt caught on something.' And as if she wished to illustrate this point, she gathered up a handful of the skirt's material and showed where it was indeed quite filthy, as if she'd taken a fall and remained writhing on the ground to savour the sensation for a while.

'No one gets that battered falling in the garden,' Barbara said.

'Alas, I do,' the woman replied. 'As I said before, my son isn't at home. But I expect him back before the children eat this evening. He doesn't miss their meals if he can help it. If you would like to call back then, Muhannad will be happy –'

'You don't speak for Muni,' another woman's voice said.

Barbara swung round to see that Muhannad's wife had come down the stairs. She too was abraded on the face. And long scratches down her left cheek suggested a fight. A fight with another woman, Barbara concluded, since she knew only too well that when men fought, they used their fists. She gave another speculative glance at Mrs Malik's injuries. She considered how the relationship between the two women might be turned to her advantage.

'Only Muhannad's wife speaks for Muhannad,' the younger woman announced.

And that, Barbara decided quickly, might be a blessing in disguise.

'He says,' Taymullah Azhar reported, 'that his papers were stolen. They were in his chest of drawers yesterday. He claims that he informed you of this when you were in his room. And when the detective constable asked for those papers this afternoon, he went to fetch them from the drawer, only to find they were missing.'

Emily was on her feet for the interrogation this time, in the airless cupboard that passed for one of the station's two interview rooms. The tape recorder was running on the table and after switching it on, she had planted herself by the door. From this location, she was able to look down upon Fahd Kumhar, which was useful in establishing for the man who had power and who hadn't.

Taymullah Azhar sat at the end of the table that served as one of the room's four pieces of furniture, with Kumhar at his right on the table's far side. So far, he had at least *appeared* to be relaying to his fellow Pakistani only what Emily allowed him to relate.

They had begun the interview with another round of babbling on the part of Kumhar. He'd been on the floor of the room when they'd entered, crouched into one of its corners like a mouse who knows that the final swipe of the cat's paw is imminent. He'd looked beyond Emily and Azhar, as if seeking another member of their party. When it became apparent to him that they constituted the whole of his inquisitors, he began the gibberish.

Emily had demanded to know what he was saying.

Azhar had listened closely without comment for some thirty seconds before replying. 'He's paraphrasing parts of the Qur'aan. He's saying that among the people of Al-Madinah there are hypocrites whom

Muhammad doesn't know. He's saying that they'll be chastised and doomed.'

'Tell him to stow it,' Emily said.

Azhar said something gently to the man, but Kumhar continued in much the same vein.

'"Others have acknowledged their faults. Even though they mixed a righteous action with another that was bad, Allah might still relent towards them. Because Allah —"'

'We went this route yesterday,' Emily interrupted. 'We're not playing the prayer game today. Tell Mr Kumhar that I want to know what he's doing in this country without proper documents. And did Querashi know that he's here illegally?'

Which was when Kumhar told her – through Azhar – that his papers had been stolen sometime between yesterday afternoon when he'd been taken from Clacton and today when he'd been returned.

'That's complete rubbish,' Emily said. 'DC Honigman informed me not five minutes ago that the other boarders in Mrs Kersey's house are English nationals who have no need of his papers and even less interest in them. The front door of the house is always kept locked, day and night, and there's a twelve-foot drop from Mr Kumhar's window to the back garden with no means of access to that window. Bearing all this in mind, does he want to explain how someone nicked his papers, let alone why?'

'He has no explanation for how it occurred,' Azhar said after listening to a lengthy commentary from the other man. 'But he says that documents are valuable items, to be sold on the black market to desperate souls wishing to avail themselves of the greater opportunities for employment and advancement that are found in this country.'

'Right,' Emily drawled, narrowing her eyes speculatively as she examined the Pakistani man from across the room. His hands, she saw, left visible streaks of damp on the table when he moved them. 'Tell him,' she said pointedly, 'that he's not to worry a bit about his papers. London will be happy to supply him with duplicates. This would have been a tough order years ago, naturally, but with the advent of computer technology, the government will be able to determine that he entered the country in possession of the appropriate visa in the first place. It *would* help if he supplied us with his port of entry, though. What was it? Heathrow? Gatwick?'

Kumhar licked his lips. He swallowed. As Azhar translated Emily's words, he gave a little mewl.

Emily persisted in this line, saying reasonably, 'Of course, we'll need to know exactly what *sort* of visa was stolen from Mr Kumhar's room. Otherwise, we won't be able to get him a duplicate, will we? So do ask him under what understanding was he given entry clearance into the country. Is he someone's relative? A working holidaymaker? Perhaps he's come to be a domestic? Or is he a doctor? Or a minister of some sort? Of course, he could be a student or someone's spouse, couldn't he? Except that he has a wife and children in Pakistan, so I suppose that isn't likely. What about having come to this country for private medical treatment? Except that he doesn't look like he has the funds for that sort of thing, does he?'

Kumhar writhed in his chair as he heard Azhar's translations. He didn't respond directly.

'"Allah promises hellfire to hypocrites and disbelievers,"' Azhar translated. '"Allah curses them and sends them to lasting torment."'

More bloody praying, Emily thought. If the little bastard actually *thought* that prayers were going to do a single thing to save him in his current situation, he was more of a fool than he looked. She said, 'Mr Azhar, tell this man that –'

'May I try something with him?' Azhar interrupted. He'd been examining Kumhar in his quiet way when Emily spoke. Now he looked at her, his gaze even and guileless.

Emily snapped suspiciously, 'What?'

'My own . . . prayer, as you call it.'

'If I know the translation.'

'Of course.' He turned back to Kumhar. He spoke and then offered the English translation. '"Triumphant are those who turn repentant to Allah, those who serve Him, those who praise Him . . . those who enjoin the right and who forbid the wrong."'

'Yes, right,' Emily said. 'That's quite enough of duelling prayer mats.'

But Azhar said, 'If I might tell him one thing more: that there is little point to hiding within a maze of lies since one can so easily lose one's way.'

'Tell him,' she said, 'but add this as well: the game is up. He can tell the truth or be on the first plane back to Karachi. It's his decision.'

Azhar relayed this information. Tears sprang into Kumhar's eyes. His lower teeth gnawed at his upper lip. And a torrent of words poured out of him.

'What's he saying?' Emily demanded when Azhar did not translate at once.

Azhar seemed to turn from the other man with difficulty. But he finally did so, slowly. 'He's saying that he doesn't want to lose his life. He's asking for protection. Roughly, he's saying what he said yesterday afternoon. "I am no one. I am nothing. Protect me, please. I am friendless in this land. And I have no wish to die like the other."'

Finally, Emily felt the sweet rush of triumph. 'Then he *does* know something about Querashi's death.'

'That appears to be the case,' Azhar said.

Barbara decided that a nice little round of Divide and Rule might be what was needed. Mrs Malik either didn't know where her son was, or she was unwilling to hand him over to the police. Muhannad's wife, on the other hand, seemed to be so intent upon illustrating that she and her husband thought each other's thoughts and wore each other's knickers that she was likely to impart one or more valuable titbits of information, all in the name of proving her own importance to the man she'd married. But to get her to do this, Barbara knew that she had to separate the younger from the older woman. This proved easier than she'd anticipated. Muhannad's wife made the suggestion that they conduct their interview alone.

'There are things between husbands and wives,' she said smugly to Barbara, 'that are not for the hearing of mothers-in-law. And as I am the wife of Muhannad and the mother of his sons –'

'Yeah. Right.' The last thing Barbara wanted was another rendition of the song and dance she'd had from this woman on her first day in Balford. She had the impression that whatever her religion, Yumn could get positively biblical when it came to the begetting and begatting game. 'Where can we talk?'

They would talk upstairs, Yumn told her. She had to bathe the sons of Muhannad prior to their tea, and the sergeant could speak to her as she did so. The sergeant would want to see this activity anyway. The naked sons of Muhannad were a sight to give the heart its greatest joy.

Right, Barbara thought. She could hardly wait.

Mrs Malik said, 'But, Yumn, don't you wish Sahlah to bathe them today?' She spoke in so quiet a fashion that the fact that her question was far more pointed than Yumn's previous comments had been was something that could easily be overlooked by anyone unused to subtleties.

Barbara was unsurprised when Yumn's reply indicated that only an axe driven between her eyes would get her attention. A scalpel between the ribs went largely unfelt. She said, 'She may read to them in the evening, *Sus-jahn*. If, of course, they are not too tired. And if her choice of material will not give my Anas further nightmares.' And to Barbara, 'Come along with me.'

Barbara followed the woman's large backside up the stairs. Yumn was chatting away happily. 'How people deceive themselves,' she confided. 'My mother-in-law believes that she's the vessel that holds my husband's heart. It's unfortunate, isn't it? He's her only son – she could have only the two children, you know, my Muni and his sister – so she's tied to him too strongly for her own good.'

'Is she?' Barbara said. 'I'd think she'd be tied more to Sahlah. Both of them being women. You know.'

'Sahlah?' Yumn tittered. 'Who would seek to be tied to such a worthless little thing? My sons are in here.'

She led the way into a bedroom where two small boys were playing on the floor. The younger child wore only a nappy – whose sagging in the direction of his knees indicated its sodden condition – while the elder was completely naked. His discarded clothing – nappy, T-shirt, shorts, and sandals – lay in a pile that appeared to be serving as an obstacle course for the lorries he and his brother were pushing round.

'Anas. Bishr.' Yumn sang their names. 'Come to *ammī-gee*. Time for our bath.'

The boys continued playing.

'And Twisters afterwards, darling ones.'

That got their attention. They set aside their toys and allowed themselves to be scooped up by their mother. Yumn said gaily, 'This way,' to Barbara and carried her treasures to the bathroom. She filled the tub with an inch of water, deposited the two boys, and dropped in three yellow ducks, two boats, a ball, and four sponges. She squeezed liquid soap liberally on all the toys as well as the sponges and handed these last to the boys to play with. 'Bathing should be a delightful game,' she informed Barbara as she stood back to watch the children begin swatting each other with the soapy sponges. Bubbles drifted into the air. 'Your auntie only scrubs and rubs, doesn't she?' Yumn asked the boys. 'Tiresome auntie. But your *ammī-gee* makes bathing fun. Shall we play with the boats? Do we need more duckies? Do you love your *ammī-gee* better than anyone?'

The boys were too occupied with plastering each other's face with the sponges to pay her much attention. She ruffled their hair and then, after sighing with satisfaction over them, said to Barbara, 'These are my pride. Their father's also. And they will be just like him, men among men.'

'Right,' Barbara said. 'I can see the likeness.'

'*Can* you?' Yumn stood back from the tub and reflected on her sons as if they were works of art. 'Yes. Well, Anas has his father's eyes. And Bishr . . .' She chuckled. 'Shall we say that in time, my Bishr shall have something else quite like his father's as well? Won't you be a bullgod to your wife someday, Bishr?'

Barbara thought at first that Yumn had said *bulldog*, but when the woman reached between her son's legs to display his penis – approximately the size of Barbara's little toe – she adjusted her thinking. Nothing quite like starting the bloke out on his complexes early, she decided.

'Mrs Malik,' she said, 'I've come here looking for your husband. Can you tell me where he is?'

'What on earth can you want with my Muni?' She bent over the bathtub and ran one of the sponges up and down Bishr's back. 'He hasn't failed to pay a parking fine, has he?'

'Just some questions I'd like to put to him,' Barbara said.

'Questions? About what? Has something happened?'

Barbara knotted her brows. The woman couldn't possibly be this much out of the loop. She said, 'Haytham Querashi –'

'Oh, that. But you don't want to talk to my Muni about Haytham Querashi. He hardly knew him. You want to speak to Sahlah.'

'I do?' Barbara watched Yumn playfully dribbling soap along the plane of Anas's shoulders.

'Of course. Sahlah was up to some nasty business. Haytham discovered what it was – who knows how? – and they had words. Words led to . . . It's sad what words lead people to, isn't it? Darlings, here. Shall we float our boats on the waves?' She splashed water against their thighs. The boats bobbed and weaved. The boys laughed and struck the water with their fists.

'What sort of nasty business?' Barbara asked.

'She was busy at night. When she assumed the house was asleep, she became quite busy, our little Sahlah. She went out. And more than once, someone came in. Someone joined her in her room. She thinks that no one knows this, of course. What she doesn't know is that when my Muni goes out in the evenings, I don't sleep well until he returns to our bed. And my ears are sharp. Quite, quite sharp. Aren't they, my lovely little ones?' And she playfully poked her sons' bellies. Anas splashed water across the front of her tunic in return. She laughed gaily and splashed back. 'And little Sahlah's bed goes *squeak, squeak, squeak*, doesn't it, darlings?' More splashing followed. 'Such a restless sleeper our auntie is. *Squeak, squeak, squeak, squeak*. Haytham found out about that nasty squeaking, didn't he, boys? And he and our Sahlah had words and words.'

What a cobra, Barbara thought. Someone needed to take a cosh to the woman's head, and she expected there would be more than one volunteer in the household should she ask who would like to wield one. Well, two could play innuendo poker. Barbara said, 'Have you a *chādor*, Mrs Malik?'

Yumn's hands hesitated in the creation of more waves for her boys. She said, 'A *chādor*? How odd. Whatever makes you ask such a question?'

'You're wearing fairly traditional garb. I was wondering. That's all. Get out and about much? Go visiting friends in the evening? Stop by one hotel or another for an evening coffee? By yourself, that is? And when you do, do you wear a *chādor*? One sees them all the time in London. But I don't recall seeing any here at the sea.'

Yumn reached for a large plastic jug on the floor nearby. She took out the bath plug and filled the jug from the tap. She began pouring water over the boys, who squealed and shook themselves like wet puppies. She didn't reply until she had both of the children thoroughly rinsed and wrapped in large white towels. She lifted one to each hip and started out of the room, saying to Barbara, 'Come with me.'

She didn't lead the way back to the boys' room, however. Instead, she went to the far end of the corridor, to a bedroom at the back of the house. The door was closed, and she opened this imperiously and gestured Barbara inside.

It was a small room with a single bed against one wall, a chest of drawers and a table against another. Its diamond-paned window was open, overlooking the back garden and, beyond this garden, a brick wall with a gate that opened on to a neat, weedless orchard.

'*This* is the bed,' Yumn said, as if revealing a place of infamy. 'And Haytham knew what went on within it.'

Barbara turned from the window, but she didn't examine the object in question. She was about to say, 'And we both know how Haytham

Querashi came by that piece of information, don't we, sweetie?' when she noticed that the table across the room from the bed appeared to be a craft centre of some sort. She walked to this curiously. Yumn continued.

'You can imagine how Haytham would feel, learning that his beloved – presented to him by her father as chaste – was little more than a common . . . Well, my language is too strong, perhaps. But no stronger than my feelings.'

'Hmm,' Barbara said. She saw that three miniature plastic chests of drawers contained beads, coins, shells, stones, bits of copperas, and other small ornaments.

'Women carry our culture forward through time,' Yumn was continuing. 'Our role is not only as wives and mothers, but as symbols of virtue for the daughters that follow us.'

'Yes. Right,' Barbara said. Next to the three chests was a rack of implements: tiny spanners, long-nosed pliers, a glue gun, scissors, and two wire cutters.

'And if a woman fails in this role, she fails herself, her husband, and her family. She stands disgraced. Sahlah knew this. She knew what awaited her once Haytham broke their engagement and stated his reasons for doing so.'

'Got it. Yes,' Barbara said. And next to the rack of tools was a row of large spools.

'No man would want her after that. If she wasn't cast out of the family altogether, she'd be a prisoner of it. A virtual slave. At everyone's command.'

Barbara said, 'I need to speak to your husband, Mrs Malik,' and she rested her fingers on the prize she'd found.

Among the spools of thin chain, string, and bright yarn stood one damning spool of very fine wire. It was more than suitable for tripping an unsuspecting man in the darkness on the top of the Nez.

Bingo, she thought. Bloody flaming hell. Barlow the Beast had been right from the first.

Emily had to allow both of them to smoke. It appeared to be the only way to get Kumhar relaxed enough to spill his guts. So with her chest feeling tighter, her eyes watering, and her head beginning to pound, she endured the fumes from his Benson & Hedges. It took three fags before he came anywhere close to speaking what might have been the truth. Before that, he tried to claim he'd come through customs at

Heathrow. Then he switched to Gatwick. Then, when he was unable to produce the flight number, the airline, or even the date of entry into the country, he was finally reduced to telling the truth. Azhar translated. His face remained expressionless throughout. To his credit, however, his eyes appeared more and more pained as the interview continued. Emily was leery of this pain, though. She knew enough of these Asians to see them for the actors they were.

There were people who helped, Kumhar began. When one wanted to emigrate, there were people in Pakistan who knew the short cuts. They could cut through the waiting time and waive the requirements and ensure one of having proper papers . . . All of this for a price, of course.

'How does he define "proper papers"?' Emily asked.

Kumhar circumvented the question. He'd hoped at first to be able to come to this wonderful country legitimately, he said. He'd sought ways to do this. He'd sought sponsors. He'd even attempted to offer himself as a bridegroom to a family unaware of his marital status, with the plan of marrying bigamously. Of course, it wouldn't really have *been* a bigamous union, polygyny being not only legal but also appropriate for a man with the means to support more than one wife. Not that he had the means, but he would. Someday.

'Spare me the cultural asides,' Emily said.

Yes, of course. When his plans were not enough to get him to England legitimately, his father-in-law had informed him of an agency in Karachi that specialised in . . . Well, they called it assisting in the immigration problem. They had, he learned, offices round the world.

'In every desirable port of entry,' Emily noted, recalling the cities that Barbara Havers had listed as locales for World Wide Tours. 'And in every undesirable port of exit.'

One could look at it that way, Kumhar said. He visited the Karachi office and explained his needs. And for a fee, his problem was taken care of.

'He was smuggled into England,' Emily said.

Well, not directly into England. He hadn't the money for that, although direct entry was available to those with £5,000 to pay for a British passport, a driving licence, and a medical card. But who except the extremely fortunate could produce that amount of money? For what he'd managed to scrape together in five years of saving and doing without, he was able to purchase only an overland passage from Pakistan to Germany.

'To Hamburg,' Emily said.

Again, he offered no direct answer. In Germany, he said, he waited – concealed in a safe lodging – for passage to England, where – in time and with sufficient effort on his part, he was told – he would be given the documents he needed to remain in the country.

'You came in through Parkeston Harbour,' Emily concluded. 'How?'

By ferry, in the back of a lorry. The immigrants hid among goods being shipped from the continent: car tyre fibre, wheat, maize, potatoes, clothing, machine parts. It made no difference. All that was required was a lorry driver willing to take the risk for considerable compensation.

'And your documents?'

Here, Kumhar began to jabber, clearly unwilling to carry his story any further. He and Azhar engaged in a rapid-fire exchange that Emily interrupted with 'Enough. I want a translation. Now.'

Azhar turned to her, his face grave. 'This is more of the same that we've already heard. He's afraid to say more.'

'Then I'll say it for him,' Emily said. 'Muhannad Malik's involved in this up to his eyeballs. He's smuggling illegals into the country and holding their forged documents hostage. Translate that, Mr Azhar.' And when the man didn't speak at once, his eyes darkening with each accusation she made against his cousin, she said icily, 'Translate. You wanted to be a part of this. So *be* a part of this. Tell him what I said.'

Azhar spoke, but his voice was altered, subtly toned by something that Emily couldn't identify but strongly suspected was preoccupation. Of course. He'd be wanting to get the word out to his detestable cousin. These people stuck together like flies over cow dung no matter what the offence. But he couldn't leave the nick until he knew for certain what the real word was. And by that time they'd have Muhannad under lock and key.

When Azhar had finished the translation, Fahd Kumhar began to weep. It was true, he said. Upon arrival in England, he'd been taken to a warehouse. There, he and his fellow travellers were met by a German and two of their own countrymen.

'Muhannad Malik was one?' Emily asked. 'Who was the other?'

He didn't know. He'd never known. But this other wore gold – watches and rings – he dressed well and he spoke Urdu fluently. He did not come often to the warehouse, but when he did, the two others deferred to him.

'Rakin Khan,' Emily breathed. The description couldn't have fitted anyone else.

Kumhar hadn't known either man's name at first. He learned Mr Malik's identity only because they themselves – and here he indicated Emily and Azhar – had given it yesterday during the interview they'd already had together. Prior to that, he'd known Malik only as the Master.

'Wonderful sobriquet,' Emily muttered. 'Doubtless he invented it himself.'

Kumhar continued. They were told that arrangements had been made for them to work until such a time as they had sufficient funds to pay for the proper documents.

'What sort of work?'

Some went to farms, others to factories, others to mills. Wherever they were needed, they went. A lorry would come for them in the middle of the night. They would be taken to the location for work. They would be returned when the labour was completed, sometimes in the night of that same day, sometimes days later. Mr Malik and the other two men took their wages. From these, they extracted a payment for the documents. When the documents were paid off, the immigrant would be given them and allowed to leave.

Except, in the three months that Fahd Kumhar had been working off his debt, no one had left. At least not with the proper papers. Not a single person. More immigrants came, but no one managed to earn enough to buy his freedom. The work increased as more fruit needed picking and more vegetables needed harvesting, but no amount of work appeared to be enough to pay off their debts to the people who had arranged their entry into the country.

It was a gangmaster programme, Emily realised. The illegals were being hired by farmers, mill owners, and factory foreman. These people paid lower wages than they would have to pay legal workers, and they paid them not to the illegals themselves, but to the person who transported them. That person skimmed off as much money as he wanted and doled out to the workers what he felt like giving them. The illegals thought the scheme was to assist them with their immigration dilemmas. But the law had another word for it: slavery.

They were trapped, Kumhar said. They had only two options: to continue to work and hope that they would be given their papers eventually, or to make their escape and find their way to London, where they might hope to fade into the Asian community and avoid detection.

Emily had heard enough. She saw how they were all involved: the entire Malik clan and Haytham Querashi as well. It was a case of greed. Querashi had uncovered the scheme that night at the Castle Hotel. He'd wanted a piece of the action as a portion of the Malik girl's dowry. He'd been refused: permanently. Doubtless he'd used Kumhar as a means of blackmailing the family to do his bidding. Slice him a piece of the financial pie or he'd bring down the entire operation by having Kumhar sing to the police or to the papers. It was a clever idea. He'd been counting on the family's greed overcoming whatever inclination they may have had to call his bluff. And his request for compensation for his knowledge wasn't so illogical. He was to be a member of the family, after all. He deserved his fair share of what everyone else was enjoying. Especially Muhannad.

Well, now Muhannad could kiss goodbye to his classic car, his Rolex watch, his snake-skin boots, his diamond signet ring, and his gold chains. He wouldn't be needing them where he was going.

And this would cook Akram Malik's position in the community. Doubtless it would cook the entire Asian population as well. Most of them worked for him anyway. And when the factory closed as a result of the investigation into the Maliks' scheme, they'd have to take themselves off to seek employment elsewhere. Those that were legal, that is.

So she'd been on the right track in searching the mustard factory. She just hadn't thought to search it for people instead of inanimate contraband. There was much to do. There was SO1 to involve, to activate an investigation into the international aspects of the scheme. Then the IND would need to be informed, to make arrangements for the deportation of Muhannad's immigrants. Some of them, of course, would be needed to testify against him and his family at the trial. Perhaps in exchange for asylum? she wondered. It was a possibility.

She said to Azhar, 'One thing more. How did Mr Kumhar come to be hooked up with Mr Querashi?'

He'd appeared at a work site, Kumhar explained. One day when they rested for lunch along the side of a strawberry field, he'd appeared among them. He'd been seeking someone to use as a means of putting an end to their enslavement, he said. He promised safety and a new start in this country. Kumhar was only one of eight men who had volunteered. He was chosen and he left that very afternoon with Mr Querashi. He'd been driven to Clacton, set up in Mrs Kersey's house, and given a cheque to send back to his family in Pakistan as a sign of Mr Querashi's good intentions towards them all.

Right, Emily thought with a mental snort. It was another form of enslavement in the making, with Kumhar as the permanent sword that Querashi would hold over the heads of Muhannad Malik and his family. Kumhar had merely been too dim to work that out.

She needed to get back upstairs to her office, to see where Barbara was in her search for Muhannad. At the same time, she couldn't let Azhar leave the station lest he give his relatives the word that she was on to them all. She could hold him as an accessory, but one misspoken word out of her mouth, and he'd be on the phone demanding a lawyer so fast that her head would be spinning. Better to leave him with Kumhar, believing he was serving the good of all concerned.

She said to Azhar, 'I'm going to need a written statement from Mr Kumhar. May I ask you to stay with him as he writes it and then append a translation for me?' That should take a good two hours, she thought.

Kumhar spoke urgently, hands trembling as he lit yet another cigarette.

'What's he saying now?' Emily asked.

'He wants to know if he'll get his papers. Now that he's told you the truth.'

Azhar's look was a challenge. It irked her to see it so openly displayed on his dark face.

'Tell him all in good time,' Emily said. And she left them to hunt down Sergeant Havers.

Yumn picked up on Barbara's interest in the craft table in Sahlah's bedroom. She said, 'Her jewellery, or so she calls it. *I* call it her excuse not to do her duty when she's asked to do it.' She joined Barbara at the table and pulled out four of the drawers from their little chests. She spilled coins and beads on to the table top and sat Anas on the table's accompanying wooden chair. He became immediately enthralled with his aunt's jewellery-making bits and pieces. He pulled out another drawer and flung its contents among the coins and beads that his mother had already given him. He laughed at the sight of the colourful objects rolling and bouncing on the table. Before, they'd been arranged carefully by size, by hue, and by composition. Now, as Anas added two more drawersful, they were hopelessly mixed up with one another, promising a long evening's work sorting them out.

Yumn did nothing to stop him from continuing to empty more of the drawers. Instead, she smiled at him fondly and ruffled his hair. 'You like the colours, don't you, pretty one?' she asked him. 'Can you name these colours for your *ammī-gee*? Here's red, Anas. Can you see red?'

Barbara certainly was doing so. She said, 'Mrs Malik, about your husband. I'd like a word with him. Where can I find him?'

'Why would you want to talk to my Muni? I've already told you –'

'And I've got every word from the last forty minutes engraved on my heart. But I've one or two points to clear up with him regarding Mr Querashi's death.'

Yumn had been continuing her play with Anas's hair. Now she turned to Barbara. 'I've told you that he isn't involved in Haytham's death. You should be talking to Sahlah, not to her brother.'

'Nonetheless –'

'There *is* no nonetheless.' Yumn's voice was louder. Two spots of colour appeared on her cheeks. She had dropped her treacly wife-and-mother routine. Steel resolve replaced it. 'I've told you that Sahlah and Haytham had words. I've told you what she got up to at night. I expect that since you're the police, you can add one and one together without my having to do it for you. My Muni,' she concluded as with the need to clarify a point, 'is a man among men. And you have no need to talk to him.'

'Right,' Barbara said. 'Well, thanks for your time. I'll find my own way out.'

The other woman read the greater meaning behind Barbara's words. She said insistently, 'You have no need to talk to him.'

Barbara passed her. She went into the corridor. Yumn's voice followed her.

'You've been taken in by her, haven't you? Just like everyone. You have five words with the little bitch and all you see is a precious doe. So quiet. So gentle. *She* wouldn't hurt a fly. So you overlook her. And she gets away.'

Barbara started down the stairs.

'She gets away with everything, the whore. *Whore.* With him in her room, with him in her bed, with pretending to be what she never was. Chaste. Dutiful. Pious. Good.'

Barbara was at the door. She reached for the handle. From the top of the stairs, Yumn cried out the words.

'He was with me.'

Barbara's hand stopped, but remained outstretched for a moment as she registered what Yumn was saying. She turned. 'What?'

Carrying her younger child, Yumn came down the stairs. The colour in her face had been reduced to two medallions of red that rode high on either cheek. Her wandering eye gave her a wild air, which was heightened by the words she next spoke. 'I'm telling you what you'll hear from Muhannad. I'm saving you the trouble of having to find him. That's what you want, isn't it?'

'What are you saying?'

'I'm saying that if you think Munhannad was involved in what happened to Haytham Querashi, he couldn't have been. He was with me on Friday night. He was up in our room. We were together. We were in bed. He was with me.'

'Friday night,' Barbara clarified. 'You're certain of that. He didn't go out? Not at any time? Not, perhaps, telling you that he was going to see a chum? Maybe even to have dinner with a chum?'

'I know when my husband was with me, don't I?' Yumn demanded. 'And he was here. With me. In this very house. On Friday night.'

Brilliant, Barbara thought. She couldn't have asked for a more pellucid declaration of the Asian man's guilt.

Chapter Twenty-six

He couldn't stop the voices in his head. They seemed to be coming from every direction and from every possible source. At first he thought that he'd know what to do next if only he could silence their shouting. But when he realised that he could do nothing to drive the howl of them out of his skull – save kill himself which he certainly did *not* intend to do – he knew he would have to lay his plans while the voices attempted to lay waste to his nerves.

Reuchlein's phone call had come into the mustard factory less than two minutes after the Scotland Yard bitch had left the warehouse in Parkeston. 'Abort, Malik,' was all he said, which meant that the new shipment of goods – due to arrive this very day and worth at least £20,000 if he could keep them working long enough without doing a bunk – would not be met at the port, would not be driven to the warehouse, and would not be sent out in work parties to the Kent farmers who had already paid half in advance, as agreed. Instead, the goods would be released on their own upon their arrival, to find their way to London or Birmingham or any other city in which they could hide. And if they weren't caught by the police in advance of reaching their destination, they would fade into the population and keep their gobs shut about how they got into the country. No sense in talking when talking would lead to deportation. As to those workers already on sites, they were on their own. When no one arrived to fetch them back to the warehouse, they'd work things out.

Abort meant that Reuchlein was on his way back to Hamburg. It meant that every document pertaining to the immigration services of World Wide Tours was heading into the shredder. And it meant that he himself had to act quickly before the world as he'd known it for twenty-six years crashed in on him.

He'd left the factory. He'd gone home. He'd started to put his own plans in motion. Haytham was dead – praise whatever Divine Being was convenient at the moment – and he knew that there was no way on earth that Kumhar would talk. Talk and he'd find himself deported, which was the last thing he wanted now that his chief protector had been murdered.

And then Yumn – that ugly cow he was forced to call *wife* – had begun her business with his mother. And she'd had to be dealt with, which was when he'd learned the truth about Sahlah.

He'd cursed her, his slag of a sister. She'd *driven* him to it. What did she expect to happen when she acted like a whore with a westerner? Forgiveness? Understanding? Acceptance? What? She'd let those hands – unclean, defiled, corrupt, disgusting – touch her body. She'd willingly met that mouth with her own. She lay with that bloody piece of shit Shaw under a tree on the bare fucking ground and she expected *him* – her brother, her elder, her lord – to walk away from the knowledge? From the sound of their breathing and moaning together? From the scent of their sweat? From the sight of his hand lifting her nightgown and sliding sliding sliding up her leg?

So yes, he'd grabbed her. Yes, he'd dragged her into the house. And yes, he'd taken her because she deserved to be taken, because she was a whore, and because above all she was meant to pay the way all whores pay. And once – one night – was not enough to impress her with the knowledge of who was the real master of her fate. One word from me and you die, he'd told her. And he didn't even need to muffle her cries with his palm as he was prepared to do. She knew she had to pay for her sin.

Once Yumn had spoken, he'd gone in search of her. It was the very last thing he knew he should do, but he had to find her. He was in a fever to find her. His eyes were throbbing, his heart was thundering, and his head was pounding with all of their voices.

Abort, Malik.

Am I meant to be treated like a dog?

She's ungovernable, my son. She has no sense of –

The police were here to search the factory. They were asking for you.

Abort, Malik.

Look at me, Muni. Look at what your mother –

Before I knew it, she had ruined the plants. I don't understand why –

Abort, Malik.

. . . your father's perfect little virgin.

Abort.

Virgin? Her? In a few more weeks she won't be able to hide the –

They wouldn't say what they were looking for. But they had a warrant. I saw it myself.

Your sister's pregnant.

Abort. Abort.

Sahlah wouldn't speak of it. She wouldn't accuse him. She wouldn't dare. An accusation would ruin her because from it would arise the truth about Shaw. Because *he* – Muhannad, her brother – would speak that truth. *He* would accuse. *He* would relate exactly what he had seen pass between them in the orchard and he'd allow their parents to conclude the rest. Could they trust the word of a daughter who betrayed them by sneaking out of the house at night? Of a daughter who acted like a common slag? Who was more likely to be telling the truth? he would demand. A son who did his duty to his wife, his children, and his parents, or a daughter who daily lived a lie?

Sahlah knew what he would say. She knew what their parents would believe. So she wouldn't speak of it, and she wouldn't accuse.

Which gave him a chance to find her. But she wasn't at the factory. She wasn't at the jewellery shop with her hag-faced friend. She wasn't in Falak Dedar Park. She wasn't on the pier.

But on the pier he'd heard the news about Mrs Shaw and he'd gone to the hospital. He was just in time to see them coming out, the three of them. His father, his sister, and Theo Shaw. And the look that passed between his sister and her lover as he opened the door of their father's car for her had told him what he needed to know. She'd told. The little bitch had told Shaw the truth.

He'd spun away before they could see him. And the voices roared.

Abort, Malik.

What am I to do? Tell me, Muni.

At the moment, Mr Kumhar hasn't identified anyone he wishes to be notified.

When one among us has died, it is not up to you to see to his resurrection, Muhannad.

. . . found dead on the Nez.

I work with our people in London when they have troubles with —
Abort, Malik.
Muhannad, come and meet my friend Barbara. She lives in London.
This person you speak of is dead to us. You should not have brought him into our house.

We go for ice creams on Chalk Farm Road and we've been to the cinema and she even came to my birthday party. Sometimes we go to see her mum in —
Abort, Malik.
We told her we were going to Essex. Only Dad didn't tell me you lived here, Muhannad.
Abort. Abort.
Will you come again? Can I meet your wife and your little boys? Will you come again?

And there — there, where he least expected to find it — was the answer he was seeking. It silenced the voices and calmed his nerves.

It sent him hurtling towards the Burnt House Hotel.

'All *right*,' Emily said fiercely. Her face lit up with a radiant smile. 'Well done, Barbara. God damn. All *right*.' She shouted for Belinda Warner. The WPC came bounding into the office.

Barbara felt like crowing. They bloody well had Muhannad Malik by the short and curlies, presented to them like the Baptist to Salome with no dancing required. And by his very own dimwitted wife.

Emily began giving orders. The DC working the Colchester end — who'd been combing the streets round Rakin Khan's home in an attempt to find someone who could either corroborate Muhannad's alibi for Friday night or sink it for ever — was to be called home. The constables sent to the mustard factory to go through everyone's personnel file for an examination of their paperwork were to be taken off that trail. The blokes working on the beach hut break-ins to clear the slate of Trevor Ruddock were to put that endeavour on the back burner. Everyone was to join the search for Muhannad Malik.

'No one could be in two places at once,' Barbara had exulted to Emily. 'He forgot to tell his wife what his alibi was. And she bloody well gave him a second one. The flaming game's not afoot, Emily. It's bloody well *up*.'

And now she watched the DCI in her glory at long last. Emily fielded phone calls, constructed a battle plan, and directed her team with a calm assurance that belied the excitement which Barbara knew that she had to be feeling. Hell, she'd been right from the very first. She'd sensed something dodgy in Muhannad Malik, something not right in all of his loud protestations of being a man of his people. Indeed, there was probably some allegory or fable that emphasised the exact hypocrisy of Muhannad's life, but at the moment Barbara was too wired to dredge it up from her memory. Dog in the manger? Tortoise and the hare? Who knew? Who cared? Let's just *get* this flaming bastard, she thought.

Constables were dispatched in all directions: to the mustard factory, to the Avenues, to the town council rooms, to Falak Dedar Park, to that small meeting hall above Balford Print Shoppe where Intelligence had revealed that *Jum'a* had its gatherings. Other constables were assigned to Parkeston in the event that their quarry had headed to Eastern Imports.

Descriptions of Malik went out by fax to surrounding communities. The Thunderbird's number plates and the car's unique colour and features were relayed to police stations. The Tendring *Standard* was phoned for a front-page position for Malik's photograph in case they hadn't run him to ground by morning.

The entire station was mobilised. Everywhere was movement. Everyone worked like a cog in the greater machine of the investigation, and Emily Barlow was that machine's centre.

It was in this sort of mode that she did her best work. Barbara remembered her ability to make quick decisions and to deploy her manpower where it would have the greatest effect. She'd done this in their exercises at Maidenhead when there was nothing at stake but the approval of the instructor and the admiration of colleagues taking the course. Now, with everything at stake – from peace in the community to her very job – she was the personification of tranquillity. Only the manner in which she bit off words as she spoke them gave an indication of her tension.

'They were all in on it,' she told Barbara, tossing back a slug of water from an Evian bottle. Her face was shiny with perspiration. 'Querashi as well. It's so fucking obvious. He wanted a share of the lolly that Muhannad was having off everyone who hired his illegals. Muhannad wouldn't play. Querashi did a header down the steps.' Another slug of water. 'Look at how easily it worked, Barb. Malik was in and out of his house all the time: meetings of *Jum'a*, dealing with Reuchlein, shipping illegals all over the country.'

'Not to mention all the travelling he does for the factory,' Barbara added. 'Ian Armstrong told me as much.'

'So if he was out on this night or that night, his family would never think a thing of it, would they? He could leave the house, trail Querashi, see his set-up with Hegarty – without even knowing it was Hegarty he was meeting – and choose his moment to give him the chop. With half a dozen alibis at the ready for any night that he was able to pull it off.'

Barbara saw how all of it fitted together. 'And then he showed up with his people in tow, ready to protest the death and make himself look innocent.'

'To make it look like he was what he never could be: a brother Muslim to Muslims, intent upon getting to the bottom of Querashi's murder.'

'Because why the hell would he be dogging your heels in pursuit of Querashi's killer if *he* was the killer?'

'Or so I was intended to think,' Emily said. 'Except I never thought it. Not for an instant.'

She paced to the window where the pillowcase that she'd hung a day earlier still shielded the room from the sun. She yanked it down. She leaned out of the window and watched the street. She said, 'This is the worst part. I *hate* this part of it.'

The waiting, Barbara thought. The keeping oneself behind the lines in order to direct the troops as information flowed into the station. It was the downside of having attained Emily's position. The DCI couldn't be everywhere at once. She had to rely on the expertise and the sheer doggedness of her team.

'Guv?'

Emily spun from the window. Belinda Warner was at the door. 'Who've we heard from?' she said.

'It's that Asian bloke. He's downstairs again. He –'

'*What* Asian bloke?'

'You know. Mr Azhar. He's in reception and he's asking for you. Or the sergeant. He said the sergeant would do. Reception said he's all in a twist.'

'Reception?' Emily echoed. 'What the hell is he doing in reception? He's supposed to be with Fahd Kumhar. I left him with him. I gave express orders to –' She cut her own words off. 'Jesus,' she said, white-faced.

'What?' The idea of Azhar in a twist brought Barbara to her feet. The Pakistani was so controlled that the thought of him in a twist about anything had alerted every one of her senses. 'What's going on?'

'He wasn't supposed to leave the station,' Emily said. 'He was supposed to be kept with Kumhar till we got our mitts on his cousin. But I goddamn bloody well left the interview room and forgot to tell reception he wasn't to leave the building.'

'What do you . . . ?' Belinda was clearly looking for direction.

'I'll see to him,' Emily snapped.

Barbara followed her. They took the corridor and the stairs at a trot. On the ground floor, Taymullah Azhar paced the reception cubicle.

'Barbara!' he cried as he caught sight of their approach. All attempts at obfuscation dissolved in a moment of what was clearly panic. His face was frantic. 'Barbara, she's gone. He's taken Hadiyyah.'

'Christ,' Barbara said, and she meant it as a prayer. 'Azhar, what? Jesus. Are you sure?'

'I went back to the hotel. I'd finished here. Mr Treves told me. Mrs Porter was with her. She remembered him from the other night. She'd seen us together. You remember. In the bar. She thought it was all arranged . . .' He was two steps away from hyperventilating.

Impulsively, Barbara put an arm round his shoulders. 'We'll get her,' she said, squeezing him hard. 'Azhar, we'll get her. I swear it. I promise you, we'll get her back.'

'What the hell is going on?' Emily demanded.

'Hadiyyah's his daughter. She's eight years old. Muhannad's taken her. Obviously, she thought it was okay to go with him.'

'She knows never to go,' Azhar said. 'A stranger. She knows that. Never. *Never.*'

'Except Muhannad isn't a stranger to her,' Barbara reminded him. 'Not any longer. She told him she wanted to meet his wife and his children. Remember, Azhar? You heard her when she said it. So did I. And you had no reason to think . . .' She felt the agitated need to absolve him of the guilt that she knew he was feeling. But she couldn't do it. This was his child.

'What the hell is this?' Emily demanded once again.

'I told you. Hadiyyah –'

'I don't give a fuck for Hadiyyah, whoever she is. D'you know these people, Sergeant Havers? And if so, exactly how many of them do you know?'

Barbara saw her error. It lay in her arm that still encompassed Azhar's shoulders. It lay in the knowledge which she'd just revealed herself to possess. Frantically, she cast through her mind for something to say, but there was nothing but the truth to offer and no time to explain it.

Azhar spoke again. 'He asked her if she liked the sea. Mrs Porter heard that much. "D'you like the sea? Shall we have ourselves a sea adventure?" He said that as they were walking off. Mrs Porter heard. Barbara, he's taken –'

'Good Christ. A boat.' Barbara's glance flew to Emily. There was no time either to explain or to placate. She knew where Muhannad Malik had gone. She knew what he planned. 'He's taken a boat from the Balford Marina. From East Essex Boat Hire, just like he did with the Zodiac. Hadiyyah thinks it's a day cruise on the North Sea. But he's heading for the continent. He has to be. It's crazy. It's too far. But that's what he's doing. Because of Hamburg. Because of Reuchlein. And Hadiyyah's his insurance that we don't stop him. We need the Coast Guard after him, Em.'

Emily Barlow didn't reply in words. But her answer was written upon her features, and what her features were saying had nothing to do with tracking a killer across the sea. The realisation of Barbara's deception was playing over her face, thinning her lips and tightening her jaw.

'Em,' Barbara said, frantic to get them past the moment. 'I know them from London. Azhar. Hadiyyah. That's it. That's all. For God's sake, Em –'

'I can't believe it.' Emily's eyes seemed to burn into hers. 'You of all people.'

'Barbara . . .' Azhar's voice was anguished.

'I didn't know you were in charge of the case until I got to Balford,' Barbara said.

'You were out of line no matter who was in charge.'

'Okay. I know it. I was out of line.' In agitation, Barbara sought something to move the DCI into action. 'Em, I wanted to keep them out of trouble. I was worried about them.'

'And I played into your hands, didn't I?'

'What I did was wrong. I should have told you. You can make a report to my super if you want. But later. *Later.*'

'Please.' Azhar spoke the word like a prayer.

'So fucking unprofessional, Havers.' It was as if the DCI hadn't heard a word.

'Yes. All right,' Barbara said. 'Unprofessional. Unprofessional as hell. But the way I did my job's not the point. We need the Coast

Guard if we want to nab Muhannad. Now, Em. We need the Coast Guard now.'

No response from the DCI.

'Jesus, Em,' Barbara finally cried. 'Is this about murder, or is this about you?'

The final remark was manipulative and rotten, and Barbara despised herself the moment she said it. But the implied judgement achieved the response that Barbara sought.

Emily shot a look at Azhar, then another at Barbara. Then she took up the reins of the case.

'The Coast Guard's no good to us.' And without further explanation, she spun round and strode towards the back of the station.

Barbara said, 'Come on,' and grabbed Azhar's arm.

Emily paused at the door of a room filled with computers and communications equipment. She said tersely, 'Get on to PC Fogarty. Send the ARV to Balford Marina. Our man's on the sea, and he's taken a hostage. Tell Fogarty I want a Glock 17 and an MP5.'

And Barbara understood why Emily had vetoed the idea of the Coast Guard. Their boats carried no weapons; their officers weren't armed. And the DCI was calling for the department's Armed Response Vehicle.

Shit, Barbara thought fervently. She tried to drive from her mind the picture of Hadiyyah caught in a crossfire of bullets. 'Come on,' she said to Azhar again.

'What's she . . . ?'

'She's going after him. We're going as well.' It was, Barbara thought, the best bet she could make to keep the worst from happening to her little London friend.

Emily strode through the weight room with Azhar and Barbara hard on her heels. Behind the station, she took possession of a panda car. She had it started, its lights revolving, by the time Barbara and Azhar climbed in.

Emily looked at the two of them. 'He stays,' she said. And to Azhar, 'Get out.' And when the man didn't move fast enough, she snarled, 'Goddamn it, I said get out. I've had enough of you. I've had enough of all of you. Get out of the car.'

Azhar looked to Barbara. Barbara couldn't tell what he wanted of her and even had she known, she couldn't have given it. Compromise was the best she could offer. She said, 'We'll get her, Azhar. Stay here.'

He said, 'Please. Allow me. She's all that I have. She's all that I love.'

Emily narrowed her eyes. 'Tell that to the wife and kids in Hounslow. I'm sure they'd be thrilled to hear the news. Now get out, Mr Azhar, before I call for an officer to help you do it.'

Barbara swung round in her seat. 'Azhar,' she said. He tore his gaze from the DCI. 'I love her, too. I'll bring her back. You wait here.'

Reluctantly, as if the effort cost him everything he had, the man got out of the car. When he'd shut the door, Emily stamped on the accelerator. They shot out of the car park and into the street. Emily flipped on the siren.

'What the fuck were you thinking?' she demanded. 'What kind of cop are you?'

They roared to the top of Martello Road. Traffic in the High Street halted. They bore right and tore in the direction of the sea.

'How many times could you have told me the truth in the last four days? Ten? A dozen?'

'I would have told you, but –'

'Stuff it,' Emily said. 'Don't bother to explain.'

'When you asked me to liaise, I should have told you. But you would've pulled back, and I would've been in the dark. I was worried about them. He's a university professor. I thought he was in way over his head.'

'Oh, yeah,' Emily scoffed. 'He's in as much over his head as I am.'

'I didn't know that. How could I have known?'

'You tell me.'

She veered into Mill Lane. A delivery van was parked too far into the street, with its driver loading cardboard boxes marked *TYPOGRAPHIC* on to a dolly. Emily dodged to miss both the van and its driver. She steered the car on to the pavement with a curse. The car knocked over a dustbin and a bicycle. Barbara grabbed for the dashboard as Emily jerked the vehicle back into the street.

'I didn't know he did all this legal stuff on the side. I knew him only as my neighbour. I knew he was coming here. Yes, right. But he didn't know I'd follow him. I know his daughter, Em. She's a friend.'

'An eight-year-old friend? Jesus. Spare me this part of the tale.'

'Em –'

'Just bloody shut up, all right?'

Back at Balford Marina for the second time that day, they grabbed a loud hailer from the panda's boot and sprinted across the car park to East Essex Boat Hire. Charlie Spencer confirmed that Muhannad Malik had taken out a motor boat. 'A nice little diesel for a proper long ride. Had a cute little doll with him as well,' Charlie said. 'His cousin, she told me. Never been in a boat before. She was all in a dither about going for a spin.'

By Charlie's reckoning, Muhannad had a forty-minute start on them and had the diesel boat he'd chosen been a fishing craft, he'd have got not much farther than the point at which Pennyhole Bay met the North Sea. But the craft he had chosen had more power than a fishing boat and enough range to take him all the way to the continent. They'd need a real fighter to challenge him, and Emily saw it gleaming in the sunlight from its position above the pontoon where Charlie had it winched out of the water.

'I'll have the *Sea Wizard*,' she said.

Charlie gulped. He said, 'Hang on. I don't know –'

'You don't have to know,' Emily told him. 'You just have to get it into the water and hand over the keys. This is a police matter. You've hired a boat to a murderer. The kid's his hostage. So put the *Sea Wizard* into the water and give me a pair of binoculars as well.'

Charlie's mouth dropped open at this piece of news. He handed over the keys. By the time he'd accompanied Emily and Barbara down the pontoon and had lowered the Hawk 31 into the water, the police Armed Response Vehicle was pulling into the car park, lights flashing and siren wailing.

PC Fogarty came at the run. He had a holstered pistol in one hand and a carbine in the other.

'Give us a hand, Mike,' Emily ordered as she leaped aboard the boat. She began tearing off the protective blue canvas, exposing the cockpit. She tossed this over her shoulder and shoved the keys into the ignition. By the time PC Fogarty had gone below to scout out the nautical charts, Emily was purging the fumes from the engine compartment. Within two minutes, she was gunning the motor.

The boat was berthed bow-in. Emily reversed it into the harbour, in a cloud of exhaust fumes. Charlie paced the narrow space of the pontoon, biting the knuckles of his index finger. 'Take care of her, for God's bloody sake,' he yelled. 'She's all I have, and she's worth a King's ransom.'

A shiver ran down Barbara's spine. *She's all I have* echoed in her head. Even as she heard the repetition, she saw Azhar's Golf bearing down on the car park of the marina. He parked haphazardly in the middle of the tarmac. He left the car door hanging open. He ran to the pontoon. He didn't attempt to intercept them. But his eyes were fixed on Barbara's as Emily steered the boat into the deeper water of the Twizzle, the tributary that fed the tidal marshes to the east of the harbour, taking its source from the Balford Channel to the west.

Don't worry, Barbara told him mentally. I'll get her, Azhar. I swear it. I swear. Hadiyyah won't be harmed.

But she'd been round murder investigations long enough to know that there was no guarantee of anyone's safety when a killer was being run to ground. And the fact that Muhannad Malik had no compunction about enslaving his own people while wearing the guise of their ardent advocate suggested that he'd have even less compunction when it came to the safety of an eight-year-old girl.

Barbara raised a thumb's up at Azhar, knowing no other sign to send him. She turned away from the marina then, and faced the tributary that would take them to the sea.

The speed limit was five knots. And in the late afternoon, returning boats filled with holiday makers made the going treacherous. But Emily ignored the warnings. She fumbled her sunglasses to her face, braced her legs for balance, and took their speed up as high as she could take it and still continue to navigate the waterway in safety.

'Turn on the radio,' she told PC Fogarty. 'Get on to headquarters. Tell them where we are. See if we can get a helicopter to sight him.'

'Right.' The constable set his weapons on one of the boat's vinyl seats. He began flipping switches on the console, calling out arcane letters and numbers. He pressed a switch on the microphone as he spoke. He listened earnestly for a response to crackle back.

Barbara joined Emily. Two seats faced the bow. But neither woman sat. They stood, the better to have a wider scope as they scanned the water. Barbara grabbed the binoculars and looped them round her neck.

'We need a reading for Germany.' Emily interrupted Fogarty, who was still shouting into the radio but bringing up no one. 'The mouth of the Elbe. Find it.'

He turned up the sound on the radio's receiver, set the microphone down, and gave himself to the charts.

'You agree that's what he'll try for?' Barbara called to Emily over the boat's motor.

'It's the logical choice. He's got partners in Hamburg. He'll need documents. A safe house. A place to lie low until he can get back to Pakistan, where God only knows –'

'We've got sand banks in the bay,' Fogarty cut in. 'Watch for the buoys. After that, set your course for zero-six-zero degrees.' He tossed the chart into the galley below.

'What's that?' Emily cocked her head as if in the need to hear.

'Your reading, Guv.' Fogarty went for the radio again. 'Zero-six-zero.'

'My reading on what?'

Fogarty stared at her, nonplussed. 'You don't sail?'

'I row, goddamn it. Gary sails. You know that. Now, what the hell's supposed to be at zero-six-zero?'

Fogarty recovered. He slapped his hand on the top of the compass. 'Steer to zero-six-zero on this,' he said. 'If he's heading for Hamburg, that's the reading for the first leg of the journey.'

Emily nodded and gunned the motor, sending a wake throbbing towards both sides of the channel.

The west side of the Nez was on their right; the tidal islands of that stretch of marshland called the Wade was on their left. The tide was high, but the hour was late for sailing so the channel was congested as recreational sailors headed for their berths in the marina. Emily kept to the centre of the channel, pushing the speed as much as she dared. When they sighted the buoys marking the point at which the channel gave over to the greater channel that was Hamford Water and the outlet to the sea, she pushed forward on the throttle. The powerful engines answered. The bow of the boat lifted, then slapped against the water. PC Fogarty briefly lost his footing; Barbara grabbed on to the handrail as the *Sea Wizard* leaped into Hamford Water.

Pennyhole Bay and the North Sea yawned ahead of them: a sheet of green the colour of lichen, incised by white caps. The *Sea Wizard* shot towards it eagerly, Emily pushing ever more on the throttle. The bow hurtled out of the water, then slammed down against it with so much force that Barbara's unhealed ribs shot fire from her chest, up to her throat, and into her eyeballs.

Jesus, she thought. The last thing she needed was to peg out now.

She lifted the binoculars to her face. She straddled her seat and let its back support her as the boat bounced viciously. PC Fogarty went back to the radio, shouting over the roar of the engines.

The wind whipped them. Spray flew up from the bow in sheets. They rounded the tip of the Nez, and Emily opened the throttle wide. The *Sea Wizard* exploded into the bay. It hurtled past two jet skiers, and its wake tossed them into the water like plastic soldiers swept off a battlefield.

PC Fogarty had assumed a crouching position in the cockpit. He continued to shout into the radio's microphone. Barbara was sweeping her binoculars across the horizon when the constable finally roused someone on shore. She couldn't hear what he said, much less what was said in return. But she got the gist when he shouted to Emily, 'No go, Guv. The divisional chopper's been called as back-up for exercises in Southend-on-Sea. Special Branch.'

'*What*?' Emily demanded. 'What the *hell* are they doing?'

'Anti-terrorist exercises. Been in the planning for six months, they said. They'll radio the chopper, but they can't guarantee it'll get here in time. You want the Coast Guard?'

'What *bloody* good is the Coast Guard going to do us?' Emily shouted. 'D'you think Malik's going to surrender like a good boy just because they pull alongside and ask him?'

'Then all we can hope is that the chopper gets out here. I gave them our compass reading.'

Emily gave the boat more throttle in reply. Fogarty lost his balance. The carbine slid from the seat with a clank. Emily glanced back at the weapons. 'Give me the holster,' she called. She slung it over her shoulder, one hand on the wheel. She said to Barbara, 'See anything?'

Barbara scanned the horizon. They weren't the only craft on the sea. To the north, the rectangular forms of ferries made a squat line from Harwich and Felixstone Harbours, stretching towards the continent. To the south, the Balford pleasure pier cast lengthening shadows on the water as the sun drew lower in the afternoon sky. Behind them, wind surfers cut colourful triangles against the shoreline. And before them . . . before them was the endless stretch of open sea, and hulking at the horizon of that sea the same bank of dirty grey fog that had hung off the shore for as many days as Barbara had been in Balford.

There were boats out there. In the height of summer, even towards the end of the day, there would always be boats out there. But she didn't know what she was looking for, aside from a craft that appeared to be heading in the same direction as they were taking. She said, 'Nothing, Em.'

'Keep looking.' Emily gunned the *Sea Wizard*. The boat answered with another wild leap from the water and another pounding return to the sea. Barbara grunted as her unhealed ribs took her body's weight. Inspector Lynley, she decided, would not be chuffed with the manner in which she'd spent her holiday. The boat rose, smashed, and rose again.

Yellow-beaked gulls soared above them. Others bobbed on the swell. These burst into flight at the approach of the *Sea Wizard*, their angry screams obscured by the roar of her engines.

For thirty minutes they held the same course. They powered past sailing boats and catamarans. They flew by fishing boats that sat low in the water, their day's catches made. They drew ever closer to that low grey band of teasing fog that had promised the coast of Essex cooler weather for days.

Barbara kept the binoculars trained ahead of them. If they didn't catch Muhannad up before they reached the fog bank, their speed advantage would do them little good. He would be able to outmanoeuvre them. The sea was vast. He could change his course, taking himself miles beyond their reach, and they wouldn't be able to catch him because they wouldn't be able to see him. *If* he reached the fog bank. *If*, Barbara realised, he was even out in the open sea at all. He could have been hugging the coastline of England. He could have another hideout altogether, another plan set in place long ago should the gaff be blown on his smuggling ring. She lowered the binoculars. She rubbed her arm across her face, removing not sweat this time but a sheen of saltwater. It was, she decided, the first time she'd been cool in days.

PC Fogarty had crawled to the stern where the carbine had slid. He was checking it over, adjusting its setting: single shot or automatic fire. Barbara guessed he was opting for automatic. From her coursework, she knew that the weapon had a range of about one hundred yards. She felt the bile rise in her throat at the thought that he might actually fire it. At one hundred yards, it was as likely that the constable would hit Hadiyyah as that he'd hit Muhannad. A completely non-religious woman, she sent a fleeting prayer heavenward that one shot aimed well above his head would convince their killer that the police were pursuing him in deadly earnest. She couldn't imagine Muhannad surrendering for any other reason.

She returned to her watch. Stay focused, she told herself. But she couldn't keep her mind's eye from seeing the little girl anyway. Plaits flying joyously round her shoulders, standing flamingo-like with her small right foot scratching at her thin left calf, nose wrinkled with concentration as she learned the mysteries of a telephone answer machine, brightly putting the best possible face on a birthday party with a single guest, dancing with happiness at the discovery of a near relation when she'd thought she had none.

Muhannad had told her that they'd meet again. She must have been bursting with delight at how soon *again* had actually occurred.

Barbara swallowed. She tried not to think. Her job was to find him. Her job was to watch. Her job was to –

'There! Bloody hell! There!'

The boat was a pencil-smudge on the horizon, rapidly approaching the fog. It disappeared with a swell. It reappeared again. It was on an identical course to theirs.

'Where?' Emily shouted.

'Straight on,' Barbara said. 'Go. *Go.* He's heading into the fog.'

They roared onward. Barbara kept the other boat in sight, shouting directions, reporting what she saw. It was clear that Muhannad hadn't yet twigged that they were behind him. But it wouldn't be long before he realised that fact. There was no way they could silence the scream of the *Sea Wizard*'s engines. The moment he heard them, he'd know capture was imminent. And the desperation factor would weigh in like a boxer.

Fogarty moved up to join them, carbine in hand. Barbara scowled at him. 'You don't intend to use that thing, do you?' she shouted.

'Sure as hell hope not,' he replied, and she liked him for the answer.

The sea round them was vast, an undulating field of murky green. They'd long ago left the lesser pleasure craft behind them. Their only companions remained the distant ferries that were making for Holland, Germany, and Sweden.

'Are we still on him?' Emily shouted. 'Do I need to correct?'

Barbara raised the binoculars. She winced as the bouncing boat rattled her ribs. 'Left,' she shouted in return. 'More to the left. And Jesus – hurry.' The other boat looked inches away from the fog.

Emily guided the *Sea Wizard* to port. A moment later, she gave a cry. 'I see him! I've got him!'

And Barbara lowered the binoculars as they roared closer.

They were some one hundred and fifty yards away when it became apparent that Muhannad had realised that they were behind him. He rode a swell and looked back over his shoulder. He bent his attention to the wheel and the fog, since he couldn't possibly hope to outrun them.

He powered onward. The boat cut into the swell. Water spat over its bow in great froths. Muhannad's hair, free from the ponytail he'd worn since the first moment Barbara had seen him, flew about his head. And next to him, indeed so close that from a distance they looked like one person, Hadiyyah stood with her hands hooked into her cousin's belt.

No fool Muhannad, Barbara thought. He was keeping her close.

The *Sea Wizard* charged forward, climbing the swell, plunging into the whitecaps. When Emily had closed the gap between the two boats to forty yards, she decreased her speed and grabbed the loud hailer.

'Shut down, Malik,' she called to him. 'You can't outrun us.'

He kept moving. Steadily. No decrease in speed.

'Don't be a goddamn fool,' Emily called. 'Shut down. You're done for.'

No decrease in speed.

'God damn,' Emily said, loud hailer at her side. 'All right, you bastard. Have it that way.'

She opened the throttle and advanced on the smaller boat. She closed the distance to twenty yards.

'Malik,' into the loud hailer again, 'shut down. Police. We're armed. You've had it.'

He gunned the motor in reply. His boat shot forward. He swung the wheel to port, away from the fog. The sudden change in direction threw Hadiyyah against him. He caught her round the waist and lifted her quickly.

'Put the kid down,' Emily shouted.

And in a horrifying instant, Barbara realised that that was exactly what Malik intended to do.

She had only a moment to see Hadiyyah's face – stricken with terror where an instant before the joy of a boat ride with her cousin had been visible. Then Muhannad had her balanced on the edge of the boat. He threw her overboard.

'Bloody hell!' Barbara cried.

Muhannad spun back to the wheel. He swung the boat away from his cousin and directly towards the fog. Emily gunned the *Sea Wizard's* motor. And in a flash that seemed like an eternity of comprehension, Barbara saw that the DCI intended to give chase.

'Emily!' she shouted. 'For God's sake! The girl!'

Frantically, Barbara searched the swell and found her. A bobbing head, thrashing arms. She went down. She resurfaced.

'Guv!' Constable Fogarty cried.

'Fuck it,' Emily said. 'We've got him.'

'She'll drown!'

'No. We've goddamn bloody *got* him.'

The child went down again. Resurfaced. Thrashed in a panic.

'Jesus Christ, Emily.' Barbara grabbed her arm. 'Stop the boat! Hadiyyah'll drown.'

Emily shook her off. She shoved forward on the throttle. 'He wants us to stop,' she shouted. 'That's why he did it. Throw her a life jacket.'

'No! We can't! She's too far away. She'll drown before it gets to her.'

Fogarty dropped the carbine. He kicked off his shoes. He was on the edge of the boat when Emily shouted, 'Stay where you are. I want you on the rifle.'

'But, Guv—'

'You heard me, Mike, goddamn it. That's an order.'

'Emily! Jesus!' Barbara cried. They were already too far away from the girl for Fogarty to swim to her before she drowned. And even if he attempted it – even if she herself attempted it with him – they would accomplish nothing but drowning together while the DCI relentlessly pursued her quarry into the fog. 'Emily! Stop!'

'Not for some goddamn Paki brat,' Emily shouted. 'Not on your life.'

Paki brat. Paki brat. The words throbbed in the air. While in the water, Hadiyyah flailed and went under. That was it.

Barbara dived for the carbine. She grabbed it. She levelled it at the DCI. 'Turn this fucking boat around,' she cried. 'Do it, Emily. Or I'll blow you straight to hell.'

Emily's hand went to the holster she was wearing. Her fingers found the butt of the gun.

Fogarty shouted, 'Guv! Don't!'

And Barbara saw her life, her career, and her future pass before her in the second before she pulled back on the carbine's trigger.

Chapter Twenty-seven

━━━━◦❖◦━━━━

Emily fell. Barbara dropped the gun. But where she expected to see blood and intestines all over the DCI's tank top, she saw only water from the spray that continued to soar up on either side of the boat. The shot had gone wide.

Fogarty leaped forward. He jerked the DCI upright in her seat. He yelled, 'She's right, Guv! She's right!'

And Barbara went for the boat's controls.

She didn't know how much time had passed. It seemed like several eternities. She brought the boat about with such speed that they nearly capsized. While Fogarty disarmed Emily, she wildly scanned the water for the girl.

Shit, she thought. Oh God. Please.

And then she saw her, some forty yards off their starboard side. Not thrashing, but floating. A floating body. She shouted, 'Mike! There!' And she gunned the motor.

Fogarty was over the side the instant they were close enough to the child. Barbara killed the engine. She flung the life jackets and seat cushions into the water where they bobbed like marshmallows. And then she prayed.

It didn't matter that her skin was dark, that her mother had left her, that her father had allowed her to live eight years believing they were alone in the world. What mattered was that she was Hadiyyah: joyous and innocent and in love with life.

Fogarty reached her. Hadiyyah was floating face down. He flipped her over, caught her under the chin, and began swimming back to the boat.

Barbara's vision blurred. She whirled on Emily. 'What were you thinking?' she shrieked. 'What the goddamn hell were you thinking? She's eight years old, eight years old!'

Emily turned from the sea back to Barbara. She raised a hand as if to fend off the words. Her fingers curled into a fist. And above that fist, her eyes narrowed.

'She's not a Paki brat,' Barbara persisted. 'She's not a nameless face. She's a human being.'

Fogarty had the child at the side of the boat.

'Christ,' Barbara whispered as she dragged the fragile body inside.

As Fogarty clambered into the boat, Barbara stretched the little girl out on the floor. Scarcely breathing herself, without thinking about its use or futility, she began CPR. She moved rapidly between the kiss of life and the cardiac massage and she kept her eyes on Hadiyyah's face. But her own ribs ached from the pounding she'd taken And every breath she took seared her chest. She grunted. She coughed. She pounded the heel of her hand beneath Hadiyyah's breast.

'Get out of the way.' It was Emily's curt voice. Next to her, right into her ear.

'No!' Barbara closed her mouth around Hadiyyah's.

'Stop it, Sergeant. Get out of my way. I'll see to it.'

Barbara ignored her. And Fogarty, panting heavily from his exertions, reached for her arm. He said, 'Let the Guv, Sarge. She can do it. It's okay.'

So Barbara allowed Emily to work on the child. And Emily worked in much the same way that Emily Barlow had always worked: efficiently, seeing that there was a job to be done, allowing nothing to get in the way of her doing it.

Hadiyyah's chest gave a monumental heave. She began to cough. Emily rolled her on to her side, and her body convulsed once before it began to expel salt water, bile, and vomit all over the bottom of Charlie Spencer's prized Hawk 31.

Hadiyyah blinked. Then she looked stunned. Then she seemed to take in the three adults who were hovering over her. Face perplexed, her glance went first to Emily, then to Fogarty, then found Barbara. She smiled beatifically.

'My stomach whoopeed,' she said.

*　　*　　*

The moon had risen by the time they finally made it back to Balford Marina. But the marina was awash with light. It was aswarm with spectators as well. As the *Sea Wizard* rounded the point at which the Twizzle met the Balford Channel, Barbara could see the crowd. They were milling about the Hawk 31's berth, headed by a bald man whose pate glittered in more lights than were natural or necessary on the pontoon.

Emily was at the helm. She squinted over the *Sea Wizard*'s bow. She said, 'Brilliant,' in a disgusted tone.

In the boat's back seat, Barbara held Hadiyyah in the curve of her arm, the child swathed in a mildewed blanket. She said, 'What's going on?'

'Ferguson.' Emily spat her superintendent's name. 'He's phoned the press.'

The media were represented by photographers wielding strobes, reporters carrying notebooks and cassette recorders, and a newsvan getting ammunition for ITV's ten o'clock broadcast. Together with Superintendent Ferguson, they surged forward and scattered down the pontoons on either side of the *Sea Wizard* as Emily cut the engines and let the boat's momentum carry them into the berth.

Voices were shouting. Strobes were popping. A video cameraman jostled his way through the crowd. Ferguson was yelling, 'Where is he, goddamn it?' Charlie Spencer was crying, 'My seats! What the hell've you done with my boat seats?' Ten journalists were shouting, 'Can I have a word over here, please?' And everyone in sight was searching the boat for the obvious – and unfortunately missing – celebrity, promised to be brought to them in chains, head bowed and repentant, just in time to avert a political disaster. Except they didn't have him. All they had was a shivering little girl who clung to Barbara until a slender dark man with intense black eyes pushed past three constables and two teenaged gawkers.

Hadiyyah saw him. She cried, 'Dad!'

Azhar reached for her, grabbed her from Barbara's arms. He clutched her to him as if she carried the only hope of his salvation, as indeed she probably did. 'Thank you,' he said fervently. 'Barbara. Thank you.'

WPC Belinda Warner kept the coffee coming through the next few hours. There was much to see to.

Superintendent Ferguson had to be dealt with first, and Emily saw to him behind closed doors. To Barbara's ears, their meeting appeared to be a cross between a round of bear-baiting and a vicious colloquy on the position of women in the police force. It seemed to consist of raised voices hurling nasty accusations, aggrieved remonstrations, and angry imprecations. Much of it centred round the superintendent's demanding to know what he was supposed to report to his own superiors about 'this monumental cock-up of yours, Barlow', and Emily's responding that she didn't give a flaming one what he reported to anyone just as long as he did his bloody reporting away from her office and let her get back to the business of nabbing Malik. Their meeting ended with Ferguson storming off vowing that she'd do well to prepare herself for disciplinary action and Emily shouting that *he'd* do well to prepare a defence for sexual harassment, which was what she intended to charge him with if he damn well didn't let her get on with her job.

Waiting uneasily with the rest of the team in the conference room next door to Emily's office, Barbara knew how much of the DCI's career now lay in the palm of her hand. As did Barbara's own professional fate rest in Emily Barlow's. Neither of them had spoken a word about those moments on the *Sea Wizard* that had led up to Barbara's seizing control of the boat. Likewise, PC Fogarty had remained mum on the subject. He'd gathered the weapons when they'd returned to the marina. He'd stowed them – along with himself – in the ARV. He'd gone on his way, back to patrol or wherever he'd been when he'd first got word to report to the marina. He'd nodded at them, said, 'Sergeant, Guv, nice work,' in farewell and left Barbara with the distinct impression that what was said on the subject of the sea chase would not be up to him.

And Barbara wasn't sure what to do because she couldn't bear to think of what she'd learnt – about herself and about Emily Barlow – in just a few brief days in Balford-le-Nez.

'*We had a score of Asians . . . howling like werewolves.*'

'*One of those take-away marriages all boxed-up pretty by Mummy and Dad.*'

'*They're Asians. They wouldn't want to lose face.*'

The reality had been before her all along, but her blind admiration for the DCI had encouraged Barbara to overlook it. Now she knew that professional ethics required her to expose what she'd seen – without wanting to see – in Emily from the first. But an allegation from Barbara would most certainly be met by the DCI's levelling a more damning set of charges against her. They began with insubordination; they ended with attempted murder. A word from Emily to London and Barbara was finished in CID. One did not aim and discharge a loaded weapon at one's superior officer and hope that moment's breach of sanity would somehow be overlooked.

When Emily rejoined the team, however, her face gave no indication of her intentions. She entered the room with a down-to-business air about her, and the manner in which she gave directions to her team told Barbara that her mind was on the job, not on retribution.

Interpol needed to be involved. Balford CID would make contact with them through the Met. The request they were making was basic enough. No investigation was being required of Germany's *Bundeskriminalamt*. All that was needed was a simple arrest: as simple as anything could ever be, once more than one country became involved.

But Interpol would require reports to send on to Germany. And Emily directed several members of the team to start gathering those reports. Others were set to work on the extradition proceedings. Still others were to assemble material for the press officer's use in the morning. And others were assigned to assembling data – activity reports, transcripts of interrogations, forensic material – to be handed over to the prosecutors once the police had Muhannad Malik in hand. At this point, pushing yet another trolley of coffee into the room, Belinda Warner informed Emily that Mr Azhar was asking to see her and the sergeant.

Azhar had disappeared with his daughter almost as soon as he'd swept her into his arms. He'd shouldered his way through the milling crowd on the pontoon, making no response to the questions shouted at him, stoically facing the strobes as his picture was recorded for tomorrow's papers. He'd carried Hadiyyah to his car and he'd driven off, leaving the police to sweep up the pieces of what his cousin Muhannad had wrought.

Emily said, 'Bring him up to my office,' and she finally gave a glance towards Barbara. 'Sergeant Havers and I will meet him there.'

Sergeant Havers and I. Barbara's gaze flew to Emily's. She tried to read for substance beneath the DCI's words. But Emily's look was level, betraying nothing, and she turned on her heel and left the conference room. Barbara followed, waiting for a sign.

'How is she?' Barbara asked when Azhar joined them in the DCI's office.

'She's well,' he said. 'Mr Treves was good enough to have soup prepared. She's eaten and bathed, and I've put her to bed. She's been seen by a doctor. Mrs Porter sits with her until I return.' He smiled. 'She has the giraffe in bed with her, Barbara. The ruined one. "Poor thing," she said. "It's not his fault he got mooshed up, is it? He doesn't know he's a mess."'

'Who really does?' Barbara replied.

Azhar gazed at her a long moment and then nodded slowly before he turned to Emily. 'Inspector, I have no idea what Barbara has told you about our acquaintance. But I'm afraid you might have misunderstood her involvement with my family. We're neighbours in London. Indeed, she's been so kind as to befriend my daughter in her mother's . . .' He hesitated, shifted his eyes away, brought them back to Emily. 'In her mother's absence. And that's the extent to which we know each other. She had no idea that I came to your town to assist my family in a police matter. Equally, she had no idea that my experience isn't limited to my work at the university, as I've never told her that. So when you requested that she assist you during her holiday, she was completely innocent of any knowledge that might have –'

'I what?' Emily said. 'I did what?'

'You phoned her? You asked for her help?'

Barbara closed her eyes briefly. It *was* one hell of a tangled web. She said, 'Azhar, that's not what happened. I lied to you both about how I happened to be in Balford. I came because of you.'

He looked so perplexed that Barbara wanted to sink through the floor rather than have to explain anything further. But she muddled on.

'I didn't want you in over your head. I thought if I was here, I could keep you out of trouble. Both you and Hadiyyah. Obviously, I failed. At least in Hadiyyah's case. I completely blew it.'

'No,' Emily said. 'You got us out on the North Sea, Sergeant. Which was where we needed to be to learn the truth.'

Surprised, Barbara shot her a grateful look, embraced entirely by relief at last. No accounting to be made. What had passed between them on the sea could be forgotten. Emily's words told Barbara that the DCI had learned richly from the experience, that no report to her superior officer was going to be made. There was a moment of silence between them. Into it came the sounds of the CID team pulling information together, working through the evening and into the night. But there was a sense of lightheartedness to their work, the sound of men and women who knew a trying job was winding down.

Emily turned to Azhar. 'Until we have Malik in interrogation, we can only sketch out the details of what happened. You can help us with that, Mr Azhar. As I see it, Querashi twigged to the smuggling ring by accident when he came across Muhannad in Parkeston on the night that he himself was there at the Castle Hotel. He wanted in on the action. He threatened to talk if he wasn't included in a way that earned him big money. Muhannad stalled. Querashi grabbed Kumhar and got him to go along by telling him the plan was to put an end to the entire smuggling business. He installed Kumhar in Clacton as the lever for his scheme to make the Maliks pay up. But things didn't work out the way he'd hoped. He got the chop instead.'

Azhar shook his head. 'That cannot be.'

Emily bristled.

Back to normal indeed, Barbara thought.

'After what Kumhar said about Muhannad, you can't think Malik's not involved in this murder? The man just dumped your own daughter into the sea.'

'I'm not disagreeing about my cousin's involvement. It's Mr Querashi's that you've misunderstood.'

Emily frowned. 'How exactly?'

'By not taking our religion into account.' Azhar indicated one of the chairs in Emily's office, saying, 'May I? I find that I'm rather more exhausted than I expected to be.'

Emily nodded. All of them sat. Barbara wished – yet another time – for a cigarette and she expected that Azhar had much the same longing because his fingers went to the breast pocket of his shirt as if with the thought of finding a packet of fags therein. They would have to make do with a roll of fruit pastilles scavenged from the depths of Barbara's shoulder bag. She offered him one. He took it with a grateful nod.

'There was a passage marked in Mr Querashi's copy of the Qur'aan,' Azhar explained. 'It was about fighting for the feeble among –'

'The passage we got Siddiqi to translate,' Emily cut in.

Azhar went on quietly. As Sergeant Havers would confirm, Mr Querashi had made several phone calls to Pakistan from the Burnt House Hotel in the days leading up to his death. One was to a *mulla*, a Muslim holy man from whom he sought a definition of the word *feeble*.

'What's feeble got to do with anything?' Emily asked.

Feeble, as in helpless, Azhar told her. As in without force or effectiveness. A word that could be used to describe a friendless soul newly arrived in this country and finding himself trapped in an enslavement that appeared to have no end.

Emily nodded cautiously. But her doubtful expression telegraphed that she would still have to be convinced of the weight of Azhar's comments.

The other phone call was to a *mufti*, Azhar continued, a legal scholar. From this man he'd sought the answer to a single question: Could a Muslim, guilty of a grave sin, remain a Muslim?

'Sergeant Havers has told me all this already, Mr Azhar,' Emily pointed out.

'Then you know that one cannot remain a Muslim and live in defiance of Islam's tenets. And that's what Muhannad was doing. And that's what Haytham wished to stop.'

'But wasn't Querashi doing it as well?' Barbara asked. 'What about his homosexuality? You said that it's forbidden. Couldn't he have been phoning the *mufti* to talk about his own soul and not Muhannad's?'

'He could have been doing that,' Azhar acknowledged, 'but taken with everything else that he did, it doesn't seem likely.'

'If Hegarty's to be believed,' Emily told Barbara, 'Querashi intended to keep up his double life after his marriage, Islam or not. So he couldn't have cared much about his soul.'

'Sexuality's powerful,' Azhar admitted. 'Sometimes more powerful than personal or religious duty. We're willing to risk everything for the sake of it. Our souls. Our lives. All that we have and all that we are.'

Barbara met his glance. Angela Weston, she thought. What must it have felt like: that desperate resolve to fly in the face of all one knew, believed, and had previously upheld in order to possess the unattainable?

Azhar continued. 'My uncle – a devout man – would have known nothing about this scheme of Muhannad's, and I suggest to you that a complete search of his factory as well as a scrutiny of the papers of his Asian employees will prove this fact.'

'You're not suggesting that Muhannad's in this business alone?' Emily said. 'You heard Kumhar earlier. There were three men. A German and two Asians, he said, and there may have been more.'

'But not my uncle. Muhannad would have had partners in Germany, true. Other partners here, no doubt. I don't question Mr Kumhar's word on that. This scheme could have been in place for years.'

'He could have cooked it up at university, Em,' Barbara pointed out.

'With Rakin Khan,' Emily acknowledged. 'Mr Alibi. They were at university together.'

'My money says that a recce of Klaus Reuchlein's past will show a history between all three of them,' Barbara added.

Azhar shrugged his shoulders in acceptance of this theory. 'Whatever the genesis of the scheme, Haytham Querashi uncovered it.'

'With Hegarty, as he himself told us,' Barbara noted. 'That night when they were at the Castle Hotel.'

'Haytham's duty as a Muslim required he put a stop to it,' Azhar explained. 'He pointed out to Muhannad that his immortal soul was at risk. And at risk for the worst possible reason: his lust for money.'

'But what about Querashi's own immortal soul, if it came to that?' Barbara persisted.

Azhar looked at her directly. 'I should guess he would already have dealt with that problem, by justifying his behaviour in some way. It's easy for us to excuse our physical lust. We call it love, we call it seeking a soul mate, we call it something bigger than and beyond ourselves. We lie so that we might have what we want to have. And we call our behaviour answering the demands of the heart, preordained by a God who stimulates hungers within us that are meant to be satisfied.' He raised his hands, palm upward, a gesture of acceptance. 'No one is immune from this sort of self-deception. But Haytham would have seen Muhannad's sin as the greater one. His own sin affected only himself. People *can* do good in one area of their lives even when they're committing a wrong in another area. Murderers love their mothers; rapists treasure their dogs; terrorists blow up department stores and then go home to rock their children to sleep. Haytham Querashi could have worked for the betterment of the people enslaved by Muhannad and still lived a sinner in one small area of his life that he set aside and excused. Indeed, Muhannad himself did that, organising *Jum'a* on the one hand and the gangmaster scheme on the other.'

'*Jum'a* just kept him looking good,' Emily argued. 'He had to demand an investigation into Querashi's death *because* of *Jum'a*. If he hadn't, everyone would have wondered why.'

'But if Querashi wanted to bring an end to Muhannad's scheme,' Barbara said, 'then why didn't he just expose it, turn him in, and get the police involved? He could have done all that anonymously. It would have served the same purpose.'

'But it would also have served to destroy Muhannad. He would have gone to prison. He would have been cut off from his family. And I expect that Haytham didn't seek that. He sought a compromise instead, with Fahd Kumhar as the guarantee that he got it. If Muhannad had closed down the operation, nothing more would be said about it. If he didn't, Fahd Kumhar would come forward and expose the smuggling ring from Karachi to Hamburg to Parkeston Harbour. I expect that was the plan. And it cost Querashi his life.'

Motive, means, and opportunity. They had it all. What they didn't have was the killer himself.

Azhar rose. He would, he said, return to the Burnt House. Hadiyyah had been sleeping peacefully when he left her, but he did not wish her to awaken without finding her father at her side.

He nodded to them both. He went to the office door. Then he turned back, hesitantly. 'I've forgotten altogether why I came here,' he said apologetically. 'Inspector,' this to Emily, 'there's one thing more.'

Emily looked wary. Barbara saw a muscle move in her jaw. 'Yes?' she said.

'I wanted to say thank you. You could have kept going. You could have captured Muhannad. Thank you for stopping and saving my daughter instead.'

Emily nodded stiffly. She moved her eyes away from him to the filing cabinets along one wall. He left her office.

Emily looked dead knackered. The incident on the sea had drained them both, Barbara thought. And Azhar's words of gratitude – so completely misplaced – could only have added another weight to the DCI's conscience, in addition to the other burdens that she was already carrying. Her own character had been revealed to her on the North Sea. That exposure to her own darker side and base inclinations had to have been a painful one.

'We all grow with the job, Sergeant,' DI Lynley had said to her more than once. 'And if we don't, we need to turn in our warrant cards and walk away.'

'Em,' Barbara said to ease her load, 'we all cock up sometimes. But our mistakes –'

'What happened out there wasn't a mistake,' Emily said quietly.

'But you didn't intend to let her drown. You just weren't thinking. And you told us to throw the life jackets out. You just didn't realise that they wouldn't reach her. That's what happened. That's all that happened.'

Emily turned from her scrutiny of the filing cabinets. She levelled a cool gaze on Barbara. 'Who's your superior officer, Sergeant?'

'My . . . ? What? Who? You are, Em.'

'I don't mean here. I mean in London. What's his name?'

'DI Lynley.'

'Not Lynley. Above him. Who is it?'

'Superintendent Webberly.'

Emily picked up a pencil. 'Spell it for me.'

Barbara felt a chill pass through her. She spelled out Webberly's name and watched the DCI write it. 'Em,' she said, 'what's going on?'

'Discipline is what's going on Sergeant. Or, in more specific terms, what's going on is what happens when you pull a gun on a superior officer, when you decide to obstruct a police investigation. You're responsible for a killer's escaping justice, and I intend to see that you pay the price.'

Barbara was dumbstruck. 'But, Emily, you said . . .' Her words died away. What, indeed, had the DCI said? *You got us out on the North Sea, Sergeant. Which was where we needed to be to learn the truth.* And the DCI was living that truth. Barbara had merely failed to understand what it was, until now.

'Jesus, Emily. You're turning me in,' Barbara said hollowly.

'I am indeed.' Emily continued writing steadily, a living demonstration of those qualities that Barbara had so admired. She was competent, efficient, and completely relentless. She was, as always, Barlow the Beast. She made it to DCI so quickly on the strength of her willingness to wield the power that went with her position. No matter the circumstances, and no matter the cost. What, Barbara thought, had prompted her to conclude that she herself would be the single exception to the rule of Emily's performance on the job?

She wanted to argue with the DCI, but she realised that she didn't have it in her. And Emily's steely expression told her that even if she had, there would have been no point.

'You're a real piece of work,' Barbara finally said, 'Do what you have to do, Emily.'

'Believe me, I intend to.'

'Guv?' At the door to the DCI's office, a detective constable stood. He held a telephone chit in his hand. His expression was troubled.

'What is it?' Emily asked. Her glance sharpened on the paper he held. 'Damn it, Doug, if Ferguson's phoned again –'

'Not Ferguson,' Doug said. 'We've had a call from Colchester. Looks like it came in round eight and the chit got put with some others in communications. I got it only ten minutes ago.'

'What about it?'

'I just returned the call. Tidying up loose ends. I did Colchester the other day, about Malik's alibi, remember?'

'Get on with it, Constable.'

He flinched at her tone. 'Well, I did it again today when we were trying to track him down.'

Barbara felt her trepidation rising. She read *caution* all over the DC's features. He looked as if he was expecting a round of kill-the-messenger upon the conclusion of his remarks.

'Not everyone was home in Rakin Khan's neighbourhood when I was there either time, so I left my card. That's what this phone call was all about.'

'Doug, I'm not interested in the minutiae of your day's activities. Get to the point or get out of my office.'

Doug cleared his throat. 'He was there, Guv. Malik was there.'

'What are you talking about? He couldn't have been there. I saw him myself on the sea.'

'I don't mean today. I mean on Friday night. Malik was in Colchester. Just like Rakin Khan claimed from the first.'

'What?' Emily flung her pencil to one side. 'Are you out of your mind?'

'This,' again he indicated the chit, 'is from a bloke called Fred Medosch. He travels, in sales. He has a bed-sit in the house directly across the street from Khan's. He wasn't home the first time I was there. And he wasn't home when I was trying to track down Malik today.' The constable paused, shifting on his feet. 'But he was home on Friday night, Guv. And he saw Malik. In the flesh. At 10.15. Inside Khan's house with Khan and another bloke. Light hair, round specs, a little hunched at the shoulders.'

'Reuchlein,' Barbara breathed. 'Bloody *hell.*' Emily, she saw, had gone dead pale.

'No *way,*' she murmured.

Doug looked miserable. 'His bed-sit looks right into the front window of Khan's house. Its dining-room window, Guv. And it was hot that night, so the window was open. Malik was there. Medosch described him right down to the ponytail. He was trying to sleep, and those blokes were loud. He looked over to see what was going on. That's when he saw Malik. I've phoned Colchester CID. They're heading over with a picture of Malik, just to make sure. But I thought you'd want to know up front. Before the press office puts out word that . . . you know.'

Emily pushed away from her desk. 'It's impossible,' she said. 'He couldn't have been . . . How did he do it?'

Barbara knew what she was thinking. It was the first thought that had struck her as well. How could Muhannad Malik possibly have been in two places at once? But the answer was obvious: he hadn't been.

'No!' Emily said insistently. Doug faded from the room. Emily got up from her chair and walked to the window. She shook her head. She said, 'God *damn*.'

And Barbara thought. She thought about everything they'd heard: from Theo Shaw, from Rachel Winfield, from Sahlah Malik, from Ian Armstrong, from Trevor Ruddock. She thought about everything they knew: that Sahlah was pregnant, that Trevor had been given the sack, that Gerry DeVitt had been hard at work on Querashi's house, that Cliff Hegarty had been the murdered man's lover. She thought of the alibis, of who had them and who hadn't, of what each of them meant and where each of them fitted in the greater structure of the case itself. She thought –

'Good Christ.' She surged to her feet, snatching up her shoulder bag in the same movement and barely noticing the spearhead of pain that pierced her chest. She was too intent upon the sudden, horrifying but utterly clear realisation that had come upon her. 'Oh my God. Of course. Of *course*.'

Emily turned from the night. 'What?'

'He didn't do it. He did the smuggling, but he didn't do this. Emily! Don't you see –'

'Don't play games with me,' Emily snapped. 'If you're trying to escape a disciplinary hearing by pinning this murder on anyone but Malik –'

'Sod you, Barlow,' Barbara said impatiently. 'Do you want the real killer or don't you?'

'You're out of line, Sergeant.'

'Fine. So report it. But if you want to close this case, come with me.'

There was no need to rush, so they didn't use either the siren or the lights. As they drove up Martello Road, from there to the Crescent where Emily's house lay in darkness, from the Crescent into the upper Parade and round the back of the railway station, Barbara explained. And Emily resisted. And Emily argued. And Emily tersely presented reasons why Barbara was leaping to a false conclusion.

But in Barbara's mind, everything was there and had been all along: the motive, the means, and the opportunity. They'd merely been incapable of seeing them, blinded by their own preconceptions of what sort of woman would submit herself to an arranged marriage in the first place. She would be docile, they had thought. She would have no mind of her own. She would give her will over to the care of others – father first, husband second, elder brothers, if there were any, third – and she would be unable to take an action even when an action might have been called for.

'That's what we think when we think of a marriage being arranged, don't we?' Barbara asked.

Emily listened, tightlipped. They were on Woodberry Way, gliding past the line of Fiestas and Carltons that stood before the down-at-heel terraced houses of one of the town's older neighbourhoods.

Barbara went on. Because their western culture was so different from the eastern, she argued, westerners saw eastern women as so many willow branches, blown by any kind of wind that happened upon the tree. But what westerners never considered was the fact that the willow branch was formed – indeed, had completely evolved over time – for resilience. Let the wind blow; let the gale howl. The branch moved but still remained fixed to the tree.

'We looked at the obvious,' Barbara said, 'because the obvious was all that we had to work with. It was logical, right? We looked for Haytham Querashi's enemies. We looked for people with a bone to pick with him. And we found them. Trevor Ruddock, who'd been given the sack. Theo Shaw, who'd been entangled with Sahlah. Ian Armstrong, who'd got his job back when Querashi died. Muhannad Malik, who had the most to lose if Querashi told anyone what he knew. We considered everything. A homosexual lover. A jealous husband. A blackmailer. You name it, and there we were, running it under the microscope. What we never thought of was what it meant in the larger scheme of *everyone's* life once Haytham Querashi was out of the way. We saw his murder as having to do solely with him. *He* got in someone's way. *He* knew something he shouldn't have known. *He* gave someone the sack. So *he* had to die. What we never saw was that his murder might not have had anything to do with him at all. We never thought it could have been the means to an end having nothing to do with anything that we – as westerners, as bloody *westerners* – could possibly hope to understand.'

The DCI shook her head stubbornly. 'You're blowing smoke. This is nothing.' She'd driven them through the solidly middle-class neighbourhood that served as a boundary between old Balford and new, between the sagging Edwardian buildings that Agatha Shaw had hoped to restore to their former glory and the upmarket tree-shaded elegant homes that had been built in architectural styles that harked back to the past. Here were mock Tudor mansions, Georgian hunting lodges, Victorian summer homes, Palladian façades.

'No,' Barbara responded bluntly. 'Just look at us. Look at how we think. We never even asked her for an alibi. We never asked any one of them. And why? Because they're Asian women. Because in our eyes they allow their men to dominate them, to decide their fates, and to determine their futures. They cover their bodies cooperatively. They cook and clean. They bow and scrape. They never complain. They have, we think, no lives of their own. So they have, we think, no minds of their own. But for God's sake, Emily, what if we're wrong?'

Emily turned right into Second Avenue. Barbara directed her to the house. The downstairs lights all appeared to be on. The family would know about Muhannad's flight by now. If they hadn't had the news from a member of the town council, they'd have had it from the media, phoning with questions, eager for a response from the Maliks, their reaction to Muhannad's escape.

Emily parked, studied the house for a long moment without speaking. Then she looked at Barbara. 'We haven't a shred of evidence for this. Not one speck. Exactly what d'you propose to do?'

That was certainly the question, all right. Barbara considered its ramifications. Especially, she considered the question in the light of the DCI's intention to pillory her for Muhannad's escape. She had two options, as she saw the situation. She could let Emily walk the plank on this one, or she could move beyond her baser inclinations, beyond what she really wanted to do. She could take her revenge or assume responsibility; she could go at the DCI in kind or give her the coup that would save her career. The choice was hers.

Of course, she wanted the former. She ached for the former. But her years with Inspector Lynley in London had shown that an ugly job can be well completed and the doer can still stand whole at the end.

'*There's a lot you might learn from working with Lynley,*' Superintendent Webberly once had said.

The words were never more true than at this moment when they gave her the answer to Emily's question.

'We do exactly what you said, Emily. We just blow smoke. And we do it till the fox comes out of its den.'

Akram Malik answered their knock at the door. He seemed years older than he had when they'd seen him at the factory. He looked at Barbara, then at Emily. He said tonelessly but with such a wealth of pain underscoring his words that the tone of it wasn't necessary for them to ascertain its presence, 'Please. Do not tell me, Inspector Barlow. He could not be any more dead to me now.'

Barbara felt a surge of compassion for the man.

Emily responded. 'Your son isn't dead, Mr Malik. That's not why we've come. As far as I know, he's on his way to Germany. We'll try to apprehend him. We'll extradite him if we can. We'll put him on trial and he'll go to gaol. But we're not here to talk to you about Muhannad.'

'Then . . .' He drew his hand down over his face and examined the sweat that glistened on his palm. The night was as hot as the day had been. And not one window in the house was open.

'May we come in?' Barbara asked. 'We'd like a word with the family. With everyone.'

He stepped back from the door. They followed him into the sitting room. His wife was there, her fingers plucking uselessly at an embroidery ring that held a complicated pattern of lines and curves, dots and squiggles, that she was sewing on to gold fabric. It was a moment before Barbara realised they were Arabic words that she was fashioning into a sampler, similar to the others that hung on the wall.

Sahlah was also there. She had a photograph album open on a glass-topped coffee table. She was in the process of removing photographs from it. Round her on the bright Persian carpet lay her brother's likeness, scrupulously incised from picture after picture as his place in the family was eradicated. The sight of this gave Barbara the shivers.

She walked to the mantel, where earlier she'd seen the photographs of Muhannad, his wife, and his children. The picture of the family's son and his wife was still in place, not a victim yet of Sahlah's scissors. Barbara picked this up and saw what she hadn't noted before: where the couple had posed for the picture. They stood on the Balford Marina, a picnic basket at their feet and Charlie Spencer's Zodiacs lined up behind them.

She said, 'Yumn's home, isn't she, Mr Malik? Could you fetch her? We'd like to speak to all of you together.'

The two elder people looked at each other apprehensively, as if the request implied that more horrors were in the offing. Sahlah was the one who spoke, but she directed her words to her father, not to Barbara. 'Shall I fetch her, *Abhy-jahn*?' She held her scissors upright between her breasts, the personification of patience as she waited for her father to direct her.

Akram said to Barbara, 'I apologise, but I see no need for Yumn to face anything more tonight. She's become a widow; her children are fatherless. Her world has been shattered. She's gone to bed. So if you have something to tell my daughter-in-law, I must ask you to tell me first and allow me to judge whether she's fit enough to hear it.'

'I'm not willing to do that,' Barbara said. 'You're going to have to fetch her or DCI Barlow and I are going to have to park ourselves here until she's ready to join us.' She added, 'I'm sorry,' because she *did* feel sympathy for his position. He was so obviously caught in the middle, the human rope in a tug-of-war whose adversaries were duty and inclination. His cultural duty was to protect the women of his family. But his adopted inclination was English: to do what was proper, to accede to a reasonable request made to him by the authorities.

Inclination won. Akram sighed. He nodded at Sahlah. She set her scissors on the coffee table. She closed the photo album upon her work. She left them. An instant later, they heard her sandalled feet on the stairs.

Barbara looked at Emily. The DCI communicated wordlessly. Don't think this changes a thing between us, Emily was telling her. You're finished as a cop if I have my way.

Do what you have to do, was Barbara's silent reply. And for the first time since meeting Emily Barlow, she actually felt free.

Akram and Wardah waited uneasily. The husband bent stiffly to gather up the severed pictures of Muhannad. He tossed these into the fireplace. The wife set aside her embroidery, weaving the needle into the fabric before she folded her hands in her lap.

Then Yumn was clattering down the stairs in Sahlah's wake. They could hear her protestations, her quavering voice. 'How much more am I meant to bear in one evening? What have they come to tell me? My Muni did nothing. They have driven him from us because they hate him. Because they hate us all. Who will be next?'

'They just want to talk to us, Yumn,' Sahlah said in her gentle lamb's voice.

'Well, if I'm made to bear this, I will *not* bear it unaided. Fetch me some tea. And I want real sugar, not that sour chemical business. Do you hear me? Where are you going, Sahlah? I said fetch me some tea.'

Sahlah entered the sitting room, her face impassive. Yumn was saying petulantly, 'I asked you to . . . I am your brother's wife. You have a duty,' as she followed her sister-in-law into the room. There, she gave her attention to the two detectives. 'What more do you want of me?' she demanded of them. 'What more do you wish to do to me now? You've driven him – *driven* him – from his family. And for what reason? Because you're jealous. You're *eaten* up with jealousy. You have no men of your own, and you can't bear the thought that someone else might have one. And not just any man, but a real man, a man among –'

'Sit down,' Barbara told the woman.

Yumn gulped. She looked to her in-laws for a reprimand to the insult given her. An outsider did not tell her what to do, her expression said. But no one made this protest on her behalf.

With affronted dignity, she walked to an armchair. If she realised the significance of the photograph album and the pair of scissors lying next to it on the coffee table, she gave no sign. Barbara shot a look at Akram, realising that he'd gathered the pictures from the floor and thrown them into the fireplace in order to spare his daughter-in-law having to witness one of the initial ceremonies illustrating her husband's official banishment.

Sahlah returned to the sofa. Akram went to another armchair. Barbara stayed where she was by the mantel, Emily by one of the room's closed windows. She looked as if she wanted to throw it open. The air inside was tepid and stale.

From this moment forward, Barbara knew, the entire investigation became a crap shoot. She drew a deep breath and rattled the dice. 'Mr Malik,' she said, 'can you or your wife tell us where your son was on Friday night?'

Akram frowned. 'I see no purpose to this question, unless you have come to my home with a desire to torment us.'

The women were motionless, their attention on Akram. Then Sahlah reached forward and picked up the scissors.

'Right,' Barbara said. 'But if you thought Muhannad was innocent until he scarpered this afternoon, then you must have had a reason for thinking that. And the reason must be that you knew where he was on Friday night. Am I right?'

Yumn said, 'My Muni was –'

'I'd like to hear it from his father,' Barbara cut in.

Akram said slowly, still reflecting, 'He was not at home. I recall this much because –'

Yumn said, '*Abhy*, you must have forgotten that –'

'Let him answer,' Emily ordered.

'I can answer,' Wardah Malik said. 'Muhannad was in Colchester on Friday night. He always dines there once each month with a friend from university. Rakin Khan, he's called.'

'*Sus*, no.' Yumn's voice was high. She fluttered her hands. 'Muni didn't go to Colchester on Friday. That would have been on Thursday. You've confused the dates because of what happened to Haytham.'

Wardah looked perplexed. She glanced at her husband as if for guidance. Slowly, Sahlah's gaze moved among them.

'You've just forgotten,' Yumn continued. 'How easy to do, considering all that's happened. But surely you remember –'

'No,' Wardah said. 'My memory is actually quite accurate, Yumn. He went to Colchester. He phoned from work before he left because he was worried about Anas's nightmares, and he asked me to change what I was making for the boys' tea. He thought the food might be upsetting him.'

'Oh, yes,' Yumn said, 'but that would have been on Thursday because Anas had one of his bad dreams on Wednesday night.'

'It was Friday,' Wardah said. 'Because I'd done the shopping, which I always do on Friday. You know that yourself, because you were helping me put the groceries away, and you were the one who answered the phone when Muni rang.'

'No, no, no.' Yumn's head moved frantically, directing her gaze first to Wardah, then to Akram, then to Barbara herself. 'He wasn't in Colchester. He was with me. Here in this house. We were upstairs, so you would have forgotten. But we were in our bedroom, Muni and I. *Abhy*, you saw us. You spoke to us both.'

Akram said nothing. His face was grave.

'Sahlah. *Bahin*, you know we were here. I asked for you. I asked

Muni to fetch you. He would have done so. He would have gone to your room and instructed you to –'

'No, Yumn. That isn't how it was.' Sahlah spoke so carefully that it seemed as if she set each word on a thin sheet of ice and wished to be diligent about not fracturing it. She seemed to be realising what each of her words meant as she said them: 'Muni wasn't here. He wasn't in the house. And . . .' She hesitated. Her face was stricken as, perhaps, she understood the import of what she was about to say, and she fully comprehended how her words would devastate the lives of two innocent little boys. 'And neither were you, Yumn. You weren't here either.'

'I was!' Yumn cried. 'How dare you say that I wasn't here! What are you thinking, you stupid girl?'

'Anas had one of his nightmares,' Sahlah said. 'I went in to him. He was screaming and Bishr had started to cry as well. I thought, Where is Yumn? Why doesn't she come to them? How can she sleep so well that she doesn't hear this terrible noise in the very next room? I even thought at the time that you were just too lazy to get out of bed. But you're never too lazy when it comes to the boys. You never have been.'

'Insolent!' Yumn jumped to her feet. 'I insist that you say I was in this house. I'm your brother's wife! I command your obedience. I order you to tell them.'

And there it was, Barbara realised. The motive itself. Buried deeply within a culture she knew so little about that she had failed to see it. But she saw it now. And she saw how it had worked its desperate energy within the mind of a woman who had nothing else to recommend her to her in-laws but a sizable dowry and the ability to reproduce. She said, 'But Sahlah wouldn't have had to obey any longer if she'd married Querashi, would she? Only you would be left having to do that, Yumn. Obeying your husband, obeying your mother-in-law, obeying everyone, including your own sons eventually.'

Yumn refused to submit. She said, '*Sus*,' to Wardah. '*Abhy*,' to Akram. And 'Your grandsons' mother,' to them both.

Akram's face closed down, shuttering itself effectively and completely. Barbara felt a chill run down her spine as she saw in that instant that Yumn had simply ceased to exist in the mind of her father-in-law.

Wardah took up her embroidery. Sahlah leaned forward. She opened the photograph album. She cut Yumn's likeness from the first of the pictures. No one spoke as her image, loosened from the family group, fluttered to the carpet at Sahlah's feet.

'I am . . .' Yumn grasped for words. 'The mother . . .' She faltered. She looked to each of them. But no one met her gaze. 'The sons of Muhannad,' she said in desperation. 'All of you will listen. You will do as I say.'

Emily moved. She crossed the room and took Yumn's arm. 'You'll need to get dressed,' she told the woman.

Yumn cast a look over her shoulder as Emily drew her towards the door. She said, 'Whore,' to Sahlah. 'In your room. In your bed. I heard you, Sahlah. I know what you are.'

Barbara looked cautiously from Sahlah to her parents, breath held and waiting for their reaction. But she could see on their faces that they discounted Yumn's accusation. She was, after all, a woman who had deceived them once and would be willing to deceive them yet again.

Chapter Twenty-eight

It was after midnight when Barbara finally returned to the Burnt House Hotel. She was wrung out. But not so much so that she failed to note the blessed stirring of a breeze from the sea. It struck her cheeks as she climbed out of the Mini, wincing as the pain in her chest told her of the rough usage she'd made of her unhealed ribcage during the day. For a moment, she stood in the car park and carefully breathed in the salt air, hoping that its long-touted medicinal properties might hurry her healing along.

In the corona of silver light from one of the street lamps, she could see the first wisps of fog – so long anticipated – finally coming to the shore. Hallelujah, she thought at the sight of the fragile feathers of vapour. Never had the potential return of a damp and dreary English summer seemed so bloody good to her.

She scooped up her shoulder bag and trudged to the door of the hotel. She felt weighed down by the case, despite – or perhaps because of – having been the means of bringing it to a conclusion. She didn't have to look far to find a reason for feeling so burdened, however. She'd seen the reason first hand, and she'd heard it spoken as well.

What she'd seen had been in the faces of the elder Maliks as they sought a way to come to terms with the enormity of their beloved son's crimes against his own people. He had represented the future to his parents – their own future and the future of their family stretching out towards infinity, each generation more successful than the last. His had been the promise of security in their old age. He had been the foundation upon which they'd built the larger part of their lives. With his flight – more, with the reason for his flight – all of that had been destroyed. What they might have anticipated for him and expected from him as their only son was gone for ever. What was left in place of their hopes was ignominy, a family disaster turned into a permanent nightmare and very real disgrace by their daughter-in-law's culpability in the murder of Haytham Querashi.

What Barbara had heard was Sahlah's quiet reply to the question she'd asked the girl out of her parents' hearing. What will you do now? she'd wanted to know. What will you do ... about everything that's happened? Everything, Sahlah. It hadn't been her business, of course, but with the thought of so many lives being ruined by one man's greed and one woman's need to cement her position of superiority, Barbara had felt anxious for any indication of reassurance, telling her that something good would arise from the devastation fallen upon these people. I'll remain with my family, Sahlah had told her in reply with a voice so steady and sure that there was no doubt that nothing could move her from her resolve. My parents have no one else, and the children will need me now, she'd said. Barbara had thought, And what do *you* need, Sahlah? But she hadn't asked a question that she'd come to realise was utterly foreign to a woman of this culture.

She sighed. She realised that every time she felt she'd got a leg up on understanding her fellow man, something happened to whip the rug out from under her. And these past few days had been one long session of energetic rug-whipping, as far as she could see. She'd begun in awe of a CID diva; she'd concluded in a stunned recognition that her chosen exemplar had feet of clay.

The hotel door opened before Barbara could put her hand on the knob. She started. All the lights were out on the ground floor. In the shadows, she had failed to see that someone had been awaiting her arrival, seated in the old porter's chair that stood just inside the entry.

Oh God. *Not* Treves, she thought wearily. The idea of another round of cloaks-and-daggers with the hotelier was too much for her. But then she saw the gleam of an incandescently laundered white shirt, and a moment later she heard his voice.

'Mr Treves wouldn't hear of leaving the door unlocked for you,' Azhar said. 'I told him I'd wait and lock up myself. He didn't like that idea, but I expect that he could see no way round it other than by giving direct offence, rather than his more usual, oblique brand of insult. I do think he intends to count the silver in the morning, however.' Despite the words, there was a smile in his voice.

Barbara chuckled. 'And he'll do the counting in your presence, no doubt.'

'No doubt,' Azhar said. He closed the door behind her and turned the key in the lock. 'Come,' he said.

He led the way into the darkened lounge, where he lit a single lamp next to the fireplace and took himself behind the bar. He poured two fingers of Black Bush into a tumbler and slid this across the mahogany to Barbara. He poured a bitter lemon for himself. That done, he came round the bar and joined her at one of the tables, placing his cigarettes at her disposal.

She told him all of it, from start to finish. She left out nothing. Not Cliff Hegarty, not Trevor Ruddock, not Rachel Winfield, not Sahlah Malik. She told him the part Theo Shaw had played and where Ian Armstrong fitted into the picture. She told him what their earliest suspicions had been, where those suspicions had led them, and how they'd ended up in the Maliks' sitting room, arresting someone they'd never once suspected could be guilty of the crime.

'Yumn?' Azhar said in some confusion. 'Barbara, how can this be?'

Barbara told him how. Yumn had been to see the murdered man, and she'd done this without the knowledge of the Malik family. She'd gone in a *chādor* – either her bow to propriety or her need for disguise – and she'd managed the trip without anyone from the Malik household being aware that she'd done so. A good look at the layout of their house, particularly at the position of the driveway and the garage in relation to the sitting room and the bedrooms upstairs, demonstrated the ease with which she could have taken one of the cars without the rest of the family ever knowing. And if she'd done this when the boys were in bed, when Sahlah was occupied with her jewellery making, when Akram and Wardah were at their prayers or in the sitting room, no one would ever have been the wiser. How, after all, could Yumn have failed at what the police had concluded was simplicity itself: watching Haytham Querashi long enough to realise that he went regularly to the Nez, taking a Zodiac round to the east side of the promontory on the night in question, stringing a single wire across a crumbling stairwell, sending him to his death?

'We knew all along and we said all along that a woman could have done it,' Barbara said. 'We just failed to see that Yumn had a motive and the opportunity to carry the plan out.'

'But what need did she have to kill Haytham Querashi?' Azhar asked.

And Barbara explained that as well. But when she'd recited chapter and verse on Yumn's need to be rid of Querashi in order to keep Sahlah in her position of subordination in the household, Azhar looked doubtful. He lit a cigarette, inhaled, and examined the tip of it before he spoke.

'Does your case against Yumn rely upon this?' he asked cautiously.

'And upon the family's testimony. She wasn't in the house, Azhar. And she claimed to be upstairs with Muhannad when Muhannad was miles away in Colchester, a fact that's been confirmed, by the way.'

'But to a good defence counsel the family's testimony will be minor points. They could be attributed to confusion about the dates in question, to animosity towards a difficult daughter-in-law, to a family's desire to protect someone whom the defence might call the real killer: a man conveniently on the run in Europe. Even if Muhannad's brought back to this country for trial on smuggling charges, a prison term for smuggling would be shorter than a term for premeditated murder. Or so the defence can argue, seeking to prove that the Maliks have reason to wish guilt upon someone other than Muhannad.'

'But they've disowned him anyway.'

'Indeed,' Azhar agreed. 'But what western jury is going to understand the impact that being cast out of one's family has for an Asian?'

He looked at her frankly. There was no mistaking the invitation in his words. Now was the time that they could talk about his own story: how it had begun and how it had ended. She could learn about the wife in Hounslow, the two children he'd left behind with her. She could discover how he'd met Hadiyyah's mother and she could learn about the forces that had worked within him, making a lifetime of disjunction from his family worth the experience of loving a woman who had been deemed forbidden to him.

She remembered once reading the seven-word excuse that a film director had used to explain the betrayal of his longtime love in favour of a girl thirty years his junior. 'The heart wants what the heart wants,' he had said. But Barbara had long since wondered if what the heart wanted had, in reality, anything to do with the heart at all.

Yet had Azhar not followed his heart – if that, indeed, had been the body part involved – Khalidah Hadiyyah would not have existed. And that would have doubled the tragedy of falling in love and walking away from love's possibility. So perhaps Azhar had acted for the best when he'd chosen passion over duty. But who could really say?

'She's not coming back from Canada, is she?' Barbara settled on asking. 'If, in fact, she's even gone to Canada at all.'

'She's not coming back,' Azhar admitted.

'Why haven't you told Hadiyyah? Why're you letting her cling to hope?'

'Because I've been clinging to hope as well. Because when one falls in love, anything seems possible between two people, no matter the differences in temperament or culture. Because – most of all – hope is always the last of our feelings to wither and die.'

'You miss her.' Barbara stated the fact, so readily apparent beneath his tranquil reserve.

'Every moment of the day,' he replied. 'But this will pass eventually. All things do.'

He stubbed out his cigarette in an ashtray. Barbara tossed down the rest of her Irish whiskey. She could have done with another one, but she took that feeling as an uneasy warning sign. Getting soused wouldn't clarify anything, and feeling the need to get soused in the first place was a fairly good sign that something inside her needed clarification. But later, she thought. Tomorrow. Next week. Next month. In a year. Tonight she was just too bloody exhausted to mine her psyche for the valuable ore of understanding why she felt what it was that she felt.

She rose. She stretched. She winced at the pain. 'Yeah. Well,' she said in conclusion. 'I expect that if we wait long enough, troubles sort themselves out, don't they?'

'Or we die without understanding them,' he said. But he softened the words with his appealing smile. It was wry but warm, making an offer of friendship.

Barbara wondered fleetingly if she wanted to accept the offer. She wondered if she really wanted to face the unknown and take the risk of engaging her heart – there it was again, that flaming, unreliable organ – where it might well be broken. But then she realised that, insidious arbiter of behaviour that it was, her heart was already entirely engaged and had been so from the moment she'd encountered the man's elfin daughter. What, after all, was so terrifying about adding one more person to the crew of the largely untidy ship upon which she appeared to be sailing in her life?

They left the lounge together and started up the stairs in the darkness. They didn't speak again until they'd reached the door of

Barbara's room. Then it was Azhar who broke the silence.

'Will you join us for breakfast in the morning, Barbara Havers? Hadiyyah will want that especially.' And when she didn't answer at once, considering – with some guiltless delight – what another morning of dining with the Asians would do to throw a spanner into Basil Treves' separate but equal philosophy of innkeeping, he went on. 'And for me, too, it would be a pleasure.'

Barbara smiled. 'I'd like that,' she said.

And she meant those words, despite the complications they brought to her present, despite the uncertainty they gave to her future.

Acknowledgments

Attempting, as an American, to write about the Pakistani experience in Great Britain was an enormous undertaking that I couldn't have begun – let alone completed – without the assistance of the following individuals.

First and foremost, I owe a significant debt of gratitude to Kay Ghafoor, whose honesty and enthusiasm for this project laid the groundwork upon which I built the structure of the novel.

As always, I'm indebted to my police sources in England. I thank Chief Inspector Pip Lane of the Cambridgeshire Constabulary for providing me with information on everything from Armed Response Vehicles to Interpol. I also thank him for liaising between me and the Essex police force. I thank Intelligence Officer Ray Chrystal of the Clacton Intelligence Unit for the background information he provided, Detective Inspector Roger Cattermole for giving me access to his incident room, Gary Elliot of New Scotland Yard for an insider's tour.

I'm additionally indebted to William Tullberg of Wiltshire Trackle-ments and to Carol Irving of Crabtree & Evelyn, who assisted in my initial search for a suitable family-operated factory, to Sam Llewelyn and Bruce Lack for nautical details, and to Sue Fletcher – my editor at Hodder & Stoughton – for throwing her support, her assistance, and the resourceful and redoubtable Bettina Jamani behind this endeavour.

In Germany, I thank Veronika Kreuzhage and Christine Kruttschnitt for assisting with police procedure and Hamburg information.

In the United States, I thank Dr Tom Ruben and Dr H. M. Upton for once again supplying me with medical information. I thank my assistant Cindy Murphy for keeping the ship afloat in Huntington Beach. And I thank my writing students for challenging me in my approach to this work: Patricia Fogarty, Barbara Fryer, Tom Fields, April Jackson, Chris Eyre, Tim Polmanteer, Elaine Medosch, Carolyn Honigman, Reggie Park, Patty Smiley, and Patrick Kersey.

And for personal reasons, I thank some wonderful people for their friendship and support: Lana Schlemmer, Karen Bohan, Gordon Globus, Gay Hartell-Lloyd, Carolyn and Bill Honigman, Bonnie SirKegian, Joan and Colin Randall, Georgia Ann Treadaway, Gunilla Sondell, Marilyn Schulz, Marilyn Mitchell, Sheila Hillinger, Virginia Westover-Weiner, Chris Eyre, Dorothy Bodenberg, and Alan Bardsley.

I owe many debts to Kate Miciak, my excellent longtime editor at Bantam, and none so many as were incurred with the creation of this novel. And last, but certainly far from least, I thank my warrior agents at William Morris – Robert Gottlieb, Stephanie Cabot, and Marcy Posner – for all that they're doing to support my work in progress and to promote the finished product both in the United States and around the world.